Frommer's®
Florence, Tuscany & Umbria
8th Edition

by Stephen Keeling &
Donald Strachan

WILEY

John Wiley & Sons, Inc.

Published by:
John Wiley & Sons, Inc.
111 River St.
Hoboken, NJ 07030-5774

ISBN 978-1-118-07466-4 (paper); ISBN 978-1-118-20357-6 (ebk); ISBN 978-1-118-20358-3 (ebk); ISBN 978-1-118-20359-0 (ebk)

Editor: Jennifer Reilly
Production Editor: Michael Brumitt
Cartographer: Roberta Stockwell
Photo Editors: Cherie Cincilla and Alden Gewirtz

Design and Layout by Vertigo Design NYC

Production by Wiley Indianapolis Composition Services
Front Cover Photo: Field of sunflowers and cypress trees near Buonconvento © Nick Bonetti/Eye Ubiquitous/Alamy Images
Back Cover Photos: Left: Castello Verrazzano winery © Vanessa Berberian; Middle: Florence's Duomo © Vanessa Berberian; Right: Grapes in Montalcino © Vanessa Berberian

For information on our other products and services or to obtain technical support, please contact our Customer Care Department within the U.S. at 877/762-2974, outside the U.S. at 317/572-3993 or fax 317/572-4002.

Wiley also publishes its books in a variety of electronic formats. Some content that appears in print may not be available in electronic formats.

Manufactured in China

5 4 3 2 1

CONTENTS

LIST OF MAPS

ABOUT THE AUTHORS

Donald Strachan (chapters 1 and 4–8) is a London-based writer and journalist. He has written about Italian travel for publications including the *Sunday Telegraph*, *Independent on Sunday*, *Sydney Morning Herald*, and *Guardian*, and is the author of *Frommer's Florence & Tuscany Day by Day* and coauthor of *Tuscany & Umbria With Your Family*.

Stephen Keeling (chapters 1-3 and 9-12) grew up in England, lived briefly in Latvia, and spent 12 years as a financial journalist in Asia. Despite attempts to kick his gelato addiction, he has been to Italy many times—an incomparable knowledge of Tuscan Chinese restaurants formed while chaperoning a group of Vietnamese officials in 1994. Stephen is the coauthor of the award-winning *Tuscany & Umbria with Your Family* and currently lives in New York City.

ACKNOWLEDGMENTS

It's impossible to amass the vast amounts of information required for a guidebook like this without lots of help from tourism professionals on the ground. It's also impossible to remember everyone who has helped me along the way, but I'm grateful to you all. Above all, a huge grazie to Roberta Romoli, at the Province of Florence, for fielding countless questions, and Claudia Bolognesi and everyone at Volterratur. Once again, I'd also like to thank the fantastic staff at Frommer's, especially Jen Reilly, my editor, as well as Sue and Colin Martin for putting me up in the glorious Province of Pistoia. Finally, a big thank you to my coauthor, Stephen. It's been a pleasure to research and write with you again. —Donald Strachan

HOW TO CONTACT US

In researching this book, we discovered many wonderful places—hotels, restaurants, shops, and more. We're sure you'll find others. Please tell us about them, so we can share the information with your fellow travelers in upcoming editions. If you were disappointed with a recommendation, we'd love to know that, too. Please write to:

Frommer's Florence, Tuscany & Umbria, 8th Edition
John Wiley & Sons, Inc. • 111 River St. • Hoboken, NJ 07030-5774
frommersfeedback@wiley.com

ADVISORY & DISCLAIMER

Travel information can change quickly and unexpectedly, and we strongly advise you to confirm important details locally before traveling, including information on visas, health and safety, traffic and transport, accommodations, shopping, and eating out. We also encourage you to stay alert while traveling and to remain aware of your surroundings. Avoid civil disturbances, and keep a close eye on cameras, purses, wallets, and other valuables.

While we have endeavored to ensure that the information contained within this guide is accurate and up-to-date at the time of publication, we make no representations or warranties with respect to the accuracy or completeness of the contents of this work and specifically disclaim all warranties, including without limitation warranties of fitness for a particular purpose. We accept no responsibility or liability for any inaccuracy or errors or omissions, or for any inconvenience, loss, damage, costs, or expenses of any nature whatsoever incurred or suffered by anyone as a result of any advice or information contained in this guide.

The inclusion of a company, organization, or website in this guide as a service provider and/or potential source of further information does not mean that we endorse them or the information they provide. Be aware that information provided through some websites may be unreliable and can change without notice. Neither the publisher nor author shall be liable for any damages arising herefrom.

FROMMER'S STAR RATINGS, ICONS & ABBREVIATIONS

Every hotel, restaurant, and attraction listing in this guide has been ranked for quality, value, service, amenities, and special features using a **star-rating** system. In country, state, and regional guides, we also rate towns and regions to help you narrow down your choices and budget your time accordingly. Hotels and restaurants are rated on a scale of zero (recommended) to three stars (exceptional). Attractions, shopping, nightlife, towns, and regions are rated according to the following scale: zero stars (recommended), one star (highly recommended), two stars (very highly recommended), and three stars (must-see).

In addition to the star-rating system, we also use seven feature icons that point you to the great deals, in-the-know advice, and unique experiences that separate travelers from tourists. Throughout the book, look for:

special finds—those places only insiders know about

fun facts—details that make travelers more informed and their trips more fun

kids—best bets for kids and advice for the whole family

special moments—those experiences that memories are made of

overrated—places or experiences not worth your time or money

insider tips—great ways to save time and money

great values—where to get the best deals

The following abbreviations are used for credit cards:

AE American Express	**DISC** Discover	**V** Visa	
DC Diners Club	**MC** MasterCard		

TRAVEL RESOURCES AT FROMMERS.COM

Frommer's travel resources don't end with this guide. Frommer's website, www.frommers.com, has travel information on more than 4,000 destinations. We update features regularly, giving you access to the most current trip-planning information and the best airfare, lodging, and car-rental bargains. You can also listen to podcasts, connect with other Frommers.com members through our active-reader forums, share your travel photos, read blogs from guidebook editors and fellow travelers, and much more.

THE BEST OF FLORENCE, TUSCANY & UMBRIA

As the cradle of the Renaissance, Tuscany and Umbria boast some of the world's most mesmerizing art and architecture, from the sublime work of Michelangelo, Botticelli, and Piero della Francesca, to gorgeous hill towns and the majestic palazzi of Florence. Yet the region isn't all medieval churches and galleries. This is a land of lush landscapes, the snowcapped Apennine mountains, and olive groves and vineyards that produce rich oils and justly famous wines. The region's famed sunshine makes Elba's beaches some of the most enticing in Europe, and its modern festivals in Spoleto and Perugia are giant outdoor parties.

Sightseeing The artistic treasures of Florence have been stupefying visitors for hundreds of years; its showstopping **Duomo, Galleria dell'Accademia,** and **Uffizi** are world-class attractions. The picturesque streets of **Siena** and **San Gimignano** drip with medieval history, while **Pisa's Leaning Tower** is a mind-blowing sight. Don't overlook Umbria, with the **Basilica di San Francesco** in Assisi and **Galleria Nazionale** in cosmopolitan Perugia. Farther south, soak up the exuberant facade of **Orvieto's cathedral.**

Eating & Drinking Eating is a real joy in Tuscany and Umbria, whether you dine in one of the fine *osterias* of Florence, or just grab a crisp, fatty *porchetta sandwich* at an Umbrian farmers' market. Try the **olive oil** here—it's like sipping liquidized olives straight off the tree—and sample the mouthwatering **gelato** in Florence, **Baci chocolates** in Perugia, and Prato's crunchy *cantucci.* Then there's the wine: not just the **Chianti,** but the rich **Brunellos** of Montalcino, the **Sagrantinos** of Montefalco, and subtle whites of **Orvieto.**

History Central Italy's complex recorded history begins with the Etruscans, a heritage best explored today in the hill towns of **Volterra** and **Chiusi,** and at exceptional museums in **Cortona** and **Orvieto.** The big names of the Tuscan Middle Ages are commemorated at dedicated museums in Caprese (**Michelangelo**), Vinci (**Leonardo da Vinci**), and Florence (**Dante**). The island of Elba harbors sights associated with **Napoleon Bonaparte,** dating from his exile there in 1814.

Arts & Culture While the artistic delights of Renaissance Florence often dominate itineraries of the region, make time for the preserved medieval gems of Siena, especially its Gothic **Palazzo Pubblico** and **Duomo.** The genius of Giotto is on full display in the basilica at **Assisi,** while the legacy of Piero della Francesca is preserved in **Arezzo's San Francesco church** and a fine museum in **Sansepolcro.** The region's contemporary culture is best represented by the eclectic **Spoleto Festival** and **Perugia's annual jazz fest.**

PREVIOUS PAGE: **Florence's Duomo.**

THE most UNFORGETTABLE TRAVEL EXPERIENCES

o **A Crash Course in Painting, Sculpture & Architecture:** Tuscany and Umbria are stuffed with the planet's best art and architecture—from frescoed chapels to giant civic paintings that date back 700 years—and every turn of the corner reveals a new wonder in paint or stone. If you've ever had any curiosity about what it all means, you've just landed in the best place in the world to learn.

o **Hiking the Hills of Florence:** The walk from Florence up to Fiesole is famous enough to earn a scene in the movie adaptation of E. M. Forster's *A Room with a View* (even if they cheated and took carriages). But don't neglect the hills of San Miniato and Bellosguardo that rise south of the Arno; the views over the city here are closer at hand, and the land is less developed. For more on Fiesole, see chapter 4.

o **Biking Lucca's Walls:** The elegant Republic of Lucca is still snuggled comfortably behind its 16th-century walls, ramparts so thick they were able to be converted into a narrow city park—a tree-lined promenade running a 5km (3-mile) loop around the city rooftops. The bicycle is the preferred mode of transportation in Lucca, and you'll be in good company as you tool under the shade past parents pushing strollers, businessmen walking their dogs, and old men at picnic tables in their 40th year of a never-ending card game. See "Circumnavigating the Walls," in chapter 6.

o **An Evening Stroll in Perugia:** Perugia's wide Corso Vannucci is perfect for the early-evening stroll Italians everywhere turn out for—the *passeggiata*. It's the time to see and be seen, to promenade arm in arm with your best friend dressed in your best duds. The crowd flows up the street to one piazza and

Cycling is the best way to tour Lucca.

then turns around and saunters back down to the other end. When you tire of meandering, take a break to sip cappuccino and nibble Perugia's fine chocolates in one of the classy cafes lining the street. See "Perugia" in chapter 10.

o **Going Off the Beaten Path in Assisi:** Who would've thought you could find a primal Umbrian country experience in overtouristed Assisi? Save the basilica's frescoes for the afternoon and get up early to hike into the wooded mountains of Monte Subasio to St. Francis's old hermitage. After a morning spent in contemplation with the monks and wandering the state parkland, head back to Assisi, but be sure to stop a mile outside town for a big lunch at **La Stalla,** one of the best countryside *trattorie* in central Italy. See "Assisi" in chapter 10.

THE most CHARMING HILL TOWNS

o **San Gimignano:** The "Medieval Manhattan" bristles with more than a dozen tall stone towers, all slightly askew. It wins the "Most Densely Decorated Church" award for its old Duomo, whose interior walls are slathered with 15th-century frescoes. San Gimignano's skyline and back alleys, especially when moonlit, make it one of Italy's most atmospheric hill towns. Stay until all the tour buses have left, when you'll have the gardens and small *piazze* all to yourself. See "San Gimignano," in chapter 5.

o **Volterra:** Proud Volterra has been important in western Tuscany since the Etruscan era. From its magnificent rocky promontory, the ocher city surveys the sometimes wild, vast countryside surrounding it. Volterra is full of workshops where artisans craft the native alabaster into translucent souvenirs. See "Volterra," in chapter 5.

Shopping in San Gimignano.

- **Cortona:** This stony hill town is no longer big enough to fill its medieval walls, but it still has its museums of paintings by Fra' Angelico and local boys Luca Signorelli and Pietro da Cortona. The restaurants serve steak from the famed Chianina cattle, raised in the valley below, where Etruscan tombs hint at the city's importance in a pre-Caesar Tuscany. See "Cortona," in chapter 9.

- **Gubbio:** This ancient Umbrian stronghold is like the last outpost of civilization before the wilderness of the high Apennines. The central piazza cantilevers over the lower town like a huge terrace. The square is bounded on one end by a mighty palace, all sharp stone lines and squared-off battlements. Inside is a cluttered archaeological

Santa Maria della Consolazione in Todi.

museum and the same echoey medieval atmosphere that pervades the entire town. See "Gubbio," in chapter 10.

- **Todi:** Umbria's most picturesque hill town somehow avoids most of the tourists. Many of its streets are so steep they've been chipped with shallow staircases down the middle. Vistas across the valley open up unexpectedly, and on the perfectly proportioned medieval main piazza is a town hall sprouting a staircase perfect for an Errol Flynn sword-fight scene. See "Todi," in chapter 11.

THE best FESTIVALS

- **Florence's Calcio Storico:** First, divide the city into its traditional neighborhoods for teams, cover Piazza Santa Croce with dirt, and don Renaissance costumes. Next, combine two parts soccer, one part rugby, one part (American) football, and a heaping helping of ice-hockey attitude. Give the winners a whole calf to roast in the streets and write it all off in honor of St. John the Baptist. See the "Calendar of Events," in chapter 2.

- **Siena's Palio:** Almost anything goes at this bareback, breakneck horse race around the dirt-packed Campo, and the competitive *contrade* (neighborhood wards) usually make sure everything does. The square is filled with costumed pageantry before the race, and massive feasts are set up on long outdoor tables that can stretch for blocks on the medieval side streets. See "Siena" in chapter 5.

- **Arezzo's Giostra del Saracino:** Arezzo really comes alive for this Renaissance titling tournament where the target at which mounted jousters aim their lances swivels around and can actually hit back. See "Arezzo" in chapter 9.

Siena's Palio.

- **Gubbio's Corso dei Ceri:** In one of Italy's most ancient festivals, teams of burly, costumed men trot about town all day carrying three huge towers topped with statues of saints. After a wild invocation ceremony in the piazza, they shoulder the towers (actually giant candles) and tear up the mountainside as fast as they can. The town's patron saint invariably wins. See "Gubbio" in chapter 10.

- **Spoleto & the Spoleto Festival:** Gian Carlo Menotti's annual bash brings some of the biggest names in orchestral music, dance, and theater to this ancient hill town. Many of the events are staged outside in Piazza del Duomo or the remains of a Roman theater. See "Spoleto" in chapter 11.

THE greatest MUSEUM MASTERPIECES

- **Michelangelo's *David*** (Galleria dell'Accademia, Florence): The Big Guy himself, the perfect Renaissance nude, masterpiece of sculpture, and symbol of Tuscany itself. See p. 140.

- **Sandro Botticelli's *Birth of Venus*** (Galleria degli Uffizi, Florence): Venus on the half shell. The goddess of love is born from the sea, a beauty drawn in the flowing lines and limpid grace of one of the most elegant masters of the Renaissance. See p. 127.

- **Duccio di Buoninsegna's *Maestà*** (Museo dell'Opera Metropolitana, Siena): The genre-defining painting of the Virgin Mary in majesty, surrounded by saints, was carried through the streets of Siena in triumph when it was unveiled in the early 14th century. See p. 197.

- **Rosso Fiorentino's *Deposition*** (Pinacoteca, Volterra): Mannerism, a style of art inspired by Michelangelo and led by Andrea del Sarto, was the last truly great native Tuscan artistic movement. The prize work of Volterra's picture gallery exhibits all the hallmarks of the school: torsion, narrative tension, hyperreal colors, and the beginnings of what many centuries later would become modern art. See p. 228.

o **Piero della Francesca's *Resurrection of Christ*** (Museo Civico, Sansepolcro): Piero's dead-on geometric perspective and exquisitely modeled figures helped make this haunting work the model for all later depictions of the risen Christ. This is quite possibly the only fresco whose reputation as the "best painting in the world" actually saved it from bombardment during World War II. See p. 348.

Botticelli's *Birth of Venus*.

THE finest CHURCH ART & SCULPTURE

o **Lorenzo Ghiberti's *Gates of Paradise*** (Battistero, Florence): In 1401, young Ghiberti won a sculpture competition to craft the doors of Florence's Baptistery. Fifty-one years later, he completed his second and final set, boosting the Gothic language of three dimensions into a Renaissance reality of invented space and narrative line. Art historians consider that 1401 competition to be the founding point of the Renaissance. Michelangelo looked at the doors and simply declared them "so beautiful they would grace the entrance to Paradise." See p. 121.

o **Masaccio's *Trinità* & the Cappella Brancacci** (Santa Maria Novella and Santa Maria del Carmine, Florence): The greatest thing since Giotto. Masaccio not only redefined figure painting with his strongly modeled characters of intense emotion and vital energy but also managed to be the first painter to pinpoint precise mathematical perspective and create the illusion of depth on a flat surface. The world's first perfecter of virtual reality. See p. 139 and 153.

o **Giovanni Pisano's *Pulpit of St. Andrew*** (Sant'Andrea, Pistoia): For more than a century, the search for Gothic perfection in stone seemed almost to be a private Pisano family race. Here Giovanni's 1301 sculpted hexagonal pulpit outshines father Nicola, and is the commanding work of the genre, crammed with emotional power and narrative detail. See p. 244.

o **Filippo Lippi's *Life of St. John the Baptist*** (Duomo, Prato): The recent restoration of this dazzling fresco cycle has at last brought the city of Prato some of the recognition (and visitors) it deserves. Lippi's depiction of the *Dance of Salome* is possibly a portrait of the amorous monk's mistress, Lucrezia Buti, and certainly one of the iconic images of the early Renaissance. See p. 236.

o *Life of St. Francis* (Basilica di San Francesco, Assisi): This fresco cycle shocked the painting world out of its Byzantine stupor and thrust it full tilt on the road to the Renaissance. Did Giotto paint it, or was it the work of many artists? Whatever the answer (and we'll probably never know for sure), the frescoes blend realism, classicism, a concept of space and bulk, and pure human emotion in a way that parlayed humanist philosophy into paint. See p. 384.

THE best PLACES TO ESCAPE HIGH-SEASON CROWDS

o **Exploring the Museo Stibbert** (Florence): This former private museum of an eccentric Scottish-Italian is made up of the general clutter of more than 50,000 random items and a huge collection of armor from all eras and world cultures, including an entire regiment of armored mannequins. See p. 156.

o **Ballooning over the Chianti:** What better way to see Europe's most famous countryside than floating lazily over the olive- and vine-covered hillsides in a hot-air balloon while having a champagne breakfast? Many outfits offer this indulgent pastime. Rates start around 240€ for a sunrise 1½-hour flight. Contact **Ballooning in Tuscany** at ℂ **338-146-2994** or visit www.ballooning intuscany.com.

o **Discovering Prehistoric Statue-Stele in Pontrémoli:** These mysterious tombstone-shaped statues were carved over a 3,000-year period starting about 3000 B.C. by an extraordinarily long-lived cult isolated in the Lunigiana. Some of the abstracted figures bear a suggestive resemblance to how ancient Roman historians described Celtic warriors from Gaul. See "The Garfagnana & the Lunigiana," in chapter 6.

o **Roaming Etruscan "Sunken Roads" in the Maremma:** No one is quite sure why the Etruscans of the Maremma carved a network of passages, some more than 7m (23 ft.) deep, into the tufa surrounding Pitigliano, Sorano, and Sovana. Many stretches of these *vie cave* have survived the millennia, and you can follow them (sometimes up to 1km/⅔ mile) in what are kind of open-air cave tunnels. See "The Maremma," in chapter 7.

o **Driving the Back Roads of the Crete Senesi & Val d'Orcia:** It's never really clear to us why the spectacular winding roads southwest of Siena—past Asciano and San Giovanni d'Asso, and farther south to the balcony-like ridges around Pienza—aren't the most heavily trafficked in all Tuscany. They are as gloriously empty as the landscape they survey, a rolling terrain punctuated by farmhouses and dotted with cypress stands.

The rolling agricultural terrain of the Val d'Orcia.

Such is the beauty of the scenery that you'll still find the going slow, however: Every new bend in the road reveals another photo stop as essential as the last. See chapter 8.

THE *best* WINES & VINEYARDS

See "What to Drink," in chapter 2, for information on Italian wines.

o **Chianti Classico:** Italy's most famous wine. Chianti is as variable as it is versatile, and while there's plenty of mass-produced cheap wine out there, the vintners of the Chianti Classico zone, in the hills between Florence and Siena, craft excellent wines of the highest quality. Premier estates abound, and the top accessible ones are highlighted in chapter 5.

o **Vernaccia di San Gimignano:** In his *Divine Comedy,* Dante wrote of this dry, peppery, straw-colored white that deepens to gold with age. Tuscany's best white is available all over the Town of Towers. It was the first DOC wine in Italy, and is Tuscany's only DOCG white; see p. 43 for information on these classifications. The consortium of Vernaccia producers dates back at least to 1276; you can contact them in town at the **Villa della Rocca (✆ 0577-940-008).** See "San Gimignano" in chapter 5.

o **Brunello di Montalcino:** Brunello has the smell of mossy, damp earth and musky berries. It tastes of dark, jamlike fruits and dry vanilla. This is Tuscany's most powerful red, and perhaps the top wine in all of Italy. Break out this complex elixir to accompany a mighty *bistecca alla fiorentina* (Florentine-style steak). Visit the **Enoteca La Fortezza (✆ 0577-849-211;** www.enotecalafortezza.com) in town to taste, browse, and buy from a vast selection of the region's best bottles or **Poggio Antico (✆ 0577-848-044;** www.poggioantico.com) for the direct sales of an award-winning boutique Brunello. See "Sampling the *Vino,*" on p. 308.

o **Vino Nobile di Montepulciano:** This purple-garnet wine smells of violets and tastes of juicy red berries, dark fruits, and a hint of musty, mossy earth. Of the traditional wines (no French grape intrusions), it plays second banana to Brunello, but many people find this Noble Wine a more forgiving *vino,* and much more versatile. Although it's powerful and complex, you can drink it with just about anything but fish. The best producers are generally represented by the town's **Consorzio** (www.consorziovinonobile.it), and if you must choose just one winery to visit, make it **Gattavecchi (✆ 0578-757-110;** www.gattavecchi.it). See "Underground Tunnels & Noble Wine," on p. 324.

Wine bottles gathering dust in a Chianti *cantina.*

○ **Rubesco Riserva:** This unique and elegant Umbrian wine made by a single estate was so deliciously demanding of attention the authorities had to create a tiny DOCG zone just to incorporate the vineyard. The vintner responsible was Giorgio Lungarotti, experimenting with his grapes in Torgiano south of Perugia. Although all the **Cantine Lungarotti** (✆ **075-988-0294**) wines are excellent, the best is the Rubesco Riserva label. See "Perugia" in chapter 10.

○ **Sagrantino di Montefalco:** This dark wine with a rounded mouth feel and tannic bite—about the biggest and most complex wine you'll get in Umbria—has been recognized by the DOCG classifications. You can get a taste at top producers **Antonelli** (✆ **0742-791-5852**) and **Cantina A. Fongoli** (✆ **0742-350-359**) in San Marco di Montefalco. See "Montefalco" in chapter 11.

○ **Orvieto Classico:** Orvieto's white is an ancient wine, made at least since the days of the Etruscans. In Orvieto itself, you can get the traditional *abboccato* variety, a juicy, semisweet version hard to find elsewhere in this age that demands gallons of dry white table wines. Try smaller producers such as **Decugnano dei Barbi** (✆ **0763-308-255**) and **Barberani** (✆ **0744-950-113**). See "Orvieto's Liquid Gold," on p. 429.

THE most ABSORBING MUSEUMS

○ **Galleria degli Uffizi** (Florence): One of the world's top museums, the Uffizi houses some of the seminal works of the Renaissance, including Giotto's *Ognissanti Maestà,* Botticelli's *Birth of Venus* and *Allegory of Spring,* Leonardo da Vinci's *Annunciation,* and Michelangelo's only panel painting, the *Holy Family.* Few rooms go by without three or four masterpieces. Thoroughly brain-draining . . . but worth it. See p. 122.

○ **Museo Nazionale del Bargello** (Florence): Past early Michelangelo marbles and Giambologna bronzes, the main attraction at the primary sculpture museum of the Renaissance is a room full of famous works that survey the entire career of Donatello, in his time rightly considered the greatest sculptor since antiquity. See p. 130.

○ **San Marco** (Florence): The entire place is the *magnum opus* of Dominican artist Fra' Angelico, who painted with delicate beauty and mathematical precision. If you're not familiar with his work, it's probably because the best of it is all here—from his cycle of intimate, contemplative frescoes in the monks' cells upstairs, to the blockbuster altarpieces displayed in the former pilgrim's hospice around the cloister downstairs. See p. 143.

○ **Palazzo Pubblico** (Siena): The Museo Civico inside Siena's medieval town hall is a masterpiece of the Sienese School. Foremost among the frescoes are Simone Martini's dazzling 1315 *Maestà* and Ambrogio Lorenzetti's *Allegories of Good and Bad Government,* the most important civic paintings of medieval Tuscany. See p. 193.

○ **Galleria Nazionale** (Perugia): Umbria's National Gallery boasts more Peruginos than it knows what to do with. It also has one of the masterpieces of his teacher, Piero della Francesca, the *Polyptych of Sant'Antonio,* with its

Annunciation scene of remarkable depth. Duccio, Arnolfo di Cambio, Fra' Angelico, and Gentile da Fabriano add to the collections. See p. 368.

THE best ETRUSCAN SIGHTS

o **Volterra:** One of Dodecapolis's ancient centers, Volterra has a medieval core still surrounded in places by the old Etruscan city walls. The best section encompasses the 4th-century-B.C. Porta all'Arco gate, from which worn basalt gods' heads gaze mutely but protectively over the valley. The Museo Etrusco Guarnacci here houses hundreds of funerary caskets and the *Shadow of the Evening*, a tiny bronze youth of elongated grace. See chapter 5.

o **Populonia:** Once an important Etruscan ironmaking center, the coastal settlement of Populonia today retains some excellent *tumuli* and fascinating tombs in necropolises dotting either side of the road leading to Populonia's promontory. It's still the only Etruscan burial coast ever found beside the sea. See "Livorno & the Etruscan Coast," in chapter 7.

o **Sarteano:** To really get a feel for life and death in the Etruscan Age, visit the tiny Tomba della Quadriga Infernale just outside town, whose ancient frescoes make Renaissance art look like a recent paint job. Only unearthed a decade ago, the unique tomb was painted 300 years before Christ and remains remarkably intact. See "A Side Trip to Sarteano," in chapter 8.

o **Chiusi:** The small but well-regarded archaeological museum here contains just some of the many finds from the dozens of tombs littering the valley floor between the town and small Lake Chiusi. The town's underground Etruscan tunnels, known as the Labirinto di Porsenna, are also visitable on a daily guided tour. See "Chiusi & Sarteano," in chapter 8.

o **Orvieto:** Orvieto, Etruria's ancient religious center, contains three archaeological museums. Taken together, they make up one of the best collections of Etruscan artifacts outside Florence and include Umbria's only accessible tomb paintings, now detached, and works from the Etrusco-Roman period. The town also runs tours of some of the tunnels and caverns under the city, parts of which, including wells and a possible temple, were carved by the Etruscans. Around the edge of the city's walls is a tidy suburban-like necropolis of tombs, some still with inscriptions on the door lintels. See "Orvieto," in chapter 11.

THE best LUXURY ACCOMMODATIONS

Not all the places to stay below are officially rated as luxury hotels, but all offer luxurious accommodations and amenities.

o **Four Seasons Florence** (Borgo Pinti 99, Florence; www.fourseasons.com/florence; ✆**055-2626-250**): There was never really any doubt, when the Palazzo della Gherardesca reopened in 2009 as the Four Seasons Firenze after a 7-year restoration project—this was destined to be the most luxurious address in Tuscany. Original frescoes on the 15th-century walls, sumptuous decor, and some of the city's finest dining are just a few of the earthly delights you'll find here. See p. 91.

o **Helvetia & Bristol** (Via dei Pescioni 2, Florence; www.royaldemeure.com; ℂ055-26-651): This most central of Florence's luxury addresses was the city's leading hotel in the 19th century, and guest rooms and lounges still exude an opulent turn-of-the-20th-century air. The bright and refreshing small Winter Garden bar, with trailing ivy and a splashing fountain, doubles as the breakfast room. The location, opposite the Strozzi and a few paces from Via de' Tornabuoni, could hardly be better for a shopping- and culture-fueled visit. See p. 88.

o **Villa Vignamaggio** (near Greve in Chianti; www.vignamaggio.com; ℂ055-854-661): Leonardo da Vinci might have approved of the saturated color schemes in the minisuites of this *agriturismo* (working farm) high in the hills of the Chianti. In fact, the Mona Lisa who sat for his famous portrait grew up in the villa. Most suites are in the peasant stone outbuildings scattered across the property and come outfitted with minibars, satellite TVs, and complimentary bottles of the estate's award-winning vintage. It's the best base for a wine-buying trip. See p. 180.

o **Hotelito Lupaia** (Loc. Lupaia 74, Torrita di Siena; www.lupaia.com; ℂ0578-668-028): Southern Tuscany generally does rustic way better than it does luxe, but this "little hotel" enveloped in a rural idyll between Montepulciano and Montefollonico successfully combines the two. Bohemian decor and strong colors permeate all the individually designed units, and the pool is the ideal spot for a lazy lunch in the sun. See p. 318.

o **Fonte Cesia** (Via Lorenzo Leonj 3, Todi; www.fontecesia.it; ℂ075-894-3737): This hotel melds 13th-century *palazzo* and modern lines. The public rooms are filled with brick vaulting, and the huge terrace, planted with palms, is for taking breakfast. The suites are each themed and decorated with fine antique pieces or modern design, such as Empire-style desks and dressers or Wassily chairs. See p. 423.

Giant oak casks used to age chianti wine at Villa Vignamaggio.

THE best MODERATELY PRICED ACCOMMODATIONS

- **Residence Hilda** (Via dei Servi 40, Florence; www.residencehilda.it; ✆ **055-288-021**): Step off the Renaissance square of Santissima Annunziata right into the 21st century at this apartment building, where clean, contemporary design is complemented by high-quality modern conveniences. Add hotel amenities to those cool, airy spaces, stripped-wood floors, and cream walls and fabrics, then throw in a management team who can't do enough to help you out, and you have just about the perfect Florence accommodations package. Oh, and did we mention it's just 2 blocks from the Duomo? See p. 96.

- **L'Antico Pozzo** (Via San Matteo 87, San Gimignano; www.anticopozzo.com; ✆ **0577-942-014**): This is central San Gimignano's best hotel, set in a restored 15th-century palace built into the *palazzo* where Dante stayed during his diplomatic visit to town. Inquisition trials are no longer held here, but you can get an enormous junior suite with a canopied bed or 17th-century frescoed ceilings, or a top-floor double with views of the city's towers. See p. 219.

- **Villa de' Fiori** (Via di Bigiano e Castel Bovani 39, Pistoia; www.villadefiori.it; ✆ **0573-450-351**): Hiding amid the olive groves just north of Tuscany's most underrated little city is this former grand residence turned *agriturismo*-hotel. The place's rustic charm remains intact—few pieces of antique furniture properly match, and there are reminders everywhere that this was once the hub of a working estate. The friendly family that runs the hotel only adds to the refined, yesteryear atmosphere, and the breakfast buffet (served in the country kitchen) is one of the best in all Tuscany. See p. 245.

THE best EATING EXPERIENCES

- **Indulging in the World's Best Gelato:** Ice cream was invented (probably) in Florence in the 16th century, and today it's impossible to resist the addictive, luscious gelato flavors on offer throughout the region. The pistachio (*pistacchio*) and hazelnut (*nocciola*) taste like they've been made with nuts plucked straight from the tree, and the zesty fruit flavors explode on the tongue. See p. 106 for the planet's best *gelaterie*.

- **Sampling the Porchetta Sandwich:** Take a suckling pig, debone, roll, spit, and roast over a wood fire, with a generous stuffing of garlic, rosemary, and fennel. Then carve and serve on a crusty roll for 2.50€. Can it get any better than this? Available at most weekly markets; see chapters 5 to 11.

- **Death by Chocolate on the Perugina Factory Tour:** Perugia is the home of Baci chocolates, those sweet, velvety "kisses" with a hazelnut truffle center. The Perugina factory tour includes a chocolate buffet. Seriously. See p. 378.

- **Enjoying Aperitivo, Tuscan Style:** These days *aperitivo* means more than just a pre-dinner drink—bars in Siena, Pisa, and Florence offer rich buffets of finger food, pasta, salads, cured meats, and *pizzette,* for free, with a drink (usually between 6 and 8pm). See chapters 4 and 7.

- **Eating Seafood by the Seashore:** You'll find the freshest fish right along Tuscany's coast, but in the port city of Livorno, on the mainland, and the island of Elba's main settlement, Portoferraio, it counts as the major attraction in town. Specialties include *fritto misto* (a mixed fry of today's catches), *baccalà alla Livornese* (salt cod stewed with tomatoes), and *cacciucco,* a spicy mixed fish soup-stew similar to Marseille's *bouillabaisse.* See "Livorno & the Etruscan Coast" and "Elba" in chapter 7.

o **Dining at a Southern Tuscan Grill:** They like their meat properly reared and cooked plain and simple on the flamegrill right across southern Tuscany. Look out especially for beef sourced from white Chianina cattle and pork from the Cinta Senese breed of pig. See chapter 8.

THE best RESTAURANTS

o **Cibrèo** (Via Andrea del Verrocchio 8r, Florence; ℭ055-234-1100; www.edizioniteatrodelsalecibreofirenze.it): The amalgamated country-style decor of this restaurant belies its status as one of the city's finest kitchens, even after years at the top. The dishes are Tuscan at heart—though they buck the standard by serving no pasta and little grilled meat—with innovative touches and plenty of peperoncino for spice. You may have to wait even with a reservation, but the wait is invariably worth it. See p. 108.

o **Il Santo Bevitore** (Via Santo Spirito 66r, Florence; ℭ055-211-264; www.ilsantobevitore.com): Few places typify the new Florentine Left Bank vibe as well as this buzzing enoteca-osteria (wine bar). Service is informal, even laidback, but they take the ingredients that make up their refreshingly modern take on Tuscan food very seriously indeed. The wine list is one of the best in town. See p. 112.

o **Antica Locanda di Sesto** (Via Ludovica 1660, Sesto di Moriano, Lucca; ℭ0583-578-181; www.anticalocandadisesto.it): The food in the northern part of Tuscany is quite different to that elsewhere in the region, making more liberal use of ingredients like *farro* (emmer) and Sorano beans. Everything you'll eat at this roadside inn in the Serchio valley is freshly made on the premises, and dishes rely on seasonal and foraged ingredients, or produce from the owner family's nearby farm. Park right outside or ride the bus north from Lucca. See p. 262.

o **Osteria del Mare** (Borgo Cappuccini 12, Livorno; ℭ0586-881-027): It's almost impossible to pick a "best" from among Livorno's crop of great value seafood restaurants, but the attentive waitstaff and a proper tablecloth perhaps just edge it for this dining room. It's impossible to predict exactly what will be on the menu—catch alone determines that—but it's guaranteed to be tasty, fresh, simply cooked, and served with a smile. See p. 287.

o **La Tana del Brillo Parlante** (Vicolo Ciambellano 4, Massa Marittima; ℭ0566-901-274): Italy's smallest Slow Travel–endorsed dining room is also one of Tuscany's best. Just don't expect haute cuisine and stuffy waitstaff: The strictly local and seasonal menu is

Antipasti, a classic Tuscan appetizer.

Ristorante di Poggio Antico.

prepared with skill, and delivered with rustic informality at a price that will make you glow. See p. 299.

○ **Acquacheta** (Via del Teatro 22, Montepulciano; ✆**0578-717-086**; www. acquacheta.eu): The open flamegrill takes center stage right across southern Tuscany, nowhere more than here at Montepulciano's quintessential cellar steakhouse. Cramped tables, one set of cutlery to last the whole meal, and a chef doing the rounds armed with his meat cleaver are all part of the charm. Order your *bistecca alla fiorentina* by weight, wash it down with house red drunk from a beaker, and soak up the experience. See p. 327.

○ **Ristorante di Poggio Antico** (Loc. i Poggi, Montalcino; ✆**0577-849-200**; www.poggioantico.com): The cheap, old trattoria on this famous wine estate shocked many when it reopened with a new minimalist interior and a talented *nuova cucina* chef spearheading the kitchen. Surrounded by vines that produce some of the silkiest Brunello wines in the region, you can dine on the most refined food in this part of Tuscany, where everything from the breadsticks to the dessert is homemade. See p. 311.

○ **Zaira** (Via Arunte 12, Chiusi; ✆**0578-20-260**; www.zaira.it): Chiusi has several good informal spots, but this one just edges out the others for its *pasta del lucumone*—ziti, ham, and three cheeses baked in a ceramic bowl until a crunchy brown crust forms—and for the moldy ancient wine cellars you can tour after your meal. See p. 333.

○ **Relais Il Falconiere** (Loc. San Martino 370, Cortona; ✆**0575-612-679**; www.ilfalconiere.it): The food and service are impeccable, and the atmosphere sophisticated. Classical music floats across your table; when it's warm and the tables are set on the lawn, crickets take over for Vivaldi. The chefs marry the best fresh ingredients, many cultivated by the owners themselves, with Tuscan recipes to make this one of the most popular restaurants in Tuscany. Follow the foodies who know which turnoff leads to this culinary hideaway. See p. 359.

○ **La Stalla** (Via Eremo delle Carceri 24, Assisi; ✆**075-812-317**; www.fonte maggio.it): This is the quintessential countryside trattoria, the sort of place where scattered Italian families get together for monthly reunions. The low ceilings are black with centuries of wood smoke that has poured from the open fire over which grilled meats sizzle. At the long wooden communal tables (and outdoors in summer), you can wash down a platter of homemade pasta and another of grilled lamb with copious quantities of the house red. See p. 393.

FLORENCE, TUSCANY & UMBRIA IN DEPTH

As the cradle of the Renaissance, Florence has an abundance of significant architecture and artistic masterpieces—as do most of the smaller cities that dot the Tuscan and Umbrian countryside, such as Arezzo, Pisa, Lucca, and Perugia. This profusion of art and architecture is the direct result of historic rivalries between the inhabitants of various medieval cities. The nobility in each of these Tuscan and Umbrian cities spent centuries outdoing each other with shows of artistic wealth; they often competed to see who could procure the most elaborate and grandest artistic masterpieces. Today we are left with vivid reminders of those historic rivalries: an artistic treasure trove in nearly every city and hamlet in the region.

While historically this intercity rivalry boiled over into countless wars, today it persists in other forms: frequent clashes between soccer fans, graffiti sprayed on *palazzo* walls (*"Pisa merda"* is a favorite vulgar phrase of vandals from Livorno), and throughout the tourism sector at every level. Ask a hotel owner in Lucca how long a drive it is to Pistoia, and you'll get the response, "What do you want to go to Pistoia for?"

What would Tuscany and Umbria be today had these rivalries never existed? Brunelleschi might have continued to work as a goldsmith, instead of building his revolutionary dome in Florence's Duomo. Donatello might have eked out an existence as a stonemason and Michelangelo might have chiseled away in anonymity on his father's marble quarries, instead of becoming the legendary artists that produced some of Italy's most extraordinary works of art.

People flock to Tuscany and Umbria from all over the world to view the plethora of art that these rivalries produced, and as a result the region has become a prime tourist destination. These rivalries—and the art they produced—have permanently shaped the regions' identities and economies. Nowhere else in the world will you find as many architects and art historians who are charged with preserving and promoting this heritage.

Italians are acutely aware of their past because it is very much a part of their present. It's difficult not to be curious about history when you confront it every day, whether you're walking on 12th-century paving stones, ambling through ancient ruins, or eating in a restaurant that is housed in a medieval palace.

FLORENCE, TUSCANY & UMBRIA TODAY

Tuscany and Umbria primarily rely on two economic resources: tourism and the land—both of which are inextricably linked. Visitors flock to the region to see the

FACING PAGE: **Michelangelo's** *David.*

The medieval towers of San Gimignano.

priceless art, but also to sample the food and local wines, indulge in the bountiful harvests, and take in the beautiful landscapes.

That's not to say the region lacks an industrial and manufacturing base. Heavy industries (mining, steel, and mechanical engineering) are concentrated along the coastal strip (outside Livorno and Pisa), well away from those pretty hill towns. And behind those gorgeous facades, the economy of Florence is primarily driven by a booming fashion and textile industry. Indeed, with a GDP of around 104€ billion (2009), and a per capita GDP of over 28,000€, Tuscany is one of the richest parts of Italy (and Europe). Its economy is far bigger than nations such as Bulgaria or Croatia, and U.S. states such as Maine, New Mexico, or Kansas.

Yet mass tourism loves Tuscany and always will. Florence is an essential stop on almost every package tour, and the region is by far Italy's most famous—sometimes the only one foreigners know by name. Though the global economic crisis that started in 2008 and continued through press time had an impact on the region, visitor numbers to Florence dropped by less than 2% between 2008 to 2010, and a recovery is well under way. Cities such as Florence and Perugia also continue to attract thousands of overseas students to their language schools and universities, not just from the U.S. and U.K., but also from Japan and China in growing numbers.

Tuscany and Umbria are strongholds of Italy's center-left Democratic Party, forming with Emilia-Romagna and Marche the so-called "Red Quadrilateral" of Italian politics. This tradition of liberal government, combined with strong financial motivations to protect natural resources, has helped fuel a strong environmental movement in Tuscany and Umbria. Italy's most powerful environmentalist organization, **Legambiente** (league for the environment; www.legambiente.it) plays the role of watchdog, protecting the environment from abuse. It also offers outings and projects that are designed to safeguard the environment by teaching the public about the environment and sustainability. With a greater emphasis on sustainability the government has generated tough traffic laws, reinforced strict zoning standards, and built bicycle paths. On Sundays, some Tuscan and Umbrian cities even close their city centers to motorized traffic, leaving the public spaces open for pedestrians and cyclists.

Ironically, tourism can have detrimental effects on the environment and vitality of the cities and regions that vie for it. For example, today Florence's historic core caters almost entirely to tourists, driving locals to move to the suburbs and rent out their historic homes. (The recent boom in San Frediano's Left Bank nightlife and dining scene is in some ways a response to this.) And although the region strives for sustainability, sometimes those well-meaning efforts backfire. For example, when pedestrian-only zones started being erected across Italy's city centers over a decade ago, the plans were met with cheers. Yet today, those pedestrian-only zones have interrupted traffic flow, and have unwittingly exacerbated an already horrible traffic problem, with parking lots taking over central piazza that were once important communal gathering places. Some Umbrian cities have successfully solved this issue. By creating large parking lots underground and in the valleys below the hilltop cities and connecting them to town via elevators, escalators, and cog railways, cities such as Orvieto, Perugia, and Assisi have actually managed to make themselves blessedly traffic-free.

Immigration is a very sensitive and divisive issue in Tuscany and Umbria. There are a lot of non-Italians here: A huge community of Chinese textile laborers lives in Prato and Florence, Albanians and other Eastern Europeans live all around central Italy, and African immigrants are spread throughout the country, as well as thousands of British and North American expats. Thanks primarily to the latter two groups, house prices in many parts of the region remain at record highs.

Tuscany and Umbria were home to Dante Alighieri, the poet credited with bringing a common language to the peninsula; in many ways, this region is the heart of Italian culture. More than a few of the natives worry about what they see as the watering down of a sacred identity. The irony is that Italy depends on laborers coming from other countries, since it is simply not producing enough workers of its own. Without outsiders, the aging workforce would shrivel to a fraction of its size, since few Italian couples are having children in the numbers they once did.

While the region is diverse, there are traces of prejudice and intolerance. Take the case of American student Amanda Knox, convicted of murdering her British roommate. In 2009, Knox was sentenced to 26 years in prison after a long and highly emotive trial. The tabloids went into overdrive as "Foxy Knoxy" became demonized as the symbol of licentious American female behavior, guilty or not. Yet after 4 years in prison, Knox was released on appeal in 2011, her original conviction thrown out.

Though national politics does affect the region, Tuscany and Umbria remain fiercely independent. The former scandal-wracked prime minister of Italy, Silvio Berlusconi, was never especially popular in left-leaning Tuscany and Umbria—indeed British prime ministers spend more time vacationing in the region than most Italian leaders. And though not entirely insulated from the national government's recent growing debt woes, Tuscany looks set to weather any future recessions as well as it has in the past.

LOOKING BACK: FLORENCE, TUSCANY & UMBRIA
The Umbri and the Etruscans
(9th C. B.C.–3rd C. B.C.)

Although Neanderthals, ancient *Homo sapiens,* and Paleolithic and Bronze Age humans left some of their bones and tools lying about, things really didn't start getting lively in central Italy until the **Etruscans** rose to power.

The most widely accepted theory is that the Etruscans came from modern-day Turkey, and arrived in central Italy in the late 9th or early 8th century B.C. The fact that their language isn't Indo-European but appears similar to some Aegean dialects helps confirm this theory, but there are others who now feel the Etruscans may have risen from native peoples in central Italy. Whatever the case, these Etruschi, or Tuschi, formed the basic cultural-political force in the region that's now named for them, Tuscany.

Much of what little remains to tell us of the Etruscans consists of tombs and their contents, and it's difficult to reconstruct an entire culture simply by looking at its graveyards. While we can read their language, what script we have goes into little beyond death, divination, and the divine.

What historians are surer of is that Etruscans became enamored of the Attic culture of Greece and adopted many of the Greek gods and myths in the 6th century B.C. This era coincided with the height of their considerable power. In fact, from the late 7th century until 510 B.C., Rome was ruled by Etruscan kings of the Tarquin dynasty. Although the Etruscan empire spread south almost to Naples, east to the Adriatic, and west onto Corsica, the heart and core called Etruria covered an area from the Arno east to the Apennines and south to the Tiber, encompassing most of Tuscany, half of Umbria, and northern Lazio.

Well before this time, around 1200 B.C., Indo-European Italic peoples had wandered into Italy from the north. The Samnites and Latins continued south, but the **Umbri** tribes decided to settle in the Apennines and valleys east of the Tiber, which flows through the middle of modern-day Umbria. Their loosely defined zone of cultural hegemony encompassed what is now northern and eastern Umbria and the Marches over to the sea, as well as corners of Tuscany and Emilia-Romagna. All we really know about the Umbri is they had a highly developed religion based on reading prophecies in animal sacrifices and the flights of birds—Gubbio's famous **Eugubine Tables** bronze plaques tell us this much. When the Roman influence spread north in the 3rd century B.C., the Umbrian cities for the most part allied themselves to the Latins, were awarded Roman citizenship early, and enjoyed a large degree of autonomy from authorities in Rome. Aside from the usual city rivalries and moderate clashes between expanding empires, the Umbrians appear to have lived more or less amicably with their Etruscan neighbors.

Enter the Romans: The Founding of Florence
(3rd C. B.C.–5th C. A.D.)

In the 3rd century B.C. **Rome** began its expansion, and some of the first neighboring peoples to fall were the Etruscans. Some cities, such as Perugia and Arezzo, allied themselves with Rome and were merely absorbed, while others, including Volterra and Orvieto, were conquered outright. As the Romans gained power over the entire peninsula, the removal of political barriers and the construction of roads allowed trade to develop and flow relatively uninhibited.

Many of the old cities flourished, and the general prosperity led to the founding of new cities throughout the region, especially as retirement camps for Roman soldiers.

During the lull of the later Roman Empire, **Christianity** quickly spread throughout much of central Italy—Lucca even claims to have converted in the 1st century A.D. through the efforts of one of St. Peter's own followers, though Pisa tries to one-up its neighbors by claiming a church first built by St. Peter.

Goths, Lombards & Franks: The Dark Ages (6th C.–9th C.)

As the Roman Empire collapsed in the 5th century A.D., Germanic tribes swept down from the north and wreaked mayhem on central Italian cities as group after group fought their way down to Rome in a sacking free-for-all. The **Goths** swept down in the 6th century A.D., and one of their leaders, **Totila,** conquered Florence in A.D. 552.

Perhaps the strongest force in the Dark Ages was the **Lombards** who established two major duchies in central Italy, one based at Lucca, which governed most of Tuscany, and the other at Spoleto, which took care of most of Umbria. When their ambitions threatened Rome (now a Church stronghold) in the 8th century, the pope invited the Frankish king Pepin the Short to come clear the Lombards out. Under Pepin, and, more important, his son **Charlemagne,** the Lombards were ousted from Tuscany and Umbria.

The Lombard duchy at Lucca was merely replaced by a Frankish margrave, with Tuscany ruled by powerful figures like the **Margrave Matilda.** Charlemagne gave the lands he took from the duchy of Spoleto directly to the pope, but the pontiffs gradually lost control over the region as they busied themselves with other concerns.

With the breakup of Charlemagne's empire in the 9th century, the German Holy Roman Emperors started pressing claims over the Italian peninsula. Central Italy was plunged into political chaos, out of which emerged for the first time the independent city-state republic known as the *commune.*

The Medieval Commune

In the late 11th century, merchants became wealthier and more important to the daily economic life of the small Italian cities. They organized themselves into **guilds** and gradually became the bourgeois oligarchic leaders of the cities. The self-governing *comuni* they established weren't the perfect democracies they've often been made out to

 Looking for Etruscan Remains

If you want to check out some Etruscan remains, head to the following places: **Volterra** (a museum, a city gate, and walls), **Chiusi** (a museum, underground aqueducts to tour, and many tombs in the area), **Sarteano** (a unique frescoed tomb and a museum), **Populonia** (a coastal tomb complex), **Pitigliano and the Alta Maremma** (a tomb complex and network of sunken roads), **Arezzo** (a museum), **Cortona** (a museum and tombs), **Perugia** (a city gate and a well), and **Orvieto** (tombs, museums, underground tunnels to tour, and a well). There are also major Tuscan finds collected at the archaeological museum in **Florence**.

Saints, such as St. Ivo, painted here by Sodoma, were part of everyday medieval life.

be. While many were ruled by popularly elected **councils,** usually only the guild members of the middle class were enfranchised. The majority of city laborers, as well as rural farmers, remained powerless.

As the *comuni* stabilized their infrastructures—after dealing with blows like the 1348 Black Death, a plague that swept through Europe and left well over half of central Italy's population dead—they also set about roughing up their neighbors and traditional rivals. Battles were fought both to increase the city-states' trading power and to acquire more towns under their control (or at least secure subservient allies). To this end, instead of raising militia armies, they hired **condottieri,** professional soldiers of fortune who controlled forces of armed mercenaries.

Many of these trade wars and ancient rivalries were fought between cities that used Europe's big power struggle of the age—the Holy Roman Emperor versus the Pope—as an excuse to attack their traditional antagonists.

Guelphs & Ghibellines: A Medieval Mess

In the 12th century, the German throne of the Holy Roman Emperor sat empty. Otto IV's family, the Welf dynasty of Bavaria, fought for it against the lords of Waiblingen, where the house of Swabia ruled under the Hohenstaufen dynasty. The names were corrupted in Italian to **Guelph** and **Ghibelline,** respectively, and when the Hohenstaufens came out winners with Frederick Barbarossa being crowned emperor, the Ghibellines stuck as the supporters of the emperor while the Guelphs became the party that backed the pope.

In Italy, the old nobility, as Ghibellines, favored the imperial promise of a return to feudalism and hence their own power, while the Guelph merchant-and-banking middle class supported the pope and his free-trade attitudes. Although they all flip-flopped to some degree, Florence (plus Lucca, Arezzo, and Perugia) turned out Guelph, while rivals Pisa, Pistoia, and Siena were Ghibelline.

The Guelph-Ghibelline conflict not only spawned intercity warfare but also sparked intracity strife between rival factions. In the 13th century Florence split into Guelph and Ghibelline parties, under which names the parties waged a decades-long struggle over who'd control the city government.

At the turn of the 14th century, when the Guelphs finally came out victorious, Florence began to enjoy a fairly stable republican rule—still of the old assembly system called now the **Signoria,** a ruling council elected from the major guilds. Florence slowly expanded its power, first allying with Prato, then conquering Pistoia, and by 1406 adding Volterra, Arezzo, and Pisa to the cities under its rule.

Guelph or Ghibelline?

Though it's admittedly not the perfect measure, you can sometimes tell which a city was, at least at any given time, by looking at the battlements of the medieval town hall: The **Guelphs** favored squared-off crenellations and the **Ghibellines** swallowtail ones.

Exceptions to this are Siena's **Palazzo Pubblico,** which was built with blocky battlements during the briefly Guelph period of the Council of Nine, and Florence's **Palazzo Vecchio,** which confusingly sports both kinds.

The Renaissance: Cue the Medici

The **Medici** came from the hills of the Mugello in the early Middle Ages, quite possibly charcoal burners (or perhaps pharmacists) looking for the good life of the city. The family found moderate success and even had a few members elected to public office in the *commune* government.

At the turn of the 15th century, **Giovanni de' Bicci de' Medici** made the family fortune by establishing the Medici as bankers to the papal curia in Rome. His son, Cosimo de' Medici, called **Cosimo il Vecchio,** orchestrated a number of important alliances and treaties for the Florentine Signoria, gaining him prestige and respect. He was a humanist leader who believed in the power of the emerging new art forms of the early Renaissance, and he commissioned works from the greatest painters, sculptors, and architects of the day.

Cosimo grew so attached to the sculptor Donatello that, as Cosimo lay dying, he made sure his son, **Piero the Gouty,** promised to care for the also aging artist and to see that he never lacked for work. Piero's rule was short and relatively undistinguished, quickly superseded by the brilliant career of his son, Lorenzo de' Medici, called **Lorenzo the Magnificent.**

Under the late-15th-century rule of Lorenzo, Florence entered its golden era, during which time it became Europe's cultural and artistic focal point. It was Lorenzo who encouraged the young Michelangelo to sculpt (enrolling him in his own school), and he and Medici cousins commissioned paintings from Botticelli and poetry from Poliziano.

Although Lorenzo fought to maintain the precious balance of power

Palazzo Pitti, former home of the Medicis.

23

between Italian city-states, in doing so he incurred the wrath of the pope and the Pazzi family, Florentine rivals of the Medici. The young Medici leader's troubles came to a head in the infamous 1478 **Pazzi Conspiracy,** in which Lorenzo and his brother were attacked during High Mass. The coup failed, and the Pazzi were expelled from the city. But Lorenzo's son and successor, **Piero de' Medici,** was also forced to flee the invading armies of Charles VIII in 1494 (although Charles quickly withdrew from the Italian field).

Into the power vacuum stepped puritanical preacher **Girolamo Savonarola.** This theocrat's apocalyptic visions and book-burning (the original Bonfire of the Vanities) held the public's fancy for about 4 years, until the pope excommunicated the entire city for following him, and the Florentines put the torch to Savonarola as a heretic.

In 1512, however, papal armies set another of Lorenzo's sons, the boring young **Giuliano de' Medici,** duke of Nemours, on the vacant Medici throne. Giuliano, and later **Lorenzo de' Medici** (Lorenzo the Magnificent's grandson via the ousted Piero) were merely mouthpieces for the real brains of the family, Giuliano's brother, **Cardinal Giovanni de' Medici,** who in 1513 became **Pope Leo X** and uttered the immortal words, "God has given us the papacy, now let us enjoy it."

Pope Leo's successor as leader of the Medici was his natural cousin, **Giulio de' Medici,** illegitimate son of Lorenzo's brother Giuliano. Although blackguards such as Ippolito and **Alessandro de' Medici** held sway in Florence, they really took their orders from Giulio, who from 1523 to 1534 continued to run the family from Rome as **Pope Clement VII.**

Charles V's imperial armies sacked Rome in 1527, sending Clement VII scurrying to Orvieto for safety and giving the Florentines the excuse to boot Alessandro from town and set up a republican government. In 1530, however, the pope and Charles reconciled and sent a combined army to Florence, and eventually Alessandro was reinstated. This time he had an official title: **Duke of Florence.**

After decadently amusing himself as a tyrant in Florence for 7 years, Alessandro was murdered in bed by his distant cousin Lorenzaccio de' Medici, who plunged a dagger into the duke's belly and fled to Venice (where he was later assassinated).

The man chosen to take Alessandro's place was a Medici of a different branch, young **Cosimo de' Medici.** Contrary to his immediate Medici predecessors, Cosimo I actually devoted himself to attending to matters of state. He built up a navy, created a seaport for Florence called **Livorno,** and even conquered age-old rival Siena after a brutal war from 1555 to 1557. His greatest personal moment came in 1569 when the pope declared him **Cosimo I, Grand Duke of Tuscany.** Except for the tiny Republic of Lucca, which happily trundled along independently until Napoleon gave it to his sister in 1806, the history of Tuscany was now firmly intertwined with that of Florence.

The Risorgimento: Italy Becomes a Country (Late 19th C.)

In 1860 Florence and Tuscany became part of the newly declared Italian state. From 1865 to 1870, Florence was the capital of Italy, and it enjoyed a frenzied building boom—the medieval walls were torn down and the Jewish ghetto demolished and replaced with the cafe-lined Piazza della Repubblica.

The army that was conquering recalcitrant states on the peninsula for **Vittorio Emanuele II,** first king of Italy, was commanded by **Gen. Giuseppe**

Garibaldi, who spent much of the end of the war slowly subjugating the papal states—the pope was the last holdout against the new regime. This meant defeating the papal authorities in Umbria, whose armies, however, quickly retreated, leaving cities like Perugia to cheer on Garibaldi's troops as they freed the region from hundreds of years of papal oppression.

Fascism: Getting Roped into World War II

The demagogue **Benito Mussolini** came to power after World War I and did much to improve Italy's infrastructure—at least on the surface—and in the process won the respect of many Italians. Then Mussolini got caught up with Hitler's World War II egomania, believing that Italy should have a second empire as great as the ancient Roman one.

Although the Tuscans certainly had their share of collaborators and die-hard Fascists, many Italians never bought into the war or the Axis alliance. The partisan movement was always strong, with resistance fighters holed up, especially in the hills south of Siena. Tuscany became a battlefield as the occupying Nazi troops slowly withdrew across the landscape in the face of American and Allied advancement—but not without committing appalling massacres along the way. In 2011, three former Nazi soldiers were found guilty in absentia of the murder of 184 civilians, in August 1944, in Padule di Fucecchio.

Postwar Tuscany & Umbria

Florence was hit with disaster when a massive **flooding of the Arno** in November 1966 covered much of the city with up to 6m (20 ft.) of sludge and water, destroying or severely damaging countless thousands of works of art and literature (8,000 paintings in the Uffizi basement alone, and 1.5 million volumes in the National Library). Along with an army of experts and trained restorers, hundreds of volunteers nicknamed "Mud Angels" descended on the city, many of them foreign students, to pitch in and help dig out all the mud and salvage what they could of one of the greatest artistic heritages of any city on earth.

The political fortunes of Tuscany and Umbria have in the past 60 years mainly followed those of Italy at large, although the region remains at the heart of Italy's left-leaning "Red Quadrilateral" (p. 18). In 2008, media magnate (and the world's 29th richest man) **Silvio Berlusconi** regained control of the Italian government as part of a center-right coalition, though over 50% of Tuscans voted for Democratic Party candidate Walter Veltroni, and only 33.6% supported Berlusconi (Umbrians voted similarly). After a series of scandals and a growing debt crisis, Berlusconi was forced to resign in 2011, to be replaced by **Mario Monti,** an academic and Independent senator.

FLORENCE, TUSCANY & UMBRIA'S ART & ARCHITECTURE

From Classical to Romanesque: The 8th Century B.C. to the 12th Century A.D.

ANCIENT ART The **Etruscans** were prodigious town builders. In architecture, they used the load-bearing arch, raised rectangular temples approached by steps, and built houses with open atrium courtyards surrounded by colonnaded porticos on the inner face.

Although precious little Etruscan painting survives, the Etruscans were masters of this art form. They painted—in fresco, to boot—scenes rich in the pleasures of everyday life, especially banqueting. What we have most of is their sculpture, which went through an idiosyncratic archaic period (with some Oriental influences), through an Attic period influenced by the art of ancient Greece, and was finally subsumed under the Hellenistic Roman style. They cranked out thousands of votive bronzes—small representations of warriors, washerwomen, and farmers plowing—occasionally producing works of singular expressive beauty, such as Volterra's famed *Shadow of the Evening.*

The Etruscans' most famous forms of sculpture are their **funerary urns,** each of which was capped with a lid carved into a likeness of the deceased, half-reclining as if at an eternal banquet. Most of these have intense expressions and enigmatic smiles that have made them a popular modern image to represent Etruria in general. As Greek culture began to seep in during the 6th century B.C., the cinerary urns under these lids were increasingly carved with reliefs depicting scenes from Greek mythology, often having to do with the movement to the underworld (riding in carts, boats, chariots, and the like).

As **Rome** gained ascendancy in the 3rd century B.C., its conservative and static style of carving, architecture, and painting supplanted the more naturalized and dynamic nature of the Etruscan arts. The Romans have left us many of their Hellenistic bronze and marble statues, innumerable fragments of decorative friezes and other reliefs, and several theaters and baths in varying stages of decay (at Fiesole, Volterra, Gubbio, and Spoleto).

PALEO-CHRISTIAN ART The 4th to 11th centuries are characterized by what's often referred to as the **paleo-Christian** style. This period was marked by very simple structures; the few that survive—including churches in Spoleto,

Sant'Antimo, an elegant example of paleo-Christian architecture.

Pienza, and Perugia, and the later and much more unified Sant'Antimo—strike most moderns as hauntingly beautiful and elegant, if architecturally inharmonious. In the north of Tuscany, the architecture quickly developed into the style known as Romanesque (see below).

BYZANTINE PAINTING The political influence of the Byzantine Empire, based in Constantinople, was confined to Italy's northeastern Adriatic coast. But the artistic influence of Byzantium's stylized iconographic tradition in mosaics and panel paintings spread throughout Italy, starting from the Adriatic city of Ravenna in the 5th century.

Byzantine painting is characterized in individual works by gold-leaf backgrounds, stylized gold crosshatching in the blue and red robes of the Madonna, oval faces with large almond eyes and spoonlike depressions at the tops of sloping noses, a flattened look (due to an almost complete lack of perspective or foreshortening), and, above all, conservatism.

Byzantine art had an Oriental decorativeness and severely static rule ensuring the reproduction of icons that wavered little from past models. It kept Italian painting moribund for over 800 years. Painting didn't break out of the conservative funk until the late 13th century.

ROMANESQUE ARCHITECTURE When Pisa became a major medieval power, it did so as a huge shipping empire, and with this trade came contact with Eastern and Islamic cultures. Pisa poured its 11th-century prosperity into building a new religious core and cathedral, adapting many of the decorative elements from these Eastern contacts. The style that was developed in Buscheto's Duomo and the associated baptistery and bell tower (yes, the one that leans) came to define the Romanesque and quickly spread across northern Tuscany.

The purest, earliest form that arose in Pisa and Lucca—known, sensibly, as the **Pisan-Luccan Romanesque**—was characterized most strikingly by horizontal stripes of marbles on the facades and eventually in some interiors as well (at first they used green and white; later, in Siena, it became black and white; and in Umbria the available local stone made it pink and white). The other key elements were curving semicircular arches; blind arcades of these arches often set with diamond-shaped decorative inlays (or coffered depressions) called lozenges; open galleries supported by thin mismatched columns and often stacked three or four rows high on facades; lots of tiny detail in marble inlay; and often a nave flanked by two colonnaded aisles inside.

The later form of the movement that was adapted in Florence (the Baptistery, San Miniato al Monte, and Badia Fiesolana) and Pistoia (San Giovanni Fuoricivitas and, though later altered, the Duomo) was called the **Florentine Romanesque.** On the surface it was very similar to the Pisan-Lucchese school, but it was practiced along much stricter lines of a geometry gleaned from classical architecture, a predecessor to the mathematically proportional architecture of the Renaissance. Before that could come to pass, however, in the late 12th century a strong northern styling came into vogue called, after its supposed association with the emperors (whether German or Frankish), the Gothic.

Tuscan Gothic: The 13th & 14th Centuries

The **Gothic** first started infiltrating Italy as architecture. It was originally imported by French Cistercian monks, who in 1218 created the huge San Galgano abbey church, now roofless (and terribly romantic). Although this French style of the Gothic never caught on, the church was still at the time revolutionary in introducing some of the new forms, which were adopted when **Giovanni Pisano** overhauled Siena's cathedral and "Gothicized" it.

Thin-columned windows, along with lacelike stone tracery that the Gothic style used to fill up arch points and the crenellations it strewed across the tops of buildings, caught the Tuscan fancy and were incorporated into many palaces, especially in Siena, where the architectural forms otherwise pretty much stayed the same old solid, reliable medieval masonry. Out of this marriage were born the civic palaces of Siena and, more influential, Volterra, which served as the model for Florence's own famous Palazzo Vecchio (and similar buildings across the region).

The Palazzo Vecchio's architect was **Arnolfo di Cambio,** the Gothic master of Florence's 1290s building boom. Arnolfo was also responsible for the Franciscan church of Santa Croce and the original plans for the Duomo. The kind of Frankish Gothic building most people associate with the term "Gothic," with lots of spires and stony frills, really showed up only in the tiny carved stone jewel of Santa Maria della Spina along the banks of the Arno in Pisa. **Andrea Orcagna,** who was also a painter, gave us another bit of this sort of Gothic in miniature with his elaborate marble-inlaid tabernacle in Florence's Orsanmichele (the church is also a Gothic structure itself, but an odd one).

The Gothic style was perhaps at its most advanced in sculpture. **Nicola Pisano** probably emigrated from southern Apulia to work in Pisa, where he crowned that city's great Romanesque building project with a Gothic finale in 1260. He created for the baptistery a great pulpit, the panels of which were carved in high relief with a new kind of figurative emotion displayed in the sway of the figures and a degree of activeness in their positioning and apparent movement. By the time Nicola carved the panels on his second pulpit in Siena, along with his son **Giovanni Pisano,** the figures were moving into a radically new sort

The richly embellished facade of Siena's cathedral.

of interaction, with a multitude of squirming bodies and pronounced stylized curves to add a graceful rhythm and emotion to the characters. Giovanni went on to carve two more pulpits (in Pistoia, perhaps the apogee of the genre, and back to Pisa for the Duomo) and numerous individual large statues for niches on the facade of Siena's Duomo, on which he was working as an architect, furthering his father's innovations in descriptive storytelling. **Andrea Pisano** (no relation) picked up the thread in Florence when in 1330 he cast the first set of bronze baptistery doors in the now-established Gothic style.

Byzantine tradition kept its hold over painting for quite a while, and the Gothic didn't catch on in this medium until the end of the 13th century. When it did, humanist philosophy was also starting to catch on. Humanism was reviving academic interest in the classical world and its philosophy and architecture, and it was encouraging a closer examination and contemplation of the natural world and everyday life—as opposed to the medieval habit of chaining all intellectual pursuits to theology and religious pondering.

True, in the 1280s Florentine master painter **Cimabue** was beginning to infuse his religious art with more human pathos than Byzantine custom had ever seen, and his Sienese compatriot (some say student) **Duccio** was beginning to adapt a narrative naturalism to his decorative Byzantine style (see "The Sienese School," below). When the Gothic style finally entered the realm of painting, its avatar was Giotto.

THE TRECENTO: SEEDS OF RENAISSANCE PAINTING In the 1290s, **Giotto di Bondone**—best known as a frescoist who left us masterpiece cycles in Assisi's Basilica di San Francesco (possibly) and Florence's Santa Croce and Padua's Cappella Scrovegni (certainly)—completely broke away from the styling of his teacher, Cimabue, and invented his own method of painting, steeped in the ideas of humanism and grounded in an earthy realism. What he did was to give his characters real human faces displaying fundamental emotions; to use light and shadow to mold his figures, giving them bulk under their robes; to employ foreshortened architecture not only to provide a stage-set backdrop but also, and this was key, to give the paintings depth and real space (he let you see through painted windows to heighten the illusion); and to use simple but strong lines of composition and imbue the figures with movement to create dynamic scenes.

The Giottesque school that grew out of his workshop, and later his fame, kept some of the naturalistic elements and realistic foreshortened backdrops, but Giotto's innovations, and especially his spirit, seemed to stagnate at first. Most trecento works remained fundamentally Gothic, especially as practiced by Giotto's pupil and faithful adherent **Taddeo Gaddi,** his son **Agnolo Gaddi,** and **Andrea Orcagna.**

THE SIENESE SCHOOL Siena adapted some of the humanist elements of realism and naturalism into its Gothic painting but left by the wayside the philosophical hang-ups and quest for perfect perspective the Florentine Renaissance soon embarked on. The Sienese school ended up with a distinctive, highly decorative art form rich in colors, patterns, and gold leaf. It was often as expressive as Giotto's work, but this was achieved more through the sinuous lines of its figures and compositional interplay.

Painters like **Duccio di Buoninsegna** and **Sano di Pietro** gave the Sienese school a focus in the late 1200s, starting to adapt Gothic elements but still working in a Byzantine tradition, and **Jacopo della Quercia** became a towering figure in Sienese Gothic sculpture. One of the first great painters to come out of Duccio's workshop was **Simone Martini,** who developed a much more refined style of the Gothic flavor with his elegant lines, ethereal figures, and richly patterned fabrics. Two more of Duccio's students were **Ambrogio** and **Pietro Lorenzetti,** both masters of color and composition who infused their art with the naturalness of common life. The former left the most important cycle of civic (that is, nonreligious) art ever painted, inside Siena's Palazzo Pubblico.

The Black Death of 1348 nipped the emergent Sienese school of painting in the bud. The Lorenzetti brothers perished, and the handful of citizens who lived through the plague were more intent on simple survival than on commissioning artworks, leaving Florence's version of the Renaissance to develop and eventually reign supreme. Mannerist painter Domenico Beccafumi (see below) was perhaps the only great Sienese artist of later generations.

The Early Renaissance: The 15th Century

Tradition holds that the Renaissance began in 1401 when **Lorenzo Ghiberti** won a competition to cast Florence's new set of baptistery doors. Although confined to Gothic frames, Ghiberti still managed to infuse his figures with an entirely new kind of fluid dynamism and emotional naturalism that earned him accolades when the doors were finished more than 20 years later. (He was immediately commissioned to do another set, which became known as the "Gates of Paradise," one of the cornerstone pieces of the early Renaissance.)

One of the men Ghiberti competed against for the first commission was **Filippo Brunelleschi,** who decided to study architecture after he lost the sculpture competition. When he came back from a learning trip to Rome, where he examined the classical construction of the ancients, he was full of groundbreaking ideas. These led to his ingenious red-tiled dome over Florence's Duomo as well as to a new kind of architecture based on the classical orders and mathematical

Ghiberti's Baptistery doors.

Brunelleschi's dome and Giotto's campanile are standout features of the Florence skyline.

proportions with which he filled Florentine church interiors—all done in smooth white plaster and soft gray stone.

One of his buddies was a sculptor named **Donatello,** who traveled with him to Rome and who on his return cast the first free-standing nude since antiquity (a *David,* now in Florence's Bargello) in an anatomically exacting style of naturalness. Donatello also developed the *schiacciato* technique of carving in very low relief, using the mathematical perspective trick his architect friend Brunelleschi taught him to achieve the illusion of great depth in shallow marble.

Brunelleschi also passed this concept of perspective along to a young painter named **Masaccio,** who was working with Gothic artist Masolino. Masaccio added it to his experimental bag of tricks, which included using a harsh light to model his figures in light and shadow, bold brushstrokes and foreshortened limbs to imply movement and depth, and an unrelenting realism. He used all of these to create the unprecedented frescoes in Florence's Cappella Brancacci. Part of his secret for creating figures of realistic bulk and volume he learned from studying the sculptures of Donatello and of another friend, **Luca della Robbia,** who besides working on marble and bronze developed a new way to fuse colored enamel to terra cotta and went on to found a popular workshop in the medium that he handed down first to his nephew Andrea, and then his son Giovanni. Masaccio got the precision perspective down to a science when painting Santa Maria Novella's *Trinità* (1428), thereby inaugurating the full-blown Renaissance in painting. He died at age 27—which perhaps explains why he isn't much more famous.

Where Masaccio tried to achieve a new level of clarity and illusionistic reality with his perspective, **Paolo Uccello** became obsessed about experimenting with it, working out the math of perfect perspective and spatial geometry in some paintings and then warping it in others to see how far he could push the tenets for narrative and symbolic ends rather than making his work only representative (at its best in the *Noah* fresco in Santa Maria Novella's Green Cloister).

Though at first it was secondary to the Florentine school, color continued to be of some importance. This is best exemplified by the still somewhat Gothic **Domenico Veneziano** (Venetian artists always were and would remain supreme colorists), who is most important for teaching **Piero della Francesca,** a Sansepolcro artist whose quiet, dramatic style and exploration of the geometry of perspective created crystalline-clear, spacious, haunting paintings with an unfathomable psychology in his figures' expressions.

Lorenzo Monaco imparted what he knew of the Gothic to **Fra' Angelico,** who continued to paint beautiful religious works in the bright colors and intimate detail of a miniaturist or illuminator of Bibles. Although his art is often seen as the pinnacle of the style known as International Gothic, Angelico's tiny racks of saints are fully Renaissance if you look closely enough; they're well modeled and lifelike, set in a plane of perspective with a strong single light source.

Fra' Filippo Lippi started a long trend toward tall, thin Madonnas and mischievous angels. His sure lines, realistic depictions, and suffused color palette made him popular and brought into his *bottega* (workshop) apprentices like **Sandro Botticelli,** who would continue to paint exceedingly graceful scenes and flowing drapery that helped make his compositions some of the most fluid of the Renaissance. The son of Botticelli's teacher became Botticelli's own pupil, and **Filippino Lippi** carried on the workshop's tradition. But Filippino also seemed to add back some of the earthiness seen in the works being turned out by the high-production workshop of **Domenico Ghirlandaio.** Ghirlandaio stayed popular by producing scenes of architectural unity and firmness, figurative grace, and complex coloring—and by adding in plenty of portraits of the commissioner's family members. In 1488, one of the apprentices in his workshop was a young Michelangelo Buonarroti.

That year also saw the death of one of the more innovative sculptor/painters, **Andrea del Verrocchio,** whose quest for hyperrealism and detailing in his carefully created bronzes and marbles and his few surviving exactingly painted panels were to greatly influence a young pupil of his studio, **Leonardo da Vinci.**

The High Renaissance: The Late 15th to Mid-16th Century

One of Piero della Francesca's students was **Luca Signorelli,** a Cortonan whose mastery of the male nude in such works as his Cappella San Brizio in Orvieto had a great effect on the painting of Michelangelo. His highly modeled figures of colorful and incisive geometry shared many similarities with the works of the nearby Umbrian school being developed by another of Piero's protégés, **Perugino,** who also studied alongside Leonardo da Vinci in Verrocchio's *bottega* and whose ethereal blues and greens, beautiful landscapes, and limpid lighting would be further refined by his student **Pinturicchio.**

Back in Florence, **Leonardo da Vinci** was developing a highly realistic style in the 1480s. His patented sfumato technique revolutionized perspective by softly blurring the lines of figures and creating different planes of distance basically by throwing far-off objects out of focus. Leonardo also studied anatomy with a frightening intensity, drawing exacting models of human and animal bodies in various degrees of dissection just to find out exactly how to paint joints bending and muscles rippling in a realistic manner. He sketched swirls of water flowing and horses rearing, always trying to catch the essential inner motion of the world. In his spare time, he designed scientific inventions (usually on paper) such as parachutes, machine guns, water screws, and a few helicopters.

Michelangelo Buonarroti left Ghirlandaio's fresco studio to study sculpture under the tutelage of Donatello's protégé, **Bertoldo,** and by age 23, following his first success in Rome with the *Pietà* in St. Peter's, had established himself as the foremost sculptor of his age with the gargantuan *David.* He's considered by many to be the first artist ever to surpass the ancients in terms of creating muscu-

The Best of Michelangelo

Il Gigante, better known as *David,* was the summation of Michelangelo's greatest obsession: the perfect nude male body.

lar bodies that (besides being naturally accurate) were proportioned for the greatest symbolic impact of grace and power. Michelangelo also revolutionized painting with his frescoes on the ceiling of Rome's Sistine Chapel (also evident in Florence's *Doni Tondo*), where his twisting, muscularly modeled figures, limpid light, bold brush strokes, and revolutionary color palette of oranges, turquoises, yellows, and greens flabbergasted an entire generation of artists and established him as one of the greatest painters of his age. Before his death at the ripe old age of 89 in 1564, he went on to design innovative architecture (the Laurentian Library in Florence and St. Peter's Dome in Rome) and write some pretty good Renaissance sonnets, too.

Perugino's star pupil, **Raphael,** melded the clarity and grace he learned from the Umbrian school with the sfumato of Leonardo and the sweeping earthy realism of Michelangelo's Sistine Chapel paintings. He created paintings that carried the picture-perfect grace and penetrating emotion to new heights, but his career was cut short with an early death in 1520 at age 37.

THE MANNERIST EXPERIMENT Eventually the High Renaissance began to feed off itself, producing vapid works of technical perfection but little substance, perhaps best exemplified by the painting of **Giorgio Vasari.** As Florentine art stagnated, several artists sought ways out of the downward spiral.

Mannerism was the most interesting attempt, a movement within the High Renaissance that found its muse in the extreme torsion of Michelangelo's figures—in sculpture and painting—and his unusual use of oranges, greens, and other nontraditional colors, most especially in the Sistine Chapel ceiling. Other artists took these ideas and ran them to their logical limits, with such painters as **Andrea del Sarto, Rosso Fiorentino, Pontormo,** Sienese **Domenico Beccafumi,** and **il Parmigianino** elongating their figures, twisting the bodies in muscularly improbable ways— waifish women with grotesquely long necks and pointy heads ran rampant—and mixing increasingly garish color palettes.

The sculptors fared perhaps better with the idea, producing for the first time statues that needed to be looked at from multiple angles to be fully appreciated, such as **Giambologna**'s *Rape of the Sabines* under Florence's Loggia dei Lanzi and the *Monument of the Four Moors* at Livorno's harbor by his student, **Pietro Tacca.**

Giambologna's *Rape of the Sabines.*

The Baroque: The Mid-16th to 18th Centuries

The experiments of the Mannerists soon gave way to the excesses of the baroque. Architecturally, the baroque era rehashed and reinterpreted yet again the neoclassical forms of the Renaissance, introducing ellipses and more radically complicated geometric lines, curves, and mathematics to replace the right angles and simple arches of traditional buildings. **Bernardo Buontalenti** was the main Tuscan architect of note in the period, and he worked extensively for the Medici, building them villas and sumptuous fanciful gardens. His more accessible works in Florence include the Tribune in the Uffizi, the facade of Santa Trinita, grottoes in the Giardino Boboli, and the Medici Forte di Belvedere. His greatest single achievement, however, was the city of Livorno, a beautiful bit of city planning he performed for the Medici in 1576.

The baroque artists achieved some success in the field of church facades and altar frames. At their most restrained, they produced facades like those on Florence's Ognissanti and half a dozen churches in Siena, interiors like that of Florence's Santa Maria Maddalena dei Pazzi, and successful chapel ensembles in the cathedrals of Volterra and Siena (the latter one of master **Gian Lorenzo Bernini**'s few works in Tuscany). But mainly they acted more like interior decorators with extremely bad taste—in the era of the Medici grand dukes and other over-rich princelings, the more different types of expensive marbles you could piece together to decorate a chapel, the better. The Medici Cappella dei Principi (Chapel of the Princes) in Florence is the perfect nauseating example.

Rococo was the baroque gone awry, a world of dripping stuccoes and cotton-candy love scenes on canvas, of which you can be thankful very little has survived in Tuscany or Umbria.

From the Neoclassical to the Present

Italy didn't have a major hand in developing many new styles after the baroque, although 19th-century works by Italy's master **neoclassical** sculptor Canova are scattered around Tuscany and Umbria, and Tuscany had one great neoclassical sculptor, **Giovanni Duprè,** born in Siena in 1817.

Tuscany had a brief moment in a very localized limelight again from the 1860s to around 1900 when the **Macchiaioli,** a group of artists in Florence and Livorno, junked the old styles and concentrated on exploring the structure of light and color in painting, concerned with the effect of the individual *macchie,* or marks of paint on the canvas. In effect, it was kind of a Tuscan Impressionism.

Some 20th-century Tuscan talents are Livorno's **Modigliani,** who garnered fame in France for his innovative oblong portraits; the futurist **Gino Severini** from Cortona; and **Marino Marini,** a Pistoian sculptor known for his stylized bronze horses. In architecture, Tuscany had the privilege of hosting the only major new movement in Italy, its own variant on Art Deco called the **Liberty Style.**

As the focus of Western painting and sculpture migrated to countries like France and the United States in the 20th century, Italy turned its artistic energies mainly to the cinema, fashion (Armani, Gucci, Versace, Pucci, and the like)—an industry in which Florence shines—and the manufacture of sleek, fun, and often mind-bogglingly useful industrial design objects like Alessi teakettles, Pavoni coffee machines, Olivetti typewriters, the Vespa (created and manufactured at Pontedera, outside Pisa), and Ferraris.

FLORENCE, TUSCANY & UMBRIA IN POPULAR CULTURE
Literature

NONFICTION Aside from the more scholarly texts, the cornerstone of any traveler's education on this part of the world is Mary McCarthy's *Stones of Florence*. It is less of a political treatise along the lines of Paul Ginsborg's seminal work, *A History of Contemporary Italy: Society and Politics, 1943-1988,* and more along the lines of Luigi Barzini's brilliant social commentary, *The Italians,* but with a focus on Tuscany alone. When you have finished with McCarthy's book, you should at least leaf through the other two. Ginsborg's work is extremely readable, comical at times, and is probably the most oft-quoted history of modern Italy in the English-speaking world. Few other countries have suffered or enjoyed the same foreign examination of their national character and culture, from the works of Shelley, Keats, and D. H. Lawrence, to more pop-culture musings, a la Frances Mayes. If you haven't done so already, you could familiarize yourself with Mayes' *Under the Tuscan Sun* if only to comprehend the admiration of those who come to Cortona to re-live her bucolic lifestyle, or to understand the disbelief of locals who marvel that the seemingly mundane effort of hiring a plumber can be so fascinating. (The only book with a bigger payout for Tuscany has been Dan Brown's *Da Vinci Code,* which spawned a cottage industry of mini-museums dedicated to the Leonardo local lore.) The U.K.-born novelist Tim Parks is a little more seasoned in his assessment, and his range of nonfiction topics now extends south of the Po River with *Medici Money.* It is a fascinating tale about the rise of the family's wealth through pioneer banking methods, their struggle with religious norms, and the way they cleverly amassed power by generating loyalty.

To fill out the historical picture in a couple of less-known Tuscan periods, get hold of Iris Origo's *War in Val d'Orcia: 1943–44,* a peerless World War II memoir, and Francis Stonor Saunders' *Hawkwood: Diabolical Englishman.* The latter is more than just the biography of the English mercenary who won himself a frescoed portrait on Florence's Duomo; it's the most comprehensive account of medieval life in pre-Renaissance Tuscany.

FICTION You will miss most of the references and inside jokes in Florence if you haven't brushed up on Dante. Butchers quote him at will, the names of the people and places in the *Divine Comedy* are everywhere from paintings to dessert menus, and, aside from all this, this is the literature that gave a diverse country a language. After the days of Dante, Petrarch, and Boccaccio and beyond the Aretine artist and writer Giorgio Vasari in the 16th century, you need to dig pretty deep to find any Tuscan literary giants. One exception might be Carlo Collodi, who gave the world a brilliant tale of a wooden boy with a very long nose. The other name you might recognize when traveling there is that of Nobel Prize–winning poet Giosuè Carducci, for whom the town Castagneto Carducci, near Bolgheri, is named. Of more recent vintage, crime writer Michele Giutarri's *A Florentine Death* and *Death in Tuscany* take a more sinister look at central Italy.

Film

When asked to think of famous Tuscan filmmakers, two come to mind: Franco Zeffirelli and the inimitable Roberto Benigni. Zeffirelli profiles his native Florence in *Tea with Mussolini* (1999). It is a story of a group of expat British women during the Fascist era, who take their tea every afternoon at the Uffizi until they are driven off to San Gimignano. For his part, Benigni will be remembered mostly for *Life Is Beautiful* (1998), a tale of a Tuscan family during the Holocaust. The first half is set in Arezzo, and visitors to the city today can pick out the window on Piazza Grande where the character played by Benigni famously shouts up to Maria for the key. Two other of his pictures are unmistakably Tuscan: *Pinocchio* (2002), based of course on the mythical marionette born in the town of Collodi (p. 250), and *Il Mostro* (1994), a hysterical story of mistaken identity, and a near-parody on the real-life saga of the so-called Monster of Florence. That is the Tuscany of popular Italian film, at least. Countless foreign films use the central Italian countryside as a backdrop, including *Hannibal* (2001), the sequel to the classic horror film *Silence of the Lambs,* and most notably, a film version of Frances Mayes' book *Under the Tuscan Sun* (2003), shot mainly around Cortona and Lake Trasimeno in Umbria. The most famous Florentine backdrop is probably the 1985 classic *A Room with a View,* based on the E. M. Forster novel. The views of the Arno come from the window of room no. 414 in the Hotel degli Orafi.

Tuscan & Umbrian Music

Florence and Tuscany contributed greatly to the transformation and progress of music in Europe, starting in the 11th century with **Guido d'Arezzo,** widely regarded as the man who gave the world the musical staff. As a Benedictine monk, he was exposed to his share of Gregorian chants, and devised a way for other monks to learn them quickly; thus it is Guido whom the world can thank for first teaching aspiring musicians their *do re mis.* Four centuries later, Tuscany produced another pioneer in musical theory, a Pisan named **Vincenzo Galilei.** While his son Galileo garnered wider fame for his outlandish theories, Vincenzo advanced some heretical notions himself, notably his tolerance of dissonance throughout his pieces and his advancing of the recitative in opera, a simple delivery of the verses nearer to ordinary speech. These and other late Renaissance movements were fostered in a circle of artists and philosophers in Count Giovanni de' Bardi's court, known as the **Florentine Camerata.** Galilei concerned himself principally with madrigals, a form of singing not in Latin, but in the vernacular, which came into vogue soon after Dante started writing in the local tongue.

A statue of Puccini in Lucca.

Over the years, northern Italian cities such as Cremona, Parma, and Venice punched above their weight in producing highly touted composers, but in 1858 Tuscany put out one of the best of all time: **Giacomo Puccini.** Born in Lucca, Puccini studied in Milan but returned to a villa in northwestern Tuscany to produce his seminal works: *La Bohème, Tosca, Madama Butterfly,* and his final composition, *Turandot.* How many sopranos have pleaded their case in his aria *O mio babbino caro* (Oh my dear papa) from his opera *Gianni Schicchi?* How many tenors have brought audiences to tears with *Nessun dorma* (None shall sleep), an aria from his opera *Turandot?* (Among them is **Andrea Bocelli,** the world-renowned Italian tenor who is from Pisa, a short carriage ride away from Puccini's hometown.) The maestro's operas can be heard nightly in Lucca, at a concert series known as **Puccini e la sua Lucca,** one of a myriad of festivals here dedicated to Italian music (p. 263). Nearly every city in Tuscany and Umbria has its own international music festival, most notably the Spoleto Festival (see "Festival dei Due Mondi" on p. 407), Estate Fiesolana (p. 169), and Umbria Jazz (p. 367).

EATING & DRINKING IN FLORENCE, TUSCANY & UMBRIA
What to Eat

The genius of **Tuscan and Umbrian cooking** is in its simplicity. Fancy sauces aren't needed to hide the food because Tuscans use pure, strong flavors and the freshest of ingredients. The great dishes are in fact very basic: homemade ribbons of egg pasta in hare sauce, game or free-range domestic animal meats grilled over wood coals, and beans simmered in earthenware pots.

The most prominent cooking additives are **wine** and **olive oil.** Tuscan and Umbrian oil is some of the finest in the world—especially oil produced around Lucca, close to the hill village of Castagneto Carducci, and around the Umbrian

Cheese for sale in Pienza.

Vale of Spoleto—and comes in several gradients depending on the level of acidity. The more the olives are bruised before being pressed, the higher the acidity will be, which is why most olive picking is still done by delicate hands and not brutish machines. We don't know why they bother classifying some oils as *vergine, fino vergine,* or *soprafino vergine,* because no self-respecting Italian would use anything but *extra vergine* (extra virgin), some of which is rated DOC and DOCG, just like wine (see below). Olives are harvested and pressed in October, and the oil is best fresh.

Another popular, and expensive, Tuscan and Umbrian garnish is the *tartufo,* or **truffle.** It's a fungal tuber (read: mushroom) that grows inexplicably around the roots of certain trees in certain soils under certain conditions that have for centuries baffled a food industry desperate to farm these lucrative little buggers.

MORE ITALIAN menu terms

Agnello Lamb.

Aragosta Lobster.

Baccalà Salt-cured cod, usually reconstituted and stewed.

Braciola Loin pork chop.

Branzino Sea bass.

Bresaola Air-dried, thinly sliced beef filet, dressed with olive oil, lemon, and pepper—usually an appetizer.

Cacciucco Seafood stew of Livorno in a spicy tomato base poured over stale bread.

Cacio or Caciotto Southern Tuscan name for pecorino cheese.

Calamari Squid.

Caprese A salad of sliced mozzarella and tomatoes lightly dressed with olive oil, salt, and pepper.

Capretto Kid.

Carciofi Artichokes.

Carpaccio Thin slices of raw cured beef, pounded flat and often served topped with arugula and parmigiano shavings.

Casalinga Home cooking.

Cozze Mussels.

Faraona Guinea hen.

Fegato Liver.

Formaggio Cheese.

Frittata Thick omelet stuffed with meats, cheese, and vegetables; often eaten between slices of bread as a sandwich.

Frutte di mare A selection of shellfish, often boosted with a couple of shrimp and some squid.

Funghi Mushrooms.

Gamberi (gamberetti) Prawns (shrimp).

Granchio Crab.

Granita Flavored ice; *limone* (lemon) is the classic.

Lepre Wild hare.

Maiale Pork.

Manzo Beef.

Mascarpone Technically a cheese but more like heavy cream, already slightly sweet and sweetened more to use in desserts such as tiramisù.

Merluzzo Cod.

Minestrone A little-bit-of-everything vegetable soup, usually flavored with chunks of cured ham.

Natural truffles come in both black (rare) and white (exceedingly rare) varieties, and they turn up in only very few areas of the world. Tuscany and Umbria are blessed to have both kinds growing underfoot, the black in many areas, especially Spoleto, and the white around San Miniato in Tuscany and Gubbio in Umbria. Fall is truffle season.

We have separated restaurant listings throughout this book into four price categories, based on the average cost of a meal per person, including tax and service charge but not including drinks. The categories are **Very Expensive,** more than 50€; **Expensive,** 25€ to 49€; **Moderate,** 15€ to 24€; and **Inexpensive,** less than 15€. (Note, however, that individual items in the listings—primi, for instance—do not include the sales or service taxes.)

Mortadella A very thick mild pork sausage; the original bologna (because the best comes from Bologna).

Osso buco Beef or veal knuckle braised in wine, butter, garlic, lemon, and rosemary; the marrow is a delicacy.

Ostriche Oysters.

Pancetta Salt-cured pork belly, rolled into a cylinder and sliced—the Italian bacon.

Panettone Sweet, yellow cakelike dry bread.

Panna Cream (either whipped and sweetened for ice cream or pie; or heavy and unsweetened when included in pasta sauce).

Pecorino A rich sheep's-milk cheese; in Tuscany it's eaten fresh and soft.

Peperonata Stewed peppers and onions under oil; usually served cold.

Peperoncini Hot peppers.

Polpette Small veal meatballs.

Polpo Octopus.

Porcini Huge bolete mushrooms.

Salsicce Sausage.

Saltimbocca Veal scallop topped with a sage leaf and a slice of prosciutto and simmered in white wine.

Sarde Sardines.

Scaloppine Thin slices of meat, usually veal.

Tonno Tuna.

Torta A pie. *Alla nonna* is Grandma's style and usually is a creamy lemony pie; *alle mele* is an apple tart; *al limone* is lemon; *alle fragole* is strawberry; *ai frutti di bosco* is with berries.

Torta al testo A flat, unleavened bread baked on the hearthstone and often split to be filled with sausage, spinach, or other goodies.

Trota Trout.

Vitello Veal. A *vitellone* is an older calf about to enter cowhood.

Vongole Clams.

Zabaglione/zabaione A custard made of whipped egg yolks, sugar, and Marsala wine.

Zuppa inglese An English trifle, layered with liqueur-soaked ladyfingers and chocolate or vanilla cream.

TUSCAN & UMBRIAN CUISINE

ANTIPASTO The classic Tuscan appetizer is an *antipasto misto,* which simply means "mixed." It usually entails *affettati misti* and *crostini misti,* both of which can be ordered alone as well. The former is a plate of sliced cured meats and salami, like *prosciutto* (salt-cured ham), *capocollo* (meaty pork salami), *finocchiona* (capocollo with fennel seeds), and *sopressata* (gelatinous headcheese—better than it sounds). *Crostini* are little rounds of toast spread with various pâtés, the most popular being *di fegatini* (chicken liver flavored with anchovy paste and capers) and *di milza* (spleen), though you'll also often get mushrooms, tomatoes, a cheesy sauce, or (especially in Umbria) a truffle paste.

Another popular appetizer is simple *bruschetta* (in Tuscany often called *fettunta*), a slab of peasant bread toasted on the grill, rubbed with a garlic clove, drizzled with extra-virgin olive oil, and sprinkled with coarse salt—order it *al pomodoro* for a pile of cubed tomatoes and torn basil leaves added on top. In summer, you'll also be offered *panzanella,* a kind of cold salad made of stale bread soaked in cold water and vinegar mixed with diced tomatoes, onions, and basil, all sprinkled with olive oil. A *pinzimonio* is a selection of raw vegetables (celery, fennel, peppers, and the like) with olive oil in which to dip them.

PRIMI Tuscan first courses come in three types. Of the *zuppa* or *minestra* (soup), the top dog is *ribollita,* literally "reboiled," because it's made the day before and reboiled before serving. It's a chunky soup closer to a stew than anything else. The prime ingredients are black cabbage, bean purée, and whatever vegetables *Mamma* taught you to add in poured over stale peasant bread. *Zuppa di fagioli* (bean soup) can mean either this or a soupier breadless alternative.

Sun-ripened tomatoes are the key ingredient in a Tuscan *bruschetta.*

2

Eating & Drinking

FLORENCE, TUSCANY & UMBRIA IN DEPTH

Pasta is the most famous Italian primo, and in Tuscany the king is ***pappardelle alla lepre*** (very wide egg noodles in a strong-flavored sauce of wild hare). From somewhere around Siena and south, every town has its own name for the simple homemade pasta that's basically durum wheat mixed with water and rolled between the hands into chewy fat spaghetti. In Siena province, it's called ***pici*** or ***pinci;*** around Orvieto, order ***umbrichelli;*** and in Assisi or Spoleto, call it ***stringozzi*** (or some variant thereof). It's usually served in a basic tomato sauce or ***alla carrettiera*** (a tomato sauce spiked with peperoncini hot peppers).

Other typical pasta dishes are ***penne strascicate*** (a tomato-and-cream ragù) and ***strozzapreti,*** "priest stranglers," because clerics would supposedly choke on these rich ricotta-and-spinach dumplings (sometimes called *gnudi*—nude since they're basically ravioli filling without the clothing of a pasta pocket).

SECONDI Tuscans are unabashed carnivores, and the main course is almost always meat, usually grilled. Italians like their grilled meat as close to raw as rare can get, so if you prefer it a bit more brown, order your bistecca *ben cotta* (well done, which just might get you something close to medium).

The king is the mighty ***bistecca alla fiorentina,*** traditionally made from thick T-bone steak cut from the sirloin and enveloping the tenderloin of the snow-white muscular cattle raised in the Chiana valley, although lately the meat is just as often imported. This is grilled over glowing wood coals, then brushed with extra-virgin olive oil and sprinkled with cracked black pepper. So simple, so good. The steaks average 1 to 2 inches thick and weigh about 3 to 4 pounds.

More everyday secondi are ***grigliata mista*** (mixed grill that may include lamb, sausage, chicken, or steak), ***arista*** (they usually leave off the *di maiale* because this dish invariably consists of slices of roast pork loin), ***fritto misto*** (mix of chicken, lamb, sweetbreads, artichokes, and zucchini dipped in bready egg batter and deep-fried in olive oil), and any wild game, especially ***cinghiale*** (wild boar), which is often cooked *in umido* (stewed with tomatoes), as well as domesticated game like ***coniglio*** (rabbit) and ***anatra*** (duck). They cook ***pollo*** (chicken) *arrosto* (roasted), *alla diavola* (with hot spices), or *al mattone* (cooked under the weight of a hot brick), but usually tend to dry it out in doing so. A ***lombatina di vitello*** is a simple veal chop, prepared in myriad ways.

One Tuscan specialty to which Florentines are particularly beholden is ***trippa*** (tripe, the stomach lining of a cow), most popularly served as ***trippa alla fiorentina,*** tripe strips or cubes casseroled with vegetables and topped with tomato sauce and *parmigiano.* ***Cibrèo*** is another local Florentine dish—a mix of cockscombs and chicken livers mixed with beans and egg yolks and served on toast.

Aside from **fresh fish,** both Tuscans and Umbrians make widespread use of ***baccalà,*** salt-cured cod they soften in water before cooking and often serve *alla livornese* (cooked with tomatoes and other veggies in white wine and olive oil, occasionally with some tripe thrown in for good measure).

CONTORNI Tuscans are called the *mangiafagioli* (bean-eaters) by other Italians. And ***fagioli*** here, the Italian word for beans in general, almost invariably means white cannellini beans (sometimes red kidney beans or green broad beans will show up, increasingly as you get into Umbria). However, a simple plate filled with nothing but *fagioli* or *fagioli in fiasco,* cooked al dente with a liberal supply of olive oil poured on and

ground black pepper for taste, is somehow divine within Tuscany's borders. For something zestier, order *fagioli all'uccelletto,* in which the beans are stewed with tomatoes, garlic, and sage.

Any other vegetable—*melanzane* (eggplant), *pomodoro* (tomato), *carciofi* (artichokes), or *peperone* (bell pepper)—is usually sliced thin, grilled, and served swimming in olive oil. About the only other side dish central Italians turn to is *patate* (potatoes), either *arrosto* (roasted and covered with olive oil and rosemary) or *fritte* (the increasingly popular french fries).

DOLCI Tuscany's best sweet is the dreamy *gelato,* a dense Italian version of ice cream (see the box "A Big Step up from Ice Cream: Florentine Gelato," in chapter 4, for details), which you should ideally get at a proper gelateria and not in a restaurant. The main dish to have after dinner, however, is *cantucci con vin santo. Cantucci,* or *biscotti di Prato* in that town most famed for them, are the Tuscan variant on the twice-baked hard almond crescent cookies called *biscotti,* usually eaten by dunking them in a small glass of the sweet dessert wine vin santo.

Panforte is a very dense fruitcake. (One of Siena's specialties, *pan pepato,* is its medieval predecessor, with more exotic spices including black pepper added into the sweetness.) A *castagnaccio* is a dense cake made of chestnut flour and topped with pine nuts; *necci* are chestnut-flour crepes; and a *zuccotto* is a concentration of calories in the form of sponge cake filled with *semifreddo* moussed chocolate, cream, candied fruit, and nuts. Other cookies are **ricciarelli** of honeyed marzipan (a sugar/honey almond paste), **brutti ma buoni** (ugly but good chewy almond-sugar cookies), and **ossi dei morti** (bones of the dead—light, crumble-in-your-mouth matrices of sugar).

What to Drink

Tuscany and Umbria have been wine country for thousands of years, and the region is the most famous wine zone in Italy.

To Italians, wine is the obvious only choice of beverage with dinner, so in most restaurants your only decision will be **rosso o bianco** (red or white). Unless you want to celebrate some special occasion or are in the mood to expand your connoisseurship, the **vino della casa** (house wine) will almost invariably do wonderfully. Sparkling wine, called **spumante,** is usually imported from other Italian zones (the most famous of which are Asti and the Valdobbiadene, which produces the best *prosecco*). Those refraining from alcohol for personal or health reasons needn't worry—you won't be met with scowls or discouragement if all you order is a bottle of mineral water; wine consumption is expected at meals but certainly not required.

To test out a few glasses without the full meal, drop by an **enoteca,** a wine shop or wine bar, where you can often sample before you buy (any regular bar will also pour you a glass of house wine for 2€–3€). When tooling around the wine-heavy countryside of Tuscany or Umbria, any sign that touts **vendita diretta** means the owner of those vines will sell to you direct. We've recommended individual producers for the major wines in each relevant chapter, and for a wine-by-wine overview of the best *vini* and their producers, see "The Best Wines & Vineyards," in chapter 1.

CLASSIFICATIONS Italy's wine falls into four main classifications. **DOC** (*Denominazione di Origine Controllata*) wines are those that a government board guarantees have come from an official wine-producing area and that meet the standard for carrying a certain name on the label. A **vino di tavola** (table wine) classification merely means a bottle doesn't fit the pre-established standards for the other classifications, and is not necessarily a reflection of the wine's quality. However, *vino da tavola* is generally used for what it was originally intended to mean: simple, hearty, tasty table wines that go well with any meal but probably won't send wine snobs into ecstasies of flowery poetic description.

Good Year or Bad?

Because most producers in Tuscany and Umbria are subject to the same basic weather patterns, the generally good and bad years for most labels are, by and large, the same. 1997 is what they call a 1-year-in-50, which means you shouldn't hesitate to scoop up any '97 bottles (if you can still find any) even at what seem to be inflated prices—it'll be half a century before stuff this good comes around again. Steer clear of 2002 and, for many (but not all) producers, 2003. In the last decade or so, 2001, 2004, 2006, and 2007 are the most remarkable years. Vintages since 2007 have been generally good.

In 1980, a new category was added. **DOCG** (the *G* stands for *Garantita*) is granted to wines with a certain subjective high quality. Traditionally, DOCG labels were merely the highest-profile wines that lobbied for the status (getting DOC or DOCG vastly improves reputations and therefore sales, though the costs of putting up the wine annually for testing are high). In 1992, the laws were rewritten and Italy's original list of six DOCG wines (three of which were Tuscan) jumped to 15; the count now stands at 47. Eight of these are Tuscans (Brunello di Montalcino, Carmignano, Chianti, in several varieties, Chianti Classico, Vino Nobile di Montepulciano, Vernaccia di San Gimignano, Morellino di Scansano, and Aleatico dell'Elba) and two are Umbrian (Sagrantino di Montefalco and Torgiano Rosso Riserva).

Many respectable producers have experimented by mixing varietals with French grapes, such as cabernet and chardonnay, to produce wines that, though complex and of high quality, don't fall into the conservative DOC system. The category known as **IGT** (*Indicazione Geografica Tipica*) has since 1992 generally been applied to these, as well as to good quality "regional" wines that don't meet any specific DOC criteria. Among this classification, the highbred wines became known as **Supertuscans:** There's no guaranteeing the quality of these experimental wines, yet most self-respecting producers won't put on the market a failure or something undrinkable. If you come across a 30€ bottle with a fanciful name marked as an IGT, it's probably a Supertuscan—or aspires to be.

Perhaps the highest-profile Supertuscan is **Sassicaia,** a huge and complex cabernet blend that lives for decades and is priced accordingly. It's produced by a single estate near the coast south of Livorno and, despite the popular status of more well-known wines such as Brunello, is perhaps Italy's finest red wine. The cabernet grapevines used here were transplanted from the Château Lafite in the 1940s.

The practical upshot of all this is that DOC and DOCG wines represent the best of traditional wine formulas. IGT wines are for unique wines from even smaller specific areas or single vintners, and this is one of the fastest growing categories among the better wines and extraordinary one-offs.

TUSCAN WINES Undoubtedly, Italy's most famous wine is the easygoing and versatile **chianti,** traditionally produced all around central Tuscany. The **Chianti Classico** zone of the tall hills between Florence and Siena produces the oldest, most balanced blends; it was the world's first officially established wine area in 1716. In the 19th century, a more exacting formula for chianti was worked out in the hills between Siena and Florence by Baron Ricasoli, with 75% to 90% sangiovese with other local grapes thrown in to mellow it out and make it more drinkable. Only recently were the DOCG laws controlling chianti relaxed to allow fully sangioveto chiantis to be produced, and today, a Chianti Classico can have anywhere from 70% to 100% sangiovese, often rounded out with an imported cru such as cabernet, merlot, or pinot nero. This has led to a surge in the quality and full-bodiedness of chianti, moving most of it from being a knockabout good table wine to a complex, structured, heavyweight contender in annual wine fairs. Although quality still varies, it's usually thoroughly reliable and is one of the best everyday wines produced anywhere.

Other Chianti DOC zones are **Chianti Colli Fiorentini,** Florence's table wine; **Chianti Colli Senesi,** the largest zone, filling in gaps around Siena where yield regulations keep them from growing Brunello, Vino Nobile, or Vernaccia (the chianti can be very good but is unreliable); **Chianti Colli Aretine,** a mellow edition; **Chianti Colline Pisane** and **Chianti Montespertoli,** the featherweight contenders; **Chianti Montalbano,** the juicy-fruits of the gang; and **Chianti Rúfina**—not to be confused with Ruffino, one of the biggest Chianti Classico houses—which flexes its muscle east of Florence to make chiantis of some complexity and style.

Tuscany's powerhouse red wine—and, depending on whom you ask, the number-one or number-two wine in all of Italy—is **Brunello di Montalcino.** It was developed in the 18th century when the Biondi-Santi vineyards

Chianti Classico is the finest of the Chianti zones.

were hit with a fungus that left only the dusty slate-blue *sangiovese grosso* grapes alive. It was the first wine to be granted DOCG status. Brunello is 100% *sangiovese grosso,* aged for 4 years (5 for the *riserva* labels), most of it in oak barrels. It's a deep-ruby elixir of remarkable complexity, a full mouth feel, long flavors, and usually a good deal of tannins. It needs steak or game dishes to let it shine; for a lighter-weight adventure try the **Rosso di Montalcino,** a younger, fruitier version.

Vino Nobile di Montepulciano is Tuscany's other long-respected red, a deep-garnet liquid that rolls around the tongue with a lasting flavor of fruits, violets, and damp soil. It's good paired with meats but also with fruit, bread, and cheese on a picnic. Significantly cheaper than Brunello, it's a less complex but more versatile wine.

Two of the oldest wine zones, also founded in 1716, border Florence, and both have made use of French grapes since the 18th century. The tiny DOC **Pomino** zone to the east of Florence (abutting Chianti Rúfina territory) mixes cabernet, merlot, and sometimes pinot noir into its sangiovese for a pleasant red. DOCG **Carmignano,** near Prato between Florence and Lucca, tosses cabernet into the chianti-like brew to make some of Tuscany's freshest, yet still refined and interesting, wines. Although they age well and keep forever, these wines can also be drunk practically straight out of the barrel.

More recent phenomena, pioneered by the Antinori family in the 1970s, are the so-called Supertuscans, made predominantly of cabernet and merlot along with just a smattering of the local Sangiovese grapes. The two most famous of these are Sassicaia and Ornellaia, produced near the town of Bolgheri in southwest Tuscany. Ornellaia produces wines in the **Bolgheri** DOC zone, while **Sassicaia** has its own DOC status—it's a sort of subdivision of Bolgheri and the only Italian estate occupying its own, exclusive denomination. Consequently, Sassicaia is one of Italy's most prestigious and expensive labels.

Tuscany produces many other fine DOC reds in zones throughout the region, such as the smooth **Rosso delle Colline Lucchesi** around Lucca. One of the best is a Maremma wine, rather trendy in Italy, called **Morellino di Scansano.** Like chianti—to which it's similar but silkier—it's about 80% sangiovese, with some other Tuscan grapes thrown in the mix along with Alicante (a Spanish grape known among the French as grenache).

Tuscany's only white wine of note is **Vernaccia di San Gimignano,** a dry wine of variable quality, but it enjoys the status of being one of Italy's few DOCG whites. Few other whites stand out in Tuscany, though the area around **Pitigliano** and the **Valdichiana** both produce drinkable *vino bianco,* and the Chianti zone is making some headway with its lightweight **Galestro.** Perhaps the finest little-known white is the dry **Montecarlo,** from the hills east of Lucca.

UMBRIAN WINES **Torgiano Rosso Riserva** was made DOCG mainly through the efforts of the Lungarotti vineyards and their **Rubesco** label, a blood-red wine making a strong first impression with a musky tannic bite that fades quickly through black fruit flavors. **Sagrantino di Montefalco** is the heavyweight contender DOCG of Umbrian reds, a purple-dark liquid of long flavors with a rounded mouth feel and a strong, lasting tannic hold. Other good local DOC reds are **Colli Altoberini, Colli del Trasimeno,** and **Colli Perugini** (a young zone; also produces rosé and white).

Umbria's mighty white is the **Orvieto Classico,** an ancient wine that was once an *abboccato* semisweet wine until prevailing tastes led to the mass production of Orvieto Classico *secco,* a dry white that fills wine-store shelves across the world. Interestingly, in Orvieto you can still find the old varieties, a straw-colored wine that not only goes well with food, but actually holds its own as a treat to savor. Another good white made in many zones across Umbria is **Grechetto.**

WHEN TO GO

The best times to visit Tuscany and Umbria are in the spring and fall. Starting in late May, the summer tourist rush really picks up, and from July to mid-September the country is teeming with visitors. August is the worst month to visit. Not only does it get uncomfortably hot, muggy, and crowded, but the entire country goes on vacation at least from August 15 until the end of the month, and many Italians (especially in the cities) take off the entire month. Pisa is virtually deserted in August, and Florence's low season includes August. Many hotels, restaurants, and shops are closed—except at the spas, beaches, and islands, which are where 70% of the Italians are headed. In winter (late Oct to Easter), most sights go to shorter winter hours or are closed for restoration and rearrangement, many hotels and restaurants take a month or two off between November and February, spa and beach destinations become padlocked ghost towns, and it can get much colder than most people expect—it may even snow on occasion.

Weather

Tuscany and Umbria cover some pretty diverse terrain and climate areas. Tuscany has lowlands along the coast with the most moderate of Mediterranean climes, but there are also snowcapped Apennine mountains in the north of Tuscany and eastern Umbria that stay cooler throughout the year and can get downright frozen in winter. Both regions are made up primarily of hills, however, and the climate varies with the seasons and the landscape. It can get uncomfortably hot at the height of August in valley cities such as Florence, but the breeze-cooled hill towns are usually eminently livable in summer. The long spring is temperate and very comfortable, with occasional showers. Fall is also fairly mild, with lots of rainfall being the only drawback. Winter, though mild for most months, can get quite cold in late December or January; it can drizzle a great deal, and snowfall isn't impossible.

Holidays

Official state holidays include January 1, January 6 (Epiphany), Easter Sunday and Monday, April 25 (Liberation Day), May 1 (Labor Day), August 15 (Ferragosto and Assumption Day), November 1 (All Saints' Day), December 8 (Day of the Immaculate Conception), December 25, and December 26 (Santo Stefano). Florence also shuts down to honor its patron, St. John the Baptist, on June 24.

 Hot Tickets

For major events where tickets should be procured well before arriving on the spot, check out **Box Office** at ☎ **055-210-804** or www.boxol.it. They will only deliver tickets to an Italian address, but you can buy ahead of time and pick them up at the booth when you arrive.

Calendar of Events

No Italian village can let the year run its course without a handful of celebrations of church, history, local talent, or just good food and wine. And no visit to Italy is complete without taking part in at least one of them. Those listed below represent merely the biggest and most spectacular Tuscany and Umbria have to offer. Under the introduction to each city throughout this book, you'll find these events described in greater detail, along with dates for smaller *feste* and weekly markets.

For an exhaustive list of events beyond those listed here, check http://events.frommers .com, where you'll find a searchable, up-to-the-minute roster of what's happening in cities all over the world.

JANUARY

Regatta on the Arno, Florence. The city of the Renaissance kicks off the new year with a boat race. Call ✆ **055-23-320** for details. January 1.

FEBRUARY

Carnevale, throughout Italy. The most outstanding Tuscan Rite of Spring occurs in the coastal town of **Viareggio ★★** (for details, contact the **Fondazione Carnevale di Viareggio,** Casella Postale 317, Viareggio; ✆ **0584-58071;** www. viareggio.ilcarnevale.com), with a colorful and sophisticated parade of mechanized floats subtly lampooning political figures and celebrities. Other Carnevale festivities worth dropping in on are the costume parade in **San Gimignano** (call ✆ **0577-940-008** for details) and a similar masked procession at **Vinci** (call ✆ **0571-568-012** for details). The week before Ash Wednesday (Feb/early Mar).

MARCH

Scoppio del Carro **(Explosion of the Cart),** Florence. When the bishop inside the cathedral gets to the "Gloria" part of Easter High Mass, a mechanical dove is let loose from high over the altar, and it slides down a wire toward the front doors. Waiting for it on Piazza del Duomo outside is a tall 18th-century cart—pulled there by two snowy white oxen and loaded with fireworks—which the dove ignites (it's hoped). Contact the tourist office at ✆ **055-290-832** for details. Easter Sunday.

Torciata di San Giuseppe, Pitigliano. An ancient Maremman festival with pagan roots—watch the men of the town march to the central square with burning torches to form a giant straw effigy. After the whole thing burns to the ground, the whole town comes out to party. Visit www.comune.pitigliano.gr.it or www. maremma-tuscany.com. March 19.

APRIL

Easter is always a big event. Some of the most colorful yet solemn celebrations are held in St. Francis's Umbrian hometown, **Assisi** (call ✆ **075-812-534** for details), and in **Florence.** Easter Sunday; Sunday in March or April.

MAY

Festa del Grillo (Cricket Festival), Florence. In the Cascine Park, vendors sell crickets in decorated cages, and, after a parade of floats on the Arno, everybody releases the bugs into the grass. Contact the tourist office at Via Cavour 1r (✆ **055-290-832**) for details. First Sunday after Ascension Day (mid- to late May).

Corso dei Ceri (Candle Race), Gubbio, Umbria. One of Italy's most spectacular and oldest festivals. Color-coded teams of burly men from the city's three districts run about town all day long carrying 9m-high (30-ft.) wooden "candles" (read: phallic symbols) topped with statues of saints. After a seafood dinner, they carry the things at a dead trot more than 300m (984 ft.) up a mountain. Perhaps the tourist office can explain it:

The Corso dei Ceri in Gubbio, Umbria.

Call ✆ **075-922-0693.** May 15.

Giostra dell'Archidado (Crossbow Competition), Cortona, Tuscany. This crossbow competition is held in late-14th-century costume. Contact the tourist office at ✆ **0575-630-353** or 0575-630-352 for details. May 18.

Balestro del Girifalco (Crossbow Competition), Massa Marittima, Tuscany. Massan crossbow sharpshooters in 13th-century costume fire bolts into impossibly small targets, following all the requisite processions and flag tossing. Call the festival association (✆ **0566-903-908;** www.societaterzierimassetani.it) for details. May 20 or the following Sunday and again the second Sunday in August.

Palio della Balestra (Crossbow Competition), Gubbio, Umbria. Eugubines, all dudded up medieval-style, test their crossbow skills against teams from historical rival Sansepolcro. Call ✆ **075-922-0693** for details. Last Sunday in May.

JUNE

Corpus Christi Procession, Orvieto, Umbria. In the town where this religious holiday was first proclaimed, the holy liturgical cloth onto which a communion wafer once miraculously dripped blood is carried through town in a procession of hundreds dressed in medieval costume. Contact the tourist office at ✆ **0763-341-772** for details. Corpus Christi, early June.

Festa di San Ranieri, Pisa, Tuscany. The city celebrates its patron saint by lining the Arno River with flickering torches (la luminaria). Call ✆ **050-42-291** or visit www.giugnopisano.com for details. June 16 and 17.

Calcio Storico (Historic Soccer), Florence. St. John is Florence's patron, and what better way to celebrate his holy day than with a violent Renaissance version of soccer played in 16th-century costume? Two teams of 26 men battle each other tooth and nail on dirt-packed Piazza di Santa Croce (the first June match) and Piazza della Signoria. The teams hail from each of Florence's four historic quarters—San Giovanni in green, Santa Maria Novella in red, Santa Croce in blue, and Santo Spirito in white. The season opens on June 16, but the big game is on June 24, after which fireworks explode over the Arno at 10pm. Contact the tourist office at Via Cavour 1r (✆ **055-290-832**) for details, or visit www.calciostorico.it or www.turismo.intoscana.it. June 24 and 28.

Gioco del Ponte (War on the Bridge), Pisa, Tuscany. Pisan teams from opposite banks of the river get into Renaissance garb, stand on the city's oldest bridge, and have a push-of-war with a 7-ton cart. For details, call ✆ **050-42-291** or visit www.giugnopisano.com. Last Sunday in June.

Spoleto Festival, Spoleto, Umbria. A world-renowned festival of music and the performing arts (see chapter 11 for more information). For details, contact the **Fondazione Festival dei Due Mondi,** c/o Teatro Nuovo, Via Vaita Sant´Andrea, Spoleto (✆ **0743-221-689;** www.festivaldispoleto.com). Mid-June to mid-July.

Estate Fiesolana (Fiesolean Summer),
Fiesole, near Florence. This summertime festival of music, ballet, film, and theater is held above the oppressive Florentine heat in the ancient hill town of Fiesole. Most of the performances are staged in the remains of the 1st-century-A.D. Roman theater. You can get information and tickets in advance through **Box Office** (✆ **055-210-804;** www.boxol.it), or at the Roman Theater on the day of performance. See www.estatefiesolana.it for the program. Late June to August.

JULY

Palio delle Contrade (Horse Race),
Siena, Tuscany. The Palio between Siena's traditional neighborhoods vies with Venice's Carnevale as Italy's premier festival. It's a breakneck bareback horse race around the dirt-packed main square prefaced by 3 days of parades, trial runs, and heavy partying. The night before the race is a regular bacchanal to which visitors are often welcome. The best 150€-to-200€ grandstand seats sell out years in advance. Standing in the center of the piazza is free. Hotel rooms in the entire city are booked more than a year in advance of the July 2 event. And they do it all over again on August 16. For more information, see chapter 5, visit www.ilpalio.org, or contact Siena's **Ufficio Informazione Turistico,** Piazza del Campo 56 (✆ **0577-280-551;** www. terresiena.it). July 2.

Umbria Jazz, Perugia, Umbria. This has been one of Europe's top jazz events for more than 30 years—2 weeks of performances, concerts, and jams from top names and bands. For more information, contact the **Associazione Umbria Jazz-Perugia,** Piazza Danti 28 (✆ **075-573-2432;** www.umbriajazz.com). Mid-July.

Giostra dell'Orso (Joust of the Bear),
Pistoia, Tuscany. This medieval-costumed jousting match pits mounted knights against targets shaped like bears. Not nearly as death-defying as in the olden days when they used real bears, but still a rousing good time. Call ✆ **0573-34-326** or visit www.giostradell orso.it for details. July 25.

Settimana Musicale Senese (Sienese Music Week), Siena, Tuscany. This festival brings a week of the best concerts and opera that Siena's prestigious music center can muster. Contact the **Accademia Musicale Chigiana,** Via di Città 89 (✆ **0577-46-152;** www.chigiana .it). One week in July or August.

Puccini Festival, Torre del Lago (Lucca). The biggest annual date in a local opera lover's calendar, celebrating Lucca's beloved composer. There's a seasonal ticket office at Viale Puccini 257a, in Torre del Lago, or book tickets online. ✆ **0584-359-322;** www.puccinifestival. it. July through August.

AUGUST

Rodeo della Rosa (cowboy parade and rodeo), Alberese, Tuscany. The gateway town to the Maremma's best natural park hosts a rodeo of the top *butteri* stars of Tuscany's deep south. *Butteri* are the old-fashioned Italian cowboys who've watched over the white Maremma cattle herds for generations. The **Parco Regionale della Maremma** information office may have details at ✆ **0564-393-211** or www. parco-maremma.it. August 15.

Palio delle Contrade (Horse Race),
Siena, Tuscany. An encore of Siena's famous horse race. This edition is marginally more prestigious, and even more crowded. August 16.

Bravio delle Botti (Barrel Race),
Montepulciano, Tuscany. This is something akin to a medieval fraternity stunt. Teams of *poliziani* (the name for local residents) dress like their 14th-century ancestors in order to be the first to roll a 79-kilogram (175-lb.) barrel uphill to the top of town. Come for the pageantry and feasting afterward. Contact the tourist office at ✆ **0578-758-687** or visit www.braviodellebotti.com (✆ **075-119-0521**) for details. Late August.

SEPTEMBER

Giostra del Saracino (Saracen Joust),
Arezzo, Tuscany. This jousting tournament is between mounted knights in
13th-century armor and the effigy of a
Saracen warrior. It's held on Arezzo's
main square and is one of the few versions of this sport in which the target,
which swivels and is armed with a whip,
actually hits back. Contact the tourist
office at ✆ **0575-377-678** or visit www.
giostradelsaracino.arezzo.it for details.
First Sunday in September.

Astiludio (flag tossing), Volterra,
Tuscany. Townies in 14th-century get-
ups practice the ancient art of juggling
silken banners on one of Tuscany's
most medieval of *piazze*. The tourist
office (✆ **0588-86-150**) can tell you
more, or contact the organizers directly
(✆ **0588-85-440;** www.sbandieratori
volterra.it). First Sunday in September.

Todi Arte Festival, Todi, Umbria. This
annual bash started in the 1980s brings
theater, music, ballet, and opera to the
medieval hill town for 10 days in late
summer. Contact www.todiartefestival.
com or ✆ **075-895-6700** for details.
Early September (some years in July or
Aug).

**Festa della Rificolona (Candlelit
Procession),** Florence. Children carry
paper lanterns around town, especially
up to Piazza Santissima Annunziata. It's
a dim memory of the lanterns peasants
from the surrounding countryside carried as they filed into town on this night,
the eve of the birth of the Virgin, to pay
their respects at the church. Contact the
tourist office at Via Cavour 1r (✆ **055-
290-832**) or visit www.comune.fi.it for
details. September 7.

**Palio dei Balestrieri (Crossbow
Competition),** Sansepolcro, Tuscany.
Sansepolcro gets the home-turf advan-
tage in part two of the medieval cross-
bow competition with Umbrian rival
Gubbio. Call ✆ **0575-75-827** for details.
Second Sunday in September.

**Rassegna del Chianti Classico (Wine
Festival),** Greve in Chianti, Tuscany.
Greve's annual wine fair showcases the
newest vintages from both the top and
the smaller vineyards in the Chianti
Classico zone. Call ✆ **055-854-5243** or
visit www.chianticlassico.com for details.
September 12 to September 15.

**Luminara di Santa Croce (Candle
Night),** Lucca, Tuscany. In honor of
their highly revered Volto Santo statue
of Christ, an image blackened with age
(they hold that Nicodemus himself, present at the Crucifixion, carved it from a
Lebanon cedar), the Lucchesi hold a
solemn candlelight parade through the
streets at 8pm. Call ✆ **0583-419-689**
or visit www.luccatourist.it for details.
September 13.

**Perugia Classico (Festival of Classical
Music),** Perugia, Umbria. Perugia's
music-filled summer is finished off
with a week of classical and chamber
music. Details are available from the
Comitato Promotore Perugia Classico,
c/o Comune di Perugia, Ripartizione
XVI Economia e Lavoro, Via Eburnea 9
(✆ **075-577-2253;** turismo.comune.
perugia.it). Last week in September.

OCTOBER

Sagra del Tordo (Feast of the Thrush),
Montalcino, Tuscany. Montalcini wander
around all weekend in medieval costume
throwing archery tournaments and parades, mainly for an excuse to roast hundreds of tiny thrushes, whose passing
they toast with plenty of Brunello wine.
Call ✆/fax **0577-849-331** or visit www.
comunedimontalcino.it for details. Last
weekend in October.

**Mostra Mercato Nazionale del Tartufo
Bianco (White Truffle Fair),** Gubbio,
Umbria. The world's most expensive
form of edible fungus, highly prized by
food connoisseurs, is the centerpiece
of Gubbio's annual agricultural fair.
Call ✆ **075-922-0693** or visit www.
cmaltochiascio.it for details. Last week
of October.

Vino Novello (New Wine) Festivals,
various towns. By law, New Wine can't
be released before November 4, and
several towns celebrate the coming-out
weekend of these light, short-lived red
wines. The main event is a weekend of
tastings, along with the usual stands
lining the streets during any festival (offering everything from traditional candy
to underwear). A big dinner night is arranged in the better restaurants in town,
where you sample *vini novelli* with your
meal. Two of the larger and more easily
accessible from Florence are the festival in Montespertoli (✆ **0571-609-412;**
www.comune.montespertoli.fi.it), for
which you can take a SITA bus, and the
festival in Pontassieve (✆ **055-83-601;**
www.comune.pontassieve.fi.it), for which
you can take a train. First weekend after
November 4.

Live Nativity Procession, Barga (in the
Garfagnana north of Lucca), Tuscany.
Just before Christmas, a live procession
of locals dressed as the Holy Family
passes through town, where other

inhabitants are costumed as traditional
tradespeople. The procession starts
sometime after 7pm and arrives at the
Duomo around 11pm. For details, call
✆ **0583-723-499,** or visit www.comune.
barga.lu.it. Usually held December 23.

**Ostensione della Sacra Cintola (Display
of the Virgin's Girdle),** Prato, Tuscany.
This is the final and most sumptuous
of the five annual occasions on which
the bishop releases Mary's Sacred
Girdle—the belt she handed to Thomas
upon her Assumption—from its jewel-
encrusted treasure chest and shows it
to the people massed inside the Duomo
and crowding the piazza outside. Plenty
of Renaissance-style drummers and
fifers are in attendance. The pomp is
repeated at Easter, May 1, August 15, and
September 8. Call ✆/fax **0574-24-112**
for details. December 25.

Umbria Jazz Winter, Orvieto, Umbria.
Wine tasting and internationally renowned jazz artists come to Orvieto for
part two of Umbria's premier jazz festival. Call ✆ **075-572-1653** or check www.
umbriajazz.com for details. December 27
to January 1.

RESPONSIBLE TRAVEL

Environmentalism in Italy has always been an area of stark contrasts. Italians
conserve fuel and energy like most Europeans do, they go to great lengths to
limit air pollution, and their shopping habits of consuming locally grown vegetables and bringing a bag to the store would put a smile on just about any environmentalist's face. Meanwhile, local entities' recycling efforts can be dubious
(investigative journalism reveals that most of the recyclables and trash in Rome,
for example, recently ended up in the same place anyway).

That aside, the tourism industry here leads the charge in protecting the
resources of a country where visitor spending accounts for a whole lot of the
nation's income. Rural Tuscany might very well be the capital of the green movement in Italy, and the region is regularly credited with leading the charge for
sustainable tourism. Most hotels in Florence, Siena, and other Tuscan cities,
as well as higher-end *agriturismi* in the countryside, have implemented green
practices; farms in particular have begun to install natural wastewater treatment
systems, and guests are strongly encouraged to participate in composting and recycling programs. Organic agriculture is widespread, especially on smaller farms
around Central Italy that host visitors, so when you eat in a restaurant in Tuscany,

chances are that the food didn't travel very far to get to your table. (The insistence on bottled water, however, is one blemish on an otherwise good record.)

Italians in general are also very protective of their beaches—and their efforts have been rewarded with several Blue Flags. Each year, a **Blue Flag** (www.blueflag.org), a voluntary eco-label that honors high water quality and environmental management, is awarded to beaches throughout the world. Thirty-three beaches on Tuscany's coast have received Blue Flags, including our favorite on the mainland, Feniglia (p. 300).

Overall, as a nation that needs to import the majority of its energy, and with 60 million people living in relatively close proximity, Italians have always been a culture to live and consume at a sustainable rate and a very human scale. Towns and provinces push for more intercity cycling paths to connect tourist sites, and public transportation is generally reliable. However, there is no escaping the fact that most often a family with luggage will need a car to get around the Tuscan and Umbrian countryside.

You can do your part by reusing towels, taking public transportation whenever possible, discarding trash and recyclables in the appropriate colored bins around the region, and eating locally grown produce. And don't shy away from central Italy's tap water; it's very good. In addition to the resources for Tuscany and Umbria listed here, see www.frommers.com/planning for more tips on responsible travel. See also p. 53 for our favorite responsible travel providers in Tuscany and Umbria.

TOURS
Special-Interest Trips
ACADEMIC TRIPS & LANGUAGE CLASSES

Florence holds more foreign student programs than almost any other city in the world. The list of universities and programs operating there is endless. For adults interested in studying in Florence, the list narrows a bit. One good place to start looking is **Education First** (© 800/992-1892; www.ef.com), as they run a number of educational programs in Italy, including Italian language classes in Florence. Another private group with a Florence program is **Academic Studies Abroad** (© 888/845-4272; www.academicstudies.com), which works through Florence University of the Arts. Note that they cannot accept applications from outside the U.S. or Canada, and that all classes and programs are at the undergraduate level. One of the better schools is the **Lorenzo de Medici** (© 055-287-203; www.lorenzodemedici.org), with branches in Florence and Tuscania on the Lazio border. Smaller towns can offer a more intimate experience of Tuscan life: The **Language Center** in Todi, Umbria (© 075-894-8364; www.wellanguage.com) has a well-deserved reputation for teaching Italian.

FOOD & WINE TRIPS

Most tourist boards offer guided tours of the vineyards in their province, as will a number of local tourist agencies; see individual chapters for more information about vineyard tours in a specific region. They're often sponsored by the vintners themselves. The **Associazione Strada del Sagrantino** (© 0742-378-490; www.stradadelsagrantino.it) offers packages and can coordinate tours of the Umbrian Sagrantino region. Another good example is Brunello and chianti producer **Donatella Cinelli Colombini** (© 0577-662-108; www.cinelli colombini.it), which offers winery tours and tastings.

Local tour company **Fufluns** (© 0132-227-0495; www.fufluns.com) runs excellent custom-made wine and gourmet tours through Tuscany, and can also help arrange cooking classes. Qualified sommelier Angela Saltafuori runs **Tuscan Wine Tours** (© 0333-318-5705; www.tuscanwinetours.net), usually driving groups of 2 to 8 adults in an air-conditioned minibus (tours 120€–145€).

Cooking Schools

The most serious cooking courses in Tuscany (and there are a lot of them these days) in our opinion are at **La Petraia ★★** (© 0577-738-582; www.lapetraia. com), for a simple reason: the simplicity of it all. The ingredients you use: the eggs, the chestnuts, the peas, the ham, the spices, almost without exception come from the very property where you are staying. Classes cost around 200€.

One of Italy's most respected cookbook authors, and former TV cooking show star, **Giuliano Bugialli ★** shares his secrets in summertime weeklong classes, with lodging in Florence and classes conducted in a kitchen in the Chianti. One-week courses can run $4,800 per person, including first-class accommodations and most meals. For more info, contact "Foods of Italy" at 105 S. 12th St., Apt. 205/206, The White Building, Philadelphia, PA 19107 (© 215/922-2086; fax 215/923-3502; www.bugialli.com).

Another high profile school is the one started over 20 years ago by **Lorenza de' Medici ★**, author of 30 kitchen tomes (including the coffee-table favorite, *Tuscany: The Beautiful Cookbook*) and star of her own TV cooking series. Unfortunately, she's hung up her apron and now leaves the lessons to Florentine chef Andrea Gagnesi. March through November, 1-day (155€) and 2-day, 3-night (900€) courses take place in the 12th-century abbey and wine estate **Badia a Coltibuono** (see chapter 5 for more information). For more information call © 0577-744-831 or visit www.coltibuono.com.

March through November, **Cook Euro,** 708 Third Ave., 13th floor, New York, NY 10017 (© 212-794-1400; www.cookeuro.com), offers a weeklong course, "L'Amore di Cucina Italiana," with visits to wine estates and cultural day trips in Tuscany and Umbria, for about $3,200 per person based on double occupancy.

If a week's time or a $4,000 investment are too rich for your cooking-lesson tastes, check out Judy Witts Francini's **La Divina Cucina ★** (©/fax 055-292-578; www.divinacucina.com) for 1-day and 1-week courses designed to teach you to cook as the Florentines do. You start off each class by shopping in Florence's large central market at 11am, and by 4pm you've put together a meal based on the freshest ingredients available that day. A single Monday at the market costs 125€ per person, or a 1-week Colle Val d'Elsa program costs 2,700€.

For more local cooking classes, see "Cook Like a Tuscan," p. 113.

BIKE TOURS

The best way to experience Tuscany and Umbria just may be by bicycle. Bike-it-yourselfers should arm themselves with a good map (see "Getting Around," p. 440). You can rent a bike by the week or longer at outlets in most cities.

Several operators specialize in setting up itineraries and making some of the arrangements for you or in leading fully guided tours. **Ciclismo Classico ★★** (© 800/866-7314 in the U.S., or 781/646-3377; fax 781/641-1512; www. ciclismoclassico.com) is one of the best. A weeklong tour of Tuscany runs about

Biking is an ideal way to experience Florence, Tuscany.

$3,295 per person. May through October, the outfit runs several guided tours through Tuscany and Umbria, always van-supported, and will help you arrange a do-it-yourself tour as well. Groups average 10 to 18 people, with all ages and ability levels welcome.

VBT Bicycling Tours and Vacations ★★ (© 800/245-3868 in the U.S.; www.vbt.com), a 40-year veteran of the bike tour business and a specialist in Tuscan and Umbrian routes, makes a point of combining a great experience with excellent value. Bike tours start at $2,850 and walking tours are also available.

Experience Plus (© 800/685-4565 in the U.S., or 970/484-8489; www.experienceplus.com) offers both guided (Sept–Oct) and self-guided (Apr–Oct) biking and walking tours through Tuscany lasting 7 to 11 days (from $3,050). Florence-based **I Bike Italy** ★ (© 561/388-0783 in the U.S.; www.ibike italy.com) offers guided 1- and 2-day rides in the Tuscan countryside. The 2-day tour requires a minimum of four participants and ends in Siena. They provide a shuttle service in and out of the city, the bike, and a bilingual guide. The 1-day tour returns to Florence around 5pm. Tours cost around 80€ per person, lunch included.

WALKING TOURS

If you don't feel the need to cover so much territory, you can appreciate even more of the countryside by walking or hiking (called *trekking* in Italian). Italy's resource for everything from countryside ambles to serious mountain trekking is the **Club Alpino Italiano,** Via E. Fonseca Pimentel 7, Milan 20127 (© 02-2614-1378; fax 02-2614-1395; www.cai.it). Many outfits run walking tours in Tuscany and Umbria. Besides **Ciclismo Classico** (see above), you might want to try **Butterfield & Robinson** (© 866/551-9090; www.butterfield.com); or **Country Walkers** ★ (© 800/464-9255 in the U.S., or 802/244-1387; www.countrywalkers.com), which has a rather refined, romantic outlook on Italy and offers several Tuscan tours, one of which divides your time between exploring hill towns on foot and taking cooking and wine appreciation lessons.

For intelligent walking tours in Florence, one of the best operators is **Context Travel** ★★ (© 215/609-4888; www.contexttravel.com), whose experts in their respective fields lead guided tours and seminars on everything from Renaissance art to ceramics to cuisine.

SUGGESTED ITINERARIES

3

Tuscany and Umbria are densely populated with things to see, perhaps more so than any other region in Europe. It could take months to experience all of its art, architecture, food, and wine. Lovers of Renaissance art could spend a month in Florence and still discover new gems to admire. Wine buffs could sip and sniff their way through months in Chianti and Montalcino. Romantics could dream away that time in Lucca alone. Most of us don't have that kind of time, so we've designed the 1-week and 2-week itineraries for first-time visitors to discover the best of Tuscany and Umbria. Then there is a tour for families, and one for food-and-wine enthusiasts as well.

A car will be indispensable in every case, because public transport only connects the main towns efficiently. And the soul of Central Italy is found in its countryside, through its sunflower fields and sloping vineyards, spotted with storied castles.

It is not a large place—you could drive from the top of Tuscany to the bottom on the highway in *about* 3 hours—but the roads of the hinterland are winding, narrow, and slow. Don't be daunted by the idea of spending much of your time in the car. Getting there, in this case, is half the fun.

The following itineraries all start in Florence—the lion's share of travelers arrive there via train, plane, or from airports in Milan or Rome. You might, however, also consider flying into Pisa, a destination for many low-cost airlines, and begin your itinerary there.

Timing is everything. Avoid peak season if at all possible. So many foreigners, especially Americans and northern Europeans, descend on Florence in July that they are literally corralled through the streets. Spring and early fall are the ideal times to visit. Enotourists (wine lovers) will get the most out of a vineyard visit just before harvest, when the grapes are still on the vine.

THE REGIONS IN BRIEF

Tuscany and Umbria are divided into administrative provinces based around major cities. These official designations aren't perfect for organizing a travel guide, so the following "regions" into which this book is divided group towns and sights based on similarities, with most chapters focused on a major city. Keep in mind that none of these regions is *very* large—Tuscany is, at 22,993 sq. km (8,877 sq. miles), a bit smaller than New Hampshire, and Umbria, at 8,456 sq. km (3,265 sq. miles), makes about two Rhode Islands. For a map of the area, see the inside back cover of this guide.

FLORENCE The capital of Tuscany is **Florence,** one of Italy's most famous cities. It was once the home of the powerful Medici dynasty, which actively

PREVIOUS PAGE: **Grapes on the vine in Tuscany.**

encouraged the development of the Renaissance by sponsoring sculptors and painters such as Donatello, Leonardo, and Michelangelo. Art treasures such as those found at the Accademia (Michelangelo's *David*), the Uffizi Gallery (Botticelli's *Birth of Venus*), and the Pitti Palace (Raphael's *La Velata*) draw millions of visitors every year. Throw into the mix fabulous architecture (the Duomo with Brunelleschi's dome, Giotto's campanile, Santa Croce), fine restaurants and earthy *trattorie,* and leading designer boutiques and bustling outdoor markets, and the city of the Renaissance becomes quite simply one of the world's must-see places.

THE CHIANTI, SIENA & THE WESTERN HILL TOWNS The land of high hills stretching from Florence south to Siena is among the most vaunted countryside on earth, the vine-covered Arcadia of **Chianti.** Here you can drive along the Chiantigiana roadway, stopping to soak up the scenery and sample the *vino.* **Siena** is Tuscany's medieval foil to the Renaissance of Florence. It's a city built of brick, with Gothic palaces, excellent pastries, and its own stylized school of Gothic painting. With steep back streets and a mammoth art-packed cathedral, it's the region's second-most popular city. The hill towns west of it—medieval tangles of roads perched atop small mountains—are almost as famous: **San Gimignano,** with its medieval stone skyscrapers; and Etruscan **Volterra,** with its alabaster workshops. The province of Siena stretches south to about Umbria in a landscape of soft green hills, lone farmhouses, stands of cypress, patches of cultivated fields, and the occasional weird erosion formations known as the **Crete Senesi** and *biancane.* This area is postcard-perfect Tuscany.

LUCCA, PISTOIA & NORTHWESTERN TUSCANY The Apuan Alps, along the shore of the Tyrrhenian Sea, kick off a series of mountain chains that rides across the northern edge of Tuscany, separating it from Emilia-Romagna to the north. In their foothills lie the little-visited regions of the **Garfagnana**

The "skyscrapers" of San Gimignano.

and **Lunigiana,** empty paradises for lovers of long walks and hearty mountain cooking. In the valley below this string of mountains sit several worthy towns also little visited by most travelers rushing from Florence to Lucca or Pisa. The medieval textile center of **Prato** is one of Italy's fastest-growing cities and about the friendliest town in Tuscany. Its historic core is filled with Renaissance art treasures overlooked by many who don't realize a city just 16km (10 miles) from Florence can be so different and rewarding. Its neighbor **Pistoia,** an old Roman town, is firmly stamped with the art stylings of the Romanesque Middle Ages. Farther along in the Valdinievole (Valley of Mists) you'll find relaxation at **Montecatini Terme,** Italy's most famous spa, and **Monsummano Terme,** where a Dantean underworld of natural "steam room" caverns hides beneath an upscale hotel.

The elegant old republican city of **Lucca** is packed with Romanesque churches, livened by the music of native sons Puccini and Boccherini, and teeming with grandmothers on bicycles going shopping.

PISA, TUSCANY'S COAST & THE MAREMMA This region consists of much of Tuscany's coast, from the ancient maritime republic of **Pisa** and its tilting tower to **Livorno,** a Medici-built port city and seafood mecca, and, farther down the coastline, the **Maremma,** Tuscany's deep south. Once a stronghold of the Etruscans, the Maremma was a swamp from the Dark Ages to the 1600s and is still a highly undeveloped region. A short journey inland, the historic capital of the "High" Maremma is undersisited **Massa Marittima,** a medieval mining town with a gorgeous cathedral and fine museums. Also covered is the old iron-mining island of **Elba,** once Napoleon's reign in exile and now one of Italy's best summer seaside resorts.

SOUTHEASTERN TUSCANY "Southeastern Tuscany" is a bit of a misnomer here, because the Maremma is technically the most southerly region. The medieval hill towns of **Montalcino** and **Montepulciano** craft some of Italy's finest red wines, and **Pienza,** prodigious producer of pecorino sheep's cheese, sits like a balcony surveying the **Val d'Orcia** and is the only perfectly designed town center of the Renaissance. If the spa waters of **Chianciano Terme** don't catch your fancy, perhaps you'll enjoy the ancient Etruscan center of **Chiusi,** with its tombs, archaeological museum, and excellent restaurants, or your unforgettable first sight of **Pitigliano,** a former Jewish town which seems to sprout from living rock.

AREZZO & NORTHEASTERN TUSCANY Arezzo was once an important Etruscan city, and today

The Val d'Orcia.

boasts some exceptional Piero della Francesca frescoes and a world-class monthly antiques market. East of Arezzo, near the Umbrian border, is Piero's hometown of **Sansepolcro,** a modest industrial city with an old core devoted to preserving Piero's great works. South of Arezzo stretches the **Chiana Valley,** where the cattle for Florence's famous steaks are raised, and the thriving art city of **Cortona,** which contains some of Tuscany's finest small museums.

PERUGIA, ASSISI & NORTHERN UMBRIA Perugia, the capital of Umbria, is a refined city of soft jazz, velvety chocolates, medieval alleys, and one of Italy's top painting galleries, featuring the works of Perugino, master of the modeled figure and teacher of Raphael. Just east is one of Italy's spiritual centers, the hill town of **Assisi,** birthplace of St. Francis. The basilica raised in his honor is the nerve center of the vast Franciscan monastic movement and home to some of the greatest fresco cycles of the early Renaissance. Umbria gets even wilder to the north, where the rocky border city of **Gubbio** is home to one of Italy's wildest pagan festivals, and the oft-ignored **Città di Castello** contains its own stash of art treasures.

ORVIETO, SPOLETO & SOUTHERN UMBRIA Spoleto was once seat of the Lombard duchy that controlled most of Umbria in the Dark Ages, but it's most famous these days for its world-class music-and-dance Spoleto Festival. Spoleto's beautiful Duomo and the odd reliefs on its early Romanesque churches draw a small but select crowd of admirers. Moving west we hit **Montefalco,** home of fine Sagrantino wines, and **Todi,** a quintessential Italian hill town that just oozes medieval charm. **Orvieto,** in the far south, is an implacable city of tufa rising above the valley on its volcanic outcropping, with a giant gem of a cathedral and perhaps the best white wine in Italy.

TUSCANY IN 1 WEEK

This route brings you to Italy's must-see destinations: Florence, Siena, Pisa, Lucca, and the Chianti.

DAYS 1–2: Florence ★★★

The sights most easily tackled together are the **Cathedral,** the **Baptistery, Giotto's bell tower, Orsanmichele,** and **Santa Maria Novella.** Except on Sundays, these are open until early evening, making them suitable opening-day attractions. Then, unwind with some comfort food at the casual **Il Santo Bevitore,** a glass of wine in the **Oltrarno,** and top it off with a frozen treat at the **Gelateria dei Neri.** After waking up early with a frothy cappuccino, the second day is best suited for more stimulating sights. Not to be missed are the monastery-museum of **San Marco** and nearby, the

Giotto's bell tower.

Accademia, to view *David*; the refined landscapes of the **Boboli Garden;** and at least a brief tour of the **Uffizi.** For details on Florence attractions and restaurants, as well as a potential side trip to **Fiesole,** see chapter 4.

Be sure to check the opening hours of all museums before planning your itinerary and make reservations for the Uffizi and Accademia. Some museums are closed on Monday, and a few churches are closed during the lunch break. Because the rest of the itinerary requires a car, you should book one well ahead of time since reservations fill up quickly (especially in summer).

DAY 3: Prato & Pistoia; Lucca & the Garfagnana ★

Art and architecture buffs would be remiss to skip **Pistoia** (p. 239) and **Prato** (p. 233). Continue on to **Lucca** (p. 250) and plan to overnight here. Stroll along its walls and savor a romantic dinner of *tortelli lucchesi* in its alleyways. The next day, you have a choice of getting some more exercise in the **Garfagnana** (p. 263), one of Tuscany's most pleasant natural preserves, or more sightseeing in some of the region's lesser-known cities. The road to the caves and hiking trails of the Garfagnana is short and very scenic, but the excursion realistically will take most of the day—especially if you break your journey with a meal of typical local food at the **Antica Locanda di Sesto** (p. 262).

DAY 4: Pisa ★★

Consider getting up for a morning bicycle ride along Lucca's **medieval walls** before making the short drive to **Pisa** (p. 268). Climb the **Leaning Tower,** snap the de rigueur photo, visit the rest of the **Campo dei Miracoli,** then drink and dine in the "real" center of town.

DAY 5: Volterra & San Gimignano ★★

Visit the Alabaster City of **Volterra** (p. 221), a medieval remnant and former center of the Etruscan world. After lunch, head for **San Gimignano.** The best time to approach San Gimignano is in the late afternoon, when the hilltop city is bathed in the setting sun. Get to the **Collegiata** before it closes. See p. 214 and 216.

DAY 6: Siena ★★★

Unless you're there during the **Palio** (p. 200), the top sights in **Siena** (p. 188) can feasibly be visited in about 1 full day. The **cathedral** is one of Italy's most interesting, especially if its elaborate intarsia pavement is uncovered. The **Museo Civico** inside the town hall houses the most important secular frescoes in Tuscany. Be sure to indulge in a feast in Siena, as its food is one of its greatest draws.

Siena's Duomo.

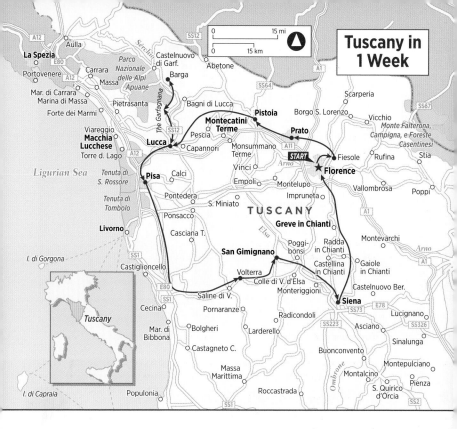

DAY 7: The Chianti ★★

Spend the day on state road SS222, which takes you through the big-name towns in Chianti, and all the way back to Florence. The three most worthy stops are **Greve, Panzano,** and **Castellina in Chianti,** all sitting at the heart of important winemaking areas. Although there are a number of great restaurants along the way, those on a tight budget might want instead to pick up picnic supplies in **Panzano,** and pay a visit to the "poet butcher," Dario Cecchini, who can recite Dante's *Inferno* in its entirety while chopping away at a rack of ribs. Be aware that many vineyards are family-run and require prebooking to tour. See p. 173.

TUSCANY & UMBRIA IN 2 WEEKS

Two weeks will give you enough time to see Tuscany's top destinations with some additional time to sample the treasures of Umbria and the pleasures of the Val d'Orcia. For the first 7 days, refer to "Tuscany in 1 Week" (see above) and then move on to Arezzo.

DAY 8: Cortona & Arezzo ★

Aside from the marvels of **Piero della Francesca** in Arezzo and the gorgeous, hilly streets of Cortona, the adopted home of *Under the Tuscan Sun* author Frances Mayes, one of the nicest parts of this day will be the ride between the two. The SS71 is studded with castles, vineyards, and sunflower fields. In fact, finding a nice bed-and-breakfast outside one of the towns will make for one of the trip's most memorable nights. See p. 351 and 336.

The narrow streets of Perugia.

DAY 9: Perugia ★

The city's **National Gallery** is a must-see on any visit to Umbria, but just hanging around the cafes of this animated medieval city makes it worth the trip. Central Italy can be rather short on nightlife for young people, but Perugia's **university** scene makes the city a welcome exception. Don't forget to sample those Perugina **Baci** chocs. See p. 363.

DAY 10: Assisi ★★

This is the most revered shrine in all of Italy, with the **Basilica di San Francesco** second in importance only to St. Peter's. It will take the entire day to explore all the city's art, from Giotto's paintings to the recently restored Rocca Maggiore fortress. Make time for the tranquil **Eremo delle Carceri** and lunch at **La Stalla.** See p. 380.

DAY 11: Montefalco, Todi & Spoleto

Wine lovers should spend most of the day in and around the capital of Sagrantino, **Montefalco** (p. 417), visiting family-owned vineyards. Otherwise **Todi,** one of the quaintest towns in all of Central Italy, is worth a quick visit. End the day in **Spoleto,** home of the country's most famous outdoor **festival** of the performing arts. Check your calendar to see if you will be there during that time. See p. 48 and 408.

DAY 12: Orvieto ★

Make a detour on the road to **Orvieto** to reach **Chiusi,** a bonanza of Etruscan urns, tombs, and other impressive remains (p. 328). Approaching Orvieto in the evening offers you a gorgeous view of the city illuminated by sunset, or spotlights at night, and is an ideal stop for dinner and some of its "liquid gold." See p. 424.

DAY 13: Montepulciano & Montalcino ★★

Make your way into the Val d'Orcia via **Montepulciano** and from there to **Montalcino.** These two wine-producing giants are worthy stops in their own right, especially the former for its handsome, *palazzo*-lined Corso. Between the two is the model Renaissance city, **Pienza,** surrounded by the kind of captivating Tuscan landscape you see in promotional photos. See p. 313.

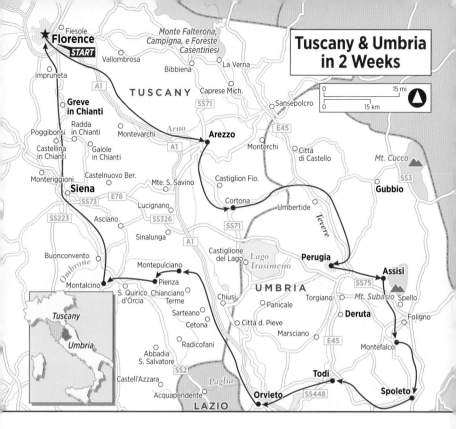

Tuscany & Umbria in 2 Weeks

DAY 14: Depart Florence

Reserve this day for last-minute leather shopping in the **Scuola del Cuoio** (p. 162) and choosing Renaissance scents from **Santa Maria Novella** (p. 159), then to catch whatever sights you missed on the first 2 days.

TUSCANY & UMBRIA FOR FAMILIES

This 10-day itinerary brings you to Tuscany's best family-oriented attractions. It's rather light on churches and art, and heavier on outdoor fun, often with parts of the day devoted to children and parts that will please the parents. In general, Italy is a family-oriented society, so kids should have fun wherever they go. Things to reserve ahead of time are Florence museum tickets, Pisa's tower, the car ferry to Elba, and possibly horseback riding in the Maremma.

DAYS 1-2: Florence ★★

Making reservations beforehand for the top-selling attractions, such as Michelangelo's *David,* will help avoid the hassle of waiting in line for hours with the little ones. But there are a number of diversions better suited to kids. Climbing Brunelleschi's **cathedral** dome will be the highlight of

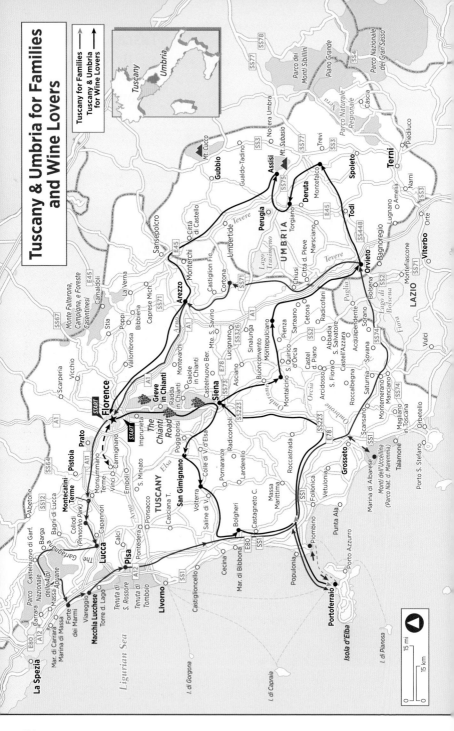

Tuscany & Umbria for Families and Wine Lovers

Tuscany for Families →
Tuscany & Umbria
for Wine Lovers →

The sandy beach at Cavoli, southwest Elba.

Florence for most, while Galileo's telescope lens (and preserved middle finger) holds court at the **Museo Galileo.** The quirky, medieval **Museo Stibbert** will thrill Harry Potter fans, while the **Specola** zoological museum is packed with an array of stuffed animals ranging from crabs to a rhinoceros. Be aware that the latter has some pretty gruesome displays on medicine, though teens will probably get a kick out of them. Then there's enough **gelato** in town to sink an aircraft carrier. See chapter 4.

DAY 3: Pinocchio Park, Spas & Lucca ★★

Pinocchio Park (p. 250), the **park** in Collodi devoted to Pinocchio's creator, isn't exactly Disneyland, but it is still a pretty good stop for imaginative little ones. Afterward, you can all unwind in the **outdoor spa pool at Monsummano Terme** (p. 248). Don't waste time on dinner here. In the late afternoon, make your way to **Lucca** for a cycle along its ramparts before sitting down to some orzo soup.

DAY 4: Caving in the Garfagnana & Beachcombing in Viareggio ★

Take a sunrise drive to the Garfagnana and start the day with a 1-hour tour of the caves and tunnels of the **Grotta del Vento.** In the morning, be sure to also visit the steep, winding streets of **Barga.** Have a seafood lunch and a sunny afternoon at the **beach in Viareggio.** Summer vacancy will be difficult to find in the beach hotels, so spend another night in enchanting Lucca. See chapter 6.

DAY 5: Pisa ★★

The best of child-friendly **Pisa** (p. 268) can be visited in half a day. Kids of all ages will want to see the famous **Leaning Tower** and climb up it, but *note that the minimum age to go up is 8 years old.* After a timeout in the Orto

Botanico, one of the world's oldest botanical gardens, continue
rolling south along the coast to
catch the ferry to your next stop,
the island of Elba.

DAY 6: Elba ★

Catch a ferry from Piombino
and spend the day touring **Napoleon's old haunts,** riding in
a cage to the summit of **Monte
Capanne,** and doing some snor-
keling at the beach—our favorite
patch of sand is at **Sant'Andrea.**
In July or August, you will need to
reserve your ferry tickets well in
advance. See "Elba," p. 288.

DAY 7: Hiking & Horseback Riding in the Maremma ★

A family photo stop at the Leaning Tower.

The southern edge of Tuscany is
cowboy country. Spend the morning hiking in the **Parco Naturale della
Maremma** (p. 300) and see wild horses, white cattle, and hopefully a wild
boar (at a distance). Contact the park's headquarters ahead of time about
horseback riding or canoeing in the area. In the evening, drive to **Orvieto**
and arrive at night to see the hilltop city awash with spotlights. It is a great
place for a late dinner of so-called "Etruscan specialties" and the town's
namesake white wine.

DAY 8: Orvieto's Tunnels, Etruscan Tombs & Cortona ★★

Scramble down Orvieto's ancient **tunnels in the tufa rock** (p. 432) and
have a look through some of the puppets in toy stores around town before lunch. Afterward, make your way up to Cortona for a hike through the
Etruscan tombs (p. 357) outside town. Cortona's reputation for hotels is
slightly better than nearby Arezzo's, though neither town has Tuscany's best
accommodations. Try to spend at least 1 night in a nearby *agriturismo* or
bed-and-breakfast. For a truly memorable experience, Cortona has a number of fantastic medieval festivals, so try to plan your visit accordingly.

DAY 9: Cortona & Arezzo ★

Spend a lazy morning wandering through the sights of Cortona, the inspiration for *Under the Tuscan Sun,* which will only take a couple of hours.
Then drive north to Arezzo. The SS71 is a curvy road through quintessential
Tuscany. Arezzo is a great place to spend any afternoon, seeing the famous
fresco cycles of Piero della Francesca, and the backdrop for Roberto Benigni's Oscar-winning film, *Life Is Beautiful.* Try to time your visit to

coincide with the **Giostra del Saracino,** a medieval joust (and a real kid-pleaser) or with one of the spectacular antiques fairs, which take place the first Sunday of every month. See p. 339 and 338.

DAY 10: Depart Florence

Take the autostrada to Florence in the morning to catch whatever sights you missed the first time around and, of course, finish up with some shopping. See "Shopping," in chapter 4 (p. 158).

TUSCANY & UMBRIA FOR WINE LOVERS

This 2-week loop includes some of the best known of Italy's winegrowing regions, a few oenological surprises, and some major artistic sights, too, as neither man nor woman can live on wine alone. To customize your tour, see the details describing local varietals in "What to Drink," in chapter 2 (p. 42).

DAY 1: Florence ★★

A good start for this tasting trip would be in Piazza Antinori, named after the vineyard barons who own the city's most refined restaurant-enoteca (wine cellar) there, the **Cantinetta Antinori.** For something more down-to-earth and local, hop around a couple of the excellent wine bars in the **Oltrarno.** (See "Florence After Dark," p. 164.) Note that most of the best bottles you will find at less expensive restaurants tend to be chianti, while highbrow places have labels from farther afield.

DAY 2: Carmignano ★

Carmignano, just outside Prato, can boast one of Tuscany's oldest winemaking traditions, and yet it is barely touched by foreign tourists. This is even more surprising considering its proximity to Florence and the potential for day trips. It produces excellent reds but is best known for its **vin santo,** enjoyed with the local, hard *cantucci* biscuits.

DAYS 3–4: The Chianti ★★

These vineyards need no introduction to wine enthusiasts, and many of them can be freely visited (the top places ask that you reserve around a week in advance). Only some, however, have accommodations for visitors. One of the finest places to stay is **Vignamaggio,** just north of Greve, a top-quality producer with excellent villas and apartments. For obvious reasons, it's wise to savor wine nearest where you plan to sleep. See "The Chianti," in chapter 5 for a complete guide.

DAY 5: San Gimignano & Volterra ★

This can almost be considered a third day in Chianti because it is so close, but this is a day for white wine: **Vernaccia di San Gimignano.** Take a respite from cork sniffing in the afternoon and visit the impressive Etruscan city of Volterra (where there's also a fine, cavelike wine bar). See chapter 5.

Chianti aged in oak barrels in a Tuscan cellar.

DAY 6: Bolgheri ★★

Home to the prestigious "Supertuscan" labels **Sassicaia** and **Ornellaia (Bolgheri DOC),** this out-of-the-way venue is worth the trip for those who are serious about wine. Book well in advance for a vineyard tour and to stay at a bed-and-breakfast or *agriturismo* (www.bolgheridoc. com). There are few hotels in the immediate vicinity.

DAYS 7–8: Elba & Siena

Take a break on the island's beaches—enjoy its seafood and try a glass of its fish-friendly, crisp white or unique sweet red **Aleatico.** You will need to organize your ferry in advance in high season. Plan to spend the second afternoon driving to Siena. Resist the temptation to explore one of the back roads as it will take much longer than you think. Instead, do as the locals do and use the highway via Grosseto. (Even if you plan to make a side trip to Massa Marittima, you'd be well advised to return to the highway afterward.) See chapters 5 and 7.

Pouring the chianti at Castello di Verrazzano.

DAYS 9–10: Montalcino & Montepulciano ★★

Brunello di Montalcino and **Vino Nobile di Montepulciano** are two of Europe's most prized reds, and the countryside that yields them is spectacular. Some of the producers have onsite apartments for rental, but wine enthusiasts may prefer to stay in one of these historic hill towns, since each of them is essentially built around the wine industry and has plenty of tasting opportunities in the center. See chapter 8.

DAY 11: Orvieto

Vintners around this hilltop Umbrian city have been cultivating their famous whites since Roman times (see "Orvieto's Liquid Gold," p. 429), but the city itself has its own treasures, gastronomic and otherwise. Explore the ancient **tunnels in the tufa rock** (which, among other uses, served as medieval wine fridges), and admire its outrageous cathedral.

DAY 12: Torgiano & Montefalco ★★★

One of the highlights of any tasting trip to Italy is the **Wine Museum** in Torgiano, near Perugia (p. 378). It is the only one of its kind, owned and operated by the area's largest producer, Lungarotti. The family also runs a tasting room just next door. Plan your meals in Perugia, or, even better, in Montefalco, which is where **Sagrantino,** the true gem of Umbrian wine, is to be found. See chapter 11.

DAY 13: Assisi ★★

No special claims to oenological fame here, but a trip to Umbria must include this spectacular shrine of Christianity. You could spend an entire morning in the **Basilica di San Francesco,** and then head back to Florence in the afternoon, stopping off in Citta' di Castello, Sansepolcro, and Arezzo along the way. See chapter 10.

DAY 14: Depart Florence

Visit whichever sights and restaurants you missed the first time around and finish up with some shopping at the city's wine stores, most notably **Enoteca Alessi** (see "Wine & Liquors," p. 164).

FLORENCE

4

otticelli, Michelangelo, and Leonardo da Vinci all left their mark on Florence, the cradle of the Renaissance and Tuscany's alfresco museum. With Brunelleschi's dome as a backdrop, follow the River Arno to the Uffizi Gallery and soak in centuries of great painting. Wander across the Ponte Vecchio as dusk descends, taking in the tangle of medieval streets. Then sample seasonal Tuscan cooking in a Left Bank trattoria. You've discovered the art of fine living in this masterpiece of a city.

Things to Do Michelangelo's *David* stands tall (literally) behind the doors of the **Accademia** and, nearby, the delicate painting of Fra' Angelico in the convent of **San Marco** enchants. Works by Florentines Donatello, Masaccio, and Ghiberti fill the city's churches and museums. Once home to the Medici, the **Palazzo Pitti** is stuffed with Raphaels and Titians, and backed by the fountains of the regal **Boboli Garden.** Climb the **Duomo's cupola** for views to the hills beyond.

Shopping Italy's leather capital strains at the seams with handmade gloves, belts, bags, and shoes sold from workshops, family-run boutiques, and high-toned stores, as well as at tourist-oriented **San Lorenzo Market.** Splurge on designer wear from glamorous fashion houses along **Via de' Tornabuoni** or Renaissance scents from the convent-turned-perfumery, **Officina Profumo-Farmaceutica Santa Maria Novella.** For authentic artisan goods, wander the alleyways of the **Oltrarno.**

Restaurants & Dining Florentine eating is more cosmopolitan than in the countryside, but flavors still have Tuscany at their core. Even in the best restaurants, meals might kick off with peasant concoctions like *ribollita* (vegetable stew) before moving onto the chargrilled delights of a *bistecca alla fiorentina* (Florentine beefsteak on the bone)—all washed down with a fine **Chianti Classico.** At lunchtime order a plate of cold cuts, or if you're feeling adventurous *lampredotto alla fiorentina* (a sandwich of cow's stomach stewed in tomatoes and garlic).

Nightlife & Entertainment Kick your evening off with *aperitivo* hour: Simple, tasty buffets are piled high for early evening drinkers to enjoy. When you've dined to your fill, retire to a wine bar in the **Oltrarno,** or to one of the edgier joints of **Santo Spirito** and **San Frediano,** where DJs play till the wee hours. If you're keen on opera, classical, theater, or jazz, you'll find it here, too.

ESSENTIALS

GETTING THERE By Plane: For flights into Florence, see "Getting There" and "Getting Around" in chapter 12. Several European airlines service Florence's Amerigo Vespucci Airport (© 055-306-1300 for the switchboard, 055-306-

FACING PAGE: **The Gates of Paradise.**

1700 or 055-306-1702 for flight info; www.aeroporto.firenze.it), also called Peretola, just 5km (3 miles) northwest of town. There are no direct flights to or from the United States, but you can make connections through London, Paris, Amsterdam, Frankfurt, and other major European cities. The half-hourly SITA-ATAF "Vola in bus" to and from downtown's bus station at Via Santa Caterina 15r (© 800-424-500), beside the train station, costs 5€ one way or 8€ round-trip. There's also a less frequent service operated by Terravision (© 050-26-080; www.terravision.eu). Metered taxis line up outside the airport's arrival terminal and charge a flat, official rate of 22€ to the city center (24€ on holidays, 25€ after 10pm). There's also a small tourist information office at the airport (© 055-315-874), open daily 8:30am to 8:30pm.

The closest major international airport with direct flights to North America is Pisa's **Galileo Galilei Airport** (www.pisa-airport.com), 97km (60 miles) west of Florence. Two to three **trains** per hour leave the airport for Florence, most requiring a change at Pisa Centrale (60–90 min.; 5.80€). Early-morning flights or lots of bags might make train connections from Florence to the airport difficult; one solution is the regular train from Florence into Pisa Centrale, with a 10-minute taxi ride around 10€ from the train station to Pisa Airport. Alternatively, 10 daily buses operated by **Terravision** (© **050-26-080;** www.terravision.eu) connect downtown Florence directly with Pisa Airport in 70 minutes. One-way ticket prices are 10€ adults, 4€ children ages 5 to 12; round-trip fares are 16€ and 8€, respectively.

By Train: Florence is Tuscany's rail hub, with regular connections to all the region's major cities. To get here from Rome, you can take high-speed Frecciarossa or Frecciargento trains (40 daily; 1½ hr.; make sure it's going to Santa Maria Novella station, not Campo di Marte; reserve tickets ahead), an IC (Intercity) train (seven daily; 2¾–3 hr.; cheaper), or a *regionale veloce* (eight daily; around 3½–4 hr.; cheapest). There are high-speed and IC trains to Milan (at least hourly; 1¾–3 hr.) via Bologna (37 min.–1 hr.). There's also a daily night-train sleeper service from Paris Bercy, operated by **Artesia** (www.artesia.eu).

Most Florence-bound trains roll into **Stazione Santa Maria Novella,** Piazza della Stazione (www.trenitalia.it), which you'll see abbreviated as **S.M.N.** The station is an architectural masterpiece in its own right—albeit one dating to Italy's Fascist period, rather than the Renaissance—and lies on the northwestern edge of the city's compact historic center, a 10-minute walk from the Duomo and a 15-minute walk from Piazza della Signoria and the Uffizi.

At the head of the tracks, the **ticketing room** (Salone Biglietti) is located through the central doors. Note that there are separate lines for making high-speed (Frecciarossa/Frecciargento) bookings and buying all other tickets, including IC and international tickets. The automatic ticket machines have taken some pressure off the ticket windows, but sometimes still attract long lines. For journeys within Tuscany, you can also buy tickets (cash only) from the newspaper vendor opposite the machines. The double-sided yellow and white sheets posted at the head of most tracks list the day's departures *(partenze)* and arrivals *(arrivi)*.

At the head of Track 16 is a **24-hour luggage depot** where you can drop your bags (4€ per piece for 5 hr., then .60€ per hr. thereafter) while you search for a hotel. The station **waiting room** is opposite Track 6.

Exit out to the left coming off the tracks and you'll find many bus lines as well as stairs down to the underground **pedestrian underpass** which leads directly to Piazza dell'Unità Italiana and saves you from the traffic of the station's piazza.

Note that occasional trains stop only at the outlying **Stazione Campo di Marte** or **Stazione Rifredi**, both of which are worth avoiding. Although there's 24-hour bus service between these satellite stations and S.M.N., departures aren't always frequent and taxi service is erratic and expensive.

By Bus: Because Florence is such a well-connected train hub, there's little reason to take the longer, less comfortable intercity coaches (one exception is if you're arriving from **Siena;** p. 188). Dozens of companies make dozens of runs here daily from all of Tuscany, much of Umbria, and the major cities in Italy. Most bus stations are near the train station; see "Getting There" and "Getting Around," in chapter 12, for details.

By Car: The A1 autostrada runs north from Rome past Arezzo to Florence and continues to Bologna. The A11 connects Florence with Lucca, and unnumbered superhighways run to Siena (the SI-FI raccordo) and Pisa (the so-called FI-PI-LI).

Driving to Florence is easy; the problems begin once you arrive. Almost all cars are banned from the historic center—only residents or merchants with special permits are allowed into this camera-patroled *zona a trafico limitato* (the "ZTL"). You may be stopped at some point by the traffic police. Have the name and address of the hotel ready and they'll wave you through. You can drop off baggage there (the hotel will give you a temporary ZTL permit); then you must relocate to a parking lot. Ask your hotel which is most convenient: Special rates are available through most hotels.

Your best bet for overnight or longer-term parking is one of the city-run garages. Although the parking lot under Santa Maria Novella (3€ per hour) is closer to the city center, the best deal if you're staying the night (better than many hotels' garage rates) is at the **Parterre parking lot** under Piazza Libertà, at Via Madonna delle Tosse 9 (**℃055-550-1994**). It's open round the clock, costing 2€ per hour, or 20€ for 24 hours; it's 65€ for up to a week's parking. There's voluminous information on Florence's parking options at **www.firenzeparcheggi.it**.

Don't park your car overnight on the streets in Florence without local knowledge; if you're towed and ticketed, it will set you back substantially—and the headaches to retrieve your car are beyond description.

4

FLORENCE | Essentials

Visitor Information

TOURIST OFFICES The most convenient **tourist office** is at Via Cavour 1r (☏ **055-290-832;** www.firenzeturismo.it), about 3 blocks north of the Duomo. The office is open Monday through Saturday from 8:30am to 6:30pm. Their free map is quite adequate for navigation purposes—there's no need to upgrade to a paid-for version.

The station's nearest **tourist office** (☏ **055-212-245**) is opposite the terminus at Piazza della Stazione 4. With your back to the tracks, take the left exit, cross onto the concrete median, and bear right; it's across the road about 30m (100 ft.) ahead. The office is usually open Monday through Saturday from 8:30am to 7pm (sometimes to 2pm in winter) and Sunday 8:30am to 2pm. This office often gets crowded; unless you're really lost, press on to the Via Cavour office, above.

Another helpful office sits under the Loggia del Bigallo on the corner of Piazza del Duomo and Via dei Calzaiuoli, open Monday through Saturday from 9am to 7pm (5pm mid-Nov through Feb) and Sunday 9am to 2pm.

PUBLICATIONS Florence has bundles of excellent, mostly free, listings publications. At the tourist offices, pick up the free monthly **_Informacittà_** (www.informacitta.net), which is strong on theater and other arts events, as well as markets. The bimonthly, bilingual **_Concierge Information_** (www.florence-concierge.it) magazine, free from the front desks of many top hotels, contains some itinerary ideas and attraction information. Younger and hipper, pocket-sized monthly **_Zero_** (http://firenze.zero.eu) is hot on the latest eating, drinking, and nightlife. It's available free from trendy cafe-bars, shops, and usually the tourist office, too. **_Firenze Spettacolo_**, a 1.80€ Italian-language monthly sold at most newsstands, is the most detailed and up-to-date listing of nightlife, arts, and entertainment. Free monthly **_iOVO_** (www.iovo.it) is good on contemporary arts and cultural goings-on in the city. **_The Florentine_** is the leading expat newspaper.

WEBSITES For events and listings, check the websites of the recommended publications, above. The official Florence information website, **www.firenzeturismo.it**, contains a wealth of up-to-date information on Florence and its province, including itineraries and a hotel search database. At **www.firenzeturismo.it/arte-musei-firenze.html** you'll find a downloadable PDF with the latest updated opening hours for all the major city sights.

AboutFlorence.com, **Firenze.net** (http://english.firenze.net), and **Florence OnLine** (www.fol.it) are all Italy-based websites with English translations and good general information on Florence. The best city blogs are generally written in Italian by locals: **Io Amo Firenze** (http://ioamo-firenze.blogspot.com) is invaluable for reviews of the latest eating, drinking, and events in town. For regularly updated Florence information and ideas, also visit **www.frommers.com/destinations/florence**.

City Layout

Florence is a smallish city, sitting on the Arno River and petering out to olive-planted hills rather quickly to the north and south but extending farther west and, to a lesser extent, east along the Arno valley with suburbs and light industry. It has a compact center best negotiated on foot. No two major sights are more than a 20- or 25-minute walk apart, and most of the hotels and restaurants in this chapter are in the relatively small **centro storico** (**historic center**), a compact tangle of medieval streets and *piazze* (squares) where visitors spend most of their time. The bulk of Florence, including most of the tourist sights, lies north of the river, with the Oltrarno, an old artisans' working-class neighborhood, hemmed in between the Arno and the hills on the south side.

STREET MAPS The tourist offices hand out two versions of a Florence *pianta* (city plan) free: Ask for the one *con un stradario* (with a street index), which shows all the roads and is better for navigation.

If you want to buy a more complete city plan, your best bets are at the newsstand in the ticketing area of the train station and at **Feltrinelli International** (see "Shopping," later in this chapter). If you need to find a tiny street not on your map, ask your hotel concierge to glance at his or her *TuttoCittà*, a complete magazine of fully indexed streets that you can't buy but residents and businesses receive with their phone books. *Note:* If you're navigating with a smartphone, Google Maps is very data hungry.

> ## Address Finding: The Red & the Black
>
> The address system in Florence and some other Tuscan cities has a split personality. Private homes, some offices, and hotels are numbered in black (or blue), while businesses, shops, and restaurants are numbered independently in red. (That's the theory anyway; in reality, the division between black and red numbers isn't always so clear-cut.) The result is that 1, 2, 3 (black) addresses march up the block numerically oblivious to their 1r, 2r, 3r (red) neighbors. You might find the doorways on one side of a street numbered: 1r, 2r, 3r, 1, 4r, 2, 3, 5r . . .
>
> The color codes occur only in the *centro storico* and other older sections of town; outlying districts didn't bother with the rather confusing system.

The Neighborhoods in Brief

We've used the designations below to group hotels, restaurants, and sights in Florence. Although the city does contain six "neighborhoods" centered on the major churches (Santa Maria Novella, Il Duomo, Santa Croce, San Lorenzo, and Santo Spirito and San Frediano in the Oltrarno), these are too broad to be useful here. We've divided the city up into visitor-oriented sections (none much more than a dozen square blocks) focused around major sights and points of reference. The designations and descriptions are drawn to give you a flavor of each area and to help you choose a zone in which to base yourself.

THE DUOMO The area surrounding Florence's gargantuan cathedral is about as central as you can get. The Duomo is halfway between the two great churches of Santa Maria Novella and Santa Croce as well as at the midpoint between the Uffizi Gallery and the Ponte Vecchio to the south and San Marco and the Accademia with Michelangelo's *David* to the north. The streets north of the Duomo are long and can be traffic-ridden, but those to the south make up a wonderful medieval tangle of alleys and tiny squares heading toward Piazza della Signoria.

This is one of the oldest parts of town, and the streets still vaguely follow the grid laid down when the city began as a Roman colony. Via degli

The Ponte Vecchio.

Strozzi/Via degli Speziali/Via del Corso was the *decumanus maximus,* the main east-west axis; Via Roma/Via Calimala was the key north-south *cardo maximus.* The site of the Roman city's forum is today's **Piazza della Repubblica.** The current incarnation of this square, lined with glitzy cafes, was laid out by demolishing the Jewish ghetto in a rash of nationalism during Italian unification in the 19th century, and (until the majority of neon signs were removed in the early 1990s) it was by and large the ugliest piazza in town. The area surrounding it, though, is one of Florence's main shopping zones. The Duomo neighborhood is, understandably, one of the most hotel-heavy parts of town, offering a range from luxury inns to student dives and everything in between.

PIAZZA DELLA SIGNORIA This is the city's civic heart and perhaps the best base for museum hounds—the Uffizi Gallery, Bargello sculpture collection, and Ponte Vecchio leading toward the Pitti Palace are all nearby. It's a well-polished part of the tourist zone but still retains the narrow medieval streets where Dante grew up. The few blocks just north of the Ponte Vecchio have reasonable shopping, but unappealing modern buildings were planted here to replace the district destroyed during World War II. The entire neighborhood can be stiflingly crowded in summer, but in those moments when you catch it off-guard and empty of tour groups, it remains the most romantic heart of pre-Renaissance Florence.

SAN LORENZO & THE MERCATO CENTRALE This small wedge of streets between the train station and the Duomo, centered on the Medici's old church of San Lorenzo and its Michelangelo-designed tombs, is market territory. The vast indoor food market is here, and most of the streets are filled daily with stalls hawking leather jackets and other wares. It's a colorful neighborhood, blessed with a good range of budget hotels, but not the quietest.

PIAZZA SANTA TRINITA This piazza sits just north of the river at the end of Florence's shopping mecca, Via de' Tornabuoni, home to Gucci, Armani,

Ferragamo, and more. Even the ancient narrow streets running out either side of the square are lined with the biggest names in high fashion. It's a pleasant, well-to-do (but still medieval) neighborhood in which to stay, even if you don't care about haute couture. But if you're an upscale shopping fiend, there's no better place to be.

SANTA MARIA NOVELLA This neighborhood, bounding the western edge of the *centro storico,* has two characters: the run-down unpleasant zone around the train station and the nicer area south of it between the church of Santa Maria Novella and the river.

In general, the train-station area is the least attractive part of town in which to base yourself. The streets, most of which lie outside the pedestrian zone, are heavily trafficked and noisy, and you're removed from the action. This area does, however, have more budget options than any other quarter. Some streets, such as Via Faenza and its tributaries, contain a glut of budget joints, with dozens of choices on every block. It's the best place to go if you can't seem to find a room anywhere else; just walk up the street and try each place you pass. Among some uninspiring flop-houses, a few (those we recommended below) seem to try twice as hard as central inns to cater to their guests and are among the friendliest hotels in town. Tip: Just avoid anything on traffic-clogged Via Nazionale.

The situation improves dramatically as you move east into the San Lorenzo area or pass Santa Maria Novella church and head toward the river. Piazza Santa Maria Novella and its tributary streets have seen a few boutique hotels open in recent years, and are attracting something of a bohemian nightlife scene (but occasionally it can still be seedy).

SAN MARCO & SANTISSIMA ANNUNZIATA These two churches are fronted by *piazze*—Piazza San Marco, now a busy transport hub, and Piazza Santissima Annunziata, the most beautiful in the city—that together define the northern limits of the *centro storico.* The neighborhood is home to the university, Michelangelo's *David* at the Accademia, the San Marco monastery, and long, quiet streets with some real hotel gems. The daily walk back from the heart of town up here may tire some, but others welcome being removed from the worst of the high-season tourist crush.

SANTA CROCE This eastern edge of the *centro storico* runs along the Arno. The bulky Santa Croce church is full of famous Florentine art and famous dead Florentines, but is also the focal point of one of the most genuine neighborhoods left in the old center. While the area's western edge abuts the medieval district around Piazza della Signoria—Via de' Bentaccordi/Via Torta actually traces the outline of the old Roman amphitheater—much of the district was rebuilt after World War II in long blocks of creamy yellow plaster buildings with residential shops and homes. Few tourists roam too far off Piazza Santa Croce, so if you want to feel like a city resident, stay here. The streets around the Mercato di Sant'Ambrogio and Piazza de'Ciompi have an especially appealing, local feel. The Santa Croce neighborhood also boasts some of the best restaurants and bars in the city.

THE OLTRARNO "Across the Arno" is the artisans' neighborhood, still packed with workshops where craftspeople hand-carve furniture and hand-stitch leather gloves. It began as a working-class neighborhood to catch the overflow from the expanding medieval city on the opposite bank, but it also

The 19th-century facade of Santa Croce.

became a rather chic area for aristocrats to build palaces on the edge of the countryside. The largest of these, the Pitti Palace, later became the home of the grand dukes and today houses a set of paintings second only to the Uffizi in scope. Behind it spreads the baroque fantasies of the Boboli Garden, Florence's best park. Masaccio's frescoes in Santa Maria della Carmine here were some of the most influential of the early Renaissance.

Florence tacitly accepted the Oltrarno when the 14th-century circuit of walls was built to include it, but the alleys and squares across the river continued to retain an edge of distinctness. It has always attracted a slightly bohemian crowd—poets Robert and Elizabeth Barrett Browning lived here from just after their secret marriage in 1847 until Elizabeth died in 1861. The Oltrarno's lively tree-shaded center, Piazza Santo Spirito, is a world unto itself, lined with bars and close to some great restaurants (and lively nightlife, too). West of here, the neighborhood of San Frediano, around the Porta Pisana, is becoming ever more fashionable for hip locals and visitors, and San Niccolò at the foot of Florence's southern hills is a buzzing nightlife spot.

IN THE HILLS From just about any vantage point in the center of Florence, you can see that the city ends abruptly to the north and south, replaced by green hills spotted with villas and the expensive modern homes of the upper-middle class. To the north rises Monte Ceceri, mined for the soft gray pietra serena that accented so much of Renaissance architecture and home to the hamlet of Settignano, where Michelangelo was wet-nursed by a stonecutter's wife. The high reaches harbor the Etruscan village of Fiesole, which was here long before the Romans built Florence below.

Across the Arno, the hills hemming in the Oltrarno—with such names as Bellosguardo (Beautiful Glimpse) and Monte Uliveto (Olive Grove Hill)—are blanketed in farmland. With panoramic lookouts like Piazzale Michelangiolo and the Romanesque church of San Miniato al Monte, these hills offer some of the best walks around the city, as Elizabeth Browning, Henry James, and Florence Nightingale could tell you. They're crisscrossed by snaking country roads and bordered by high walls over which wave the silvery-green leaves of olive trees.

Owing to the lack of public transportation, first-time visitors who plan a strenuous sightseeing agenda probably will not want to choose accommodations in the hills. But for those who don't need to be in town every day and want a cooler, calmer, and altogether more relaxing vacation, the hills can be heaven. Public transportation links with the center are fairly good, too.

Getting Around

Florence is a walking city. You can leisurely stroll between the two top sights, the Duomo and the Uffizi, in less than 5 minutes. The hike from the most northerly sights, San Marco with its Fra' Angelico frescoes and the Accademia with Michelangelo's *David,* to the most southerly, the Pitti Palace across the Arno, should take no more than 30 minutes. From Santa Maria Novella across town to Santa Croce is an easy 20- to 30-minute walk.

Most of the streets, however, were designed to handle the moderate pedestrian traffic and occasional horse-drawn cart of a medieval city. Sidewalks, where they exist, are narrow—often less than .5m (2 ft.) wide. Although the *centro storico* is increasingly being closed to traffic, this doesn't always include taxis, residents with parking permits, people without permits who drive there anyway, and the endless swarm of noisy Vespas and *motorini* (scooters). However, since the election of center-left Mayor Matteo Renzi in 2009, the city has become noticeably more pedestrian friendly, a trend that is likely to continue while he is in office.

In high season, especially June, the cars and their pollution, massive pedestrian and tourist traffic, maniac moped drivers, and stifling heat can wear you down. On some days Florence can feel like a minor circle of Dante's *Inferno.* Evenings can be cool year-round, bringing residents and visitors alike out for the traditional before-dinner *passeggiata* (stroll) up and down Via Calzaiuoli and down Via Roma and its continuations across the Ponte Vecchio.

BY BUS You'll rarely need to use Florence's efficient ATAF bus system (© 800-424-500 in Italy; www.ataf.net) since the city is so wonderfully compact. Many visitors accustomed to big cities step off their arriving train and onto a city bus out of habit, thinking to reach the center; within 5 minutes they find themselves in the suburbs. The cathedral is a mere 5- to 7-minute walk from the train station.

Bus tickets cost 1.20€ and are good for 90 minutes. A four-pack *(biglietto multiplo)* is 4.70€, a 24-hour pass 5€, a 3-day pass 12€, and a 7-day pass 18€. Tickets are sold at *tabacchi* (tobacconists), bars, and most newsstands. *Note:* Once onboard, validate your ticket in the box

 A Walking Warning

Florentine streets are mainly cobbled or flagstone, as are the sidewalks, and thus they can be rough on soles, feet, and joints after a while. Florence may be one of the world's greatest shoe-shopping cities, but a sensible pair of quality walking shoes or sneakers is highly recommended over loafers or pumps. In dress shoes or heels, forget it—unless you are an experienced stone walker.

near the rear door to avoid a steep fine. If you intend to use the bus system, you should pick up a bus map at the ATAF window through the main ticket hall in Santa Maria Novella station. Since traffic is limited in most of the historic center, buses make runs on principal streets only, save four tiny electric buses (*bussini* services C1, C2, C3, and D) that trundle about the *centro storico*. The most useful lines to outlying areas are no. 7 (for Fiesole) and nos. 12 and 13 (for Piazzale Michelangiolo).

BY TAXI Taxis aren't cheap, and with the city so small and the one-way system forcing drivers to take convoluted routes, they aren't an economical way to get about town. They are most useful to get you and your bags between the train station and your hotel in the virtually busless *centro storico*. The standard rate is .91€ per kilometer (slightly more than a half-mile), with a whopping minimum fare of 3.30€ to start the meter (which rises to 5.30€ on Sun; 6.60€ 10pm–6am), plus 1€ per bag. There's a taxi stand outside the train station; otherwise, call **Radio Taxi** at ✆ **055-4242** or 055-4390.

BY BICYCLE & SCOOTER Many of the bike-rental shops in town are located just north of Piazza San Marco, such as **Alinari,** Via San Zanobi 38r (✆ **055-280-500;** www.alinarirental.com), which rents bikes (2.50€ per hr.; 12€ per day) and mountain bikes (3€ per hr.; 18€ per day). It also rents 50cc and 100cc scooters (10€ or 15€ per hr.; 30€ or 55€ per day). Another renter with similar prices is **Florence by Bike,** Via San Zanobi 120–122r (✆ **055-488-992;** www.florencebybike.it).

Illegally parked bicycles and scooters have become such an issue in Florence that authorities have begun "towing" them—that is, breaking the locks and impounding them. Make sure you park your scooter in a marked spot (there will be dozens of others there) or your bike at a rack where it won't interfere with pedestrian traffic.

Cycling Florence's backstreets.

BY CAR Trying to drive in the *centro storico* is a frustrating, useless exercise, and moreover, unauthorized traffic is not allowed past signs marked "ZTL." On top of that, 2012 will likely see the introduction of a city charge (1€ per day or thereabouts) even to drive into the center to park. Florence is a maze of one-way streets and pedestrian zones, and it takes an old hand to know which laws to break in order to get where you need to go—plus you need a permit to do anything beyond dropping off and picking up bags at your hotel. Park your vehicle in one of the huge underground lots on the center's periphery and pound the pavement. (See "By Car" under "Getting There," earlier in this chapter.) For car-rental firms in town, see chapter 12.

[FastFACTS] FLORENCE

Business Hours Hours mainly follow the Italian norm (see chapter 12). In Florence, however, many of the larger and more central shops stay open through the midday *riposo* or nap (note the sign ORAR-IO NON-STOP).

Consulates See "Embassies & Consulates," in chapter 12.

Doctors There's a walk-in **Tourist Medical Service,** Via Lorenzo il Magnifico 59, north of the city center between the Fortezza del Basso and Piazza della Libertà (✆ **055-475-411**), open Monday to Friday 11am to noon and 5 to 6pm, Saturday 11am to noon only; take bus no. 8 or 20 to Viale Lavagnini, or bus no. 12 to Via Poliziano. **Dr. Stephen Kerr** keeps an office at Piazza Mercato Nuovo 1 (✆ **335-836-1682** or 055-288-055; www.dr-kerr.com), with office hours Monday through Friday from 3 to 5pm without an appointment (appointments are

available 9am–3pm). The consultation fee is 50€ to 60€; it's slightly cheaper if you show a valid student ID card.

Emergencies Dial ✆ **113** for an emergency of any kind. You can also call the **carabinieri** (police) at ✆ **112.** Dial an **ambulance** at ✆ **118,** and report a **fire** at ✆ **115.** All these calls are free from any phone.

Hospitals The **ambulance number** is ✆ **118.** You can walk into most any Italian hospital when ill and get taken care of with no insurance questions asked, no forms to fill out, and no fee charged. The most central hospital is **Santa Maria Nuova,** a block northeast of the Duomo on Piazza Santa Maria Nuova (✆ **055-27-581**), open 24 hours.

For a **free translator** to help you describe your symptoms, explain the doctor's instructions, and aid in medical issues in general, call the volunteers at the **Associazione**

Volontari Ospedalieri (**AVO;** ✆ **055-234-4567;** www.federavo.it) Monday, Wednesday, and Friday from 4 to 6pm and Tuesday and Thursday from 10am to noon.

Internet Access Most hotels in the city center now offer wireless Internet, for free or a small fee. Otherwise, head to the chain **Internet Train** (www.internettrain.it), with six locations in Florence, including their very first shop at Via dell'Oriuolo 40r, a few blocks from the Duomo (✆ **055-263-8968**); Via Guelfa 54r, near the train station (✆ **055-214-794**); Borgo San Jacopo 30r, in the Oltrarno (✆ **055-265-7935**); and Via de' Benci 36r (no phone). The magnetic access card you buy is good at any Internet Train store nationwide (there are three in Livorno, one in each of San Gimignano and Pisa, and two in Umbria). They also provide printing, scanning, webcam, and fax services, plus other services (bike rental, international shipping, 24-hr. film developing) at some offices. Open hours vary, but generally run at least daily from 9am to 8:30pm, often later. Alternatively, if you have your own laptop or smartphone, buy a time-limited pass from **www.wifipass. it**, a network of local Wi-Fi hotspots.

Laundry & Dry Cleaning Although there are several coin-op shops—including several in the **Wash & Dry** chain (www. washedry.it)—instead visit a pay-by-weight *lavanderia,* so you don't have to waste a morning sitting there watching it go in circles. The cheapest are around the university (east of San Marco), and one of the best is a nameless joint at **Via degli Alfani 44r** (✆ **055-247-9313**), where they'll do a load overnight for around 6€. It's closed Saturday afternoon and all day Sunday. Always check the price *before* leaving your clothes—some places charge by the item. Dry cleaning (*lavasecco*) is much more costly and available at *lavanderie* throughout the city (ask your hotel for the closest).

Mail You can buy *francobolli* (stamps) from any *tabacchi* or from the central post office. Florence's **main post office** (✆ **055-273-6481**) is at Via Pellicceria 3, off the southwest corner of Piazza della Repubblica. The post office is open Monday through Saturday from 8:15am to 7pm.

Drop postcards and letters into the boxes outside. To mail larger packages, queue inside for a *sportello* (window). You can also send packages via **UPS,** Via di Pratignone 56a in Calenzano (✆ **02-3030-3039**).

To receive mail at the central post office, have it sent to [your name], Fermo Posta Centrale, 50103 Firenze, Italia/ITALY. They'll charge you a nominal sum when you come to pick it up; bring your passport for ID. They hold mail for 30 days.

Pharmacies For pharmacy information, dial ✆ **800-420-707** (in Italy only). There are 24-hour pharmacies (also open Sun and state holidays) in **Stazione Santa Maria Novella** (✆ **055-216-761;** ring the bell btw. 1 and 4am); at **Piazza San Giovanni 20r,** just behind the baptistery at the corner of Borgo San Lorenzo (✆ **055-211-343**); and at **Via dei Calzaiuoli 7r,** just off Piazza della Signoria (✆ **055-289-490**).

On holidays and at night, look for the sign in any pharmacy window telling you which ones are open.

Police For emergencies, dial ✆ **112** for the *carabinieri.* To report lost property or passport problems, call the *questura* (urban police headquarters) at ✆ **055-49-771. *Note:*** It is illegal to knowingly buy fake goods anywhere in the city (and, yes, a Rolex watch at 20€ counts as *knowingly*). You may be served a hefty on-the-spot fine if caught.

Post Offices See "Mail," above.

Safety Central Italy is exceedingly safe with practically no random violent crime. As in any city, plenty of pickpockets are out to ruin your vacation, and in Florence you'll find light-fingered youngsters (especially around the train station), but otherwise you're safe. Do steer clear of the Cascine Park after dark, when it becomes somewhat seedy and you may run the risk of being mugged; and you probably won't want to hang out with the late-night heroin addicts shooting up on the Arno mud flats below the Lungarno embankments on the edges of town. See chapter 12 for more safety tips.

WHERE TO STAY

In the past few years, thanks to growing competition, the recent financial crises, and unfavorable euro-dollar and euro-pound exchange rates, the trusty forces of supply and demand have brought hotel prices in Florence down for the first time in memory, but it is still difficult to find a high-season double you'd want to stay in for much less than 100€. In addition, some of the price drops have been added back in taxes: Since July 2011, Florence's city government levies an extra 1€ per person per night per government-rated hotel star, for the first 5 nights of any stay. The tax is payable on arrival.

Because hotel prices had previously outpaced inflation, the hoteliers stockpiled some surplus cash, and over the last decade reinvested in their properties. In many hotels, the amenity levels are now at or above what travelers expect to find at home, and the days of the bathroom-down-the-hall cheap *pensioni* are fading—or at least, those properties are now mostly student dives. Almost everyone seems to have put in satellite TV, new bathrooms, and Wi-Fi. In the past few years, the trend has been to trade quantity of rooms for quality, eliminating small doubles to create larger suites and attract a higher-rolling clientele. There's been a flourishing of *residenze d'epoca,* historic palaces and characterful buildings transformed into not-quite-full-service hotels and comfortable, upscale B&Bs. The city also now boasts a fair share of contemporary boutique hotels that wear their lack of "Renaissance character" almost as a badge of honor. We've tried to balance our selections to suit all tastes and budgets.

For help finding a room, inquire at the tourist office (see earlier) or see the subsection on accommodations at **www.firenzeturismo.it**, a site sponsored by the province that lists virtually every hotel and other type of accommodations in town.

Peak hotel season is mid-March through early July, September through early November, and December 23 through January 6. May, June, and September are particularly popular; January, February, and August are the months to grab a bargain—never be shy to haggle if you're coming in these months.

To help you decide which area you'd like to base yourself in, consult "The Neighborhoods in Brief," earlier in this chapter. Note that we've included parking information only for those places that offer it. As indicated below, many hotels offer babysitting services; note, however, these are generally "on request." A couple of days' notice is advisable.

Near the Duomo
VERY EXPENSIVE
Hotel Savoy ★★ This 1896 hotel underwent a complete transformation by Sir Rocco Forte and his sister, who designed the warm, stylishly minimalist modern interiors. Rooms are standardized, with walk-in closets, marble bathrooms, and mosaics over the tubs. The different room "styles"—classic, executive, and deluxe—really refer to size. Among the four suites (two rooms, two TVs, leather easy chairs, white marble bathrooms), two include a Turkish bath. Rooms on the fifth floor, added in 1958, just peep over the surrounding buildings for spectacular views, especially those on the Duomo (back) side. You're just a few steps from all the city's sights and shopping.

Piazza della Repubblica 7, 50123 Firenze. www.hotelsavoy.it. © **800/223-6800** in the U.S., or 055-27-351 in Italy. Fax 055-273-5888. 102 units. 530€ double; 620€ executive double; 830€ studio; 1,250€–2,700€ suite. Breakfast 32€. AE, DC, MC, V. Valet garage parking 29€. Bus: C2, 6, 11, 22, 36, or 37. **Amenities:** Restaurant; bar; babysitting; concierge; gym; room service; Wi-Fi (20€ per 24 hr). *In room:* A/C, TV, fax on request, hair dryer, minibar.

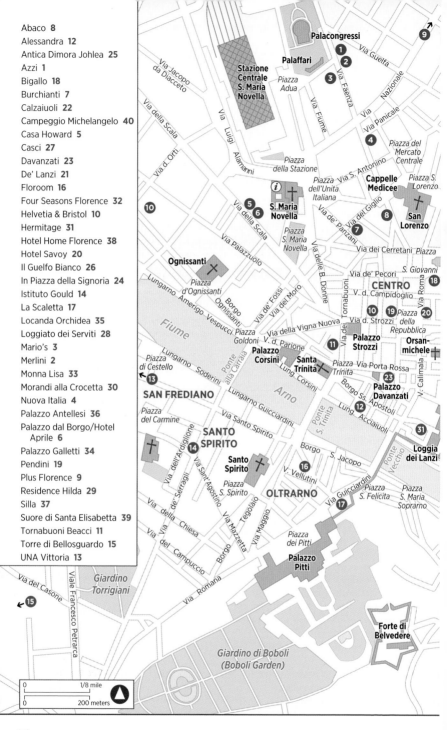

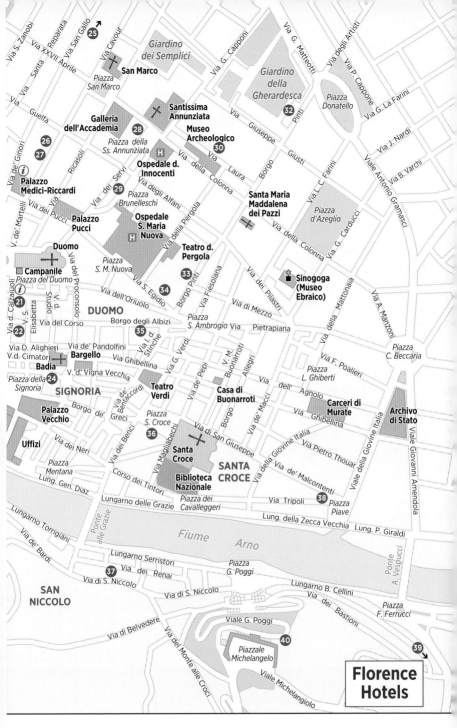

Florence Hotels

EXPENSIVE

Calzaiuoli ★ As central as you can get, the Calzaiuoli offers comfortable, well-appointed rooms on the main strolling drag halfway between the Uffizi and the Duomo. The halls' rich runners lead up a *pietra serena* staircase to the midsize and largish rooms decorated with painted friezes and framed etchings. The firm beds rest on patterned carpets; the bathrooms range from huge to cramped, but all have fluffy towels (and a few have Jacuzzis). The rooms overlook the street, with its pedestrian carnival and some of the associated noise, or out the back—either over the rooftops to the Bargello and Badia towers or up to the Duomo's cupola.

Via Calzaiuoli 6 (near Orsanmichele), 50122 Firenze. www.calzaiuoli.it. ✆ **055-212-456.** Fax 055-268-310. 53 units. 120€–490€ double. Rates include breakfast. AE, DC, MC, V. Valet garage parking 26€. Bus: C2. **Amenities:** Bar; babysitting; concierge. *In room:* A/C, TV, hair dryer, minibar, Wi-Fi (free).

MODERATE

Bigallo In the competition for best location, the Bigallo is hard to beat, sitting on the corner of Piazza del Duomo. Request one of the few rooms facing the Duomo to guarantee a view like no other, within poking distance of Giotto's bell tower, although the decor is a little bland. Suites all have the Duomo view as well as a mezzanine space—well worth the extra 30€ to 40€. The traffic-free zone doesn't mean you won't have significant pedestrian noise that drifts up from the cobbled street below, as this is the city's most tourist-trammeled intersection.

Vicolo degli Adimari 2 (off Via Calzaiuoli by Piazza del Duomo), 50122 Firenze. www.hotelbigallo. it. ✆/fax **055-216-086.** 17 units. 104€–199€ double; 133€–271€ suite. Rates include breakfast. AE, DC, MC, V. Garage valet parking 21€. Bus: C2. **Amenities:** Concierge. *In room:* A/C, TV, hair dryer, minibar, Wi-Fi (5€/day).

Burchianti ★★ 🏠 In 2002, rising rents forced the kindly owner of this venerable inn (established in the 19th c.) to move up the block into the *piano nobile* of a neighboring 15th-century *palazzo*. She definitely traded up. Incredible frescoes dating from 17th century and later decorate virtually every ceiling. This is one of the most sought-after little hotels in Florence, so be sure to book well in advance.

Via del Giglio 8 (off Via Panzani), 50123 Firenze. www.hotelburchianti.it. ✆ **055-212-796.** Fax 055-272-9727. 12 units. 100€–130€ double; 115€–155€ triple; 140€–170€ junior suite. Rates include breakfast. AE, DC, MC, V. Garage parking 25€. Bus: C2, 6, 14, 22, 36, or 37. **Amenities:** Concierge. *In room:* A/C, TV, hair dryer, minibar, Wi-Fi (free).

De' Lanzi A quieter alternative to the Hotel Bigallo, its sister hotel around the corner (see above), the De' Lanzi is just as centrally located and more comfortable; it just doesn't have those drop-dead views of the Duomo and bell tower, and the entrance is not particularly photogenic. Still, the beds have firm mattresses and spreads embroidered in an antique Florentine pattern. The accommodations, in fact, are done tastefully for a hotel of this price. A few rooms on the front get a window-filling side view of the Duomo, but for silence request a room overlooking the central courtyard.

Via delle Oche 11 (off Via Calzaiuoli), 50122 Firenze. www.hoteldelanziflorence.com. ✆/fax **055-288-043.** 44 units. 100€–150€ double; 130€–180€ triple. Rates include breakfast. AE, DC, MC, V. Garage parking 21€–26€. Bus: C2. **Amenities:** Bar; concierge; Internet. *In room:* A/C, TV, hair dryer, minibar.

Pendini 😊 Built during the heyday of the 1880s, when Florence was briefly the capital of the newly unified Italy, the Pendini rises above the arcades of Piazza della Repubblica. The entrance is not very welcoming and the furniture has seen better days, but it is clean and a great value for the location, poised next to the top shops in the city, and it retains a certain old-fashioned charm. The rather large accommodations on the piazza have the best views, over the bustle of the cafe-lined square, but they also pose a real risk of a noisy night. One child stays free in a parent's room.

Via Strozzi 2 (on Piazza della Repubblica), 50123 Firenze. www.hotelpendini.it. ✆ **055-211-170.** Fax 055-281-807. 42 units. 90€–189€ double; 120€–240€ triple. Rates include breakfast. AE, MC, V. Bus: C2, 6, 11, 22, 36, or 37. **Amenities:** Bar; concierge. *In room:* A/C, TV, hair dryer on request, Wi-Fi (free).

INEXPENSIVE

Abaco ★ Owner Bruno continues to please his guests with a clean, efficient little hotel in a prime location, albeit short on creature comforts. The Abaco has inherited a few nice touches from its 15th-century *palazzo,* including high wood ceilings, stone floors (some parquet), and even a carved *pietra serena* fireplace. Each room is themed after a Renaissance artist, with framed reproductions of the painter's works; this hotel is more beatnik, less Bulgari, and has been done up with quirky antique-style pieces such as gilded frame mirrors and rich half-testers over the beds. It's at a busy intersection, but the double-paned windows help. Those who are not okay with lugging suitcases up stairs should look elsewhere.

Via dei Banchi 1 (off Via de' Panzani), 50123 Firenze. www.abaco-hotel.it. ✆ **055-238-1919.** Fax 055-282-289. 7 units. 45€–75€ double without bathroom; 60€–90€ double with bathroom; extra 20€ per person to make a triple or quad. Rates include breakfast. AE, MC, V. Garage parking 24€. Bus: C2, 6, 14, 22, 36, or 37. **Amenities:** Bar; concierge. *In room:* A/C, TV, hair dryer, Wi-Fi (free).

Near Piazza Della Signoria

The best B&B close to this bustling civic heart of the city is aptly-titled **In Piazza della Signoria ★**, Via dei Magazzini 2, 50122 Firenze (www.inpiazza dellasignoria.com; ✆ **055-239-9546**). The 10 refined rooms, named after famous Florentines through the ages and embellished in the *residenza d'epoca* style with antique furnishings, cost between 160€ and 220€ without a view; it's an extra 30€ to 40€ per night for one of the best views in Florence.

EXPENSIVE

Hermitage ★ This ever-popular hotel is located right at the foot of the Ponte Vecchio. The rooms are of moderate size, occasionally a bit dark, but they're full of 17th- to 19th-century antiques and boast double-glazed windows to cut down on noise. Rooms have either wood floors or thick rugs, and superior room bathrooms have Jacuzzis; those that don't face the Ponte Vecchio are on side alleys and quieter. Their famous roof terrace is covered in bright flowers that frame postcard views of the Arno, Duomo, and Palazzo Vecchio. The charming breakfast room full of picture windows gets the full effect of the morning sun. The owners and staff excel in doing the little things that help make your vacation go smoothly—but prices are a bit inflated.

Vicolo Marzio 1/Piazza del Pesce (to the left of the Ponte Vecchio as you're facing it), 50122 Firenze. www.hermitagehotel.com. ✆ **055-287-216.** Fax 055-212-208. 28 units. 120€–220€ double; 160€–250€ triple. Rates include breakfast. AE, MC, V. Valet garage parking 25€. Bus: C1, 3, 12, 13, or 23. **Amenities:** Bar; babysitting; concierge; Wi-Fi (2€/hr.). *In room:* A/C, TV, hair dryer.

Near San Lorenzo & the Mercato Centrale
MODERATE

Il Guelfo Bianco ★★ Once you enter this refined hotel you'll forget it's on busy Via Cavour. Its windows are triple-paned, blocking out nearly all traffic noise, and many rooms overlook quiet courtyards and gardens out back. The interior successfully combines modern comforts with antique details. Some rooms have retained such 17th-century features as frescoed or painted wood ceilings, carved wooden doorways, and the occasional parquet floor—deluxe rooms 101, 118, 228, and 338 have a separate seating area. The friendly staff is full of advice.

Via Cavour 29 (near the corner of Via Guelfa), 50129 Firenze. www.ilguelfobianco.it. ✆ **055-288-330.** Fax 055-295-203. 40 units. 99€–250€ double; 133€–300€ triple. Rates include breakfast. AE, DC, MC, V. Valet garage parking 26€–32€. Bus: C1, 14, or 23. **Amenities:** Restaurant; bar; babysitting; concierge; room service. *In room:* A/C, TV, hair dryer, minibar, Wi-Fi (free).

INEXPENSIVE

Casci ★ ☺ 🍴 This clean hotel in a 15th-century *palazzo* is run by the Lombardis, one of Florence's most accommodating families. It's patronized by a host of regulars who know a good value when they find it. The frescoed bar room was, from 1851 to 1855, part of an apartment inhabited by Gioacchino Rossini, composer of the *Barber of Seville* and *William Tell Overture*. The rooms ramble on toward the back forever, overlooking the gardens and Florentine rooftops, and are mouse-quiet except for the birdsong. Ask for a double with a bath and shower, as those units are the most recently updated. A few family suites in back sleep four to five. The central location means some rooms (with double-paned windows) overlook busy Via Cavour, so if you're seeking quiet ask for a room facing the inner courtyard.

Via Cavour 13 (btw. Via dei Ginori and Via Guelfa), 50129 Firenze. www.hotelcasci.com. ✆ **055-211-686.** Fax 055-239-6461. 25 units. 80€–150€ double; 100€–190€ triple; 120€–230€ quad. Rates include buffet breakfast. 10% discount for cash payment; check website for offers, including one free museum ticket per guest Nov–Feb. AE, DC, MC, V. Garage parking 15€–23€. Bus: C1, 14, or 23. Closed 2 weeks in Dec and 3 weeks in Jan. **Amenities:** Bar; babysitting; concierge. *In room:* A/C, TV/DVD, DVD library, fridge, hair dryer, Wi-Fi (free).

Near Piazza Santa Trinita
VERY EXPENSIVE

Helvetia & Bristol ★★ This classy Belle Epoque hotel is the most central of the top luxury properties in town, host in the past to the Tuscan Macchiaioli painters as well as De Chirico, playwright Pirandello, and atom-splitting Enrico Fermi. The attentive staff oversees the rather cushy accommodations outfitted with marble bathrooms, large, firm beds, and heavy curtains. Most rooms have at least one antique work of art on the fabric-covered walls, and all are well insulated from the sounds of the outside world. The large 17th-century canvases add an air of dignity.

Via dei Pescioni 2 (opposite Palazzo Strozzi), 50123 Firenze. www.royaldemeure.com. ✆ **055-26-651.** Fax 055-288-353. 67 units. 285€–475€ classic double; 325€–540€ executive double;

396€–660€ deluxe double. AE, DC, MC, V. Valet garage parking 45€. Bus: C2, 6, 11, 22, 36, 37, or 68. **Amenities:** Restaurant; bar; babysitting; bikes; concierge; room service. *In room:* A/C, TV, hair dryer, minibar, Wi-Fi (18€/day).

EXPENSIVE

Tornabuoni Beacci ★ From the Renaissance until the 19th century this was the sumptuous guesthouse of the Strozzi family. It later became a sort of luxury *pensione,* and then a grand hotel. The staff greets return guests and new friends alike with genuine warmth. Everything is a bit worn, but there's a concerted effort to furnish the rooms with period pieces—and the real treasure is the roof deck. In summer, you can take breakfast on this terrace bursting with a view of the Bellosguardo hills. Off the terrace is a bar, and there's an atmospheric reading room with a 17th-century tapestry and a large fireplace that roars to life in winter.

Via Tornabuoni 3 (off the north corner of Piazza Santa Trínita), 50123 Firenze. www.tornabuoni hotels.com. ✆ **055-212-645.** Fax 055-283-594. 28 units. 90€–350€ double; 130€–380€ triple. Rates include buffet breakfast. AE, DC, MC, V. Garage valet parking 230€. Bus: 6, 11, 36, 37, or 68. **Amenities:** Restaurant; bar; babysitting; concierge; room service. *In room:* A/C, TV, hair dryer, minibar, Wi-Fi (free).

MODERATE

Alessandra ★ 🍴 This old-fashioned *pensione* in a 1507 *palazzo* just off the river charges little for its simple comfort and kind hospitality. The rooms differ greatly in size and style, and while they won't win any awards from *Architectural Digest,* there are a few antique pieces and parquet floors to add to the charm. The bathrooms are outfitted with fluffy white towels, and the shared bathrooms are ample, clean, and numerous enough that you won't have to wait in line in the morning.

Borgo SS. Apostoli 17 (btw. Via dei Tornabuoni and Via Por Santa Maria), 50123 Firenze. www.hotel alessandra.com. ✆ **055-283-438.** Fax 055-210-619. 27 units (20 with private bathroom). 110€ double without bathroom; 150€–175€ double with bathroom; 150€ triple without bathroom; 195€ triple with bathroom; 160€ quad without bathroom; 215€ quad with bathroom. Rates include buffet breakfast. AE, MC, V. Valet garage parking 22€–27€. Bus: 6, 11, 36, 37, or 68. **Amenities:** Bar; concierge. *In room:* A/C, TV, hair dryer, minibar (in some), Wi-Fi (free).

Davanzati ★★ ☺ 🍴 A dizzying array of recently renovated rooms, each equipped to a high specification, plus a great location at an unbeatable value make this one of our favorite moderately priced hotels in the *centro storico.* No two units in the sympathetically converted, 15th-century *palazzo* are the same: Your best bet is to tell the friendly staff your party size and requirements, and let them advise. Our personal favorite is no. 100, in light wood with cream fabrics and multiple split levels that have private sleeping areas, ideal if you're traveling with kids (who will also like the laptop and PlayStation that are standard in every room).

Via Porta Rossa 5 (on Piazza Davanzati), 50123 Firenze. www.hoteldavanzati.it. ✆ **055-286-666.** Fax 055-265-8252. 21 units. 120€–188€ double; 150€–312€ superior sleeping up to 4; 190€–352€ suite. Rates include breakfast. Valet garage parking 26€. AE, MC, V. Bus: C2, 6, 11, 22, 36, 37, or 68. **Amenities:** Bar; babysitting; concierge. *In room:* A/C, TV, hair dryer, minibar, Wi-Fi (free).

South of Santa Maria Novella

MODERATE

Casa Howard ★★ 🍴 Quirky, midsize, individual rooms in this *palazzo* turned chic, contemporary guesthouse come with stylized themes: If you're the intellectual type, you'll enjoy the Library Room, which is filled with wall-to-wall reading. Our other favorite rooms include the Fireplace Room, with two picture windows. The three different rooms that comprise the Oriental Room are filled with objects collected by the owners in Asia, including a gigantic lacquer red shower. The Black and White Room lives up to its name, right down to a zebra armchair, and the small, cozy Hidden Room is dressed in sensual red. **Note:** The surroundings are plush and refined, and the welcome is friendly, but this is *not* a hotel. If you require hotel-type services to enjoy a stay, look elsewhere.

Via della Scala 18, 50123 Firenze. www.casahoward.com. © **0669-924-555.** Fax 0667-94-644. 13 units. 120€–240€ double. Rates include breakfast. AE, MC, V. Bus: 11, 36, 37, or 68. **Amenities:** Concierge. *In room:* A/C, TV, hair dryer, minibar, no phone, Wi-Fi (free).

Palazzo dal Borgo/Hotel Aprile The friendly Aprile fills a semi-restored 15th-century *palazzo* on this busy hotel-laden street near the station. Aside from their antique touches, the pleasant guest rooms are nothing to write home about. The street noise gets through even the double glazing, so light sleepers will want to request a room off the road—besides, some of the back rooms have a breath-taking view of Santa Maria Novella. Historical footnote: Cavernous room no. 3 has had a bathroom attached to it since the 15th century, one of the first "rooms with bathroom" ever!

Via della Scala 6 (1½ blocks from the train station), 50123 Firenze. www.hotelaprile.it. © **055-216-237.** Fax 055-280-947. 34 units. 150€–320€ double; 180€–350€ triple. Rates include buffet breakfast. AE, DC, MC, V. Garage parking 26€. Bus: 11, 36, 37, or 68. **Amenities:** Bar; concierge. *In room:* A/C, TV, hair dryer, minibar, Wi-Fi (free).

Between Santa Maria Novella & Mercato Centrale

MODERATE

Mario's ★★ In a traditional Old Florence atmosphere, the Masieri and Benelli families run a first-rate ship. Your room might have a wrought-iron headboard and massive reproduction antique armoire, and look out onto a peaceful garden. The beamed ceilings in the common areas date from the 17th century, although the building became a hotel only in 1872. The only major drawback is its location—it's a bit far from the Duomo nerve center. Hefty discounts during off-season months "de-splurge" this lovely choice.

Via Faenza 89 (1st floor; near Via Cennini), 50123 Firenze. www.hotelmarios.com. © **055-216-801.** Fax 055-212-039. 16 units. 80€–150€ double; 110€–185€ triple. Rates include breakfast. AE, DC, MC, V. Bus: 1, 2, 12, 13, 28, 29, 30, 35, 57, or 70. **Amenities:** Bar; babysitting; concierge. *In room:* A/C, TV/DVD, hair dryer, Wi-Fi (free).

INEXPENSIVE

Azzi ★ Musicians Sandro and Valentino, the owners of this ex-*pensione* (also known as the Locanda degli Artisti/Artists' Inn), have created here a haven for artists, artist *manqués*, and students. It exudes a relaxed bohemian feel—not all the doors hang straight and not all the bedspreads match, though strides are being made (and they've even discovered some old frescoes in a couple of the rooms). You'll love the open terrace with a view where breakfast is served in warm weather, as well as the small library of art books and guidebooks. Only two rooms face the noisy street out front—you don't want either of those.

Via Faenza 88r (1st floor), 50123 Firenze. www.hotelazzi.com. © **055-213-806.** Fax 055-239-8322. 16 units. 80€–130€ double; 85€–140€ triple. Rates include breakfast. AE, DC, MC, V. Garage parking 16€. Bus: 1, 2, 12, 13, 28, 29, 30, 35, 57, or 70. **Amenities:** Bar; concierge; Wi-Fi (free). *In room:* A/C, TV, hair dryer, no phone.

Merlini ★ Run by the Sicilian Gabriella family, this cozy third-floor walk-up renovated in 2010 is a notch above your average budget place, the best in a building full of tiny *pensioni*. The optional breakfast is served on a sunny glassed-in terrace decorated in the 1960s with frescoes by talented American art students and overlooking a leafy large courtyard. Room nos. 1, 4 (with a balcony), 6 through 8, and 11 all have views of the domes topping the Duomo and the Medici Chapels across the city's terra-cotta roofscape.

Via Faenza 56 (3rd floor), 50123 Firenze. www.hotelmerlini.it. © **055-212-848.** 10 units. 50€–80€ double without bathroom; 50€–100€ double with bathroom. Garage parking 20€. AE, DC, MC, V. Bus: 1, 2, 12, 13, 28, 29, 30, 35, 57, or 70. **Amenities:** Bar. *In room:* A/C, TV, hair dryer, no phone, Wi-Fi (free).

Nuova Italia A Frommer's fairy tale: With her trusty Arthur Frommer's *Europe on $5 a Day* in hand, the fair Eileen left the kingdom of Canada on a journey to faraway Florence. At her hotel, Eileen met Luciano, her baggage boy in shining armor. They fell in love, got married, bought a castle (er, hotel) of their own called the Nuova Italia, and their clients live happily ever after . . . The rooms are medium to small, and a little characterless, but the attention to detail and impeccable service makes the Nuova Italia stand out. Every room has triple-paned windows, though some morning rumble from the San Lorenzo market still gets through. The family's love of art is manifested in framed posters and paintings, and staff here really puts itself out for guests, recommending restaurants, shops, and day trips.

Via Faenza 26 (off Via Nazionale), 50123 Firenze. www.hotel-nuovaitalia.com. © **055-287-508.** Fax 055-210-941. 20 units. 54€–139€ double; 74€–149€ triple. Rates include breakfast. AE, MC, V. Garage parking 24€. Bus: 1, 2, 12, 13, 28, 29, 30, 35, 57, or 70. **Amenities:** Bar; concierge. *In room:* A/C, TV, hair dryer, Wi-Fi (free).

Near San Marco & Santissima Annunziata
VERY EXPENSIVE

Four Seasons Florence ★★★ If the Medici should miraculously return to Florence, surely the clan would move in here. Installed in the overhauled historic Palazzo della Gherardesca and a former convent, this spa hotel offers spectacular frescoes, museum-worthy sculptures, and Florentine artisanal works, with its oldest wing dating from the 1440s. Its grounds are on one of the largest private gardens in the city. Damask draperies, regal appointments in all the bedrooms, fabric-trimmed walls, ceramic floors, an elegant spa, rich marble bathrooms, luxurious beds and furnishings, and pools equipped with phones are just some of the features that make this perhaps the finest Four Seasons in Europe.

Borgo Pinti 99, 50121 Firenze. www.fourseasons.com/florence. © **055-2626-250.** Fax 055-2626-500. 116 units. 550€–850€ double. AE, DC, MC, V. Free valet parking. Bus: 8 or 70. **Amenities:** 4 restaurants; 2 bars; concierge; gym; outdoor pool; room service; spa. *In room:* TV/DVD, CD player, fax (on request), fridge (on request), hair dryer, MP3 docking station, Wi-Fi.

EXPENSIVE

Loggiato dei Serviti ★ There's no mistaking the Renaissance aura: The Loggiato is installed in the building designed by Antonio da Sangallo the Elder in 1527 to mirror the Ospedale degli Innocenti across the piazza, forming part of one of Italy's most beautiful squares. High vaulted ceilings in soft creams abound throughout and are supported by the gray columns of the bar/lounge. The wood or brick-tiled floors in the rooms are covered with rugs, and most of the beds have wood frames and fabric canopies for an antique feel. The rooms along the front can be a bit noisy in the evenings because traffic is routed through the edges of the piazza, but we usually reserve one anyway, just for the magical view.

Piazza Santissima Annunziata 3, 50122 Firenze. www.loggiatodeiservitihotel.it. © **055-289-592.** Fax 055-289-595. 38 units. 120€–205€ double. Rates include breakfast. AE, DC, MC, V. Valet garage parking 20€. Bus: C1, 6, 14, 23, 31, 32, or 71. **Amenities:** Babysitting; concierge; Wi-Fi. *In room:* A/C, TV, hair dryer, minibar.

MODERATE

Antica Dimora Johlea ★★ A *"dimora"* is a refined residence, and that's exactly what this boho B&B feels like—a regal, but still homey and comfortable Florentine home. Rooms are midsize with parquet floors and four-poster beds, and come embellished with rich fabrics; the interior decor draws inspiration from East and West. Space throughout is at a premium, but that just makes it all the cozier. We're docking one star for a rather bland location 15 minutes' walk north of Piazza della Signoria, but adding it right back on again for Florence's best roof terrace in this price category—a little eyrie that looks right at Brunelleschi's dome.

Antica Dimora Johlea is part of a mini *residenza* empire that's grown up in the surrounding streets. All offer a similar take on a Florence city break—see the website for details of four more comfortable, characterful *dimore* if this place is full.

Via San Gallo 80, 50129 Firenze. www.johanna.it. © **055-463-3292.** Fax 055-463-4552. 6 units. 100€–170€ double. Rates include buffet breakfast. No credit cards. Bus: C1, 1, 7, 20, or 25. **Amenities:** Honesty bar. *In room:* A/C, TV/DVD, DVD library, hair dryer, Wi-Fi (free).

Morandi alla Crocetta ★ This subtly elegant hotel belongs to a different era, when travelers stayed in private homes filled with family heirlooms and well-kept antiques. Although the setting is indeed historical (it was a 1511 Dominican nuns' convent), many of the old-fashioned effects, such as the wood-beam ceilings, 1500s artwork, and antique furnishings, are the result of a redecoration. It has all been done in good taste, however, and there are still plenty of echoes of the original structure, from exposed brick arches to one room's 16th-century fresco fragments.

Via Laura 50 (a block east of Piazza Santissima Annunziata), 50121 Firenze. www.hotelmorandi. it. © **055-234-4747.** Fax 055-248-0954. 10 units. 100€–150€ double; 150€–180€ triple. Rates include breakfast. AE, DC, MC, V. Garage parking 20€. Bus: 6, 14, 23, 31, 32, or 71. **Amenities:** Bar; babysitting; concierge. *In room:* A/C, TV, hair dryer, minibar, Wi-Fi (8€/day; free in low season).

Near Santa Croce

EXPENSIVE

Hotel Home Florence ★★ Minimalist chic meets dazzling bright-white (like an ultra-fashionable ski resort) at this 2009 addition to Florence's crop of design hotels. A harmonious colonial villa on the eastern fringe of the *centro storico* was transformed in 2009 into the ultimate city bolthole for anyone seeking sleek design at a reasonably sensible price. Rooms are kitted out to a top contemporary spec: all-white homewares and furnishings are by the Cyrus Company (which owns the hotel); there's Nespresso machines and iPods in all the rooms and a free bar (alcoholic drinks extra) throughout. If money is no object, the suite has a terrace that surveys the city skyline, and there's an unforgettable rooftop Jacuzzi rentable by the night (250€) with a 360-degree panorama of Florence.

A Soothing Central Spa

If you can't stretch to one of Florence's upscale spa hotels, book a session at **Soulspace,** Via Sant'Egidio 12 (🕾 **055-200-1794; www.soulspace.it). This calm, contemporary spot has a heated pool and hammam (Turkish bath), and a range of modern spa treatments for women and men including aromatherapy massages. Day spa packages cost from 50€ upward.

Piazza Piave 3, 50122 Firenze. www.hhflorence.it. 🕾 **055-243-668.** Fax 055-200-9852. 38 units. 150€–300€ double; 300€–450€ suite. Rates include breakfast. AE, DC, MC, V. Garage parking 30€. Bus: 8, 12, 13, 14, 23, 31, 32, 33, 70, or 71. **Amenities:** Bar; airport transfer; babysitting; bikes; concierge; gym; Jacuzzi; room service. *In room:* A/C, TV, hair dryer, minibar (free), Wi-Fi (free).

Monna Lisa ★★ There's a certain old-world elegance, reminiscent of an English country manor, to the richly decorated common rooms and the gravel-strewn garden of this 14th-century *palazzo*. Among the potted plants and framed oils, the hotel has Giambologna's original rough competition piece for the *Rape of the Sabines,* along with many pieces by neoclassical sculptor Giovanni Duprè, whose family's descendants own the hotel. They try their best to keep the entire place looking like a private home, and many rooms have the original painted wood ceilings, as well as antique furniture and richly textured wallpaper and fabrics, although the Jacuzzi tubs in superior units are very much 21st-century additions. Outbuildings known as "La Scudera" and "La Limonaia" overlook a peaceful garden.

Borgo Pinti 27, 50121 Firenze. www.monnalisa.it. 🕾 **055-247-9751.** Fax 055-247-9755. 45 units. 139€–289€ double. Rates include buffet breakfast. AE, DC, MC, V. Garage parking 20€. Bus: C1, C2, 14, 23, or 71. **Amenities:** Bar; babysitting; concierge; small gym. *In room:* A/C, TV, hair dryer, minibar, Wi-Fi (5€/30 min.).

MODERATE

Palazzo Galletti ★★ 🏛 *Palazzo* living doesn't come much more refined than in the restored 18th-century surrounds of this *residenza d'epoca* B&B. Elegant rooms are arranged around a tranquil atrium, and named after the planets (which themselves are named after Roman gods). Doubles are on the big side for Florence, with tall ceilings, but if you can stretch to a suite such as Giove or Cerere, you'll have a memorable stay surrounded by original 18th-century frescoes restored by the owners. Breakfast is served in a vaulted former kitchen that predates the *palazzo*—it originally belonged to a building that stood here in the 1500s.

Via Sant'Egidio 12, 50122 Firenze. www.palazzogalletti.it. 🕾 **055-390-5750.** Fax 055-390-5752. 11 units. 100€–160€ double; 170€–240€ suite. Rates include breakfast. MC, V. Bus: C1, C2, 14, 23, or 71. **Amenities:** Concierge. *In room:* A/C, TV, hair dryer, Internet (free).

INEXPENSIVE

Locanda Orchidea ★ ☺ ✦ If you need to flop on a tight budget, but don't want to compromise on location, there's nowhere cleaner or friendlier at the price. Units are compact, but plenty big enough if you're here to see the city, not your bedroom, and arranged around a communal sitting area with free tea and coffee. Rooms at the back are the most desirable, as they overlook a peaceful courtyard. Bathrooms are shared, but each room has a sink. The large family room with its own shower is a great deal.

Borgo degli Albizi 11 (close to Piazza San Pier Maggiore), 50122 Firenze. www.hotelorchidea florence.it. ℂ/fax **055-248-0346.** 7 units. 50€–80€ double; 65€–100€ triple; 75€–120€ quad. No credit cards. Bus: C1, C2, 14, 23, or 71. **Amenities:** Wi-Fi (free).

In the Oltrarno & San Frediano

MODERATE

Floroom ★ This hybrid between boutique hotel and contemporary premium B&B, overlooking a tiny Oltrarno piazza, is aimed squarely at a new, younger generation of visitor to the city. Rooms are small and monochrome, with privacy screens separating the sleeping and bathroom areas, and hung with striking black-and-white photography. Clever use of reclaimed materials, occasional exposed wood beams, and furniture in a 1950s style custom built for the space, ensure the design never veers to the cold. There's a small communal mezzanine where you can help yourself to drinks and snacks. Travel light, bring an iPad, and settle in.

Opened in 2010 by the same owners, four-room **Floroom 2** ★, Via del Sole 2 (www.floroom.com; ℂ**055-216-674**), provides equally chic, stripped-down neoclassical style in the *centro storico,* just off Via de' Tornabuoni.

Via del Pavone 7 (behind Piazza della Passera), 50125 Firenze. www.floroom.com. ℂ/fax **055-230-2462.** 4 units. 120€–160€ double. Rates include Italian breakfast. MC, V. Minimum stay 2 nights. No children 14 and under. Bus: C3, D, 11, 36, 37, or 68. **Amenities:** Honesty bar. *In room:* A/C, TV, Wi-Fi (free).

La Scaletta Three partners, Andrea, Paolo, and Fabrizi, took over this well-worn old shoe of a place in 2005, one of the only remaining *palazzo* on this block between the Pitti Palace and Ponte Vecchio. The inn's star is the flower-bedecked, sun-kissed terrace offering a 360-degree vista over the Boboli Garden, the Oltrarno rooftops, and (beyond a sea of antennas) the monumental heart of Florence. Return visitors book months in advance for the homey rooms that have tiny bathrooms and old tiled floors. Street-side accommodations have double-paned windows that really do block the noise, and the worn, dark-wood lacquer furniture is pleasantly unassuming.

Via Guicciardini 13 (2nd floor; near Piazza de' Pitti), 50125 Firenze. www.hotellascaletta.it. ℂ **055-283-028.** Fax 055-283-013. 13 units. 75€–140€ double; 90€–165€ triple. AE, MC, V. Bus: C3 or D. **Amenities:** Restaurant (May–Oct); bar (May–Oct); concierge. *In room:* A/C, TV, hair dryer, mini-bar, Wi-Fi (free).

Silla ★ On a shaded riverside piazza, this 15th-century *palazzo*'s second-floor patio terrace is one of the city's nicest breakfast settings (in winter, there's a breakfast salon with chandeliers and oil paintings). Many rooms overlook the Arno and, when winter strips the leaves off the front trees, the spire of Santa Croce on the opposite bank. The friendly, skilled staff should make this hotel better known; word-of-mouth keeps it regularly full in pricey Florence, despite its refreshing low profile.

Via de' Renai 5 (on Piazza Demidoff, east of Ponte delle Grazie), 50100 Firenze. www.hotelsilla. it. © **055-234-2888.** Fax 055-234-1437. 35 units. 89€–220€ double; 120€–270€ triple. Rates include breakfast. AE, DC, MC, V. Garage parking 19€. Bus: C3, D, 12, 13, 23, or 71. **Amenities:** Bar; babysitting; concierge. *In room:* A/C, TV, hair dryer, minibar, Wi-Fi (free).

UNA Vittoria ★★ Is this a boutique hotel or a disco? Either way, this out-post of the small Italian chain UNA is in a class of its own when it comes to contemporary styling at an affordable price. The second you step into the floor-to-ceiling mosaic in the reception area, you realize this is no ordinary Florentine inn. Midsize rooms are bold and contemporary (quite un-chainlike), and all come equipped with modern amenities like 32-inch plasma TVs. A rolling program of renovations ensures interiors never grow tired. Executive rooms come with super-sexy all-in-one rainfall tub/shower combos.

Via Pisana 59 (at Piazza Pier Vettori), 50143 Firenze. www.unahotels.it. © **055-22-771.** Fax 055-22-772. 84 units. 109€–306€ double. Rates include breakfast. MC, V. Garage parking 20€. Bus: 6. **Amenities:** Restaurant; bar; bikes; concierge. *In room:* TV, hair dryer, Wi-Fi (free).

In the Hills

EXPENSIVE

Torre di Bellosguardo ★★★ 🏨 This castle was built around a 13th-century tower sprouting from a hillside on the southern edge of Florence. Spend a few days here above the city heat and noise, lounging by the pool, hiking the olive groves, or sitting on a garden bench to enjoy the intimate close-range vista of the city. Don't come expecting a climate-controlled and carpeted bastion of luxury, however. With its echoey halls, airy loggias, and imposing stone staircases, the Bellosguardo feels just a few flickering torches shy of the Middle Ages—exactly its attraction. It's packed with antiques, and the beds from various eras are partic-ularly gorgeous. Some rooms have intricately carved wood ceilings, others sport fading frescoes, and many have views, including a 360-degree panorama in the romantic tower suite.

Via Roti Michelozzi 2, 50124 Firenze. www.torrebellosguardo.com. © **055-229-8145.** Fax 055-229-008. 16 units. 250€–290€ double; 290€–340€ suite. AE, MC, V. Free parking. Bus: D, 12, or 13 to Piazza Tasso (then taxi up hill). **Amenities:** Bar; airport transfer; babysitting; concierge; exercise room; Jacuzzi; outdoor pool (June–Sept); small indoor pool; room service; sauna; Wi-Fi (free). *In room:* A/C (in some), TV, hair dryer, minibar.

MODERATE

Pensione Bencistà ★ ☺ This comfortable and quiet family-run *pensione* in a rambling 14th-century villa gets you the same drop-dead view and escape from the city as the local celeb hangout, Villa San Michele, at one-fifth the price—plus owners who are friendly and truly consider you a guest in their home. Antiques abound in aging, elegantly cluttered salons that are straight out of an E. M. Forster novel. Many accommodations have big old chests of drawers, and some open onto the pretty little garden. If the budget will stretch, go for a superior with a balcony and much more space. Some rooms, bathrooms especially, are getting a little tired for this price category, but that million-dollar view is irreplaceable.

Via Benedetto da Maiano 4 (just below Fiesole off the main road.), 50014 Fiesole (FI). www. bencista.com. ©/fax **055-59-163.** 40 units. 143€–158€ double; 160€–178€ double with view; 180€–192€ triple. Half-board 13€ per person. MC, V. Free parking. Bus: 7. **Amenities:** Restaurant; bar; airport transfer; babysitting; children's play area; concierge; Internet (free). *In room:* Hair dryer.

Apartments

Many of the agencies listed under "Tips on Accommodations," in chapter 12, also handle villas in Florence's hills and apartments in town. One of the most reputable city specialists is **Florence and Abroad,** Via San Zanobi 58 (℃**055-487-004;** www.florenceandabroad.com), which matches different tastes and budgets to a wide range of apartments. Another reputable agency for short-term apartment and house rentals (weekly and monthly) is **Windows on Tuscany,** Via de' Serragli 6r (℃**055-268-510;** www.windowsontuscany.com). Online agencies **Cross Pollinate** (www.cross-pollinate.com) and **RentXpress** (℃**02-8734-4500** in Italy; www.rentxpress.com) also have good apartment portfolios covering Florence.

For basic grocery shopping, try **Conad City,** Via dei Servi 56r (℃**055-280-110**) or any central branch of **Supermercato il Centro:** There's a map at **www.ilcentro.biz**.

Palazzo Antellesi ★ Many people passing through Piazza Santa Croce notice Giovanni di Ser Giovanni's 1620 graffiti frescoes on the overhanging facade of no. 21, but few realize they can actually stay there (weeklong bookings only). The 16th-century *palazzo* is owned by Signora Piccolomini, who rents them out to anyone who has dreamed of lying in bed next to a roaring fire under a 17th-century frescoed ceiling, or sipping tea in a living room surrounded by *trompe l'oeil* Roman ruins with a 16th-century wood ceiling above (the Donatello, which sleeps six to seven). Even in the more standard units the furnishings are tasteful, with wicker, wood, or wrought-iron bed frames; potted plants; and the occasional 18th-century inlaid wood dresser to go with the plush couches. Author R. W. B. Lewis wrote about the Antellesi in the final chapter of *City of Florence.*

Piazza Santa Croce 21, 50122 Firenze. www.palazzoantellesi.com. ℃ **845/704-2426** in the U.S., or 055-244-456. Fax 055-234-5552. 13 units (sleeping 2–7). $2,100–$5,500 per week (all priced in U.S. dollars). Final cleaning and utilities extra. No credit cards. Garage parking 16€. Bus: C1, 3, or 23. **Amenities:** Babysitting; exercise room. *In room:* A/C, TV/DVD, CD player, fridge, hair dryer, kitchen, Wi-Fi.

Residence Hilda ★★★ ☺ The best place in the city to combine apartment convenience with hotel services. What these elegant apartments lack in period charm they comfortably make up for with space, crisp, contemporary design, and modern facilities—and the fact that they are available from a single night upward. All units have large living areas, with a double or twin sofa bed, big bathrooms, well-equipped kitchens, and a double bedroom; family suites are big enough to set up home in. The airy, cool design includes stripped and polished floors, cream walls, and sliding divider doors. The location, between the Duomo and Santissima Annunziata, is ideal. Child equipment like highchairs and cots are included in the price.

Via dei Servi 40 (2 blocks north of the Duomo), 50122 Firenze. www.residencehilda.it. ℃ **055-288-021.** Fax 055-287-664. 12 units. 150€–450€ per night for apartments sleeping 2–5. Breakfast 7.50€ (served next door). AE, MC, V. Valet garage parking 30€. Bus: C1, 6, 14, 23, 31, 32, or 71. **Amenities:** Airport transfer; babysitting; concierge; room service. *In room:* A/C, TV, DVD player (on request), CD player (on request), hair dryer, kitchen, Wi-Fi (free).

Hostels, Camping & Convents

Florence's central hostels are immensely popular, especially in summer. If you aren't able to e-mail or call to reserve a space—months ahead, if possible—show up when they open with your fingers crossed.

An alternative budget option is to stay in a religious house. A few monasteries and convents in the Florence area are happy to receive guests for a modest fee. The **Suore di Santa Elisabetta,** Viale Michelangiolo 46, 50125 Firenze (close to Piazza Ferrucci; www.csse-roma.eu; ✆/fax **055-681-1884**) occupy a colonial villa a short walk south of Ponte San Niccolò. Simple en suite singles (for either sex), doubles, and family rooms are on offer; there's no need for you to be religious, merely respectful. Bus nos. 12, 13, and 39 drop you almost at the door, and the sisters also have a small, free, locked car park. The easiest way to build a monastery and convent itinerary in the city and beyond is via agent **Monasterystays.com**. Note that most religious houses have a curfew, generally 11pm or midnight.

Campeggio Michelangelo ☺
Here you can sleep with a select 1,000 of your fellow campers and have almost the same vista that the tour buses get up above on Piazzale Michelangiolo. (Sadly, a stand of trees blocks the Duomo.) Of course, you're packed in like sardines on this small plateau with very little shade (in Aug, arrive early to fight for a spot along the tree-lined fringe), but you get a bar, a minimart, a laundromat, cheap prices, and that killer view.

Viale Michelangelo 80 (just east of Piazzale Michelangiolo), 50125 Firenze. www.ecvacanze.it/en/campingmichelangelo. ✆ **055-681-1977.** Fax 055-689-348. Open camping (sleeps 1,000). 9.50€–12€ per adult, plus 12€–14€ per pitch. Campers 13€–15€. Rented tents (sleep 2) 36€. MC, V. Free parking. Bus: 12 or 13. **Amenities:** Restaurant; bar; children's play area.

Istituto Gould ☺
These are the most characterful hostel-like accommodations in Florence, without a curfew, but with new furnishings in plain but immaculate rooms inside a *palazzo* that dates to the 1600s—like a Renaissance college dorm that's never seen a frat party. It's technically not a hostel, though it operates like one (most rooms are doubles or triples, but there's no housekeeping). The institute's real work is caring for needy or troubled youth, and the proceeds from your room fee go to help them. Reception is open Monday through Friday from 8:45am to 1pm and 3 to 7:30pm, Saturday from 9am to 1:30pm and 2:30 to 6pm; you can stay over and prepay in order to check out during Sunday, but you can't check in.

Via de' Serragli 49 (near Santo Spirito), 50124 Firenze. www.istitutogould.it/foresteria. ✆ **055-212-576.** Fax 055-280-274. 39 units (37 with private bathroom). 45€ single; 56€–68€ double; 75€–90€ triple; 88€–110€ quad. No credit cards. Bus: C3, 11, 36, 37, or 68. *In room:* No phone.

Plus Florence ☺ 💣
It's an ugly, functional building, and a 10-minute walk in the wrong direction from San Lorenzo, but the services and facilities at Florence's newest "flashpacking" hostel put hotels at five-times the price to shame. Rooms are ample in size and clean, and come with hotel-style accoutrements (towels, linen, small private shower room). Triples have a three-berth bunk (double down, single up) if you're traveling as a small family; there are also female-only accommodations. If you're a light sleeper, avoid rooms that face the busy street out front. The phenomenal services beat those at most hotels in town: There's an indoor pool, a Turkish bath, a mini-spa and beauty salon, and free Wi-Fi throughout. There's no curfew.

Via Santa Caterina d'Alessandria 15, Firenze. www.plusflorence.com. ✆ **055-462-8934.** 110 units. Dorm room from 19€ per person; 55€–65€ double; 75€–85€ triple. Breakfast 6€. MC, V. Bus: 8, 20, or 70. **Amenities:** Restaurant; bar; concierge; gym; indoor pool; sauna; small spa. *In room:* A/C (in some), TV, no phone, Wi-Fi (free).

WHERE TO EAT

Florence is thick with restaurants, though many in the most touristy areas (around the Duomo and Piazza della Signoria) are of low quality, charge high prices, or both. We'll point out the few that are worth a visit. The highest concentrations of excellent *ristoranti* and *trattorie* are around Santa Croce and across the river in the Oltrarno. For a more complete Florentine dining primer, see "Eating & Drinking in Florence, Tuscany & Umbria," in chapter 2. Bear in mind that menus at restaurants in Tuscany can change weekly or even daily.

For food delivery to your hotel or apartment, try **The Food** (*©***055-6812-477;** www.thefood.it), which for a small delivery fee services a handful of central restaurants, including a couple of our favorite places below. You can order online or by phone.

Near the Duomo

MODERATE

Ganino FLORENTINE The tiny family-run Ganino continues its tradition of friendly service and good *osteria* food, from the big ol' chunk of mortadella that accompanies your bread basket through the tasty *ribollita* or *gnocchi al pomodoro* (ricotta-and-spinach gnocchi in tomato sauce) to the *filetto all'aceto balsamico* (veal filet cooked in balsamic vinegar) or *coniglio in umido* (stewed rabbit with boiled potatoes on the side) that rounds out your meal.

Piazza de' Cimatori 4r (near the Casa di Dante). *©* **055-214-125.** Reservations recommended. Primi 9€–12€; secondi 12€–23€. AE, DC, MC, V. Mon–Sat 12:30–3pm and 7:30–10pm. Closed Aug. Bus: C1 or C2.

Paoli TUSCAN Paoli has one of the most *suggestivo* (oft-used Italian word for "evocative") settings in town, with tables under a 14th-century vaulted ceiling whose ribs and lunettes are covered with fading 18th-century frescoes. The *ravioli con burro e salvia* (with butter and sage) may not be especially creative, but it's freshly made and tasty. In mushroom season you can order *risotto ai funghi,* and

A cafe in the Oltrarno.

New York has the hot dog. London has pie and mash. Florence has . . . cow's intestine in a sandwich. The city's traditional street food, *lampredotto* (the cow's fourth stomach) stewed with tomatoes, has made a big comeback over the last decade, including on the menus of some fine-dining establishments. However, the best places to sample it are still the city's *trippai,* tripe vendors who sell it from takeaway vans around the center, alongside other, more "regular" sandwiches. The most convenient are in Piazza de' Cimatori and on Via de' Macci at the corner of Piazza Sant'Ambrogio. A hearty, nutritious lunch should come to around 4€. Most are open Monday through Saturday, but close in August, when Florentines flee their city.

a year-round offering is the scrumptious *secondo entrecôte di manzo arlecchino* (a thick steak in cognac-spiked cream sauce with peppercorns and sided with mashed potatoes).

Via dei Tavolini 12r. 🕾 **055-216-215.** www.casatrattoria.com. Reservations recommended. Primi 9€–12€; secondi 14€–22€. AE, DC, MC, V. Daily noon–3:15pm and 7–11pm. Bus: C1 or C2.

INEXPENSIVE

Cantinetta dei Verrazzano ★ WINE BAR Owned by the Castello di Verrazzano, one of Chianti's best-known wine-producing estates (p. 177), this wood-paneled *cantinetta* with a full-service bar/*pasticceria* and seating area helped spawn a revival of stylish wine bars as convenient spots for fast-food breaks. It promises a delicious self-service lunch or snack of focaccia, plain or studded with rosemary, onions, or olives; buy it hot by the slice or as *farcite* (sandwiches filled with prosciutto, arugula, cheese, or tuna). Platters of Tuscan cold cuts and aged cheeses are also available.

Via dei Tavolini 18r (off Via dei Calzaiuoli). 🕾 **055-268-590.** www.verrazzano.com. Tasting plates 4.50€–8€; glass of wine 4€–8€. AE, DC, MC, V. Mon–Sat 8am–9pm. Bus: C1 or C2.

I Due Fratellini ★ WINE BAR Just off the busiest tourist thoroughfare lies one of the last of a dying breed: a *fiaschetteria* (derived from the word for a flask of wine). It's the proverbial hole in the wall, a doorway about 1.5m (5 ft.) deep with rows of wine bottles against the back wall and the cheapest tasty lunch in town. You stand, munching and sipping, on the cobblestones of the narrow street surrounded by Florentines on their lunch break and a few bemused tourists. The *cinghiale piccante con caprino* (spicy cured wild boar sausage with creamy goat cheese) is excellent.

Via dei Cimatori 38r (2 blocks from Piazza della Signoria, off Via Calzaiuoli). 🕾 **055-239-6096.** www.iduefratellini.com. Sandwiches from 2.50€; wine from 2€ a "shot." No credit cards. Daily 9am–8pm (July–Aug closed Sat–Sun). Closed 2 weeks in mid-Aug. Bus: C1 or C2.

Le Mossacce ★ 🍴 FLORENTINE Delicious, cheap, abundant, fast home cooking: This tiny *osteria,* filled with lunching businesspeople, farmers in from the hills, locals who've been coming since 1942, and a few knowledgeable tourists, is authentic to the bone. The waiters hate breaking out the printed menu, preferring to rattle off a list of Florentine faves like *ribollita, crespelle,* and *lasagne al forno.* Unlike in many cheap joints catering to locals, the secondi are pretty good. You could try the *spezzatino* (goulashy veal stew) or a well-cooked, reasonably priced *bistecca alla fiorentina,* but I put my money on the excellent *involtini*

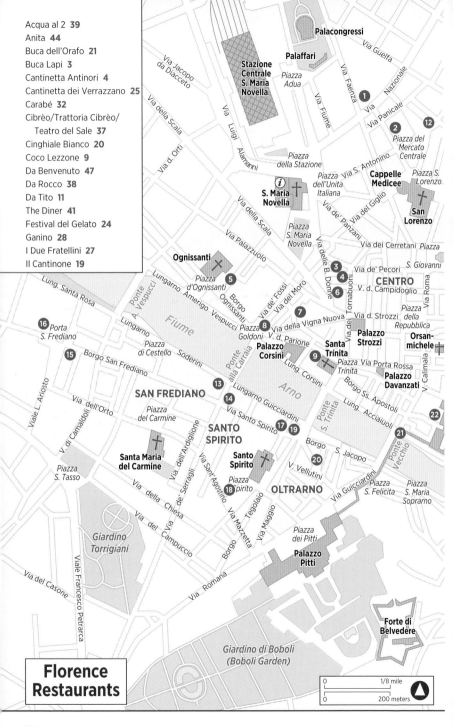

Acqua al 2 **39**
Anita **44**
Buca dell'Orafo **21**
Buca Lapi **3**
Cantinetta Antinori **4**
Cantinetta dei Verrazzano **25**
Carabé **32**
Cibrèo/Trattoria Cibrèo/
  Teatro del Sale **37**
Cinghiale Bianco **20**
Coco Lezzone **9**
Da Benvenuto **47**
Da Rocco **38**
Da Tito **11**
The Diner **41**
Festival del Gelato **24**
Ganino **28**
I Due Fratellini **27**
Il Cantinone **19**

Florence
Restaurants

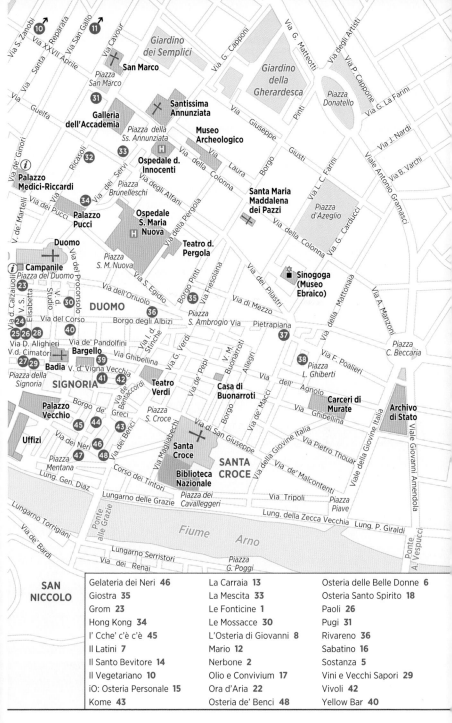

Gelateria dei Neri **46**	La Carraia **13**	Osteria delle Belle Donne **6**
Giostra **35**	La Mescita **33**	Osteria Santo Spirito **18**
Grom **23**	Le Fonticine **1**	Paoli **26**
Hong Kong **34**	Le Mossacce **30**	Pugi **31**
I' Cche' c'è c'è **45**	L'Osteria di Giovanni **8**	Rivareno **36**
Il Latini **7**	Mario **12**	Sabatino **16**
Il Santo Bevitore **14**	Nerbone **2**	Sostanza **5**
iO: Osteria Personale **15**	Olio e Convivium **17**	Vini e Vecchi Sapori **29**
Kome **43**	Ora d'Aria **22**	Vivoli **42**
	Osteria de' Benci **48**	Yellow Bar **40**
Il Vegetariano **10**		

(thin slices of beef wrapped tightly around a bread stuffing and artichoke hearts, then cooked to juiciness in tomato sauce).

Via del Proconsolo 55r (a block south of the Duomo). ℂ **055-294-361.** www.trattoria lemossacce.it. Reservations recommended for dinner. Primi 5.50€–6.50€; secondi 9€–11€. AE, MC, V. Mon–Fri noon–2:30pm and 7–9:30pm. Bus: C1 or C2.

Near Piazza Della Signoria
VERY EXPENSIVE

Ora d'Aria ★★ CONTEMPORARY TUSCAN Marco Stabile is a celebrated young Tuscan chef at the very height of his creative powers, and the 2010 relocation of his signature restaurant right into the heart of the *centro storico* has only seen his fame grow. Seasonality and a modern interpretation of Tuscan food traditions are the overarching themes of his cooking. You'll need to book ahead (and save up) to enjoy the delights of *gnocchetti di patate con pomodorini confit e guancia affumicata* (gnocchi with confit tomatoes and smoked pig's cheek) or *maialino con sottobosco, aglio e lavanda* (piglet with berries, garlic, and lavender).

Via dei Georgofili 11r (off Via Lambertesca). ℂ **055-200-1699.** www.oradariaristorante.com. Primi 18€–20€; secondi 32€–34€. AE, MC, V. Tues–Sat 12:30–2:30pm; Mon–Sat 7:30–10:30pm. Closed Aug. Bus: C1 or C2.

MODERATE

Acqua al 2 ★ ITALIAN Under a barrel-vaulted ceiling and dim sconce lights, diners sit elbow-to-elbow at tightly packed tables to sample this innovative restaurant's *assaggi* (tastings) courses. Acqua al 2 is proud of its almost cultish status, attained through the success of its *assaggio di primi,* which offers you a sampling of five flavorful pastas or *risotti.* If you order the *assaggio* for two, you both just may have room left over for a grilled portobello mushroom "steak," one of the many veal dishes, or something more cross-cultural, like *couscous d'agnello* (lamb). They also offer *assaggi* of salads, cheese, and desserts. Tour companies have started bringing in tourists by the busload on occasion, but the crowd still remains a good mix of locals and travelers.

Via della Vigna Vecchia 40r (at Via dell'Acqua). ℂ **055-284-170.** www.acquaal2.it. Reservations recommended. Primi 9€; secondi 9€–18€; *assaggio* 10€ for pasta, 5.50€ for dessert. AE, MC, V. Daily 7pm–1am. Closed 1 week in Aug. Bus: C1 or C2.

Buca dell'Orafo FLORENTINE A *buca* is a cellar joint with half a dozen crowded tables serving good, seasonal Florentine fare. A few locals come here every night, but Orafo's years in the guidebooks have made Americans its primary customers—Florentines aren't willing to give this place up yet, though, and you can still find a smattering of locals if you reserve a late seating. Alas, the heavy tourism has jacked its prices substantially above what you'd expect for peasant food. That food is still very well prepared, however, and the location can't be beat. If it's on the menu, go for the *paglia e fieno alla boscaiola* (a "hay and straw" mix of both egg and spinach fettuccine in mushroom-meat sauce). Orafo's best secondo is *arista di maiale con patate* (roast pork loin with potatoes), while candied stewed pears round out the meal nicely.

Volta dei Girolami 28r (under the arched alley left of the Ponte Vecchio). ℂ **055-213-619.** www. bucadellorafo.com. Reservations strongly recommended. Primi 10€–15€; secondi 16€–22€. No credit cards. Tues–Sat noon–2:30pm and 7:30–9:45pm. Bus: C1, 3, 6, 11, 36, 37, or 68.

l' Cche' c'è c'è ★★ TUSCAN The name is a dialect variant on "What you see is what you get." What you see is a room with modern art prints and shelves of ancient wine bottles on the walls. What you get is good Tuscan cooking from Gino Noci, who trained in the kitchens of London. There's no telling what he might come up with for an appetizer: One recent treat was a *sformatino* with pears, while for a first dish, the scrumptious *ravioli rosée* (in creamy tomato sauce) faces serious competition from the *tagliatelle alla boscaiola* (same sauce with giant slices of forest mushrooms added). Follow up with the grilled salmon or one of their specialties, *stracotto al chianti* (beef stuffed with celery and carrot and smothered in a chianti gravy served with fried polenta and an artichoke heart).

Via de' Magalotti 11r (off Borgo de' Greci). *© **055-216-589.** Reservations recommended. Primi 7€–12€; secondi 8€–16€. AE, MC, V. Tues–Sun 12:30–2:30pm and 7:30–10:30pm. Closed 1 week in Jan and 1 week in Aug. Bus: C1, 3, or 23.

Vini e Vecchi Sapori FLORENTINE/TUSCAN Within sight of the Palazzo Vecchio is this authentic *osteria* with a wood-beamed ceiling, brick floor, the end of a giant chianti barrel embedded in one wall, and a handwritten menu that starts *Oggi C'è* ("Today we got . . ."). As the sign proudly proclaims, this buzzing one-room joint is devoted to "wine and old flavors," which means lunch could consist of anything from a rib-sticking stewlike *ribollita* and a *frittata rustica* (a darkly fried omelet thick with potatoes and vegetables) to an excellent crostini assortment and *scamorza e speck al forno* (smoked mozzarella melted with ham in a bowl, to scoop out and slather onto bread). The paunchy owner will continue

 FAMILY-FRIENDLY eating

It'd be a sin for any family to visit Florence and not drop by one of its premier **gelato** parlors to sample the rich Italian equivalent of ice cream. (See "A Big Step Up from Ice Cream: Florentine Gelato," on p. 106.) If the kids mutiny and absolutely insist on a hamburger, you could try the slightly American-style restaurant **Yellow Bar,** Via del Proconsolo 39r (*© **055-211-766**). But be warned: The hamburger doesn't come with a bun (a form of blasphemy among certain preteens). The Yellow Bar also serves pizzas. It's closed on Tuesday evening. A slightly more authentic

sizzling taste of the West is to be found at **The Diner** (see review, p. 104). **Il Cantinone** (p. 112) is popular with students, and has long tables where your family can spread out and bite deep into *crostoni* (slabs of peasant bread piled with your choice of toppings, like a pizza). **Il Latini** (p. 107) can be one of the most fun places to eat in Florence with kids—you're seated at communal tables under battalions of hanging ham hocks and treated to huge portions of the Tuscan bounty. No food is too fancy or oddball to offend suspicious young palates, the waiters love to ham it up, and a festive atmosphere prevails. It's much lower-key at **Da Benvenuto** (p. 104): The dishes are simple and homey, and they're sure to have a plate of plain spaghetti and tomato sauce to please finicky youngsters. If your little ones like Chinese food, **Hong Kong,** Via dei Servi 35r (*© **055-239-8235;** www.ristorantehongkong.com) is a reliable central choice for Cantonese staples like sizzling stir-fry platters.

pacing back and forth, passing around the lone menu, and welcoming people in off the street until he feels like going home.

Via dei Magazzini 3r (the alley off the northeast corner of Piazza della Signoria). ℂ **055-293-045.** Primi 7€–9€; secondi 10€–14€. No credit cards. Tues–Sat 9am–11pm; Sun noon–2:30pm. Bus: C1 or C2.

INEXPENSIVE

Da Benvenuto ★ ☺ ✦ TUSCAN/ITALIAN This is a no-nonsense trattoria, simple and good, a neighborhood hangout that somehow found its way into many a guidebook over the years. Yet it continues to serve adequate helpings of tasty Florentine home cooking to travelers and locals seated together in two brightly lit rooms. This is often our first stop on any trip to Florence, where we usually order ravioli or *gnocchi*—both served in tomato sauce—and follow with a *scaloppa di vitello al vino bianco* (veal escalope cooked in white wine).

Via della Mosca 16r (at the corner of Via dei Neri). ℂ **055-214-833.** Primi 4.50€–8€; secondi 6€–18€. AE, MC, V. Daily 12:30–3pm and 7–10:30pm. Bus: C1, 3, 13, 23, or 71.

The Diner ☺ AMERICAN/FAST FOOD If you or the kids are craving something familiar, then roll up for breakfast, lunch, or dinner at this tiny American-style diner between Santa Croce and Piazza della Signoria. Squeeze into fun, informal booth seating for Californian eggs Benedict (with avocado and tomato) or a pancake stack at breakfast, omelets anyway you like them at lunch, and a fine array of burgers with fries—go for the Pica Burger, served with a spicy pesto for a (small) concession to your Italian hosts. If you like your burger well cooked (*ben cotto*) be sure to ask: They usually arrive pink. There's free Wi-Fi, too.

Via dell'Acqua 2 (behind the Bargello). ℂ **055-290-748.** www.theflorencediner.com. Breakfast 6€–7€; lunch 6€–8€; burgers 7€–10€. AE, DC, MC, V. Daily 8am–10:30pm. Bus: C1 or C2.

Near San Lorenzo & the Mercato Centrale

MODERATE

Le Fonticine BOLOGNESE/TUSCAN Modern paintings carpet the walls like a jigsaw puzzle here, but even with the art, this place still feels a bit like a country trattoria. Ask to sit in the back, if only so you get to walk past the open kitchen and grill. There are so many good primi it's hard to choose, but you can't go wrong with *tagliatelle al prosciutto e asparagi* (with diced prosciutto and asparagus tips), or in season, *tagliatelle al radicchio rosso e groviera* (with radicchio and gruyere cheese). Afterward, you just might change your mind about liver if you try their *fegato di vitello alla salvia*.

Via Nazionale 79r (at Via dell'Ariento). ℂ **055-282-106.** www.lefonticine.com. Reservations recommended. Primi 6€–13€; secondi 10€–20€. AE, MC, V. Tues–Sat noon–2:30pm and 7–10pm. Closed July 25–Aug 25. Bus: 1, 2, 12, 13, 28, 29, 30, 35, 57, or 70.

INEXPENSIVE

Mario ★ ✦ FLORENTINE This is down-and-dirty Florentine lunchtime at its best, a trattoria so basic the little stools don't have backs and a communal spirit so entrenched the waitresses will scold you if you try to take a table all to yourself. Since 1953, their stock in trade has been feeding market workers, and you can watch the kitchen through the glass as they whip out a wipe-board menu of simple dishes at lightning speed. Hearty primi include *tortelli di patate al ragù* (ravioli stuffed with potato in meat ragù), *minestra di farro e riso* (emmer-and-rice soup), and *penne al pomodoro* (pasta quills in fresh tomato sauce). The secondi are basic but good; try the *coniglio arrosto* (roast rabbit) or go straight for the fiorentina steak, often priced to be the best deal in town.

Via Rosina 2r (north corner of Piazza Mercato Centrale). ✆ **055-218-550.** www.trattoria-mario. com. Reservations not accepted. Primi 4.50€–6.50€; secondi 7.50€–11€. No credit cards. Mon–Sat noon–3:30pm. Closed Aug. Bus: C1.

Nerbone ★ 📷 FLORENTINE Nerbone has been stuffing stall owners and market patrons with excellent Florentine *cucina povera* ("poor people's food") since the Mercato Centrale opened in 1874. You can try *trippa alla fiorentina, pappa al pomodoro,* or a plate piled with boiled potatoes and a single fat sausage. But the mainstay here is a *panino con bollito,* a boiled beef sandwich that's *bagnato* (dipped in the meat juices). Eat standing with the crowd of old men at the side counter, sipping glasses of wine or beer, or arrive early to fight for one of the few tables.

In the Mercato Centrale, entrance on Via dell'Ariento, stand no. 292 (ground floor). ✆ **055-219-949.** All dishes 4€–7€. No credit cards. Mon–Sat 7am–2pm. Bus: C1.

Near Piazza Santa Trinita

VERY EXPENSIVE

Buca Lapi TUSCAN Prices at this vaulted basement eatery have risen astronomically, and for no apparent reason, but the quality is still spot-on. An interesting start is the *filetto di cinghiale al rosmarino* (wild boar slices cured like prosciutto and served with rosemary-scented olive oil). Specialty primo is the *cannelloni gratinati alla Buca Lapi* (pasta canapés stuffed with ricotta and spinach served in a cream sauce of boar and mushrooms). A light secondo could be *coniglio disossato ripieno* (stuffed rabbit), or you can go all out on a masterful *bistecca chianina* (grilled steak, for two only).

Via del Trebbio 1r (just off Piazza Antinori at the top of Via de' Tornabuoni). ✆ **055-213-768.** www.bucalapi.com. Reservations recommended. Primi 14€–18€; secondi 20€–40€. AE, MC, V. Mon–Sat 7–11pm. Bus: C1, 6, 11, 22, 36, 37, or 68.

Cantinetta Antinori TUSCAN The Antinori *marchesi* started their wine empire 26 generations ago, and, taking their cue from an ancient vintner tradition, installed a wine bar in their 15th-century *palazzo* 30 years ago. Most ingredients come fresh from the Antinori farms, as does all the fine wine. Start with the *fettuccine all'anatra* (noodles in duck sauce) and round out the meal with the mighty *gran pezzo* (a thick slab of oven-roasted Chianina beef). If you choose this worthy splurge as a secondo, skip the first course and instead follow your steak with *formaggi misti,* which may include pecorino made fresh that morning. Their *cantucci* (Pratese biscotti) come from Tuscany's premier producer.

Palazzo Antinori, Piazza Antinori 3 (at the top of Via Tornabuoni). ✆ **055-292-234.** www. cantinetta-antinori.com. Reservations recommended. Primi 14€–18€; secondi 24€–30€. AE, DC, MC, V. Mon–Fri noon–2:30pm and 7–10:30pm. Closed Aug and Dec 24–Jan 6. Bus: C1, 6, 11, 22, 36, 37, or 68.

EXPENSIVE

L'Osteria di Giovanni ★★ TUSCAN Giovanni Latini comes from one of Florence's best-known culinary clans, whose eponymous eatery on Via del Palchetti is a household name in Florence, but he and his daughters Caterina and Chiara have made quite a name for themselves in the same neighborhood. Their *osteria* features a sophisticated but social atmosphere, with well-dressed

Italians and tourists sharing either the quiet front room or the more communal back room. If they are in season, you may be offered some fresh, garden-raised fava beans with pecorino, followed by sautéed squid with asparagus and cherry tomatoes. Don't miss the *involtini di vitello con pecorino fresco, melanzane e funghi* (sliced veal wrapped around fresh pecorino, eggplant, and mushrooms). Save room for chocolate mousse.

Via del Moro 22 (near the Ponte alla Carraia). ☎ **055-284-897.** www.osteriadigiovanni.com. Reservations recommended. Primi 11€–16€; secondi 19€–26€. AE, MC, V. Tues–Sat noon–2:30pm and 7–11pm; Mon 7–11pm. Closed Aug. Bus: C3, 6, 11, 36, 37, or 68.

A BIG STEP UP FROM ICE CREAM: FLORENTINE gelato

Gelato is a Florentine institution—a creamy, sweet, flavorful food item on a different level entirely from what the English-speaking world calls "ice cream." Making fine Florentine gelato is a craft taken seriously by all except the tourist-pandering spots around major attractions that serve air-fluffed bland "vanilla" and nuclear-waste pistachio so artificially green it glows.

A couple of high-quality national chain vendors have opened up Florence branches. You'll see the lines before you see the goods at **Grom ★**, Via del Campanile (☎ **055-216-158;** www. grom.it), famous for using only natural and seasonal ingredients in its gelato. **Rivareno,** Borgo degli Albizi 46r (☎ **055-011-8039**) offers a small range of predictably excellent flavors—mandarin is a big hit here. Both are open daily. **Festival del Gelato,** Via del Corso 75r, just off Via dei Calzaiuoli (☎ **055-239-4386;** www.festivaldelgelato.com), is one of the few serious contenders right in the center, offering about 50 flavors along with pounding pop music and colorful neon. It's open daily, but closed all January.

Vivoli ★★, Via Isole delle Stinche 7r, a block west of Piazza Santa Croce (☎ **055-239-2334;** www.vivoli.it), is still the city's institution. Exactly how renowned is this bright gelateria? Taped to the wall is a postcard bearing only "Vivoli, Europa" for the address, yet it was successfully delivered to this world capital of ice cream. It's open all day Tuesday through Sunday. Nearby **Gelateria dei Neri ★★**, Via dei Neri 20–22r (☎ **055-210-034**) gets less acclaim, but plenty of locals think this is up there with Vivoli. Their ricotta and fig gelato is divine. It's open daily. The best of the "new breed" of Florentine gelateria is **Carapina ★★**, Via Lambertesca 18R (☎ **055-291-128;** www.carapina.it), where a serious commitment to sourcing and seasonality is rewarded with some sensational fruit flavors. It's also open daily.

A block south of the Accademia (pick up a cone after you've gazed upon *David*'s glory) is **Carabé**, Via Ricasoli 60r (☎ **055-289-476;** www.gelatocarabe. com). It offers genuine Sicilian gelato in the heart of Florence, with ingredients shipped in from Sicily by the Sicilian owners. May 16 through September, it's open daily; February 15 through May 15 and October through November 15, it's open Tuesday through Sunday only.

South of the Arno, plenty of Florentines swear by unassuming **La Carraia ★**, Piazza N. Sauro 25r (☎ **055-280-695**). It's open daily.

MODERATE

Coco Lezzone FLORENTINE This tiny trattoria hidden in a tangle of alleys near the Arno consists of long communal tables in a couple of pocket-size rooms wrapped around a cubbyhole of a kitchen whose chef, according to the restaurant's dialect name, is a bit off his rocker. While enjoying your *ribollita* (known here as a "triumph of humility") or *rigatoni al sugo* (in a chunky ragù), look at where the yellow paint on the lower half of the wall gives way to white: That's how high the Arno flooded the joint in 1966. Friday is *baccalà* (salt cod) day, and every day their *involtini* (thin veal slice wrapped around vegetables) and *crocchette di filetto* (veal-and-basil meatloaf smothered in tomato sauce) are good.

Via del Parioncino 26r (at the corner of Via Purgatorio). ✆ **055-287-178.** www.cocolezzone.it. Reservations recommended. Primi 8€–12€; secondi 10€–18€. No credit cards. Mon and Wed–Sat noon–2:30pm and 7–10:30pm; Tues noon–2:30pm. Closed late July through Aug and Dec 23–Jan 7. Bus: C3, 6, 11, 36, 37, or 68.

Il Latini ★ ☺ FLORENTINE Arrive here at 7:30pm to join the crowd massed at the door, for even with a reservation you'll have to wait as they skillfully fit parties together at the communal tables. In fact, sharing a common meal with complete strangers is part of the fun here. Under hundreds of hanging prosciutto ham hocks, the waiters try their hardest to keep a menu away from you and suggest something themselves. This usually kicks off with *ribollita* and *pappa al pomodoro* or *penne strascicate* (in a ragù mixed with cream). If everyone agrees on the *arrosto misto,* you can get a table-filling platter heaped high with assorted roast meats. Finish off with a round of *cantucci con vin santo* for all the adults.

Via del Palchetti 6r (off Via della Vigna Nuova). ✆ **055-210-916.** www.illatini.com. Reservations strongly recommended. Primi 5€–9€; secondi 14€–22€. AE, DC, MC, V. Tues–Sun 12:30–2:30pm and 7:30–10:30pm. Closed 15 days in Aug and Dec 24–Jan 6. Bus: 1, 6, 36, 37, or 68.

Osteria delle Belle Donne ★ TUSCAN Tucked away on a narrow street (whose name refers to the women of the night who once worked this then-shady neighborhood) parallel to exclusive Via de' Tornabuoni, this packed-to-the-gills lunch spot immediately drew the area's chic boutique owners and sales staff. It now tries to accommodate them and countless others in a rather brusque style—no lingering over lunch; dinner isn't as rushed. Tuscan cuisine gets reinterpreted and updated by the talented chef, who placates the local palate without alienating it: Traditional dishes appear in the company of innovative specials such as cream of zucchini and chestnut soup or lemon-flavored chicken.

Via delle Belle Donne 16r. ✆ **055-238-2609.** www.casatrattoria.com. Reservations recommended. Primi 9€–16€; secondi 12€–18€. DC, MC, V. Daily noon–3pm and 7pm–midnight. Closed most of Aug. Bus: C1, 6, 11, 22, 36, 37, or 68.

Near Santa Maria Novella
MODERATE

Sostanza FLORENTINE This trattoria is popularly called "Il Troia" (the trough) because people have been lining up at the long communal tables since 1869 to enjoy huge amounts of some of the best traditional food in the city. The primi are very simple: pasta in sauce, *tortellini in brodo* (meat-stuffed pasta in chicken broth), and *zuppa alla paesana* (peasant soup *ribollita*). The secondi don't steer far from Florentine traditions either, with *trippa alla fiorentina* or their mighty specialty *petti di pollo al burro* (thick chicken breasts fried in butter).

We've never seen an empty seat in the place while walking by at dinnertime, so it's certainly worth calling ahead.

Via Porcellana 25r (near the Borgo Ognissanti end). ☎ **055-212-691.** Reservations strongly recommended. Primi 9€; secondi 10€–16€. No credit cards. Mon–Fri noon–2:15pm and 7:30–9:45pm. Closed Aug. Bus: 11, 36, 37, or 68.

Near San Marco & Santissima Annunziata

If you're staying north of San Marco and don't fancy the walk into the center, locals swear by **Da Tito ★**, Via San Gallo 112r (☎ **055-472-475;** www.trattoria datito.it), where you'll find traditional Florentine cooking, fresh pasta handmade daily, and a friendly welcome. It's popular, so book ahead. San Marco is also the place to head for *schiacciata alla fiorentina,* sweetish olive-oil flatbread loaded with savory toppings. You'll find the best in the city at **Pugi ★**, Piazza San Marco 9b (☎ **055-280-981;** www.focacceria-pugi.it), open 7:45am (8:30am Sat) to 8pm Monday to Saturday, but closed most of August.

INEXPENSIVE

La Mescita LIGHT FARE This tiny *fiaschetteria* is immensely popular with local businesspeople and students from the nearby university. Lunch can be a crushing affair, and they have signs admonishing you to eat quickly to give others a chance to sit. You'll be eating with Italians, and it's not for the timid because you have to take charge yourself: securing a seat, collecting your own place setting, and getting someone's attention to give your order before going to sit down. They offer mainly sandwiches, though there are always a few simple meat and pasta dishes ready as well. *Melanzana* (eggplant) is overwhelmingly the side dish of choice, and you can look to the cardboard lists behind the counter to select your wine, although the house wine is very good, and a quarter liter of it is cheaper than a can of soda.

Via degli Alfani 70r (near the corner of Via dei Servi). ☎ **347-795-1604.** Sandwiches and simple dishes 4€–7€. No credit cards. Mon–Sat 11am–4pm. Closed Aug. Bus: C1.

Il Vegetariano VEGETARIAN Come early to one of Florence's best vegetarian restaurants and use your coat to save a spot at one of the communal wood tables before heading to the back to get your food. The self-service menu changes constantly but uses only fresh produce in such dishes as risotto with yellow squash and black cabbage; a quichelike *pizza rustica* of ricotta, olives, tomatoes, and mushrooms; and a plate with *farro* (emmer) and a hot salad of spinach, onions, sprouts, and bean-curd chunks sautéed in soy sauce. There's a nice patio in back.

Via delle Ruote 30r (off Via Santa Reparata). ☎ **055-475-030.** www.il-vegetariano.it. Reservations not accepted. Primi 5€–6€; secondi 7.50€–9€. No credit cards. Tues–Fri 12:30–3:30pm; Tues–Sun 7:30pm–midnight. Closed 3 weeks in Aug and Dec 24–Jan 2. Bus: C1 or anything to San Marco.

Near Santa Croce

VERY EXPENSIVE

Cibrèo ★★ TUSCAN There's no pasta and no grilled meat—can this be Tuscany? Rest assured that while Fabio Picchi's culinary creations are a bit out of the ordinary, most are based on antique recipes. Picchi's fan-cooled main restaurant room, full of intellectual babble, is where the elegance is in the substance of the food and the service, not in surface appearances. Waiters pull up a chair to explain the list of daily specials, and those garlands of hot peppers hanging in

4

Where to Eat

FLORENCE

the kitchen window are a hint at the cook's favorite spice. All the food is spectacular, and dishes change regularly, but if they're available try the yellow pepper soup drizzled with olive oil; the soufflé of potatoes and ricotta spiced and served with pecorino shavings and ragù; or the roasted duck stuffed with minced beef, raisins, and pinoli.

Via Andrea del Verrocchio 8r (next to Sant'Ambrogio Market). ✆ **055-234-1100.** www.edizion iteatrodelsalecibreofirenze.it. Reservations required. Primi 20€; secondi 36€. AE, DC, MC, V. Tues–Sat 1–2:30pm and 7:30–11:15pm. Closed July 26–Sept 6. Bus: C2, C3, 14, or 71.

EXPENSIVE

Giostra ★ TUSCAN The chef/owner is Dimitri d'Asburgo Lorena, a Habsburg prince (with some local Medici blood for good measure) who opened this restaurant merely to indulge his love of cooking. They start you off with a complimentary flute of *spumante* before you plunge into the tasty *crostini misti* and exquisite primi. Among the more enlightened are *ravioli di brie con carciofini Morelli* (ravioli stuffed with brie and dressed with artichokes), and homemade *taglierini* with white truffles. For an encore, try the *nodino di vitella ai tartufi bianchi* (veal slathered in eggy white truffle sauce with fresh truffle grated on top) or the lighter *spianata alle erbe aromatiche di Maremma* (a huge platter of spiced beef pounded flat and piled with a salad of rosemary sprigs, sage, and other herbs). Don't leave without sampling the sinfully rich Viennese Sacher torte, made from an old Habsburg family recipe.

Borgo Pinti 12r (off Piazza Salvemini). ✆ **055-241-341.** www.ristorantelagiostra.com. Reservations recommended. Primi 10€–18€; secondi 16€–24€. AE, DC, MC, V. Daily noon–2:30pm and 7pm–midnight. Bus: C1, 14, 23, or 71.

Kome ★ 🏮 JAPANESE/SUSHI There's something refreshingly cosmopolitan about perching in a *kaiten*, grazing on *hosomaki* made by a skilled Japanese chef right in front of you. Florence's best sushi joint gets the formula about right: Nigiri with octopus, cuttlefish, prawn, or tuna are light and fresh straight from the conveyor. An excellent mixed tempura of seasonal vegetables, prawn, and

PANEM ET cultura

Fabio Picchi was always something of a virtuoso in his restaurant, **Cibrèo,** where the kitchen is virtually his stage. So it came as little surprise when he actually did open a stage, across Via de' Macci at the **Teatro del Sale** (✆ **055-200-1492;** www.teatrodelsale.com), where one virtuoso on stage accompanies another in his glassed-in kitchen. It is a members-only dining club (membership costs just

5€) where the 30€ price of admission includes not only a dinner buffet of inventive Tuscan specialties but also a performance by an artist, often a jazz performer or dancer with the same disdain for rules and normalcy that pervades Picchi's persona.) Under the guidance of artistic director Maria

Cassi, Picchi's wife and a theatrical talent in Italy, the Teatro del Sale aims to bring contemporary culture to a city most often associated with the past. Less dramatic, but equally tasty are the breakfast (9–11am; 7€) and lunch buffet (noon–2:15pm; 20€).

anchovy is the best among five or six hot dishes cooked to order. Keep track of your total as you eat, however: The check soon mounts up, especially if you wash it all down with a Kirin or two. They also offer delivery via **www.thefood.it**.

Via de' Benci 41r. © **055-200-8009.** Reservations not accepted. Sushi 3.50€–8€. AE, MC, V. Mon–Sat noon–3pm; daily 7–11pm. Bus: C3 or 23.

MODERATE

Osteria de' Benci MODERN TUSCAN This popular trattoria serves enormous portions (especially of secondi) on beautiful hand-painted ceramics under high ceiling vaults echoing to a slightly obtrusive, jazzy soundtrack. The menu changes monthly, but you can always be assured of excellent *salumi*—they come from Falorni, the famed butcher from the Chianti (see chapter 5). The *eliche del profeta* are fusiloni tossed with ricotta, olive oil, oregano, and fresh tomatoes sprinkled with *parmigiano*. The unique *spaghetti dell'ubriacone* is bright crimson spaghetti that takes its color from being cooked in red wine, sauced with garlic, pepperoncino, and parsley sautéed in olive oil. And the *cibrèo delle regine* is a traditional rich Florentine dish of chopped chicken livers and gizzards served on toast.

Via de' Benci 13r (corner of Via de' Neri). © **055-234-4923.** www.osteriadeibenci.it. Reservations recommended. Primi 10€; secondi 13€–22€. AE, DC, MC, V. Daily 12:30–3pm and 7:30–11pm. Bus: C3, 12, 13, 23, or 71.

Trattoria Cibrèo ★★ 🗲 FLORENTINE This is the casual trattoria of celebrated chef-owner Fabio Picchi; its limited menu comes from the same creative kitchen that put on the map his premier and more than twice as expensive *ristorante* next door. Picchi takes his inspiration from traditional Tuscan recipes, and the first thing you'll note is the absence of pasta. After you taste the velvety *passata di peperoni gialli* (yellow bell-pepper soup), you won't care much. The stuffed roast rabbit demands the same admiration.

Via de' Macci 122r. © **055-234-1100.** Primi 7€; secondi 14€. AE, DC, MC, V. Tues–Sat 1–2:30pm and 7–11:15pm. Closed July 26–Sept 6. Bus: C2, C3, 14, or 71.

INEXPENSIVE

Anita FLORENTINE You're unlikely to find too many surprises on the menu at this backstreet trattoria; what you will find, however, is proper Florentine cooking with friendly service just a stone's throw from the city's marquee monuments. A typical trip through the courses might start with Tuscan *crostini* with chicken livers and pecorino cheese, followed by *pici al cinghiale* (hand-rolled, thick pasta with boar sauce), then *lombatino di vitello all'aceto balsamico* (thick veal steak with a creamy balsamic vinegar sauce). It's hearty and delicious local cooking at fair prices.

Via del Parlascio 2r (corner of Via Vinegia). © **055-218-698.** Reservations recommended for dinner. Primi 6€–8€; secondi 8€–14€. MC, V. Mon–Sat noon–2:30pm and 7–10:15pm. Bus: C1, C2, C3, or 23.

Da Rocco 🗲 FLORENTINE This tiny trattoria, one of the best bargains in the city, is tucked away inside Sant'Ambrogio Market. It's a great place to get acquainted with a proper local eating experience, with simple food served to hungry workers without the show. Behind the takeaway counter is an enclosed seating area with booths big enough for four. Staff is friendly, but also rushed off their feet, so don't expect any special treatment (there is a menu in English, if you're struggling). Hearty dishes of lasagne, various other pasta dishes, or roast meats such as *coniglio* (rabbit) straight from the market rarely cost more than 5€. Get here by 1pm if you want a table.

Mercato di Sant'Ambrogio. No phone. Reservations not accepted. Primi 3.50€; secondi 5€. MC, V. Mon–Sat noon–2:30pm. Bus: C2, C3, or 14.

In the Oltrarno & San Frediano

EXPENSIVE

iO: Osteria Personale ★★★ 📔 CONTEMPORARY TUSCAN The stripped brick and sleek banquette seating wouldn't be out of place in Brooklyn or Shoreditch, but the exceptional food here is resolutely Tuscan. Not Tuscan like you've tasted before, though: There's no pasta on a modular dinner menu that's divided into seafood, meat, and vegetarian dishes—a "renewal" of Tuscan food tradition, is how proprietor Matteo Fantini describes it. You buy by the dish, in any sequence you fancy, or go for a multidish tasting menu. The likes of raw squid ribbons served with sage-infused garbanzo cream or spelt with artichoke, cocoa beans, and robiola cheese deliver traditional flavors, but are served up in a clean, deconstructed style. There's even a chalkboard on the wall with diagrams showing how some of the dishes are built—Fantini's equivalent of the football coach's playbook.

Borgo San Frediano 167r. ✆ **055-933-1341.** www.io-osteriapersonale.it. Reservations highly recommended. Vegetable dishes 13€; meat and fish dishes 14€–20€; tasting menus 40€ 4 dishes, 55€ 6 dishes. AE, DC, MC, V. Mon–Sat 8–10:45pm; also open for *aperitivo* from 7pm. Closed 1st 10 days in Jan and all Aug. Bus: 6 and D.

Olio e Convivium ★★ CONTEMPORARY ITALIAN This slightly fussy, but nevertheless thoroughly satisfying little restaurant is set in tiled surrounds inside one of the Oltrarno's best delicatessens. Its menu eschews the style and content of "typical Florence." You can choose one of their creative, skillfully presented pasta combinations like *tagliolini con capesante, carciofi e calamari* (thin pasta with scallops, artichokes, and squid). Or order one of their "gastronomy tasting plates," built straight from the deli counter. The wines-by-the-glass list is short, creative, and a little pricey; the soft classical music soundtrack makes for a refined atmosphere.

Via Santo Spirito 6. ✆ **055-265-8198.** www.conviviumfirenze.it. Primi 12€–16€; secondi 14€–28€. MC, V. Mon–Sat noon–2:30pm; Tues–Sat 7–10:30pm. Closed 3 weeks in Aug. Bus: C3, D, 6, 11, 36, 37, or 68.

Osteria Santo Spirito MODERN TUSCAN The cool kids have moved on, and on occasion the wait can be extraordinarily long, but the food at this former fashionable hangout is as interesting as ever. You can start with a salad such as *insalatina tiepida di polpo con patate* (warm octopus salad with potato), or for pasta try *rigatoni Santo Spirito* (pasta in spicy tomato sauce with ricotta) or *gnocchi gratinati ai formaggi* (oven-baked gnocchi swimming in a bubbling-hot mix of soft cheeses flavored with truffle). Afterward, fill up on *tagliata di manzo* (beef filet). Lunchtime set menus at 10€ and 19€ offer good value.

Piazza Santo Spirito 16r. ✆ **055-238-2383.** www.osteriasantospirito.it. Reservations recommended. Primi 7€–15€; secondi 14€–25€. AE, DC, MC, V. Daily 12:45–2:30pm and 8pm–midnight. Bus: D, C3, 11, 36, 37, or 68.

MODERATE

Cinghiale Bianco TUSCAN Massimo Masselli will sooner turn people away at the door than rush you though your meal. His *osteria* does a good repeat business of locals and tourists alike who come for the delicious *taglierini* (wide pasta) with pesto or the famous *strozzapreti* ("priest-chokers" made of the spinach-and-ricotta mix normally found inside ravioli, served with melted butter). You can't go wrong ordering anything made of the restaurant's namesake *cinghiale* (wild boar)—from the cold boar slices as an appetizer to *cinghiale alla maremmana con polenta* (wild boar stew cozied up to creamy, firm polenta) as a main course. Set in the base of a 12th-century tower, the air-conditioned dining room milks its medieval look with exposed stone, odd iron implements hanging everywhere, and lights hidden in suspended cauldrons over the pigeonholed walls.

Borgo San Jacopo 43r. ℂ **055-215-706.** Reservations recommended on weekends. Primi 7€–10€; secondi 10€–17€. MC, V. Thurs–Tues 6:30–10:30pm (Sat–Sun also noon–3pm). Closed 3 weeks in July. Bus: C3 or D.

Il Cantinone ☺ TUSCAN With tourists and large groups of locals all seated at long tables under the low arc of a brick ceiling, the convivial noise can sometimes get a bit overwhelming. But the feeling of having walked into a party is part of the charm of this place. The specialty is *crostini,* slabs of peasant bread that act as vehicles for toppings such as prosciutto, tomatoes, mozzarella, and Tuscan sausage—plenty big enough for young children to share. The *ribollita* is also great, but is usually only served in winter, when black cabbage is in season.

Via Santo Spirito 6r. ℂ **055-218-898.** www.ilcantinonedifirenze.it. Primi and *crostini* 4€–8€; secondi 9€–16€. AE, MC, V. Daily 12:30–2:30pm and 7:30–10:30pm. Bus: C3, D, 6, 11, 36, 37, or 68.

Il Santo Bevitore ★★ CONTEMPORARY ITALIAN Encapsulating all that's best about the new generation of Florentine eateries, this restaurant-enoteca (wine cellar) takes the best of Tuscan tradition and sprinkles it with some contemporary fairy dust. A buzzing, candlelit interior is the setting for clever combinations presented with style—and a smile. Best of the *antipasti* are the tasting platters, including cured meats sliced right at the bar and an *assaggio di sott'olio* (a trio of preserved vegetables in olive oil). Pastas skew to the unusual, pulling in influences from across Italy, such as in the *tortelloni* filled with cavolo nero cabbage and pancetta served with a pecorino cream sauce. Seasonal mains might include a tartare of Chianina beef or roast *baccalà* (salt cod) with late-harvest radicchio. The wine list is similarly intriguing. Lunch is a daily menu only.

Via Santo Spirito 66r (corner of Piazza N. Sauro). ℂ **055-211-264.** www.ilsantobevitore.com. Reservations highly recommended. Primi 7.50€–10€; secondi 8.50€–25€. MC, V. Mon–Sat 12:30–3pm; daily 7–11pm. Closed 10 days in Aug. Bus: C3, D, 6, 11, 36, 37, or 68.

INEXPENSIVE

Sabatino ★ ✦ FLORENTINE It feels a long way off the tourist trail—and, in a way, it is—but a mere 10-minute walk from the Cappella Brancacci and you're eating in Florence before the arrival of mass tourism. Sabatino is the kind of San Frediano trattoria where local families and work colleagues meet to eat good food in simple surrounds, for a modest outlay. Dishes are straightforward and Florentine: *tortellini in brodo* (meat-filled pasta parcels in a clear broth), a selection of pasta dishes for around 4€, and a daily-changing roster of roasts such as *pollo ripieno* (herb-stuffed chicken), *faraona* (guinea hen), or *vitello* (veal). Whitewashed walls hung with farming implements remind you that it's all about the produce.

Via Pisana 2r (just outside the Porta Pisana). ℂ **055-225-955.** Primi 4€–5€; secondi 5€–7€. AE, MC, V. Mon–Fri noon–2:30pm and 7:15–10pm. Bus: 6 or D.

In the Hills

MODERATE

Le Cave di Maiano ★ TUSCAN This converted farmhouse is the countryside trattoria of choice for Florentines wishing to escape the city heat on a summer Sunday afternoon. You can enjoy warm-weather lunches on the tree-shaded stone terrace with a bucolic view. In cooler weather, you can dine inside rustic rooms with haphazard paintings scattered on the walls. The *antipasto caldo* of varied *crostini* and fried polenta is a good way to kick off a meal, followed by a *misto della casa* that gives you a sampling of primi. This may include *penne strascicate* (stubby pasta in cream sauce and tomato ragù) or *riso allo spazzacamino* (rice with beans and black cabbage). The best secondo is the *pollastro al mattone* (chicken roasted under a brick with pepper) or the *lombatina di vitello alla griglia* (grilled veal chop).

Via Cave di Maiano 16 (in Maiano, halfway btw. Florence and Fiesole east of the main road). ℂ **055-59-133.** www.trattoriacavedimaiano.it. Reservations recommended. Primi 8€–12€; secondi 10€–18€. AE, DC, MC, V. Daily 12:30–3pm and 7:30pm–midnight. Bus: 7 (get off at Villa San Michele, then turn around and take the road branching to the left of the winding one your bus took; continue on about 1.2km/¾ mile up this side road, past the Pensione Bencistà); a taxi is a better idea.

COOK **LIKE A TUSCAN**

Take a walk down Via dei Velluti in the Oltrarno, peek into the furniture restoration studios, watch the artisans practicing their ancient craft, and soon you'll stumble upon another studio devoted to a time-honored art: cooking. For 55€ per person, for example, **"In Tavola,"** Via dei Velluti 18r (ℂ **055-217-672;** www.intavola.org), will get you started on your culinary quest by showing you how to prepare an easy Tuscan lunch (3 hr.) or a full 4-course dinner (4 hr.; 65€).

In Tavola has taken to the city what *agriturismi* have been doing for a few years now in the countryside, especially in Chianti. Another good beginner's course is offered by the **Villa Rosa di Boscorotondo,** near Panzano (p. 180). For 95€ per person, Vincenzo Regoli shows you the ins and outs of bruschetta, panzanella, spezzatino del Chianti, handmade pasta, and tiramisù. **Villa Bordoni,** outside Greve (p. 179) offers professional-level classes covering such subjects as *"La Cucina Povera."* Your 150€-per-person fee covers dinner in the outstanding restaurant, with wine and a guided wine tasting. See **www. chianticookingschool.com.**

For a full-immersion course in a place that raises its own meat and vegetables, also check out **La Petraia,** 53017 Radda-in-Chianti (ℂ **0577-738-582;** www.lapetraia.com), where award-winning chef Susan McKenna Grant will help you make an elegant Tuscan dish with whatever vegetables and herbs are in season. The price is 200€ for a cooking and foraging class that includes a multicourse lunch, an apron, and a copy of her book.

Most farm resorts and luxury hotels throughout Tuscany and Umbria are affiliated with some sort of cooking class these days—be sure to inquire when you book.

EXPLORING FLORENCE
On Piazza Del Duomo

The cathedral square is filled with tourists and caricature artists during the day, strolling crowds in the early evening, and knots of students strumming guitars on the Duomo's steps at night. Though it's always crowded, the piazza's vivacity and the glittering facades of the cathedral and the baptistery doors keep it an eternal Florentine sight. The square's closure to traffic in 2009 has made it a more welcoming space than ever for strolling.

At the corner of the busy pedestrian main drag, Via Calzaiuoli, sits the pretty little **Loggia del Bigallo** (1351–58). Inside is a small museum of 14th-century works, which is unfortunately often closed. Call ℂ **055-233-9406** if you're interested in trying to make an appointment to get in to see the 1342 *Madonna della Misericordia* by the school of Bernardo Daddi, which features the earliest known cityscape view of Florence.

Note that just south of the Duomo, hidden in the tangle of medieval streets toward Piazza della Signoria, is a 14th-century Florentine house restored and converted into the **Casa di Dante** (ℂ **055-219-416**), a small museum chronicling the life and times of the great poet. But, this isn't likely the poet's actual house. The entrance is in Via Santa Margherita, and it's open Tuesday to Sunday from 10am to 5pm. Admission is 4€.

Battistero (Baptistery) ★★★ In choosing a date to mark the beginning of the Renaissance, art historians often seize on 1401, the year Florence's powerful wool merchants' guild held a contest to decide who would receive the commission to design the **North Doors** ★★ of the Baptistery to match the Gothic **South Doors,** cast 65 years earlier by Andrea Pisano. The era's foremost Tuscan sculptors each cast a bas-relief bronze panel depicting his own vision of the *Sacrifice of Isaac.* Twenty-two-year-old Lorenzo Ghiberti, competing against the likes of Donatello, Jacopo della Quercia, and Filippo Brunelleschi, won. He spent the next 21 years casting 28 bronze panels and building his doors. Although limited by his contract to design the scenes within Gothic frames as on Pisano's doors, Ghiberti infused his figures and compositions with an unmatched realism and classical references that helped define Renaissance sculpture. (Ghiberti stuck a self-portrait in the left door, the fourth head from the bottom of the middle strip, wearing a turban.)

Florence's octagonal Battistero.

The result so impressed the merchants' guild—not to mention the public and Ghiberti's fellow artists—they asked him in 1425 to do the **East Doors** ★★★, facing the Duomo, this time giving him the artistic freedom to realize his Renaissance ambitions.

Twenty-seven years later, just before his death, Ghiberti finished 10 dramatic life-like Old Testament scenes in gilded bronze, each a masterpiece of Renaissance sculpture and some of the finest examples of low-relief perspective in Italian art. The panels now mounted here are excellent copies; the originals are in the Museo dell'Opera del Duomo (see below). Years later, Michelangelo was standing before these doors and someone asked his opinion. His response sums up Ghiberti's accomplishment as no art historian could: "They are so beautiful that they would grace the entrance to Paradise." They've been called the Gates of Paradise ever since.

The Baptistery is one of Florence's oldest, most venerated buildings. Florentines long believed it was originally a Roman temple, but it most likely was raised somewhere between the 4th and 7th centuries on the site of a Roman palace. The octagonal drum was rebuilt in the 11th century, and by the 13th century it had been clad in its green-and-white Romanesque stripes of marble and capped with its odd pyramid-like dome.

The interior is ringed with columns pilfered from ancient Roman buildings and is a spectacle of mosaics above and below. The floor was inlaid in 1209, and the ceiling was covered between 1225 and the early 1300s with glittering **mosaics ★★**. Most were crafted by Venetian or Byzantine-style workshops, which worked off designs drawn by the era's best artists. Coppo di Marcovaldo drew sketches for the over 7.8m-high (26-ft.), ape-toed *Christ in Judgment* and the *Last Judgment* that fills over a third of the ceiling.

 DISCOUNT tickets **FOR THE CITY**

Florence at last has a *biglietto cumulativo* worthy of the name. Launched in 2011, the **Firenze Card ★** includes free entrance to around 25 of the city's leading museums and monuments, including the Uffizi, Accademia, Cappella Brancacci, Palazzo Pitti, San Marco, and lots, lots more. It also gets you into shorter lines at the Uffizi and other busy places, thereby making prebooking tickets unnecessary. Any E.U. citizen under 18 accompanying a cardholder also enters all the sites free. The card is valid for 72 hours from first activation, includes bus transport while valid, and

costs 50€ from the tourist offices on Piazza della Stazione and Via Cavour, as well as a handful of the major museums themselves. If you intend to pack as much into a 3-day visit as possible, the card offers good value. For the latest information on the card, and to order online, see **www.firenzecard.it**. If you're here for a longer visit, and prefer to take things slower, an **Amici degli Uffizi membership ★** (*(**©** 055-285610; www.amicidegliuffizi.it) costs about the same—60€ adults, 40€ anyone 25 years and under, 100€ family—and is valid for a calendar year, but only

secures entrance (without queuing) into 15 or so state museums in Florence, including the Uffizi, Accademia, San Marco, Bargello, Medici Chapels, and Pitti Palace. The card makes sense for families from outside the E.U. (children who are E.U. citizens always get in free), as two children go free with a family ticket, and for anyone who wishes to make multiple visits to museums (very useful for the Uffizi). Arrange instant membership Tuesday through Saturday at the dedicated office inside Uffizi entrance #2 (no need to queue, just ask for access); take your passport.

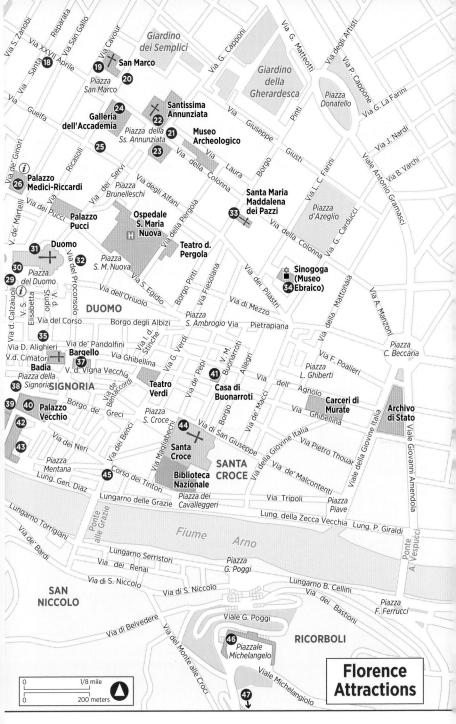

Florence Attractions

To the right of the altar is the 1425 wall **tomb of Antipope John XXIII,** designed by Michelozzo and Donatello, who cast the bronze effigy of the deceased, deposed pontiff.

Piazza di San Giovanni. ℂ **055-230-2885.** www.operaduomo.firenze.it. Admission 4€. Mon–Sat 12:15–7pm; Sun and 1st Sat of month 8:30am–2pm. Bus: C2, 14, 23, or 71.

Campanile di Giotto (Giotto's Bell Tower) ★★ In 1334, Giotto started the cathedral bell tower (clad in the same three colors of marble gracing the Duomo) but completed only the first two levels before his death in 1337. He was out of his league with the engineering aspects of architecture, and the tower was saved from falling in on itself by Andrea Pisano, who doubled the thickness of the walls. Andrea, a master sculptor of the Pisan Gothic school, also changed the design to add statue niches—he even carved a few of the statues himself—before quitting the project in 1348. Francesco Talenti finished the job between 1350 and 1359—he exchanged the heavy solidness of the base for a lighter, airier effect.

The **reliefs** and **statues** in the lower levels—by Andrea Pisano, Donatello, and others—are all copies; the weatherworn originals are now housed in the Museo dell'Opera del Duomo (see below). You can climb the 414 steps to the top of the tower. What makes this 84m-high (276-ft.) **view** ★★ different are great views of the Baptistery as you ascend, and the best close-up shot in the entire city of Brunelleschi's dome.

Piazza del Duomo. ℂ **055-230-2885.** www.operaduomo.firenze.it. Admission 6€. Daily 8:30am–6:50pm. Bus: C2, 14, 23, or 71.

Duomo (Cattedrale di Santa Maria del Fiore) ★★ For centuries, people have commented that Florence's cathedral is turned inside out, its exterior boasting Brunelleschi's famous dome and a festive cladding of white, green, and pink marble, but its interior left spare, almost barren.

Florence's massive Duomo, topped by Brunelleschi's dome.

By the late 13th century, Florence was feeling peevish: Its archrivals Siena and Pisa sported huge new Duomos filled with art while it was saddled with the tiny 5th- or 6th-century Santa Reparata as a cathedral. So, in 1296, the city hired Arnolfo di Cambio to design a new Duomo, and he raised the facade and the first few bays before his death in 1302. Work continued under the auspices of the Wool Guild and architects Giotto di Bondone (who concentrated on the bell tower) and Francesco Talenti (who finished up to the drum of the dome). The facade we see today is a neo-Gothic composite designed by Emilio de Fabris and built from 1871 to 1887 (for its story, see "Museo dell'Opera del Duomo," below).

The Duomo's most distinctive feature is its enormous **dome ★★★**, which dominates the skyline and is a symbol of Florence itself. The raising of this dome, the largest in the world in its time, was no mean architectural feat, tackled admirably by Filippo Brunelleschi between 1420 and 1436 (see "A Man & His Dome," below). You can climb up between the two shells of the cupola for one

A MAN & HIS dome

Filippo Brunelleschi, a diminutive man whose ego was as big as his talent, managed in his arrogant, quixotic, suspicious, and brilliant way to invent Renaissance architecture. Having been beaten by Lorenzo Ghiberti in the contest to cast the Baptistery doors (see above), Brunelleschi resolved he'd rather be the top architect than the second-best sculptor and took off for Rome to study the buildings of the ancients. On returning to Florence, he combined subdued gray *pietra serena* stone with smooth white plaster to create airy arches, vaults, and arcades of classically perfect

proportions in his own variant on the ancient Roman orders of architecture. He designed San Lorenzo, Santo Spirito, and the elegant Ospedale degli Innocenti, but his greatest achievement was erecting the dome over Florence's cathedral.

The Duomo, then the world's largest church, had already been built, but nobody had been able to figure out how to cover the daunting space over its center without spending a fortune and without filling the church with the necessary scaffolding—plus no one was sure whether they could create a dome that would hold up under its own weight. Brunelleschi insisted he knew how, and once granted the commission, revealed his ingenious plan—which may have been inspired by close study of Rome's Pantheon.

He built the dome in two shells, the inner one thicker than the outer,

both shells thinning as they neared the top, thus leaving the center hollow and removing a good deal of the weight. He also planned to construct the dome of giant vaults with ribs crossing over them, with each of the stones making up the actual fabric of the dome being dovetailed. In this way, the walls of the dome would support themselves as they were erected. In the process of building, Brunelleschi found himself as much an engineer as architect, constantly designing winches, cranes, and hoists to carry the materials faster and more efficiently up to the level of the workmen.

His finished work speaks for itself, 45m (148 ft.) wide at the base and 90m (295 ft.) high from drum to lantern. For his achievement, Brunelleschi was accorded a singular honor: He's the only person ever buried in Florence's cathedral.

of the classic panoramas across the city (not recommended for claustrophobes or anyone lacking a head for heights). At the base of the dome, just above the drum, Baccio d'Agnolo began adding a balcony in 1507. One of the eight sides was finished by 1515, when someone asked Michelangelo—whose artistic opinion was by this time taken as cardinal law—what he thought of it. The master reportedly scoffed, "It looks like a cricket cage." Work was halted, and to this day the other seven sides remain rough brick.

The Duomo was actually built around **Santa Reparata** so it could remain in business during construction. For more than 70 years, Florentines entered their old church through the free-standing facade of the new one, but in 1370 the original was torn down when the bulk of the Duomo—minus the dome—was finished. Ever the fiscal conservatives, Florentines started clamoring to see some art as soon as the new front door was completed in the early 1300s—to be sure their investment would be more beautiful than rival cathedrals. Gaddo Gaddi was commissioned to mosaic an *Enthronement of Mary* in the lunette above the inside of the main door, and the people were satisfied. The stained-glass windows set in the facade were designed by Lorenzo Ghiberti, and Paolo Uccello, a painter obsessed by the newly developed perspective, frescoed the huge *hora itálica* clock with its four heads of prophets in 1443.

At a right-aisle pier are steps leading down to the excavations of the old Santa Reparata. In 1972, a tomb slab inscribed with the name Filippo Brunelleschi was discovered there (visible through a gate). Unless you're interested in the remains of some ancient Roman houses and parts of the paleo-Christian mosaics from Santa Reparata's floor, the 3€ admission isn't worth it.

Against the left-aisle wall are the only wall frescoes in the Duomo. The earlier one to the right is the greenish *Memorial to Sir John Hawkwood* ★ (1436), an English *condottiere* (mercenary commander) whose name the Florentines mangled to Giovanni Acuto when they hired him. Before he died, or so the story goes, the mercenary asked to have a bronze statue of himself riding his charger to be raised in his honor. Florence solemnly promised to do so, but, in typical tightwad style, after Hawkwood's death the city hired the master of perspective and illusion, Paolo Uccello, to paint an equestrian monument instead—much cheaper than casting a statue in bronze. Andrea del Castagno copied this painting-as-equestrian-statue idea 20 years later when he frescoed a *Memorial to Niccolò da Tolentino* next to Uccello's work. Near the end of the left aisle is Domenico di Michelino's *Dante Explaining the Divine Comedy* (1465).

In the back left corner of the sanctuary is the **New Sacristy.** Lorenzo de' Medici was attending Mass in the Duomo one April day in 1478 with his brother Giuliano when they were attacked in the infamous Pazzi Conspiracy. The conspirators, egged on by the pope and led by a member of the Pazzi family, old rivals of the Medici, fell on the brothers at the ringing of the sanctuary bell. Giuliano was murdered on the spot—his body rent with 19 wounds—but Lorenzo vaulted over the altar rail and sprinted for safety into the New Sacristy, slamming the bronze doors behind him. Those doors were cast from 1446 to 1467 by Luca della Robbia, his only significant work in the medium. Earlier, Luca had provided a lunette of the *Resurrection* (1442) in glazed terra cotta over the door, as well as the lunette *Ascension* over the south sacristy door. The interior of the New Sacristy is filled with beautifully inlaid wood cabinet doors.

The frescoes on the **interior of the dome** were designed by Giorgio Vasari but painted mostly by his less talented student Federico Zuccari by 1579. The frescoes were subjected to a thorough cleaning that was completed in 1996, which brought out Zuccari's only saving point—his innovative color palette.

Piazza del Duomo. © **055-230-2885.** www.operaduomo.firenze.it. Admission to church free; Santa Reparata excavations 3€; cupola 8€. Church Mon–Wed and Fri 10am–5pm; Thurs 10am–4:30pm (Jul–Sept till 5pm, May and Oct till 3:30pm); Sat 10am–4:45pm; Sun 1:30–4:45pm. Free tours every 40 min. daily; times vary. Cupola Mon–Fri 8:30am–7pm; Sat 8:30am–5:40pm. Bus: C1, C2, 14, 23, or 71.

Museo dell'Opera del Duomo (Duomo Works Museum) ★

This museum exists mainly to house the sculptures removed from the niches and doors of the Duomo group for restoration and preservation from the elements.

The courtyard is enclosed to show off—under natural daylight—Lorenzo Ghiberti's original gilded bronze panels from the Baptistery's *Gates of Paradise* ★★★, which are displayed on rotation as they're restored. Ghiberti devoted 27 years to this project (1425–52), and you can admire up close his masterpiece of *schiacciato* (squished) relief—using the Donatello technique of almost sketching in perspective to create the illusion of depth in low relief.

On the way up the stairs, you pass **Michelangelo's *Pietà*** ★ (1548–55), his second and penultimate take on the subject, which the sculptor probably had in mind for his own tomb. The face of Nicodemus is a self-portrait, and Michelangelo most likely intended to leave much of the statue group only roughly carved, just as we see it. Art historians inform us that the polished figure of Mary Magdalene on the left was finished by one of Michelangelo's students, while storytellers relate that part of the considerable damage to the group was inflicted by the master himself when, in a moment of rage and frustration, he took a hammer to it.

The museum also houses the **Prophets** carved for the bell tower, the most noted of which are the remarkably expressive figures carved by Donatello: the drooping, aged face of the *Beardless Prophet*; the sad, fixed gaze of *Jeremiah*; and the misshapen ferocity of the bald *Habakkuk* ★ (known to Florentines as *Lo*

A detail from the della Robbia marble choirs at the Duomo museum.

Zuccone—pumpkin head). Mounted on the walls above are two putty-encrusted marble *cantorie* (**choir lofts**). The slightly earlier one (1431) on the entrance wall is by Luca della Robbia. His panels are in perfect early Renaissance harmony, both within themselves and with each other, and they show della Robbia's mastery of creating great depth on a shallow piece of stone. Across the room, Donatello's *cantoria* ★ (1433–38) takes off in a new artistic direction as his singing cherubs literally break through the boundaries of the "panels" to leap and race around the entire *cantoria* behind the mosaicked columns.

The room off the right stars one of Donatello's more morbidly fascinating sculptures, a late work in polychrome wood of the *Magdalene* ★ (1453–55), emaciated and veritably dripping with penitence.

Also here are some of the **machines** used to build the cathedral dome, **Brunelleschi's death mask** as a grisly reminder of its architect, and the **wooden model proposals** for the cupola's drum and for the facade. The original Gothic facade was destroyed in 1587 to make room for one done in High Renaissance style, but the patron behind the work—Grand Duke Francesco de' Medici—died before he could choose from among the submissions by the likes of Giambologna and Bernardo Buontalenti. The Duomo remained faceless until purses of the 19th century, heavy with money and relentless bad taste, gave it the neo-Gothic facade we see today.

Piazza del Duomo 9 (behind the back of the cathedral). ☏ **055-230-2885.** www.operaduomo. firenze.it. Admission 6€. Mon–Sat 9am–7:30pm; Sun 9am–1:45pm; last admission 40 min. before close. Bus: C1, C2, 14, 23, or 71.

Around Piazza della Signoria & Santa Trinita

Galleria degli Uffizi (Uffizi Gallery) ★★★ The Uffizi is one of the world's great museums, and the single best introduction to Renaissance painting, with works by Giotto, Masaccio, Paolo Uccello, Sandro Botticelli, Leonardo da Vinci, Perugino, Michelangelo, Raphael Sanzio, Titian, Caravaggio . . . and the list goes on. The museum is deceptively large. What looks like a small stretch of gallery space can easily gobble up half a day—many rooms suffer the fate of containing nothing but masterpieces.

Know before you go that the Uffizi regularly shuts down rooms for crowd-control reasons—especially in summer, when the bulk of the annual 1.5 million visitors stampede the place. Of the more than 3,100 artworks in the museum's archives, only about 1,700 are on exhibit.

The painting gallery is housed in the structure built to serve as the offices (*uffizi* is Florentine dialect for *uffici,* or "offices") of the Medici, commissioned by Cosimo I from Giorgio Vasari in 1560—perhaps his greatest architectural work. The painting gallery was started by Cosimo I as well and is now housed mostly in the second-floor rooms that open off a long hall lined with ancient statues and frescoed with grotesques.

 How to See the Uffizi

If you have the time and budget, make two trips to the museum. On your first, concentrate on the first dozen or so rooms and pop by the "Greatest Hits of the 16th Century," with works by Michelangelo, Raphael, and Titian. Return later for a brief recap and continue with the rest of the gallery. If you're planning a "slow" visit like this, consider getting an **Amici degli Uffizi** membership; see p. 115.

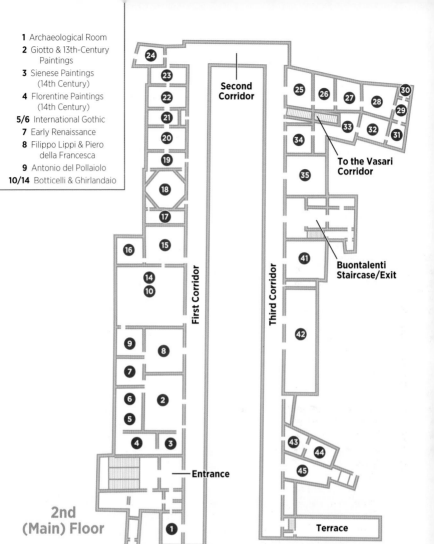

1 Archaeological Room
2 Giotto & 13th-Century Paintings
3 Sienese Paintings (14th Century)
4 Florentine Paintings (14th Century)
5/6 International Gothic
7 Early Renaissance
8 Filippo Lippi & Piero della Francesca
9 Antonio del Pollaiolo
10/14 Botticelli & Ghirlandaio

Second Corridor

25
26
27
28
30
29
33
32
31
34

To the Vasari Corridor

35

First Corridor

Third Corridor

41

Buontalenti Staircase/Exit

42

43
44
45

Entrance

2nd (Main) Floor

Terrace

The Uffizi

15 Leonardo da Vinci
16 Geographic Maps
17 Ermafrodito
18 The Tribune
19 Perugino & Signorelli
20 Dürer & German Artists
21 Giovanni Bellini & Giorgione
22 Flemish & German Paintings
23 Mantegna & Correggio
24 Miniatures

25 Michelangelo & Florentine Artists
26 Raphael & Andrea del Sarto
27 Pontormo & Rosso Fiorentino
28 Titian & Sebastiano del Piombo
29 Parmigianino & Dosso
30 Emilian Paintings
31 Veronese

32 Tintoretto
33 16th-Century Paintings
34 Lombard School
35 Barocci
41 Rubens & Flemish Paintings
42 Roman Statues
43 17th-Century Painters
44 Rembrandt
45 18th-Century Paintings

The first room off to your left after you climb Vasari's monumental stairs (**room 2;** room 1 houses Roman reliefs) presents you with a crash course in the Renaissance's roots. It houses three huge altarpieces by Tuscany's greatest late-13th-century masters. On the right is Cimabue's *Santa Trínita Maestà* (1280), still rooted in the Byzantine traditions that governed painting in the early Middle Ages—gold-leaf crosshatching in the drapery, an Eastern-style inlaid throne, spoonlike depressions above the noses, highly posed figures, and cloned angels with identical faces stacked up along the sides. On the left is Duccio's **Rucellai Maestà ★★** (1285), painted by the master who founded the Sienese school of

PIAZZA DELLA signoria

When the medieval Guelph party finally came out on top of the Ghibellines, they razed part of the old city center to build a new palace for civic government. It's said the Guelphs ordered architect Arnolfo di Cambio to build what we now call the Palazzo Vecchio in the corner of this space, but to be careful that not 1 inch of the building sat on the cursed former Ghibelline land. This odd legend was probably fabricated to explain Arnolfo's quirky off-center architecture.

The space around the *palazzo* became the new civic center of town, the L-shaped **Piazza della Signoria ★★**, named after the oligarchic ruling body of the medieval city. Today, it's an outdoor sculpture gallery, teeming with tourists, postcard stands, horses and buggies, and very expensive outdoor cafes.

The statuary on the piazza is particularly beautiful, starting on the far left (as you're facing the Palazzo Vecchio) with Giambologna's equestrian statue of *Grand Duke Cosimo I* (1594). To its right is one of Florence's favorite sculptures to hate, the **Fontana del Nettuno (Neptune Fountain; 1560–75),** created by Bartolomeo Ammannati as a tribute to Cosimo I's naval ambitions but nicknamed by the Florentines *Il Biancone,* "Big Whitey" (see picture). Michelangelo, to whom many a quip is attributed, took one look at it and shook his head, moaning "Ammannati, Ammannati, what a beautiful piece of marble you've ruined." The highly Mannerist bronzes surrounding the basin are much better, probably because a young Giambologna had a hand in most of them.

Note the **porphyry plaque** set in the ground in front of the fountain. This marks the site where puritanical monk Savonarola held the Bonfire of the Vanities: With his fiery apocalyptic preaching, he whipped the Florentines into a reformist frenzy, and hundreds painting. The style is still medieval but introduces innovations into the rigid traditions. There's a little more weight to the Child and the Madonna's face has a more human, somewhat sad, expression.

In the center of the room is Giotto's incredible ***Ognissanti Maestà*** ★★★ (1310), by the man who's generally credited as the founding father of Renaissance painting. It's sometimes hard to appreciate just how much Giotto changed when he junked half the traditions of painting to go his own way. It's mainly in the very simple details, the sorts of things we take for granted in art today, such as the force of gravity, the display of basic emotions, the individual facial expressions,

filed into this piazza, arms loaded with paintings, clothing, and other effects that represented their "decadence." They consigned it all to the flames. However, after a few years the pope (not amused by Savonarola's criticisms) excommunicated first the monk and then the entire city for supporting him. On May 23, 1498, Florentines decided they'd had enough of the rabid-dog monk, dragged him and two followers to the torture chamber, pronounced them heretics, and led them into the piazza for one last day of fire and brimstone. In the very spot where they once burned their luxurious belongings, they put the torch to Savonarola himself. The event is commemorated by an anonymous painting kept in Savonarola's old cell in San Marco (p. 143) and by the plaque here.

To the right of the Neptune Fountain is a long, raised platform fronting the Palazzo Vecchio known as the *arringheria,* from which soapbox speakers would lecture to crowds before them (we get our word "harangue" from this). On its far left corner is a copy (original in the Bargello) of Donatello's ***Marzocco,*** symbol of the city, with a Florentine lion resting his raised paw on a shield emblazoned with the city's emblem, the *giglio* (lily). To its right is another Donatello replica, ***Judith Beheading Holofernes.*** Farther down is a man who needs little introduction, Michelangelo's ***David,*** a

19th-century copy of the original now in the Accademia. Near enough to David to look truly ugly in comparison is Baccio Bandinelli's ***Heracles*** (1534). Poor Bandinelli was trying to copy Michelangelo's muscular male form but ended up making his Heracles merely lumpy.

At the piazza's south end, beyond the long U that opens down the Uffizi, is one of the square's earliest and prettiest embellishments, the **Loggia dei Lanzi** ★★ (1376–82), named after the Swiss guard of lancers *(lanzi)* Cosimo de' Medici stationed here. The airy loggia was probably built on a design by Andrea Orcagna—spawning another of its many names, the Loggia di Orcagna (another is the Loggia della Signoria). The three huge arches of its simple, harmonious form were way ahead of the times, an architectural style that really belongs to the Renaissance. At the front left corner stands Benvenuto Cellini's masterpiece in bronze, ***Perseus*** ★★★ (1545), holding out the severed Medusa's head before him. On the far right of the loggia is Giambologna's ***Rape of the Sabines*** ★★, one of the most successful Mannerist sculptures in existence, and a piece you must walk all the way around to appreciate, catching the action and artistry from different angles. Talk about moving it indoors, away from the elements, continues . . . but for now, it's still here.

and the figures that look like they have an actual bulky body under their clothes. Giotto's Madonna sways slightly to one side, the fabric of her off-white shirt pulling realistically against her breasts as she twists. Instead of floating in mysterious space, Giotto's saints and angels stand on solid ground.

Room 3 pays homage to the 14th-century Sienese school with delicately crafted works by Simone Martini and the Lorenzetti brothers. Here is Martini's *Annunciation* ★★★ (1333). Mary, who in so much art both before and after this period is depicted as meekly accepting her divine duty, looks reluctant at the news of her imminent Immaculate Conception. Pietro and Ambrogio Lorenzetti helped revolutionize Sienese art and the Sienese school before succumbing to the Black Death in 1348. Of their work here, Ambrogio's 1342 *Presentation at the Temple* ★ is the finest, with a rich use of color and a vast architectural space painted with some understanding of perspective—whose depiction is usually thought of as a 15th-century Florentine "discovery."

Room 4 houses the works of the 14th-century Florentine school, where you can clearly see the influence Giotto had on his contemporaries. **Rooms 5 and 6** represent the flourishing of International Gothic, still grounded in medievalism but admitting some of the emergent naturalism and humanist philosophy into their highly decorative works. Gentile da Fabriano's *Procession of the Magi* ★ (1423) is especially resplendent, and loaded with detail and caricature.

In **room 7,** the Renaissance proper starts taking shape, driven primarily by the quest of two artists, Paolo Uccello and Masaccio, for perfect perspective. On the left wall is Uccello's *Battle of San Romano* (1456), famously innovative but also rather ugly. This painting depicts one of Florence's great victories over rival Siena, but for Uccello it was more of an excuse to explore perspective—with which this painter was, by all accounts, obsessed. In the far corner is the only example of Masaccio's art here (he died at 27), the *Madonna and Child with St. Anne,* which he helped his master, Masolino, paint in 1424. Masaccio's earthy realism and sharp light are evident in the figures of Mary and the Child, as well as in the topmost angel peeking down.

In the center of **room 8** is Piero della Francesca's *Portrait of Federico da Montefeltro and Battista Sforza* ★★, painted around 1465 or 1470 and the only work by this remarkable Sansepolcran to survive in Florence. The fronts of the panels depict the duke of Urbino and his wife, while on the backs are horse-drawn carts symbolic of the pair's respective virtues. Piero's lucid style and the detailed Flemish-style backgrounds need no commentary, but do note that he purposefully painted the husband and wife in profile—without diluting the realism of a hooked nose and moles on the duke—and mounted them face to face, forever gazing into each other's eyes.

The rest of room 8 is devoted to Filippo Lippi, with more than half a dozen works by the amorous monk who turned out rich religious paintings with an earthy quality and a three-dimensionality that make them immediately accessible. His most exquisite Madonna here is the *Madonna and Child with Two Angels* ★★ (1455–66)—also a tender portrait of his mistress, Lucrezia Buti. Nearby are a few works by their illegitimate son, Filippino. **Room 9** is an interlude of virtuoso paintings by Antonio del Pollaiolo, plus a number of large Virtues by his less-talented brother, Piero. These two masters of anatomical verisimilitude greatly influenced the young Botticelli.

The walls separating **rooms 10 to 14** were knocked down in the 20th century to create one large space to accommodate the resurgent popularity of Sandro

Filipepi—better known by his nickname, Botticelli ("little barrels")—master of willowy women in flowing gowns. Fourteen of his paintings line the walls, along with works by his pupil (and son of his former teacher) Filippino Lippi, and by Domenico Ghirlandaio, Michelangelo's first artistic master. But most flock here for just two paintings, Botticelli's *Birth of Venus* and his *Primavera (Allegory of Spring)*. Though in later life Botticelli was influenced by the puritanical preachings of Savonarola and took to cranking out boring Madonnas, the young painter began in grand pagan style. Both paintings were commissioned between 1477 and 1483 by a Medici cousin for his private villa, and they celebrate not only Renaissance art's love of naturalism but also the humanist philosophy permeating 15th-century Florence, a neo-Platonism that united religious doctrine with ancient ideology and mythological stories.

In the **Birth of Venus** ★★, the love goddess is born of the sea on a half shell, blown to shore by the Zephyrs. Ores, a goddess of the seasons, rushes to clothe her. Some say the long-legged goddess was modeled on Simonetta Vespucci, a renowned Florentine beauty, cousin to Amerigo (the naval explorer after whom America is named) and not-so-secret lover of Giuliano de' Medici, Lorenzo the Magnificent's brother. The **Primavera** ★★ is harder to evaluate, since contemporary research indicates it may not actually be an allegory of spring influenced by the humanist poetry of Poliziano but rather a celebration of Venus, who stands in the center, surrounded by various complicated references to Virtues through mythological characters. Also check out Botticelli's *Adoration of the Magi,* where the artist painted himself in the far right side, in a great yellow robe and golden curls.

Room 15 boasts Leonardo da Vinci's **Annunciation** ★★★, which the young artist painted in 1472 or 1475 while still in the workshop of his master, Andrea del Verrocchio; however, he was already fully developed as an artist. The solid yet light figures and *sfumato* airiness blurring the distance render remarkably lifelike figures somehow suspended in a surreal dreamscape; view it from the lower-right to appreciate his mastery of perspective. Leonardo helped Verrocchio on the *Baptism of Christ*—most credit the artist-in-training with the

Leonardo da Vinci's *Annunciation.*

angel on the far left as well as the landscape, and a few art historians think they see his hand in the figure of Jesus as well. The *Adoration of the Magi* ★★, on which Leonardo didn't get much beyond the sketching stage, shows how he could retain powerful compositions even when creating a fantasy landscape of ruinous architecture and incongruous horse battles. The room also houses a *Pietà* that shows Perugino's solid plastic style of studied simplicity. (This Umbrian master would later pass it on to his pupil Raphael.)

Alas, visitors are no longer permitted in **room 18, the Tribune,** where mother-of-pearl discs line a domed ceiling; antique statues, such as the famous *Medici Venus* (a 1st-c.-B.C. Roman copy of a Greek original), are housed; and Medici portraits wallpaper the room. The latter include many by the talented early baroque artist Agnolo Bronzino, whose portrait of *Eleonora of Toledo* ★, wife of Cosimo I, with their son Giovanni de' Medici (1545), is particularly well worked. It shows her in a satin dress embroidered and sewn with velvet and pearls. When the Medici tombs were opened in 1857, her body was found buried in this same dress.

Room 19 is devoted to both Perugino, who did the luminous *Portrait of Francesco delle Opere* (1494), and Luca Signorelli, whose *Holy Family* (1490–95) was painted as a tondo set in a rectangle, with allegorical figures in the background and a torsion of the figures that were to influence Michelangelo's version (in a later room). **Room 20** is devoted to Dürer, Cranach, and other German artists who worked in Florence, while **room 21** takes care of 16th-century Venetians Giovanni Bellini, Giorgione, and Carpaccio. In **room 22** are Flemish and German works by Hans Holbein the Younger, Hans Memling, and others, and **room 23** contains Andrea Mantegna's triptych of the *Adoration of the Magi, Circumcision, and Ascension* ★ (1463–70), showing his excellent draftsmanship and fascination with classical architecture. **Room 25** is overpowered by Michelangelo's *Holy Family* ★★ (1506–08), one of the few panel paintings by the master. The glowing colors and shocking nudes in the background seem to pop off the surface, and the torsion of the figures was to be taken up as the banner of the Mannerist movement. Michelangelo also designed the elaborate frame.

Room 26 is devoted to Andrea del Sarto and High Renaissance darling Raphael. Of Raphael we have the *Madonna of the Goldfinch* ★ (1505), a work he painted in a Leonardesque style for a friend's wedding, more vivid than ever after a 2009 restoration. Also here are important portraits including *Pope Leo X with Cardinals Giulio de' Medici and Luigi de' Rossi* ★★ and *Pope Julius II,* as well as a famous *Self-Portrait.* Del Sarto was the most important painter in Florence in the early 16th century, while Michelangelo and Raphael were in Rome. His consciously developed Mannerist style is evident in his masterful *Madonna of the Harpies* (1515–17).

Room 27 is devoted to works by Del Sarto's star Mannerist pupils, Rosso Fiorentino and Pontormo, and by Pontormo's adopted son, Bronzino. Fiorentino's *Moses Defends the Daughters of Jethro* ★ (1523) owes much to Michelangesque nudes but is also original in the use of harsh lighting that reduces the figures to basic shapes of color.

Room 28 honors the great Venetian Titian, of whose works you'll see include a warm full-bodied *Flora* ★★ and a poetic, somewhat suggestive *Venus of Urbino* ★ languishing on her bed.

Tiny **rooms 29 and 30,** ostensibly honoring works by several Emilian artists, are totally dominated by late Mannerist master Il Parmigianino, who carried the Mannerist movement to its logical extremes with the almost grotesquely elongated bodies of the *Madonna of the Long Neck* ★ (1534). **Room 31** continues to chart the fall of painting into decorative grace with Paolo Veronese's *Martyrdom of St. Justine* (1573), which is less about the saint being stabbed than it is a sartorial study in fashion design.

Room 32 is a nice break provided by the dramatic and visible brush strokes that boldly swirled rich, somber colors of several lesser works by Venetian master Tintoretto. All the better, as these must see you through the treacle and tripe of **rooms 33 to 34,** stuffed with substandard examples of 16th-century paintings by the likes of Vasari, Alessandro Allori, and other chaps who grew up in Michelangelo's shadow and desperately wished they could paint like him. (*Note:* They couldn't.)

Room 35 features the taffeta, cotton-candy oeuvre of baroque weirdo Federico Barocci. Continue right past that exit staircase, because they save a few eye-popping rooms for the very end.

Room 41 is all about Rubens and his famously ample nudes, along with some works by his Flemish cohorts (Van Dyck, Sustermans). **Room 42** is a lovely side hall flooded with sunlight and graced by more than a dozen Roman statues that are copies of Hellenic originals, most of them of the dying Niobids.

Pay your respects to Rembrandt in **room 44,** where he immortalized himself in two *Self-Portraits,* one done as a youth and the other as an old man. If you need to pause for breath, prices at the Uffizi's terrace **cafe** are no worse than in the piazza below. It's a nice spot to catch a new angle on the Palazzo Vecchio's facade.

Downstairs is a space used to house temporary exhibitions that, at their best, provide some added context to the permanent collection, but at worst are just a way to slap a few more euros onto your entrance fee. However, it's certainly worth visiting the space devoted to Caravaggio and the *Caravaggeschi*. Caravaggio was the baroque master of *chiaroscuro*—painting with extreme harsh light and deep shadows. The Uffizi preserves his painting of the severed head of *Medusa,* a *Sacrifice of Isaac,* and his famous **Bacchus** ★. Caravaggio's work influenced a generation of artists—the *Caravaggeschi* (painters who followed his style) included Artemisia Gentileschi, the only female painter to make a name for herself in the early baroque. Artemisia was eclipsed in fame by her less talented father, Orazio, and was the victim in a sensational rape trial brought against Orazio's one-time collaborator. It evidently affected her professional life; the violent *Judith Slaying Holofernes* ★ is featured here, in all its gruesome detail.

The precise configurations of the other rooms here are in flux, but look out for other European students of Caravaggio, including Matthias Stomer, Francesco Rustici, Nicolas Regnier, and

 Reserving Tickets for the Uffizi & Other Museums

You should bypass the hours-long ticket line at the Uffizi Gallery by reserving a ticket and an entry time in advance by calling **Firenze Musei** at ✆ **055-294-883** (Mon–Fri 8:30am–6:30pm; Sat until 12:30pm) or visiting **www.firenzemusei.it** (you may need to have patience with their website, however). You can also reserve for the Accademia Gallery (another interminable line, to see *David*), as well as the Galleria Palatina in the Pitti Palace, the Bargello, and several others. There is a 3€ fee (4€ for the Uffizi or Accademia, where a reservation is essential); you can pay by credit card.

Guido Reni, perhaps best known for his collaboration with Annibale Carracci on the Farnese Palace in Rome, but also noted for his paintings betraying the influence of Caravaggio. His rendering of a triumphant David admiring the slain head of Goliath, upon your exit, is a fitting tribute to your conquest of this overwhelming gallery—because that's it. The Uffizi is finished. Navigate the (at last count) five gift shops and then treat yourself to a cappuccino alfresco. You've earned it.

Piazzale degli Uffizi 6 (off Piazza della Signoria). ✆ **055-238-8651.** www.uffizi.firenze.it. (Reserve tickets at ✆ 055-294-883 or www.firenzemusei.it.) Admission 6.50€ (10€–11€ with compulsory temporary exhibition). Tues–Sat 8:15am–6:50pm; also same hours 1st, 3rd, and 5th Sun of month. Ticket window closes 45 min. before museum. Bus: C1 or C2.

Museo Galileo ★ The laptop computer and smartphone don't hold a candle to the beautifully engraved intricate mechanical instruments from Florence's history of science museum. Galileo and his peers practiced a science that was an art form of the highest aesthetic order. The cases display such beauties from the original Medici collections (begun by Cosimo I) as a mechanical calculator from 1664—a gleaming bronze sandwich of engraved disks and dials—and an architect's compass and plumb disguised as a dagger, complete with sheath.

In the field of astronomy, the museum has the lens with which Galileo discovered four of the moons of Jupiter (which he prudently named after his Medici patrons) and, alongside telescopes of all sizes and complexity, a tiny "lady's telescope" made of ivory that once came in a box of beauty products. There's also a somewhat grisly section of the Lorraine Collections (room 10) devoted to medicine, with disturbingly realistic wax models of just about everything that can go wrong during childbirth. And what Italian institution would be complete without a holy relic? In this case, it's the middle finger of Galileo's right hand, swiped while he was en route to reinternment in Santa Croce. He was allowed burial in a Christian church only in the 18th century, after he was posthumously vindicated for supporting a heliocentric view of the universe.

Piazza dei Giudici 1 (just east of the Uffizi along the riverside). ✆ **055-265-311.** www.museogalileo.it. Admission 8€ adults, 5€ for ages 7–18 and 65 and over. Mon and Wed–Sun 9:30am–5pm; Tues 9:30am–1pm. Bus: C1.

Museo Nazionale del Bargello (Bargello Museum) ★★ Inside this 1255 Gothic *palazzo* is Florence's premier sculpture museum, with works by Michelangelo, the della Robbias, and Donatello.

In the *palazzo*'s old **armory** are 16th-century works, including some of Michelangelo's earliest sculptures. Carved by a 22-year-old Michelangelo while he was visiting Rome, ***Bacchus ★*** (1497) was obviously inspired by the classical antiquities he studied there but is also imbued with his own irrepressible Renaissance realism—here is a (young) God of Wine who's actually drunk, reeling back on unsteady knees and holding the cup aloft with a distinctly tipsy wobble. (The statue was rejected by its original patron.) Michelangelo polished and finished his *Bacchus* in the traditional manner, but from 1503 to 1505, soon after finishing his famous *David* with a high polish, he carved the ***Pitti Tondo ★*** here, a *schiacciato* Madonna and Child scene in which the artist began using the textures of the partially worked marble itself to convey his artistic message. Also in this room is Giambologna's ***Flying Mercury ★*** (ca. 1564), looking for all the world as if he's on the verge of taking off from the ground—justifiably one of this Mannerist's masterpieces.

The *palazzo*'s inner **courtyard**—one of the few medieval *cortile* in Florence to survive in more-or-less its original shape—is studded with the coats of arms of past *podestà* (mayors) and other notables. The grand stairwell leads up to a second-story loggia filled with a flock of whimsical bronze birds cast by Giambologna for the Medici's gardens. The doorway leads into the old **Salone del Consiglio Generale (General Council Room) ★★**, a vast space with a high ceiling filled with glazed terra-cotta Madonnas by Luca della Robbia and his clan, and some of the most important sculptures of the early Renaissance.

Donatello dominates the room, starting with a mischievously smiling *Cupid* (ca. 1430–40). He sculpted the *Marzocco,* lion symbol of the Florentine Republic, out of *pietra serena* between 1418 and 1420. The marble *David* (1408) is an early Donatello, but the bronze ***David* ★★** (1440–50)—or perhaps *Mercury,* opinion is divided—is a much more mature piece, the first freestanding nude since antiquity. The figure is an almost erotic youth, with a shy, detached air that has little to do with the giant severed head at his feet. Against the far wall is **St. George ★**, carved in 1416 for a niche of Orsanmichele. The relief below it of the saint slaying his dragon is the first example of the sculptor's patented *schiacciato* technique, using thinly etched lines and perspective to create great depth in a very shallow space.

In the back right corner of this room are two bronze relief panels by Brunelleschi and Ghiberti of the *Sacrifice of Isaac,* finalists in the famous 1401 competition for the commission to cast the Baptistery's doors (see p. 114). Ghiberti's panel won for the greater dynamism and flowing action in his version.

Upstairs are rooms with glazed terra cottas by Andrea and Giovanni della Robbia and another room devoted to the sculptural production of Leonardo da Vinci's teacher Verrocchio, including yet another *David* (1465), a haughty youth with a tousle of hair inspired by the Donatello version downstairs.

Via del Proconsolo 4. ☎ **055-238-8606.** www.firenzemusei.it/bargello. Admission 4€. Daily 8:15am–1:50pm. Closed 2nd and 4th Mon and 1st, 3rd, and 5th Sun of each month. Bus: C1 or C2.

Orsanmichele ★★ This bulky structure halfway down Via dei Calzaiuoli looks more like a Gothic warehouse than a church—which is exactly what it was, built as a granary and grain market in 1337. After a miraculous image of the Madonna appeared on a column inside, however, the lower level was turned into a chapel. The city's merchant guilds each undertook the task of decorating one of the outside nichelike Gothic tabernacles around the lower level with a statue of their guild's patron saint. Masters such as Ghiberti, Donatello, Verrocchio, and

St. Mark, in one of the niches that surround Orsanmichele.

Giambologna all cast or carved masterpieces to set here. The originals have been replaced by casts and are cleaned and exhibited (sometimes) up on the second story.

In the chapel's dark interior, the elaborate Gothic ***Tabernacle*** ★ (1349–59) by Andrea Orcagna looks something like a miniature church, covered with statuettes, enamels, inset colored marbles and glass, and reliefs. It protects a luminous 1348 *Madonna and Child* painted by Giotto's student Bernardo Daddi, to which miracles were ascribed during the Black Death of 1348–50. The prominent statue of the *Madonna, Child, and St. Anne* to its left is by Francesco da Sangallo (1522).

Across Via dell'Arte della Lana from the Orsanmichele's main entrance is the 1308 Palazzo dell'Arte della Lana. This Gothic palace was home to medieval Florence's most powerful body, the guild of wool merchants, which employed about one-third of Florence in the 13th and 14th centuries. Up the stairs inside you can cross over the hanging walkway to the first floor (American second floor) of Orsanmichele. These are the old granary rooms, now housing a **museum of the statues** ★ that once surrounded the exterior. Many of the original sculptures are here, well labeled, including Donatello's marble *St. Mark* (1411–13); Ghiberti's bronze *St. John the Baptist* (1413–16), the first life-size bronze of the Renaissance; and Verrocchio's *Incredulity of St. Thomas* (1473–83). Alas, the room is rarely open—Monday is the day you'll most likely get lucky.

Via Arte della Lana 1. ✆ **055-210-305.** Free admission. Daily 10am–5pm. Bus: C2.

Palazzo Vecchio ★ Florence's fortresslike town hall was built from 1299 to 1302 on the designs of Arnolfo di Cambio, Gothic master builder of the city. Arnolfo managed to make it solid and impregnable-looking yet still graceful, with thin-columned Gothic windows and two orders of crenellations—square for the main rampart and swallow-tailed on the 94m-high (308-ft.) bell tower.

The Palazzo Vecchio towering over Piazza della Signoria.

The palace was once home to the various Florentine republican governments (and today to the municipal government). Cosimo I and his ducal Medici family moved to the *palazzo* in 1540 and engaged in massive redecoration. Michelozzo's 1453 **courtyard ★**, just through the door, was left architecturally intact but frescoed by Vasari with scenes of Austrian cities to celebrate the 1565 marriage of Francesco de' Medici and Joanna of Austria. The grand staircase leads up to the **Sala dei Cinquecento,** named for the 500-man assembly that met here in the pre-Medici days of the Florentine Republic and site of the greatest fresco cycle that ever wasn't. Leonardo da Vinci was commissioned in 1503 to paint one long wall with a battle scene celebrating a famous Florentine victory. He was always trying new methods and materials and decided to mix wax into his pigments. Leonardo had finished painting part of the wall, but it wasn't drying fast enough, so he brought in braziers stoked with hot coals to try to hurry the process. As others watched in horror, the wax in the fresco melted under the intense heat and the colors ran down the walls to puddle on the floor. Michelangelo never even got past making the preparatory drawings for the fresco he was supposed to paint on the opposite wall—Pope Julius II called him to Rome to paint the Sistine Chapel, and the master's sketches were destroyed by eager young artists who came to study them and took away scraps. Eventually, the bare walls were covered by Vasari and assistants from 1563 to 1565 with blatantly subservient frescoes exalting Cosimo I de' Medici and his dynasty.

Against the wall of the Sala dei Cinquecento, opposite the door you enter, is Michelangelo's statue of *Victory* ★, carved from 1533 to 1534 for the Julius II tomb but later donated to the Medici. Its extreme torsion—the way the body twists and spirals upward—was to be a great influence on the Mannerist movement.

The first series of rooms on the second floor is the **Quartiere degli Elementi,** again frescoed by Vasari. Crossing the balcony overlooking the Sala dei Cinquecento, you enter the **Apartments of Eleonora di Toledo,** decorated for Cosimo's Spanish wife. Her small private chapel is a masterpiece of mid-16th-century painting by Bronzino. Farther on, under the coffered ceiling of the **Sala dei Gigli,** are Domenico Ghirlandaio's fresco of *St. Zenobius Enthroned* with ancient Roman heroes and Donatello's original *Judith and Holofernes* ★ bronze (1455), one of his last works.

Piazza della Signoria. ✆ **055-276-8325.** Admission 6€. Fri–Wed 9am–7pm; Thurs and public holidays 9am–2pm. Bus: C1 or C2.

Ponte Vecchio (Old Bridge) ★ The oldest and most famous bridge across the Arno, the Ponte Vecchio was built in 1345 by Taddeo Gaddi to replace an earlier

Vasari's Corridor

The enclosed passageway that runs along the top of Ponte Vecchio is part of the **Corridoio Vasariano (Vasari Corridor) ★**, a private elevated link between the Palazzo Vecchio and Palazzo Pitti, and now hung with the world's best collection of artists' self-portraits. Duke Cosimo I found the idea of mixing with the *hoi polloi* on the way to work rather distressing, and so commissioned Vasari to design his VIP route in 1565. It's often possible to walk the corridor, although closures for restoration work are common. Inquire at the tourist office. **Context Travel** (p. 54) operates a guided walk through the corridor, costing 100€ per person.

Rowers on the Arno, passing under the Ponte Vecchio.

version. The characteristic overhanging shops have lined the bridge since at least the 12th century. In the 16th century, it was home to butchers until Cosimo I moved into the Palazzo Pitti across the river. He couldn't stand the stench as he crossed the bridge from on high in the Corridoio Vasariano every day, so he evicted the meat cutters and moved in the classier gold- and silversmiths, tradesmen who occupy it to this day.

A bust of the most famous Florentine goldsmith, the swashbuckling autobiographer and *Perseus* sculptor Benvenuto Cellini, stands off to the side of the bridge's center, in a small piazza overlooking the Arno. From this vantage point Mark Twain, spoiled by the mighty Mississippi, wryly commented of the Arno, "They call it a river, and they honestly think it is a river . . . They even help out the delusion by building bridges over it. I do not see why they are too good to wade."

The Ponte Vecchio's fame saved it in 1944 from the Nazis, who had orders to blow up all the bridges before retreating out of Florence as Allied forces advanced. They couldn't bring themselves to reduce this span to rubble—so they blew up the ancient buildings on either end instead to block it off. The Great Arno Flood of 1966 wasn't so discriminating, however, and severely damaged the shops. Apparently, a private night watchman saw the waters rising alarmingly and called many of the goldsmiths at home, who rushed to remove their valuable stock before it was washed away.

Via Por Santa Maria/Via Guicciardini. Bus: C3 or D.

Santa Trínita ★★ Beyond Bernardo Buontalenti's late-16th-century **facade** lies a dark church, rebuilt in the 14th century but founded by the Vallombrosans before 1177. The third chapel on the right has what remains of the detached frescoes by Spinello Aretino, which were found under Lorenzo Monaco's excellent 1422 frescoes covering the next chapel down.

In the right transept, Domenico Ghirlandaio frescoed the **Cappella Sassetti** ★ in 1483 with a cycle on the *Life of St. Francis,* but true to form he set all the

Catching an Exhibition at the Strozzi

The two spaces inside the Renaissance **Palazzo Strozzi** ★★, Piazza Strozzi—known as the **Piano Nobile** and the basement **Strozzina**—are Florence's major spaces for temporary and contemporary art shows, and have been experiencing a 21st-century renaissance of their own under new and energetic directorship. Major hits of recent years have included the likes of 2011's "Picasso, Miró, Dalí." There's always lots going on around the shows too, including talks, late-night events, and even discovery trails aimed at 5- to 9-year-olds. Check www.palazzostrozzi.org for the latest exhibition news.

scenes against Florentine backdrops and peopled them with portraits of contemporary notables. The most famous is *Francis Receiving the Order from Pope Honorius,* which in this version takes place under an arcade on the north side of Piazza della Signoria—the Loggia dei Lanzi is featured in the middle, and on the left is the Palazzo Vecchio. (The Uffizi between them hadn't been built yet.) In the little group on the far right, the unhandsome man with the red cloak is Lorenzo the Magnificent.

The chapel to the right of the main altar houses the miraculous **Crucifix** that once hung in San Miniato al Monte. One day the nobleman Giovanni Gualberto was storming up the hillside in a rage, on his way to wreak revenge on his brother's murderer. Gualberto paused at San Miniato and after some reflection decided to pardon the assassin, whereupon this crucifix bowed its head in approval. Gualberto went on to found the Vallombrosan order of monks, who later established this church.

The south end of the piazza leads to the **Ponte Santa Trínita,** Florence's most graceful bridge. In 1567, Ammannati built a span here that was set with four 16th-century statues of the seasons in honor of the marriage of Cosimo II. After the Nazis blew up the bridge in 1944, it was rebuilt, and all was set into place again—save the head on the statue of Spring, which remained lost until a team dredging the river in 1961 found it by accident. From the bridge you get a great view upriver of the Ponte Vecchio and downriver of the **Ponte alla Carraia** (another postwar reconstruction), where in 1304 so many people gathered to watch a floating production of Dante's *Inferno* that it collapsed and all were drowned. Florentine wits were quick to point out that all the people who went to see Hell that day found what they were looking for.

Piazza Santa Trínita. 🕐 **055-216-912.** Free admission. Mon–Sat 8am–noon and 4–6pm; Sun 4–6pm. Bus: C3, 6, 11, 36, or 37.

Around San Lorenzo & the Mercato Centrale

Michelangelo's *New Sacistry* in the Medici Chapels.

The church of San Lorenzo is practically lost behind the leather stalls and souvenir carts of Florence's vast **San Lorenzo street market** (see "Shopping," later in this chapter). In fact, the hawking of wares and bustle of commerce characterize all the streets of this neighborhood, centered on both the church and the nearby **Mercato Centrale food market.** This is a colorful scene, but one of the most pickpocket-happy in the city, so be wary. *Note:* You are liable for a fine if you knowingly buy counterfeit goods in the city.

Cappelle Medicee (Medici Chapels) ★★ When Michelangelo built the New Sacristy between 1520 and 1533 (finished by Vasari in 1556), it was to be a tasteful monument to Lorenzo the Magnificent and his generation of fairly pleasant Medici. When work got underway on the Chapel of the Princes in 1604, it was to become one of the world's most god-awful and arrogant memorials, dedicated to the grand dukes, some of Florence's most decrepit tyrants. The **Cappella dei Principi (Chapel of the Princes)** is an exercise in bad taste, a mountain of cut marbles and semi-precious stones—jasper, alabaster, mother-of-pearl, agate, and the like—slathered onto the walls and ceiling with no regard for composition and still less for chromatic unity. The pouring of ducal funds into this monstrosity began in 1604 and lasted until the rarely conscious Gian Gastone de' Medici drank himself to death in 1737 without an heir—but teams kept doggedly at the thing, and they were still finishing the floor in 1962. The tombs of the grand dukes in this massive marble mistake were designed by Pietro Tacca in the 17th century, and off to the left and right of the altar are small treasuries full of gruesome holy relics in silver-bedecked cases. The dome of the structure, seen from the outside, is one of Florence's landmarks, a kind of infant version of the Duomo's.

Michelangelo's **Sagrestia Nuova (New Sacristy)** ★★, built to jibe with Brunelleschi's Old Sacristy in San Lorenzo proper, is much calmer. (An architectural tidbit: The windows in the dome taper as they get near the top to fool you into thinking the dome is higher.) Michelangelo was supposed to produce three tombs here (perhaps four) but ironically got only the two less important ones done. So Lorenzo de' Medici the Magnificent—wise ruler of his city, poet of note, grand patron of the arts, and moneybags behind much of the Renaissance—ended up with a mere inscription of his name next to his brother Giuliano's on a plain marble slab against the entrance wall. Admittedly, they did get one genuine Michelangelo sculpture to decorate their slab, a *Madonna and Child* that's perhaps the master's most beautiful version of the theme.

On the left wall of the sacristy is Michelangelo's ***Tomb of Lorenzo*** ★, duke of Urbino (and Lorenzo the Magnificent's grandson), whose seated statue symbolizes the contemplative life. Below him on the elongated curves of the tomb stretch *Dawn* (female) and *Dusk* (male), a pair of Michelangelo's most famous sculptures, where he uses both high polish and rough cutting to impart strength, texture, and psychological suggestion to the allegorical works. This pair mirrors the similarly fashioned and equally important *Day* (male) and *Night* (female) across the way. One additional point *Dawn* and *Night* brings out is that Michelangelo really wasn't too adept at the female body—he just produced softer, less muscular men with slightly elongated midriffs and breasts sort of tacked on at funny angles.

Piazza Madonna degli Aldobrandini (behind San Lorenzo, where Via Faenza and Via del Giglio meet). ✆ **055-238-8602.** Admission 6€. Daily 8:15am–4:50pm. Closed 1st, 3rd, and 5th Mon, and 2nd and 4th Sun of each month. Bus: C1, C2, 6, 11, 14, 22, 23, 36, or 37.

Palazzo Medici-Riccardi ★ The Palazzo Medici-Riccardi was built by Michelozzo in 1444 for Cosimo de' Medici il Vecchio; it's the prototype Florentine *palazzo,* on which the more overbearing Strozzi and Pitti palaces were later modeled. It remained the Medici private home until Cosimo I more officially declared his power as duke by moving to the city's traditional civic brain center, the Palazzo Vecchio. A door off the right of the entrance courtyard leads up a staircase to the **Cappella dei Magi,** the oldest chapel to survive from a private Florentine palace; its walls are covered with gorgeously dense and colorful Benozzo Gozzoli **frescoes** ★★ (1459–63). Rich as tapestries, the walls depict an extended *Journey of the Magi* to see the Christ child, who's being adored by Mary in the altarpiece. Gozzoli is at his decorative best here, inheriting an attention to detail in plants and animals from his teacher Fra' Angelico. The remainder of the palace is steadily being opened up to visitors.

Via Cavour 3. ℂ **055-276-0340.** www.palazzo-medici.it. Admission 7€ adults, 4€ ages 6–12. Thurs–Tues 9am–7pm. Bus: C1, 14, or 23.

San Lorenzo ★ A rough brick anti-facade and the undistinguished stony bulk of a building surrounded by market stalls hide what is most likely the oldest church in Florence, founded in A.D. 393. San Lorenzo was the city's cathedral until the bishop's seat moved to Santa Reparata (later to become the Duomo) in the 7th century. More importantly, it was the Medici family's parish church, and as those famous bankers began to accumulate a vast fortune, they started a tradition of lavishing it on the church that lasted until the 18th century. (The Medici Chapels, listed above, have a separate entrance around the back of the church, and keep different hours.)

The first thing Giovanni di Bicci de' Medici, founder of the family fortune, did for the church was hire Brunelleschi to tune up the **interior,** rebuilding according to the architect's plans in 1426. At the end of the right aisle is a Desiderio da Settignano marble tabernacle that's a mastery of *schiacciato* relief and carefully incised perspective. Across the aisle is one of the two bronze 1460 **pulpits** ★★—the other is across the nave—that were Donatello's last works. His patron and the first great consolidator of Medici power, which at this early stage still showed great concern for protecting the interests of the people, was Cosimo il Vecchio, Lorenzo the Magnificent's grandfather. Cosimo, whose wise behind-the-scenes rule made him popular with the Florentines, died in 1464 and is buried in front of the high altar. The plaque marking the spot is simply inscribed PATER PATRIE—father of his homeland.

Off the left transept is the **Sagrestia Vecchia (Old Sacristy)** ★, one of Brunelleschi's purest pieces of early Renaissance architecture. The focal sarcophagus contains Cosimo il Vecchio's parents, Giovanni di Bicci de' Medici and his wife, Piccarda Bueri, and a side chapel is decorated with an early star map that shows the night sky above the city in the 1440s.

On the wall of the left aisle is Bronzino's huge fresco of the *Martyrdom of San Lorenzo* ★. The 3rd-century namesake saint of this church, St. Lawrence was a flinty early Christian and the treasurer of the Roman church. When commanded by the Romans to hand over the church's wealth, Lorenzo appeared before Emperor Valerian's prefect with "thousands" of sick, poor, and crippled people saying: "Here is all the church's treasure." The Romans weren't amused and decided to martyr him on a gridiron over hot coals. Feisty to the last, while Lorenzo lay there roasting he called out to his tormentors through gritted teeth, "Turn me over, I'm done on this side."

Left of the church's main door is an entrance to the cloister and inside it a stairwell leading up to the **Biblioteca Laurenziana (Laurentian Library)** ★★. Michelangelo designed this library in 1524 to house the Medici's manuscript collection, and it stands as one of the most brilliant works of Mannerist architecture. The vestibule is a whacked-out riff on the Renaissance, all *pietra serena* and white plaster walls like a good Brunelleschi piece, but turned inside out.

Piazza San Lorenzo. ℂ **055-214-042.** Admission to church 3.50€; admission to library 3€; combined admission 6€. Church Mon–Sat 10am–5:30pm; Sun Mar–Oct 1:30–5:30pm. Laurentian Library Mon–Sat 9:30am–1pm. Bus: C1, 14, or 23.

On or Near Piazza Santa Maria Novella

Piazza Santa Maria Novella boasts patches of grass and a central fountain. The two squat obelisks, resting on the backs of Giambologna tortoises, once served as the turning posts for the "chariot" races held here from the 16th to the mid–19th century. Once a depressed and down-at-heel part of the center, the area is now on the up, but the night can still lean toward the seedy. The **Officina Profumo-Farmaceutica di Santa Maria Novella** is a sight on its own; see "Shopping," later in this chapter.

Museo di Santa Maria Novella ★ The cloisters of Santa Maria Novella's convent are open to the public as a museum. The **Chiostro Verde,** with a cypress-surrounded fountain and chirping birds, is named for the greenish tint in the pigment used by Paolo Uccello in his **frescoes ★★**. His works line the right wall as you enter; the most famous is the confusing, somewhat disturbing first scene you come to, where the *Flood and Recession of the Flood and the Drunkenness and Sacrifice of Noah* (1446) are all squeezed onto one panel as the story lines are piled atop one another and Noah appears several times. The two giant wooden walls on either side are meant to be the Ark, shown both before and after the Flood, seen in extreme, distorting perspective. Ironically, it owes its poor condition to severe damage during the Great Arno Flood of November 4, 1966.

The **Cappella degli Spagnoli (Spanish Chapel)** ★ got its name when it became the private chapel of Eleonora of Toledo, recently arrived in Florence to be Cosimo de' Medici's bride. The chapel was frescoed by Andrea di Bonaiuto and his assistants with allegories on the preaching of the Dominicans, whose Florence base this was.

Piazza Santa Maria Novella (entrance behind gate left of the church facade). ✆ **055-282-187.** www.museicivicifiorentini.it/en/smn. Admission 2.70€ adults, 1€ ages 4–17. Fri–Mon 10am–4pm. Bus: C2, 6, 11, 22, 36, or 37.

Ognissanti ★ Founded in 1256 by the Umiliati, a wool-weaving sect of the Benedictines whose trade helped establish this area as a textile district, the present Ognissanti was rebuilt by its new Franciscan owners in the 17th century. It has the earliest baroque **facade** in Florence, designed by Matteo Nigetti in 1627 and rebuilt in travertine in 1872.

Ognissanti was the parish church of the Vespucci family, agents of the Medici bank in Seville. A young Domenico Ghirlandaio portrayed several of the family members in his *Madonna della Misericordia* (1470) on the second altar to the right. The lady under the Madonna's left hand may be Simonetta Vespucci, renowned beauty of her age, mistress of Giuliano de' Medici (Lorenzo's brother), and the possible model for Venus in Botticelli's *Birth of Venus.* The young man with black hair to the Madonna's right is said to be Amerigo Vespucci (1454–1512), whose letters about exploring the New World in 1499 and again from 1501 to 1502 would become so popular that a cartographer used a corruption of Amerigo's name on an influential set of maps to describe the newly discovered continent. The family tombstone (America's namesake rests in peace underneath) is to the left of this altar.

Between the third and fourth altars is Botticelli's fresco of a pensive *St. Augustine in His Study* (1480), a more intense work than its matching *St. Jerome in His Study* by Ghirlandaio across the nave. Botticelli, whose real name was Sandro Filipepi, is buried under a round marker in the second chapel in the right transept. You can enter the convent to the left of the church facade at Borgo Ognissanti 42. In the refectory here is Domenico Ghirlandaio's **Last Supper ★**, or *Cenacolo,* painted in 1480 with a background heavy on Christian symbolism.

Piazza Ognissanti. ✆ **055-239-8700.** Free admission. Church Mon–Wed and Sat 8am–12:30pm and 4–6pm. Cenacolo Mon–Tues and Sat 9am–noon. Bus: C3.

Santa Maria Novella ★★ Of all Florence's major churches, the home of the Dominicans is the only one with an original **facade** ★ that matches its era of greatest importance. The lower Romanesque half was started in the 14th century by architect Fra' Jacopo Talenti, who had just finished building the church itself (started in 1246). Leon Battista Alberti finished the facade, adding a classically inspired Renaissance top that not only went seamlessly with the lower half but also created a Cartesian plane of perfect geometry.

Looking down the nave at Santa Maria Novella.

The church's interior underwent a massive restoration in the late 1990s, returning Giotto's restored *Crucifix* to pride of place, hanging in the nave's center—and becoming the first church in Florence to charge admission. Against the second pillar on the left of the nave is the pulpit from which Galileo was denounced for his heretical theory that the earth revolved around the sun. Just past the pulpit, on the left wall, is **Masaccio's *Trinità*** ★★★ (ca. 1428), the first painting ever to use perfect linear mathematical perspective. Florentine citizens and artists flooded in to see the fresco when it was unveiled, many remarking in awe that it seemed to punch a hole back into space, creating a chapel out of a flat wall. The **transept** is filled with spectacularly frescoed chapels. The **sanctuary** ★ behind the main altar was frescoed after 1485 by Domenico Ghirlandaio with the help of his assistants and apprentices, probably including a young Michelangelo. The left wall is covered with a cycle on the *Life of the Virgin* and the right wall with a *Life of St. John the Baptist.* The works have a polished decorative quality and are less biblical stories than snapshots of the era's fashions and personages, full of portraits of the Tornabuoni family who commissioned them.

The **Cappella Gondi** to the left of the high altar contains the *Crucifix* carved by Brunelleschi to show his buddy Donatello how it should be done (see the Santa Croce review, p. 146, for the story). At the end of the left transept is another **Cappella Strozzi,** covered with restored **frescoes** ★ (1357) by Nardo di Cione, early medieval casts of thousands where the saved mill about Paradise on the left and the damned stew in a Dantean inferno on the right.

Piazza Santa Maria Novella. ✆ **055-219-257.** Admission 3.50€. Mon–Thurs 9am–5:30pm; Fri 11am–5:30pm; Sat 9am–5pm; Sun noon–5pm. Bus: C2, 6, 11, 22, 36, or 37.

Near San Marco & Santissima Annunziata

Cenacolo di Sant'Apollonia ★ There are no lines at this former convent and no crowds: Few people even know it's here. What they're missing is one vast wall covered with the vibrant colors of Andrea del Castagno's masterful *Last Supper* (ca. 1450). Castagno used his paint to create the rich marble panels that checkerboard the *trompe l'oeil* walls and broke up the long white tablecloth with the dark figure of Judas the Betrayer, whose face is painted to resemble a satyr, an ancient symbol of evil.

Via XXVII Aprile 1. ✆ **055-238-8607.** Free admission. Daily 8:15am–1:50pm. Closed 1st, 3rd, and 5th Sun and 2nd and 4th Mon of each month. Bus: 1, 6, 11, 14, 17, or 23.

Galleria dell'Accademia ★★ Although day-trip crowds flock here just for Michelangelo's *David*, anyone with more than a day in Florence can take the time to peruse some of the Accademia's paintings as well.

The first long hall is devoted to Michelangelo and, although you pass his *Slaves* and the entrance to the painting gallery, most visitors are immediately drawn down to the far end, a tribune dominated by the most famous sculpture in the world: **Michelangelo's *David* ★★★**. A hot young sculptor fresh from his success with the *Pietà* in Rome, Michelangelo offered in 1501 to take on a slab of marble that had already been worked on by another sculptor (who had taken a chunk out of one side before declaring it too strangely shaped to use). The huge slab had been lying around the Duomo's work yards so long it earned a nickname, *Il Gigante* (the giant), so it was with a twist of humor that Michelangelo, only 29 years old, finished in 1504 a Goliath-size David for the city.

There was originally a spot reserved for it high on the left flank of the Duomo, but Florence's republican government soon wheeled it down to stand on Piazza della Signoria in front of the Palazzo Vecchio to symbolize the defeated tyranny of the Medici, who had been ousted a decade before (but would return with a vengeance). During a 1527 anti-Medicean siege on the *palazzo,* a bench thrown at the attackers from one of the windows hit David's left arm, which reportedly came crashing down on a farmer's toe. (A young Giorgio Vasari came scurrying out to gather all the pieces for safekeeping, despite the riot going on around him, and the arm was later reconstituted.) Even the sculpture's 1873 removal to the Accademia to save it from the elements (a copy stands in its place) hasn't kept it entirely safe—in 1991, a man threw himself on the statue and began hammering at the right foot, dislodging several toes. The foot was repaired, and *David*'s Plexiglas shield went up.

The hall leading up to *David* is lined with perhaps Michelangelo's most fascinating works, the four famous *nonfiniti* ("unfinished") **Slaves,** or **Prisoners ★★★**. Like no others, these statues symbolize Michelangelo's theory that sculpture is an "art that takes away superfluous material." The

David at the Accademia.

great master saw a true sculpture as something that was inherent in the stone, and all it needed was a skilled chisel to free it from the extraneous rock. That certainly seems to be the case here, as we get a private glimpse into Michelangelo's working technique: how he began by carving the abdomen and torso,

Seeing *David* Without a Reservation

The wait to get in to see *David* can be an hour or more if you didn't reserve ahead. Try getting there before the museum opens in the morning or an hour or two before closing time.

going for the gut of the sculpture and bringing that to life first so it could tell him how the rest should start to take form. The result, no matter what the sculptor's intentions, is remarkable, a symbol of the master's great art and personal views on craft as his *Slaves* struggle to break free of their chipped stone prisons.

Nearby, in a similar mode, is a statue of **St. Matthew** ★★ (1504–08), which Michelangelo began carving as part of a series of Apostles he was at one point going to complete for the Duomo. (The *Pietà* at the end of the corridor on the right is by one of Michelangelo's students, not by the master as was once thought.)

Off this hall of *Slaves* is the first wing of the painting gallery, which includes a panel, possibly from a wedding chest, known as the **Cassone Adimari** ★, painted by Lo Scheggia in the 1440s. It shows the happy couple's promenade to the Duomo, with the green-and-white marbles of the baptistery prominent in the background. Other rooms house a fine collection of pre-Renaissance panels dating to the 1200s and 1300s.

Via Ricasoli 60. (✆ **055-238-8609.** www.polomuseale.firenze.it/english. (Reserve tickets at (✆ 055-294-883 or www.firenzemusei.it; booking fee 4€; admission 6.50€; 11€ with temporary exhibition). Tues–Sun 8:15am–6:50pm; last admission 30 min. before close. Bus: C1, 6, 7, 11, 14, 23, 31, or 32.

Museo Archeologico (Archaeological Museum) ★ This embarrassingly rich collection, in an apparently permanent state of reorganization, is often overlooked by visitors in full-throttle Renaissance mode. It conserves Egyptian sarcophagi and hieroglyphs, Roman remains, and an important Etruscan *bucchero* pottery collection. The relics to be on the lookout for include an early-4th-century-B.C. bronze **Chimera** ★★, a mythical beast with a lion's body and head, a goat head sprouting from its back, and a serpent for a tail. (The tail was incorrectly restored in 1785.) The beast was found near Arezzo in 1553 and probably made in a Chiusi or an Orvieto workshop as a votive offering.

Such is the chaos that it's impossible to predict what you'll find next, but do track down an extraordinarily rare **Hittite wood-and-bone chariot** from the 14th century B.C. Room XVI upstairs had at time of writing a cast bronze **Arringatore,** or orator, found near Perugia. It was made in the 1st century B.C. and helps illustrate how Roman society was having a great influence on the Etruscan world—not only in the workmanship of the statue but also in the fact that the Etruscan orator Aule Metele is wearing a Roman toga. The focus of the top floor is the **Idolino** ★. The history of this nude bronze lad with his outstretched hand is long, complicated, and in the end a bit mysterious. The current theory is that he's a Roman statue of the Augustan period (around the time of Christ), with the head perhaps modeled on a lost piece by the Greek master Polyclitus. The rub: *Idolino* was originally probably part of a lamp stand used at Roman banquets.

Piazza Santissima Annunziata 9b. (✆ **055-23-575.** www.firenzemusei.it. Admission 4€. Tues–Sun 8:15am–6:50pm. Bus: C1, 6, 14, 23, 31, or 32.

Museo di Mineralogia e Litologia (Mineral Museum) 😊 🎁 This little visited outpost of Florence's multicenter Museo di Storia Naturale (Natural History Museum) is a treasure trove for aspiring (or actual) gemologists and geologists—displays will appeal to rock hunters of all ages suffering from a little Renaissance fatigue. The collection was begun by the later members of the Medici family, among whose few saving graces was their patronage of the sciences. Hundreds of curious, colorful rocks from all corners of the planet are displayed in detailed, illuminated cross-section—kids are free to touch and handle some of them. These astounding exhibits were revamped in 2009 and are well labeled in English.

Via La Pira 4. ☎ **055-234-6760.** www.msn.unifi.it. Admission 6€ adults, 3€ ages 6–14, 12€ family ticket. Sun–Tues and Thurs–Fri 10am–1pm (opens 9am Oct–May); Sat 9am–5pm (10am–6pm Oct–May). Bus: C1, 1, 7, 20, or 25.

michelangelo: THE MAKING OF A RENAISSANCE MASTER

Irascible, moody, and manic-depressive, Michelangelo was quite simply one of the greatest artists of all time. Many feel he represents the pinnacle of the Italian Renaissance, a genius at sculpture, painting, and architecture, even poetry.

In 1475, Michelangelo Buonarroti was born near Arezzo in the tiny town of Caprese, where his Florentine father was serving a term as a *podestà* (visiting mayor). He was apprenticed to the fresco studio of Domenico Ghirlandaio who,

while watching him sketching, once remarked in shock, "This boy knows more about it than I do." After just a year at the studio, Michelangelo was recruited by Lorenzo the Magnificent de' Medici into his new school for sculptors.

Michelangelo learned quickly, and soon after his arrival at the school took a chunk of marble and carved it to copy the head of an old faun from a statue in the garden. Lorenzo saw the skill with which the head was made, but when he saw that Michelangelo had departed from his model and carved the mouth open and laughing with teeth and a tongue, he commented only, "But you should have known that old people never have all their teeth and there are always some missing." The young artist reflected on this. When Lorenzo returned a while later, he found Michelangelo waiting anxiously, eager to show he had not only chipped out a few

teeth but also gouged down into the gums of the statue to make the tooth loss look more realistic.

After success at age 19 with his *Pietà* sculpture in Rome, Michelangelo was given the opportunity to carve the enormous block of marble that became *David.* Legend has it that when Soderini, the head of the city council, came to see the finished work, he remarked the nose looked a tad too large. Michelangelo, knowing better but wanting to please Soderini, climbed up to the head (out of view), grabbed a handful of leftover plaster dust, and while tapping his hammer lightly against his chisel, let the dust sprinkle down gradually as if he were actually carving. "Much better," remarked Soderini when Michelangelo climbed down again and they stepped back to admire it. "Now you've really brought it to life."

Museo Opificio delle Pietre Dure In the 16th century, Florentine craftsmen perfected the art of *pietre dure*, piecing together cut pieces of precious and semi-precious stones in an inlay process, and the Medici-founded institute devoted to the craft has been in this building since 1796. Long ago misnamed "Florentine mosaic" by the tourism industry, this is a highly refined craft in which skilled artisans (artists, really) create scenes and boldly colored intricate designs in everything from cameos and tabletops to never-fade stone "landscape paintings." The collection in this museum is small, but the pieces are uniformly excellent. Souvenir shops all over town sell modern *pietre dure* items—much of it mass-produced junk. The authentic stuff is very expensive: If you're paying less than hundreds of euros for a piece, it's not *pietre dure*. One of the best contemporary maestros is Ilio de Filippis, whose workshop is called Pitti Mosaici (see "Shopping," later in this chapter).

Via degli Alfani 78. © **055-265-111.** www.firenzemusei.it. Admission 4€. Mon–Sat 8:15am–2pm (Thurs until 7pm). Bus: C1.

San Marco ★★★ ♥ In 1437, Cosimo de' Medici il Vecchio, grandfather of Lorenzo the Magnificent, had Michelozzo convert a medieval monastery here into a new home for the Dominicans, in which Cosimo also founded Europe's first public library. From 1491 until he was burned at the stake on Piazza della Signoria in 1498, this was the home base of puritanical preacher Girolamo Savonarola. The monastery's most famous friar, though, was "International Gothic" painter Fra' Angelico, and he left many of his finest works, devotional images painted with the technical skill and minute detail of a miniaturist or an illuminator but on altarpiece scale. While his works tended to be transcendently spiritual, Angelico was also prone to filling them with earthly details with which any peasant or stonemason could identify.

The museum rooms are entered off a pretty cloister. The old **Pilgrim's Hospice** ★★ is full of his altarpieces and painted panels, notably an exquisite **Deposition** ★, the 2011-restored *Tabernacolo dei Linaioli* (1435) whose predella scenes are especially enchanting, and the 1443 **San Marco Altarpiece** ★★, with Medici saints Cosmas and Damian. Also off the cloister is the **Refettorio Grande (Large Refectory),** with 16th- and 17th-century paintings, and the **Sala del Capitolo (Chapter House),** frescoed from 1441 to 1442 with a huge *Crucifixion* by Fra' Angelico and his assistants. The door next to this leads past the staircase up to the Dormitory (see below) to the **Sala del Cenacolo (Small Refectory),** now the gift shop, with a *Last Supper* frescoed by Domenico Ghirlandaio.

The **Dormitorio (Dormitory)** ★★ of cells where the monks lived is one of Fra' Angelico's masterpieces and his most famous cycle of frescoes. In addition to the renowned **Annunciation** ★★ at the top of the stairs to the monks' rooms, Angelico painted the cells themselves with simple works to aid his fellow friars in their meditations. One of these almost anticipates surrealism—a flagellation where disembodied hands strike at Christ's face and a rod descends on him from the blue-green background. Angelico's assistants carried out the repetitive *Crucifixion* scenes in many of the cells. At the end of the left corridor is the suite of cells occupied by Savonarola when he was here prior, housing an anonymous 16th-century painting of *Savonarola Burned at the Stake* on Piazza della Signoria. The **Biblioteca (Library)** off the corridor to the right of the stairs was designed by Michelozzo in 1441.

If you're traveling on a budget, San Marco represents the city's most absorbing art experience for the price, but beware the slightly odd opening hours.

Piazza San Marco 1. © **055-238-8608.** Admission 4€. Mon–Fri 8:30am–1:50pm; Sat–Sun 8:15am–4:50pm. Closed 1st, 3rd, and 5th Sun and 2nd and 4th Mon of month. Bus: C1, 1, 6, 7, 10, 11, 14, 17, 20, 25, 31, 32, or 33.

Santissima Annunziata ★ In 1230, seven Florentine nobles had a spiritual crisis, gave away all their possessions, and retired to the forests to contemplate divinity. They returned to what were then fields outside the city walls and founded a small oratory, proclaiming they were Servants of Mary, or the Servite Order. The oratory was enlarged by Michelozzo (1444–81) and later redesigned in the baroque. Under the facade's **portico,** you enter the **Chiostro dei Voti (Votive Cloister),** designed by Michelozzo with Corinthian-capitaled columns and decorated with some of the city's finest Mannerist **frescoes** ★★ (1465–1515). Rosso Fiorentino provided an *Assumption* (1513) and Pontormo a *Visitation* (1515) just to the right of the door, but the main works are by their master, Andrea del Sarto, whose *Birth of the Virgin* (1513), in the far right corner, is one of his finest works. To the right of the door into the church is a damaged but still fascinating *Coming of the Magi* (1514) by del Sarto, who included a self-portrait at the far right, looking out at us from under his blue hat.

The **interior** is excessively baroque. Just to the left as you enter is a huge tabernacle hidden under a mountain of *ex votos* (votive offerings). It was designed by Michelozzo to house a small painting of the *Annunciation.* Legend holds that this painting was started by a friar who, vexed that he couldn't paint the Madonna's face as beautifully as it should be, gave it up and took a nap. When he awoke, he found an angel had filled in the face for him. Newlywed brides in Florence don't toss their bouquets—they head here after the ceremony to leave their flowers at the shrine for good luck.

The large circular **tribune** was finished for Michelozzo by Leon Battista Alberti. You enter it from its left side via the left transept, but first pause to pay your respects to Andrea del Sarto, buried under a floor slab at the left-hand base of the great arch.

From the left transept, a door leads into the **Chiostro dei Morti (Cloister of the Dead;** sometimes closed), where over the entrance door is another of Andrea del Sarto's greatest frescoes, the ***Madonna del Sacco*** ★, illustrating the rest on the flight into Egypt, that got its name from the sack Joseph is leaning against to do a little light reading as he takes a breather. Also off this cloister is the **Cappella di San Luca (Chapel of St. Luke),** evangelist and patron saint of painters. It was decorated by late Renaissance and Mannerist painters, including Pontormo, Alessandro Allori, Santi di Tito, and Giorgio Vasari.

On the **piazza** ★★ outside, flanked by elegant porticos (see Spedale degli Innocenti, below), is an equestrian statue of *Grand Duke Ferdinando I,* Giambologna's last work; it was cast in 1608 after his death by his student Pietro Tacca, who also did the two little fountains of fantastic mermonkey-monsters. The piazza's beauty is somewhat ruined by the car and bus traffic routed through both ends, but it's kept lively by students from the nearby university, who often sit on the loggia steps at lunchtime.

Piazza Santissima Annunziata. © **055-266-181.** Free admission. Daily 7:30am–12:30pm and 4–6:30pm. Bus: C1, 6, 14, 23, 31, or 32.

Spedale degli Innocenti ☺ 🎁 Europe's oldest foundling hospital, opened in 1445, is still going strong as a convent orphanage, though times have changed a bit. The Lazy Susan set into the wall on the left end of the arcade—where once people left unwanted babies, swiveled it around, rang the bell, and ran—has since been blocked up. The colonnaded **portico** ★ (built 1419–26) was designed by Filippo Brunelleschi when he was still an active goldsmith. It was his first great achievement as an architect and helped define the new Renaissance style he was developing. Its repetition by later artists in front of other buildings on the piazza makes it one of the most exquisite squares in Tuscany. The spandrels between the arches of Brunelleschi's portico are set with glazed **terra-cotta reliefs** of swaddled babes against rounded blue backgrounds—hands-down the masterpieces of Andrea della Robbia.

If you're traveling with young children, next door (and run by the Institute) is **La Bottega dei Ragazzi,** Via de' Fibbai 2 (℃ **055-247-8386;** www.labottegadeiragazzi.it) a *ludoteca* (play space) where parents with children aged 3 to 11 can drop in to make use of the play area, books, and toys. It's open Monday to Saturday 9am (10am Sat) to 1pm and 4 to 7pm; it is closed mid-July through early September. On Saturdays the Bottega stages child-only 1½-hour creative activities, for which you have to book (10€), focusing on themes in art, local history, or music. About once a month they are in English; e-mail or check the program online.

Piazza Santissima Annunziata 12. ℃ **055-203-7308.** Admission 5€. Daily 10am–7pm. Bus: C1, 6, 14, 23, 31, or 32.

Around Piazza Santa Croce

Piazza Santa Croce is pretty much like any in Florence—a nice bit of open space ringed with souvenir and leather shops and thronged with tourists. Its unique feature (aside from the one time a year it's covered with dirt and violent Renaissance soccer is played on it; see p. 48) is **Palazzo Antellesi** on the south side. This well-preserved, 16th-century patrician house is owned by a contessa who rents out her apartments (p. 96).

Casa Buonarroti ★ Although Michelangelo never actually lived in this modest *palazzo*, he did own the property and left it to his nephew Lionardo. Lionardo named his own son after his famous uncle, and this younger Michelangelo became devoted to the memory of his namesake, converting the house into a museum and hiring artists to fill the place with frescoes honoring the genius of his great uncle.

The good stuff is upstairs, starting with a display rotating pages from the museum's collection of original drawings. In the first room off the landing are Michelangelo's earliest sculptures: the Donatello-esque *Madonna of the Steps,* carved before 1492 when he was a 15- or 16-year-old student in the Medici school. A few months later, the prodigy was already finished carving another marble, a confused, almost Pisano-like tangle of bodies known as the *Battle of the Centaurs and Lapiths.* The sculptural ideals that were to mark his career are already evident: a fascination with the male body to the point of ignoring the figures themselves in pursuit of muscular torsion and the use of rough "unfinished" marble to speak sculptural volumes.

Via Ghibellina 70. ℃ **055-241-752.** www.casabuonarroti.it. Admission 6.50€; combined ticket with Santa Croce 8€. Wed–Mon 9:30am–2pm. Bus: C2, C3, 14, or 23.

Museo Horne Of the city's several small private collections, the one formed by Englishman Herbert Percy Horne and left to Florence in his will has perhaps the best individual pieces, although the bulk of it consists of lesser paintings by marquee artists, including Pietro Lorenzetti, Simone Martini, and Filippino Lippi. In a 15th-century *palazzo* designed by Cronaca (not Sangallo, as was once believed), the collections are left, unlabeled, as Horne arranged them; the idea was to re-create as faithfully as possible the atmosphere and layout of a wealthy Renaissance home. The best works are a *St. Stephen* by Giotto and Sienese Mannerist Domenico Beccafumi's weirdly colored tondo of the *Holy Family.*

Via dei Benci 6. ☏ **055-244-661.** www.museohorne.it. Admission 6€ adults, 4€ per person for family groups. Mon–Sat 9am–1pm. Bus: C1, 3, 12, 13, or 23.

Santa Croce ★★ The center of the Florentine Franciscan universe was begun in 1294 by Gothic master Arnolfo di Cambio in order to rival the church of Santa Maria Novella being raised by the Dominicans across the city. The church wasn't consecrated until 1442, and even then it remained faceless until the neo-Gothic **facade** was added in 1857. The cloisters are home to Brunelleschi's Cappella Pazzi, the convent partially given over to a famous leather school (see "Shopping," later in this chapter), and the church itself a shrine of 14th-century frescoes and a monument to notable Florentines, whose tombs and memorials litter the place like an Italian Westminster. It's a vast complex that demands 2 hours of your time, at least, to see properly.

The Gothic **interior** is vast, with huge, pointed stone arches creating the aisles and an echoing nave trussed with wood beams, in all feeling vaguely barn-like (an analogy the occasional fluttering pigeon only reinforces). The floor is paved with worn tombstones—because being buried in this hallowed sanctuary got you one step closer to Heaven, the richest families of the day paid big bucks to stake out small rectangles of the floor. Starting from the main door, immediately on the right is the first tomb of note, a mad Vasari contraption containing the bones of the most venerated Renaissance master, **Michelangelo Buonarroti,** who died of a fever in Rome in 1564 at the ripe age of 89. The pope wanted him buried in the Eternal City, but Florentines managed to sneak his body back to Florence. Close to Michelangelo's monument is a pompous 19th-century cenotaph to Florentine **Dante Alighieri,** one of history's great poets, whose *Divine Comedy* codified the Italian language. He died in 1321 in Ravenna after a bitter life in exile from his hometown (on trumped-up embezzlement charges), and that Adriatic city has never seen fit to return the bones to Florence.

Against a nave pillar farther up is an elaborate **pulpit** (1472–76) carved by Benedetto di Maiano with scenes from the life of St. Francis. Next comes a monument to **Niccolò Machiavelli,**

The interior of Santa Croce.

the 16th-century Florentine statesman whose philosophical tract *The Prince* was the perfect practical manual for a powerful Renaissance ruler.

Past the next altar is an ***Annunciation*** ★ (1433) carved in low relief of *pietra serena* and gilded by Donatello. Nearby is Antonio Rossellino's 1446 tomb of the humanist scholar and city chancellor **Leonardo Bruni** (d. 1444). Beyond this architectural masterpiece of a tomb is a 19th-century knockoff honoring **Gioacchino Rossini** (1792–1868), composer of the *Barber of Seville* and the *William Tell Overture*.

Around in the right transept is the **Cappella Castellani** frescoed by Agnolo Gaddi, with a tabernacle by Mino da Fiesole and a *Crucifix* by Niccolò Gerini. Agnolo's father, Taddeo Gaddi, was one of Giotto's closest followers, and the senior Gaddi is the one who undertook painting the **Cappella Baroncelli** ★ (1332–38) at the transept's end. The frescoes depict scenes from the *Life of the Virgin,* and include an *Angel Appearing to the Shepherds* that constitutes the first night scene in Italian fresco. The altarpiece *Coronation of the Virgin* is by Giotto.

Also in the right transept, Giotto frescoed the two chapels to the right of the high altar. The frescoes were whitewashed over during the 17th century but uncovered from 1841 to 1852 and inexpertly restored. The **Cappella Peruzzi** ★★, on the right, is a late work and not in the best shape. The many references to antiquity in the styling and architecture of the frescoes reflect Giotto's trip to Rome and its ruins. Even more famous, including as the setting for a scene in the film *A Room with a View,* is the **Cappella Bardi** ★★. Key panels here include the *Trial by Fire Before the Sultan of Egypt* on the right wall, full of telling subtlety in the expressions and poses of the figures. In one of Giotto's most well-known works, the *Death of St. Francis,* monks weep and wail with convincing pathos. Alas, big chunks of the scene are missing from when a tomb was stuck on top of it in the 18th century. Most people miss seeing *Francis Receiving the Stigmata,* which Giotto frescoed above the outside of the entrance arch to the chapel.

At the end of the left transept is another Cappella Bardi, this one housing a legendary ***Crucifix*** ★ by Donatello. According to Vasari, Donatello excitedly called his friend Filippo Brunelleschi up to his studio to see this *Crucifix* when he had finished carving it. The famed architect, whose tastes were aligned with the prevailing view of the time that refinement and grace were more important than realism, criticized the work with the words, "Why Donatello, you've put a peasant on the cross!" Donatello sniffed, "If it were as easy to make something as it is to criticize, my Christ would really look to you like Christ. So you get some wood and try to make one yourself." Secretly, Brunelleschi did just that, and one day he invited Donatello to come over to his studio for lunch. Donatello arrived bearing the food gathered up in his apron. Shocked when he beheld Brunelleschi's elegant *Crucifix,* he let the lunch drop to the floor, smashing the eggs, and after a few moments turned to Brunelleschi and humbly offered, "Your job is making Christs and mine is making peasants." Tastes change, and to modern eyes this "peasant" stands as the stronger work. If you want to see how Brunelleschi fared with his Christ, visit it at Santa Maria Novella (p. 139).

Back up the left aisle is the roped-off floor tomb of Lorenzo Ghiberti, sculptor of the Baptistery doors. The final tomb at the main door by the end of the nave is that of **Galileo Galilei** (1564–1642), the Pisan scientist who figured out everything from the action of pendulums and the law of bodies falling at the same rate (regardless of weight) to discovering the moons of Jupiter and asserting that the earth revolved around the sun. This last one got him in trouble with the Church, which tried him and—when he wouldn't recant—excommunicated him. At the urging of friends frightened his obstinacy would get him executed, Galileo eventually kneeled in front of an altar and "admitted" he'd been wrong. He lived out the rest of his days under house arrest near Florence and wasn't allowed a Christian burial until 1737. Giulio Foggini designed this tomb for him, complete with a relief of the solar system—the sun, you'll notice, is at the center. The pope finally got around to lifting the excommunication in 1992.

Outside in the cloister is the **Cappella Pazzi** ★, one of Filippo Brunelleschi's architectural masterpieces (faithfully finished after his death in 1446). Giuliano da Maiano probably designed the porch that now precedes the chapel, set with glazed terra cottas by Luca della Robbia. The rectangular chapel is one of Brunelleschi's signature pieces and a defining example of (and model for) early Renaissance architecture. Light gray *pietra serena* is used to accent the architectural lines against smooth white plaster walls, and the only decorations are della Robbia roundels of the *Apostles* (1442–52). The chapel was barely finished by 1478, when the infamous Pazzi Conspiracy got the bulk of the family, who were funding this project, either killed or exiled.

From back in the cloister enter the **Museo dell'Opera** where, in the long hall of the former refectory, hangs the painting that became emblematic of the 1966 flood, Cimabue's **Crucifix** ★, by the artist who began bridging the gap between Byzantine tradition and Renaissance innovation, not least by teaching Giotto to paint. Look out here for Bronzino's *Christ in Limbo* and fresco fragments by Orcagna.

Piazza Santa Croce. ✆ **055-246-6105.** www.santacroceopera.it. Admission 5€ adults, 3€ ages 11–17; combined ticket with Casa Buonarotti 8€. Mon–Sat 9:30am–5pm; Sun 1–5pm. Bus: C1, 3, or 23.

Santa Maria Maddalena dei Pazzi The entrance to this church is an unassuming, unnumbered door on Borgo Pinti that opens onto a pretty cloister designed in 1492 by Giuliano da Sangallo, open to the sky and surrounded by large *pietra serena* columns topped with droopy-eared Ionic capitals. The interior of the 13th-century church was remodeled in the 17th and early 18th centuries and represents the high baroque at its restrained best. At the odd hours listed below, you can get into the chapter house to see the church's main prize, a wall-filling fresco of the **Crucifixion and Saints** ★ (1493–96) by Perugino, grand master of the Umbrian school. Typical of Perugino's style, the background is drawn as delicately in blues and greens as the posed figures were fleshed out in full-bodied volumes of bright colors.

Entrance next to Borgo Pinti 58. ✆ **055-247-8420.** Free admission to church; Perugino *Crucifixion* 1€ "donation." Church daily 9am–noon and 4:30–6:30pm; *Crucifixion,* enter at Via della Colonna 9, Tues and Thurs 2:30–5:30pm. Bus: C1, 6, 14, 23, 31, or 32.

Sinagoga (Synagogue) and Jewish Museum The center of the 1,000-strong Jewish community in Florence is this imposing Moorish-Byzantine synagogue, built in 1882. In an effort to create a neo-Byzantine building, the architects ended up making it look rather like a church, complete with a dome, an apse, a pulpit, and a pipe organ. The intricate polychrome arabesque designs, though, lend it a distinctly Eastern flavor, and the rows of prayer benches facing each other, and the separate areas for women, hint at its Orthodox Jewish nature. Though the synagogue is technically Sephardic, the members of the Florentine Jewish community are Italian Jews, a Hebrew culture that has adapted to its Italian

Florence's Sinagoga.

surroundings since the 1st century B.C. when Jewish slaves were first brought to Rome. (The Florentine community dates from the 14th c.)

Via Farina 6. ℂ **055-234-6654.** www.firenzebraica.net. Admission 5€ adults, 3€ students. Apr–Sept Sun–Thurs 10am–6pm; Oct–Mar Sun–Thurs 10am–3pm; also every Fri 10am–2pm.; obligatory 45-min. guided tour. Bus: C1, 6, 14, 23, 31, or 32.

The Oltrarno, San Niccolò & San Frediano

Museo Zoologia "La Specola" ★ ☺ Italy has few zoos, but this is its largest zoological collection, with rooms full of insects, crustaceans, and stuffed birds and mammals—everything from ostriches and apes to a rhinoceros. The museum was founded here in 1775, and the collections are still displayed in the style of an old-fashioned natural sciences museum, with specimens crowded into beautiful old wood-and-glass cases. The last 10 rooms contain an important collection of **human anatomical wax models** ★ crafted between 1775 and 1814 by Clemente Susini for medical students. The life-size figures are flayed, dissected, and disemboweled to varying degrees and are truly disgusting, but fascinating. The final room is even more grisly, showcasing three lurid tableaux created by Gaetano Zumbo for Cosimo III (1670–1723) depicting Florence during the plague, complete with rats, rotting flesh, and heaps of the dead.

Via Romana 17. ℂ **055-234-6760.** www.msn.unifi.it. Admission 6€ adults, 3€ children 6–14 and seniors 65 and over. Tues–Sun 10:30am–5:30pm. Bus: C3, D, 11, 36, or 37.

Palazzo Pitti & Giardino di Boboli (Pitti Palace & Boboli Garden) ★★ Although the original, much smaller Pitti Palace was a Renaissance affair probably designed by Filippo Brunelleschi, that *palazzo* is completely hidden by the enormous Mannerist mass we see today. Inside is Florence's most extensive set of museums, including the Galleria Palatina, a huge painting gallery second in scope only to the Uffizi, with works by Raphael, Andrea del Sarto, Titian, and Rubens. When Luca Pitti died in 1472, Cosimo de' Medici's wife, Eleonora of Toledo, bought this property and unfinished palace to convert into the new Medici home—she hated the dark, cramped spaces of the Palazzo Vecchio. They hired Bartolomeo Ammannati to enlarge the *palazzo,* which he did starting in 1560 by creating the courtyard out back, extending the wings out either side, and incorporating a Michelangelo architectural invention, "kneeling windows," on the ground floor of the facade. (Rather than being visually centered between the line of the floor and that of the ceiling, kneeling windows' bases extend lower to be level with the ground or, in the case of upper stories, with whatever architectural element delineates the baseline of that story's first level.) Later architects finished the building off by the 19th century, probably to Ammannati's original plans, in the end producing one of the masterpieces of Florentine Mannerist architecture.

The Galleria Palatina at the Pitti Palace.

The painting gallery—the main, and for many visitors, most interesting of the Pitti museums—is off Ammannati's excellent **interior courtyard ★** of gold-tinged rusticated rock grafted onto the three classical orders. The ticket office is outside the main gate, on the far right as you face it from the piazza.

GALLERIA PALATINA ★★★ If the Uffizi represents mainly the earlier masterpieces collected by the Medici, the Pitti Palace's painting gallery continues the story with the High Renaissance and later eras, a collection gathered by the Medici, and later the Grand Dukes of Lorraine. The works are still displayed in the old-world fashion, which hung paintings according to aesthetics—how well, say, the Raphael matched the drapes—rather than that boring academic chronological order. Just after the first long **Galleria delle Statue (Hall of Statues)** is a 19th-century tabletop inlaid in *pietre dure*—an exquisite example of the famous "Florentine mosaic" craft.

While the first batch of rooms have decorative interest, the art-historical meat starts later: Filippo Lippi's 1452 *Madonna and Child* and a minor Botticelli in the **Sala di Prometeo (Room of Prometheus)** are a mere appetizer for the **Sala dell'Educazione di Giove (Room of Jupiter's Education).** Here you'll find a 1608 *Sleeping Cupid* ★★ that Caravaggio painted while living in exile from Rome (avoiding murder charges) on the island of Malta; and the other Cristofano Allori's *Judith with the Head of Holofernes* ★, a Freudian field day where the artist depicted himself in the severed head, his lover as Judith holding it, and her mother as the maid looking on.

The **Sala dell'Iliade (Iliad Room)** has Raphael's portrait of a *Pregnant Woman* ★, along with some Titian masterpieces. Don't miss *Mary Magdalene* and *Judith* ★, two paintings by one of the only female artists of the late Renaissance era, Artemisia Gentileschi, who often turned to themes of strong biblical women. Raphael is also the focus of the **Sala di Saturno (Saturn Room)** ★★, where the transparent colors of his *Madonna*s and probing portraits show the strong influence of both Leonardo da Vinci (the *Portrait of Maddalena Strozzi Doni* owes much to the *Mona Lisa*) and Raphael's old master Perugino, whose *Deposition* and a *Mary Magdalene* hang here as well.

The star of the **Sala di Giove (Jupiter Room)** is Raphael's **La Velata ★★**, one of the crowning achievements of his short career and a summation of what he had learned about color, light, naturalism, and mood. It's probably a portrait of his Roman mistress called La Fornarina, a baker's daughter who sat for many of his Madonnas.

The **Sala di Marte (Mars Room)** is dominated by Rubens, including the enormous **Consequences of War ★★**, which an aged Rubens painted for his friend Sustermans at a time when both were worried that their Dutch homeland was on the brink of battle.

The **Sala di Apollo (Apollo Room)** has a masterful early *Portrait of an Unknown Gentleman* by famed early-16th-century Venetian painter Titian as well as his sensual, luminously gold **Mary Magdalene ★**, the first in a number of takes on the subject the painter was to make throughout his career. There are several works by Andrea del Sarto, whose late *Holy Family* and especially *Deposition* display the daring chromatic experiments and highly refined spatial compositions that were to influence his students Pontormo and Rosso Fiorentino as they went about mastering Mannerism.

The **Sala di Venere (Venus Room)** is named after the neoclassical *Venus,* which Napoleon had Canova sculpt in 1810 to replace the *Medici Venus* the emperor had appropriated for his Paris digs. Two masterpieces by Titian hang on the walls. Art historians still argue whether **The Concert ★** was wholly painted by Titian in his early 20s or by Giorgione, in whose circle he moved. However, most now attribute at most the fop on the left to Giorgione and give the rest of the canvas to Titian. There are no such doubts about Titian's *Portrait of Julius II,* a copy of the physiologically penetrating work by Raphael in London's National Gallery (the version in the Uffizi is a copy Raphael himself made). The room also contains Rubens's *Return from the Hayfields,* famous for its classically harmonious landscape.

APPARTAMENTI REALI The other wing of the *piano nobile* is taken up with the Medici's private apartments, which have been restored to their late-19th-century appearance when the kings of the House of Savoy, first rulers of the Unified Italy, used the suites as their Florentine home. The over-the-top sumptuous fabrics, decorative arts furnishings, stuccoes, and frescoes reflect the neo-baroque tastes of the Savoy kings. Amid the general interior-decorator flamboyance are some thoroughly appropriate baroque canvases, plus Caravaggio's **Portrait of a Knight of Malta ★** and lots of works by Flemish painter Sustermans, on whom the Medici were unfathomably keen.

GALLERIA D'ARTE MODERNA ★ Modern art isn't what draws most people to the capital of the Renaissance, but the Pitti's collection includes some important works by the 19th-century Tuscan school of art known as the Macchiaioli, who painted a kind of Tuscan Impressionism, concerned with the *macchie* (marks of color on the canvas and the play of light on the eye). Most of the scenes are of the countryside or peasants working, along with the requisite lot of portraits. Some of the movement's greatest talents are here, including Silvestro Lega, Telemaco Signorini, and Giovanni Fattori, the genius of the group. Don't miss his two white oxen pulling a cart in the **Tuscan Maremma ★**.

GALLERIA DEL COSTUME & MUSEO DEGLI ARGENTI These aren't the most popular of the Pitti's museums, and the **Museo degli Argenti** has what seem like miles of the most extravagant and often hideous objets d'art and house-wares the Medici and Lorraines could put their hands on. If the collections prove anything, it's that as the Medici became richer and more powerful, their taste declined proportionally. Just be thankful their **carriage collection** has been closed for years. The **Costume Gallery** is marginally more interesting. The collections concentrate on the 18th to 20th centuries but also display outfits from back to the 16th century. The dress in which Eleonora of Toledo was buried, made famous by Bronzino's intricate depiction of its velvety embroidered silk and in-sewn pearls on his portrait of her in the Uffizi, is sometimes on display.

GIARDINO DI BOBOLI (BOBOLI GARDEN) ★★ The statue-filled park behind the Pitti Palace is one of the earliest and finest Renaissance gardens, laid out mostly between 1549 and 1656 with box hedges in geometric patterns, groves of ilex, dozens of statues, and rows of cypress. In 1766, it was opened to the Florentine public, who still come here with their families for Sunday-morning strolls. Just above the entrance through the courtyard of the Palazzo Pitti is an oblong **amphitheater** modeled on Roman circuses. Today, we see in the middle a **granite basin** from Rome's Baths of Caracalla and an **Egyptian obelisk** of Ramses II, but in 1589 this was the setting for the wedding reception of Ferdinando de' Medici's marriage to Christine of Lorraine. For the occasion, the Medici commissioned entertainment from Jacopo Peri and Ottavio Rinuccini, who decided to set a classical story entirely to music and called it *Dafne*—the world's first opera. (Later, they wrote a follow-up hit *Erudice,* performed here in 1600; it's the first opera whose score has survived.)

Around the park (which is overlooked by the **Forte di Belvedere**), don't miss the rococo **Kaffehaus,** with bar service in summer, and, near the high point, the **Giardino del Cavaliere ★**, the Boboli's prettiest hidden corner— a tiny walled garden of box hedges with private views over the hills of Florence's outskirts. Toward the south end of the park is the **Isolotto ★**, a dreamy island marooned in a pond full of huge goldfish, with Giambologna's *L'Oceano* composition at its center. At the north end, down around the end of the Pitti Palace, are some fake caverns filled with statuary, attempting to invoke a classical sacred grotto. The most famous, the **Grotta Grande,** was designed by Giorgio Vasari, Bartolomeo Ammannati, and Bernardo Buontalenti between 1557 and 1593, dripping with phony stalactites and set with replicas of Michelangelo's unfinished *Slave* statues. (The originals were here before being moved to the Accademia.) You can usually get inside on the hour (but not every hour) for 15 minutes.

The Isolotto, part of the Giardino di Boboli.

Near the exit to the park is a Florentine postcard fave, the **Fontana di Bacco** (**Bacchus Fountain;** 1560), a pudgy dwarf sitting atop a tortoise. It's actually a portrait of Pietro Barbino, Cosimo I's court jester.

Piazza de' Pitti. **Galleria Palatina and Apartamenti Reali:** © 055-238-8614; reserve tickets at © 055-294-883 or www.firenzemusei.it. Admission (with Galleria d'Arte Moderna) 8.50€ (13€ with temporary exhibition). Tues–Sun 8:15am–6:50pm. **Galleria d'Arte Moderna:** © 055-238-8616. Admission (with Galleria Palatina) 8.50€. Tues–Sun 8:15am–6:50pm. **Museo degli Argenti and Galleria del Costume:** © 055-238-8709. Admission (with Giardino di Boboli) 7€ (9€ with temporary exhibition). Nov–Feb daily 8:15am–4:30pm; Mar and Oct daily 8:15am–5:30pm; Apr–May and Sept daily 8:15am–6:30pm; June–Aug daily 8:15am–6:50pm. Closed 1st and last Mon of month. **Giardino di Boboli:** © 055-238-8791. Admission (with Museo degli Argenti) 7€. Nov–Feb daily 8:15am–4:30pm; Mar and Oct daily 8:15am–5:30pm; Apr–May and Sept daily 8:15am–6:30pm; June–Aug daily 8:15am–7:30pm. Closed 1st and last Mon of month. Cumulative ticket for everything, valid 3 days. 12€. E.U. citizens ages 18 and under or 65 and over enter free. Bus: C3, D, 11, 36, or 37.

Piazzale Michelangiolo This panoramic piazza is a required stop for every tour bus. The balustraded terrace was laid out in 1885 to give a sweeping **vista** ★★ of the entire city, spread out in the valley below and backed by the green hills of Fiesole beyond. The bronze replica of *David* here points right at his original home, outside the Palazzo Vecchio.

Viale Michelangelo. Bus: 12 or 13.

San Felice This tiny Gothic church just south of the Pitti Palace sports a High Renaissance facade by Michelozzo (1457) and a *Crucifixion* over the high altar recently attributed to the school of Giotto.

At no. 8 on the piazza, on the corner of Via Maggio, is the entrance to the **Casa Guidi,** where from 1846 English poet Elizabeth Barrett Browning lived with her husband, Robert, moving in just after their secret marriage. When the unification of Italy became official in Florence, Elizabeth recorded the momentous event in a famous poem, "Casa Guidi Windows": "I heard last night a little child go singing / 'Neath Casa Guidi windows, by the church, / O bella libertà, O bella!" Mrs. Browning died in this house on June 18, 1861.

Piazza di San Felice. No phone. Free admission. Bus: C3, D, 11, 36, or 37.

Santa Felícita ★ The 2nd-century Greek sailors who lived in this neighborhood brought Christianity to Florence with them, and this little church was probably the second to be established in the city, the first edition of it rising in the late 4th century. The current version was built in the 1730s. The star works are in the first chapel on your right—paintings by Mannerist master Pontormo (1525–27). His *Deposition* ★★ and frescoed *Annunciation* are rife with his garish color palette of oranges, pinks, golds, lime greens, and sky blues, and exhibit his trademark surreal sense of figure. The four round paintings of the *Evangelists* are also by Pontormo, except for *St. Mark* (with the angel), which was probably painted by his pupil Bronzino.

Piazza Santa Felícita (2nd left off Via Guicciardini across the Ponte Vecchio). © 055-213-018. Free admission. Daily 8am–noon and 3:30-6:30pm. Bus: C3 or D.

Santa Maria del Carmine ★★★ Following a 1771 fire that destroyed everything but the transept chapels and sacristy, this Carmelite church was almost entirely reconstructed and decorated in high baroque style. Ever since a long and expensive restoration of the famous frescoes of the **Cappella Brancacci**

The Cappella Brancacci at Santa Maria del Carmine.

★★★ in the right transept, they've blocked off just that chapel and you have to enter through the cloisters (doorway to the right of the church facade) and pay admission. The frescoes were commissioned by an enemy of the Medici, Felice Brancacci, who in 1424 hired Masolino and his student Masaccio to decorate it with a cycle on the *Life of St. Peter.* Masolino probably worked out the cycle's scheme and painted a few scenes along with his pupil before taking off for 3 years to serve as court painter in Budapest, during which time Masaccio kept painting, quietly creating the early Renaissance's greatest frescoes. Masaccio left for Rome in 1428, where he died at age 27. The cycle was completed between 1480 and 1485 by Filippino Lippi.

The frescoes were an instant hit. People flocked from all over the city to admire them, and almost every Italian artist of the day came to sketch and study Masaccio's mastery of perspective, bold light and colors, and unheard-of touches of realism. Even much later painters like Michelangelo came to learn what they could from the young artist's genius. A 1980s restoration cleaned off the dirt and dark mold that had grown in the egg-based pigments used to "touch up" the frescoes in the 18th century, and removed additions like the prudish ivy leaves trailing across Adam and Eve's privates.

Masolino was responsible for the *St. Peter Preaching,* the upper panel to the left of the altar, and the two top scenes on the right wall, which shows his fastidiously decorative style in a long panel of *St. Peter Healing the Cripple* and *Raising Tabitha,* and his *Adam and Eve.* Contrast this first man and woman, about to take the bait offered by the snake, with the **Expulsion from the Garden ★★,** opposite it, painted by Masaccio. Masolino's figures are highly posed models, expressionless and oblivious to the temptation being offered. Masaccio's Adam and Eve, on the other hand, burst with intense emotion and forceful movement. The top scene on the left wall, the **Tribute Money ★★,** is also by Masaccio, and it showcases both his classical influences and another of his innovations, linear perspective. On the end wall, Masaccio painted the lower scene to the left of the altar of *St. Peter Healing the Sick with His Shadow,* unique at the time for its realistic portrayal of street beggars and crippled bodies. The two scenes to the right of the altar are Masaccio's as well, with the ***Baptism of the Neophytes*** ★★ taking its place among his masterpieces. Most of the rest was painted by Lippi.

Piazza del Carmine. ✆ **055-276-8224.** Free admission to church; Brancacci Chapel 4€, cumulative ticket with Palazzo Vecchio 8€. Wed–Sat and Mon 10am–5pm; Sun 1–5pm. Bus: D, 6, 11, 36, or 37.

San Miniato al Monte ★★ High atop a hill, its gleaming white-and-green facade visible from the valley below, San Miniato is one of the few ancient churches of Florence to survive the centuries virtually intact. The titular St. Minias was an eastern Christian who settled in Florence and was martyred during Emperor Decius's persecutions in A.D. 250. The legend goes that the decapitated saint picked up his head, walked across the river, climbed up the hillside, and didn't lie down to die until he reached this spot. He and other Christians were buried here, and a shrine was raised on the site as early as the 4th century.

The current building began to take shape in 1013, under the auspices of the powerful Arte di Calimala guild, whose symbol, a bronze eagle clutching a bale of wool, perches atop the **facade** ★★. This Romanesque facade is a particularly gorgeous bit of white Carrara and green Prato marble inlay. Above the central window is a 13th-century mosaic of *Christ Between the Madonna and St. Miniato* (a theme repeated in the apse).

The **interior** has a few Renaissance additions, but they blend in well with the overall medieval aspect—an airy, stony space with a raised choir at one end, painted wooden trusses on the ceiling, and tombs interspersed with inlaid marble symbols of the zodiac paving the floor.

Below the choir is an 11th-century **crypt** with small frescoes by Taddeo Gaddi. Off to the right of the raised choir is the **sacristy,** which Spinello Aretino covered in 1387 with cartoonish yet elegant frescoes depicting the *Life of St. Benedict* ★. Off the left aisle of the nave is 15th-century **Cappella del Cardinale del Portogallo** ★★, a collaborative effort by Renaissance artists built to honor young Portuguese humanist Cardinal Jacopo di Lusitania, who was sent to study in Perugia but died an untimely death at age 25 in Florence. Brunelleschi's student Antonio Manetti started the chapel in 1460 but soon died, and Antonio Rossellino finished the architecture and carving by 1466. Luca della Robbia provided the glazed terra-cotta dome, a cubic landscape set with tondi of the four *Virtues* surrounding the *Holy Spirit* to symbolize the young scholar's devotion to the church and to humanist philosophy. It stands as one of della Robbia's masterpieces of color and classical ideals. The unfinished **bell tower** seen from the outside was designed by Baccio d'Agnolo. In 1530 the combined troops of Charles V and Medici Pope Clement VII, who had recently reconciled with each other, lay siege to the newly declared Republic of Florence in an attempt to reinstate the Medici dukes. San Miniato al Monte was one of the prime fortifications, and an artilleryman named Lapo was stationed up in the tower with two small cannons—he was basically bait, stuck there to draw the fire of the enemy where it would do little harm. The man in charge of the defenses was Michelangelo, who, the authorities figured, was so good at everything else, why not military fortifications? After throwing up dirt ramparts and cobbling together defensible walls out of oak timbers, Michelangelo helped poor Lapo out by devising an ingenious way to protect the tower: He hung mattresses down the sides to absorb the shock of the cannonballs fired at it and left the tower (and, more important, Lapo) still standing. The siege was eventually successful, however, and the Florentine Republic fell.

Around the back of the church is San Miniato's **monumental cemetery** ★, one enormous "city of the dead," whose streets are lined with tombs and mausoleums built in elaborate pastiches of every generation of Florentine architecture (with a marked preference for the Gothic and the Romanesque). It's a peaceful spot soundtracked only by birdsong and the occasional tolling of the church bells.

Via Monte alle Croci/Viale Galileo Galilei (behind Piazzale Michelangiolo). ✆ **055-234-2731.** Free admission. Daily 8am–12:30pm and 3–5:30pm (closed some Sun afternoons); sometimes open through *riposo* in summer. Bus: 12 or 13.

Santo Spirito ★ One of Filippo Brunelleschi's masterpieces of architecture, this 15th-century church doesn't look like much from the outside (no true facade was ever built), but the **interior** ★ is a marvelous High Renaissance space—an expansive landscape of proportion and mathematics worked out in classic Brunelleschi style, with coffered vaulting, tall columns, and the stacked perspective of arched arcading. Good late-Renaissance and baroque paintings are scattered throughout, but the best stuff lies up in the transepts and in the east end, surrounding the extravagant **baroque altar** with a ciborium inlaid in *pietre dure* around 1607.

The **right transept** begins with a *Crucifixion* by Francesco Curradi. Two chapels down is one of Filippino Lippi's best works, a *Madonna and Child with Saints and Donors.* In the **left transept,** the first chapel on the right side is a late-15th-century *Madonna Enthroned with Child and Saints.* Next to this is the highly skilled *St. Monica and Augustinian Nuns,* an almost monochrome work of black and pale yellow, faintly disturbing in its eerie monotony and perfection of composition. It's now usually attributed to the enigmatic Andrea del Verrocchio, who taught Leonardo da Vinci.

The famed **piazza** outside is one of the focal points of the Oltrarno, shaded by trees and lined with trendy cafes that see some bar action in the evenings.

Piazza Santo Spirito. ✆ **055-210-030.** Free admission. Mon–Tues and Thurs–Sat 10am–12:30pm and 4–5:30pm; Sun 4–5:30pm. Bus: C3, D, 11, 36, or 37.

North of the Center

Museo Stibbert ☺ Half Scotsman, half Italian, Frederick Stibbert was nothing if not eccentric. A sometime artist, intrepid traveler, voracious accumulator, and even hero in Garibaldi's army, he inherited a vast fortune and this villa from his Italian mother. He connected the house to a nearby villa to create an eclectic museum housing his extraordinary collections, including baroque canvases, fine porcelain, Flemish tapestries, Tuscan crucifixes, and Etruscan artifacts. The museum was partially rearranged to try and make some sense out of 57 rooms stuffed with over 50,000 items.

Stibbert's greatest interest and most fascinating assemblage is of **armor** ★ —Etruscan, Lombard, Asian, Roman, 17th-century Florentine, and 15th-century Turkish. The museum has the largest display of Japanese arms and armor in Europe. The high point of the house is a remarkable grand hall filled with an entire cavalcade of mannequins in 16th-century armor (mostly European, but with half a dozen samurai foot soldiers thrown in for good measure). Stibbert even managed to get some seriously historic Florentine armor, that in which Medici warrior Giovanni delle Bande Nere was buried. Visits are by 1-hour accompanied tour only.

Via Stibbert 26. ✆ **055-475-520.** www.museostibbert.it. Admission 6€ adults, 4€ children 4–11. Mon–Wed 10am–2pm; Fri–Sun 10am–6pm; last visit starts 1 hr. before closing. Bus: 4.

Organized Tours

If you want to get under the surface of the city, **Context Travel** ★ (✆ **800/691-6036** in the U.S. or 06-976-25-204 in Italy; www.contexttravel.com), offers insightful tours led by academics and other experts in their field in a variety of specialties, from the gastronomic to the archeological. Tours are limited to six people and cost between 40€ and 75€ per person. Context also conducts a guided walk through the Vasari Corridor (subject to availability; p. 133). **CAF Tours,** Via Roma 4 (✆ **055-283-200;** www.caftours.com), offers two half-day bus tours of town (47€), including visits to the Uffizi, the Accademia, and Piazzale Michelangiolo, as well as several walking tours and cooking classes from 25€ to 80€. **ArtViva** (✆ **055-264-5033;** www.italy.artviva.com) has a huge array of walking tours and museum guides for every budget, starting at 25€. Websites such as **Viator.com** and **Isango.com** have a vast range of locally organized tours and activities, reviewed and rated by users.

Call **I Bike Italy** (✆ **055-012-3994;** www.ibikeitaly.com) to sign up for 1-day rides through Chianti for 80€, or 2 days to Siena for 329€.

Outdoor Activities

Florence's best park is the Medici grand dukes' old backyard to the Pitti Palace, the **Giardino di Boboli** (p. 152). Less scenic, but free and more jogger-friendly, is the **Parco delle Cascine** along the Arno at the west end of the historic center. Originally a wild delta of land where the Arno and Mugnone rivers met, the area later became a Medici hunting reserve and eventually a pasture for the grand duke's milk cows. Today, the Cascine is home to tennis courts, pools, a horse racetrack, and some odd late-18th- and early-19th-century features like an incongruous pyramid and funky neoclassical fountains. There's a flea market here every Tuesday morning. Although perfectly safe in the daylight, this park becomes a hangout for drug addicts after dark, as do many sections of the Arno's banks away from the center, so steer clear.

For **bike rental** information, see p. 80.

Spectator Sports

There's only really one game in town when it comes to spectator sports: *calcio.* To Italians, soccer/football is something akin to a second religion, and an afternoon at the stadium can offer you as much insight (if not more) into local culture as a day in the Uffizi. The local team, **Fiorentina** (nicknamed *i viola,* "the purples"), plays in Italy's top league, Serie A. You can usually catch them alternate Sundays from September through May at the Stadio Comunale Artemio Franchi, Via Manfredo Fanti 4 (www.violachannel.tv). Tickets are best bought ahead of time from **Chiosco degli Sportivi,** Via degli Anselmi 1 (an alley off Piazza della Repubblica; ✆ **055-292-363**). To reach the stadium from the center, take a train from Santa Maria Novella to Campo di Marte (5 min.) or bus no. 10 from San Marco.

Shopping along Via de' Tornabuoni.

SHOPPING
The Shopping Scene

The cream of the crop of Florentine shopping lines both sides of elegant **Via de' Tornabuoni,** with an extension along **Via della Vigna Nuova** and other surrounding streets. Here you'll find big names like Gucci, Armani, and Ferragamo ensconced in old palaces or modern minimalist boutiques.

On the other end of the shopping spectrum is the haggling and general fun of the colorful and noisy **San Lorenzo street market.** Antiques gather dust by the truckload along **Via Maggio** and other Oltrarno streets. Another main corridor of stores somewhat less glitzy than those on Via de' Tornabuoni begins at **Via Cerretani** and runs down **Via Roma** through the Piazza della Repubblica area; it keeps going down **Via Por Santa Maria,** across the **Ponte Vecchio** with its gold jewelry, and up **Via Guicciardini** on the other side. Store-laden side tributaries off this main stretch include **Via della Terme, Borgo Santissimi Apostoli,** and **Borgo San Jacopo** (which becomes **Via Santo Spirito** as it heads west). Over in the east of the center, **Borgo degli Albizi** has seen a flourishing of one-off, independent stores, with an emphasis on young, independent fashions.

General Florentine **shopping hours** are Monday through Saturday from 9:30am to noon or 1pm and 3 or 3:30 to 7:30pm, although increasingly, many shops are staying open on Sunday and through that midafternoon *riposo* or nap (especially the larger stores and those around tourist sights).

Shopping A to Z

Here's **what to buy in Florence:** leather, fashion, shoes, marbleized paper, hand-embroidered linens, artisan craft goods, Tuscan wines, jewelry, *pietre dure* (known also as "Florentine mosaic," inlaid semiprecious stones), and antiques.

ART & ANTIQUES

The antiques business is clustered where the artisans have always lived and worked: the Oltrarno. Dealers' shops line Via Maggio, but the entire district is packed with venerable chunks of the past. On "this side" of the river, Borgo Ognissanti has the highest concentration of aging furniture and art collectibles.

The large showrooms of **Gallori-Turchi,** Via Maggio 14r (✆**055-282-279**), specialize in furnishings, paintings, and weaponry (swords, lances, and pistols) from the 16th to 18th centuries. They also offer majolica and ceramic pieces and scads of hand-carved and inlaid wood. Nearby you'll find **Guido Bartolozzi Antichità,** Via Maggio 18r (✆**055-215-602**), under family management since 1887. This old-fashioned store concentrates on the 16th to 19th centuries. They might be offering a 17th-century Gobelin tapestry, an inlaid stone tabletop, or wood intarsia dressers from the 1700s. The quality is impeccable. For the serious collector who wants his or her own piece of Florence's cultural heritage, the refined showroom at **Gianfranco Luzzetti,** Borgo San Jacopo 28A (✆**055-211-232**), offers artwork and furniture from the 1400s to 1600s. They have a gorgeous collection of 16th-century Deruta ceramics and majolica, canvases by the likes of Vignale and Bilivert, and even a glazed terra-cotta altarpiece from the hand of Andrea della Robbia. Bring sacks of money.

BEAUTY PRODUCTS

You may never in your life have been inside anywhere quite like the **Officina Profumo-Farmaceutica Santa Maria Novella** ★★, Via della Scala 16 (✆**055-216-276**), an old-style pharmacy, herbalist, bookstore, and even museum, opened in 1612 and still part of the Dominican convent attached to the church. In an atmosphere of subdued reverence, choose your favorite scents, soaps, remedies, and essences for your body, mind, child, or even pet dog.

BOOKS

Even the smaller bookshops in Florence these days have at least a few shelves devoted to English-language books. **Feltrinelli International,** Via Cavour 12 (✆**055-219-524;** www.lafeltrinelli.it), is one of the few of any size. For English-only reading, hit **Paperback Exchange,** Via delle Oche 4r (✆**055-293-460;** www.papex.it), the best for books in English, specializing in titles relating in some way to Florence and Italy. Much of their stock is used, and you can't beat the prices locally—Italy is generally an expensive place to buy books. **G. Vitello,** Via dei Servi 94–96r (✆**055-292-445**), sells coffee table–worthy books on art and all things Italian at up to half off the price you'd pay in a regular bookstore.

CERAMICS

La Botteghina del Ceramista, Via Guelfa 5r (✆**055-287-367**), is about the most reasonably priced city outlet for artisan ceramics. Daniela Viegi del Fiume deals in hand-painted ceramics from the best traditional artisans working in nearby Montelupo and the famed Umbrian ceramics center of Deruta.

If you can't make it to the Chianti workshop of **Giuseppe Rampini** ★ (p. 184 in chapter 5), visit his classy showroom at Borgo Ognissanti 32–34 (right at Piazza Ognissanti; ✆ **055-219-720;** www.rampiniceramics.com).

For big-name production-line china and tablewares, visit **Richard Ginori,** Via Giulio Cesare 50 (✆**055-420-49;** www.richardginori1735.com). Colorful rims and whimsical designs fill this warehouselike salesroom of the firm that has sold Florence's finest china since 1735.

CRAFTS

Florentine traditional "mosaics" are actually works of inlaid semiprecious stone called *pietre dure*. The creations of Ilio de Filippis and his army of apprentices at **Pitti Mosaici ★**, Piazza Pitti 23–24r (**℃ 055-282-127;** www.pittimosaici.com), reflect traditional techniques and artistry. Ilio's father was a *pietre dure* artist, and his grandfather was a sculptor. (The family workshop was founded in 1900.) There's another store at Via Guicciardini 80r.

Professore Agostino Dessi and his daughter Alice preside over the traditional Venetian Carnevale and *Commedia dell'arte*–style maskmaking at **Alice Atelier ★**, Via Faenza 72r (**℃ 055-287-370;** www.alicemasks.com). All masks are made using papier-mâché, leather, and ceramics according to 17th-century techniques, hand-painted with tempera, touched up with gold and silver leaf, and polished with French lacquer.

DEPARTMENT STORES

Florence's central branch of the national chain **Coin,** Via Calzaiuoli 56r (**℃ 055-280-531;** www.coin.it), is a stylish multifloored display case for upper-middle-class fashions—a vaguely chic Macy's. **La Rinascente,** Piazza della Repubblica 2 (**℃ 055-219-113;** www.rinascente.it), is another of Italy's finer department stores. This six-floor store serves as an outlet for top designers (Versace, Zegna, Ferré, and so on). It also has areas set up to sell traditional Tuscan goods (terra cotta, alabaster, olive oils, and wrought iron).

FASHION & CLOTHING

Although Italian fashion reached its pinnacle in the 1950s and 1960s, the country has remained at the forefront of both high (Armani, Gucci, Pucci, Ferragamo, just to name a few) and popular (evidenced by the spectacular success of Benetton in the 1980s) fashion. Florence plays second fiddle to Milan in today's Italian fashion scene, but the city has its own cadre of well-respected names, plus, of course, outlet shops of all the hot designers. The epicenter of the city's high fashion is **Via de' Tornabuoni.** Serious clothes shoppers should also consider visiting one of the outlet malls clustered around the city. Best of the bunch is **The Mall** (www.themall.it), a half-hour south-east of Florence in Leccio Reggello. Units include Bottega Veneta, Stella McCartney, Gucci, Armani, Dior and about 20 others—with steep discounts off last season's threads for women, men, and kids. With one day's notice, you can pre-book a shuttle bus to collect you from any Florence hotel (**℃ 055-865-7775** or e-mail info@themall.it; 25€ per person), or take the train from Santa Maria Novella to Rignano sull'Arno and then a short cab ride.

FOR MEN & WOMEN Luisa Via Roma, Via Roma 19–21r (**℃ 055-906-4116;** www.luisaviaroma.com), is a famed gathering place for all the top names in avant-garde fashion, including Jean Paul Gaultier, Dolce & Gabbana, and Julien Macdonald. Men can hand over their wallets upstairs, and women can empty their purses on the ground floor. There's also an outlet store at Via Silvio Pellico 9 (**℃ 055-217-826**) and a professional online shopping setup.

Marchese **Emilio Pucci**'s ancestors have been a powerful banking and mercantile family since the Renaissance, and in 1950 Marchese suddenly turned designer and shocked the fashion world with his flowing silks in outlandish colors. His women's silk clothing remained the rage into the early 1970s and had a renaissance in the 1990s club scene. Drop by the flagship store at Via dei Tornabuoni 20–22r (**℃ 055-265-8082;** www.pucci.com).

Bags at Salvatore Ferragamo.

Then there's **Giorgio Armani,** Via Tornabuoni 48r (✆ **055-219-041;** www.giorgioarmani.com), Florence's outlet for Italy's top fashion guru. The service and store are surprisingly not stratospherically chilly. The **Emporio Armani** branch at Piazza Strozzi 16r (✆ **055-284-315;** www.emporioarmani.com) is the outlet for the more affordable designs. The merchandise is slightly inferior in workmanship and quality but considerably less expensive. The rest of the Via dei' Tornabuoni is fleshed out with the mainstays of Italian style, notably **Salvatore Ferragamo** (✆ **055-292-123;** www.salvatoreferragamo.it) at no. 4r.

But the biggest name to walk out of Florence onto the international catwalk has to be **Gucci ★**, with the world flagship store at Via de' Tornabuoni 73r (✆ **055-264-011;** www.gucci.com). This is where this Florentine fashion empire was started by saddlemaker Guccio Gucci in 1904. You enter through a phalanx of their trademark purses and bags. Forget the cheesy knockoffs sold on street corners around the world; the stock here is elegant.

Florence has caught the vintage fashion bug, and on the two floors of **Pitti Vintage ★**, Borgo degli Albizi 72r (✆ **055-234-4115;** www.pittivintage.com), you'll find classic threads, stylish men's shirts and ties, and accessories for women such as silk scarves, 1980s bags, and haute couture dresses. Prices are fair and the welcome is friendly.

FOR WOMEN Loretta Caponi, Piazza Antinori 4r (✆ **055-213-668;** www. lorettacaponi.com), is world famous for her high-quality intimates and embroidered linens made the old-fashioned way. Under Belle Epoque ceilings are nightgowns of all types, as well as underwear, bed, and bath linens of the highest caliber. There's also a section for the little ones in the back. There's another branch at Via delle Belle Donne 28r (✆ **055-211-074**).

JEWELRY

If you've got the financial clout of a small country, the place to buy your baubles is the Ponte Vecchio, famous for its gold- and silversmiths since the 16th century. The craftsmanship at the stalls is usually of a high quality, and so they seem to compete instead over who can charge the highest prices. **Aprosio** ★, Via Santo Spirito 11 (✆ **055-290-534;** www.aprosio.it), is a glass and crystal jewelry designer without equal in the city. The store is arranged like a temple to creativity. Semiprecious stones are crafted into elaborate necklaces, classy earrings, and simple brooches at **Tharros Bijoux,** Via Condotta 2r (corner of Via de' Cerchi; ✆ **055-284-126;** www.tharros.com).

Florence is also a good place to root around for interesting costume jewelry. The audacious bijoux at **Angela Caputi,** Via Santo Spirito 58r (✆ **055-212-972;** www.angelacaputi.com), aren't for the timid. Much of Angela's costume jewelry is at least oversize and bold and often pushes the flamboyance envelope. Tradition goes out the window at **Falsi Gioelli** ★, Via dei Tavolini 5r (✆ **055-293-296**). Prepare to be assaulted by primary colors the minute you step into this funky "false" jeweler, where everything from hairbands and bracelets to necklaces and earrings in bright shades of acrylic is handmade on the premises. Items are inexpensive. There's another branch at Via de' Ginori 34r (✆ **055-287-237**).

LEATHER, ACCESSORIES & SHOES

It has always been a buyers' market for leather in Florence, but these days it's tough to sort out the jackets mass-produced for tourists from the high-quality artisan work. The most fun you'll have leather shopping, without a doubt, is at the outdoor stalls of the **San Lorenzo** market, even if the market is rife with mediocre goods (see "Markets," below). Never accept the first price they throw at you; sometimes you can bargain them down to almost half the original asking price.

Our favorite spot, where we get to watch the artisans at work before buying, is at the **Scuola del Cuoio (Leather School) of Santa Croce** ★. It's around the back of the church: Enter through Santa Croce itself (right transept) or on Via San Giuseppe 5r (✆ **055-244-533;** www.scuoladelcuoio.com). The very fine quality soft-leather merchandise isn't cheap.

In the imposing 13th-century Palazzo Spini-Feroni lording over Piazza Santa Trínita are the flagship store, museum, and home of **Ferragamo,** Via de' Tornabuoni 4–14r (✆ **055-292-123;** www.ferragamo.it). Salvatore Ferragamo was the man who shod Hollywood in its most glamorous age and raised footwear to an art form. View some of Ferragamo's funkier shoes in the second-floor museum or slip on a pair yourself in the showrooms downstairs—if you think your wallet can take the shock.

If you prefer to buy right from the cobbler, head across the Arno to **Calzature Francesco da Firenze,** Via Santo Spirito 62r (✆ **055-212-428**), where handmade shoes run 120€ to 300€, and you can see the cobbler tap-tapping away on soles in the back room.

For more made-in-Florence accessorizing, head to **Madova Gloves,** Via Guicciardini 1r (✆ **055-239-6526;** www.madova.com). Gloves are all they sell in this tiny shop, and they do them well. The grandchildren of the workshop's founders do a brisk business in brightly colored, supple leather gloves lined with cashmere and silk.

MARKETS

Somewhere in the center of the mercantile whirlwind of Florence hides the indoor **Mercato Centrale food market** ★ (btw. Via dell'Ariento and Piazza del Mercato Centrale). Downstairs you'll find meat, cheese, dry goods, tripe, *baccalà* (dried salt cod), and a good cheap eatery, **Nerbone** (p. 105). The upstairs is devoted to fruits and veggies—a cornucopia of fat eggplants, long yellow peppers, artichokes, and peperoncini bunched into brilliant red bursts. In all, you couldn't ask for better picnic pickings. The market is open Monday through Saturday from 7am to 2pm (until 5pm Sat Sept–June).

As if two names weren't enough, the **Mercato Nuovo,** or **della Paglia (Straw Market),** is also known as Mercato del Porcellino or Mercato del Cinghiale because of the bronze wild boar statue at one end, cast by Pietro Tacca in the 17th century after an antique original now in the Uffizi. Pet the well-polished *porcellino*'s snout to ensure a return trip to Florence. Most of the straw stalls disappeared by the 1960s. These days, the loggia hawks mainly tourist trinkets. Beware of pickpockets. It's open daily.

Produce at the Mercato Centrale.

For more of a local flavor, head east beyond Santa Croce to find the daily flea market, the **Mercato delle Pulci** ★, in Piazza de' Ciompi, which specializes in a bit of everything, from costume jewelry, ornaments, and vintage buttons to silver, antique bric-a-brac, and yesteryear postcards. The nearby food market where Florentines shop (Mon–Sat), the **Mercato di Sant'Ambrogio,** is also home to one of the city's best cheap lunch spots, **Da Rocco** (see p. 110).

PAPER & JOURNALS

Il Papiro, Via dei Tavolini 13r (☏**055-213-823;** www.ilpapirofirenze.it), is a small Tuscan chain of jewel box–size shops specializing in marbled and patterned paper, as plain gift-wrap sheets or as a covering for everything from pens and journals to letter openers or full desk sets. There are further branches at Via Cavour

Florence's Famous Street Market

The queen of Florentine markets is the daily **San Lorenzo market,** filling Piazza San Lorenzo, Via del Canto de' Nelli, Via dell'Ariento, and other side streets around the basilica. It's a wildly chaotic and colorful array of hundreds of stands hawking T-shirts, silk scarves, marbleized paper, souvenirs, and lots and lots of leather. However, almost all of the buyers here are tourists, and you'll find plenty of lemons among the occasional deals on quality goods. By all means have a browse—San Lorenzo in full swing is quite a sight—but it's not worth committing to half a day of picking through it all and fending off sales pitches. *Note:* Haggling is accepted, and even expected, at most of Florence's outdoor markets (but don't try it in stores). It's also an offense (punishable with a hefty fine) to knowingly buy counterfeit goods. And, yes, buying a "Rolex" for 20€ does count as *knowingly.*

49r (☏**055-215-262**), Piazza del Duomo 24r (☏**055-281-628**), Lungarno Acciaiuoli 42r (☏**055-264-5613**), and Via Porta Rossa 76r (☏**055-216-593**).

Scriptorium, Via dei Servi 5–7r (☏**055-211-804**), is our favorite journal supplier, and one of the few fine stationery stores in Florence with little marble-ized paper. Come here for hand-sewn notebooks, journals, and photo albums made of thick paper—all bound in soft leather covers. With classical music or Gregorian chant playing in the background, you can also shop for calligraphy and signet wax sealing tools.

PRINTS

Bottega delle Stampe, Borgo San Jacopo 56r (☏**055-295-396;** www.bottega dellestampe.com), carries prints, historic maps, and engravings from the 1500s through the Liberty-style and Art Deco prints of the 1930s. You might dig out some Dürers here, or original Piranesis and plates from Diderot's 1700 *Encyclopedia.* There are also Florence views from the 16th to 19th centuries.

TOYS

Since 1977, Florence's branch of national chain **La Città del Sole,** Via del-lo Studio 23r (☏**055-277-6372;** www.cittadelsole.it), has sold old-fashioned wooden brain teasers, construction kits, hand puppets, 3-D puzzles, science kits, and books. There's nary a video game in sight.

WINE & LIQUORS

The front room of **Enoteca Alessi,** Via dell'Oche 27–31r (☏**055-214-966;** www.enotecaalessi.it), sells boxed chocolates and other sweets, but in the back and in the large cellars, you can find everything from prime vintages to a simple-quality table wine.

FLORENCE AFTER DARK
The Performing Arts

Florence doesn't have the musical cachet or grand opera houses of Milan, Venice, or Rome, but there are two symphony orchestras and a fine music school in Fiesole. The city's public theaters are certainly respectable, and most major tour-ing companies stop in town on their way through Italy. Get tickets to all cultural and musical events online (they'll send an e-mail with collection instructions) or in person at **Box Office,** Via delle Carceri 1 (☏**055-210-804;** www.boxol.it). In addition to tickets for year-round events of all genres, they handle the sum-mertime Calcio Storico folkloric festival.

Many concerts and recitals staged in major halls and private spaces are sponsored by the **Amici della Musica** (☏**055-607-440;** www.amicimusica. fi.it), so check their website to see what "hidden" concert might be on while you're here.

CHURCH CONCERTS Many Florentine churches fill the autumn with organ, choir, and chamber orchestra concerts, mainly of classical music. The tiny **Santa Maria de' Ricci** (☏**055-215-044**) on Via del Corso has a free organ concert most nights, starting at 7 or 9:15pm (pass by during the day to check). Technically it's free, but contributions to the church's upkeep, as well as that of the nearby Chiesa di Dante, are appreciated. The **Orches-tra da Camera Fiorentina (Florentine Chamber Orchestra;** ☏**055-**

Centro Storico nightlife.

783-374; www.orcafi.it), also runs a season at historic sites around the city; tickets are available from Box Office. **St. Mark's,** Via Maggio 18 (✆ **340-811-9192;** www.concertoclassico.info) hosts regular, often nightly, operas and operatic music concerts inside its church in the Oltrarno. Tickets cost 15€ to 30€.

CONCERT HALLS & OPERA One of Italy's busiest stages, Florence's contemporary **Teatro Comunale,** Corso Italia 12 (✆ **055-277-9350;** www.maggio fiorentino.com), offers everything from symphonies to ballet to plays, opera, and concerts. The main theater seats 2,000, with orchestra rows topped by horseshoe-shaped first and second galleries. Its smaller Piccolo Teatro, seating 500, is rectangular, offering good sightlines from most any seat. The Teatro Comunale is the seat of the prestigious annual Maggio Musicale Fiorentino.

The **Teatro Verdi,** Via Ghibellina 99r (✆ **055-212-320;** www.teatro verdionline.it), is Florence's opera and ballet house, with the nice ritual of staging Sunday-afternoon shows during the January-through-April season. The **Orchestra della Toscana** (www.orchestradellatoscana.it) plays classical concerts here November through May, and occasionally plays cheap Saturday afternoon shows aimed at children. The Verdi also hosts a bit of theater, but not of the caliber of Teatro della Pergola (see below).

THEATER The biggest national and international touring companies stop in Florence's major playhouse, the **Teatro della Pergola,** Via della Pergola 12 (✆ **055-226-4353;** www.teatrodellapergola.com). La Pergola is the city's chief purveyor of classical and classic plays from the Greeks and Shakespeare through Pirandello, Samuel Beckett, and Italian modern playwrights. Performances are professional and of high quality—and, of course, in Italian.

The Club & Music Scenes

Italian clubs are rather cliquey—people usually go in groups to hang out and dance only with one another. There's plenty of flesh showing, but no meat market.

Singles hoping to find random dance partners will often be disappointed.

LIVE MUSIC Florence's best jazz venue is the aptly titled **Jazz Club,** Via Nuova de' Caccini 3 (𝒞**055-247-9700;** www.jazzclubfirenze. com). You need to join, online or at the venue, which costs 8€ for the year and entitles you to free entry to all concerts. It's closed Sunday, Monday, and all summer. The forthcoming program is posted on their website. New kid on the block is **Volume ★**, Piazza Santo Spirito 5r (𝒞**055-2381-460;** www.volume.fi.it), which opened in 2010; it's an artsy cafe cum creperie cum gelateria by day, with contemporary art hanging on the walls. When night falls, Left Bank revelers stop in for cocktails

A street musician in Florence.

(around 6€), followed by live acoustic music 4 or 5 nights a week (Thurs night is a blues jam).

DANCE BARS & NIGHTCLUBS Any guide to nightclubbing should come with a health warning: What's hot (and what's not) can change from month to month. If you're clubbing at the cutting edge, we suggest you consult the listings magazines recommended on p. 74, or check the websites for **Zero** (http://firenze.zero.eu) and **Firenze Spettacolo** (www.firenzespettacolo.it).

It's not exactly cutting edge, but the most centrally located nightclub is **Yab,** Via Sassetti 5r (𝒞**055-215-160;** www.yab.it), just behind the post office on Piazza della Repubblica. This dance club for 20-somethings is a perennial favorite, an archetypal 1980s disco complete with velvet rope, bouncers, and eclectic, upbeat music policy.

Much more fashionable is **Dolce Vita,** Piazza del Carmine (𝒞**055-284-595;** www.dolcevitaflorence.com), still going strong after 3 decades leading Florence's nightlife scene, and, these days attracting clued-up 30-somethings who have grown up with the city's iconic DJ bar.

Bars, Pubs & Wine Bars

BARS & PUBS **Via dei Benci ★**, which runs south from Piazza Santa Croce toward the Arno, is the *centro storico*'s cool-bar central, and a great place to kick off a night with *aperitivo* hour. (Wander in from around 7pm, buy a drink, and help yourself to any of the food laid out buffet style.) **Moyo,** at no. 23r (𝒞**055-247-9738;** www.moyo.it) does some of the best *aperitivo* in Florence, and is frequented by beautiful people drinking cocktails. **Oibò,** up the road at Borgo de' Greci 1A (corner of Via dei Benci; 𝒞**055-263-8611;** www.oibo.net) is also popular with fashionable 20- and 30-somethings. They mix a decent cocktail and after 10pm DJs spin house and dance sounds.

cafe CULTURE

Florence no longer has a glitterati or intellectuals' cafe scene, and when it did—from the late-19th-century Italian *Risorgimento* era through the *dolce vita* of the 1950s—it was basically copying the idea from Paris. Although they're often overpriced tourist spots today, Florence's high-toned cafes are fine if you want designer pastries served to you while you sit on a piazza and people-watch.

At the refined, wood-paneled, stucco-ceilinged, and very expensive 1733 cafe **Gilli,** Via Roma 1r (© **055-213-896;** www.gilli.it), tourists gather to sit with the ghosts of Italy's *Risorgimento,* when the cafe became a meeting place of the heroes and thinkers of the unification movement from the 1850s to the 1870s. The red-jacketed waiters at **Giubbe Rosse,** Piazza della Repubblica 13–14r (© **055-212-280;** www.giubbe rosse.it), must have been popular during the 19th-century glory days of Garibaldi's red-shirt soldiers. This was once a meeting place of the Futurists, but today it too is mainly a tourists' cafe with ridiculous prices.

Once full of history and now mainly full of tourists, **Rivoire,** Piazza della Signoria/Via Vacchereccia 4r (© **055-214-412;** www.rivoire.it), has a chunk of prime real estate on Piazza della Signoria. Smartly dressed waiters serve smartly priced sandwiches to cappuccino-sipping patrons.

At **Sei Divino ★**, Borgo Ognissanti 42r (© **055-217-791**), you'll find artisan beers, Tuscan wines by the glass, and some interesting cocktails, as well as *aperitivo* plates piled high from 7pm every night. **Caffe Sant'Ambrogio,** Piazza Sant'Ambrogio 7 (© **055-247-7277;** www.caffe santambrogio.it) is a funky cafe-bar by day and a popular wine bar after dark. Just across the Ponte Vecchio, **Golden View Open Bar,** Via de' Bardi 58r (© **055-214-502;** www.goldenviewopenbar.com) is a sleek, minimalist cocktail bar with plenty of chrome, great river views, dressed-up clientele, a renowned *aperitivo* buffet, and jazz 5 nights a week from 9pm. On nearby Via dei Renai, **Zoe** (no. 13; © **055-243-111**) and **Negroni** (no. 17r; © **055-243-647**) are buzzing on a weekend, pumping out music and fashionable chatter until late.

There's an unsurprising degree of similarity among Florence's several **Irish-style pubs'** dark, woody interiors—usually frequented by a crowd (stuffed to the gills on weekends) of students and 20- and 30-something Americans and Brits along with their Italian counterparts. Our favorites are **Lion's Fountain,** Borgo Albizi 34r (© **055-234-4412;** www.thelions fountain.com), on the tiny but lively Piazza San Pier Maggiore near Santa Croce, and **Kikuya,** Via dei Benci 43r (© **055-234-4879;** www.kikuya pub.it), where you'll find draft ales and soccer on the screens.

For a swanky cocktail with a panoramic view of the city, check out the rooftop **Sky Lounge** of the Hotel Continentale, Vicolo dell'Oro 6r (next to Ponte Vecchio; © **055-2726-4000;** www.lungarnohotels.com; open Apr–Oct). Sunset is the best time to visit. The million-dollar view is amortized by the steep price of a martini.

WINE BARS The most traditional wine bars are called *fiaschetterie,* after the word for a flask of chianti. The best wine lists focusing on handpicked labels, most offered with plates of cheese and other snacks, tend to be in the Oltrarno. **Il Volpe e L'Uva ★**, Piazza de' Rossi, by Santa Felícita (✆ **055-239-8132**; www.levolpieluva.com), is popular with visitors and locals, and has a compelling by-the-glass list. Nearby, a great little wine bar right across from the Pitti Palace called **Pitti Gola e Cantina,** Piazza de' Pitti 16 (✆ **055-212-704**), sells glasses of fine wine from 7€ to 12€. The kitchen also serves light dishes for 8€ to 15€. We also love the buzzy little corner of the Oltrarno known as San Niccolò, a 10-minute walk from the Ponte Vecchio, where the wine bars serve substantial Tuscan dishes alongside *antipasti* platters to share. Our favorite well-stocked cantinas are at **Bevo Vino ★**, Via San Niccolò 59r (✆ **055-200-1709**); **Il Rifrullo,** Via San Niccolò 57r (✆ **055-234-2621**; www.ilrifrullo.com); and **Fuori Porta ★**, Via Monte alle Croci 10 (✆ **055-234-2483**). Partying goes on here till late.

The Gay & Lesbian Scene

The gay nightlife scene in Florence is gradually growing, but for lesbians it's still fairly limited. The best place for a predisco drink in the company of a young and friendly gay, lesbian, bisexual, and trans crowd is **YAG Bar ★**, Via de' Macci 8r (✆ **055-246-9022**; www.yagbar.com). It's open nightly from 9pm all year.

One of Florence's dark rooms is the **Crisco Club,** Via Sant'Egidio 43r, east of the Duomo (✆ **055-248-0580**; www.criscoclub.it), for men only. Its 18th-century building contains a bar and a dance floor open Tuesday through Saturday from 9pm to 3am (until 5am weekends). Check the website for one-off events and performances.

The city's major gay dance floor is **Tabasco,** Piazza Santa Cecilia 3r (✆ **055-213-000**; www.tabascogay.it). Italy's first gay disco attracts crowds of men (mostly in their 20s and 30s) from all over the country. The music is generally techno, disco, and retro rock, but entertainment offerings also include cabaret, art shows, and the occasional transvestite comedy. In summer, foreigners arrive in droves.

The owners of the Tabasco Bar also run **Bar 85** at Via Guelfa 85r (✆ **055-264-5461**; www.tabascogay.it/bar85), which every night lives by their motto "Free your fantasies." Directly next door is **Florence Baths,** Via Guelfa 93r (✆ **055-216050**), which has saunas for men only. It's open daily from 2pm to 2am.

A SIDE TRIP TO FIESOLE

Although it's only a city bus ride away from Florence, Fiesole is very proud of its status as an independent municipality. In fact, this hilltop village high in the wash of green above Florence predates that city in the valley by centuries.

An Etruscan colony from Arezzo probably founded a town here in the 6th century B.C. on the site of a Bronze Age settlement. By the time Caesar set up a Roman retirement colony on the banks of the Arno below, Faesulae was the most important Etruscan center in the region. It butted heads with the upstart Fiorenza in the valley almost right from the start. Although it eventually became a Roman town, building a theater and adopting Roman customs, it always retained a bit of the Etruscan otherness that has kept it different from Florence throughout the ages. Following the barbarian invasions, it became part of Florence's administrative district in the 9th century, yet continued to struggle for self-government. Medieval Florence put an end to it all in 1125 when it attacked and razed the entire city, save the cathedral and bishop's palace.

Becoming an irrelevant footnote to Florentine history has actually aided Fiesole in the end. Modern upper-middle-class Florentines have decided it's posh to buy an old villa on the hillside leading up to the town and maintain the villa's extensive gardens. This means that the oasis of cultivated greenery separating Florence from Fiesole has remained. Even with Florence so close by, Fiesole endures as a Tuscan small town to this day, entirely removed from the city at its feet and hence the perfect escape from summertime crowds. It stays relatively cool all summer long, and while you sit at a cafe on Piazza Mino, sipping an iced cappuccino, it might seem as though the lines at the Uffizi and pedestrian traffic around the Duomo are very distant indeed.

Essentials

GETTING THERE Take bus no. 7 from Florence, from the station or down the right flank of San Marco, on Via La Pira. A scenic 25-minute ride through the greenery above Florence takes you to Fiesole's main square, Piazza Mino.

VISITOR INFORMATION The **tourist office** is at Via Portigiani 3, 50014 Fiesole (℃ **055-596-1323;** www.comune.fiesole.fi.it; daily 10:30am–1pm and 1:30–5pm).

FESTIVALS & MARKETS Fiesole's biggest event is cultural: 2 months of music, ballet, film, and theater from late June to August called the **Estate Fiesolana** ★—sit back under the stars in the restored 1st-century-A.D. Roman theater and listen to Mozart and Verdi. You can get information and tickets in Florence at Box Office (see "Florence After Dark," earlier in this chapter) or via Fiesole's tourist office; see **www.estatefiesolana.it** for details of the program. The **Festa di San Romolo** on July 6 brings processions and partying all day and fireworks in the evening. There's a market every Saturday in Piazza Mino, and an artisan fair on the first Sunday of each month in the same place.

Exploring Fiesole

Fiesole's two museums and its Teatro Romano archaeological site keep the same hours and use a single admission ticket, costing 10€ adults, 6€ students age 7 to 25 and seniors 65 and over, and free for children 6 and under. A family ticket costs 20€. They all open April through September daily from 10am to 7pm, March and October daily from 10am to 6pm, and in winter Wednesday through Monday from 10am to 2pm. For more information, call ℃ **055-596-1293** or visit www.museidifiesole.it.

Cattedrale di San Romolo The cathedral's 13th-century **bell tower,** with its comically oversize crenellations added in the 18th century, can be spotted for miles around. The cathedral is a pleasingly bare-walled medieval church, built in 1028 using columns from nearby Roman buildings. The **crypt** is supported by slender columns with primitive carvings on the capitals. The remains of St. Romolo, Fiesole's patron, reside under the altar, and 15th-century lunette frescoes tell his story. There's a spot near the front of the crypt where you can see through the floor to a bit of Roman road and column bases, discovered during restoration in the early 1990s.

Piazzetta della Cattedrale. ✆ **055-599-566.** Free admission. Daily 8am–noon and 3–6pm (2–5pm in autumn and winter). Bus: 7.

Museo Bandini Newly restructured, this modest museum to the left of the Roman Theater entrance has a small collection of 13th- to 15th-century Florentine paintings by the likes of Bernardo Daddi, Taddeo and Agnolo Gaddi, Nardo di Cione, Bicci di Lorenzo, Sandro Botticelli, and Neri di Bicci, plus a couple of ringers by the likes of Umbrian Luca Signorelli.

Via Duprè 1. ✆ **055-59-118.** For admission and hours, see the section intro above.

San Francesco The road up here is intimidating, rising steeply to a sharp bend, which you round only to discover you're not even near the end. You can take a break halfway up in the small ilex-planted **panoramic gardens ★★**, which offer a postcard view of Florence. This garden is called the Park of Remembrance, and there's an odd, dangerously sharp-looking modern memorial set up near the edge in honor of three *carabinieri* who laid down their lives before a Nazi firing squad in exchange for the safety of Fiesole's inhabitants.

At the top of the hill, the ancient focal point of the Etruscan and Roman cities, are the church and convent of **San Francesco.** The 14th-century church has been largely overhauled, but at the end of a small nave hung with devotional works—Piero di Cosimo and Cenni di Francesco are both represented—is a fine *Crucifixion and Saints* altarpiece by Neri di Bicci. Off the cloisters is a quirky but interesting little ethnographic museum.

Via San Francesco (off Piazza Mino). ✆ **055-59-175.** Free admission. Daily 9am–noon and 3–5pm (7pm in summer). Bus: 7.

Teatro Romano (Roman Theater & Archaeological Museum) ★ If you're in the Florence area during the summertime Estate Fiesolana music concerts, by all means try to get a ticket for a night of music under the stars in this 1st-century-B.C. **Roman Theater.** The *cavea,* of which the right half is original and the left rebuilt in the 19th century when this area was first excavated, seats 3,000. This

A COUNTRYSIDE stroll IN THE CITY

Take the afternoon to **walk back down to Florence from Fiesole ★**. As you exit Piazza Mino, just as the main road makes its big downward curve to the left, look straight ahead where Via Vecchia Fiesolana, the narrow old road linking the two cities, forks right. It's steep, winding, and banked by high walls along many parts over which occasionally peek olive trees or more exotic plantings that are from

the gardens of rich eccentrics from the 18th century. A few of these gardens are open to the public and admission is free. Among them are the **Villa Medici** (entrance on main road only; no phone; open Mon–Fri 9am–1pm; 6€—prebooking essential by e-mailing: com.toscana@airc.it); and the **Villa Le**

Balze (✆ **055-59-208;** 5€; call Mon–Fri 9am–noon and 2–4pm to reserve a visit) at no. 26, now owned by Georgetown University. Every so often along the road is a break in the cypress where a Florence panorama opens before you—a scene you share only with yourself and the occasional passing nun.

archaeological area is romantically overgrown with grasses, amid which sit sections of column, broken friezes, and other remnants of architectural elements. Beyond the theater to the right, recognizable by its three rebuilt arches, are the remains of the 1st-century-A.D. **baths.** Near the arches is a little cement balcony over the far edge of the archaeological park. From it, you get a good look at the best stretch that remains of the 4th-century-B.C. **Etruscan city walls.** At the other end of the park from the baths are the floor and steps of a 1st-century-B.C. **Roman Temple** built on top of a 4th-century-B.C. Etruscan one. To the left are some oblong **Lombard tombs** from the 7th century A.D., when this was a necropolis.

Among the collections in the modest **Museum** are the bronze "she-wolf," a fragment of the back of what was probably a statue of a lion, lots of Etruscan urns and Roman architectural fragments, and Bronze Age remains found atop the hill now occupied by San Francesco.

Via Portigiani 1. ✆ **055-59-118.** For admission and hours, see the section intro above.

En Route from Florence to Fiesole

San Domenico ★ Halfway between Fiesole and Florence's outskirts, this crossroads hamlet grew around two religious buildings: the **Badia** and the 15th-century **church and convent of San Domenico.** Soon after the convent opened, one Giovanni da Fiesole came knocking on the door wanting to put on the Dominican habit, take his vows, and start painting altarpieces. He moved along with many other friars to San Marco in Florence a little later, and we now know him as Fra' Angelico. He did leave his old convent a few works, such as a beautiful *Crucifixion* (1430) and a detached *Madonna and Child* in the Chapter House. (Ring at no. 4, to the right of the church, to ask to see those two.)

Inside the church are *pietra serena*–accented chapels. In the first chapel on the left is a rich ***Madonna and Saints*** ★ by Fra' Angelico, recently restored to its fully ripe colors and modeling. Lorenzo di Credi filled in the background landscape in 1501.

Via San Domenico. ✆ **055-59-230.** http://sandomenicodifiesole.op.org. Free admission. Mon–Sat 8am–noon and 4–6pm; Sun 8–10:30am. Bus: 7.

THE CHIANTI, SIENA & THE WESTERN HILL TOWNS

5

Central Tuscany is the bit that looks like it's supposed to—the wondrous region of a million postcards and wall-calendars, where corrugated, vine-crowned hills roll their way to a hazy horizon. The principal "city" of the area is Siena, a great banking and textile rival of Florence in the Middle Ages that has preserved dozens of noble palaces and art-filled churches, none greater than its Gothic-Romanesque Duomo. Its museums are filled with a distinctive and decorative style of painting quite outside the Florentine tradition. Between there and Florence lies one of the region's most picturesque parts: the castle-topped hills and Arcadian vineyards of the Chianti, Tuscany's internationally famous winelands.

Siena is also the epicenter of hill-town territory, a landscape of small mountains and river-fed valleys watched over by stony medieval towns perched on the taller peaks. (Those towns south of Siena are covered in chapter 8.) West of the city, in bucolic, idyllic countryside, hide two of the more famous and visited towns: **San Gimignano** still sprouts more than a dozen medieval towers, and **Volterra** is an ancient Etruscan center and modern workshop of alabaster artisans.

THE CHIANTI

You can find many people's idea of earthly paradise in the 167 sq. km (64 sq. miles) of land between Florence and Siena, known as the Chianti. In fact, the British have such a history of buying up old farmhouses and settling here it's often referred to as "Chiantishire." It isn't hard to see why people come—the tall, closely gathered hills are capped by ancient cities and medieval castles, and the stream-fed valleys are dotted with jovial winemaking and market towns. All is often shrouded in a light mist that renders the blue-gray distance inscrutable and cloaks the hills in a mysterious rural magic. Many of the rolling slopes are planted with olive groves that shimmer dark green and dusty silver, but some 4,000 hectares (9,884 acres) are blanketed with vines.

This is the world's definitive wine region, in both history and spirit; these hills have been an oenological center for several thousand years. Indeed, one local grape, the canaiolo nero—one of the varietals that traditionally goes into Chianti Classico—was known to the ancients as the "Etruscan grape." The name Chianti, probably derived from that of the local noble Etruscan family Clantes, has been used to describe the hills between Florence and Siena for centuries, but it wasn't until the mid–13th century that Florence created the **Lega del Chianti** to unite the region's three most important centers—Castellina, Radda, and Gaiole—which chose the black rooster as their symbol. By 1404, the red wine long produced here was being called chianti as well, and in 1716 a grand ducal decree defined the boundaries of the Chianti and laid down general rules for its

Sangiovese grapes hanging from vines near Greve.

wine production, making it the world's first officially designated wine-producing area. In the 19th century, one vintner, the "Iron Baron" Ricasoli, experimented with varietals using the sangiovese grape as his base. Working off centuries of refinement, he eventually came up with the perfect balance of grapes that became the unofficial standard for all chianti.

Soon the title "chianti" was being used by hundreds of poor-quality, *vino*-producing hacks, both within the region and from far-flung areas, diminishing the reputation of the wine. To fight against this, Greve and Castelnuovo Berardenga joined the original Lega cities and formed the **Consorzio del Gallo Nero** in 1924, reviving the black rooster as their seal. The *consorzio* (still active—their members produce about 80% of the Chianti Classico that's bottled) pressed for laws regulating the quality of chianti wines and restricting the Chianti Classico name to their production zone. When Italy devised its DOC and DOCG laws in the 1960s, chianti was one of the first to be defined as DOCG, guaranteeing its quality as one of the top wines in Italy. Today, of the 100 sq. km (39 sq. miles) of vineyards in the hills between Florence and Siena, some 6,972 hectares (17,228 acres) are devoted to the grapes that will eventually become Chianti Classico and carry the seal of the black rooster.

Essentials

GETTING AROUND The only way to explore the Chianti effectively is **by car.** But know that many of the roads off the major SS222 (known as the *Chiantigiana*) are unpaved and sometimes heavily potholed (so-called *strade bianche,* or "white roads"). More importantly, wine tasting presents its own obstacles to driving, and so oenophiles might consider joining a wine tour. Local tourist offices, especially Siena, have a number of them from which to choose. One wine tour guide in particular is memorable: **Dario Castagno,** who wrote a well-received book called *Too Much Tuscan Sun,* in response to Frances Mayes' bestseller of a similar name. Track him down at **www. dariocastagno.com**.

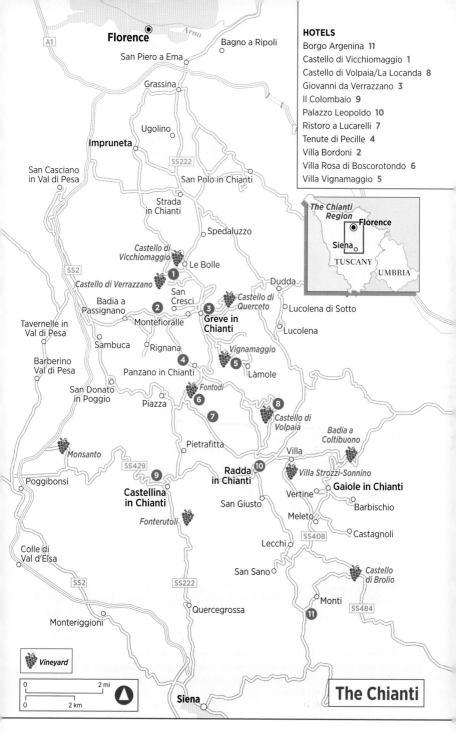

HOTELS

Borgo Argenina **11**
Castello di Vicchiomaggio **1**
Castello di Volpaia/La Locanda **8**
Giovanni da Verrazzano **3**
Il Colombaio **9**
Palazzo Leopoldo **10**
Ristoro a Lucarelli **7**
Tenute di Pecille **4**
Villa Bordoni **2**
Villa Rosa di Boscorotondo **6**
Villa Vignamaggio **5**

Florence

Arno

Bagno a Ripoli

San Piero a Ema

Grassina

Ugolino

Impruneta

San Casciano
in Val di Pesa

San Polo in Chianti

Strada
in Chianti

Spedaluzzo

The Chianti Region

Florence

Siena

TUSCANY

UMBRIA

Castello di Vicchiomaggio

Le Bolle

❶

Castello di Verrazzano

San
Cresci

Dudda

Badia a
Passignano

❷

Montefioralle

❸

Castello di Querceto

Greve in Chianti

Lucolena di Sotto

Tavernelle in
Val di Pesa

Sambuca

Rignana

Vignamaggio

Lucolena

❹

❺

Barberino
Val di Pesa

Panzano in Chianti

Làmole

San Donato
in Poggio

Fontodi

Piazza

❻

❽

❼

*Castello di
Volpaia*

*Badia a
Coltibuono*

Pietrafitta

Villa

Monsanto

SS429

❾

Villa Strozzi-Sonnino

Poggibonsi

**Radda
in Chianti**

❿

Gaiole in Chianti

**Castellina
in Chianti**

Vertine

Barbischio

San Giusto

Meleto

Fonterutoli

Castagnoli

Lecchi

SS408

Colle di
Val d'Elsa

San Sano

*Castello
di Brolio*

SS2

SS222

Quercegrossa

Monti

⓫

SS484

Monteriggioni

🍇 *Vineyard*

0 ——— 2 mi
0 ——— 2 km

Siena

The Chianti

On the other hand, **biking** through the Chianti can be one of Tuscany's most rewarding and scenic workouts. See "Special-Interest Trips," in chapter 2, for tour companies, or go on your own by renting a bike in central Greve at **Ramuzzi,** Via Italo Stecchi 23 (© **055-853-037;** www.ramuzzi. com); the cost is 20€ per day for a road bike or mountain bike, and 55€ a day for a scooter. (There are discounts for multiple days.) The region's low mountains and stands of ancient forest are also excellent for **hiking.** For exploring by any means, you'll need an appropriate **map,** available in book and souvenir stores in the Chianti, Siena, and Florence. The free maps distributed by tourist offices aren't sufficient for veering far off the beaten path.

You can visit the major towns by **bus,** but be prepared to stay awhile until the next ride comes along. **SITA** (© **055-214-721;** www.sitabus. it) from Florence services Strada (40 min. from Florence), Greve (1 hr.), Panzano (65–80 min.), Radda or Castellina (95 min.), and Gaiole (2 hr.); it leaves approximately hourly for stops up through Greve and Panzano and between one to three times a day all the way to Gaiole. Monday through Saturday, different lines of **TRA-IN** buses (© **0577-204-111;** www.train-spa.it) from Siena hit Radda (55 min. from Siena), Gaiole (50 min.–1 hr.), and Castellina (35 min.).

VISITOR INFORMATION You can pick up some information on the Chianti at the **Florence tourist office** (see "Essentials," in chapter 4, for details) or the **Siena tourist office** (see "Siena," later in this chapter). The unofficial capital of the area is Greve in Chianti, and its **tourist office** (© **055-854-6299**), on the main square at Piazza Matteotti 11, makes an effort to provide some Chianti-wide info. From Easter to October, it's open daily from 10am to 1pm and 2 to 7pm, although out of season you may find that the place is closed. You can also try **www.chianti.it,** or **www.chiantinet.it** for more information on the region.

WINE FESTIVALS The second weekend in September, Greve in Chianti hosts the annual **Rassegna del Chianti Classico,** a bacchanalian festival of food and dancing that showcases wine from all the region's producers. **Radda** sponsors its own wine festival, **Radda nel Bicchiere** in early June, where buying the commemorative glass lets you sample 50 to 60 wines for free.

The Florentine Chianti: En Route to Greve

From Florence, follow the signs from Piazza Ferrucci on the Arno's south side toward Grassina and the SS222, the "Chiantigiana." At **Ponte a Ema,** take a 1km (⅔-mile) detour to the left, following the brown road signs to the **Oratorio di Santa Caterina dell'Antella,** which has a wall fresco cycle of the *Life of St. Catherine of Alexandria* (1390) by Spinello Aretino. The apse frescoes are also of St. Catherine and were painted by the "Master of Barberino" around 1360. *Note:* It closes over lunchtimes most days.

At the bend in the road called Le Bolle beyond Strada is a right turnoff for the **Castello di Vicchiomaggio** ★ (© **055-854-079;** www.vicchiomaggio.it). This A.D. 957 Lombard fortress was modified in the 15th century and is today one of the best preserved of the typical Chianti castles. Its estate produces well-regarded wines, including Ripa delle More, a sangiovese/cabernet sauvignon. You can taste for free at the roadside Cantinetta San Jacopo wine shop (on the SS222 right at the turnoff for the castle) daily from 10am to 6pm. One-hour tours of the cellars, parts of which date to the 10th century, depart at 11:30am and 4:30pm daily between March and October, costing 8€ per person. Booking is essential. They also offer cooking courses (anywhere from 1–2 hr. to several days) and rent rooms (see "Where to Stay in the Florentine Chianti," below).

A bit farther along on the right is the turnoff for the **Castello di Verrazzano** ★★ (✆ **055-854-243** or 055-290-684; www.verrazzano.com), the 12th-century seat of the Verrazzano family. Young Giovanni Verrazzano, born here in 1485, sailed out of the Chianti to discover New York. The estate has been making wine at least since 1170, and you can sample it daily from 10am to 1pm and 2 to 7pm at the roadside shop; tasting is free. Their "jewel" is a 100% sangiovese called Sasello, while the "Bottiglia Particolare" ("Particular [Special] Bottle") is in the Supertuscan style, at 70% sangiovese and 30% cab. Four daily tours of the gardens and cellars run Monday through Friday starting at 10am (last one goes at 3pm); book ahead at least a day in advance, a week or more in advance in high season. Each is different, and prices range from 14€ for a tour and tasting of three wines to 48€ for a tour, wine tasting, and a four-course lunch (you'll get a few more wines, too) and 85€ to 110€ depending on group size to include transportation to and from Florence. Booking is essential for all tours.

Greve in Chianti

Throughout the Middle Ages, the Chianti princelings and their heavily fortified castles ruled the patchwork of fiefdoms that made up this area. As alliances sweetened castle-to-castle relations in the later Middle Ages, trade began flowing. Valley crossroads became market towns, and one such town began growing along the tiny river Greve in the 13th or 14th century. As trade became increasingly important, so did that market town. Today, as **Greve in Chianti** ★, the oversize village is the center of the wine trade and the unofficial capital of Chianti.

The central **Piazza Matteotti** is a rough triangle surrounded by a mismatched patchwork arcade—each merchant had to build the stretch in front of his own shop. The statue in the center is of the intrepid explorer **Giovanni Verrazzano** (for whom the bridge in New York is named), and the narrow end of the piazza spills into the tiny **Piazzetta Santa Croce,** whose pretty little church houses an *Annunciation* by Bicci di Lorenzo and a 13th-century triptych.

Greve is the host of Chianti's annual September wine fair, and there are, naturally, dozens of wine shops in town. The best is the **Enoteca del Chianti Classico,** Piazzetta Santa Croce 8 (✆ **055-853-297**). At Piazza Matteotti 69–71 is one of Italy's most famous butchers, **Macelleria Falorni** (✆ **055-854-363;** www.falorni.it), established in 1700 and still containing a cornucopia of hanging prosciutti and hundreds of other cured meats, along with a decent wine selection. It's open daily. For **visitor information,** see the beginning of this chapter.

Near Greve

One kilometer (⅔ mile) west of (and almost as high above) Greve perches the solid stone 14th-century medieval hamlet of **(Castello di) Montefioralle** ★, where the circular main street and enticing alleyways have only a few electric cables to remind you you're still in the 21st century.

The road beyond Montefioralle continues over several miles of winding, often potholed dirt roads to the **Badia a Passignano** ★, dramatically situated

Badia a Passignano.

amid a cypress grove atop its vineyards and olive groves. The monastery was established in 1049 by Benedictine St. Giovanni Gualberto, who founded the Vallombrosan order. Gualberto died here in 1073 and is buried in what was originally the small Romanesque church of San Michele. The church is usually the meeting spot for tours of the rest of the monastery, but restoration work has closed it through 2012 at least; thereafter call ✆ 055-807-1622 for information. The tour's highlight is the Ghirlandaio brothers' (Davide and Domenico) fresco of the *Last Supper* (1476) in the refectory. The Antinori family now runs the small burg and the **Osteria di Passignano** ★ (✆ 055-807-1278; www.osteria dipassignano.com) out of the monks' old wine cellars, where refined Tuscan primi cost 15€ and secondi 28€. Booking is recommended; it's closed Sunday.

South of Greve, the SS222 takes you past the left turn for Lamole. Along that road you'll find **Villa Vignamaggio** ★★ (✆ 055-854-661; www.vignamaggio. com), a russet-orange villa surrounded by cypress and elegant gardens that might seem suspiciously similar to Signor Leonato's home in the 1993 movie *Much Ado About Nothing*. Kenneth Branagh's choice of movie sets wasn't the first time this 14th- or 15th-century villa garnered fame: Lisa Gherardini, who grew up to pose for Leonardo da Vinci's *Mona Lisa,* was born here in 1479. The estate's wine was famous in the past and in 1404 became the first red wine of these hills to be referred to as "chianti" in written record. Long derelict in reputation, Vignamaggio wines have been stunningly revived in recent years, becoming one of the top local vineyards. Book ahead at least a week in advance and you can tour the cellar and ornate gardens and sample the wines; the tasting tour with simple snacks costs 25€, with lunch priced at 50€, and with dinner priced at 58€. They also rent rooms (see "Where to Stay in the Florentine Chianti," below).

The Chiantigiana next cuts through the town of **Panzano in Chianti** ★. The town is known for its embroidery and for another famed butcher, **Antica Macelleria Cecchini** ★, Via XX Luglio 11 (✆ 055-852-020), where Dario Cecchini loves to entertain visitors with classical music and tastes of his products, while he recites the entirety of Dante's *Inferno* from memory. (A local character,

Dario has been featured on more than one TV program in Italy.) There's clearly something in Panzano's water supply, because the proprietor of the Old Town's exceptional enoteca (wine cellar), **Accademia del Buon Gusto** ★, Piazza Ricasoli 11 (✆ **055-856-0159;** www.accademiadelbuongusto.com), is also something of a philosopher. An hour with Stefano Salvadori provides a unique wine education, and a particular insight into the smaller Chianti estates—which produce tiny quantities "for love, not money." Tasting is "without obligation," but we guarantee you'll end up buying something special.

Just south of town is the turnoff for the Romanesque **Pieve di San Leolino.** Beyond the 16th-century portico, this simple, atmospheric church conserves several 14th- and 15th-century Sienese altarpieces, plus on the left aisle a *Madonna with Sts. Peter and Paul* (1260–80), attributed to Meliore di Jacopo. The SS222 continues south toward Castellina (see "The Sienese Chianti: Castellina & the Road to Siena," below).

Where to Stay in the Florentine Chianti

If you really need to stay in a town—for transport links, for example— the **Giovanni da Verrazzano,** Piazza Matteotti 28, 50022 Greve in Chianti (www.ristoranteverrazzano.it; ✆ **055-853-189**), hotel-restaurant sits across from its namesake's statue on Greve's triangular piazza. Rooms are on the smallish side, but are pleasantly decorated in a simple Tuscan style. Those on the front overlook the piazza, while the back rooms have terraces with late-morning sun and a view over lichen-spotted roof tiles to the Chianti hills. Prices range from 90€ to 105€ for a double.

EXPENSIVE

Tenute di Pecille ★★ 🎒 The Conca d'Oro, or "Golden Shell," is one of the Chianti's most scenic stretches, and precisely one rental property has a prime perch amid the vines surveying it all. The magnificent stone *casa colonica* known as Villa Pecille has been converted into five spacious apartments, decorated in a traditional Tuscan style with terra-cotta floors, antique furniture, high ceilings, and firm beds. The largest unit, four-bedroom La Loggia, comes with its own mezzanine terrace that catches the morning sun. A cook and a driver are available on request, and there's also a free tour of Fontodi winery offered to all guests. Nearby Villa La Rota and Villa I Canonici have also been converted to guest accommodations. All this, of course, comes at a price, but everything here is done to a high spec, and the location is unbeatable.

50022 Panzano in Chianti (FI). www.tenutedipecille.com. ✆/fax **055-852-805.** 10 units (in 3 sites). 160€–490€ apartment. MC, V. Free parking. **Amenities:** Babysitting; bikes; cooking classes; outdoor pool; smoke-free rooms. *In apartments:* TV, CD player, hair dryer, kitchen, MP3 docking station, Wi-Fi (free).

Villa Bordoni ★★★ Our favorite luxury hotel along the Chianti Road is this restored wisteria-smothered inn and restaurant, marooned in the vines west of Greve and run by two Scottish expats. A stay in one of its rustic, chic bedrooms and a gourmet dinner at its intimate restaurant is one of the highlights of the wine country. Originally a 16th-century villa with an olive mill and chapel, today this vineyard-ringed hotel evokes an English country house with beautifully furnished bedrooms, filled with original Italian antiques and beamed ceilings.

Via San Cresci, 31–32 Loc. Mezzuola, 50022 Greve in Chianti (FI). www.villabordoni.com. ✆ **055-854-6230.** Fax 055-851-9114. 11 units. 170€–310€ double; 260€–340€ junior suite. Rates include breakfast. AE, MC, V. Free parking. Closed Jan–Feb. **Amenities:** Restaurant (daily mid-Apr to Oct, closed Mon otherwise); bar; babysitting; bikes (free); concierge; cooking classes; outdoor pool (Apr–Oct); smoke-free rooms. *In room:* A/C, TV/DVD, hair dryer, minibar, MP3 docking station (in suites), Wi-Fi (free).

MODERATE

Castello di Vicchiomaggio ★★ This fine wine estate (see "The Florentine Chianti: En Route to Greve," above) has always had a few recommendable apartments, but the conversion in 2007 of the old priest's house into 10 bed-and-breakfast units upped the quality ante considerably. Quarters each comprise two large (for Tuscany) rooms with cool tile floors, decorated in antique creams for a clean, modern take on country styling. The sitting area can be converted to sleep one child or adult; two units have small outdoor spaces. The outdoor pool is terraced into the hill with sensational views over the vineyards, and the tiny adjacent chapel hosts occasional recitals in summer.

Via Vicchiomaggio 4, 50022 Greve in Chianti (FI). www.vicchiomaggio.it. ☏ **055-854-079.** Fax 055-853-911. 16 units (10 rooms and 6 apartments). 120€–158€ double; apartments from 118€ per night. Rates include breakfast (rooms only). AE, MC, V. Free parking. **Amenities:** Restaurant (lunch daily; dinner 3 days/week.); babysitting; outdoor pool (June–Sept); smoke-free rooms. *In room:* A/C (rooms only), TV, hair dryer, Wi-Fi (free; rooms only).

Villa Rosa di Boscorotondo ★ 🍴 This hotel offers countryside seclusion at modest prices—a rarity in the Chianti for a place retaining its original features and roominess yet modernized with an elegance that lends it a rustic air. The curtained beds on wrought-iron frames rest under beamed ceilings, and rooms along the front open onto two terraces with views of the small valley in which the villa nestles. There are a series of small drawing rooms, a pool with a view, and a path that leads through the vineyards all the way to San Leolino church above Panzano.

Via San Leolino 59 (by SS222 btw. Panzano and Radda), 50022 Loc. Panzano in Chianti (FI). www.resortvillarosa.it. ☏ **055-852-577.** Fax 055-856-0835. 14 units. 80€–130€ double; 100€–120€ triple. Rates include breakfast. AE, MC, V. Free parking. Closed mid-Nov to Easter. **Amenities:** Restaurant; bar; babysitting; concierge; outdoor pool; room service; smoke-free rooms; Wi-Fi (free). *In room:* A/C (some), TV, hair dryer (on request), minibar.

Villa Vignamaggio ★ You can't actually stay in the room where Mona Lisa grew up, but you can certainly make do with the apartments and suites here, many with a tiny kitchenette and complimentary bottle of the estate's award-winning chianti. This is one of the most hotel-like *agriturismi* in the area, offering amenities such as daily maid service. The heavy wood-beam ceilings and the comfortable rustic furnishings mesh well with the contemporary designer lights and cast-iron bed frames; five units even have Jacuzzi tubs and air-conditioning. You can stay in one of several suites in the villa, rent the small cottage next door, or shack out in a suite in one of the old stone peasant houses dotting the property on either side of the road.

Villa Vignamaggio (5km/3 miles southeast of Greve), 50022 Greve in Chianti (FI). www. vignamaggio.com. ☏ **055-854-661.** Fax 055-854-4468. 26 units (14 apts, 12 rooms). 150€ double; 200€–275€ apt. Minimum 2-night stay; 10% discount for stays of a week or longer. DC, MC, V. Free parking. Closed mid-Dec to mid-Mar. Turn off the SS222 just south of Greve onto the Lamole road, then follow the signs. **Amenities:** Restaurant (closed Tues and Sun); babysitting; bikes (free); children's playground; concierge; small exercise room; 2 outdoor pools (1 heated); outdoor tennis court; Wi-Fi (free). *In room:* A/C, TV, hair dryer, kitchenette in apts, minibar.

Where to Eat in the Florentine Chianti

Also in Greve, the **Enoteca Bar Gallo Nero,** Via C. Battisti 9 (*©* **055-853-734**), is a good grill and pasta joint (order the *affettati misti* appetizer) popular with families—and reasonably priced at 8€ to 12€ for primi, 8€ to 20€ for secondi. It's open Friday through Wednesday from noon to 10pm (closed Jan 6–31).

La Cantinetta di Rignana ★★ TUSCAN A medieval ramble of stone houses at the end of a long dirt road hides La Cantinetta, one of the Chianti's most refined countryside trattorie. The outdoor tables take in a sweeping view, while inside, a congregation of reproduction Madonna and Child icons on one wall stare down. The staff is given to warbling snatches of folk songs and opera as they prepare handmade pasta (ravioli, gnocchi, or tagliolini) with your pick of rich sauces—the thick, pasty noci (nut) sauce is excellent. In season, be sure to start with the artichokes from their garden, soaked all day outside and then served roasted with olive oil. Grilled meats top the main courses (try the pheasant if it's on), and the tagliata with sea salt and balsamic is excellent. The white-chocolate mousse is legendary.

Loc. Rignana, Greve in Chianti. *©* **055-852-601.** www.lacantinettadirignana.it. Reservations strongly recommended. Primi 8€–12€; secondi 9€–18€. AE, DC, MC, V. Wed–Mon (daily in summer) noon–3:30pm and 6:30–11pm.

Nerbone di Greve ★ FLORENTINE/TUSCAN You don't expect traditional cuisine served right on the piazza of a busy wine and tourism town to taste this good—but then, this is the Chianti outpost of Nerbone, the legendary lunch joint in Florence's Mercato Centrale. The stripped brick vault decorated with simple wooden furniture is surprisingly stylish. The menu cleaves to the ultra-traditional, kicking off with pasta staples and *crostini* topped with pork cheek (*guancia*). Nerbone's real strength, however, is its meat secondi: steak tartare is constructed at your table, to taste; *arista di maiale con mele* (sliced pork with rosemary and a caramelized apple) is overflowing with succulent flavor; and of course, there's a proper Florentine selection of offal, such as *collo ripieno* (stuffed chicken neck) and *lingua bollita* (boiled ox tongue). It's Tuscan fare done properly.

Piazza Matteotti 22, Greve in Chianti. *©* **055-853-308.** www.nerbonedigreve.it. Reservations recommended. Primi 8€–9€; secondi 12€–16€. MC, V. Wed–Mon 11:30am–3:30pm and 7:30–10:30pm.

Oltre Il Giardino ★ TUSCAN Here you can dine on the terrace in warm weather or ensconce yourself in the intimate second-floor dining room, lit by table candles and a fireplace, with great Chianti-side views (so long as you don't look straight down from the window, where Panzano's mini-sprawl festers). The monthly menu usually includes primi like *tagliatelle al ragù di anatra* (they don't skimp on the duck) and *maltagliati ai carciofi* (sheets of fresh-cut pasta with artichoke hearts, tomatoes, celery, and carrots). The meat that goes into the excellent *stracotto al chianti* (beef strewed in chianti wine and served with sautéed spinach) and *maiale al senape* (suckling pig with mustard and pearl onions) comes from neighbor and famed "poet butcher" Dario Cecchini.

Piazza G. Bucciarelli 42, Panzano in Chianti. *©* **055-852-828.** www.ristoranteoltreilgiardino.com. Reservations recommended. Primi 8€; secondi 12€–13€. DC, MC, V. Tues–Sun noon–2:30pm and 7–10pm. Closed some evenings in winter and all Nov.

DINING WITH dario

Panzano's famous opera-singing butcher, Dario Cecchini, brings his own meat, love of conviviality (large, shared tables are a feature), and Dantesque sense of humor to three celebrated (m-)eateries in the village—any of which is worth the trip here on its own. **Solociccia** ★★ opened in 2007 right across from his butcher shop, at Via XX Luglio 11. As the name ("only flesh") suggests, this is not a place for vegetarians: Among the six meat courses, look out for *ramarino in culo,* "rosemary up the you-know-what," which are little peach-shaped balls of tartare impaled with a sprig of rosemary. The menu is fixed (30€) and sitting times are 7 and 9pm Thursday through Saturday and 1pm Sunday.

Above the shop itself, the **Officina della Bistecca** ★ is Dario's multicourse homage to all-things-cow, including the sacred *bistecca alla Fiorentina,* of course. The fixed menu costs 50€, including house wine, and sittings are Tuesday, Friday, and Saturday at 8pm and Sunday at 1pm. The same space at lunchtimes Monday through Saturday hosts **Dario+** ★★, offering fast food, Tuscan style. For 10€, McDonald's-starved children (and adults) can feast on a fresh, breadcrumbed beef burger, oven-cooked "fries," sides of pickles and shredded red onion, and two great relishes. The atmosphere is communal and fun, but the quality of the food is as serious as his two "grown-up" restaurants. For information and to reserve (advisable at Solociccia and the Officina), call ✆ **055-852-727** (for Soliciccia) or ✆ **055-852-176** (for the Officina), or see www.dariocecchini.com.

The Sienese Chianti: Castellina & the Road to Siena

An Etruscan center later fortified by the Florentines as an outpost against rival Siena, **Castellina in Chianti** ★ is one of the more medieval-feeling hill towns of the region and a triumvirate member of the old Lega del Chianti. The **tourist office,** at Via Ferruccio 40 (✆**0577-741-392**), is open Monday through Saturday 9am to 1pm and each of those afternoons except Wednesday 2 to 6pm. Castellina's medieval walls survive almost intact, and central Piazza del Comune is dominated by the imposing crenellated **Rocca** fortress, which now houses the **Museo Archeologico del Chianti Senese** (✆**0577-742-090;** www.museoarcheologicochianti.it). Inside is a modest collection of finds from nearby Etruscan tombs and displays on Etruscan wine culture, as well as access to the Torre (tower) for views over the surrounding woods and winelands. Admission costs 5€ adults, 3€ for children 7 to 14, students, and seniors 65 and over; it's open 11am to 7pm daily April through October and 11am to 5pm on weekends only November to March. The nearby **Via delle Volte** is an evocative tunnel street with open windows facing out to the valley—it's a soldiers' walk from the town's days as a Florentine bastion. You can taste a few drops of *vino* at **La Castellina**'s enoteca in the ground floor of the family *palazzo* at Via Ferruccio 26 (✆**0577-740-454**). The **Bottega del Vino,** Via della Rocca 13 (✆**0577-741-110;** www.enobottega.it), is another good wine outlet. Castellina's gelateria, **L'Antica Delizia** ★, Via Fiorentina 4 (by the SS222; ✆**0577-741-337;** www.anticadelizia.it), sells the best ice cream within a day's cycle in any direction. It's closed Tuesday.

Just outside town (follow signs marked *tombe etrusche* on the SS222 just north of the Castellina junction) is a 6th-century-B.C. Etruscan tomb, the **Ipogeo Etrusco di Montecalvario** ★. It's a perfect example of its type, a little green beanie of a hill surrounded by pines, topped with a pair of cypress, and slashed with stone-walled tunnels leading to the burial chambers beneath. You're free to wander.

From Castellina, you can take a long but rewarding detour on the road toward Poggibonsi into the Val d'Elsa to visit the vineyards of **Monsanto** ★★ (✆ **055-805-9000;** www.castellodimonsanto.it), which produces one of our favorite chianti wines. (Their Classico Riserva 1995 is among the best we've ever tasted.) At this medieval estate, Dr. Laura Bianchi carries on her father Fabrizio's iconoclastic oenological traditions—after buying Monsanto in 1961, he was among the first to produce a 100% sangiovese chianti, and using only *sangiovese grosso* grapes at that. (Because this was illegal back in 1974, they still listed all the unused grapes on the labels.) Aside from an exquisite "chardonnay" (aged half in steel and half in wood, so that its fruitiness isn't overpowered with oak but still has its body and longevity), they use native grapes as much as possible. The result is a suite of remarkable and singular wines. They do tastings and direct sales Monday through Friday from 9am to 5pm (until 6pm in summer); or, reserve a 1-hour tasting tour of the cellars for 18€ per person a few days in advance, which you can extend with outstanding vintages and add a plate of local salami and cheese to accompany the wine for 35€ a head. Visits don't run in December or January.

If you're tired of these wine-sodden hills, you can shoot down the Chiantigiana from here to Siena, an 18km (11-mile) trip. It takes you past the medieval hamlet of **Fonterutoli** ★ (✆ **0577-741-385;** www.fonterutoli.com), a working *borgo* (village) that has been supporting the winemaking business of the Mazzei Marquis since 1435. Fonterutoli produces some of the most highly regarded wines in the

The wine village of Fonterutoli, in the Sienese Chianti.

region, including an excellent Chianti Classico and Chianti Classico Riserva, Supertuscans Siepi and Brancaia (the latter a sangiovese and merlot cru), and the superb fruity IGT Badiola, a sangiovese wine (with 3% each of merlot and cabernet) that's among Tuscany's best 10€ bottles. The roadside enoteca is open Monday to Saturday 10am to 7pm and Sunday 10am to 1pm and 3 to 7pm.

The road continues on to Siena, passing through **Quercegrossa,** the birthplace of Siena's great sculptor Jacopo della Quercia.

Radda in Chianti & Environs

Radda in Chianti ★, one of the three players in the original Lega del Chianti and still an important wine center, retains its medieval street plan and a bit of its walls. The center of town is the 15th-century **Palazzo del Podestà,** studded with the mayoral coats of arms of past *podestà;* there's an information board explaining who's who outside **San Niccolò** opposite. Radda's **tourist office,** Piazza del Castello (✆ **0577-738-494**), is open Monday to Saturday 10:30am to 12:30pm and 3:15 to 6pm between November and Easter; in high season, hours are slightly longer and it's open Sunday morning. The local butcher here is a true artisan; **Porciatti** will give you a taste of traditional salami and cheeses at their *alimentari* on Piazza IV Novembre 1 at the gate into town (✆ **0577-738-055;** www.casaporciatti.it). They also sell local products, from wines to pasta.

Seven kilometers (4⅓ miles) north of Radda on a secondary road is the **Castello di Volpaia** ★★ (✆ **0577-738-066;** www.volpaia.com), a first-rank wine estate with a medieval stone heart. The castle here was a Florentine holding buffeted by Sienese attacks and sieges from the 10th to 16th centuries. The still-impressive central keep is all that remains, but it's surrounded by an evocative 13th-century *borgo* (village) containing the Renaissance La Commenda church. You can tour the winery daily at 11am and 3pm—installed in a series of buildings throughout the little village (with an eye to preserving its medieval visual charm; there is nonetheless high-tech plumbing, through which the wine flows, buried seamlessly inside the stone walls)—for 16€ per person; the tour includes a tasting of the wines and their fantastic olive oil. Call ahead, preferably a week in advance. The central tower has an enoteca (daily 10am–1pm and 4–7pm) for drop-in tastings (5€ for three wines) and direct sales of some of the wines that helped found the Chianti Consorzio in 1924, plus award-winning (and scrumptious) olive oils and farm-produced white and red vinegars. They also rent accommodations (see "Where to Stay in the Sienese Chianti," below).

Beside a side-road to just east of Radda, you'll see the workshop and showroom of **Ceramiche Rampini** ★★, Casa Beretone di Vistarenni (✆ **0577-738-043;** www.rampiniceramics.com). The artisan family originates in Gubbio, in Umbria, and here create spectacular hand-painted ceramics based on antique Florentine motifs or inspired by the Renaissance art of Venetian painter Arcimboldo.

From Radda, an 8km (5-mile) eastward trip brings you to the beautifully isolated **Badia a Coltibuono** ★ (✆ **0577-74-481;** www.coltibuono.com). The abbey's core was founded in A.D. 770, but the monastery was owned and expanded by the Vallombrosan Order from the 12th century to 1810, when the Napoleonic suppressions passed it into private hands and it became an agricultural estate. You can visit the 11th-century San Lorenzo church, but the rest is via a 45-minute guided tour only (afternoons only May–Oct; 5€). The wine estate is owned by the Stucchi-Prinetti family; Chianti Classico comes in a light style here, but the Riserva is a mouth-filling delight. The family's most famous member, international cookbook maven Lorenza de' Medici, started a famed (and egregiously overpriced) culinary school here in summers, though it's now run by an acolyte (see "Special-Interest Trips," in chapter 2, for details), and her son, Paolo, runs the acclaimed on-site **Ristorante Badia a Coltibuono** (✆ **0577-749-424;** closed Nov–Feb; primi around 10€, secondi 18€). There's a direct-sales office for their products called the **Osteria** (✆ **0577-749-479**) down at the main road. March through December, it's open daily 10am to 7pm. Tasting is free, but in the friendly proprietor's words, "It's not a bar!"

To Gaiole & Beyond

Heading south directly from Badia a Coltibuono on the SS408 will take you through **Gaiole in Chianti,** the third member of the Lega del Chianti. The tourist office is beside the main road, at Via Galileo Galilei 1 (✆ **0577-749-411;** www.chiantistorico.com; daily in season 10am–1pm and 3–6pm). An ancient market town like Greve, Gaiole is now basically modernized without much to see, aside from the wine shops: the **Cantina Enoteca Montagnani,** Via B. Bandinelli 13–17 (✆ **0577-749-517**), and **La Cantinetta del Chianti,** Via Ricasoli 33 (✆ **0577-749-125;** www.lacantinettadelchianti.it).

A side road here leads west past the 12th-century Castello di Spaltenna (now a hotel) 3km (1¾ miles) to the 13th-century **Castello di Vertine,** an imposing castle surrounded by a 9th-century village.

East of Gaiole, an unfinished road winds up to the fortified medieval hamlet of **Barbischio.** For more castle viewing, head south of Gaiole to the turnoff for Meleto and Castagnoli. **Castello di Meleto**'s twin circular towers stand mighty at either expanse of a long blank wall to watch over the estate's vineyards. The poor castle-cum-villa was built in the 1100s, partially dismantled by the Sienese in the 15th century, rebuilt by the Florentines, and then smashed by the Sienese again in the 16th century before a 1700s restoration transformed it into the villa we see today.

Farther south of Gaiole, the SS484 branches east toward Castelnuovo Berardenga and the famous **Castello di Brolio ★★** (✆ **0577-749-066;** www.ricasoli.it). The Chianti as a region may date to the 1200s, but Chianti Classico as a wine was born here in the mid–19th century. The Brolio castle has been in the Ricasoli family since 1141, though its vineyards date from at least 1007; the current fortress was rebuilt in 1484. "Iron Baron" Bettino Ricasoli inherited it in 1829 at age 20 and, before he went off in 1848 to help found a unified Italy and become its second prime minister, spent his days here, teaching—really dictating—scientific farming methods to his workers. He also whiled away the time tinkering with grape varietals. By the mid–19th century, he'd arrived at a quaffable formula balancing sangiovese, canaiolo, trebbiano, and malvasia grapes that was used when Italy's wine-governing DOC and DOCG laws were written in the 1960s. You can visit the castle grounds, including the small chapel (Bettino rests in peace in the family crypt) and the gardens, and walk along the wall for a good view of the lower Chianti valleys. Admission is 5€, and includes a taste of the estate wine on departure. Between March and November, the gardens are open daily 10am to 6pm, or dusk if it falls earlier.

After years of being passed from larger to larger corporate ownership, Brolio declined as a winery; then in 1993 the Baron Francesco Ricasoli brought it back into the family. He effected a drastic turnaround, investing, replanting vines, and rigorously revising the philosophy to rocket Brolio back to respect on the Italian wine scene, winning acclaim and awards once again. They now produce several wines, including the newest—a single Castello di Brolio, 100% sangiovese Chianti Classico. They're going for the French châteaux concept, where the wine is associated with a place, not a brand. To buy their award-winning wines, visit the wine shop (℡ 0577-730-220) between April and October from Monday to Friday 9am to 7:30pm, Saturday and Sunday from 11am to 7pm. They offer a range of tours (advance booking obligatory) with a wine tasting at the end.

The westerly byroad out of here leads most quickly to join the SS408 as it heads south, out of the land of the black rooster and into Siena.

Where to Stay in the Sienese Chianti

Besides the choices below, the medieval **Castello di Volpaia** (www.volpaia.com; ℡ 0577-738-066), recommended above for its wine, rents out apartments with kitchenettes and TVs and, in a few, working fireplaces in the stony buildings of its 13th-century village for 95€ to 150€ per night for two people (plus a sofa bed for children if required), or 180€ to 340€ per night for one that sleeps seven. Guests can take part in various programs, from self-guided hikes to cooking lessons and of course tastings. They also rent lovely villas (sleeping up to 8 or 11) with private gardens and pools with views (Sat–Sat rental only), and lease a *casa colonica* on a nearby hillock amid the estate's vineyards to a hotelier who operates it as an exquisite rustic-chic hotel, **La Locanda ★** (www.lalocanda.it; ℡ 0577-738-832), with 220€-to-290€ double rooms. To stay in Radda itself, the best lodgings are at the **Palazzo Leopoldo,** Via Roma 33 (www.palazzoleopoldo.it; ℡ 0577-735-605), where the ambience is traditional and the panoramic terrace will knock you out. Doubles range from 119€ to 226€.

Borgo Argenina ★★ From the flagstoned terrace of Elena Nappa's hilltop B&B (she bought the whole medieval hamlet), you can see the farmhouse where Bertolucci filmed *Stealing Beauty* in 1996. Against remarkable odds (she'll regale you with the anecdotes), Elena has created the rural retreat of your dreams. Since the place isn't easy to find, English-speaking Elena will send you directions when you reserve. In addition to four doubles, she offers accommodations in two suites, two small houses (for two or three people), and the Villa Oliviera (for four). When faced with all the questions guests often inundate her with when booking (Do you have air-conditioning? Is there parking? How much of a deposit do I need to make?), Elena replies, "Don't worry. Just come!" Great advice.

Loc. Argenina (near San Marcellino Monti), 53013 Gaiole in Chianti. www.borgoargenina.it. ℡ 0577-747-117. Fax 0577-747-228. 10 units. 170€ double; 200€–240€ suite; 240€–300€ house. 3-night minimum stay. Rates include breakfast. DC, MC, V. Free parking. Closed Nov–Feb. **Amenities:** Restaurant (3 days/week.); smoke-free rooms. *In room:* Hair dryer, minibar, Wi-Fi (free).

Il Colombaio ★ This modest, excellently priced hotel sits in a 16th-century stone house at the edge of Castellina (near the

Etruscan tomb and a 5-min. walk into town) and once housed shepherds who spent the night after selling their sheep at market. The good-size rooms with their sloping beam-and-tile ceilings, terra-cotta floors, and iron bed frames seem to belong to a well-to-do 19th-century farming family. Upstairs accommodations are lighter and airier than the ground-floor rooms (formerly stalls) and enjoy better views over the vineyards (a few overlook the road). You breakfast in winter under stone vaults and in summer on a terrace sharing its countryside vistas with the pool.

Via Chiantigiana 29, 53011 Castellina in Chianti (SI). www.albergoilcolombaio.it. ✆ **0577-740-444.** Fax 0577-740-402. 13 units. 85€–100€ double. Rates include breakfast. AE, MC, V. Free parking. **Amenities:** Babysitting; concierge; outdoor pool (June–Sept); smoke-free rooms. *In room:* TV, hair dryer, minibar, Wi-Fi (free).

Where to Eat in the Sienese Chianti

Albergaccio di Castellina ★★ CONTEMPORARY TUSCAN This renowned place offers an excellent mix of fine cuisine and rustic timbered atmosphere with valley views, and a changing roster of dishes steeped in local traditions but enlivened by the creativity of chef Sonia Visman. Strict seasonality is the key to the cooking here, but among the tasty combinations we've sampled, we heartily recommend the *bavette con timo e pecorino di fossa* (thin noodles with tomatoes, thyme, and aged pecorino cheese) and *gnocchi di ricotta con tartufo marzolo* (dollops of ricotta with shaved truffles and thyme leaves). The *rollé di maiale con cavolo nero* (pork *involtini* made with black cabbage, tomatoes, and wild fennel) and *piccione sfumato al marsala con fichi caramellati* (Marsala-perfumed pigeon with caramelized figs) are fine secondi.

Via Fiorentina 63, Castellina in Chianti (beside the road toward San Donato). ✆ **0577-741-042.** www.albergacciocast.com. Reservations highly recommended. One/two/three/four courses 26€/42€/54€/64€; tasting menus 58€ and 65€. MC, V. Mon–Sat 12:30–2pm and 7:30–9:30pm (lunch only Wed–Thurs). Closed last 2 weeks of Nov and 1st week of Dec; call ahead in winter.

La Bottega TUSCAN The Barucci family takes care of hospitality in Volpaia's main square: Carla runs this cozy tavern with outdoor seating in a garden, and her sister owns the bar across the piazza. The cuisine is simple and honest, with Tuscan classics such as *ribollita* and *pici con ragù* and rabbit with white wine and olives, plus just about anything with wild boar in it. They make their own cold cuts and offer a nice wine list of local labels, all at fair prices.

Piazza della Torre 1, Volpaia. ✆ **0577-738-001.** Primi 7€–9€; secondi 7€–10€. AE, DC, MC, V. Wed–Mon noon–3pm and 7–10pm.

Le Vigne TUSCAN The aptly named Le Vigne is tucked between the rows of vines covering the slopes southeast of Radda. You can watch vintners working the vines as you sip your wine and sample such well-turned dishes as *pici all'aglione* (hand-rolled spaghetti with tomatoes, leeks, and a dab of pancetta), bready *ribollita*, boned duck stuffed with porchetta, and excellent *arrosto misto*, a mixed roast which might include a trio like pigeon, chicken, and pork, served with seasonal vegetables.

Podere Le Vigne (off SS408 to Villa just east of Radda in Chianti). ✆ **0577-738-301.** www. ristorantepoderelevigne.com. Reservations recommended. Primi 6€–10€; secondi 10€–18€. AE, MC, V. Wed–Mon noon–2:30pm and 7:15–9:30pm (daily in summer). Closed Nov 15–Mar 15.

SIENA ★★★

70km (43 miles) S of Florence; 232km (144 miles) N of Rome

Siena is a medieval city of brick. Viewed from the summit of the Palazzo Pubblico's tower, its sea of roof tiles blends into a landscape of steep, twisting stone alleys. This cityscape hides dozens of Gothic palaces and pastry shops galore, unseen neighborhood rivalries, and painted altarpieces of unsurpassed beauty.

Siena is proud of its past. It trumpets the she-wolf as its emblem, a hold-over from its days as *Saena Julia*, the Roman colony founded by Augustus about 2,000 years ago (though the official Sienese myth has the town founded by the sons of Remus, younger brother of Rome's legendary forefather). Siena still parcels out the rhythms of life, its rites of passage and communal responsibilities, to the 17 *contrade* (neighborhood wards) formed in the 14th century. Compared with its old medieval rival, Siena is as inscrutable in its culture, decorous in its art, and festive in its life attitude as Florence is forthright, precise, and serious on all counts. Where Florence produced hard-nosed mystics such as Savonarola, Siena gave forth saintly scholars like St. Catherine (1347–80) and St. Bernardino (1380–1444).

Its bankers, textile magnates, and wool traders put 12th-century Siena in competition with Florence, and the two cities kept at each other's throats for more than 400 years. When Florence went Guelph, Siena turned Ghibelline and thrashed Florence at the 1260 Battle of Montaperti; see "Guelphs & Ghibellines: A Medieval Mess," in chapter 2. Unfortunately for Siena, the battle was fought in alliance with ousted Florentine Ghibellines, who refused to allow the armies to press the advantage and level Florence. Within 10 years, Charles of Anjou had crushed the Sienese Ghibellines.

With Siena now Guelph again, Sienese merchants established in 1270 the Council of Nine, an oligarchy that ruled over Siena's greatest republican era, when civic projects, the middle-class economy, palace building, and artistic prowess reached their greatest heights.

Artists like Duccio, Simone Martini, and the Lorenzetti brothers invented a distinctive Sienese art style, a highly developed Gothicism that was an artistic foil to the emerging Florentine Renaissance (see "Florence, Tuscany & Umbria's Art & Architecture," in chapter 2).

Then, in 1348, the Black Death hit the city, killing perhaps three-quarters of the population, decimating the social fabric, and devastating the economy. The Council of Nine soldiered on, but Charles IV attacked Siena from 1355 to 1369, and although Siena again trounced Florence in 1526, the Spanish took control in 1530 and later handed Siena over to Ducal Florence.

To subdue these pesky Sienese once and for all, Cosimo I sent the brutal marquis of Marignano, who

Piazza del Campo.

besieged the city for a year and a half, destroying its fields and burning its buildings. By the time he stormed the city in 1555, the marquis had done more damage than even the Black Death—only 8,000 out of a population of 40,000 had survived—and the burned and broken city and countryside bore an uncanny resemblance to the *Effects of Bad Government,* half of Ambrogio Lorenzetti's fresco in Siena's Palazzo Pubblico. Some 2,000 fiercely independent Sienese escaped to Montalcino, where they kept the Sienese Republic alive, in name at least, for another 4 years. Then Montalcino, too, was engulfed by Florence. Siena became, on paper and in fact, merely another part of Grand Ducal Tuscany. Since the plague of the 14th century, Siena was so busy defending its liberty it had little time or energy to develop as a city. As a result, it offers your best chance in Tuscany to slip into the rhythms and atmosphere of the Middle Ages.

Essentials

GETTING THERE By Train: The bus is often more convenient, because Siena's rail station is outside town. Some 19 trains daily connect Siena with **Florence** (90 min.), via Empoli. There's also a line to **Chiusi–Chianciano Terme** (75–90 min.) passing through **Asciano** and **Montepulciano** (see chapter 8). Siena's **train station** is at Piazza Roselli, about 3km (1¾ miles) north of town. Take the no. 9 or 10 bus to Piazza Gramsci in Terza di Camollia or a taxi.

By Car: There's a fast highway direct from **Florence** (it has no route number; follow the green signs toward Siena), or take the more scenic route, down the Chiantigiana SS222 (see "The Chianti," earlier in this chapter). From **Rome** get off the A1 north at the Val di Chiana exit and follow the SS326 west for 50km (31 miles). The SS223 runs 70km (43 miles) here from **Grosseto** in the Maremma. From **Pisa** take the highway toward Florence and exit onto the SS429 south just before Empoli (100km/62 miles total). The easiest way into the center is from the *Siena Ovest* highway exit.

Trying to drive into the one-way and pedestrian-zoned center isn't worth the headache. Siena **parking** (✆ **0577-228-711;** www.sienaparcheggi.com) is now coordinated, and lots charge between .50€ and 1.60€ per hour (most at the top end of that scale). Luckily, many hotels have a discount deal with the nearest lot; around 15€ per day is standard. All lots are well signposted, with locations just inside city gates Porta Tufi (the huge and popular Il Campo lot, though it's a 20-min. uphill walk to the Campo!), Porta San Marco, and Porta Romana; under the Fortezza (another large lot) and around La Lizza park (the latter closed market Wed and soccer Sun); and at Piazza Amendola (just outside the northern gate Porta Camollia). You can **park for free** a bit farther away around the unguarded back (northwest) side of the Fortezza all week long. There's also free parking outside the southeast end of town at Due Ponti (beyond Porta Pispini) and Coroncina (beyond Porta Romana); from both you can get a *pollicino* (minibus; 4 per hour) into the center.

By Bus: Because buses from **Florence** are faster and let you off right in town, they're more convenient than trains. **TRA-IN** and **SITA** (www.sitabus.it) codeshare express (*corse rapide;* around 25 daily; 75 min.) and slower buses (*corse ordinarie;* 14 daily; 95 min.) from **Florence**'s SITA station to Siena's Piazza Gramsci. Siena is also connected with **San Gimignano** (at least hourly Mon–Sat; 10 direct, rest change in Poggibonsi; 65–80 min. not

Siena

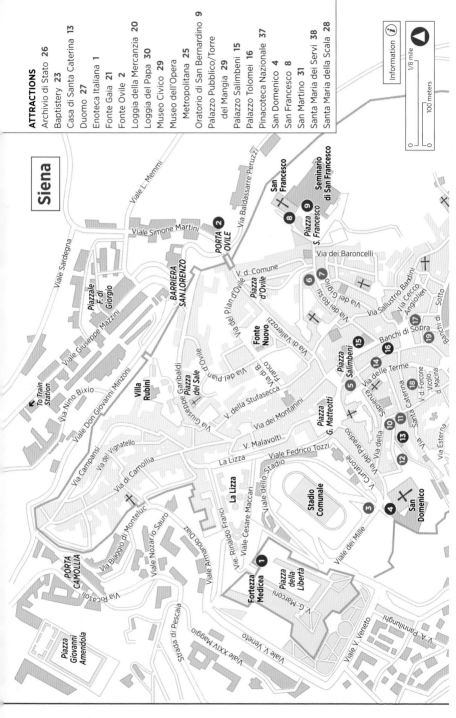

ATTRACTIONS

Archivio di Stato **26**
Baptistery **23**
Casa di Santa Caterina **13**
Duomo **27**
Enoteca Italiana **1**
Fonte Gaia **21**
Fonte Ovile **2**
Loggia della Mercanzia **20**
Loggia del Papa **30**
Museo Civico **29**
Museo dell'Opera Metropolitana **25**
Oratorio di San Bernardino **9**
Palazzo Pubblico/Torre del Mangia **29**
Palazzo Salimbeni **15**
Palazzo Tolomei **16**
Pinacoteca Nazionale **37**
San Domenico **4**
San Francesco **8**
San Martino **31**
Santa Maria dei Servi **38**
Santa Maria della Scala **28**

Information *i*

0 — 1/8 mile
0 — 100 meters

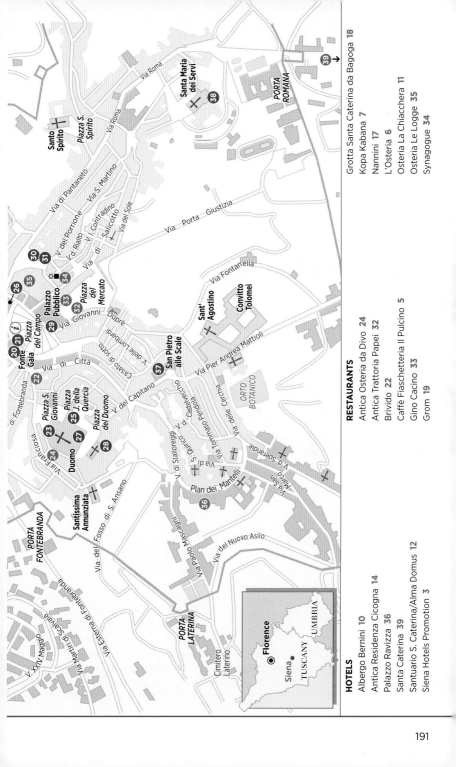

HOTELS

Albergo Bernini **10**
Antica Residenza Cicogna **14**
Palazzo Ravizza **36**
Santa Caterina **39**
Santuario S. Caterina/Alma Domus **12**
Siena Hotels Promotion **3**

RESTAURANTS

Antica Osteria da Divo **24**
Antica Trattoria Papei **32**
Brivido **22**
Caffè Fiaschetteria Il Pulcino **5**
Gino Cacino **33**
Grom **19**

Grotta Santa Caterina da Bagoga **18**
Kopa Kabana **7**
Nannini **17**
L'Osteria **6**
Osteria La Chiacchera **11**
Osteria Le Loge **35**
Synagogue **34**

191

including layover), **Volterra** (four daily; change in Colle di Val d'Elsa; 80 min. plus layover), **Massa Marittima** (two daily; 100 min.), **Perugia** (two to four daily; 90 min.), **Arezzo** (eight daily; 90 min.), and **Rome**'s Tiburtina station (five to nine daily; 3 hr.).

Siena's **TRA-IN bus ticket office** is underneath Piazza Gramsci in the pedonale della Lizza (© 0577-204-246 or 0577-204-225; www.train spa.it), and there's another small office in the city's train station (© 0577-204-328).

CITY LAYOUT Siena is splayed out like a "Y" along three ridges with deep valleys in between, effectively dividing the city into thirds, called *terzi.* The *terzi* are each drawn out along three main streets following the spines of those ridges. The southern arm, **Terzo di San Martino,** slopes gently down around Via Banchi di Sotto (and the various other names it picks up along the way). To the west is **Terzo di Città** (home to the Duomo and Pinacoteca), centered on Via di Città. **Terzo di Camollia** runs north along and beyond Via Banchi di Sopra. These three main streets meet at the north edge of **Piazza del Campo,** Siena's gorgeous scallop-shaped central square.

Tip for the footsore: Each *terzo*'s main ridge-top street is relatively flat—for Siena—while off either side medieval alleyways drop precipitously. If you hate hills, the shortest (or at least less strenuous) distance between two points in Siena isn't a straight line but a curve that follows the three main drags as much as possible.

GETTING AROUND Although it often looks and feels like a small Tuscan hill town, Siena truly is a city (albeit a small one), and its sites are relatively spread apart. There is no efficient public transport system in the center, so it's up to your feet to cover the territory. There are plenty of steep ups and downs and no shortcuts from one *terzo* to another without a serious workout.

The city does run **minibuses,** called *pollicini* (© 0577-204-246; www.sienamobilita.it), which run quarter-hourly (every half-hour Sat afternoon and all day Sun) into the city center from 6:30am to 8:30pm. The B services the Terzo di San Martino and heads out from the Porta Pispini gate. Confusingly, there are four A buses, differentiated by color. *A pink* goes around Terzo di San Martino (and out the Porta Romana gate); *A green* and *A yellow* cover Terzo di Città (green from Porta Tufi to the Duomo, yellow from Porta San Marco to the Duomo); and *A red* serves the southerly part of Terzo di Camollia (from Piazza della Indipendenza out Porta Fontebranda).

You can call for a radio **taxi** at © 0577-49-222 (7am–9pm only); they also queue at the train station and in town at Piazza Matteotti.

VISITOR INFORMATION The **tourist office,** where you can get a useless free map or pay .50€ for a useful one, is at Piazza del Campo 56, 53100 Siena (© 0577-280-551; www.terresiena.it). It's open daily 9am to 7pm.

FESTIVALS & MARKETS Aside from the two annual **Palio races** ★★★ (see "The Palio delle Contrade," later in this chapter), Siena throws a **pottery fair** in honor of the Festa di Santa Lucia on December 13. The prestigious **Accademia Musicale Chigiana** music center, Via di Città 89 (© 0577-22-091; www.chigiana.it), sponsors concerts and opera year-round (the website has a schedule), culminating in the week of the **Settimana Musicale Senese** in July. **St. Cecilia** is celebrated on November 22 with church concerts. The extensive main city **market** is held Wednesday from 8am to 1pm, filling the streets around La Lizza.

Il Campo: The Heart of Siena

Via Banchi di Sopra, Via Banchi di Sotto, and Via di Città all meet at the **Loggia della Mercanzia,** begun from Sano di Matteo's plans in 1417. Here Siena's merchants argued cases before a commercial tribunal so impartial that foreign governments came to have them settle financial differences.

From here, several tunnel-like stepped alleys lead down into **Piazza del Campo (Il Campo)** ★★★, arguably the most beautiful piazza in Italy. Crafted like a sloping scallop shell, the Campo was first laid out in the 1100s on the site of the Roman forum. The herringbone brick pavement is divided by white marble lines into nine sections representing the city's medieval ruling body, the Council of Nine. The Campo's tilt, fan shape, and structure are all a calibrated part of the city's ancient water system and underground canal network. At the top of the Campo is a poor 19th-century replica of Jacopo della Quercia's 14th-century fountain, the **Fonte Gaia** ★★. Some of the restored, but badly eroded original panels are in Santa Maria della Scala (discussed later).

The only surviving medieval buildings on the square are, at the top, the curving facade of the battlemented 13th-century **Palazzo Sansedoni** and at the fan's base, the city's focal point, the **Palazzo Pubblico** ★★ (1297–1310). This crenellated town hall is the city's finest Gothic palace, and the Museo Civico inside is home to Siena's best artworks (see below). When the Black Death finally abated in 1348, the city built a loggia chapel, the **Cappella della Piazza,** at the left end of the *palazzo's* base to give thanks that at least parts of the city had been spared. Rising above it is the slender 100m-tall (328-ft.) brick **Torre del Mangia** ★ (1338–48), crowned with a Lippo Memmi–designed cresting in white travertine. It was the second-tallest tower in medieval Italy and was named after a slothful bell ringer nicknamed *Mangiaguadagni,* or "profit eater." (There's an armless statue of him in the courtyard.)

If you fancy climbing 503 steps and aren't particularly claustrophobic, the tower is a great place to check out the unforgettable view across Siena's cityscape and the rolling countryside beyond. Admission is 8€. The tower (entrance in the courtyard) is open from October 16 through February from 10am to 4pm, otherwise from 10am to 7pm.

Museo Civico ★★★ Don't be put off by the first rooms of mediocre 16th- to 18th-century works; the museum's pride comes later with the masterpieces of Sienese painting giants Simone Martini and Ambrogio Lorenzetti. The fifth room, the **Sala del Risorgimento,** was painted (1887–90) to celebrate the career of Italy's first king, Vittorio Emanuele II.

The **Sala di Balìa** ★ beyond the foot of the stairs was frescoed (1407) by Spinello Aretino and his son Parri, with scenes from the *Life of Pope Alexander III,* including an exceptional naval battle. The **Anticamera del Concistoro** has a detached Ambrogio Lorenzetti fresco on the entrance wall and a Matteo di Giovanni *Madonna and Child.* The **Sala del Concistoro** was frescoed (1529–35) by Domenico Beccafumi in his Mannerist style, illustrating the heroic feats of ancient Greece and Rome in order to give the government authorities who met here a backbone.

The **vestibule** has a 1429 gilded bronze she-wolf, Siena's republican symbol and link to its Roman founding. The *Anticappella* was frescoed by Taddeo di Bartolo with ancient Greek and Roman heroes, along with the *Virtues* and a giant *St. Christopher*. The **Cappella** is difficult to see through Jacopo della Quercia's iron screen, but it was also frescoed by Domenico di Bartolo (1407–08). The altarpiece is a dark *Madonna and Child with Saints* by Sodoma.

The **Sala del Mappamondo** off the chapel—named after a now-lost Ambrogio Lorenzetti painting of the world—contains two of Simone Martini's greatest works. On the left is his masterpiece, **Maestà ★★★**. Incredibly, this was his very first painting, finished in 1315 (he went over it again in 1321). Cleaned and restored in the early 1990s, it's the next generation's answer to Duccio's groundbreaking work on the same theme painted just 4 years earlier and now in the Museo dell'Opera Metropolitana (p. 197). Martini's paintings tend to be characterized by richly patterned fabrics, and the gown of the enthroned Mary is no exception.

Those fabrics can be seen again across this great hall in Simone Martini's other masterwork, the fresco of **Guidoriccio da Fogliano ★★**, where the captain of the Sienese army rides his charger across the territory he has just conquered (Montemassi, in 1328). Recently, iconoclastic U.S. art historians have disputed the attribution of this work to Martini, claiming that it was either a slightly later work or even a 16th-century fake. Part of what sparked the debate was the 1980 discovery of another, slightly older, scarred fresco lower on the wall here. This earlier painting depicts two figures standing in front of a wooden-fenced castle. Some claim this is the fresco Martini painted, while those who support the authenticity of the *Guidoriccio* attribute this older fresco to Duccio, Pietro Lorenzetti, or Memmo di Filippuccio.

The **Sala della Pace** was where the Council of Nine met, and to keep them mindful of how well they needed to govern, the city commissioned Ambrogio Lorenzetti (1338) to fresco the walls with his masterpiece and the single most important piece of secular art to survive from medieval Europe, the **Allegory of Good and Bad Government and Their Effects on the Town and Countryside ★★★**. Good government is represented by a bearded old man surrounded by virtues. The good effects of this government are played out on the entrance wall. A prosperous 14th-century Siena is pictured here—recognizable by its towers, battlemented houses, and the Duomo squeezed into the corner. The painted city wall breaks the scene in half so that the countryside—with its cultivated hillsides watched over by winged Serenity—runs the length of the Sienese territory all the way to their seaport Talamone.

The *Bad Government* frescoes are, perhaps appropriately, in a high state of ruin. Monstrous Tyranny reigns with the help of such henchmen as Cruelty, Fraud, and the creaturelike Deceit. The city under their rule is literally falling into ruin, soldiers must patrol constantly, the shops are abandoned, and citizens

---

Siena's Cumulative Tickets

Siena has a bewildering range of **reduced-price cumulative ticket** combos you can pick up at any of the participating museums or sites. The **Musei Comunali** pass, valid for 2 days, covers civic museums—Museo Civico and Santa Maria della Scala—for 11€. The **S.I.A.**, valid for 7 days and available March 15 through October only, gives you access to those sites plus the Museo dell' Opera Metropolitana, Baptistery, Sant'Agostino, and Museo Diocesano for 17€. In winter months, it's 3€ cheaper, but excludes the last two. The **OPA Pass** costs 10€ and offers entry to the Duomo, Museo dell'Opera Metropolitana, Baptistery, Cripta, and Oratorio di San Bernardino.

are robbed on the streets. The countryside, over which flies Terror, fares as badly, with scorched, lifeless fields and armed highwaymen scaring travelers off the roads. Unfortunately, in the aftermath of the Black Death of 1348, *Bad Government* pretty much came to pass.

Palazzo Pubblico, Piazza del Campo. © **0577-292-226.** Admission on cumulative ticket with Torre del Mangia 13€; or 7.50€ adults with reservation, 8€ adults without reservation; 4€ students and seniors 65 and over with reservation, 3.50€ students and seniors without reservation; free for ages 11 and under. Nov–Mar 15 daily 10am–6pm; Mar 16–Oct daily 10am–7pm. Bus: A (pink) or B.

On Piazza Del Duomo

Baptistery ★ The Duomo's baptistery was built between 1355 and 1382 beneath the cathedral's choir and supports a Gothic facade left unfinished by Domenico di Agostino. The upper walls and vaulted ceilings inside were **frescoed by Vecchietta** and his school in the late 1440s (look for the alligator) but "touched up" in the 19th century. What you're principally here to see, though, is the **baptismal font** ★★ (1417–30). The frames are basically Gothic, but the gilded brass panels were cast by the foremost Sienese and Florentine sculptors of the early Renaissance. Starting on the side facing the altar, Siena's master Jacopo della Quercia did the *Annunciation to Zacharias*. Giovanni di Turino did the next two, the *Birth of the Baptist* and the *Preaching of the Baptist*. The *Baptism of Christ* is by the author of the Baptistery doors in Florence, Lorenzo Ghiberti, who collaborated with Giuliano di Ser Andrea on the *Arrest of St. John*. The final panel is perhaps the greatest, Donatello's masterful early study of precise perspective and profound depth in the *Feast of Herod*.

Piazza San Giovanni (down the stairs around the rear right flank of the Duomo). © **0577-283-048.** Admission on cumulative ticket, or 3€. Mid-June to mid-Sept daily 9:30am–8pm; mid-Sept to Oct and Mar to mid-June daily 9:30am–7pm; Nov–Feb daily 10am–5pm.

Cripta ★ Beneath the cathedral is the latest major artistic discovery in Siena, in a room widely referred to as the "crypt," although no bodies have been found here. In fact, this subterranean room is part of the pre–14th-century Romanesque church. What the 21st-century restoration workers scraped up was a cycle of frescoes painted between 1270 and 1275, shedding some light on the early development of the Sienese school. The crypt has only been viewable since 2004, and scholars have yet to attribute the cycle to a particular artist. Some have speculated it may be the work of Duccio, though he would have been exceedingly young at the time. What is more or less certain is that the style and composition, such as the way Christ's feet are oddly crossed on the crucifix, have been mirrored—almost copied—by later painters. Though chipped and still a little rough around the edges, the vibrant blue, gold, and burgundy colors have been impressively preserved thanks to the lack of light and humidity since the 1300s.

Piazza del Duomo. © **0577-283-048.** Admission on cumulative ticket, or 6€. Mid-June to mid-Sept daily 9:30am–8pm; mid-Sept to Oct and Mar to mid-June daily 9:30am–7pm; Nov–Feb daily 10am–5pm.

Duomo ★★★ Siena's cathedral is a rich treasure house of Tuscan art. Despite being an overwhelmingly Gothic building, the Duomo has one eye-popping Romanesque holdover: its 1313 **campanile** with its black-and-white banding. The Duomo was built from around 1215 to 1263, involving Gothic master Nicola Pisano as architect at some point. His son, Giovanni, drew up the plans for the lower half of the **facade,** begun in 1285. Giovanni Pisano, along with his studio, also carved many of the statues adorning it (most of the originals are now in the Museo dell'Opera Metropolitana; see below). The facade's upper half was added in the 14th century and is today decorated with 19th-century Venetian mosaics.

The city was feeling its oats in 1339. Having defeated Florence 80 years earlier, Siena was by now its rival's equal. It began its most ambitious project yet: to turn the already huge Duomo into merely the transept of a new cathedral, one that would dwarf St. Peter's in Rome and trumpet Siena's political power, spiritual devotion, and artistic prowess. The city started the new nave off the Duomo's right transept but completed only the fabric of the walls when the Black Death hit in 1348, decimating the population and halting building plans forever. The **half-finished walls** remain—a monument to Siena's ambition and one-time wealth.

The interior of Siena's Gothic Duomo.

You could wander inside for hours, just staring at the **flooring ★★★**, a mosaic of 59 etched and inlaid marble panels (1372–1547). The top artists working in Siena lent their talents, including Domenico di Bartolo, Matteo di Giovanni, Pinturicchio, and, especially, Beccafumi, who designed 35 scenes (1517–47)— his original cartoons are in the Pinacoteca. The ones in the nave and aisles are usually uncovered, including the *Sibyls,* mythical Greek prophetesses, but the most precious ones under the apse and in the transepts are protected by cardboard flooring and uncovered from mid–August to early October in honor of the Palio. The only floor panel usually visible in the Duomo's center, in the left transept, is Matteo di Giovanni's powerful 1481 *Massacre of the Innocents* (a theme with which the painter was obsessed, leaving us disturbing paintings in Santa Maria della Scala and Santa Maria dei Servi).

At the entrance to the right transept, the small octagonal **Cappella Chigi ★** was designed by Roman baroque master Gian Lorenzo Bernini in 1659. It houses the *Madonna del Voto,* a fragmentary late–13th-century painting by a follower of Guido da Siena. The work fulfilled a vow the Sienese made on the eve of the Montaperti battle that they would devote their city to the Madonna should they win the fight against Florence (they did). Five times since, in times of dire need, the Sienese have placed the keys to the city in front of the miraculous Madonna and prayed for deliverance, most recently in June 1944 during Nazi occupation. Two weeks later, the city was liberated. The *St. Jerome* and *St. Mary Magdalene* statues cradling their heads in the niches nearest the door are also by Bernini, who did the organ outside the chapel as well.

At the entry to the left transept is Nicola Pisano's masterpiece **pulpit ★★** (1265–68), on which he was assisted by his son, Giovanni, and Arnolfo di Cambio. The elegantly Gothic panels depict the life of Christ in crowded, detailed turmoil, divided by figures in flowing robes. The columns are supported on the backs of lions with their prey and cubs, and the base of the central column is a seated congregation of philosophers and figures representing the liberal arts.

Umbrian master Pinturicchio is the star in the **Libreria Piccolomini** ★★★, built in 1485 by Cardinal Francesco Piccolomini (later Pope Pius III— for all of 18 days before he died in office) to house the library of his famous uncle, Pope Pius II. The marble entrance was carved by Marrina in 1497, above which Pinturicchio was commissioned to paint a large fresco of the *Coronation of Pius III* (1504). Pinturicchio and assistants covered the ceiling and walls with 10 giant frescoes (1507) displaying rich colors, delicate modeling, limpid light, and fascination with mathematically precise, but somewhat cold, architectural space. The frescoes celebrate the life of Aeneas Silvio Piccolomini, better known as the humanist Pope Pius II.

Next door to the library's entrance is the **Piccolomini Altar** ★, designed by Andrea Bregno around 1480. The *Madonna and Child* above may be Jacopo della Quercia's earliest work (1397–1400). A young Michelangelo carved the statuettes of *Sts. Peter, Pius, Paul,* and *Gregory* in the other niches here (1501–04).

Piazza del Duomo. ✆ **0577-283-048.** Admission on cumulative ticket, or 3€, except when floor uncovered 6€. Mar–May and Sept–Oct Mon–Sat 10:30am–7:30pm, Sun 1:30–5:30pm; Nov–Feb Mon–Sat 10:30am–6:30pm, Sun 1:30–5:30pm; June–Aug Mon–Sat 10:30am–8pm, Sun 1:30–6pm.

Museo dell'Opera Metropolitana ★★ Housed in the walled-up right aisle of the Duomo's abortive new nave, Siena's outstanding Duomo museum contains all the works removed from the facade for conservation as well as disused altarpieces, including Duccio's masterpiece. It also offers one of the city's best views. The **ground floor** has the fascinating but weather-beaten facade **statues by Giovanni Pisano** and his school (1284–96), remarkable for their Gothic plasticity and craned, elongated necks. (When they were 15m/50 ft. up in niches, these protruding necks made sure their faces were visible from the ground.) The focus of the room, however, is Duccio's restored 30-sq.-m (323-sq.-ft.) **stained glass window** ★★ made in the late 1280s for the window above the cathedral's apse. Nine panels depict the Virgin Mary, Siena's four patron saints, and the four Biblical Evangelists.

Upstairs is the museum's (in fact, the city's) masterpiece, **Duccio's** *Maestà* ★★★. It's impossible to overstate the importance of this double-sided altarpiece, now separated and displayed on opposite sides of the intimate room. Not only did it virtually found the Sienese school of painting, but it has also been considered one of the most important medieval paintings in Europe since the day it was unveiled. When Duccio finished the

The Torre del Mangia and Siena's rooftops as seen from atop the Museo dell'Opera Metropolitana.

work on June 9, 1311, it was reportedly carried in procession from the painter's workshop on Via Stalloreggi to the Duomo's altar by the clergy, government officials, and every last citizen in Siena. The centuries have, all told, been kind to it. Although eight of the predella panels are in foreign museums and one is lost (12 pinnacle angels suffered similar fates), it's otherwise remarkably intact. The central scene of the *Maestà*, or Virgin Mary in Majesty enthroned and surrounded by saints, became the archetypal grand subject for a Sienese painter. Her dark bulk and the gorgeous inlaid throne contribute to the Madonna's majesty, while the soft folds of her robes and her gentle features bring out her humanity.

On a side wall is an early Duccio *Madonna and Child*. Almost overlooked here is Pietro Lorenzetti's incredible **Birth of the Virgin ★★**. Lorenzetti broke traditions and artistic boundaries with his fabrics, his colors, and (most important) the architectural space he created. Instead of painting a triptych with a central main scene and two unrelated side panels, as was the norm, Lorenzetti created a single continuous space by painting vaulted ceilings that seem to grow back from the pointed arches of the triptych's frame. This is the last work Pietro painted before succumbing to the plague.

The upper floor's **Treasury Room** has the Bernini-designed *Golden Rose* (1653) and a 13th-century gilded silver reliquary containing the head of St. Galgano. In the **Sala della Madonna degli Occhi Grossi,** the namesake *Madonna of the Big Eyes,* which got nudged off the cathedral's high altar by Duccio's *Maestà*, was painted in the 1220s by the "Maestro di Tressa." Also here is Sano di Pietro's iconic image of St. Bernardino preaching in front of the instantly recognizable Palazzo Pubblico (note the gender segregation of the audience, which was standard practice).

If you take the stairs (past rooms of baroque canvases and a couple of Matteo di Giovanni altarpieces) that lead up to the walkway atop the would-be facade of the "New Duomo," the **Facciatone ★★**, you get the best visualization of how the enlarged Duomo would have looked as well as sweeping views across the city's rooftops with the Torre del Mangia towering over the Campo.

Piazza del Duomo 8. ℂ **0577-283-048.** www.operaduomo.siena.it. Admission on cumulative ticket, or 6€. Mid-June to mid-Sept daily 9:30am–8pm; mid-Sept to Oct and Mar to mid-June daily 9:30am–7pm; Nov–Feb daily 10am–5pm.

Santa Maria della Scala ★★ ☺ The hospital across from the Duomo entrance cared for the infirm from the 800s up until the 1990s, when its wards, halls, and chapels began to be restructured as a diverse and constantly changing museum complex and exhibition space. The original decorations of the hospital itself, inside, also merit a visit on their own.

The **Sala del Pellegrinaio ★★**, which held hospital beds until just a few years ago, has walls frescoed in the 1440s with scenes from the history of the hospital and its good works (all well labeled). Most are vivid works by Domenico di Bartolo, richly colored and full of amusing details of hospital life in the 1400s. However, Vecchietta did the upwardly mobile orphans over the exit door; Jacopo della Quercia's less talented and little known brother, Priamo, did a cartoonish scene on the left wall; and a pair of Mannerist hacks filled in the spaces at the room's end. An adjacent hall houses **Bambimus,** Siena's Museum of Children's Art, where paintings are hung at tot-friendly heights and there's usually something crafty for them to explore themselves. Elsewhere on the ground floor, the recently restored **Sagrestia Vecchia (Old Sacristy) ★** has a damaged and complex fresco cycle completed by Vecchietta in 1449, and the adjacent **Cappella della Madonna** a surreal and rather gruesome *Massacre of the Innocents* ★ (1482), by (of course) Matteo di Giovanni.

Downstairs are Jacopo della Quercia's original **Fonte Gaia** ★ alongside plaster casts and explanations of its 20-year restoration process, and the **Oratorio di Santa Caterina della Notte** ★, where St. Catherine prayed at night. This latter was decorated mainly in the 17th century by Rustici and Rutilio Manetti but also contains a rich *Madonna and Child with Saints, Angels, and Musicians* by Taddeo di Bartolo (ca. 1400) in the back room. Still farther down, Siena's **Museo Archeologico** is small, and while there's nothing of earth-shattering significance, there are some surprisingly good pieces for a museum hardly anyone knows exists—local Etruscan bronzes, black *bucchero* vases, funerary urns in terra cotta and alabaster, and some Roman coins.

Piazza del Duomo 2. ✆ **0577-534-571.** www.santamariadellascala.com. Admission on cumulative ticket, or 5.50€ with reservations, 6€ without reservations, free for ages 11 and under. Mar 17–Oct 15 daily 10:30am–6:30pm; Oct 16–Mar 16 daily 10:30am–4:30pm.

Exploring the Rest of Siena
IN TERZO DI CITTÀ

Pinacoteca Nazionale ★ Siena's painting gallery houses the most representative collection of the Sienese school of art. It wouldn't be fair to label it a museum of second-rate paintings by first-rate artists, but the supreme masterpieces of Siena do lie elsewhere. It's laid out more or less chronologically starting on the second floor, though the museum is constantly rearranging (especially the last bits).

Room 1 contains the first definite work of the Sienese school, a 1215 altar frontal by the "Maestro di Teresa," and one of the earliest known paintings on canvas, Guido da Siena's *Scenes from the Life of Christ* (late 1200s). Rooms 3 and 4 have works by the first great Sienese master, Duccio, including an early masterpiece showing Cimabue's influence, the tiny 1285 *Madonna dei Francescani* (in poor condition, it's kept under glass). Rooms 5 to 8 pay homage to the three great early-14th-century painters, Simone Martini and the brothers Pietro and Ambrogio Lorenzetti. Of Martini, be sure to look at the four charming narrative panels from the *Altar of Beato Agostino Novello.* Martini's brother-in-law Lippo Memmi weighs in with a fresco fragment of the *Madonna and Child with Saints.* The best Lorenzetti works are in the small side rooms off room 7, including a *Madonna Enthroned* and a *Madonna of the Carmelites* by Pietro; also look for Ambrogio's tiny landscapes in room 12, an expressive but much deteriorated *Crucifixion,* and his last dated work, a 1343 *Annunciation.*

Rooms 13 to 19 feature 15th-century Sienese paintings by the likes of Giovanni di Paolo, including two attempts at the *Presentation at the Temple* (his attempts at mastering perspective work in neither). Matteo di Giovanni is also represented here by a sophisticated *Madonna and Child* before passing to lots of Sano di Pietro, as well as Vecchietta and Francesco di Giorgio Martini.

Among the paintings on the first floor are a Pinturicchio *Holy Family* and Girolamo Genga's 1509 frescoes *Ransom of Prisoners* and the *Flight of Aeneas from Troy.* The museum usually displays in the next rooms its many works by local Mannerist Domenico Beccafumi, including a 1530 *Birth of the Virgin* and a fine *Christ Descending into Limbo.* Also look for Beccafumi's huge **cartoons** ★★,

THE palio DELLE CONTRADE

No other festival in Italy is as colorful, as intense, or as spectacular as **Siena's Palio** ★★★. Twice a year, Siena packs the Piazza del Campo with dirt and runs a no-holds-barred bareback horse race around it, the highlight of a week of trial runs, feasts, parades, and solemn ceremonies. The tradition, in one form or another, goes back to at least 1310. The Palio is a deadly serious competition, and while Siena doesn't mind if visitors show up, the Palio is for the Sienese.

To understand the Palio—really, to understand Siena—you must know something of the *contrada* system. In the 14th century there were about 42 *contrade,* neighborhood wards that helped provide militia support for Siena's defense. The number of wards was successively reduced until the current 17 *contrade* were fixed in 1675. Each ward is named after an animal or object—*Drago* (Dragon), *Giraffa* (Giraffe), *Bruco* (Worm), *Onda* (Wave), and so on—and each has its own head-quarters, social club, museum, and church.

You are born into the *contrada* of your parents, are baptized in your *contrada*'s open-air font, learn your *contrada*'s allies and enemies at an early age, go to church in your *contrada*'s oratory, almost invariably marry within your *contrada,* spend your free time hanging out in the *contrada* social club, and help elect or serve on your *contra-da*'s governing body. Even your funeral is sponsored by the *contrada,* which mourns your passing as family. It's like a benevolent form of Hollywood's mythi-cal Mafia—but no *contrada* tolerates unlawfulness, and as a result Siena has a shockingly low crime rate.

Ten *contrade* are chosen each year to ride in the **July 2** Palio di Provenzano (established in 1659)—the seven that didn't ride the previous July 2 plus three chosen by lot. A similar process decides the runners for the even big-ger Palio dell'Assunta, in honor of the Assumption of the Virgin, on **August 16** (which dates from 1310), meaning it's technically possible for your *contrada* to compete in neither race in a year. The horse you're given and the order you're lined up on the track are also chosen by separate lots. Jockeys are hired guns, and usually imported—traditionally a Maremma horseman, but many come from Sardegna or Sicily—and you'll never know how well he'll ride, whether the bribe one of your rival *contrade* may slip him will outweigh the wages you paid, or if he'll even make it to the race without being ambushed. If your jockey does turn on you, you'd better hope he's thrown quickly. The Palio, you see, is a true horse race—the horse is the one that wins, whether there's a rider still on it or not (both editions in 1989 were won by riderless steeds). The jockey's main job is to hang onto the horse's bare back and thrash the other horses and their riders with the stiff ox-hide whip he's given for the purpose. The Palio may at this point seem pretty law-less, but there actually is one rule: No jockey can grab another horse's reins.

At the two 90-degree turns of the Campo, almost every year a rider or two goes flying out of the racetrack to land among the stands or slams up against the mattresses prudently padding the palazzi walls. Sienese lore, however, maintains that no one has ever died in the running of a Palio. What is the prize for all this? A *palio,* a banner painted with the image of the Virgin Mary, in whose name the race is run. That, and the honor of your *contrada.*

The Palios really start on June 29 and August 13, when the lots are drawn to select the 10 racers and the trial races begin. Over the next 2 days, morning and afternoon trial runs are held, and on the evening before each Palio, the *contrade* hold an all-night feast and party lasting more or less until the 7:45am Jockey's Mass in the Cappella della Piazza on the Campo. There's a final heat at 9am, then everybody dissolves to his or her separate *contrada* for last-minute preparations. The highlight is the 3pm (3:30pm in July) Blessing of the Horse in each *contrada*'s church—a little manure dropping at the altar is a sign of good luck—at which the priest ends with a resounding command to the horse: "Go forth, and return a winner!"

Unless invited by a *contrada,* you're probably not going to get into any of the packed churches for this, so your best strategy is to stick around the Campo all day. Because standing in the center of the Campo for the race is free (the grandstands require tickets; see below), you should ideally stake out a spot close to the start-finish line before 2pm. Just before 5pm, the pageantry begins, with processions led by a contingent from Montalcino in honor of it harboring the last members of the Sienese Republic in the 16th century. The *palio* banner is drawn about the piazza in the War Chariot (a wagon drawn by two snowy white oxen), and *contrada* youths in Renaissance garb juggle colorful banners in the *sbandierata* flag-throwing display.

At 7:30pm (7pm in July) the horses start lining up between two ropes. Much care is taken to get the first nine in perfect order. After countless false starts and equine finagling, suddenly the 10th horse comes thundering up from behind, and as soon as he hits the first rope the second one is dropped and the race is on. Three laps and fewer than 90 seconds later, it's over. The winning *contrada* bursts into songs celebrating its greatness, losers cry in each other's arms, and those who suspect their jockeys of double-crossing them chase the hapless men—whose horses don't stop running at the finish line—through the streets, howling for blood. The winners truly live it up—their party goes on for several days.

If standing in the middle of the hot and crowded Campo doesn't attract you—and anyone with a small bladder might want to think twice, as there are no facilities and no one is allowed in or out from just before the procession until the race is over (about 3½ hr.)—you can try to buy a ticket for a seat in the grandstands or at a window of one of the buildings surrounding the piazza. These are controlled by the building owners and the shops in front of which the stands are set up and cost anywhere from 350€ for a single seat to about 1,500€ for a window seating four people. They can sell out a year in advance; the tourist office has contacts for the individual shops and buildings if you want to negotiate directly for a seat. If you show up late and sans ticket, make your way up Via Giovanni Duprè to Piazza del Mercato behind the Palazzo Pubblico; the police stationed there will sometimes allow people into the Campo between the processions and the race itself.

from which many of the panels in the Duomo floor were made. Beccafumi's 16th-century rival, who painted more in the classicist branch of the High Renaissance rather than in the Mannerist style, was Sodoma, whose works are generally brighter with a more precise use of color, but lack Beccafumi's weird mastery of light and experimentation with form. The detached fresco of Sodoma's *Christ at the Column* is remarkably realistic and has a fascinating use of rich colors, as does his large and detailed *Deposition,* where parts of the scene are reflected in the soldier's armor and helm.

Via San Pietro 29. © **0577-286-143.** Admission 4€. Sun–Mon 9am–1pm; Tues–Sat 8:15am–7:15pm.

IN TERZO DI SAN MARTINO

Archivio di Stato ★ The 1469 **Palazzo Piccolomini** is a touch of Florence peeking into the southeast corner of the Campo. It was designed by Bernardo Rossellino in the Florentine Renaissance style and is now home to the *Archivio di Stato* (head down the corridor off the left of the courtyard to grab the elevator to the fourth floor). The State Archive preserves, among other notable documents, Boccaccio's will and Jacopo della Quercia's contract for the Fonte Gaia. But the main thing to see is a remarkable set of wooden covers dating back to 1258 and made for the city's account books, called the ***Tavolette di Biccherna*** ★, painted from the 13th to 17th centuries with religious scenes, daily working life in the civic offices, and important events in Siena's history—Sano di Pietro, Vecchietta, and Ambrogio Lorenzetti even did a few.

Via Banchi di Sotto 52 (facing Loggia del Papa). © **0577-241-745.** Free admission. Mon–Sat hourly viewings at 9:30, 10:30, and 11:30am. Bus: A (pink) or B.

San Martino Beyond a 1613 facade by Giovanni Fontana, this little church, whose founding dates from before the 8th century, retains a few good late-Renaissance paintings. The second altar on the right has a Guido Reni *Circumcision* (1636), and beyond it is a severely darkened Il Guercino *Martyrdom of St. Bartholomew.* The high altar is a fair baroque job by Giuseppe Mazzuoli, and as you leave take a good look at Domenico Beccafumi's Mannerist *Nativity* on the third altar of the left aisle.

Just to the facade's left is the Renaissance **Loggia del Papa** (1462), built for Pope Pius II. When you exit San Martino, head left down Via delle Scotte to no. 14 to see the 18th-century **Synagogue,** a remnant of the Jewish ghetto that existed behind the Campo from 1571 to 1796. It doesn't keep regular hours, but you can ring the bell anytime outside the Sabbath for a tour costing 3€ per person. For information, call © **0577-284-647.**

Off Via Banchi di Sotto. No phone. Free admission. Bus: A (pink) or B.

Santa Maria dei Servi Beyond some cypress and a small patch of green grass, this huge 13th-century church sits facadeless, with mute rough brick climbing up the front next to an enormous campanile. The second chapel on the right aisle houses the church's masterpiece, a late Byzantine-style **Madonna del Bordone ★** by Coppo di Marcovaldo, signed in 1261. The third chapel jumps ahead to the baroque with Rutilio Manetti's 1625 *Birth of the Virgin,* and the Renaissance is represented in the fifth chapel with Matteo di Giovanni's frightening *Massacre of the Innocents* (1491). The right transept has another take on the subject in the second chapel to the right of the altar; this *Massacre* was probably frescoed by Francesco di Segna with the help of Niccolò di Segna and Pietro

Lorenzetti. Across the transept are a painted *Crucifix* by Niccolò di Segna in the chapel and an *Annunciatory Angel* by Francesco Vanni (the *Mary Annunciate* half is in the left transept). The second chapel to the left of the high altar has frescoed scenes from the *Life of St. John the Baptist*, again by the di Segnas and Pietro Lorenzetti; Taddeo di Bartolo did the *Nativity* altarpiece in 1404.

Piazza A. Manzoni. No phone. Free admission. Bus: A (pink) or B.

IN TERZO DI CAMOLLIA

Siena's northern third spreads off either side of palace-lined **Via Banchi di Sopra.** Two blocks up on the left is Siena's oldest Gothic palace, the **Palazzo Tolomei,** begun in 1208 and now home to the Cassa di Risparmio di Firenze bank. The piazza out front is where the city council met from the 11th century until the Palazzo Pubblico was built. Two blocks farther is the piazza formed by the Gothic **Palazzo Salimbeni** and its tributary palaces, linked to form the seat of the Monte di Paschi di Siena, Siena's powerhouse bank founded in 1472 and still a strong player in Italian finance.

Casa di Santa Caterina ★ The remarkable Caterina Benincasa, daughter of a rich Sienese dyer, took a nun's veil (but never an order's vows) in 1355 at the age of 8 after her first of many visions of Christ. In 1375, a crucifix in Pisa cinched her holiness by giving her the stigmata of Christ's wounds. Her name and reputation for devout wisdom and saintly life spread, and in 1378 she was chosen as Siena's ambassador to Pope Gregory XI in Avignon. There, her eloquent letter writing and sharp, argumentative mind eventually succeeded in doing what 73 years of political finagling had not been able to accomplish: She persuaded the pope to leave civilized Avignon and return the papal seat to Rome, which was then a backwater rife with the armed squabbles of noble clans. Caterina died in Rome in 1380, at age 33, and was canonized 80 years later. In 1939, she was declared patron saint of Italy, and in 1970, together with St. Teresa of Avila, received the highest honor the church can bestow: Saints Catherine and Teresa became the first women elevated to Doctors of the Church.

The house where she was born was converted into a sanctuary in 1466, and it remains a peaceful, reflective spot. The entrance is a small brick-lined courtyard where you can occasionally see a pair of Oca (Goose) *contrada* teenagers practicing the art of flag tossing. To the left is the old family kitchen transformed into an **oratory** and decorated in the 16th and 19th centuries with paintings by Il Pomarancio, Il Riccio, Francesco Vanni, and others. The majolica-tiled floor is 16th century. The **church** opposite the oratory was built in 1623 over Catherine's orchard to house the 12th-century Pisan-school *Crucifixion,* in front of which the saint received the stigmata. Back under the loggia, the stairs lead down past Catherine's **cell,** frescoed in 1896, toward the Goose *contrada*'s church, the **Oratorio dell'Oca** (seldom open, but containing works by Sodoma).

At the bottom of Via Santa Caterina below, nestled amid the remaining green of the narrow valley between San Domenico and the Duomo, is the brick 1246 **Fonte Branda,** a public wash house battlemented like a tiny fortress.

Costa di San Antonio (btw. Via della Sapienza and Via Santa Caterina). ℂ **0577-280-801.** www. caterinati.org. Free admission. Easter–Oct daily 9am–12:30pm and 3–6pm; winter daily 9am– 12:30pm and 3:30–6pm. Bus: A (red).

Enoteca Italiana ★★ The 16th-century Fortezza Medicea di Santa Barbara has been turned into a (slightly untidy) public park. Its courtyard is an open-air theater, its ramparts are a place for a stroll and a view, and its vaults are filled with Italy's **national wine museum.** Here you can sample a choice selection of Italian wines by the glass or go all out on an entire bottle from their extensive *cantina* (around 1,600 labels cool their heels here), or just roam the vaulted basement armed with a barcode reader that can access information on all the bottles. It wouldn't be fair to say this is a truly representative collection, because not all vintners choose to take part, but it has been Italy's official state-mandated *museo del vino* since 1950. Out of Italy's some 4,000 wines, it preserves at least all 266 kinds of DOC, each of the 17 DOCG labels, and every last one of Italy's 128 IGT wines.

Fortezza Medicea. ✆ **0577-228-843.** www.enoteca-italiana.it. Free admission; glass of wine 3€–6.50€; cold plate of typical regional foods 8€–10€. Mon noon–8pm; Tues–Sat noon–1am.

Oratorio di San Bernardino e Museo Diocesano ★ The church of San Francesco was where St. Bernardino first donned his monkish robes. The exact spot where he prayed and began preaching is now marked by the **Oratory of San Bernardino,** built in the late 15th century. The lower of the oratory's two levels was frescoed by the best 17th-century Sienese artists—including Francesco Vanni, Rutilio and Domenico Manetti, and Ventura Salimbeni—and houses a little *Madonna* by Sano di Pietro. The upper level has higher-quality **frescoes** ★ depicting the *Life of the Virgin* by 16th-century artists Sodoma, Domenico Beccafumi, and Girolamo del Pacchia. The rooms that make up the **Diocesan Museum** contain minor panel paintings (including a couple by Matteo di Giovanni) and detached fresco fragments.

Via del Comune doglegs off Via dei Rossi just down from Piazza San Francesco and leads to the 14th-century double city gate **Porta Ovile,** which preserves a tabernacle frescoed by Sano di Pietro. Just outside the gate you'll find the 1262 **Fonte Ovile,** one of the city's most picturesque public fountains.

Piazza San Francesco 18. ✆ **0577-283-048.** Admission on cumulative ticket, or 3€. Mar 15–Oct daily 1–7pm.

San Domenico ★ The Dominican's Siena home is an enormous, severe, and vaguely unattractive pile of bricks (1226), jutting above a modern section of town. There are good views here, though, of the Duomo and Siena's rooftops. The raised chapel off the west end (to the right as you enter) preserves the only genuine *Portrait of St. Catherine,* painted by her friend and contemporary Andrea Vanni.

The **Cappella di Santa Caterina (Chapel of St. Catherine)** halfway down the right wall was frescoed with scenes from the saint's life. All except the right wall (where in 1593 Francesco Vanni painted Catherine performing an exorcism) were frescoed by Sodoma in 1526. The large work on the left wall of her interceding on behalf of a condemned man as well as the other scenes of her in ecstasy and swooning are some of Sodoma's best work. The focal point of the chapel, however, is Catherine's venerated head, in a gilt reliquary case, on the altar.

At the end of the nave, on the right, is an *Adoration of the Shepherds* ★ by Francesco di Giorgio Martini, dominated by a crumbling Roman triumphal arch in the background and a *Pietà* above. The first chapel to the right of the altar is home to a *Madonna and Child with Saints* by Matteo di Giovanni, one of whose masterpieces, *St. Barbara Enthroned with Angels and Sts. Mary Magdalene and Catherine* (1479), is in the second chapel of the left transept.

Piazza San Domenico. No phone. Free admission. Daily 7am–12:55pm and 3–6:30pm. Bus: A (red).

San Francesco ★ A late Gothic church (1326–1475), Siena's Franciscan barn was badly damaged in a 1655 fire and used as a military barracks for a long time before being reconstructed in the 1880s. On the inside of the entrance wall you can see what happens to frescoes that are left out under the elements. Remounted here are heavily deteriorated works that once graced tabernacles at the Porta Romana (on the left, painted by Sassetta and Sano di Pietro) and the Porta Pispini (on the right, by Sodoma). In the second chapel to the right of the altar is a tomb with a *schiacciato* effigy carved by Urbano da Cortona (1462–87); the chapel to its left has a 14th-century *Madonna and Child* by St. Catherine's friend Andrea Vanni. The first chapel left of the altar contains a detached *Crucifixion* by Pietro Lorenzetti, whose brother Ambrogio did the excellent frescoes, now in poor condition, in the third chapel down. What's left of these early 1330s works, Ambrogio's first fresco attempt, depict the *Martyrdom of Franciscan Missionaries at Ceuta* and *St. Louis d'Anjou Taking Leave of Pope Boniface VIII*, where Lorenzetti makes the viewer part of the onlooking papal court.

Piazza San Francesco. No phone. Free admission. Daily 7am–noon and 3:30–7pm.

Shopping

ANTIQUES You may not find any real bargains at **Antichità Monna Agnese** (✆ 0577-282-288), Via di Città 45, but you will find spectacular period homewares aimed at those with deep pockets.

BOOKS & PAPER **Libreria Senese,** Via di Città 62–66 (✆ 0577-280-845), has the largest selection of English-language books, though it's now getting competition from chain store **Feltrinelli,** Via Banchi di Sopra 52 and 64–66 (✆ 0577-271-104 or 0577-44-009; www.lafeltrinelli.it). If you enjoyed browsing the leather-bound journals and quality stationery at **Il Papiro** in Florence, you have a second chance to buy that literary someone a gift at the Siena branch, Via di Città 37 (✆ 0577-284-241; www.ilpapirofirenze.it).

CERAMICS & CRAFTWARES Once upon a time there were countless ceramic stores lining Via di Città, few of them offering any real quality. The most authentic ceramics feature only black, white, and—surprise—the reddish-brown Crayola color of "burnt sienna," or *terra di Siena*. **Ceramiche Artistiche Santa Caterina,** with showrooms at Via di Città 74–76 (✆ 0577-283-098) and a workshop outside town at Via Mattioli 12 (✆ 0577-45-006), sells high-quality ceramics, courtesy of Maestro Marcello Neri, who trained at Siena's premier art and ceramics institutions, and his son, Fabio. **Sator Print** ★, Via Stalloreggi 70 (✆ 0577-247-478; www.satorprint.com), sells hand-decorated prints and original art and calligraphy based on historic Sienese designs. Nothing inside is cheap, but you'll find an affordable, authentic gift or souvenir with little trouble. Or just stop by to see the maestro at work.

CLOTHING At **Tessuti a Mano,** Via San Pietro 7 (✆ 0577-282-200), weaver Fioretta Bacci will do the hard work for you, creating old-school sweaters and other outerwear on her giant looms.

FOOD At **Consorzio Agrario Siena,** Via Pianigiani 9 (✆ 0577-2301), local restaurateurs stock up on ingredients for their classic dishes, as most of the produce comes directly from the farm, and many of the packaged goods are produced locally. The **Antica Drogheria Manganelli,** Via di Città

71–73 (✆ **0577-280-002**), is a little more upscale but just as authentic: It has made its own *panforte* and soft *ricciarelli* almond cookies since the 19th century. Our favorite food stop is more proletarian, however: **Gino Cacino** ★, Piazza del Mercato 31 (✆ **0577-223-076**; www.ginocacinosiena.it; closed Wed afternoon) sells all manner of fresh and preserved delights, and will even load you a sandwich with pecorino aged in olive oil, Tuscan salami, anchovies, or anything else you fancy from his top-quality deli counter.

Siena After Dark

If the sheer spectacle of an evening lounging in the Campo isn't enough, the **Enoteca Italiana** (p. 203) is the only state-sponsored wine bar in Italy, in vaults that were built for Cosimo de' Medici in 1560. Drink by the glass or buy one of 1,600 bottles on sale. **Enoteca I Terzi**, Via dei Termini 7 (✆ **0577-44-329**; www.enotecaiterzi.it) is under the vaulted ceiling of a 12th-century tower, and sells fine wine by the glass. For something younger and more local, head down **Via Pantaneto** ★ toward the university buildings. Names may change, but bars down here go on till late.

GLASSWARE At **Vetrate Artistiche Toscane,** Via della Galluzza 5 (✆ **0577-48-033**; www.glassisland.com; closed Sat) everything from souvenir trinkets to photo frames and simple jewelry is handmade on the premises. Prices are reasonable.

Where to Stay

For help finding a room, stop by the **Siena Hotels Promotion** booth on Piazza San Domenico (✆ **0577-288-084**; www.hotelsiena.com), where for 1.50€ to 4€, depending on the category of hotel, they'll find you a room and reserve it. The booth is open Monday through Saturday from 9am to 7pm (until 8pm in summer). The city **tourist office** (p. 192) also books accommodations.

EXPENSIVE

Aia Mattonata ★★ 🛍 This tiny, tranquil boutique inn, crafted from an old stone farmhouse renovated in 2009, is enveloped by the gently rolling Tuscan hills just a 10-minute ride from central Siena. Both the midsize guest rooms and the classy common areas (where you'll find an honesty snack bar) remain true to their Tuscan roots, but add a touch of rustic refinement. Two rooms have romantic *baldacchino* (canopy) beds, but the smallest (not by much) shares with the garden a sublime view towards the Torre del Mangia and Siena's ochre rooftops.

Strada del Ceraiolo 1, 53100 Siena. www.aiamattonata.it. ✆ **0577-592-677.** Fax 0577-392-073. 6 units. 155€–240€ double. Rates include breakfast. AE, MC, V. Free parking. No children 11 and under. Closed Nov–Feb. From Siena Ovest junction, head toward Roccastrada then after 1km/½ mile follow SS46 left toward Casciano di Murlo; after 2km Strada del Ceraiolo is on left. Bus: 31. **Amenities:** Bar; bikes (free); concierge; exercise room; outdoor pool; room service; smoke-free rooms; small spa. *In room:* A/C, TV, hair dryer, Wi-Fi (free).

Palazzo Ravizza ★ The Santi-Ravizza family has run this hotel in a 17th-century Renaissance *palazzo* since the 1920s. The rooms tend to be large, with high ceilings—some gorgeously frescoed, a few with painted details around the wood beams. Those on the front catch some traffic noise, but on the back you'll hear only birdsong and the splashing fountain in the garden with sublime countryside vistas. The Ravizza is just outside the center of Siena, but still inside the city walls, offering a good Sienese neighborhood experience away from the tourist bustle.

Pian dei Mantellini 34 (near Piazza San Marco), 53100 Siena. www.palazzoravizza.it. ✆ **0577-280-462.** Fax 0577-221-597. 35 units. 90€–150€ double. Rates include breakfast. AE, DC, MC, V. Free parking. Bus: A (green, yellow). Closed early Jan to early Feb. **Amenities:** Bar; babysitting; concierge; room service; smoke-free rooms; Wi-Fi (free). *In room:* A/C, TV, hair dryer, minibar.

MODERATE

Santa Caterina ★ You'll find some of the friendliest hoteliers in Siena here, and they've been slowly reinvesting in the place. The characterful rooms have tile floors (antique terra-cotta flooring in some), soft beds, and chunky furniture made of old wood. Ask for a room with a view down a verdant, unspoiled valley south of Siena. In summer you can breakfast in the pretty little garden; a glassed-in breakfast veranda is used for winter dining.

Via Enea Silvio Piccolomini 7 (just outside the Porta Romana), 53100 Siena. www.hscsiena.it. ✆ **0577-221-105.** Fax 0577-271-087. 22 units. 85€–195€ double. Rates include buffet breakfast. AE, DC, MC, V. Free parking along street or 10€–15€ in rear lot. Bus: A (pink) or 2. **Amenities:** Babysitting; bikes; concierge; smoke-free rooms. *In room:* A/C, TV, hair dryer, minibar, Wi-Fi (free).

INEXPENSIVE

Albergo Bernini ★ 🌴 ☺ Mauro and Nadia and their son Alessandro oversee a homey set of clean and, for the price, surprisingly comfortable rooms decorated with the odd antique. The firm beds rest on patterned tiling and are surrounded by whitewashed walls curving into the ceilings. If you can live without an internal bathroom (it's right across the hall), room 11 has a stupendous view of the Duomo's flank, and sleeps five at a seriously good price. All the rooms are mouse quiet, as the place sits atop St. Catherine's house-cum-convent. If you ask, they'll let you go up on the terrace for views of the city and valley. This is a family environment; there is a midnight curfew.

Via della Sapienza 15 (near San Domenico), 53100 Siena. www.albergobernini.com. ✆/fax **0577-289-047.** 10 units. 65€ double without bathroom; 85€ double with bathroom. Breakfast 3.50€–7.50€. No credit cards. Closed 1 month in winter. Bus: A (red). **Amenities:** Babysitting (requires notice); smoke-free rooms. *In room:* Hair dryer on request, no phone, Wi-Fi (free).

Antica Residenza Cicogna ★★ 🌴 This friendly, family-run B&B has established itself as one of the most desirable pads in the center of town—and you'll need to book ahead in peak season to secure one of the handful of rooms. Units are compact, but the place is dripping with character, and its location (a 5-min. walk from the Campo) could hardly be better. Among the neat doubles, all of which come with textured wallpaper and carefully matched fabrics, our favorite is "Liberty," which comes with slightly more space (including for an extra bed if necessary) and a *baldacchino* (canopy) bed.

Via dei Termini 67, 53100 Siena. www.anticaresidenzacicogna.com. ✆ **0577-285-613.** 7 units. 80€–100€ double; 110€–150€ suite. Rates include buffet breakfast. MC, V. Garage parking 18€. **Amenities:** Smoke-free rooms. *In room:* A/C, TV, hair dryer, Wi-Fi (free).

Santuario S. Caterina/Alma Domus ☺ Terraced into the hill below San Domenico church in a relatively untouristy part of Siena, this simple, cheap hotel is run by the nuns of St. Catherine, so there's a certain monastic quality—but also a kindly hospitality and meditative calm. Many of the midsize rooms have tiny balconies with great views of the Duomo across the little valley. The furnishings are a mix of modular and old-fashioned, with a few wrought-iron bed frames (but soft mattresses), giving some rooms a slightly institutional feel—units modernized in 2011 are of a much higher standard. Guests can use a common living room and a TV room.

Via Camporegio 37 (the steep street down off Piazza San Domenico), 53100 Siena. www.hotel almadomus.it. ✆ **0577-44-177.** Fax 0577-47-601. 28 units. 65€–75€ double; 80€–95€ triple; 95€–110€ quad. Rates include breakfast. MC, V. Bus: A (red). **Amenities:** Smoke-free rooms. *In room:* A/C, TV (some), hair dryer on request, Wi-Fi (8€/6 hr.).

Where to Eat

Siena has a good **cafe culture,** and during the *passeggiata* (ritual evening stroll), Sienese cozy up to the bar of the cafes lining Via Banchi di Sopra and Via di Città to gulp down espresso and sample finger-size pastries and slices of *panettone* (**dry cake**) and Siena's dense, barlike *panforte.* (It comes in many types, most a variation on a thick honey paste binding nuts and candied fruit, a holdover from the cane sugar–less Middle Ages.)

For pastry makers and specialty food shops, see "Shopping," above. Or, sample the bounty at Siena's top cafe, the bustling **Nannini,** Via Banchi di Sopra 22–24 (✆**0577-41-591**). The cafe is open Monday through Saturday from 7:30am to 9pm, and Sunday from 8am to 9pm.

An alternative to our favorites below, for a quick lunch, is **Caffè Fiaschetteria Il Pulcino,** Via dei Termini 91 (✆**0577-289-068**), where homemade pasta dishes cost 5€ and simple secondi between 6€ and 8€.

EXPENSIVE

Antica Osteria da Divo ★★ CONTEMPORARY SIENESE This former trattoria has thrived since it went midscale and greatly improved its menu to offer excellent innovative dishes rooted in Sienese traditions in a classy, but not frosty, atmosphere of soft jazz. The main dining room is a crazy medieval mélange of stone, brick, wood supports, and naked rock, while the rooms in back and in the basement are actually Etruscan tombs carved from the tufa. *Pici al ragout di lepre* (thick hand-rolled pasta in hare ragù) and *gnocchetti di patate con erbe cipollina e pecorino di fossa* (gnocchi with chives swimming in melted pecorino cheese) are palate-pleasing primi. For the main course, they ascribe to the growing school of Italian cooking wherein a side dish is included with each secondo (making a meal here less costly than the prices below would suggest). A perfect example: the exquisite *petto d'anatra al vin santo con patate allo zafferano* (duck breast with crisp balls of saffron-kissed mashed potatoes).

Via Franciosa 25–29 (2 streets down from the left flank of the Duomo). ✆ **0577-284-381.** www.osteriadadivo.it. Reservations recommended. Primi 10€; secondi with side dish 20€–24€. MC, V. Wed–Mon noon–2:30pm and 7–10:30pm. Closed 2 weeks Jan–Feb. Bus: A (green, yellow).

 The Perfect Sienese Gelato

Superstar high-quality chain gelateria **Grom** hit Siena in 2010, grabbing a prime site at Via Banchi di Sopra 11–13 (✆ **0577-289-303;** www.grom.it). Queues are long and the cold stuff is tasty, but we still make the short detour down Via de' Rossi to **Kopa Kabana ★,** at no. 52–54 (✆ **0577-223-744**), for a daily-changing range of flavors, including *panpepato,* based on the peppery Sienese cake. Closer to the Campo, **Brivido,** Via dei Pellegrini 1 (no phone), is another reliable choice.

Osteria Le Logge ★ CONTEMPORARY SIENESE Prices are creeping up here, but this former pharmacy is still many a local's choice for a special night out, offering excellent cooking in a sedate—yet not sedated—atmosphere. Stars of a regularly rotated menu include *taglierini al tartufo* in a light butter sauce that doesn't mask the delicate flavor of the black truffles. Heavier primi include *malfatti all'Osteria* (spinach-and-ricotta balls in a creamy tomato sauce) and *ravioli ripieni di pecorino e menta* (ravioli stuffed with sheep's-milk cheese and mint in a sauce flavored with port). The staff is friendly and very accommodating: I once visited with a vegetarian, and our waitress quickly established his eating parameters, proceeded to indicate what he could order, and then had the kitchen concoct for him a suitable secondo of all the veggies they had on hand.

Via del Porrione 33 (just off the Campo). ℂ **0577-48-013.** www.osterialelogge.it. Reservations recommended. Primi 10€–15€; secondi 20€–25€. AE, DC, MC, V. Mon–Sat noon–2:45pm and 7–10:30pm. Closed Jan 1–Feb 20. Bus: A (pink) or B.

MODERATE

Antica Trattoria Papei ★ 🍴 SIENESE Although tourists now know to filter behind the Palazzo Pubblico to this large family-run trattoria, locals still hang on vigorously, returning for the simple but good Sienese fare. In summer, you can dine alfresco on the trafficked piazza. If you're eating inside, head to the left of the door or upstairs for wood-ceilinged ambience. The *pappardelle al sugo di cinghiale* (in wild boar sauce) is a traditional dish, while the *pici alla cardinale* (chewy fat spaghetti in tomato sauce with hot peppers and chunks of pancetta) is a bit more original. Keep it spicy with *coniglio all'arrabbiata* (rabbit cooked in white wine, rosemary, and sage with a pinch of *peperoncino*), or try *anatra alla Tolomei* (duck stewed with tomatoes).

Piazza del Mercato 6 (behind Palazzo Pubblico). ℂ **0577-280-894.** Primi 7€; secondi 8€–15€. AE, MC, V. Tues–Sun noon–3pm and 7–10:30pm.

Grotta Santa Caterina da Bagoga ★★ SIENESE This tiny, brick-vaulted dining room in a quiet corner of the center is run by former Palio-winning jockey "Bagoga"—check out the race memorabilia hung on the walls. Primi generally stick to the usual *pici* and *papperdelle* pasta sauces, but things get interesting when the mains come around. There's plenty of classic Southern Tuscan grills, but the kitchen is especially strong on stews, such as *coniglio alla Senese* (rabbit stewed on the bone with capers, tomatoes, and herbs), *peposo* (spicy beef stew), and even unusual dishes like *filetto alla birra scura* (beef in dark beer). From a spectacular selection of desserts, each is paired with an appropriate sweet wine, including *Panpepato* (sticky Sienese cake dusted with pepper) with *vinpepato* (fortified chianti with herbs and spices) and a *bavarese* with a Moscadello from Montalcino. The romantically inclined should book ahead to secure one of four snug outdoor tables.

Via della Galluzza 26. ℂ **0577-282-208.** www.bagoga.it. Reservations recommended. Primi 7€–10€; secondi 7€–15€. AE, MC, V. Tues–Sun 12:30–2:30pm and 7:30–10:30pm. Bus: A (pink).

L'Osteria ★★ TUSCAN/GRILL The mission at this boisterous grill in Bruco *contrada* is straightforward: to turn out tasty cooking using local ingredients whenever possible. The menu is short and focused, emphasizing simple, ingredient-led dishes. Primi include the classic *pici cacio e pepe* (hand-rolled pasta with pecorino cheese and black pepper), but the grill is the star with flavor packed into seared beef, wild boar, *bistecca di vitello* (veal steak), and (our favorite) a

5

CHIANTI, SIENA & WESTERN HILL TOWNS

Siena

succulent *tagliata* of the local Cinta Senese breed of pig. Pair any of the above with a simple side of *patate fritte* (fries) or garbanzo beans dressed with olive oil and you have yourself a Tuscan taste sensation.

Via de' Rossi 79–81. ℂ **0577-287-592.** Reservations highly recommended. Primi 6€–8€; secondi 7.50€–18€. AE, MC, V. Mon–Sat 12:30–2:30pm and 7:30–10:30pm.

INEXPENSIVE

Osteria La Chiacchera 🗲 SIENESE This is a tiny joint with worn wooden tables, terra-cotta floors, and barrel ends embedded everywhere. "The Chatterbox" proudly serves Sienese "poor people's food." Young couples come here to save money on the date (not only is it cheap, but there's no cover charge or service fee—though tips are greatly appreciated). A choice first course is the *pici boscaiola* (long strands of fat, hand-rolled pasta in tomato-and-mushroom sauce), though the *penne arrabbiata* (in piquant tomato sauce) goes pretty quickly, too. Secondi are simple peasant dishes such as *salsicce e fagioli* (grilled sausages with beans) and *stracotto* (beef and boiled potatoes in piquant tomato sauce). They also do a mean chocolate pie.

Costa di Sant'Antonio 4 (near San Domenico, off Via della Sapienza under the Albergo Bernini). ℂ **0577-280-631.** Reservations recommended. Primi 6€–7€; secondi 7€–8€. MC, V. Daily noon–3pm and 7pm–midnight. Bus: A (red).

North into the Val d'Elsa

Monteriggioni ★, 14km (8½ miles) northwest of Siena along the SS2, is one of the most perfectly preserved fortified villages in all of Italy. (You've probably seen aerial photos of its stone streets at postcard stands.) The town was once a Sienese outpost; the city's soldiers patrolled the walls and kept an eye out for Florentine troops from the towers. All 14 of these vantage points have survived more or less intact since the day Dante likened them to the circle of Titans guarding the lowest level of Hell. Between April and September, you can climb up to a couple to admire the view; the ticket booth is open daily 9:30am to 1:30pm and 2 to 7:30pm, and access costs 1.50€. The **tourist office** is at Piazza Roma 23, 53035 Monteriggioni (ℂ **0577-304-810;** www.monteriggioniturismo.it).

Although more day-trippers are stopping by every year, Monteriggioni remains a sleepy little place. There's a board-rated four-star hotel (**Hotel Monteriggioni;** www.hotelmonteriggioni.net; ℂ **0577-305-009;** doubles 230€) hidden in one of the buildings, but you'll find a better value at one of the three central, characterful rooms, decorated in the Tuscan style with modern bathrooms, let by **Ristorante da Remo** (ℂ **0577-304-370**), at 80€ to 100€ a night. The quad with a mezzanine, ideal for families, costs the same as the doubles. Much of the village is taken up with quiet gardens and a few olive trees. Monteriggioni is content to offer you a lunch at one of its two restaurants, and sell you a few postcards from the shops on the central piazza.

Another 11km (7 miles) along a secondary road takes you to **Colle di Val d'Elsa** ★, the medieval birthplace of master Gothic architect Arnolfo di Cambio, who designed Florence's Palazzo Vecchio and Duomo. The **tourist office** is at Via Campana 43, 53034 Colle di Val d'Elsa (ℂ **0577-922-791;** www.comune. collevaldelsa.it). Regular buses run here from Siena and San Gimignano. Don't enter Colle's old city at the east end; instead, circle around the small center to come in the west side for the proper introduction, passing under the yawning arch of Baccio d'Agnolo's Mannerist **Palazzo Campana** gate (1539).

The intact walled village of Monteriggioni.

The main road of the Old Town, Via del Castello, leads to **Piazza del Duomo.** The cathedral contains one of the nails supposedly used to crucify Christ in a Mino da Fiesole tabernacle and a bronze *Crucifix* designed by Giambologna and cast by his student Pietro Tacca over the high altar. Next door is the **Palazzo Pretorio,** which houses a small **Museo Archeologico** (*©* 0577-922-954; www.museocolle.it) with a rather bland Etruscan collection and some 14th- and 15th-century frescoes. The communists jailed here in the 1920s scrawled political graffiti on some of the walls. May through September, it's open Tuesday through Sunday from 10:30am to 12:30pm and 4:30 to 7:30pm; October through April, hours are Tuesday through Friday from 3:30 to 5:30pm and weekends from 10am to noon and 3 to 6pm. Admission is 3€, 2€ for children and seniors. A fine set of Sienese-school paintings resides in the nearby **Museo Civico e d'Arte Sacra,** Via del Castello 31 (*©* 0577-923-888), housed in the **Palazzo dei Priori.** It's open April through October Tuesday through Sunday from 10am to 12:30pm and 4:30 to 7:30pm; November through March, hours are weekends only from 10am to noon and 3:30 to 6:30pm. Admission here is also 3€, 2€ for children and seniors. If you can find time to dine, the **Officina della Cucina Popolare** ★, Via Gracco del Secco 86 (*©* 0577-921-796; www.cucina-popolare.com), serves the best seasonal Tuscan food for miles in any direction.

ASCIANO & THE CRETE SENESI

Asciano is 106km (66 miles) S of Florence; 29km (18 miles) SE of Siena

Asciano

The SS438 winds a gloriously scenic 26km (16 miles) from Siena to **Asciano** ★, a small town still partially girded by its 1351 walls. The town's **tourist office** is by the main road on Via delle Fonti, 53041 Asciano (*©* 0577-718-811). April to October hours are Tuesday through Sunday from 10:30am to 1pm, plus Tuesday,

Friday, and Saturday 3 to 6pm. November to March it's Friday and Saturday only 10:30am to 1pm.

The 14th-century **Museo Palazzo Corboli** ★, Corso Matteotti 122 (✆ **0577-719-524**), has charming frescoes on humanist themes and allegories, a 1410 *Annunciation* carved in wood by Francesco di Valdambrino, Matteo di Giovanni's altarpiece from the town's church of Sant'Agostino, and Ambrogio Lorenzetti's *St. Michael* altarpiece. The Etruscan collections were gleaned from tombs discovered in the area and include a couple of nicely painted 3rd- to 5th-century-B.C. vases, funerary urns, and the standard pile of pottery bits. Between March and October, the *palazzo* is open Tuesday through Sunday from 10:30am to 1pm and 3 to 6:30pm; November to February it's Friday through Sunday 10:30am to 1pm and 3 to 5:30pm. Admission is 4.50€ adults, 3€ for students and seniors 65 and over.

At the town's **Museo Cassioli,** Via Fiume 8, is a collection of late-19th- and early-20th-century art by a local artist and his son (open Wed–Sun in summer, weekends only otherwise). Admission prices are the same as for the Palazzo Corboli, or there's a 7€ ticket covering both. Asciano's Romanesque and Gothic **Collegiata,** built of travertine between the 10th and 13th centuries, has, unusually, three apses and a 15th-century Sienese-school crucifix over the altar. You'll find the best lunch in town at **La Mencia** ★, Corso Matteotti 85 (✆ **0577-718-227;** www.lamencia.it), where star primi include the likes of *fusilli con zucca gialla, porri e pecorino* (pasta spirals with squash, leeks, and pecorino cheese) and secondi includes such dishes as *bistecca di cinta senese con salsa di mele* (local pork steak with apple sauce). Primi cost around 9€, secondi range from 12€ to 16€, and there's also a pizza list (5€–8€). It's closed Monday.

The Crete Senesi

Asciano is surrounded by *biancane,* land formations where erosion has left emerald lawns, sitting like toupees atop knobby white hills. These blend to the south with the *Crete Senesi,* a similarly eerie landscape of eroded clay and

Monte Oliveto Maggiore.

limestone hillsides with farmhouses perched atop deep washed-out gullies and cypress crowded along sheer ridges. In the center of these weird badlands, accessible by a spectacular minor road out of Asciano, the abbey of **Monte Oliveto Maggiore** ★ (✆ **0577-707-611**) is hidden in its own womb of pines.

Founded in 1313 by a group of wealthy Sienese businessmen who wanted to devote themselves to the contemplative life, the red-brick monastic complex was built by the early 15th century. The Olivetans, still an active order within the Benedictines, were trying to restore some of the original simplicity and charity of the Benedictine rule, and the monks cared for victims during the 1340s Black Death. What draws most visitors today is the 36-scene **fresco cycle** by Luca Signorelli and Sodoma, one of the masterpieces of High Renaissance narrative painting and Sodoma's greatest work. After parking, walk under the gate tower with its small cafe and through the cool woods for about 5 minutes to the bulky brick heart of the complex. The entrance to the monastery is around to the right: A signed doorway leads into the **Chiostro Grande** ★★ and puts you right at the frescoes' start.

Signorelli started the job of illustrating the *Life of St. Benedict* here in 1497. He finished nine of the scenes before skipping town the next year to work on Orvieto's Duomo. Antonio Bazzi arrived in 1505 and finished the cycle by 1508 in his own inimitable style. Bazzi was known as "Il Sodoma," a derogatory nickname that Vasari suggests was due to Bazzi's predilection for young men. Sodoma was married at least three times, however, and may have had in the neighborhood of 30 children. To follow the cycle's narrative, start in the back-left corner as you enter. On the third, or west, wall are the Signorellis. Scene 20, *Benedict Sending Mauro to France and Placido to Sicily,* is an interlude by Il Riccio. Scenes 21 to 28, starting with *Florenzo's Death,* are by Signorelli (his last work, no. 29, was destroyed when a door was installed). Sodoma did most of the rest of the painting in this part of the monastery, including the grotesques and monotone details on the pilasters between the scenes, a self-portrait (with pet badger; panel 3), and two fine separate frescoes: a small *Christ at the Column* and *St. Benedict Confers the Rule on the Olivetans,* both in the passage leading from the church. Afterward, pop into the **church** to see some gorgeous intarsia choir stalls by Giovanni da Verona (1505) with scenes including cityscapes modeled in precise perspective. Monte Oliveto is open daily from 9am to noon (12:30pm Sun) and 3 to 6pm (until 5pm from the last Sun in Oct to the last Sun in Mar). Admission is free.

The SS451 leads southwest out of the Crete 9km (5½ miles) to the Via Cassia SS2 and **Buonconvento.** Hidden within a ring of plain suburbs are Buonconvento's pretty medieval core and an excellent small museum of Sienese-school art, the **Museo d'Arte Sacra della Val d'Arbia,** Via Soccini 18 (✆ **0577-807-190;** www.museoartesacra.it), with works by Duccio, Sano di Pietro, Andrea di Bartolo, and Matteo di Giovanni. It's open April through September Wednesday from 3 to 6pm and Thursday through Sunday from 10am to 1pm and 3 to 6pm; winter hours are generally weekends only from 10am to 1pm and 3 to 5pm. Admission is 3.50€. Before leaving town, drop by the 14th-century **Santi Pietro e Paolo,** where you'll see a pair of 15th-century *Madonna and Child* paintings, one with saints by Pietro di Francesco degli Orioli and one without by Matteo di Giovanni. For more itineraries in and around the town, see **www.turismobuonconvento.it**.

The best hotel accommodations for miles in any direction are to be found at the **Locanda del Castello** ★, Piazza Vittorio Emanuele II 4, 53020 San Giovanni d'Asso (www.lalocandadelcastello.com; ✆ **0577-502-939**), set 13km

(8 miles) northeast of Buonconvento in the pedestrian center of a tiny, silent little Crete village. Each of the nine rooms is decorated simply, in a refined take on the Tuscany rustic style, and the restaurant serves similarly sophisticated Tuscan flavors. Doubles cost around 120€.

SAN GIMIGNANO ★★

40km (25 miles) NW of Siena; 57km (35 miles) SW of Florence; 270km (168 miles) NW of Rome

The scene that hits you when you pass through the Porta San Giovanni gate, inside the walls of San Gimignano, and walk the narrow flagstone Via San Giovanni is thoroughly medieval. Okay, so the crossbows, flails, and halberds in shop windows are miniature souvenir versions, and the small Romanesque church facade halfway up the street today hides a modern wine shop. But, if you can mentally block out the racks of postcards, you've got a stage set straight out of the history books.

The center is peppered with the tall medieval towers that have made San Gimignano, "city of the beautiful towers," the poster child for Italian hill towns everywhere. No one can agree how many stone skyscrapers remain—so many have been chopped down it's a tough call whether they're still officially towers or merely tall, skinny buildings—but the official tower count the tourist office gives is 14. There were at one time somewhere between 70 and 76 of the things spiking the sky above this little village. The spires started rising in the bad old days of the 1200s, partly to defend against outside invaders but mostly as command centers for San Gimignano's warring families. Several successive waves of the plague that swept through (1348, 1464, and 1631) caused the economy (based on textiles and hosting passing pilgrims) to crumble, and San Gimignano became a provincial backwater. Because there was no impetus for new construction, by the time tourism began picking up in the 19th century, visitors found a preserved medieval village of crumbling towers.

San Gimignano's towers.

San Gimignano is by far the most popular Tuscan hill town, a day-trip destination for masses of tour buses coming from Siena and Florence. Therefore, the town is best enjoyed in the evening, after the tour buses leave, especially in the off season and on spring nights: The alleyways are empty, and you can wander in the yellow light of street lamps.

Essentials

GETTING THERE By Train: The approximately 30 daily trains on the line between **Siena** (trip time: 25–40 min.) and Empoli, where you can connect from **Florence** (1 hr.), stop at Poggibonsi. From **Poggibonsi,** over 30 buses make the 25-minute run to San Gimignano Monday through Saturday, but only six buses run on Sunday.

By Car: From the north, take the *Poggibonsi Nord* exit off the **Florence-Siena** highway or the SS2. San Gimignano is 12km (7½ miles) from Poggibonsi. From the south, including Siena, exit at *Colle di Val d'Elsa Sud* and follow signs. Colle is 15km (9½ miles) from San Gimignano.

By Bus: You almost always have to transfer buses at **Poggibonsi** (see "By Train," above). SITA (✆ 055-47-821; www.sitabus.it) and TRA-IN (✆ 0577-204-111; www.trainspa.it) codeshare hourly (at least, fewer on Sun) buses for most of the day from both **Florence** (50 min.) and **Siena** (45 min.) to Poggibonsi, many of which meet right up with the connection to San Gimignano (a further 20–25 min.). From **Siena** there are also 10 direct buses (1¼ hr.) Monday through Saturday, most stopping at **Colle di Val d'Elsa** on the way. In San Gimignano, buy tickets at the tourist office.

VISITOR INFORMATION The **tourist office** is at Piazza Duomo 1 (✆ 0577-940-008; www.sangimignano.com). It's open daily March through October from 9am to 1pm and 3 to 7pm, and November through February from 9am to 1pm and 2 to 6pm.

FESTIVALS & MARKETS The citizens dress up in elaborate masks and costumes for a **Carnival** parade just before Lent. **Dentro e Fuori le Mura** has, since 1924, brought some lightweight culture to town on the last weekend in July, with open-air opera recitals, classical concerts, and film screenings in the ruins of the Rocca fortress. Thursday and Saturday morning see a bustling **market** on Piazza del Duomo.

Exploring San Gimignano

Anchoring the town, at the top of Via San Giovanni, are its two interlocking triangular *piazze*: **Piazza della Cisterna ★★**, centered on a 1237 well, and **Piazza del Duomo,** flanked by the city's main church and civic palace. The town also has some fascinating outdoor frescoes that you can view for free. The archway to the left of the Collegiata's facade leads to a pretty brick courtyard called Piazza Pecori. On the right, under brick vaulting, is a fresco of the *Annunciation* painted in 1482 by either Domenico Ghirlandaio or his brother-in-law and pupil, Sebastiano Mainardi. The door to the right of the tourist office leads into a courtyard of the Palazzo del Comune, where Taddeo di Bartolo's 14th-century *Madonna and Child* is flanked by two works on the theme of justice by Sodoma, including his near-monochrome *St. Ivo.*

Collegiata ★★ The main church in town—it no longer has a bishop, so it's no longer officially a *duomo* (cathedral)—was started in the 11th century and took its present form in the 15th century. It's not much from the outside, but the interior is smothered in 14th-century frescoes, making it one of Tuscany's most densely decorated churches.

The right wall was frescoed from 1333 to 1341—most likely by Lippo Memmi—with three levels of **New Testament scenes** (22 in all) on the life and Passion of Christ along with a magnificent *Crucifixion.* In 1367, Bartolo di Fredi frescoed the left wall with 26 scenes out of the **Old Testament,** and Taddeo di Bartolo provided the gruesome *Last Judgment* frescoes around the main door in 1410. Benozzo Gozzoli wins the "Prickliest **St. Sebastian** in Tuscany" prize for his colorful and courtly 1464 rendition on the entrance wall.

In 1468, Giuliano da Maiano built the **Cappella di Santa Fina ★★** off the right aisle, and his brother Benedetto carved the relief panels for the altar. Florentine Renaissance master Domenico Ghirlandaio decorated the tiny chapel's walls with some of his finest, airiest works. With the help of assistants (his brother Davide and Sebastiano Mainardi), Ghirlandaio in 1475 frescoed two scenes summing up the life of Santa Fina, a local girl who, though never officially canonized, is one of San Gimignano's patron saints. Little Fina, who was very devout and wracked with guilt for having committed the sin of accepting an orange from a boy, fell down ill on a board one day and didn't move for 5 years, praying the entire time. Eventually, St. Gregory appeared to her and foretold her death, whereupon the board on which she lay miraculously produced flowers. When her corpse was carried solemnly to the church for a funeral, the city's towers burst forth with yellow pansies and angels flew up to ring the bells. At the church, a blind choirboy and Fina's

Gozzoli's *Martyrdom of St. Sebastian* at the Collegiata.

nurse, who had a paralyzed hand, found themselves miraculously cured merely by touching her body. The town still celebrates their child saint every year on March 12, when the pansies on San Gimignano's towers naturally bloom.

Piazza del Duomo. ✆ **0577-940-316.** Admission 3.50€ adults, 1.50€ ages 6–18. Feb–Mar, Nov, Dec–Jan Mon–Sat 10am–4:40pm, Sun 12:30–4:40pm; Apr–Oct Mon–Fri 10am–7:10pm, Sat 10am–5:10pm, Sun 12:30–7:10pm. Closed 1st Sun in Aug, Mar 12, Nov 16–30, and Jan 16–31.

Museo Archeologico & Spezieria di Santa Fina San Gimignano's modest Etruscan collection proves the town's roots run deeper than the Middle Ages. Atop one of the funerary urns, a reclining figure representing the deceased is holding the cup of life—now empty of all but a single coin to pay his way into the afterlife. This museum is now installed in the 1253 Spezieria, the pharmacy branch of the medieval Santa Fina hospital (though the painted druggery vases and other accouterments on display are largely 15th–18th c.). Upstairs is a surprisingly large and sporadically interesting **Galleria di Arte Moderna e Contemporanea,** usually deserted.

Via Folgore 11. ✆ **0577-940-348.** Admission on cumulative ticket, or 3.50€ adults, 2.50€ ages 6–18 and 65 and over. Daily 11am–6pm.

Museo Civico & Torre Grossa ★★ In the late 13th century, the city government moved from the Palazzo del Podestà, across from the Collegiata, to the brand-new **Palazzo del Comune** (or del Popolo). You can climb its **Torre Grossa ("Big Tower")** ★★, finished in 1311, for one of the best tower-top views of the cityscape and rolling countryside in Tuscany. Before the step workout, though, check out the **civic painting gallery.**

The small museum was built around a large fresco in the Sala del Consiglio of the *Maestà* ★★ (1317) by the Sienese Lippo Memmi. Up the stairs is the

Pinacoteca, but before entering it, duck through the door to the Camera del Podestà to see perhaps San Gimignano's most famous **frescoes** ★. Painted in the 14th century by Memmo di Filippuccio, they narrate a rather racy story of courtship and love in quite a departure from the usual religious themes of the era. The most oft-reproduced scenes are of a couple bathing together and then getting into bed for their wedding night.

A Discount Pass

You can buy a **cumulative ticket** that covers the Torre Grossa and Museo Civico; the tiny Museo Archeologico, Spezieria Santa Fina (a preserved Renaissance pharmacy), and Galleria di Arte Moderna modern art gallery; and the weird little **Museo Ornitologico** (✆ **0577-941-388**), a couple of glass cases containing stuffed birds in the dimly lit confines of a tiny, deconsecrated church. The ticket costs 7.50€ for adults and 5.50€ for ages 6 to 18 and 65 and over.

The first major work in the painting gallery that's especially strong on pre-Renaissance works is a Coppo di Marcovaldo Crucifix, immediately on the right, surrounded by Passion scenes, one of the masterpieces of 13th-century Tuscan art. Benozzo Gozzoli's *Madonna and Child with Saints* (1466) has an almost surreal *Pietà* with a delicate landscape running the length of the predella. A 25-year-old Filippino Lippi painted the matching tondi of the *Annunciation* in 1482, and the huge early-16th-century *Madonna in Glory with Sts. Gregory and Benedict,* with its wild Umbrian landscape, is a late work by Pinturicchio. That psychedelic almond-shaped rainbow of cherub heads over which Mary is hovering was one of Pinturicchio's favorite painterly devices to symbolize virginity.

Two works in the rooms to the right tell the stories of the city's most popular patron saints. Lorenzo di Niccolò Gerini did a passable job in 1402 on the *Tabernacle of Santa Fina,* built to house the teen saint's head and painted with scenes of the four most important miracles of her brief life. In the late 14th century, Taddeo di Bartolo painted the *Life of St. Gimignano* as an altarpiece for the Collegiata; the saint himself sits in the middle, holding in his lap the town he was constantly invoked to protect.

This city, you see, was founded by the Etruscans and originally called Castel di Selva. When Totila the Goth was rampaging through the area in the 6th century A.D., the town decided to pray—no one is quite sure why—to Gimignano, an obscure martyred bishop from the distant city of Modena. The sanctified bishop came riding out of the clouds clad in golden armor, and the Goths took to their heels and left the city alone (the lower-left panels illustrate this). The town gratefully changed its name and has kept St. Gimignano on call ever since.

Piazza del Duomo. ✆ **0577-990-312.** Admission on cumulative ticket, or 5€ adults, 4€ ages 6–18 and 65 and over. Apr–Sept daily 9:30am–7pm; Oct–Mar daily 10am–5:30pm.

Museo della Tortura (Torture Museum) ☺ The Torture Museum (the original one in town, not to be mistaken with

A Great Point of View

Behind the Collegiata, the remains of the city's 14th-century fortress, the **Rocca,** are now a public park. Climb atop the crumbling ramparts for a view of the surrounding farmland and the best panorama of San Gimignano's towers. There's also a little **Museo del Vino** (✆ **0577-941-267**) inside, where you can taste Tuscany's only DOCG white wine, Vernaccia di San Gimignano (3.50€–5€ a glass).

poorer imitations) is serendipitously installed in the medieval **Torre del Diavolo (Devil's Tower).** Its iron maidens, racks—both the spiked and unspiked varieties—chastity belts, various bone-crunching manacles, breast-rippers, and other medieval party favors are accompanied by engrossingly dispassionate descriptions of their uses and history. If nothing else, older kids might think it's cool (though the historical etchings and watercolors showing the torture instruments at work are potentially upsetting).

Via del Castello 1 (just off Piazza della Cisterna). *C* **0577-942-243.** Admission 8€ adults, 5.50€ students. Mar daily 10am–5pm; Apr–Oct daily 10am–7pm; Nov–Feb Mon–Fri 10:30am–4:30pm, Sat–Sun 10am–6pm.

San Gimignano 1300 ★ ☺ It took a team of five skilled craftsmen (two named Michelangelo and Raffaello, honestly) 3 years and a ton of clay to build the 800 structures that make up this 1:100 scale model of San Gimignano around 1300, with its 72 towers intact. It's not just a child-size model of this enchanting place; serious historical archive research by the universities at Florence and Pisa contributed to what is a unique reproduction of a medieval walled town, by digging up details of buildings long lost to history. Make sure to stick around long enough until night falls over the model, too.

Via Berignano 23. *C* **0577-941-078.** www.sangimignano1300.com. Admission 5€ adults, 3€ children. Jun–Aug daily 8am–11pm; Sept–May daily 8am–8pm.

Sant'Agostino ★ This 13th-century church at the north end of town is full of accomplished 15th-century frescoes. In 1464, a plague swept the town and the citizens prayed to their patron saint to end it. When the sickness passed, they dutifully hired Benozzo Gozzoli to paint a thankful scene, on the nave's left wall, showing St. Sebastian and his cloak full of angels stopping and breaking the plague arrows being thrown down by a vengeful God and his angelic hosts. The city liked the results, so they commissioned Gozzoli to spend the next 2 years frescoing the choir behind the main altar floor-to-ceiling with scenes rich in architectural detail from the *Life of St. Augustine* ★★.

Against the main entrance wall is a chapel filled with an elaborate marble tomb (1495) by Benedetto di Maiano. Sebastiano Mainardi painted the frescoes on the chapel's vaults and the *Saints Gimignano* (holding his city), *Lucy, and Nicholas of Bari* to the left of the tomb. Next to the cloister door on the nave's left wall is another fresco by Sebastiano Mainardi, of an enthroned St. Gimignano blessing three city dignitaries.

Piazza Sant'Agostino. *C* **0577-907-012.** Free admission. Daily 7am–noon and 3–7pm (Nov–Apr closes at 6pm, and Jan to mid-Apr closed Mon mornings).

Where to Stay

Hotels here aren't cheap, nor are they by any measure the finest lodgings in Tuscany. However, there is a special ambience about the center of San Gimignano at dusk, when the tour groups are gone, so below we recommend our favorites in the town itself. If you prefer to find a farmhouse bed-and-breakfast or *agriturismo* nearby, of which there are dozens, the San Gimignano tourist office (see above) has an extensive selection and can book on your behalf.

L'Antico Pozzo ★ L'Antico Pozzo is the choicest inn within the walls, a 15th-century *palazzo* converted to a hotel in 1990 with careful attention to preserving the structural antiquity without sacrificing convenience. Over the building's colorful history it has hosted Dante, the Inquisition trials, a religious community, and an 18th-century salon. Accommodations vary in size and decor, but none is small, and the large junior suites have wood ceilings and spumante waiting for you. Throughout, the furnishings are simple wooden 19th-century pieces, and the firm beds are surrounded by cast-iron frames—the junior suites come with canopies. "Superior" doubles have 17th-century ceiling frescoes and the smaller "standard" rooms on the third floor have wood floors and a view of the Rocca and a few towers.

Take a Hike

The tourist office sponsors 6km (4-mile) guided walks through the countryside on weekend afternoons March through October, costing 20€ per person (walks occur if at least two people make reservations). Because the country edges right up to San Gimignano's walls, you could also easily set out on your own to wander with a good map—the tourist office sells an excellent 1:25,000 map for 7€, marked with suggested hikes and walks, or you can pick one up from any local souvenir stand.

Via San Matteo 87, 53037 San Gimignano. www.anticopozzo.com. ✆ **0577-942-014.** Fax 0577-942-117. 18 units. 110€–140€ double; 165€–180€ superior double. Rates include breakfast. DC, MC, V. Garage parking 20€. Closed for 20 days Jan–Feb. **Amenities:** Bar; babysitting; bikes; concierge; smoke-free rooms. *In room:* A/C, TV, hair dryer, minibar, Wi-Fi (1 hr. daily free).

La Cisterna The rooms in this friendly hotel, installed in the bases of 14th-century tower stumps, vary in size; some are quite large and others seem almost cramped, but all are comfortable, with firm beds and a tastefully uncluttered decor. The place was scenic enough to serve as a set for the film version of E. M. Forster's novel *Where Angels Fear to Tread.* You have a choice of views: the bustling piazza side or the expansive valley view out back (including from our favorite unit, no. 59). Don't go for the cheapest rooms with no view at all; you get a vista starting around 100€, and can add a balcony for another 10€. Skip the restaurant—there's better eating in town.

Piazza della Cisterna 23, 53037 San Gimignano. www.hotelcisterna.it. ✆ **0577-940-328.** Fax 0577-942-080. 48 units. 85€–150€ double. Rates include buffet breakfast. AE, DC, MC, V. Closed Jan 7–Mar 7. **Amenities:** Restaurant (closed Tues and lunch Wed); bar; babysitting; concierge; Wi-Fi (free). *In room:* A/C, TV, hair dryer, minibar (some).

Leon Bianco ★ Typical of a 500-year-old building turned hotel, the rooms here can't seem to agree on a style or decor scheme, but most retain some element from the 14th-century *palazzo*—a painted wood-beam ceiling here, an old stone wall in a bathroom there, or a brick barrel vault filling one room. Accommodations overlook the pretty well of the tower-lined piazza out front or across rooftops to the countryside. (A few, however, overlook the partially glassed-in courtyard of the lobby.) "Superior" rooms are larger and come with minibars. The rooms are perhaps less well appointed than those at the Antico Pozzo (see above), but along with La Cisterna (see above), this place has the most central location in town.

Piazza della Cisterna, 53037 San Gimignano. www.leonbianco.com. ✆ **0577-941-294.** Fax 0577-942-123. 26 units. 85€–118€ standard double; 115€–138€ superior double. Rates include breakfast. AE, DC, MC, V. Closed Nov 10 until just before Christmas and Jan 10 to early Feb. **Amenities:** Bar; concierge; exercise room; Jacuzzi; room service; smoke-free rooms. *In room:* A/C, TV, hair dryer, minibar (.50€/hr.).

Where to Eat

Few of San Gimignano's restaurants are outstanding, but its white wine certainly is. **Vernaccia di San Gimignano,** the only DOCG white wine in Tuscany, is a slightly peppery, dry wine old enough to have been cited in Dante's *Divine Comedy.* Our favorite place to sip a glass or two is on the couple of panoramic tables at **diVinorum ★**, Via degli Innocenti 5 (✆ **0577-907-192;** www.divino rumwinebar.com). There are over 20 wines by the glass and *bruschettone* (large bruschetta) to accompany them cost around 8€. The town's essential foodie stop is **Gelateria di Piazza ★★**, Piazza della Cisterna 4 (✆ **0577-942-244**), for creative combinations like raspberry and rosemary (it works) and the signature crema di Santa Fina, made with saffron.

Chiribiri ☺ 🍴 ITALIAN This cramped, eight-table trattoria in a tiny cellar at the southern tip of town is an oasis of value among some distinctly overpriced competition. The food is straight-up Italian classics with a Tuscan twist: lasagne or spaghetti with a choice of sauces to start; beef in chianti, cinghiale in umido (wild boar stew), and *osso buco* are among the well-executed mains. Handily for families, it's also open all day, so kids can eat when they want.

Piazzetta della Madonna 1. ✆ **0577-941-948.** Reservations recommended. Primi 6€–7€; secondi 8€–12€. No credit cards. Daily 11am–11pm.

Dorandò ★★ TUSCAN Dorandò is an elegant splurge tucked away just off Piazza Duomo, where the stone-walled rooms, alabaster platters, and knowledge-able waiters create a backdrop for San Gimignano's best fine dining. The chef attempts to keep the oldest traditions of Sangimignanese cooking alive—many of the recipes purport to be medieval, some even Etruscan, in origin—while balancing Slow Food philosophy with hearty home-cooking quality. The menu varies with the season and market, but if the excellent *cibrèo* (chicken livers and giblets scented with ginger and lemon) is offered, by all means order it. Desserts are excellent, too.

Vicolo dell'Oro 2. ✆ **0577-941-862.** www.ristorantedorando.it. Reservations highly recommended. Primi 14€–15€; secondi 20€–24€; tasting menu 50€. AE, MC, V. Tues–Sun (daily Easter–Sept) noon–2:30pm and 7–9:30pm. Closed Dec 10–Jan 31.

Osteria delle Catene ★ TUSCAN This is an *osteria* true to its name, a small gathering place offering ultra-traditional dishes to accompany its well-priced se-lection of local wines. The decor can only be described as minimalist medieval, with contemporary paintings and modern lighting in concert with an abbrevi-ated barrel vault made of hand-cast bricks. A great appetizer to pair with your Vernaccia is the *piatto misto di prosciutto* (with both pig and boar ham) along with *formaggi Toscani* (Tuscan cheeses). The *ribollita* adds a purée of cannellini beans to the usual mix, and the *penne al porro* (stubby pasta quills in cheesy leek sauce) is an eminent pasta choice. If you're still hungry, try a Tuscan standby like *salsicce con fagioli all'uccelletto* (grilled sausage with beans stewed with tomatoes).

Via Mainardi 18 (near Porta San Matteo). ✆ **0577-941-966.** www.osteriadellecatene.it. Reser-vations recommended. Primi 8€–10€; secondi 13€–14€; fixed-price menu without wine 22€. MC, V. Thurs–Tues noon–2pm and 7–9pm (closed Sun evenings). Closed occasionally Dec–Feb.

VOLTERRA

29km (18 miles) SW of San Gimignano; 50km (31 miles) W of Siena; 72km (45 miles) SW of Florence; 300km (186 miles) NW of Rome

Volterra is, in the words of the writer D. H. Lawrence, "on a towering great bluff that gets all the winds and sees all the world." The city seems to rear higher than any other in Tuscany, rising a precipitous 540m (1,772 ft.) above the valley below. It's a fortresslike town, drawn out thinly along a narrow ridge with a warren of medieval alleys falling steeply off the main piazza.

Lawrence came here to study the Etruscans, who took the 9th-century-B.C. town established by the Villanovan culture and by the 4th century B.C. had turned it into Velathri, one of the largest centers in Etruria's 12-city confederation. The Etruscans left some haunting bronzes and a stupefying collection of alabaster funerary urns. The art of carving the translucent white alabaster still flourishes today in artisan workshops scattered throughout the city, but modern Volterra has only recently moved beyond the shrunken womb of its medieval inner circle of walls to fill in the abandoned extent of Velathri's 4th-century-B.C. defensive belt. These days it's as likely to be known as the fictional home of the Volturi, from Stephanie Meyer's teen vampire trilogy, *Twilight*.

Essentials

GETTING THERE By Train: Volterra isn't very convenient by train, with a station only at **Saline di Volterra** 10km (6¼ miles) away, to which six daily trains run from Cécina (trip time: 30 min.) on the coast. Buses meet the incoming trains for the 20-minute ride up to the center. From points north, take the train to **Pontedera** (on the Pisa-Florence line) then switch to a 1¼-hour bus connection (10 per day Mon–Sat).

By Car: Driving by car is comfortably the simplest option for getting here: Volterra is on the SS68 about 30km (19 miles) from where it branches off the Colle di Val d'Elsa exit on the Florence-Siena highway. From San Gimignano, head southwest on the secondary road to Castel di San Gimignano, which is on the SS68. The most convenient free parking is at **Vallebuona,** by the Teatro Romano (not Sat 6am–3pm).

By Bus: From **Siena,** there are 16 daily TRA-IN buses (www.trainspa. it) that make the 20- to 30-minute trip to **Colle di Val d'Elsa,** from which there are four daily buses to Volterra (50 min.). From **San Gimignano,** you have to first take a bus to Poggibonsi (20 min.), four of which daily link up with buses to Colle di Val d'Elsa for the final transfer. From **Florence,** take one of five daily buses (three on Sun) to Colle di Val d'Elsa and transfer there (2½–3 hr. total). Six to 10 **CPT** (www.cpt.pisa.it) buses run here Monday through Saturday from **Pisa** (change in Pontedera; 2–2½ hr. total). **Tickets** and information in Volterra are available at the tourist office.

VISITOR INFORMATION Volterra's helpful **tourist office,** Piazza dei Priori 19–20, 56048 Volterra (© 0588-87-257; www.volterratur.it), offers both tourist information and free hotel reservations. It's open daily from 9:30am to 1pm and 2 to 6pm.

FESTIVALS & MARKETS Volterrateatro is the town's July theater festival. The best local event for families is **Volterra AD1398** (© 0588-86-099; www. volterra1398.it), on the final two Sundays in August. The town dresses head-to-toe in medieval garb, and kids don 14th-century dress and get to play as wool merchants or craftspeople. On the first Sunday of September, Volterrans dress up in medieval costume to engage in a bit of flag-tossing on Piazza dei Priori, an event known as the **Astiludio.** The sizable **weekly market** is Saturday morning adjacent to the Teatro Romano.

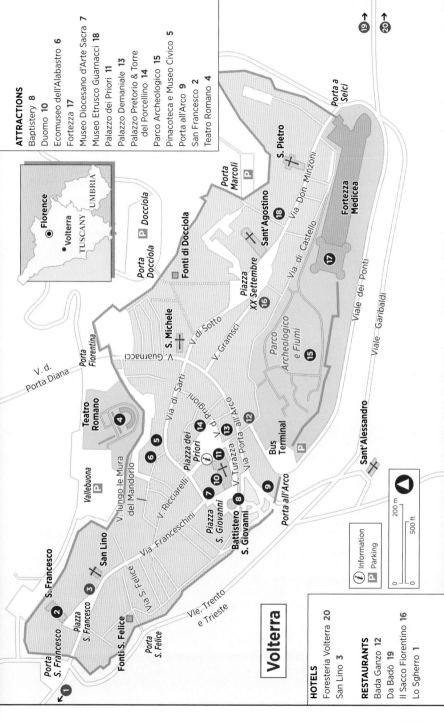

Volterra

ATTRACTIONS
Baptistery 8
Duomo 10
Ecomuseo dell'Alabastro 6
Fortezza 17
Museo Diocesano d'Arte Sacra 7
Museo Etrusco Guarnacci 18
Palazzo dei Priori 11
Palazzo Demaniale 13
Palazzo Pretorio & Torre del Porcellino 14
Parco Archeologico 15
Pinacoteca e Museo Civico 5
Porta all'Arco 9
San Francesco 2
Teatro Romano 4

HOTELS
Foresteria Volterra 20
San Lino 3

RESTAURANTS
Bada Ganzo 12
Da Badò 19
Il Sacco Fiorentino 16
Lo Sgherro 1

(i) Information
P Parking

223

Exploring Volterra

One **cumulative admission ticket** covers all three major museums—the Museo Etrusco Guarnacci, Museo Diocesano d'Arte Sacra, and Pinacoteca e Museo Civico. It costs 10€ adults, 6€ students and seniors 60 and over, 20€ family of five (children 5 and under are admitted free). All museums' summer hours run March 16 through November 1.

You only need walk the narrow streets at night to appreciate that Volterra does spooky pretty well. Appropriately, it served as the backdrop to pivotal scenes in Stephenie Meyer's 2006 teen-vampire novel *New Moon,* part of the smash *Twilight* trilogy (although the 2009 movie was shot in Montepulciano). Fans of the story can take an excellent guided walking tour to follow in the footsteps of Edward and Bella to some of Volterra's secret places, and enjoy a theatrical "surprise finale" in the creepy confines of a 1st-century Roman well. The tour costs a slightly expensive 30€ per person, runs irregularly, and lasts about 1½ hours. Book before 1pm at the tourist office (see above); nonfans are discouraged, but there is a discount for family groups (four tickets for the price of three) if you show this guidebook. See **www.newmoonofficialtour.com** for dates. If your budget won't stretch, the tourist office issues a special *New Moon* version of its town map, with key locations marked.

IN SEARCH OF craftsmanship

Volterrans have been working the watery, translucent calcium sulfate stone found around their mountain for almost 3,000 years. The Etruscans turned the **alabaster** into the sarcophagi that fill the Guarnacci museum; the industry revived in the late 19th century, mainly to crank out lampshades for the exploding market in electric lights. The working of alabaster is taken very seriously in town, and you can major in it at the local art school.

The *comune* has put Plexiglas plaques at the workshops of some of the best traditional artisans, who still handwork every stage. The large **Rossi Alabastri** (✆ **0588-86-133**) outfit works out of a shop at Piazzetta della Pescheria, at one end of the Roman theater panoramic walk. At **alab'Arte** ★, Via Orti S. Agostino 28 (✆ **0588-87-968;** www.alabarte.com), you can roam the open sculptural workshop and buy finished pieces that catch your eye. Via Porta all'Arco has several fine shops, including the town's top artiste, **Paolo Sabatini** ★, at no. 45 (✆ **0588-87-594**). For some of the better craft objects, the **Società Cooperativa Artieri Alabastro,** Piazza dei Priori 4–5

(✆ **0588-87-590**), has since 1895 been a cooperative showroom and sales outlet for artisans who don't have big enough operations to open their own.

The town's rep for workmanship goes beyond alabaster, too. **Fabula Etrusca,** Via Lunga le Mura del Mandorlo 10 (✆ **0588-87-401;** www.fabulae trusca.it), sells exquisite (but expensive) handcrafted jewelry, much of it made to Etruscan-influenced designs. Prints and lithographs created from hand-engraved zinc plates are another specialty. Our two favorite workshops, where everything is created on-site, are **L'Istrice** ★, Via Porta all'Arco 23 (✆ **0588-85-422;** www.laboistrice.it) and **Bubo Bubo** ★, Via Roma 24 (✆ **0588-80-307**).

Baptistery The baptistery drum, with its one side of distinctive black-and-white marble bands, was built in 1283, but the dome was added in the 16th century. Just inside the door is an Etruscan funerary urn recycled as a holy water stoup, and in the center is an 18th-century font. This polychrome affair replaced the smaller, more elegant **marble font** Andrea Sansovino carved with simple reliefs in 1502, now against the right wall.

Piazza San Giovanni. No phone. Free admission. Summer daily 7am–7pm; winter daily 8am–12:30pm and 3–6pm.

Duomo ★ Beyond the 13th-century Pisan-style facade, the first thing that strikes you in this 12th-century church is its coffered **ceiling.** It was carved and embossed with gold and azure in 1580 and is filled with portraits of

Volterra's Duomo.

Volterran saints, including St. Linus, a venerable native son who became the world's second pope, filling St. Peter's shoes in A.D. 67.

Volterra's Duomo is filled with well-done baroque paintings, but few stand out. Among those that do is the first altarpiece on the right, Belgian Mannerist Pieter de Witte's *Presentation of Volterra to the Virgin,* with a 1578 view of the city. In the right transept, above the door to the Chapel of the Holy Sacrament, is a 1611 *Crucifixion* by Francesco Curradi—a good baroque study of light and fabric. Across the transept from this chapel is a life-size sculpted wood group of the **Deposition ★**, painted in bright primaries and heavy gold. It looks vaguely mid-20th-century but was actually carved around 1228 by anonymous Pisan masters, artists who were bridging the gap between stiff Byzantine traditions and the more fluid, emotional art of the Romanesque era.

In the left aisle of the church is a **pulpit** assembled from 13th-century Pisan relief panels in the 16th century; the *Last Supper* facing the nave is particularly arresting for its visual style and whimsical detail. Next up the left aisle is a magnificently restored 1497 *Annunciation ★* by Fra' Bartolomeo.

In the **Cappella dell'Addolorata (Lady Chapel) ★**, off the end of the left aisle, in the niche housing the *Nativity* terra cottas, Benozzo Gozzoli frescoed an intimate backdrop for the scene, placing it in a rocky pass bursting with foliage and the horse train of the Magi riding in from the distance.

Piazza San Giovanni. No phone. Free admission. Summer daily 8am–12:30pm and 3–6pm; winter daily 8am–12:30pm and 3–5pm.

Ecomuseo dell'Alabastro Start with the first disc laid for the Tower of Pisa, kept at this small museum, and you'll start to get a feel for the importance of this porous stone in western Tuscany. The most significant highlight is the collection of 19th-century hand-carved cameos by Luigi Albino Funaioli: delicate bas-reliefs and portraits of the ladies and gentlemen of the era. Upstairs is a description of how the stone is formed, and later extricated and carved, as well as a sweeping view of the valley below from the third-floor tower.

A Cappuccino, a Gelato & a Glass of Wine

Right on the main square, with a few tables outside, sits the very friendly little **Bar Priori,** Piazza Priori 2 (no phone), our regular coffee-break stop. There's nowhere better than **L'Incontro** ★, Via Matteoti 18 (② **0588-80-500**), for a gelato or relaxed pit stop, with home-made pastries. Their artisan chocolate is also pretty good. Our favorite enoteca in town is grottolike **La Vena di Vino,** Via Don Minzoni 30 (② **0588-81-491;** www. lavenadivino.com), which has an especially good range of reds plus cheese platters to accompany them. Glasses range from 2€ to 6€.

Piazza Minucci. ② **0588-875-80.** Admission 3.50€ adults, 2.50€ children aged 6–18, students, and seniors 65 and over, 8€ family. Summer daily 11am–5pm; winter Sat–Sun 9am–1:30pm.

Museo Diocesano d'Arte Sacra The medieval and early Renaissance fragments salvaged from an older version of the cathedral and other Volterran churches along with a few good paintings make this small museum a good half-hour bonus if you've bought the town's cumulative admission ticket. Among the sculptural pieces are some works by Tino di Camaino and Romanesque elements fitted with Roman friezes. Giovanni della Robbia may have crafted the painted terra-cotta *Bust of San Lino,* while Antonio Pollaiolo created the hyper-realist silver-and-gilt reliquary *Bust of San Ottaviano.* Of the paintings, keep an eye out for Rosso Fiorentino's Mannerist *Madonna of Villamagna* (1521) and a *Madonna of Ulignano* (1545) by Daniele "da Volterra" Ricciarelli.

Palazzo Vescovile, Via Roma 13. ② **0588-86-290.** Admission by cumulative ticket. Daily 9am–1pm (summer also 3–6pm).

Museo Etrusco Guarnacci ★★ Volterra has managed to hold on to a horde of valuable remains from its rich past: Presentation at this museum is a little dry, but this is without doubt one of the world's leading Etruscan collections. Besides the prehistoric section with its Villanovan tombs and some Roman busts and mosaic floors, the lion's share of this three-floor museum is taken up with more than 600 **Etruscan funerary urns** ★. Most of these date from the 3rd century B.C., but there are some entire tomb finds gathered from as early as the 9th century B.C. The urns—rectangular boxes about 3 feet long, the oldest ones in plain terra cotta, but most carved of alabaster or other stones with a relief on the front and capped with a lid sculpted with the reclining figure of the deceased—are grouped by their many styles and types. The effect of room after room lined with these intricate studies on the Etruscans' views of life and death is fascinating.

The reliefs and reclining effigies often show a primitive naturalism unmatched even by the Renaissance, and because many of the panels depict the symbolic departure of the deceased to the realm of the dead—on horseback, in wagons, aboard ships, riding centaurs, driving chariots—there's room for plenty of touching episodes where friends and family are shown waving their last goodbyes. One of the finest, the **Urna degli Sposi** ★ is a striking bit of portraiture: an early-1st-century-B.C. sarcophagus lid carved with the figures of a husband and wife, both very old, somewhat dour-faced and full of wrinkles, but staying together even in death. Also here, among the bronzes, is an early-3rd-century-B.C. votive figure of an exceedingly elongated young boy known as the *Ombra della Sera (Shadow of the Evening)* ★★.

Via Don Minzoni 15. ☎ **0588-86-347.** Admission by cumulative ticket, or 8€. Summer daily 9am–7pm; winter daily 8:30am–1:45pm.

Palazzo dei Priori The Palazzo dei Priori (1208–57) is the oldest building of its kind in Tuscany, the Gothic town hall on which Florence's Palazzo Vecchio and most other civic buildings in the region were modeled. Walk up to the first floor to see the town council chamber, which aside from getting a new vaulted ceiling in 1516 has pretty much looked the same over its 740 years of continuous use. The end wall was frescoed with an *Annunciation* by Jacopo di Cione or his brother Orcagna in 1383.

Volterra's civic palace sits on a medieval rectangle of a piazza. The **Piazza dei Priori** ★ is laid with mason-cut stone and surrounded on all sides with 13th- and 14th-century buildings, some crenellated, some with Gothic two-light windows, and some just implacably old and stony. It's particularly evocative under the moonlight. Across from the Palazzo dei Priori is the **Palazzo Pretorio,** sprouting the rough old **Torre del Porcellino**—a tower named after the weather-beaten little sculpted boar jutting out near the top window. The only impostor on this perfectly medieval piazza was built to blend in very well—the modern **Palazzo Demaniale** on the southeast end.

Piazza dei Priori. ☎ **0588-86-050.** Admission 1.50€. Mid-Mar to Oct daily 10:30am–5:30pm; Nov to mid-Mar Sat–Sun 10am–5pm.

Parco Archeologico ☺ Volterra's public park calls itself "archaeological" after the jumbled remains of a Roman-era *piscina* reservoir partially excavated in one corner, but it's really just a pleasant, grassy space spotted with trees, crossed by hedge-lined gravel paths, and kitted out with a small children's play area. It's ideal for picnics and napping in the sun. Guarding it at one end is the **Fortezza** (1343–1475), used since the Medici times as a prison, a function it still performs admirably.

Via del Castello. No phone. Free admission. Summer daily 8:30am–8pm; winter daily 8:30am–5pm.

Palazzo dei Priori.

Pinacoteca e Museo Civico ★ Volterra's worthy painting gallery contains some pick-of-the-litter works by artists working in Volterra between the 12th and 17th centuries, as well as a coin collection stretching back to the 7th century. Room 4 has a remarkably intact polyptych of the **Madonna with Saints** ★ (1411), complete with pinnacles, predella, and all, signed by Taddeo di Bartolo; the guy in the red cape and beard in the tiny left tondo is Santa Claus (St. Nicholas of Bari). Room 5 preserves a polyptych by Cenni di Francesco, and in the following room hangs a polyptych by Portuguese immigrant Alvaro Pirez d'Evora (1430), who mixed Spanish traditions with early Renaissance Sienese styles. In room 11 is a *Christ in Glory with Saints* (1492), the last great work from the brush of Florentine Domenico Ghirlandaio. The figures create a perfectly oval architectural frame for the Flemish-inspired landscape detailing of the background—if you look hard, you can spot a giraffe, recently acquired by the Medici for their menagerie, being led along the road.

Room 12 pulls out all the stops and hits you with two large 1491 Luca Signorelli paintings, including a remarkably colored **Annunciation** ★, and an early masterpiece by Rosso Fiorentino. A 26-year-old Rosso Fiorentino painted the **Deposition** ★★★ here (1521). The late Renaissance instruction of his teacher Andrea del Sarto shows through in the young artist's work, as do the influences of other contemporary masters, like Filippino Lippi, from whom Rosso lifted the basic composition, and Michelangelo, from whom he copied the pose of the mourning St. John on the right. (It's Eve expelled from the garden on the Sistine Chapel ceiling.) But Rosso's supremely odd color palette and exaggerated use of light are purely his own, and the work's tense action and the rhythm created by the ladders and alternately calmly posed or violently contorted figures have helped set it among the masterpieces of the Mannerist movement. Try to picture it hanging amid the bright Cenni frescoes in San Francesco church, where it originally sat atop the altar. A highlight of the less satisfying upper floor is a detached fresco depicting *Justice*, by Daniele da Volterra.

Via dei Sarti 1. ℂ **0588-87-580.** Admission by cumulative ticket, or 6€ adults, 4€ students and seniors 60 and over. Summer daily 9am–7pm; winter daily 8:30am–1:45pm.

Porta all'Arco ★ At the end of Via Porta all'Arco stands the main gateway to Etruscan Volterra, a huge arch of a gate that has survived since the 4th century B.C.—with a bit of Roman-era rebuilding in the 1st century B.C. On the outside of the arch are mounted three basalt heads—worn by well over 2,000 years of wind and rain to featurelessness—said to represent the Etruscan gods Tinia (Jupiter), Uni (Juno), and Menrva (Minerva). In 1944, just before intense fighting began against the Germans laying siege to the city, Volterran partisans saved the gate from destruction by filling it overnight with stones—both for structural support and to keep it from being a focus of attack.

No phone. Free admission.

San Francesco Just inside the 14th-century Porta San Francesco, Volterra's 13th-century Franciscan church has one overwhelming reason to visit: Halfway up the right aisle is the **Cappella Croce del Giorno** ★★, frescoed with the *Legend of the True Cross* in medieval Technicolor by Cenni di Francesco. (The light switch is outside the chapel entrance.) Cenni painted this story in 1410, creating an unmatched example of early-15th-century narrative art. His vivid and unusual color palette, eye for detail, and painterly tailoring have also left us a valuable record of the dress and architecture of his era.

Teatro Romano.

Piazza San Francesco (off Via San Lino). No phone. Free admission. Daily 8:30am–6:30pm.

Teatro Romano (Roman Theater & Baths) A left turn off Via Guarnacci as you head steeply down toward Porta Fiorentina takes you to a walkway atop the medieval ramparts overlooking the impressive remains of Volterra's Roman theater and baths. These are some of the best-preserved Roman remains in Tuscany, dating back to the 1st century B.C. The view from up here is the best way to see it all, but there's an entrance down on Viale Francesco Ferrucci if you want to wander among the stones.

Viale Francesco Ferrucci. ✆ **0588-86-050.** Admission 3.50€ adults, 2.50€ students. Summer daily 10:30am–5:30pm; winter Sat–Sun 10am–4pm.

Where to Stay

A budget alternative to our favorites below is the **Foresteria Volterra,** Borgo San Lazzero, 56048 Volterra (www.foresteriavolterra.it; ✆ **0588-80-050**), in a quiet wood about 1km (.6 mile) east of the center. Rooms are slightly institutional, but spotless, cheery, and well-equipped, and come in all configurations from single up to quad. A double room costs between 62€ and 82€ depending on the season.

Podere Marcampo ★★ 📖 This restored brick-and-stone *agriturismo,* opened in 2010, commands unmatched 360-degree views of Volterra, Le Balze, and the enveloping silence of the Valdicecina. Despite a 5-year conversion, the place has retained its traditional farmhouse feel, with terra-cotta flooring, exposed beams, and dark-wood fittings keeping the large, fully equipped apartments and hotel-style doubles firmly rooted in their Tuscan heritage. Of the rooms, La Ginestraia is our favorite, with a large bathroom and double shower. The same family owners run the Ristorante Del Duca in Volterra, and can build half-board packages on request. Apartments must be booked by the week in summer, at a small discount on the daily rate.

Signposted by road, 1½km (1 mile) northwest of Volterra. www.agriturismo-marcampo.com. ℰ **0588-85-393.** 6 units. 80€–118€ double; 105€-160€ apartment. Rates include breakfast (rooms only). AE, MC, V. Free parking. **Amenities:** Outdoor pool; cookery courses; smoke-free rooms. *In room:* A/C, TV/DVD, hair dryer, hydromassage shower (rooms only), minibar, Wi-Fi (free).

San Lino ★ Volterra isn't blessed with a dazzling range of hotels inside the historic center, but the San Lino is probably the best, a 13th-century *palazzo* 5 minutes' downhill walk from Piazza dei Priori that until 1978 was a cloistered convent. The standard rooms on the first floor, reserved mainly for students and groups, have functional furniture and subcompact bathrooms: It's well worth upgrading to a superior room on the second floor, for more space, more character, and the choice of a view of the large rear sun terrace with a small pool or the atmospheric street outside. There are a couple of well-priced quads for family travelers.

Via San Lino 26 (near Porta San Francesco), 56048 Volterra (Pisa). www.hotelsanlino.com. ℰ **0588-85-250.** Fax 0588-80-620. 44 units. 90€–105€ double; 110€-125€ triple; 125€–140€ quad. Rates include breakfast. AE, DC, MC, V. Garage parking 11€. Closed Dec–Feb. **Amenities:** Restaurant; bar; outdoor pool; smoke-free rooms. *In room:* A/C, TV, hair dryer, minibar, Wi-Fi (free).

Where to Eat

Opened in 2011, tiny **Bada Ganzo,** Via dei Marchesi 13 (ℰ **0588-80-508**) offers a contemporary take on Volterran cuisine. Primi such as ravioli with *pecorino Volterrano e noci* (local sheep's milk cheese and hazelnuts) range from 7€ to 8.50€; secondi such as *pollo arrosto al vino e uvetta* (chicken roasted with wine and raisins) cost between 8€ and 12€.

Da Badò ★ TUSCAN The small and simple Badò is loved and respected by locals for its unwavering commitment to Volterran cuisine—though popularity and plaudits have pushed prices a couple of euros per dish beyond the norm. The thick-sliced prosciutto in the *antipasto* of local meat is gorgeously soft and salty (note, some cuts come with plenty of fat attached). The *zuppa alla Volterrana* is a ribollita with fresh veggies, and the *pappardelle alla lepre* are wide homemade egg pasta in hare sauce. There's a selection of delicious meat and *baccalà* (salt cod) dishes for the main, but Badò's specialty secondo, for those who can stomach tripe, is *trippa alla Volterrana,* stewed with tomatoes and herbs.

Borgo San Lazzero 9 (just east of the walls). ℰ **0588-86-477.** www.trattoriadabado.com. Reservations recommended. Primi 10€-12€; secondi 13€-16€. MC, V. Thurs–Tues 12:30–2pm and 7-9:30pm. Closed Feb 10-28 and Nov 15-30.

Il Sacco Fiorentino TUSCAN This inventive establishment features a Tuscan menu with international touches while remaining a moderately priced and friendly neighborhood hangout. The traditional *pappardelle* (wide pasta) with wild boar and porcini *ragù* is excellent, as is the odd *tagliatelle con pollo, peperoni e curry,* noodles enveloped in curry-chicken sauce with fresh peppers. For a secondo, try *piccione al forno con radicchio e vin santo* (roast pigeon with bitter leaves and sweet wine).

Piazza XX Settembre 18. ℰ **0588-88-537.** Reservations recommended. Primi 6.50€–8.50€; secondi 11€-16€. AE, DC, MC, V. Thurs–Tues noon–3pm and 7–10pm. Closed Jan.

Lo Sgherro ★ 🍴 TUSCAN There's no ceremony at this neighborhood trattoria—just solid, regional cooking at prices that have gone out of fashion elsewhere in Tuscany—where your order is hollered through a hole-in-the-wall at *mamma* in the kitchen. Pasta staples are all present—*lepre* (hare) and *cinghiale* (boar), as well as the usual tomato or meat *ragù*—but the house special *penne allo sgherro* (with minced pork, mushrooms, and artichokes) tops them all. A long list of tasty secondi might include *capriolo in salmi* (deer stew) or *coniglio alla Vernaccia con olive* (rabbit cooked in Vernaccia wine with olives). The dining room could use a lick of paint, and if you know Tuscan food there are few surprises here, but you won't find a more authentic eating experience this close to the lair of the Volturi.

Borgo San Giusto 74 (a 10-min. downhill walk from Porta San Francesco). ℂ **0588-86-473.** Primi 4.50€–7€; secondi 7.50€–17€. MC, V. Tues–Sun noon–2pm and 7–10pm.

6

LUCCA, PISTOIA & NORTHWESTERN TUSCANY

The strip of Tuscany riding along the Apennines and the Emilia-Romagna border remains relatively uncrowded despite its being wedged between Florence and Pisa, favorites of guided tours. Florence's close neighbors—Prato, with its Lippi frescoes, renowned theater, and the best biscuits in Tuscany, and Pistoia, known in the Middle Ages for its murderous inhabitants but today for Pisano's most accomplished Gothic pulpit and a slew of Romanesque churches—have rich histories and artistic patrimonies that can keep you steeped in Tuscan culture just a few dozen kilometers from Florence . . . but a world away from its tourist traffic. Both are also blessed with fine, great-value eating establishments.

Beyond them stretches a land of serene hills smothered in olive groves and vines, genteel spas such as **Montecatini Terme,** and tall alpine mountains buried in green forest and capped with snow all winter long. Tuscany's northern coast catches some of the Riviera attitude in resort towns like Viareggio, but of more interest just inland are the jagged peaks of the **Garfagnana.** It was in these hills that Michelangelo quarried his marble, and where today you can explore one of the most extensive cave systems in Italy.

Lucca, the northwest's main *città*, lies in the plains just south of these mountains. This regally refined burg of few cars and many bicyclists is home to beautiful Romanesque churches, towers, and the mightiest set of walls of any medieval Tuscan town—now tamed into a city park and planted with trees to shade Sunday strollers.

PRATO

17km (11 miles) NW of Florence; 333km (207 miles) N of Rome

Poor Prato is unwisely overlooked by many sightseers: What they're missing is one of northern Tuscany's most open, friendly, and lively cities, one with heavyweight art treasures courtesy of Donatello and Filippo Lippi, as well as a glittering collection of early Renaissance altarpieces. The city was probably an Etruscan campsite and later meadow (*prato* in Italian) market site that quickly developed into a stable Lombard town around A.D. 900. Now the region's fastest-growing city, it has always been a thriving trade center and was a free commune from 1140 until 1351, when Florence bought it from its nominal lord and set it up as an ally state. The textile industry has been important since the Middle Ages and was the foundation of the medieval wealth of early Pratese capitalists like Francesco Datini, the famous "Merchant of Prato"; it's going stronger than ever today, as is other light industry. The Pratese also know how to enjoy themselves, and have perhaps Tuscany's top theater.

FACING PAGE: **Lucca's ancient skyline.**

Essentials

GETTING THERE By Train: Prato is on the Florence-Pistoia-Lucca-Viareggio and the Florence-Bologna lines, with more than 50 trains daily from Florence (trip length: 20–40 min. depending on interim stops). From Pisa, change at Lucca or Florence Rifredi. All trains stop at **Prato Centrale,** a 10-minute walk southeast from the center, but only some halt at the more convenient **Prato Porta al Serraglio,** outside the gate just a couple of blocks north of the Duomo (head straight down Via Magnolfi and you're there).

By Car: If you're taking the A11 from Florence or Pistoia, exit at either Prato Est or Prato Ovest and follow signs. The best place to **park** is on Piazza Mercatale, where there are a small number of free spaces (indicated by white markings) along the southeastern edge, and payment by the hour in the rest of the lot.

By Bus: Buses make the trip from Florence in about 45 minutes. The quarter-hourly (hourly on Sun) **CAP** bus will drop you on Via Pomeria or terminates at the train station (✆ **0574-608-218** in Prato, 055-214-637 in Florence; www.capautolinee.it). From Siena, change in Florence; from points west of Prato, take the more convenient train.

VISITOR INFORMATION The helpful **tourist office** (✆ **0574-24-112;** www. pratoturismo.it; Mon–Sat 9am–1pm and 3–6pm, Sun 10am–1pm), is at Piazza Duomo 8. The free monthly **events guide,** *Pratomese,* available here and at many hotels, faces an uncertain future due to budget cuts—inquire locally. Thankfully, Prato's tourism website (www.pratoturismo.it) features an event search by date, so you can learn what's happening during your visit. A **cumulative ticket** for the Museo di Pittura Murale (in San Domenico), the Castello dell'Imperatore, and the Museo dell'Opera del Duomo costs 8€.

FESTIVALS & MARKETS The town's main event is the **display of the Virgin's girdle ★★**, which is done five times yearly—Easter Sunday, May 1, August 15, September 8, and December 25. This girdle is supposedly Mary's belt, which she removed and passed down to that ever-doubting St. Thomas while she was being Assumed into Heaven (rather than have Mary suffer a mortal death, God decided to assume her, or lift her bodily, up into the afterlife right at the point of her death; Thomas, as usual, didn't believe his eyes, and Mary did this to convince him—you'll see the moment captured in paint, marble, and inlaid wood all over town).

The holy artifact came to Prato at the time of the Crusades, when a local boy fighting in the Holy Land married Thomas's descendant and got the girdle as part of her dowry. The strip of dark green cloth is now preserved in a glass-and-gilt case that's kept inside nesting boxes within its own chapel in the Duomo under a series of locks that only keys held by the bishop, mayor, and local chief of *carabinieri* can open—and they do this with much pomp and Renaissance-style ceremony during the five yearly High Masses to celebrate the relic. The prelate, amid swirling incense and chanting, shows the girdle three times each to the parishioners inside the church and to the crowds massed on the piazza outside (there's a special exterior pulpit solely for this purpose), the faithful chosen to be so blessed line up to kneel and kiss the case with the girdle in it, and the relic is then locked away until the next celebratory Mass. A costumed parade with lots of drumming and fifing then follows.

The **Festa degli Omaggi** is a costumed historical pageant on September 8. The renowned **Teatro Metastasio's season** runs October through April, and the main **market** is held on Mondays at the Mercato Nuovo.

Exploring Prato

Castello Imperatore Hohenstaufen Emperor Frederick II's sharp-lined and blindingly white stone citadel was inspired by the Norman-style fortresses of Puglia. Frederick II built it here in the 1240s to remind the Pratese who was boss, and to defend the route from his homelands in Germany to his realm in southern Italy. While these days the inside is bare, you can climb onto what's left of the broken-toothed ramparts for a view of the city. Nearby is the newly restored 14th-century keep, the **Cassero,** Viale Piave (✆ **0574-26-693**), once connected to the defensive wall by a viaduct until modern roads cut through it.

Piazza Santa Maria delle Carceri. ✆ **0574-38-207.** Castello: Admission on cumulative ticket, or 2.50€ adults, 1.50€ children. Apr–Oct Mon, Wed–Fri 4–7pm, Sat–Sun 10am–1pm and 4–7pm; Nov–Mar Fri 3–5pm, Sat–Sun 10am–1pm and 3–5pm. Cassero: Free admission. Apr–Oct Wed–Mon 4–7pm.

Duomo ★★ There was once the Pieve di Santo Stefano in the center of the Prato of the 900s, but between 1211 and 1457 a new building with Romanesque green-and-white striping rose on the site to become Prato's Duomo. The facade has a glazed terra-cotta *Madonna and Sts. Stefano and Lorenzo* (1489) by Andrea della Robbia above the main door. The beautiful *Pulpit of the Sacred Girdle* hangs off the facade's right corner, from which Prato's most revered relic, the Virgin Mary's girdle, is displayed five times yearly (see above). The pulpit is a Michelozzo (design) and Donatello (sculpted friezes) collaborative effort (1434–38). The frolicking cherubs around the base are casts of Donatello's originals, now kept in the Museo dell'Opera (see below).

Inside the church on the left is the **Cappella della Cintola (Chapel of the Sacred Girdle),** entirely frescoed (1392–95) by Agnolo Gaddi. On top of the altar stands one of Giovanni Pisano's finest sculptures, a small marble *Madonna and Child* (1317). Popping 2€ in the box buys you 5 minutes of light. The nave **pulpit** was carved by Mino da Fiesole and Antonio Rossellino (1469–73).

To access the church's prized, frescoed chapels, you have to pay a small fee. To the right of the high altar is the **Cappella dell'Assunzione (Chapel of the Assumption) ★,** frescoed by Paolo Uccello and Andrea di Giusto with the *Lives of St. Stephen*

Prato's Duomo.

235

and the Virgin (1436). St. Stephen was the first Christian martyr—his death by stoning is the subject of the middle panel of the left-hand wall.

The **frescoes ★★★** (1452–66) covering the walls of the choir behind the high altar—the *Life of St. Stephen* on the left wall (spot his martyrdom again to the left of the stained glass) and *St. John the Baptist* on the right—comprise one of the masterpieces of Filippo Lippi, and indeed the early Renaissance. The amorous, monk-painter asked if a certain Lucrezia Buti, a beautiful young novice from the nearby convent, could model for his Madonnas. The nuns agreed, Filippo promptly seduced her, and the two ran off, eventually having a son, Filippino Lippi, who became an important painter in his own right. Supposedly Filippo did actually use Lucrezia in the paintings—she's the graceful flowing figure of Salome dancing into the *Feast of Herod* on the right wall's lower register. Lippi portrayed himself, along with Fra' Diamante and the assistants who helped him here, on the left wall among the crowd mourning the passing of St. Stephen. (They're the little red-hatted group on the far right; Filippo is third in from the end.)

Piazza Duomo. ☎ **0574-26-234.** Free admission to nave; 3€ to altar chapels (3.50€ with audio guide). Mon–Sat 7:30am–7pm, Sun 7:30am–noon and 1–7pm; access to altar chapels Mon–Sat 10am–5pm, Sun 1–5pm.

Galleria degli Alberti Just up the street from the Palazzo Datini, the pinkish Palazzo degli Alberti houses the Cassa di Risparmio di Prato bank, which keeps its painting collection above the pit where they carry on Datini's money-making tradition. Giovanni Bellini crucified his beautifully modeled *Christ* ★ in the middle of a Jewish graveyard and painted an amalgamated fantasy city in the background. Next to this masterpiece hangs a small *Madonna col Bambino* against a scallop-shelled niche by Filippo Lippi, and a few paintings later we get the large canvas of *Christ Crowned with Thorns* (1604), the crowning apparently being done by Roman soldier triplets—Caravaggio must have used the same model in different poses.

Via Alberti 2. ☎ **0574-617-359.** www.galleriapalazzoalberti.it. Free admission, but you must book ahead. Mon–Fri 8:30am–12:30pm and 3–5pm.

Museo Civico & Galleria Comunale ★ Inside the crenellated, 14th-century Palazzo Pretorio in Prato's civic heart, is the city's communal museum—or at least, it will be when it finally reopens after a seemingly interminable renovation project that's currently scheduled to complete in 2013 or 2014. The fine collection's highlights include a World War II–damaged 1498 **Filippino Lippi tabernacle** he frescoed for his mother, Lucrezia, and a *Nativity* by his father Filippo, that's obviously another portrait of her. The museum also houses one of the finest collections of **polyptych altarpieces** ★ in Tuscany. Among the masterpieces is a predella by Bernardo Daddi telling the story of the Holy Girdle cartoon-strip style. Most of the works, though, are various takes on the Madonna theme (with Child, with Saints, Enthroned, and so on) by Pietro di Miniato, Lorenzo Monaco, Luca Signorelli, both Filippo and Filippino Lippi, Raffaelino di Garbo, Andrea di Giusto, and Botticini. The collection's best works are on display at the Museo di Pittura Murale in San Domenico (see below) while the museum is undergoing renovations.

On the piazza outside is a **statue of Francesco Datini** (see Palazzo Datini, below) with bronze plaques showing the man's life accomplishments.

Piazza del Comune. ☎ **0574-1836-302.** Admission and opening times to be announced.

Museo dell'Opera del Duomo ★ The collection here is fairly limited, although the admission price is worth it for the worn originals of Donatello's beautifully detailed friezes of dancing putti from the Duomo's outdoor *Pulpit of the Sacred Girdle.* The Michelozzo bronze capital for the pulpit also returned to the collection in 2011, after restoration. First, however, you pass through a room with early-14th-century works, including Bettino di Corsino's *Madonna del Parto*—the pregnant Mary is an extremely rare subject in early Italian art. The remainder is arranged around a pretty cloister; look out for a *St. Lucy* sprouting a huge sword from her neck by Filippino Lippi, dad Filippo's 1453 *Funeral of St. Jerome,* and a 15th-century reliquary case for the Holy Girdle by Maso di Bartolomeo. The atmospheric vaults across the cloister house fragmentary frescoes dating to the 14th and 15th centuries.

Piazza Duomo 49 (left of the cathedral entrance). © **0574-29-339.** Admission on cumulative ticket, or 5€ adults, 3€ children. Mon, Thurs, Fri 9am–1pm and 2:30–6:30pm, Wed 9am–1pm, Sat 10am–1pm and 2:30–6:30pm, Sun 10am–1pm.

Museo di Pittura Murale in San Domenico Inside this barnlike Dominican church finished by Giovanni Pisano in 1322 is a Niccolò Gerini *Crucifix* on the second altar on the right and a pair of Matteo Rosselli works (*Madonna and St. Filippo Neri* on the second altar on the left and an *Annunciation* on the fifth altar). Across the cloister is the **Museo di Pittura Murale,** which alongside the outstanding 14th- and 15th-century altarpieces from the Museo Civico (see above) houses fresco fragments and *sinopie,* many of them damaged, by Niccolò Gerini, Pietro di Miniato, Agnolo Gaddi, and a nice Taddeo Gaddi *San Domenico,* along with anonymous 15th-century graffiti decorations saved from the gardens of the Palazzo Vaj.

---

italy's best BISCOTTI, TUSCANY'S TOP THEATER & FINE CONTEMPORARY ART

Prato is known throughout Italy for making the finest of those twice-baked hard almond crescent cookies called *cantucci.* To pick up a bag of these **biscotti di Prato,** as they are known here, stop by the city's venerable *biscottificio* (biscuit-maker), **Antonio Mattei,** Via Ricasoli 20–22 (© **0574-257-56;** www.antoniomattei.it), which has been selling Prato's famous *cantucci* and the *vin santo* in which to dunk them since 1858. It is open Tuesday through Friday from 8am to 7:30pm, Saturday from 8am to 1pm and 3:30 to 7:30pm, Sunday from 8am to 1pm (closed Sun in July and completely for 3 weeks in Aug).

For an evening at one of Tuscany's most innovative theaters, head to the **Teatro Metastasio** ★, Via Cairoli 59 (© **0574-608-501** for tickets; www.metastasio. it). The program features mostly prose theater in Italian, but there are also regular jazz events. The box office is open Tuesday through Saturday from 9:30am to 12:30pm and 4 to 7pm.

Lovers of *contemporary* art have also come to the right city: The Centro per l'Arte Contempopranea, the **Pecci** for short, outside the center at Viale Repubblica 277 (© **0574-53-17;** www. centropecci.it) has a varied and important permanent collection (closed for major building works through late 2012) and runs themed shows (which continue through renovations). See the website for info.

Piazza San Domenico 8. ℂ **0574-440-501.** Church: Free admission. Daily 7am–noon and 4–7pm. Museo: Admission on cumulative ticket, or 5€ adults, 3€ children. Apr to mid-Sept Mon, Thurs–Sat 9am–1pm and 2:30–6:30pm, Wed 9am–1pm, Sun 10am–1pm; mid-Sept to Mar Wed–Mon 9am–1pm (Fri–Sat also 3–6pm).

Palazzo Datini ★ This was the home of Francesco di Marco Datini (1330–1410), a textile magnate and secular patron saint of capitalism whose life was drawn so vividly by Italian-American author Iris Origo that he's become known by the title of her book, *The Merchant of Prato.* Datini invented the promissory note, and he kept scrupulous records of all his business activities—the basis for Origo's book—and inscribed each one of his ledgers with an accountant's battle cry: "For God and Profit."

One of the few places he allowed himself to spend money was on the decoration of his home, hiring Niccolò Gerini and Arrigo di Niccolò di Prato for the job. The outside frescoes have faded to reveal fascinating *sinopie* (preparatory sketches) underneath—though what you see on the facade is a copy (originals are in the archive). However, many paintings on the interior walls remain. The ticket room retains bucolic scenes bubbling with plant and animal life, and a side room contains a portrait of Datini. Next to the door, as in many medieval houses, is a giant St. Christopher, which Datini glanced at daily to protect against sudden death while he was out conducting business.

Via Mazzei 43 (corner of Via Rinaldesca). ℂ **0574-21-391.** Free admission. Mon–Fri 9am–12:30pm and 3–6pm (mornings only July–Aug); Sat 9am–12:30pm.

Santa Maria delle Carceri ★ This was the first centrally planned temple-like church of the High Renaissance (1485–1506), a not entirely successful exercise in Brunelleschian theoretical architecture by Giuliano da Sangallo. The light plaster walls with *pietra serena* accents and Andrea della Robbia friezes and tondi are pleasantly evocative, but the monumental space can leave you a little cold. The interior contains a St. John the Baptist statue over the font by the architect's son Francesco and the miraculous 14th-century fresco of the *Madonna with Child and Two Saints* that the church was built to house. The stained glass was designed by Domenico Ghirlandaio.

Piazza Santa Maria delle Carceri. ℂ **0574-27-933.** Free admission. Daily 7am–noon and 4–7pm.

Where to Stay

With tourist juggernaut Florence just a few kilometers down the road, Prato doesn't offer much in the way of hotels aimed at leisure travelers. In fact, the city makes a better day trip than an overnight destination. Besides our favorite below, you could also try the **Wall Art,** Viale della Repubblica 8 (www.wallart.it; ℂ **0574-596-600**), a brutal-looking business-oriented hotel on the fringes of the center. Rooms are spacious and contemporary, with some style, but the hotel is not well located for strolling the *centro storico;* doubles run 100€ to 160€, including overnight parking in a secure garage. (Better rates are available through Booking.com and agents.)

Hotel Giardino The Giardino is right on the corner of Piazza del Duomo (but you can't see the Duomo itself), just a short walk from Porta al Serraglio station. It is the center's most modern hotel, with good-size rooms for the price and location, quality built-in furniture, and large, firm beds. Another plus is the Risaliti family who run it: an extremely friendly bunch who have kept their little inn in great shape since the 1930s.

Via Magnolfi 2–6, 59100 Prato. www.giardinohotel.com. ☎ **0574-606-588.** Fax 0574-606-591. 28 units. 70€–135€ double. Rates include breakfast. AE, DC, MC, V. Garage parking 11€. Closed Christmas and 2 weeks in Aug. **Amenities:** Bar; concierge; room service. *In room:* A/C, TV, hair dryer, minibar, Wi-Fi (6€/day).

Where to Eat

Compared to many Tuscan destinations, Prato's family-run *trattorie* offer plenty of bang for your euro. Besides the places listed below, you could try **Osteria Cibbé,** Piazza Mercatale 49 (☎ **0574-607-509;** www.cibbe.it), an informal, friendly place with plenty of home-cooked regional staples at value prices. The *ragù di coniglio e faraona* (with rabbit and guinea hen) is especially tasty. Dishes cost around 8€; it's closed Sunday. For a sweet treat, be sure to stop by **Chocolat,** Via Magnolfi 83 (☎ **0574-27-308**), home to an arsenal of chocolate goodies and tasty pastries. It's just across from the main entrance to Porta al Serraglio train station (and makes for a great, air-conditioned lobby while waiting for a train in the summer.)

Il Piraña ★★ SEAFOOD Hard to believe, but this modern restaurant land-locked in a residential suburb is one of Tuscany's bastions of fine seafood. They leave you no doubt about their purpose: When you open the door you come face-to-fish with an aquarium of the flesh-eating critters after which the place is named. After you target the fresh specimen you want grilled, steamed, or baked for a second course from the ample selection, start with one of the superb *antipasti,* such as "fantasy of crustaceans" with asparagus and tartar sauce. Select primi might include *gnocchetti con scampi e fiori di zucca* (potato dumplings with shrimp and stuffed squash blossoms) or *riso con crema di scampi* (a large portion of shrimpy, creamy rice). The Piraña is popular enough to warrant reservations even midweek, but service, while very competent, can sometimes make a glacier look speedy. If you don't like fish, don't come.

Via Valentini 110 (south of the walls). ☎ **0574-25-746.** www.ristorantepirana.it. Reservations strongly recommended. Primi 12€; secondi 20€–30€. AE, DC, MC, V. Mon–Fri 12:30–2:30pm and 8–10:30pm; Sat 8–10:30pm. Closed 1 week in Jan and Aug 5–Sept 5.

Soldano ★ 🥄 TUSCAN No-nonsense food at unfashionably cheap prices in the city backstreets—this is what Tuscany was like before mass tourism arrived, and at Soldano the clock hasn't moved on an inch. The dining room, hung with nostalgic, black-and-white photos and featuring checked tablecloths, is plucked right from trattoria central casting. The dishes are too: Primi favorites include *tortellini in brodo* (filled pasta in clear broth) and *pici* (hand-rolled long pasta) with any number of sauces. Secondi like *osso buco* (braised veal shank) and *papero in umido* (duck stew) are accompanied by seasonal vegetables. It's an overall fantastic value in a genuinely authentic setting.

Via Pomeria 23 (corner of Via Simintendi). ☎ **0574-34-665.** Primi 4€–6€; secondi 6€–8.50€. MC, V. Mon–Sat noon–2:30pm and 7:30–10pm.

PISTOIA ★

17km (11 miles) NW of Prato; 35km (22 miles) NW of Florence; 336km (209 miles) N of Rome

An ancient Roman town (Catiline and his conspirators were defeated here in 62 B.C.) built against the foothills of the Apennines, Pistoia has retained its pretty churches, small but worthy art collections, and well-preserved dark medieval alleyways. Halfway between rivals Pisa and Florence, it inherited Romanesque architecture and Gothic sculpture through the influence of the former and the best of the Renaissance from proximity to the latter.

However, the machinations of these eternally feuding Tuscan rivals, with some 14th-century meddling by Lucca thrown in, also left their mark on Pistoia's medieval character. After the city's Ghibelline *comune* was conquered by Guelph Florence in 1254, the Pistoiese were reportedly the ones who began the schism between Black and White Guelphs. One day, a Pistoiese child of the ancient Neri (Black) family was playing at wooden swords with a friend from the Bianchi (White) household and one—the legend doesn't say which—was injured. When the perpetrator was sent by his father to apologize to the other boy, the hurt child's father responded by hacking off the offending youth's hand, declaring, "Iron, not words, is the remedy for sword wounds." The ensuing conflict spread to Florence as noble households waged secret wars and occasional all-out street battles against one another.

The Pistoiese already had a nasty reputation. Political arguments here were historically decided by secret assassinations, performed with the aid of the daggers, called *pistolese,* produced by the city's famous metalworking industry (which ironically, also once led the world in the manufacture of medical instruments). As advances in science allowed people to kill one another in increasingly effective ways, the city began producing hand-held firearms that adopted the dagger's old name: pistol.

The town's biggest modern industry is horticulture, and Pistoia's peripheral "industrial zone" is a miniature landscape of ornamental trees and shrubbery lined up in orderly rows at the city's famous plant nurseries, or *vivai.* Many of the cypresses that stud the ridges and decorate the postcards of rural Tuscany began their lives here.

Essentials

GETTING THERE By Train: Pistoia is on the Florence-Lucca-Viareggio line, with more than 35 trains daily from **Florence** (45–55 min.). Pistoia's **train station** is on Piazza Dante Alighieri. To reach the center from there, walk right ahead on Via XX Settembre for about 5 blocks as far as Via Cavour, in Pistoia's pedestrian heart.

By Car: From east or west, take the A11: from **Florence,** past Prato, and from **Pisa** or **Lucca** past Montecatini. From the south, a slower but **panoramic drive ★** heads north from Empoli through olive groves and past **Vinci** (p. 282). The most convenient free parking is signposted "Cellini," and lies just southeast of the city walls.

By Bus: Lazzi/COPIT buses (✆0573-363-243; www.blubus. it) run to Via XX Settembre 71 (opposite the train station). To and from Florence, the fast Lazzi *"via autostrada"* nonstop service links the two in around 50 minutes. Montecatini Terme is also well linked by bus, but from just about anywhere with a rail station, you're better off taking the train (see above).

VISITOR INFORMATION The helpful **tourist information office** (✆0573-21-622; www.turismo.pistoia.it, though you'll find as much info regarding museums and such at www.comune.pistoia.it) is open daily 9am (10am Sun) to 1pm and 3 to 6pm at Via Roma 1/Piazza del Duomo 4 (inside the Antico Palazzo dei Vescovi).

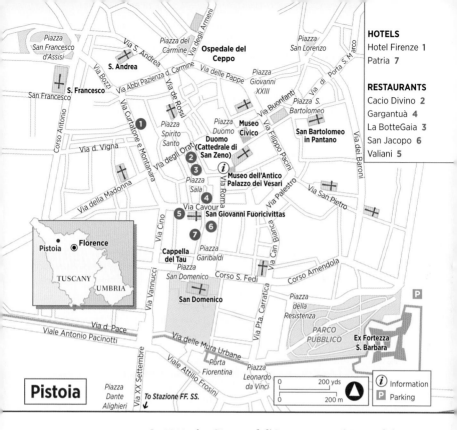

Pistoia

HOTELS
Hotel Firenze 1
Patria 7

RESTAURANTS
Cacio Divino 2
Gargantuà 4
La BotteGaia 3
San Jacopo 6
Valiani 5

FESTIVAL & MARKETS In 1300, the **Giostra del'Orso** was a real Joust of the Bear, a bearbaiting event in which horsemen ceremonially took on a captive ursine. Revived in 1947, the wildly popular July 25 event is now more humane. The highlight in a day of costumed pageantry is the joust, when mounted knights circle around a track and score points by slamming their lances into stylized bear targets. There are **daily fruit and veggie markets** (except Sun) on Piazza della Sala and Via Ciliegiole, and a thriving **Wednesday and Saturday morning market** on Piazza del Duomo.

Exploring Pistoia

Baptistery This baptistery was built in those strong Pistoian bands of dark green and white by Cellino di Nese from 1337 to 1359, based on a design by Andrea Pisano. The Gothic pulpit to the right of the entrance was added in 1399, and the *Madonna* above the door is the work of Tommaso and Nino Pisano. The spare interior, with bare bricks showing off the bulk of the dome, contains a reconstituted baptismal font (1226) of carved and intarsia marble panels by Lanfranco da Como.

Piazza del Duomo. No phone. Free admission. Tues–Wed and Fri–Sat 10am–1pm and 3–5pm; Sun 10am–1pm and 3–6pm.

Cappella del Tau ★★ This remarkable chapel was built in 1360 by a branch of the Franciscan order that cared for the sick and those with disabilities, and whose members wore a Greek Tau as their symbol. In the 1500s a private citizen bought it and whitewashed over the 1372 **fresco cycle by Niccolò di Tommaso** that covered every inch of the walls and ceiling. In the process of stripping the whitewash in 1968, many of the frescoes were seriously damaged, but what remains illustrates the *Life of St. Anthony Abbot* (lower register), *Stories from the New Testament* (middle register), and *Stories from the Old Testament* (upper register and vaults). The wall facing the door is covered by a huge *Last Judgment:* The colors of the images in the upper back corners give some idea of how vivid the original effect must have been. The space is now shared, somewhat incongruously, with giant bronzes by Pistoiese sculptor Marino Marini (1901–80).

Corso Silvano Fedi 28 (at Piazza Garibaldi). ✆ **0573-32-204.** Free admission. Mon–Sat 8:30am–1:30pm.

Duomo (Cattedrale di San Zeno) ★ The current incarnation of San Zeno dates from 1220, soon after which an old defensive tower close by, bristling with Ghibelline swallowtail crenellations, was given a respectable church clothing of Romanesque striped arches and converted to the cathedral bell tower. The glazed terra-cotta decorations of the **barrel vault** ★ in the entrance arcade and the lunette above the main door are Andrea della Robbia creations.

On the inside right wall is a tomb by Cellino di Nese (1337), beyond which is the Cappella di San Jacopo and the Duomo's greatest treasure, the **Altare di San Jacopo (Altar of St. James)** ★. Close to a ton of partially gilded silver is molded into medieval saints (the upper half), early Renaissance biblical scenes (the front and flanks), and a pair of Brunelleschi prophets around on the left side. Started in 1287 and not finished until the 15th century, this altar outlasted a number of silversmiths, including a handful, such as Leonardo di Ser Giovanni, who also worked on the only other comparable altar, a similar pile of silvery holiness now in Florence's Museo dell'Opera del Duomo.

Pop down into the **crypt** for the remains of the 5th-century church and marvelously medieval bits of a **Guido da Como pulpit** (1199), dismembered in the 17th century. On the right-hand wall of the chapel to the left of the high altar is the 1485 *Madonna di Piazza,* a brightly colored work, including a fantastically rich carpet under the Virgin's feet, that has been declared the only documented painting by Verrochio (though some are now trying to credit it to his protégé Leonardo da Vinci—or even Leonardo's student Lorenzo di Credi).

Piazza del Duomo. ✆ **0573-25-095.** Admission to Duomo free; Cappella di San Jacopo 2€ adults, .50€ children. Duomo daily 8:30am–12:30pm and 3:30–7pm. Cappella di San Jacopo Mon–Sat 10am–12:30pm and 3:30–5:30pm; Sun 8–9:30am, 11–11:30am, and 4–5:30pm.

Museo Civico Pistoia's most worthwhile museum is housed in the 1294 **Palazzo del Comune,** which sprouts a basalt black head from the early 14th century above the entrance that local legends take to be either a Moorish king of Mallorca, enslaved by pirating Pistoiese, or a traitorous citizen who sold his city out to Lucca. The museum's first floor boasts a Lucchese-style panel of *St. Francis* surrounded by his life story (1270s), a 14th-century *Lamentation* by Lippo di Benivieni, a polyptych of the *Madonna and Child with Saints* by the anonymous Master of 1310, and four early-16th-century *Sacred Conversations* with colors of deep saturation. Two of the conversations are by local boy Gerino Gerini, and one each came from the brushes of Florentine's Lorenzo di Credi and Ridolfo del Ghirlandaio. (There's also one almost surrealist attempt painted in 1523 by Pistoiese painter Bernardino Detti.) The collection continues upstairs but goes downhill from here, with a glut of 17th- to 19th-century efforts on the third floor—including Empoli's 1624 *Justice of Midas.*

Piazza del Duomo. ✆ **0573-371-296.** www.comune.pistoia.it/museocivico. Admission 3.50€ adults, free children 17 and under or seniors 60 and over. Thurs–Sun 10am–6pm.

Museo dell'Antico Palazzo dei Vescovi A local bank now owns the old Bishop's Palace wedged between the Duomo and the Baptistery, but they keep their archaeological and Duomo-related collections open to the public via a guided tour. The ancient highlights are bits of a **Roman house** and an **Etruscan furnace,** as well as a pair of **Etruscan tomb markers** and a precious **alabaster funerary urn** carved with a chariot scene in high relief. There's also a **gold reliquary case** (1407) by Lorenzo Ghiberti and his workshop in the room that was once used as the Duomo's sacristy and treasury. In the 13th century, Vanni Pucci—one of those bad seeds who helped cement Pistoia's evil reputation—broke into this room looking for politically damaging documents. While inside, Pucci also helped himself to some of the church's riches, a despicable act that caused Dante to stick Pucci, surrounded by snakes and a cursing God, in a fairly low circle of Hell.

Palazzo dei Vescovi, Piazza del Duomo. ✆ **0573-36-91.** Admission 4€ adults, 2€ children 1m (3¼ ft.) tall and over and seniors. Guided tour only: Tues and Thurs–Fri 10am, 11:30am, and 3pm.

Ospedale del Ceppo/Pistoia Sotterranea ★ Pistoia's star outdoor attraction is the **facade** ★★ of the Ospedale del Ceppo, one of the best works by the often disappointing Giovanni della Robbia and Pistoia's answer to the Ospedale degli Innocenti in Florence, which was decorated by Giovanni's father, Andrea. Here, Giovanni was in top form, creating a frieze (1514–25) of glazed terra-cotta panels to surmount a Michelozzo-designed loggia. The six well-preserved della Robbia panels, plus a decaying one added later by Filippo Paladini, represent the seven acts of mercy, divided by the cardinal and theological virtues.

The hospital is also the jumping-off point for the **Pistoia Sotterranea** ★ tour, inaugurated in mid-2010. The 1-hour guided visit follows the path of a diverted stream, under a couple of intact bridges now below the hospital's foundations, that over the centuries has served as a power source for an olive press, a public laundry, a refuse dump, and a source of water—often simultaneously. The

Pistoia's Duomo.

The della Robbia frieze on the Ospedale del Ceppo.

fascinating tour takes in the history of the hospital above (founded in 1277 and still going strong), and ends at the tiny, frescoed teaching and autopsy theater that was built in the mid-1700s and used to teach medical students until its replacement by the Medical Academy in 1844. Tours in English are available.

A Cappuccino Break

Valiani, Via Cavour 55 (℃ **0573-23-034**), is a cafe and pastry shop installed in 1831 under high, vaulted ceilings behind a striped Romanesque facade next to San Giovanni Fuorcivitas. There are also a few tables outside; it's closed Tuesday.

Piazza Giovanni XXIII 13. ℃ **0573-368-023.** www.irsapt.it. Tour 9€ adults, 8€ children, 30€ family. Tours (1 hr.) daily at 10:30am, 11:30am, 12:30pm, 2pm, 3pm, 4pm, 5pm (Apr–Sept also 6pm).

Sant'Andrea ★ Pistoia's undisputed artistic heavyweight is Giovanni Pisano's **pulpit ★★★** (1298–1301) inside this 12th-century church. The third of the four great Pisano pulpits (the others are in Pisa and Siena) and the first carved by Giovanni without the help of his dad, Nicola, this is the work with which the Pisan sculptor brought his art to absolute Gothic perfection. The reliefs are so deeply carved that the figures seem to come out at us. Because the naturalism of the Renaissance hadn't yet come into vogue, Giovanni relied on narrative density and power (the Annunciation, two takes on the Nativity, and the angels averting the shepherds in their fields are all crammed into the first panel) and exaggerated expression to bring his works to life. But the reliefs do foreshadow later movements, especially where Giovanni breaks the borders of the panels to carry the artistic narrative across real space. Notice how the angel of the Magi panel is pointing back to the Nativity scene as it wakes the three wise men to go adore the baby Jesus. There are also two **wood crucifixes,** one behind the pulpit by Gerino Gerini (early 1500s) and another by Giovanni Pisano across the nave. Bring a .50€ coin for the light box.

Piazzetta Sant'Andrea. ℃ **0573-21-912.** Free admission. Daily 8am–12:30pm and 3–6pm.

San Domenico This 1280 church squats a block inside the southern walls of town. The first item on the right as you enter is the **tomb of Filippo Lazzari ★,** one of Dante's best friends. The scholar lectures on eternally in the relief panel below. (We like to think his young follower Boccaccio, said to be one of the students here, is the kid stifling a yawn on the right.) The chapel to the left of the high altar contains a Cristofano Allori canvas of *St. Domenic Receiving the Rosary,* interesting not so much for the painting itself, but for the argument in the background between the artist and the church sacristan over payment for the picture. Benozzo Gozzoli, who died of the plague while on a fresco job here in 1497, is buried in the cloister, which also (when open) gives access to several rooms housing detached **13th-century frescoes.** The refectory and attached tiny museum house the remaining fragments of Gozzoli's last work, a *Journey of the Magi,* and a possible early Verrochio *St. Jerome.*

Piazza San Domenico. ℃ **0573-28-158.** Free admission. Daily 7–11:50am and 3:30–6pm (Sun to 8pm).

San Francesco Pistoia's barnlike Franciscan church contains lots of good **14th-century frescoes,** the best of which are in the transept chapels. Behind the high altar is a fresco cycle on the *Life of St. Francis* by a Giotto copycat (perhaps a student) who mimicked his master's formulae for most of the scenes.

The chapel to the left has a Sienese cycle of an *Allegory of the Triumph of St. Augustine*. After giving a nod to the frescoes in the second chapel to the right of the high altar, go through the door at the transept's end for a peek at more 14th-century works in the **sacristy**. If it's open, pass through the door into the **chapter house** beyond for even better frescoes, including a giant *Tree of Life* that just might be by the hand of Sienese master Pietro Lorenzetti.

Piazza San Francesco. ☏ **0573-368-096.** Free admission. Daily 8am–noon and 5–6:30pm.

San Giovanni Fuorcivitas ★ The **side facade** of this small, supremely Romanesque church is an orderly festival of blind arcades, inlaid diamond lozenges, and stripes to put a zebra to shame. Inside are a giant 13th-century crucifix, a *Visitation* in white terra cotta by Luca della Robbia, and a Giovanni Pisano holy-water stoup. The main attraction, however, is the **pulpit** ★ (1270) by Fra' Guglielmo da Pisa (a student of Nicola Pisano). Of the three major pulpits in Pistoia (see Sant'Andrea, above), this is the most solidly Romanesque.

Via Cavour. ☏ **0573-24-784.** Free admission. Daily 8:30am–noon and 5–6:30pm.

Where to Stay

With just a few business travelers and a handful of tourists staying the night, central Pistoia doesn't have a particularly scintillating crop of hotels. An additional choice to the ones below, especially well adapted to budget travelers, is the **Hotel Firenze,** Via Curtatone e Montanara 42, 51100 Pistoia (www.hotel-firenze.it; ☏/fax **0573-23-141**), where spacious, plain rooms come with air conditioning and are kept spotlessly clean. Doubles are a value at 55€ to 88€ per night (extra beds for family groups range from 15€–25€).

Patria ★ Completely renovated and reopened in 2011, this is the most striking option in the historic center, a modern hotel with midsize, contemporary yet warm rooms sporting parquet flooring and shiny chrome rainfall shower units. Its location can't be beat: just a few blocks from the train station but also only three doors down from the Romanesque stripes of San Giovanni Fuorcivitas and a minute's walk from the Duomo. Weekend rates offer the best value.

Via.Crispi 8–12, 51100 Pistoia. www.patriahotel.com. ☏ **0573-358-800.** Fax 0573-977-236. 27 units. 110€–250€ double. Rates include breakfast. AE, DC, MC, V. Free parking on street; ask hotel for overnight permit. **Amenities:** Bar; airport transfer; babysitting; bikes; concierge. *In room:* A/C, TV, hair dryer, minibar, Wi-Fi (free).

Villa de' Fiori ★★ 🛏 To label this refined, secluded colonial villa set amid olive groves north of the center a mere *"agriturismo"* appears to do it a grave injustice—but strictly speaking, that's what it is. There's been no conversion as such, just a re-equipping of the structure to receive 21st-century hotel guests in comfort: Rooms come in all shapes and configurations, from suite-style family units divided by period screens, to romantic doubles with canopy beds, to mini-apartments suited to long stays. There's also nothing fake-antique-chic about the handsome wood furniture that embellishes the warren of bedrooms and comfortable common areas on both floors of the villa. Service is impeccable: You'll feel like a guest in an aristocratic home.

Via di Bigiano e Castel Bovani 39 (3km/2 miles north of center), 51100 Pistoia. www.villadefiori. it. ☏ **0573-450-351.** Fax 0573-452-669. 9 units (7 rooms, 2 apartments). 94€–152€ double, plus 30€ per stay cleaning charge; 90€–165€ apartment (July–Aug weekly Sat–Sat only). Room rates include buffet breakfast. AE, DC, MC, V. Free parking. Closed Jan and weekdays

Feb–Mar. **Amenities:** Restaurant; bar; babysitting; outdoor pool; Wi-Fi (free). *In room:* A/C, TV, hair dryer.

Where to Eat

At groovy enoteca (wine cellar) **Gargantuà ★**, Piazza dell'Ortaggio 12 (✆**0573-23-330;** www.tavernagargantua.com), a lengthy wines-by-the-glass list is complemented by large mixed tasting platters (7€–10€) of bruschetta, cheese, salami, and seafood. Tables outside enjoy a fine spot on a buzzing little piazza. For excellent midpriced meals under brick vaults, you could also try reliable **San Jacopo,** Via Crispi 15 (✆**0573-27-786;** Wed–Sun 12:15–2:30pm and 7–10pm, Tues 7–10pm), for well-cooked dishes that make use of local and seasonal ingredients.

Cacio Divino ★★ 🔪 CONTEMPORARY TUSCAN This fun, friendly, and tiny enoteca with outside tables close to Pistoia's produce market offers a menu of surprisingly daring, contemporary Tuscan flavors at fair prices. There's also an unusual (for Tuscany, in this price bracket) amount of care taken with the presentation of each dish. For primi, expect the likes of *pici alla lepre sul cacao amaro* (hand-rolled pasta with hare sauce on bitter chocolate) or *paccheri al tonno fresco con melanzane e pesto rosso* (pasta tubes with fresh tuna, eggplant, and tomato pesto). Many secondi are equally unusual, with the *pollo in crosta di mandorle* (chicken in an almond crust) among the more conservative options. The superlative wine list is as thick as a novella—there's a whole page just on reds from the Pistoiese hills. The two-course weekday lunch special is a steal at 13€.

Via del Lastrone 13. ✆ **0573-194-1058.** www.cacio-divino.it. Reservations recommended. Primi 9€–11€; secondi 9€–11€; set weekday lunch 8€ one course, 13€ two courses. MC, V. Daily 11am–3pm and 7–11pm (mid-June to mid-Sept closed Sun lunch).

La BotteGaia ★ MODERN TUSCAN This popular restaurant opened in 2001 to great fanfare in the gastronomic community after the success of the owners' nearby wine shop, **I Sapori della BotteGaia,** Via di Stracceria 4 (✆**0573-358-450**). It serves classic local cuisine, elevated a notch above the norm, alongside some more daring Tuscan specialties, such as the *lampredotto trippato all fiorentina*—which, even for someone who normally steers clear of tripe, is a tasty stew—and supremely succulent slow-cooked, milk-fed veal. The tables in the back look across to Piazza del Duomo.

Via del Lastrone 17 (also an entrance behind the Baptistery). ✆ **0573-365-602.** www.labotte gaia.it. Reservations recommended. Primi 7€; secondi 10€–14€. AE, DC, MC, V. Tues–Sat noon–3pm and 7–11pm; Sun 7–11pm. Closed 2 weeks in Aug.

MONTECATINI TERME & MONSUMMANO TERME

15km (9⅓ miles) W of Pistoia; 46km (29 miles) W of Florence; 330km (205 miles) N of Rome

The curative powers coursing through the sulfurous underground hot springs and steaming vaporous caverns of the Valdinievole west of Pistoia have been renowned for centuries. This "Valley of Mists" is home to Montecatini Terme, the grande dame of Italian spas, as well as Monsummano Terme, with eerie natural sauna caves. Although modern thermal centers aimed at relaxing your body and emptying your wallet have begun filling the valley, the hillsides remain beautiful. Capped with tiny medieval villages, they are a joy to wander—the SS633 twists its way into the mountains north of Montecatini, providing a gorgeous route for Sunday drivers. If you're heading here hell-bent on heavy relaxation, know that both Montecatini and Monsummano become veritable ghost towns from mid-October to Easter.

Essentials

GETTING THERE By Train: The Florence-Lucca-Viareggio train, which pauses at Pistoia and Prato on the way, stops at Montecatini (19 daily; 50 min. from Florence, 10 min. from Pistoia). **Montecatini Centro** is the most convenient station for most of the town. However, if you're heading to Monsummano Terme, get off at **Montecatini Terme–Monsummano** and take a **taxi** (© 0572-75-100).

By Car: Take the A11 from Florence or Lucca to the Montecatini exit. There's plenty of pay parking in the center. Monsummano Terme has a free car park.

By Bus: Hourly **Lazzi/BluBus** (© 055-363-041 or 0572-911-781; www.blubus.it) buses run from Florence (50 min. by *autostrada*) to Piazza Italia in Montecatini. There are also hourly weekday buses to/from Lucca (55 min.), but it's easier to take the train.

VISITOR INFORMATION Montecatini Terme's **tourist office** is at Viale Verdi 66 (© 0572-772-244; www.montecatiniturismo.it). It's open Monday through Friday from 9am to 1pm and 3 to 6pm, Saturday 9am to 1pm only. For Monsummano information, see **www.grottagiustispa.com**.

Exploring Montecatini & Monsummano

MONTECATINI TERME Montecatini is a quiet and aging town that seems to long for its heyday as a "ville d'eau" where the wealthy came to "take the waters." It is still a mecca for well-heeled seniors who like to do a bit of shopping to unwind after drinking mineral-laden, laxative waters, getting radioactive vapors steamed into various parts of their body, and generally lying about doing nothing. This town's on permanent *riposo,* and its nucleus is the **Parco delle Terme,** a long park of neoclassical temples each expanding over the sources of various underground hot springs and vaporous crevices.

The oldest is **Terme Tettuccio,** Viale Verdi 71 (© 0572-778-501), written of as early as 1370 and visited by the high-strung merchant of Prato, Francesco Datini, in 1401. The spa wasn't really exploited until Grand Duke Leopold I took an interest in developing the *termi* of the town in the 1700s. Reconstructed from 1919 to 1927, the neoclassical facade opens onto the 20th-century ideal of a Roman bathhouse, decorated with murals, ceramics, and statues by Art Nouveau Liberty masters, like Galileo Chini and Ezio Giovannozzi. Drinking the waters here will supposedly do wonders for the intestines and liver you've been rotting with all that Chianti Classico: A ticket to imbibe the waters morning and afternoon costs 14€. Tourist visits (after 11am) cost 6€.

The **Terme Leopoldina,** Viale Verdi 67 (© 0572-778-551) at the park's entrance goes so far as to dedicate itself as a neoclassical (1926) temple to Asclepius, the god of medicine, as if its mineral mud baths could cure all ills. These and most of the other spas are open Easter through October only, but one remains open to the ailing, aching public year-round: the neo-Renaissance-meets-modernism **Excelsior,** Viale Verdi 61 (© **0572-778-511**). It costs anywhere from 22€ to 115€ for thermal baths, mud soaks, ayurvedic massages, and more serious treatments. Tickets for all the spas, and a brochure with details of Montecatini's various treatments, are available at the **Società delle Terme** office, Viale Verdi 41 (© **0572-7781;** www.termemontecatini.it). An open-air thermal pool, like that at Monsummano Terme (see below) is scheduled to open by 2013.

Neoclassical Terme Tettuccio in Montecatini.

Perhaps most interesting for younger visitors is **Montecatini Alto,** reachable in the summer via a funicular railway (© **0572-766-862;** www.funicolare1898.it), which makes a 10-minute trip from Viale Diaz every half-hour daily from 9:30am to midnight. It costs 4€ one-way and 7€ round-trip (2€/4€ for children aged 6–10). For a bite to eat, stop by **La Torre,** Piazza Giusti 8 (© **0572-706-50;** closed Tues), built around a medieval tower, where you'll find reliably tasty but (like everywhere else here) slightly pricey food: primi cost 10€ to 12€, secondi 14€ to 18€, and the cover charge is a steep 3€. The Old Town offers fine views across the Valdinievole, and makes a pleasant break from the languorous, wallet-draining hedonism and general flatness of the modern spa town below. It's also a base for short hikes, especially to visit the stalactites of the **Grotta Maona** caverns nearby (© **0572-74-581**), open April through October Monday to Saturday from 9am to noon and 3 to 6pm. Admission is 6€ adults, 4€ for kids 6 to 12. The surrounding complex includes a bar that becomes a disco some evenings.

MONSUMMANO TERME One of the eeriest spas in Italy lies just south of Montecatini at Monsummano Terme. In 1849, the Giusti family discovered on their lands a series of stalactite- and stalagmite-laden caves with a sulfurous lake at the bottom and hot mineral-laden vapors permeating the air. By 1852, they had built a spa around it dubbed the **Grotta Giusti Terme ★** and converted their adjacent villa into a luxury hotel (see below).

You don't have to stay at the inn to visit the **spa** at Via Grotta Giusti 1411 (© **0572-90-771;** www.grottagiustispa.com), where you can don a white shift and a dun-colored robe—like a member of some monastic order—and descend through a series of increasingly hot and steamily dripping caverns named, of course, Paradiso, Purgatorio, and Inferno, after Dante (the scalding sulfur pool below is the Lake of Limbo). It costs 40€ to steam in the caves for 50 minutes, but you can also go in for a massive array of treatments (such as full-body massages, starting at 30€ for 20 min.; or 20€ for a "thermal nasal irrigation"; or 40€ to soak in anti-inflammatory thermal mud). Less serious (and more fun, especially if you're traveling with kids) is the **outdoor thermal pool ★**, where you can soak and splash in the 95°F (35°C) waters, whatever the weather, looking out at the wilderness. All-day pool entry costs 20€ on weekdays, 24€ on weekends (13€/11€ for kids 12 and under). There's a few euros off in low season, and after 2pm on weekdays adults pay just 13€. The *terme* are open from 10am to 6pm (mid-May to mid-Oct closes 3pm Wed).

Where to Stay & Eat

IN MONTECATINI TERME

We sometimes wonder where Montecatinians live, because almost every building that isn't a restaurant, store, or spa seems to be an *albergo* (hotel). With more than 300 hotels in town, you should have no difficulty finding a room—Montecatini's tourist office spends half its time rounding them up for vacationers. Many hotels require you to take half or full board, and several are closed completely from mid-October until just before Easter. If you can escape your hotel's pension requirement, head to the refined **Enoteca Giovanni,** Via Garibaldi 25 (✆ **0572-71-695;** www.enotecagiovanni.it), for an excellent, but far from cheap, meal of innovative Tuscan fare. Primi cost around 19€, with secondi ranging from 25€ to 30€.

If you're seeking old-fashioned Belle Epoque grandeur for your Montecatini base, consider the **Grand Hotel & La Pace,** Via della Torretta 1 (www.grand hotellapace.it; ✆ **0572-9240**). Rooms, alas, don't quite deliver on the promise of the palatial lobby, but staying here gives a flavor of Montecatini in its pomp. For a real splurge, however, we prefer options in Monsummano Terme (see below) or Pistoia (p. 239).

IN MONSUMMANO TERME

There's nothing hugely surprising about the menu at **La Cantina (da Caino),** Via Picasso 3 (✆ **0572-53-173**), but you're assured a friendly welcome and are in the capable hands of a kitchen staff that knows what it's doing with Tuscan flavors from land or sea. In warm weather, you can dine in the arbor-covered garden. Primi range from 8€ to 10€ and secondi from 10€ to 25€. It's closed Monday. To find it from the Grotta Giusti, exit the property and take the first left (just before Albergo La Speranza). La Cantina is the last building on the right.

Grotta Giusti ★ Converted from a family villa in the 1850s, this hotel has hosted Garibaldi, Verdi, and Liz Taylor, and provides a greater sense of escape than the supposedly "grander" hotels of nearby Montecatini. Rooms are well sized if bland, but they're comfortable and have thermal bathwater on tap. A few accommodations downstairs have frescoed ceilings, and some on the third floor have balconies, but steer clear of the boring modern rooms in the new wing. The ceiling frescoes are repeated in the sunny breakfast rooms and in the vaulted lounges off the lobby. They also have a 42-hectare (104-acre) forest with a fitness path.

Via Grotta Giusti 1411, 51015 Monsummano Terme (PT). www.grottagiustispa.com. ✆ **0572-90-771.** Fax 0572-907-7200. 64 units. 260€–300€ "comfort" double; 296€–356€ "charm" double; 310€–626€ superior. AE, DC, MC, V. Rates include breakfast. Free parking. **Amenities:** Restaurant; bar; babysitting; bikes; concierge; gym and health spa; outdoor pool; room service; outdoor tennis court; Wi-Fi. *In room:* A/C, TV, hair dryer, Internet, minibar.

pinocchio's **PARK**

Another 5km (3 miles) along the road from Pescia takes you to **Collodi,** family home village of 19th-century Florentine novelist Carlo Lorenzini, who visited often as a child and took the pen name Collodi when he wrote *The Adventures of Pinocchio* (1881). Although it's one of the world's most beloved children's stories (translated into more than 60 languages), Italians of all ages have an especially fierce love of and devotion to the tale. The **Parco di Pinocchio** (© **0572-429-342;** www.pinocchio.it) was built here in 1956

to celebrate it, with a bronze *Pinocchio* by Emilio Greco, mosaic scenes from the story by Futurist Venturino Venturini, a restaurant designed by Giovanni Michelucci, and a hedge maze and some diversions for the kids. The park is open daily from 8:30am to sunset; admission is 11€ adults, 8€ children ages 3 to 14 and seniors 65 and over. Negotiate some tricky first impressions (overpriced, needs a lick of paint), and imaginative little ones will enjoy the old-fashioned style. *Note:* It gets *very* busy on holiday weekends.

En Route to Lucca: Pescia & Pinocchio

Pescia, stretched along the Pescia River 12km (7½ miles) west of Montecatini along the SS435, is Tuscany's capital of cut flowers. Its huge market still ships out carnations, gladioli, lilies, and chrysanthemums, in commercial quantities daily before 8am. Pescia's horticulture industry also produces excellent asparagus, olive oil, and sorano beans (a prized local pulse). Art aficionados will enjoy 13th-century **San Francesco,** frescoed by Bonaventura Berlinghieri (1235) with a cycle of the *Life of St. Francis*—Berlinghieri was a close friend of Francis, who had died a mere 9 years earlier, and many believe that these may be some of the most accurate portraits of Assisi's famous mystic.

LUCCA ★

26km (16 miles) W of Montecatini; 72km (45 miles) W of Florence; 335km (208 miles) NW of Rome

Lucca is apparently the most civilized of Tuscany's small cities, a stately grid of Roman roads snug behind a mammoth belt of tree-topped battlements. It's home to Puccini and soft pastel plasters, an elegant landscape of churches and palaces, delicate facades, and Art Nouveau shop fronts. The sure lines of the churches here inspired John Ruskin to study architecture, and although the center isn't the traffic-free Eden many guidebooks would lead you to believe, car access is restricted. Everyone from rebellious teens to fruit-shopping grandmothers tools around this town atop bicycles.

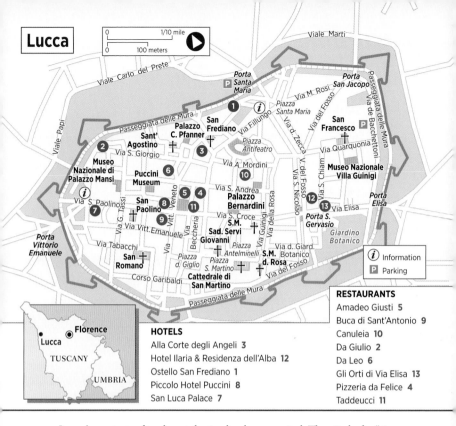

Lucca

0 — 1/10 mile
0 — 100 meters

Viale Marti

Viale Carlo del Prete

Porta Santa Maria **P**

Porta San Jacopo

Via M. Rosi

Via del Fosso

Passeggiata delle Mura

Passeggiata delle Mura de Bacchettoni

Piazza Santa Maria **❶** **ℹ**

Via Fillungo

Via d. Zecca

San Francesco **P**

Via Quarquonia

Passeggiata delle Mura

San Frediano
Palazzo
C. Pfanner

Sant'
Agostino

Viale Papi

❷
Museo
Nazionale di
Palazzo Mansi

Via S. Giorgio

❸

Piazza Antifeatro

Via A. Mordini

V. del Fosso

V. S. Nicolao

Via S. Chiam

Museo Nazionale
Villa Guinigi

ℹ
Via S. Paolino

Via G. Tassi

Puccini
Museum **❻**

San
Paolino **❽**

Vitt. Veneto

❺ **❹**

❾

❼

Via Becctheria

Via Vitt. Emanuele

Via S. Andrea

Via S. Croce

❿
Palazzo
Bernardini **⓫**

Via della Rosa

Via S. Guinigi

⓬
⓭ Via Elisa

Porta Elisa

Porta S. Gervasio

Sad. Servi
S.M.
Giovanni

Piazza Antelminelli

S.M.
Botanico
d. Rosa

Via d. Giard.

Giardino Botanico

ℹ Information

P Parking

Porta
Vittorio
Emanuele

Via Tabacchi

San
Romano

Corso Garibaldi

Piazza
d. Giglio

Piazza
S. Martino

Via del Fosso

Cattedrale di
San Martino

Passeggiata delle Mura

Florence
Lucca

TUSCANY

UMBRIA

HOTELS
Alla Corte degli Angeli **3**
Hotel Ilaria & Residenza dell'Alba **12**
Ostello San Frediano **1**
Piccolo Hotel Puccini **8**
San Luca Palace **7**

RESTAURANTS
Amadeo Giusti **5**
Buca di Sant'Antonio **9**
Canuleia **10**
Da Giulio **2**
Da Leo **6**
Gli Orti di Via Elisa **13**
Pizzeria da Felice **4**
Taddeucci **11**

Lucca's greatest cultural contribution has been musical. The city had a "singing school" as early as A.D. 787, and this crucible of musical prodigies gave the world Luigi Boccherini (1743–1805), the composer who revitalized chamber music in the 18th century with such compositions as his Minuet no. 13, and most famously the operatic genius Giacomo Puccini (1858–1924), whose *Tosca, Madame Butterfly, Turandot,* and *La Bohème* have become some of the world's favorite operas.

Lucca boasts some pretty heavyweight history. Its plains were inhabited more than 50,000 years ago, and as a Roman *municipium,* it was the site of the First Triumvirate between Julius Caesar, Pompey, and Crassus in 56 B.C. Bishop Paulinus, one of St. Peter's disciples, brought a third-generation Christianity here in A.D. 47, making Lucca the first Tuscan city to convert. It was a major pit stop for pilgrims and crusaders coming from northern Europe along the Via Francigena pilgrim route from Canterbury to Rome, and in 588 local clergy shanghaied one passing Irish pilgrim, the abbot Finnian, and pronounced him bishop "Frediano."

When Pisa conquered Lucca in 1314, hometown adventurer Castruccio Castracani fought back until Lucca regained its liberty. Over the next 10 years, Castracani went on to conquer Pisa and expanded a Luccan empire over western Tuscany. Both Pistoia and Volterra fell, but in 1328, just as Castracani was training his sights on Florence, malaria struck him down. Disgruntled Pisa took over again until 1369, when Charles IV granted Lucca its independence. The proud, if relatively unimportant, city stayed a free *comune*—occasionally under powerful bosses such as Paolo Guinigi (1400–30)—for 430 years. Napoleon gave it to his sister Elisa Baciocchi as a principality in 1805, and in 1815 it was absorbed into the Tuscan Grand Duchy.

Essentials

GETTING THERE   By Train: Lucca is on the Florence-Viareggio train line, with about 30 trains daily (fewer on Sun) connecting with **Florence** (trip time: 75–90 min.), **Pistoia** (40 min.–1 hr.), and **Montecatini Terme** (25–40 min.). A similar number of trains make the short hop to/from **Pisa** (30 min.). The **station** is a short walk south of Porta San Pietro.

   By Car: The A11 runs from Florence past Prato, Pistoia, and Montecatini before hitting Lucca. The SS12 runs straight up here from Pisa, a pleasant drive through the olive groves of the Monti Pisani. The closest free parking is outside the walls (follow signs for the Palazzetto dello Sport, a short walk north of the center). Inside the walls, you'll usually find a pay-parking space underground at **Mazzini** (enter from east, through the Porta Elisa, and take an immediate right).

   By Bus: Lucca's former two bus companies, Lazzi and CLAP, have merged to become **VaiBus** (www.vaibus.it). A service runs hourly from Florence (70 min.) and one from Pisa (50 min.) to Lucca's Piazzale Verdi. Head for the same terminus for services to Bagni di Lucca, the Versilia coast (including Viareggio), Livorno, Pescia, and the Garfagnana. Buy tickets from the office on the south side of the piazza.

GETTING AROUND   A set of *navette* (electric minibuses) whiz dangerously down the city's peripheral streets, but the flat center is easily traversable on foot. To really get around like a Lucchese, though, you need to **rent a bike.** There's the **city-sponsored stand** on Piazzale Verdi (✆0583-442-937; closed Nov to mid-Mar); **Antonio Poli,** Piazza Santa Maria 42 (✆0583-493-787; www.biciclettepoli.com; daily 8:30am–7:30pm; closed Sun mid-Nov to Feb and Mon mornings year-round); and **Cicli Bizzarri** next door at Piazza Santa Maria 32 (✆0583-496-031; www.ciclibizzarri.net; Mon–Sat 8:30am–1pm and 2:30–7:30pm and same hours Sun Mar to mid-Sept). The going rates are 3€ an hour for a regular bike, 4€ to 4.50€ for a mountain bike, and 6.50€ for a tandem.

   Taxis line up at the train station (✆0583-494-989), Piazza Napoleone (✆0583-491-646), and Piazzale Verdi (✆0583-581-305).

VISITOR INFORMATION   The main **tourist office** is inside the north side of the walls at Piazza Santa Maria 35, 55100 Lucca (✆0583-919-931; www.luccaturismo.it; daily 9am–7pm, sometimes later in summer). It provides an excellent free map and good pamphlets on Lucca and the Garfagnana. The *comune* also has a small **local info office** on Piazzale Verdi (✆0583-442-944), which keeps similar hours.

   For **events** and theater, pick up the English-language monthly *Grapevine* for 2€ at most newsstands.

FESTIVALS & MARKETS   Musical festivals celebrate the town's melodious history. In addition to the town's nightly Puccini concerts (see "Lucca After Dark," later), all September long, **Settembre Lucchese** brings concerts and operas by the city's favorite son to the theater where many premiered, the Teatro Comunale on Piazza del Giglio. The shore of nearby Lago di Massaciuccoli provides the backdrop to the summer **Puccini Festival** ★ (*℡0584-359-322;* www.puccinifestival.it), the biggest annual date in a local opera lover's calendar. There's a seasonal ticket office at Viale Puccini 257a, in Torre del Lago, or book tickets online. Prices range from 35€ to 125€. With every year that passes, Lucca's July **Summer Festival** (www.summer-festival.com) grows in size and profile. Recent headline acts to grace the outdoor stage in Piazza Napoleone have included Grammy winners Arcade Fire, Elton John, and the late Amy Winehouse. On September 13, an 8pm candlelit procession from San Frediano to the Duomo honors Lucca's most prized holy relic, the **Volto Santo** statue of Christ that tradition holds was carved by Nicodemus himself.

A huge **antiques market,** one of Italy's most important, is held the third Sunday (and preceding Sat) of every month in Piazza Antelminelli and the streets around the Duomo. It's great fun but it makes hotel rooms hard to find and restaurants booked, especially at lunch (even those normally closed Sun reopen for this one). It's spawned a local **art market** on Piazza del Arancio on the same dates, and the final Sunday of the month sees an **artisans' market** on Piazza San Giusto.

Exploring Lucca

The most curious feature of Lucca's street plan is **Piazza Anfiteatro** ★ near the north end of Via Fillungo, where a series of houses were built during the Middle Ages into the remains of a 1st- or 2nd-century-A.D. Roman amphitheater, which had been used for centuries as a quarry for raw materials to raise the city's churches and palaces. The outline was still visible in the 1930s when Duke Ludovico asked local architect Lorenzo Nottolini to rearrange the space and bring out the ancient form better. Nottolini pulled down the few structures that had been built inside the oval, restructured the ground floors of each building, and inserted four tunneled entryways.

Cattedrale di San Martino ★★ The **facade** ★ of Lucca's Duomo is an eye-catching example of the Pisan–Lucchese Romanesque school of architecture. Long lines of baby columns—every variety imaginable—backed by discreet green-and-white Romanesque banding are stacked into three tiers of arcaded loggias. Signed in 1204 by Guidetto da Como, the facade is technically unfinished, lacking the topmost loggia and a tympanum. The carved great arches making up the portico underneath include a dwarfish third partner, probably made smaller to accommodate the preexisting (1060) base of the bell tower, the crenellated marble top half of which was finished in 1261. The pillar abutting the tower is carved with a circular 12th-century **labyrinth,** a symbol of the long, torturous road to salvation. Such mazes once graced the entrance to many medieval churches.

The 13th-century **reliefs under the portico** ★★ are beautiful examples of medieval stonework, a few of them carved by Guido da Como. Around the central door are the months of the year and stories from the life of St. Martin. Martin of Tours was a 4th-century Hungarian soldier in the Roman army who famously divided his cloak to share with a beggar and, after converting, preached against capital punishment (panel 1, starting right of the door), cured lepers with kisses (panel 2, though here he's not puckering), raised a few dead (panel 3), and was made bishop (panel 4) before becoming the first saint to die of natural causes. Bedecking the left portal are an *Adoration of the Magi* and *Deposition* that may be early Nicola Pisano works.

In the 14th- to 15th-century **interior,** talented local sculptor Matteo Civitali designed the **pavement** as well as the holy-water stoups and the **pulpit.** Against the entrance wall is the original 13th-century statue of St. Martin dividing his cloak to give to a beggar (outside is a replica). Among the fine baroque works in the right aisle is (third altar) a ***Last Supper*** (1590–91) by Tintoretto and his assistants.

Halfway down the left aisle is Civitali's octagonal **Tempietto** (1482), built of white Carrara and red porphyry marble, with a St. Sebastian on the backside. It houses Lucca's most holy relic, the **Volto Santo ★**. This thick-featured, bug-eyed, time-blackened wooden statue of Jesus crucified was rumored to have been started by Nicodemus—who would've known what he was carving since he was the one who actually took Jesus off the Cross—but was miraculously completed. Hidden during the persecutions and eventually stuck on a tiny boat by itself and set adrift, it found its way to the Italian port of Luni in 782, where the local bishop was told in a dream to place it in a cart drawn by two wild oxen, and wherever they went, there the Holy Image would stay. The ornery beasts, submitting meekly to the yoke, wandered over to Lucca and hit the brakes, and the miraculous image has been planted here ever since. In truth, however, the simple sculpture was probably carved in a 13th-century Lombard workshop to replace a lost 11th-century version that may have been copied from a Syrian statue of the 700s. Every September the Luccans dress their Christ up in kingly jewel-encrusted medieval vestments (kept in the Museo della Cattedrale; see below) and hold a solemn procession in its honor.

To access the area beyond the crossing, you must pay an admission fee (see below). On the right aisle just past a few steps is the entrance to the former sacristy, containing a 1479 altarpiece of the ***Madonna Enthroned with Saints*** by Domenico Ghirlandaio over a predella by his pupil Bartolomeo di Giovanni and surmounted by a lunette of the *Deposition* by a follower of Filippo Lippi. The sacristy is also home to the Duomo's masterpiece, Jacopo della Quercia's **Tomb of Ilaria Carretto Guinigi ★★**. Married in 1403 to Paolo Guinigi and dead 2 years later at age 26, Ilaria had only been in the limelight for a brief moment. But her rich husband also happened to be the town boss, so she was guaranteed everlasting fame as the subject of Jacopo della Quercia's masterpiece in marble. Della Quercia's International Gothic style is influenced here by French models—the lying-in-state look with folded hands and with a little pug dog at her feet to symbolize fidelity. But he also started to introduce Renaissance elements that look back to antiquity, such as the sarcophagal friezes of putti and garlands around the sides; the natural and accurate representation of Ilaria's face; and the flowing, limpid lines full of grace and repose. The tomb is famous—if for nothing else—because the young lady was obviously very beautiful, and Jacopo's chisel has kept her beauty alive. Incidentally, Ilaria is actually buried, and always has been, in the Guinigi chapel of Santa Lucia in San Francesco; Paolo Guinigi had the tomb placed in the cathedral just to show off what he could buy.

In the right transept are more Matteo Civitali works, including the 1472 **tomb of Pietro Noceto** and the tomb of Domenico Bertini. In the far right transept chapel, Civitali did the two praying angels flanking the tabernacle, and the chapel next to the choir has his *Altar of St. Regolo* (1484).

Piazza San Martino. ✆ **0583-957-068.** Admission to church free; transepts and Ilaria tomb 2€ adults, 1.50€ children 6–14. Cumulative ticket for tomb, Museo, and San Giovanni 6€ adults, 4€

children 6–14. Mon–Fri 9:30am–5:45pm (closes 4:45pm Nov–Mar), Sat 9:30am–6:45pm, Sun 9:30–10:45am and noon–6pm.

Chiesa e Battistero di San Giovanni e Santa Reparata ★ The Duomo's Romanesque neighbor has a 16th-century facade and a 12th-century body, but excavations have revealed the structure is actually five layers (and several more centuries) deep. It sits atop a much older Lombard church that served until the early 700s as Lucca's cathedral, which in turn was built atop a 5th-century-A.D. paleo-Christian church and 6th-century cemetery, which took the place of a Roman temple built atop Roman houses (from which some mosaic fragments survive). In the 9th century, a crypt was added. In all, 12 centuries of history jumble together in a confusing but interesting mélange beneath the pavement inside. You're free to wander a well-signed route in the church's bowels.

Piazza San Giovanni. © **0583-490-530.** Admission 2.50€ adults, 1.50€ children 6–14. Cumulative ticket for Ilaria tomb, Museo, and San Giovanni 6€ adults, 4€ children 6–14. Hours same as Museo della Cattedrale; see below.

Museo della Cattedrale The highly successful architectural marriage of the town's 12th- to 15th-century buildings with the steel-and-glass modernity of this new museum is almost more interesting than the exhibits themselves. The small collection kicks off with the gold ornament, jewelry, and baubles the Volto Santo wears on the days he's specially venerated. Upstairs Sala III contains a bit of Matteo Civitali's late-15th-century **choir screen,** removed from the Duomo in 1987 despite vehement local protest. The second floor starts with a pair of too-realistic wooden carvings of St. John the Baptist's head on a plate. Past an early-17th-century Francesco Vanni *Crucifixion* and a stretch of priestly vestments is a room with sculptures from the Duomo's facade, such as Jacopo della Quercia's huge early-15th-century *St. John the Evangelist* ★.

Piazza Antelminelli (next to the cathedral). © **0583-490-530.** Admission 4€ adults, 2.50€ children 6–14. Cumulative ticket for Ilaria tomb, Museo, and San Giovanni 6€ adults, 4€ children 6–14. Apr–Oct daily 10am–6pm; Nov–Mar Mon–Fri 10am–2pm, Sat 10am–6pm, Sun 10am–5pm.

Museo Nazionale Palazzo Mansi This museum is worth the admission price if only to see the ridiculously sumptuous tapestries, frescoes, and other decorations of this 16th- to 19th-century palace. The painting collection isn't large or particularly spectacular, but be on the lookout for Luca Giordano's *St. Sebastian,* Domenico Beccafumi's wildly colored *Scipio,* Jacopo Vignali's *Tobias and the Angel,* and Rutilio Manetti's *Triumph of David.* In the second room is one of several versions of Agnolo Bronzino's definitive *Portrait of Cosimo I* and Pontormo's Mannerist *Portrait of a Young Man.* The third room has a *Madonna and Child* by Correggio and Il Sodoma's *Christ with the Cross,* along with portraits by Tintoretto and Luca Giordano.

Via Galli Tassi 43. © **0583-55-570.** www.luccamuseinazionali.it. Admission 4€ adults, 2€ students 18–25, free for children 17 and under and seniors 65 and over. Cumulative ticket with Museo Nazionale Villa Guinigi 6.50€ adults, 3.25€ students 18–25. Tues–Sat 8:30am–7:30pm; Sun 8:30am–1pm.

Museo Nazionale Villa Guinigi The early-15th-century palace built for Paolo Guinigi on the occasion of his second marriage is now home to the best gallery in Lucca's relatively poor museum crop. The collections start with **archaeological finds** that are well labeled—alas, only in Italian. Among the scraps from the Iron Age of the 10th century B.C. through the 8th-century-B.C. Villanovan period and

6th- to 3rd-century-B.C. Etruscan era are some reconstructed 3rd-century-B.C. Ligurian tombs that look like miniature versions of Fred Flintstone's suburban Bedrock home.

Upstairs are some fascinating **medieval carvings** and capitals, and **14th- and 15th-century paintings,** arranged roughly chronologically. Highlights of the collection include a Berlinghieri *Crucifix* (ca. 1230), a Spinello Aretino *Crucifixion with Saints* triptych, a couple of Matteo Civitali marble reliefs, and two *Madonna and Child* terra cottas recently proven to have been by the hand of Donatello (before 1425). The **15th-century wood inlays** show Luccan scenes as well as the Devil's Bridge at Borgo a Mozzano (see "The Garfagnana & the Lunigiana," later in this chapter). Fra' Bartolomeo is represented by three panels, including a classically simple *Eternal Father with Saints* and a Raphael-influenced *Madonna della Misericordia.*

Via della Quarquonia. ⓒ **0583-496-033.** www.luccamuseinazionali.it. Admission 4€ adults, 2€ students 18–25, free children 17 and under and seniors 65 and over. Cumulative ticket with Museo Nazionale di Palazzo Mansi 6.50€ adults, 3.25€ students 18–25. Tues–Sat 8:30am–7:30pm; Sun 8:30am–1pm.

San Frediano ★ Particularly on a sunny day, San Frediano's **facade** vies with those of the Duomo and San Michele as the most attention-grabbing in town, with a glittering 13th-century mosaic two stories high taking the place of the other churches' stacks of columns. Berlinghiero Berlinghieri designed it in a Byzantine/medieval style and threw just enough color into the apostles and ascending Christ to balance the tens of thousands of gold-leaf tiles for a truly eye-popping effect. The original church here was built by Irish Bishop Frediano in the 6th century, and when the current structure was rebuilt (1112–47), it was rededicated to the by-then-sanctified Frediano.

All the interior works are well labeled, and the highlight is just inside the entrance, a Romanesque **baptismal font** in the right aisle from around the 12th century, dismantled and squirreled away in the 18th century and reassembled only a few decades ago. A Lombard sculptor gave us the stories of Moses on the large lower basin, and one Maestro Roberto signed the last two panels of the Good Shepherd and six prophets. The small tempietto sprouting out of the top was carved by a Tuscan master, with the apostles and months of the year on

The Patron Saint of Ladies-in-Waiting

Just beyond the font inside San Frediano is the **Cappella di Santa Zita (Chapel of St. Zita),** built in the 17th century to preserve the glass-coffined body of the saint and painted with her miracles by Francesco del Tintore. Zita is the patron saint of ladies-in-waiting and maids everywhere who, as a serving girl in the 13th-century Fatinelli household, was caught sneaking out bread in her apron to feed beggars on the street. Her suspicious master demanded to know what she was carrying, to which she answered, "Roses and flowers." She opened her apron and, with a little divine intervention, that's what the bread had become. Every April 26, the Lucchesi carpet the piazza of the nearby amphitheater with a dazzling flower market to commemorate the miracle and bring out the glass coffin containing her shrunken body to the front of the church to venerate.

circumnavigating THE WALLS

The walls are Lucca's defining characteristic, and they make up a city park more than 4km (2½ miles) long but in parts only about 18m (59 ft.) wide, filled with avenues of plane, chestnut, and ilex trees planted by Marie Louise Bourbon in the 19th century. The shady, paved paths of Lucca's formidable bastions are busy year-round with couples walking hand in hand, tables of old men playing unfathomable card games, families strolling, children playing, and hundreds of people on bicycles, from tykes to octogenarians.

Rent a bike ★★ (see "Getting Around," above) and take a spin, peering across Lucca's rooftops and down into its palace gardens and narrow alleys, gazing toward the hazy mountains across the plane, and checking out the 11 bastions and six gates. The 1566 **Porta San Pietro,** the southerly and most important gate into town, still has a working portcullis, the original doors, and Lucca's republican motto, "Libertas," carved above the entrance.

The defensive walls you see today—a complete kidney-shaped circuit built from 1544 to 1654—are Lucca's fourth and most impressive set and perhaps the best preserved in Italy. About 12m (39 ft.) high and 30m (98 ft.) wide at their base, the ramparts bristled with

126 cannons until the Austrian overlords removed them. The walls were never put to the test against an enemy army, though it turned out they made excellent dikes—there's no doubt the walls saved the city in 1812 when a massive flood of the Serchio River inundated the valley. Elisa Bonaparte Baciocchi was governing Lucca at the time from her villa outside the walls, and when she tried to get into the city for safety, the people didn't want to open the gates for fear of the surging waters. Lest they let their princess—and, more important, the sister of Europe's emperor—drown, however, they hoisted her highness over the walls rather unceremoniously with the help of a crane.

the lid. High up on the wall is a glazed terra-cotta lunette attributed to Andrea dell Robbia of the *Annunciation* framed by garlands of fruit and a chorus line of winged putti heads. Matteo Civitali carved the 15th-century polychrome *Madonna Annunciata* in the corner.

Up to the left of the high altar is a massive **stone monolith,** probably pilfered from the nearby Roman amphitheater. The Cappella Trenta, fourth in the left aisle, contains another Jacopo della Quercia masterpiece, an **altar** carved with the help of his assistant Giovanni da Imola (1422) as well as a pair of tombstones from the master's chisel.

Lucca's finest fresco cycle ★ is in the second chapel of the left aisle, painted by Amico Aspertini (1508–09): In the *Miracles of St. Frediano,* the Irish immigrant bishop saves Lucca from a flood—although he symbolically performs a miracle in the middle ground by raking a new path for the water to be diverted away from the city, naked-torsoed workmen take the prudent, pragmatic step of building a dam as well; the group of noblemen on the left (who aren't doing the least bit to help) are probably portraits of Luccan bigwigs of the day. In the *Arrival in Lucca of the Volto Santo,* opposite, the legend says the pair of heifers drag the holy statue, which washed ashore at the port of Luni in the background, to Lucca of their own volition, accompanied only by Luni's bishop. But here they're joined by a crowd of singing monks, townsfolk, and a stooped old lady in voluminous red robes who steals the show down in front.

Around the left side of the church and down Via Battisti, at Via degli Asili 33, is the 17th-century **Palazzo Pfanner** (✆ **0583-491-243**), whose sumptuous 18th-century walled garden out back was featured in Jane Campion's 1996 film *Portrait of a Lady*. Admission is 4€ each to visit the gardens *or* the *palazzo* (or 5.50€ for both). It's open March to October daily from 10am to 6pm. If you walk around the city's ramparts you can look down into the gardens for free.

Piazza San Frediano. ✆ **0583-493-627.** Free admission. Mon–Sat 8:30am–noon and 3–5:30pm; Sun 9–11:30am and 3–5:30pm.

Mosaics on the facade of San Frediano.

Santa Maria Forisportam This church was built in the 12th century outside the gates, hence the name, with a Pisan-style facade from the 1200s. Inside are two late-17th-century Guercino paintings: *St. Lucy* on the fourth altar on the right, a simple composition with Lucia holding her eyes daintily on a plate, and a smoke-blackened *Assumption* in the left transept. There's also a ciborium in *pietre dure* in the right transept (1680) and a 1386 Giottesque *Assumption* by Angelo Puccinelli with angels emerging from cocoonlike clouds in the sacristy (ring for the custodian).

Via Santa Croce and Via della Rosa. ✆ **0583-467-769.** Free admission (donation appreciated). Mon–Sat 9am–noon and 3:15–6:30pm.

San Michele in Foro ★ The exterior of this church is as beautiful as a 12th-century Romanesque church can get. It boasts a Pisan-inspired **facade** ★★ of blind arches with lozenges and colonnaded arcades stacked even higher than San Martino's, and it's smack in the center of town—on top of the ancient Roman forum, in fact, hence the name—and yet this isn't the Duomo. Past the marvelous facade, with its orderly rows of doggedly unique columns topped by a Romanesquely flattened St. Michael, however, the **interior** is a little disappointing. The original Matteo Civitali *Madonna and Child* sculpture from the facade is wedged in the right corner as you enter. (Its replacement doppelgänger basks in gilded beams of holy light on the outside corner of the church.) Another take on the same theme in glazed **terra cotta** by Andrea della Robbia (some now say it was by his uncle Luca) is inset on the first altar on the right. The church's best art hangs on the far wall of the right transept, a painting of **Sts. Roch, Sebastian, Jerome, and Helen** ★ by Filippino Lippi, whose figures are more humanly morose but every bit as graceful as those of his famous teacher Sandro Botticelli. As you leave, check out the **medieval graffiti drawings** scratched on the columns of the left aisle (especially the third and fourth from the door).

Two generations of Puccinis played the organ in this church, and the third, one young master Giacomo, sang in the choir as a boy. He didn't have far to walk,

San Michele in Foro.

for the young **Giacomo Puccini,** who was to become one of Italy's greatest operatic composers, was born in 1858 just down the block at Via Poggio no. 30 (a plaque marks the site). Around the corner at Corte San Lorenzo 9 is the entrance to a small museum installed in his birth home (✆ **0583-584-028**). Along with the usual composer memorabilia, it includes the piano on which he composed *Turandot.* It reopened in September 2011 after a long and controversial restoration. The nearby heavily baroque church of **San Paolino** is where the boy Puccini got his first crack at twiddling an organ's keyboard.

Piazza San Michele. ✆ **0583-48-459.** Free admission. Summer daily 7:40am–noon and 3–6pm; winter daily 9am–noon and 3–5pm.

Torre Guinigi ★ Only one of the two towers sprouting from the top of the 14th-century palace, home of Lucca's iron-fisted ruling family, still stands, but it certainly grabs your attention. Historians tell us that many of Lucca's towers once had little gardens like this on top—the city was civilized even in its defenses—but that doesn't diminish the delight at your first glance at this stack of bricks 44m (144 ft.) high with a tiny forest of holm oaks overflowing the summit. For a closer look, climb the 230 steps for a spectacular **view ★★** of Lucca's skyline with the snowcapped Apuan Alps and the Garfagnana in the distance. Up here, you can also see the oval imprint the Roman amphitheater left on the medieval buildings of Piazza Anfiteatro (see above).

Via Sant'Andrea 14 (at Via Chiavi d'Oro). ✆ **347-627-0423.** Admission 3.50€ adults, 2.50€ children 6–12 and seniors 65 and over. Cumulative ticket with Torre delle Ore, on Via Fillungo, 5€ adults, 4€ children and seniors. Apr–May daily 9am–7:30pm; June–Sept daily 9am–6:30pm; Oct and Mar daily 9:30am–5:30pm; Nov–Feb daily 9:30am–4:30pm.

Shopping

Lucca's main shopping promenades are the elite **Via Fillungo ★★** and more proletarian **Via Santa Lucia,** both epicenters of the evening *passeggiata.* Cross-street **Via Buia** also has a number of chic boutiques. While you're here, drop by the ultra-traditional dried beans and seed shop **Antica Bottega di Prospero,** Via Santa Lucia 13 (no phone; www.bottegadiprospero.it). Since 1965, the best wine cellar in town has been **Enoteca Vanni ★,** Piazza San Salvatore 7 (✆ **0583-491-902;** www.enotecavanni.com), with hundreds of bottles lining the cryptlike rooms under the tiny storefront. For heavenly rich chocolates, stop by **Cioccolateria Caniparoli,** Via San Paolino 96, at the corner of Via Galli Tassi (✆ **0583-53-456**).

Lucca has lots of jewelry stores but none more gorgeous than **Carli,** Via Fillungo 95 (✆ **0583-491-119**), specializing in antique jewelry, watches, and silver from its high-vaulted room frescoed in 1800. The best bookshop (with some titles in English) is **Edison,** Via Cenami (at Via Roma; ✆ **0583-492-447;** www.edisonlucca.it).

Where to Stay

An economical alternative to our favorite hotels below is the delightful **Ostello San Frediano,** Via della Cavallerizza, 55100 Lucca (www.ostellolucca.it; ✆ **0583-469-957**), which has 140 beds in multibed rooms, standard doubles, and family rooms sleeping six. The cost is 19€ to 22€ per day for a bunk in a multibed room. Private units cost 60€ for two people, 78€ for three, and 100€ for four. The **San Luca Palace** ★, Via San Paolino 103, 55100 Lucca (www. sanlucapalace.com; ✆ **0583-317-446**), opened in 2007 and immediately raised the bar for the upscale or business traveler looking to stay within the walls. The characterful 16th-century *palazzo* has large, air-conditioned units that have retained some antique character. Doubles officially cost from 170€ to 290€, and junior suites suited to families between 250€ and 350€, depending on season—but always check the website for discounted offers.

Alla Corte degli Angeli ★★ This welcoming, warrenlike *palazzo* just off Via Fillungo is blessed with the most romantic rooms in town. The individually restored bedrooms are well proportioned, although not enormous, and simply kitted out with Italian antique furniture. The design flourish is provided by a unique, hand-painted fresco adorning the walls and ceiling of each, carefully coordinated with the room's fabrics and moniker: Each unit is named after a flower and our favorites include Orchidea and Ortensia, both of which come with large hydromassage tubs.

Via degli Angeli 23 (off Via Fillungo), 55100 Lucca. www.allacortedegliangeli.com. ✆ **0583-469-204.** Fax 0583-991-989. 10 units. 130€–210€ double. Rate includes buffet breakfast. AE, DC, MC, V. Garage parking 15€. Closed 2 weeks in Jan. **Amenities:** Bikes; concierge. *In room:* A/C, TV, minibar, MP3 docking station, Wi-Fi (free).

Fattoria Maionchi ★ ☺ Fitted into the olive-blanketed hills where Lucca's valley rises to the Pizzorne hills, this *agriturismo* offers you the chance to stay in an outbuilding of a 17th-century farming estate—with concessions to modernity such as fully outfitted kitchens and a pool overlooking the grapevines. A motley assortment of antiques acquired over the centuries is scattered throughout the spacious multifloor apartments, but the overall scheme manages to remain rustic. A stay here (which must be at least a week) makes a perfect escape in the country; you're close enough for easy excursions into Lucca (15 min. by car) as well as trips into the Garfagnana mountains.

Loc. Tofori (13km/8 miles northeast of Lucca), 55012 Camigliano (LU). www.fattoriamaionchi. it. ✆ **0583-978-194.** Fax 0583-978-345. 11 apartments (sleeping 2–6). Weekly rates July–Aug, Easter, and Christmas 670€–990€; June and Sept 530€–890€; May and Oct 415€–570€; otherwise 370€–570€ per week (Sat afternoon–Sat morning). AE, DC, MC, V. Free parking. **Amenities:** Restaurant; babysitting; bikes (free); outdoor pool. *In room:* TV, kitchen, no phone.

Hotel Ilaria & Residenza dell'Alba ★★ The former stables in the gardens of the Villa Bottini these days provide deluxe, businesslike accommodations with modern rooms, where all guests enjoy such complimentary perks as a snack bar (free beer and fresh pastries, anyone?) and free use of bikes. (The deconsecrated medieval church across the street is now an annex called Residenza dell'Alba.) The rooms are fitted simply but stylishly with cherry veneer built-in units and double-paned windows—though you don't need them on this quiet street—and standard rooms had new parquet flooring added in 2011. The rooms opening onto the little canal out front are nice, but even better views are over the rear terrace dotted with potted camellias and shaded by a sycamore. The same group owns three restaurants in town, including Buca di Sant'Antonio (see below), and you can work out a pension deal for 30€ to 40€ per person extra.

Via del Fosso 26, 55100 Lucca. www.hotelilaria.com. ☎ **0583-47-615.** Fax 0583-991-961. 41 units. 110€–260€ double. Rates include buffet breakfast. AE, DC, MC, V. Garage parking 10€. **Amenities:** Bar; babysitting; bikes (free); concierge; Jacuzzi (outdoor). *In room:* A/C, TV, hair dryer, minibar, Wi-Fi (free).

Piccolo Hotel Puccini ★ 🐾 This tiny hotel boasts Lucca's best location: just off the central piazza of San Michele. Your neighbor is the ghost of Puccini, who grew up across the street. The prices are fantastic for the location and comfort, and Paolo and his staff are the friendliest hoteliers in town. Most of the rooms are smallish, but they have firm beds, compact bathrooms, carpeting, and reproduction opera playbills framed on the walls. Be sure to request one of the lighter rooms along the front (this street sees little traffic), from where you can lean out and see a sliver of the fabulous San Michele facade. The Puccini fills quickly, so book ahead.

Via di Poggio 9 (off Piazza San Michele), 55100 Lucca. www.hotelpuccini.com. ☎ **0583-55-421.** Fax 0583-53-487. 14 units. 95€ double. AE, MC, V. Garage parking 15€. **Amenities:** Bar; babysitting; bikes; concierge. *In room:* TV, hair dryer, Wi-Fi (1.50€/day).

Where to Eat

Gastronomically, Lucca is famous above all for its divine extra-virgin olive oil, a light-green elixir with a fresh olive taste that's drizzled on just about every dish in these parts. The most typically Luccan dish is the creamy, filling *zuppa di farro,* a soup made with spelt, an emmer- or barley-like grain cooked al dente. The Lucca area is also known for its asparagus, strawberries, and honey. Accompany any dish with Lucca's excellent and little-known DOC **wines,** Rosso delle Colline Lucchesi and Montecarlo.

If you just want to grab a pizza slice and a Coke for 5€, try the **Pizzeria da Felice,** Via Buia 12 (☎ **0583-494-986;** Tues–Sat 9:30am–2pm and 4–8:30pm, Mon 11am–2pm and 4–8:30pm), where you can also sample two more Lucchese specialties: *cecina* (a flat bread made of garbanzo bean flour) and *castagnaccio* (a sort of chestnut-flour pita, split with each half wrapped around sweetened fresh ricotta).

People line up to wait for the bakery **Amadeo Giusti,** Via Santa Lucia 18–20 (☎ **0583-496-285**), to reopen at 4:30pm (it's open daily 7am–1pm and 4:30–7:45pm, but closed Sat afternoons), whose popular focaccia is used by many local restaurants in their bread baskets. *Buccellato,* a dense, sweet bread flavored with raisins and fennel seeds, is equally in demand at **Taddeucci,** Piazza San Michele 34 (☎ **0583-494-933;** www.taddeucci.com).

Buca di Sant'Antonio ★ LUCCHESE Since before 1782, this has been the premier gastronomic pit stop inside Lucca's walls. It's attracted the likes of Puccini, Ezra Pound, and others who in times past just wanted to read the restaurant's secret stock of banned books. The menu changes regularly, but expect exciting lineups like *sella di coniglio lardellata su radicchietti di campo* (a cold rabbit salad), followed by ravioli filled with ricotta and lightly sautéed in butter and zucchini, and then move to one of their signature dishes, *capretto allo spiedo con patate arrosto e sformato di carciofi* (tender spit-roasted kid with roast potatoes and artichoke pudding). Finish it off with a green apple sorbet and smile the rest of the day.

Via della Cervia 3 (a side alley just west of Piazza San Michele). ☎ **0583-55-881.** Reservations highly recommended. Primi 10€; secondi 15€. AE, DC, MC, V. Tues–Sat 12:30–3pm and 7:30–10:30pm; Sun 12:30–3pm.

Canuleia ★ MODERN ITALIAN This little restaurant may only carry the humble "trattoria" sign above its door, but the kitchen can justly claim to be among Lucca's most creative. You will find traditional Lucchese items on the menu, but Canuleia's strength lies in taking the best of the Italian peninsula—and beyond—and combining it in creative ways. Start, perhaps, with *sformatino di pecorino con salsa di pere* (pecorino cheese soufflé with pear salsa), followed by a risotto *alla pernice* (with partridge) and *petto d'anatra salsa teriyaki* (duck breast with teriyaki sauce). The informal shaded garden is a delightful spot in warmer months.

Via Canuleia 14. ℰ **0583-467-470.** www.ristorantecanuleia.it. Reservations recommended. Primi 8€–10€; secondi 12€–20€. AE, MC, V. Mon–Sat 12:30–2pm and 7:30–10pm.

Da Giulio LUCCHESE/TUSCAN This cavernous and popular trattoria is short on antique charm but long on antique tradition. Don't let the modern decor dissuade you—the friendly service and genuine peasant cuisine are as trattoria as they come. The soups are superb, such as the *farro con fagioli* (emmer and beans), or you can try the *maccheroni tortellati* (large pasta squares in ricotta, tomatoes, and herbs). *Pollo al mattone* (chicken breast roasted under a heated brick) is the secondo most in demand, but they also have plenty of local "extreme eating" specialties—tripe, horse tartar, and veal lung—to challenge your appetite.

Via Conce 45, Piazza San Donato (nestled in the very northwest corner of the walls). ℰ **0583-55-948.** Reservations recommended. Primi 5€–7€; secondi 6€–13€. MC, V. Mon–Sat noon–3pm and 7:30–10:30pm. Closed 10 days in Aug and 10 days around Christmas.

Da Leo ★★ 🍴 LUCCHESE/TUSCAN This authentic Lucchese dining spot run by the amiable Buralli family has the best value meals in the center—locals swear you can pay twice as much for inferior food at many of Lucca's other popular spots, and it has retained a devoted following of shopkeepers, students, and solitary art professors sketching on the butcher-paper place mats between bites. The food isn't fancy, but they execute traditional dishes well: *minestra di farro, ravioli alla crema di spinaci* (with spinach cream), *arrosto di maialino con patate* (roast piglet and potatoes), and the excellent *zuppa ai cinque cereali* (a soup with emmer, red and green lentils, barley, and cannellini beans).

Via Tegrimi 1 (just north of Piazza San Salvatore). ℰ **0583-492-236.** www.trattoriadaleo.it. Reservations recommended. Primi 6.50€–7€; secondi 9€–16€. No credit cards. Daily noon–2:30pm and 7:30–10:30pm.

Gli Orti di Via Elisa ★ ☺ PIZZA/LUCCHESE The proprietor Samuele wakes up every morning before 5am to bake the bread for this artistic pizzeria and trattoria, which has the feel of a 1930s Parisian bistro. Musical instruments line the wall, while homestyle Lucchese favorites line the menu. The *capretto al forno con verdure stufate* is a scrumptious dish of roasted goat with thinly sliced roasted carrots, celery, zucchini, and red peppers, dressed with the perfect amount of rosemary. The pizzas are reason enough to come, as are some of the best home-baked cakes in Tuscany for dessert.

Via Elisa 17 (near the eastern city gate). ℰ **0583-491-241.** www.ristorantegliorti.it. Reservations recommended. Primi 7€; secondi 10€–16€. AE, DC, MC, V. Mon–Tues and Thurs–Sat noon–3pm and 7:30pm–midnight; Wed noon–3pm.

NORTH OF THE CITY

Antica Locanda di Sesto ★★★ 🏠 LUCCHESE There's been a roadside restaurant here serving the finest Lucchese dishes since the 1300s—and it's still going strong under family ownership. Local and seasonal specialties permeate the menu, which is delivered in a relaxed country dining room where friendly staff nevertheless preserve a welcome nod to old-fashioned restaurant formalities. Among the primi, Lucchese soups like *farro* (spelt wheat) and *garmugia* (spring vegetables and ground meat) stand out. For secondi, there's plenty of choices from the grill (Cinta senese pork, cuts of beef) or oven (piglet, rabbit, kid), as well as *gran fritto toscano* (deep-fried mixed meats on the bone and seasonal vegetables). Unusually for Tuscany, there's also fare for vegetarians beyond the usual pastas, with dishes like grilled tomino cheese drizzled in balsamic vinegar and served with shredded radicchio and pine nuts. The fine house wines and olive oil hail from the family estate.

Via Ludovica 1660, Sesto di Moriano (signposted off SS12, 11km/7 miles north of Lucca; or take Garfagnana bus from Lucca, journey time 30 min.). ✆ **0583-578-181.** www.anticalocanda disesto.it. Reservations highly recommended. Primi 8€–12€; secondi 12€–18€. MC, V. Sun–Fri 12:30–2:30pm and 8–10pm.

Lucca After Dark

The **Teatro del Giglio,** Piazza del Giglio 13–15 (✆ **0583-465-320;** www.teatro delgiglio.it), is where Rossini premiered his *William Tell* in 1831 (Paganini was in the orchestra, little realizing that the dramatic Overture he was playing would one day be better known as the theme song from *The Lone Ranger*). Today it presents opera, plays, and ballet in the fall, winter, and spring months, and concerts in the summer, with a rare orchestral performance in the winter as well. Tickets cost from 14€ to 65€. Every evening at 7pm, the Chiesa di San Giovanni hosts an opera recital or orchestral concert dedicated to hometown composer Giacomo Puccini, in a series called **Puccini e la sua Lucca** (www.puccinielasualucca .com). Tickets are 17€ (13€ for those 22 and under) and can be purchased all day inside San Giovanni.

If you're seeking somewhere livelier than the street cafes that line every piazza, DJ bar **Zero,** Via San Paolino 58 (no phone), is where Lucca's twenty-somethings gather for evening *aperitivos* and to drink cocktails and socialize until late.

THE GARFAGNANA & THE LUNIGIANA

The Garfagnana region north of Lucca along the Serchio River is heavily wooded and mountainous, peppered with Romanesque churches, medieval Alpine villages, and good hiking trails. It's home to the eastern slopes of the **Parco Regionale delle Alpi Apuane,** now a natural park protecting the wildlife of the massive Apuan Alps. Over one-quarter of the plants known in Italy grow here; it's also a good bird-watching region, with more than 165 species wheeling in the skies above the mountains, including peregrine falcons and golden eagles. The **Lunigiana** to the northwest, a Ligurian land that's part of Tuscany in name only, preserves some remarkable prehistoric carvings in a museum at Pontrémoli.

Getting There by Bus & Train

VaiBus (www.vaibus.it) services most of the Garfagnana and the major towns north of Lucca, including **Bagni di Lucca** (trip time from Lucca: 50 min.), **Barga** (70 min.), and **Castelnuovo** (80 min.). In Lucca, buy tickets and hop aboard at Piazzale Verdi. A slow **scenic railway line** ducks in and out of tunnels alongside the Serchio River—you ride under an arch of the Devil's Bridge—and goes out onto the Lunigiana plain to Aulla (seven direct runs daily from Lucca, plus a couple with changes at Piazza al Serchio), where you can change for a train to Pontrémoli.

A Drive up the Garfagnana

The main SS12 road north toward Barga and Castelnuovo splits to go up either side of the steep-valleyed Serchio just south of Ponte a Moriano. You want to stay on the east (right) branch because there's no parking on the other side of the river when you get to Borgo a Mozzano (20km/12 miles) and just beyond it, the **Ponte del Diavolo (Devil's Bridge),** also called the Ponte della Maddalena. This impossibly narrow humpbacked 11th-century bridge of fitted stone was built under the auspices of the area's iron-fisted ruler, Countess Matilda. Much more fun to believe, however, is the legend that Satan agreed to build the span for the townspeople if they'd grant him the first soul to cross it. The morning after the bridge was completed—diabolical work crews move fast—the villagers outwitted Lucifer by sending a hapless dog trotting over.

Two and a half kilometers (1½ miles) farther along, the SS12 diverges east up the Lima valley for **Bagni di Lucca.** This was one of Europe's most famous spas in the 19th century. It hosted nobles and moneyed princes from the 17th century onward and a veritable stampede of British Romantics at the height of its popularity. Napoleon's sister Elisa Baciocchi, whom he made the princess of Lucca, helped its heyday along by turning it into her summer residence. As you enter the lower part of town, known as **Ponte a Serraglio,** take the lower road to the left along the tree-shaded river to see the neoclassical, riverside **Casino,** Europe's first licensed gaming house and the birthplace of roulette. For information on the town, see **www.prolocobagnidilucca.it.** Up the hill behind the Casino, past the ruined shells of once popular *terme,* is the town's last remaining thermal spa, the **Terme Bagni di Lucca,** Piazza San Martino (© **0583-87-221;** www.termebagnidilucca.it). A vast range of treatments includes several kinds of massage and beauty therapy, soaks in thermal mud, a natural steam cave (20€ for 20 min.), a thermal swimming pool (admission 12€–15€), and more. Day spa packages, with a selection of treatments, cost 120€.

Back in the Serchio valley, the main road now becomes the SS445 and runs another 18km (11 miles) to the turnoff to **Barga** ★ set high on the mountainside; the tourist office is at Via di Mezzo 47 (at Piazza Garibaldi; © **0583-724-743**), open Monday through Saturday 9am to 1pm, Saturday also 3 to 5:30pm, and Sunday 10:30am to 12:30pm and 3 to 5:30pm. Bilingual hyperlocal site **www.barganews.com** is another excellent source of information (the same folks run an English-language book exchange at Via di Mezzo 37). Barga is home to a gaggle of **della Robbian terra cottas:** On the inside of the Porta Mancianella, in the 15th-century Conservatorio di Sant'Elisabetta, at Via del Pretorio 22 (an *Assumption* ★), and in the Collegiata. The facade of the 9th- to 14th-century **Collegiata** is made from local white stone called albarese and covered with medieval and Romanesque low reliefs. The interior houses a reddish-toned 13th-century **pulpit** ★ by the quirky Lombard carver Guido Bigarelli da Como, full of medieval symbolism. The red marble columns are supported by a pug-nosed dwarf (evil) and the Lion of Judea (representing Jesus), who under one pillar conquers a dragon (evil) and under another is simultaneously killed and stroked worshipfully by a man (supposedly representing the fact that man, who once crucified Christ, later came to love him). Don't miss the 12th-century painted wooden St. Christopher in an apse niche, the della Robbian terra cottas in a right-hand chapel, and the view from the terrace outside. If you're feeling hungry, there are plenty of dining choices along Via di Mezzo, which snakes through the town. Our favorite spot is cheery, funky bar-trattoria **Scacciaguai,** Via di Mezzo 23 (✆ **0583-711-368;** www.scacciaguai.it), where local and seasonal dishes go for between 9€ and 14€. It's closed Monday. Our favorite accommodations in these parts are the rustic apartments at **Agriturismo Al Benefizio,** Loc. Ronchi 4 (www.albenefizio.it; ✆ **0583-722-201**), just north of town. All three comfortable units on this working olive oil farm are bookable per night, plus there's an outdoor pool with fine views. Prices range from 70€ to 110€ (cash only) for an apartment sleeping four.

From Barga take the road heading directly back down to the Serchio, cross under the railroad tracks, cross over the river and under the main road on the other side, proceed through the hamlet of Gallicano, and climb alongside the Turrite stream into the **Parco Naturale delle Alpi Apuane.** After about 9km (5½ miles) up the slopes of the 1,800m (5,906-ft.) "Queen of the Apuan Alps," Pania della Croce, you'll come to Fornovolasco and the **Grotta del Vento (Cave of the Wind)** ★ (✆ **0583-722-024;** www.grottadelvento.com). It's one of the best and most easily visited caverns of a system that honeycombs these mountains, a grotto network offering some of the best caving in Italy. The Grotta is a fascinating subterranean landscape of tunnels, stalactites, bottomless pits, eerie pools of water, and polychromatic rivers of rock that seem to flow in sheets and cascade down stony shoots. April through October, it's open daily with 1-hour guided tours (9€ adults, 7€ children 10 and under) on the hour from 10am to noon and 2 to 6pm; 2-hour visits (14€ adults, 11€ children) at 11am, 3, 4, and 5pm; and 3-hour explorations (20€ adults, 16€ children) leaving at 10am and 2pm. November through March, only the shortest itinerary is available Monday through Saturday, with a regular service on Sunday. Go as early as possible to miss the crowds in high season.

The stony capital of the Garfagnana, **Castelnuovo di Garfagnana,** lies about 11km (7¾ miles) north of Barga. For information on nearby outdoor activities or to book accommodations, visit the **Centro Visite Parco Apuane,** Piazza delle Erbe (✆ **0583-644-242**); Castelnuovo itself is covered by the **Pro-Loco tourist office** opposite the Centro Visite office (✆ **0583-641-007;** www.castel nuovogarfagnana.org). Both are

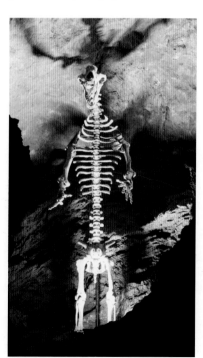

A bear skeleton at the Grotta del Vento.

open daily. There's not much to see other than the 14th-century **Rocca** castle, a stronghold of the Este dukes of Ferrara, so the best Castelnuovo is good for are views of the mountains and valley, and as an information office for wilderness hikes, climbs, or via ferrata (a mountain route equipped with fixed cables and bridges). Just north of town, you can branch off into the **Parco Naturale dell'Orecchiella (Orecchiella Natural Park)** on the east (Apennine) side of the valley by heading up one of the most scenic winding roads in this part of Tuscany, toward Villa, San Pellegrino in Alpe, and the Emilia-Romagna border. Fit walkers of most abilities will be able to tackle the marked 10km (6-mile) hike around the nearby **Pania di Corfino ★**, which takes in an alpine botanic garden and fine mountain views. The jumping-off point is the village of Corfino, 13km (8 miles) north of Castelnuovo. Park on the right as you enter and follow the signs that begin by the Albergo La Baita. Take a map.

Into the Lunigiana

Following the main Garfagnana road for another 58km (36 miles), or the more direct A12-A15 *autostrada* route from Lucca via Carrara, brings you to **Aulla,** lorded over by the 16th-century Brunella fort. You're now in the **Lunigiana,** a northern spur of Tuscany wedged between Liguria and Emilia-Romagna. The main interest here is the sleepy, partly medieval town of **Pontrémoli** on the Magra River 22km (14 miles) north of Aulla; the tourist office is at Piazza della Repubblica (© **0187-832-000**). Tuscany's northernmost sizable habitation has the baroque church of **San Francesco,** the rare Tuscan rococo church of **Nostra Donna,** and a baroque **Duomo** hitched up to the **Torre del Campanone,** the only remnant of the fortress Castruccio Castracani built in 1322 to keep two feuding factions from ripping each other to shreds.

The town's most important attraction, though, almost worth the whole trip up here, is the **Museo delle Statue Stele Lunigianesi ★★**, Castello del Piagnaro (© **0187-831-439;** www.statuestele.org), housed in a 14th-century castle and created to show off some 20-odd prehistoric **statue-stele** and casts of 30 or so others whose originals are elsewhere. The stylized menhirs look sort of like tombstones carved to resemble humans and were created by a long-lived Lunigiana cult that existed from about 3000 to 200 B.C. The earliest (3000–2000 B.C.) have just a "U" for a head and the mere suggestion of arms and a torso; the next group (2000–800 B.C.) has more features and realism; and the most recent (700–200 B.C.) are developed to the point where many of them carry weapons in both hands. That so many have been decapitated is a sure sign the Catholic Church got here before the archaeologists. The museum is open Monday to Saturday from 9am to 12:30pm and 3 to 6pm (Oct–Apr afternoon hours are 2:30 to 5:30pm). Admission is 4€ for adults, 2€ for children ages 6 to 16. Pontremoli's warren of ancient streets is also home to one of northern Tuscany's best *trattorie,* **Da Bussè ★★**, Piazza del Duomo 31 (© **0187-831-371**). This restaurant's dishes, served in an informal country-kitchen style dining room, have more than a whiff of Liguria about them—don't miss the *testaroli* (pasta discs) with basil pesto, if it's on. Main courses cost around 10€, but pasta dishes run less. It's open for lunch only Monday through Thursday; lunch and dinner are served on weekends.

PISA, TUSCANY'S COAST & THE MAREMMA

T he ancient maritime republic of **Pisa** is one of Italy's must-see cities. This lively university town boasts one of the most beautiful *piazze* in the world, an expansive grassy lawn studded with serene Gothic-Romanesque buildings of white- and gray-banded marble and delicate colonnaded arcading. But it'll forever be known chiefly for that square's cathedral bell tower: It just refuses to stick straight up.

Strung out along the river back toward Florence, the historic towns of the Valdarno, including **San Miniato** and **Vinci,** birthplace of Renaissance master Leonardo, make excellent day trips from Pisa. The brawny Medici-created port of **Livorno,** to the south, is Tuscany's second-largest city, but is perhaps unique in the region for its lack of art (beyond some Tuscan "Impressionists") and dearth of decorative churches. The seafood in its restaurants, though, is reason alone to visit, and its canal quarter adds some quasi-Venetian romance.

The green islands of the Tuscan archipelago sitting off the **Etruscan Coast** shoreline are dotted with some fine beaches and fantastic nature preserves. The granddaddy of the group, **Elba,** is a high-power summer tourist destination. It's Italy's third-largest island and a veritable mineral horde that has been mined since the Etruscan Age. Elba is famous as the short-lived kingdom of exiled ex-emperor Napoleon and popular for its colorful fishing towns, island cuisine, inland hiking, and beaches.

The **Maremma** is Tuscany's far south, a little-visited province with deep Etruscan roots, crumbling hill towns built atop dramatic tufa outcrops, and snow-white cattle watched over by the *butteri,* some of the world's last true-grit cowboys. The principal art stop here is **Massa Marittima,** a two-story stone town that's home to a fine Lorenzetti altarpiece and a stately Sienese-Gothic piazza. Inland, **Pitigliano** seems to sprout straight from its tufa rock perch—and curiously for Tuscany, has preserved a fascinating Jewish heritage.

PISA ★★

22km (14 miles) S of Lucca; 81km (50 miles) W of Florence; 334km (208 miles) NW of Rome

Nothing says Pisa more than its Leaning Tower, keystone of the Romanesque Campo dei Miracoli, but this city of ancient architectural wonders goes against type with its young and upbeat feel. Native son Galileo may be long gone but students still come here to study at the prestigious university where he taught and enjoy the city's vibrant vibe.

Things to See & Do Seeing the **Leaning Tower**'s lopsided beauty may satisfy, but to do it justice you can climb the 294 steps at a five-degree angle to the top for views over the Campo's other spectacular Romanesque monuments: the **Duomo, Baptistery,** and **Camposanto.** The underrated collection at the **Museo Nazionale di San Matteo** is another essential stop.

PREVIOUS PAGE: **Pisa's Leaning Tower.**

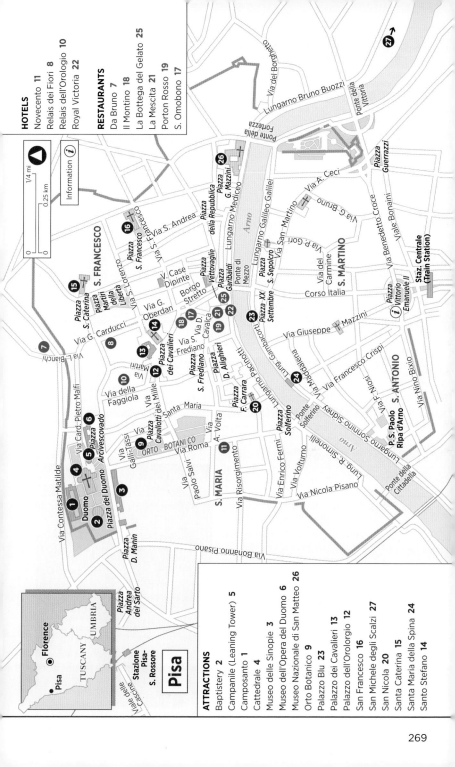

Pisa

Relaxation For a relaxing break from the Campo's bustle, roam the streets around arcaded **Borgo Stretto** as they burst into life every morning during the market, then head for the **Orto Botanico,** one of the oldest botanical gardens in Italy. Regular boat trips also depart from the center, cruising the Arno as far as the empty **Tenuta di San Rossore,** wedged between the city and the sea.

Restaurants & Dining In Pisa's medieval center, plenty of simple *trattorie* keep the locals well fed. Pisa's maritime history means that a traditional menu here specializes in fishy delights such as *baccalà alla pisana,* salt cod stewed in tomato sauce. **La Mescita,** in the heart of the produce market, serves the freshest ingredients.

Nightlife & Entertainment Pisa is probably Tuscany's liveliest city when night falls. Locals and students while away their evenings in the bars and nightclubs around **Piazza Garibaldi,** and along **Borgo Stretto** and the banks of the River Arno. On a warm evening here you'll find groups gathering outside to sip beer and *aperitivi* from chic bars, then heading to laid back haunts with live music or DJ sets.

Essentials

GETTING THERE **By Train:** There are around 20 direct trains daily from **Rome** (2¾–4 hr.). From **Florence,** 50 daily trains make the trip (60–90 min.). Three trains an hour run from nearby **Livorno** (18 min.); there are trains approximately every hour from **Siena** (change at Empoli; 100 min. total). **Lucca** offers over 25 runs here every day (25–35 min.). On the Lucca line, day-trippers (and anyone staying in any of the hotels listed below *except* the Royal Victoria) should get off at **San Rossore station,** a few blocks west of Piazza del Duomo and the Leaning Tower. All other trains—and eventually the Lucca one—pull into **Pisa Centrale** station. From here, bus no. 4 or the **LAM Rossa** bus will take you close to Piazza del Duomo.

By Car: There's a Florence-Pisa fast highway (the so-called *FI-PI-LI*) along the Arno valley. Take the SS12 or SS12r from Lucca; the A12 comes down the coast from the north (and up from Livorno), and the SS1 runs north and south along the coast. There's plenty of pay parking on the city streets: Park for free at **Park Pietrasantina,** a 10-minute walk or short bus ride (on the LAM Rossa) north of the Campo, or to get closer to the action, the **Parcheggio Piazza di Miracoli** lot at Via C. S. Cammeo 51 charges 2€ per hour. For more details on locations and charges, see **www.pisamo.it.**

By Bus: From most places with a rail station, the train is usually more convenient, but **VaiBus** (www.vaibus.it) runs services from Pisa Airport, Via Bonanno, and the Porta a Lucca to Lucca (at least hourly; 25–55

Pisa's Leaning Tower at night.

PISAN history 101

The city began as a seaside settlement around 1000 B.C. and was expanded into a naval trading port by the Romans in the 2nd century B.C. By the 11th century, Pisa had grown into one of the peninsula's most powerful maritime republics, along with Venice, Amalfi, and Genoa. Its extensive trading in the Middle East helped import advanced Arabic ideas (decorative and scientific), and its wars with the Saracens led it to create an offshore empire of Corsica, Sardegna, and the Balearics. It lay waste to rival Amalfi in 1135 and, riding a high tide of wealth in the late Middle Ages, created its monumental buildings. In 1284, Pisa's battle fleet was destroyed by Genoa at Meloria (off Livorno), a staggering defeat allowing the Genoese to take control of the Tyrrhenian Sea and forcing Pisa's long slide into twilight. Its Ghibelline nature gave Florence the excuse it needed to take control in 1406. Despite a few small rebellions, Florence stayed in charge until Italian unification in the 1860s.

Pisa's main claim to fame since has been its university, one of Italy's top schools, established in 1343. Pisa was also the birthplace of one of Western history's greatest physicists and astronomers, Galileo Galilei (1564–1642), a man prone to dropping uneven weights from the Leaning Tower and making blasphemous statements about Earth revolving around the sun, and it was home in the 12th century to St. Bona, who (among other things) is the patron saint of flight attendants.

min.). **CPT** (✆ 050-505-511 or 800-012-773 in Italy; www.cpt.pisa.it), has routes to/from **Volterra** (6–10 daily connect through Pontedera for a 2- to 2½-hr. total trip), **Livorno** (hourly; 55 min.), and towns along the coast. The CPT bus **station** and ticket office is in Piazza Sant'Antonio, just north of Centrale station.

By Plane: Tuscany's main international airport, **Galileo Galilei** (www.pisa-airport.com), is just 3km (2 miles) south of the center. Trains zip you downtown to Centrale station in 5 minutes; the LAM Rossa bus departs every 9 minutes for Centrale station and then the Campo. A metered taxi ride to town will cost 10€ to 15€ (drivers accept credit cards). For more on air connections, see "Getting There" and "Getting Around," in chapter 12.

GETTING AROUND By Bus: CPT (see above) runs the city's buses. Bus no. 4 and the LAM Rossa bus run to near the Campo dei Miracoli from Centrale station.

By Taxi: Taxis can be found on Piazza della Stazione and Piazza del Duomo. Call a radio taxi at ✆ 050-541-600 or 055-555-330.

VISITOR INFORMATION The main city **tourist office** is at Piazza Vittorio Emanuele II 16, Pisa (✆ 050-42-291; www.pisaunicaterra.it; Mon–Sat 9am–7pm, Sun 9am–4pm). There's also a helpful desk inside the arrivals hall at the airport (✆ 055-502-518; daily 9:30am–11:30pm). Either can hand out street maps and a good selection of pamphlets about the city and wider province.

To find out what's going on in town, pick up a copy of the monthly *ToDo* (often in bars and cafes), or check it online at **www.todomagazine. it**. Privately operated **www.pisaonline.it** is also useful.

FESTIVALS & MARKETS Since the 1400s, teams from the north and south sides of the Arno have dressed in Renaissance costumes and tried their darnedest to run one another over with a giant 7-ton (14,000-lb) decorated cart on the Ponte di Mezzo, site of the city's old Roman bridge. This inverse tug-of-war, the **Gioco del Ponte ★**, is held on the last Sunday in June. Also in June is the **Festa di San Ranieri,** when Pisans honor their patron saint by lining the Arno with torches on the 16th, then running a boat race on the 17th. There's an excellent **food market** Monday through Saturday on and around Piazza delle Vettovaglie.

Exploring the Campo dei Miracoli

On a grassy lawn wedged into the northwest corner of the city walls, medieval Pisans created one of the most dramatic squares in the world. Historically dubbed the **Campo dei Miracoli (Field of Miracles) ★★★**, Piazza del Duomo contains an array of elegant buildings that heralded the Pisan-Romanesque style.

But Piazza del Duomo isn't the central plaza in town as in most Tuscan cities. When it was built between the 11th and 13th centuries, the square was against the city walls, surrounded by farmland. But this peripheral location also somehow plays a role in the piazza's uniqueness. A very large but hidden part of its appeal, aside from the beauty of the buildings, is its spatial geometry. The piazza's medieval engineers knew what they were doing. If you take an aerial photo of the square and draw connect-the-dot lines between the centers, doors, and other focal points of the buildings and the spots where streets enter the piazza, you'll come up with all sorts of perfect triangles, tangential lines of mathematical grace, and other unfathomable hypotenuses.

Incidentally, only the tourist industry calls it the "Campo dei Miracoli." Pisans think that's just a bit too much and refer to it as Piazza del Duomo. We recommend visiting the Camposanto after the two museums, since both contain exhibits that'll help you appreciate the loss of the Camposanto frescoes.

Baptistery ★★ Italy's biggest baptistery (104m/341 ft. in circumference) was begun in 1153 by Diotisalvi, who gave it its lower Romanesque drum. Nicola and Giovanni Pisano "Gothicized" the upper part from 1277 to 1297 and Cellino di Nese capped it with a Gothic dome in the 1300s. Most of the exterior statues and decorative elements by Giovanni Pisano are now kept in the Museo dell'Opera del Duomo (see below), and only a few have been replaced here with casts. It may not look it, but if you include the statue on top, this building is marginally taller than the Leaning Tower across the square. The interior is surprisingly plain but features the first of the

Campo dei Miracoli Admissions

Admission charges for the monuments and museums of the Campo are tied together in a complicated way. The Cattedrale alone costs 2€ (though it's free Nov–Feb). Any other single sight is 5€; any two sites cost 6€. To access everything except the Leaning Tower costs 8€ between November and February and 10€ otherwise. Children 9 and under enter free. For more information, visit their website at **www.opapisa.it**. Admission to the Leaning Tower is separate, costing 15€, or 17€ if you reserve a timed slot in advance at www.opapisa.it (essential in peak periods). Children 7 and under are not permitted; see also "Pisa's Perpendicularly Challenged Tower," below.

The interior of Pisa's Baptistery.

great Pisano pulpits as well as a large baptismal **font,** carved and inlaid by the idiosyncratic Guido Bigarelli da Como and sprouting a 20th-century statue of St. John.

Nicola Pisano was the founder of a great line of Gothic sculptors who liberated their art from the static iconography of medievalism to a new level of dynamic action and intense expressiveness that would influence Ghiberti and Donatello and so pave the road for the Renaissance. The **pulpit ★★** Nicola carved for the baptistery (1255–60) is perhaps his masterpiece and the prototype for a series he and his son Giovanni carried out over the years (the last is in Pisa's Duomo; the other two are in Pistoia and Siena). Heavily influenced by classical works—including the Roman sarcophagi and Greek vase now in the Camposanto—Nicola's high-relief panels (a synopsis of Christ's life) include pagan gods converted to Christianity as Madonnas and saints.

The other main attraction of the baptistery is its renowned **acoustics.** When it's crowded in summer, you may have to ask a guard to warble, but when there are fewer people (come early in the morning), lean over the ropes to get as near to center as possible and let fly a clear loud note, listening to it echo around the room as it fades. Even better, sing two notes a half-octave apart and listen for their echoing atonal mingling. When a choir sings here, you can hear it for miles.

Piazza del Duomo. ✆ **050-835-011.** www.opapisa.it. For prices, see "Campo dei Miracoli Admissions," above. Apr–Sept daily 8am–8pm; Mar daily 9am–6pm; Oct daily 9am–7pm; Nov and Feb daily 9am–5pm; Dec–Jan daily 9:30am–4:30pm. Bus: E, 4, or LAM Rossa.

Camposanto Begun in 1278 by Giovanni di Simone to house the shiploads of holy Golgotha dirt (the mount where Christ was crucified) brought back by an archbishop from the Crusades, the Camposanto has been burial ground for Pisan bigwigs ever since. Most funerary monuments are recycled Roman sarcophagi or neoclassical confections installed in the peacefully arcaded corridor encircling the patches of green in the center.

The walls were once covered with important 14th- and 15th-century frescoes by Taddeo Gaddi, Spinello Aretino, and Benozzo Gozzoli, among others. On July 27, 1944, however, American warplanes launched an attack against the city (which was still in German hands) and the cemetery was bombed. The wooden roof caught fire, and its lead panels melted and ran down over the frescoes, destroying many of the paintings and severely damaging the few that remained—a couple of sides of the walls have been returned, however. When the surviving frescoes were detached to be moved, workers discovered the artists' preparatory sketches (*sinopie*) underneath. These, along with the *sinopie* of some of the destroyed frescoes, are housed in the Museo delle Sinopie (see below).

A doorway off one corridor leads to an exhibit of some frescoes that made it through the bombing. The most fascinating is the 1341 ***Triumph of Death ★***,

273

attributed to Florentine Buonamico Buffalmacco. Liszt was so moved by it that he sat down and wrote his famous *Totentanz*.

Piazza del Duomo. ℂ **050-835-011**. www.opapisa.it. For prices, see "Campo dei Miracoli Admissions," above. Same hours as the Baptistery; see above. Bus: E, 4, or LAM Rossa.

Cattedrale ★★ Buscheto, the architect who laid the cathedral's first stone in 1063, kicking off a new era in art by building what was to become the model for the Pisan-Romanesque style, is buried in the last blind arch on the left of the facade. All the elements of the nascent Romanesque style are here on the **facade ★**, designed and built by Buscheto's successor, Rainaldo: alternating light and dark banding, rounded blind arches with Moorish-inspired lozenges at the top and colored marble inlay designs, and Lombard-style open galleries of tiny mismatched columns stacked to make the facade much higher than the church roof. A disastrous 1595 fire destroyed most of the works inside the church, but luckily the 16th-century Pisans recognized and hired some of the better late- and post-Renaissance artists for the refurbishing.

The **main door** is one of three cast by students of Giambologna after the 1595 fire destroyed the originals. On the back of the right transept, across from the bell tower, is a 2008 cast of the bronze **Door of San Ranieri ★★★**; the

PISA'S PERPENDICULARLY CHALLENGED tower

The problem with the Leaning Tower **★★★**, Pisa's *Torre Pendente*—and the bane of Pisan engineers for 8 centuries—is that you can't stack that much heavy marble on shifting subsoil and keep it all upright. It was started in 1173—the date on the wall of 1174 owes to an old quirk of dating from the Virgin's conception—by Guglielmo and Bonnano Pisano, who also cast the Duomo's original doors. They reached the third level in 1185 when they noticed a lean, at that point about 3.8 centimeters (1½ in.).

Work stopped and wasn't resumed until 1275 under Giovanni di Simone. He tried to correct the tilt by curving the structure back toward the perpendicular, giving the tower its slight banana shape. In 1284, work stopped yet again. In 1360, Tommaso di Andrea da Pontedera capped it off at about 51m (167 ft.) with a vaguely Gothic belfry.

Excavations around the base in the early 19th century caused the tower to start falling faster than ever (about 1mm/.04 in. a year), and by 1990 the lean was about 4.6m (15 ft.), so Pisa's mayor closed the tower. Stabilization work continued until December 2001 when, righted to its lean of 1838 (when it was a mere 4m/13 ft. off), the tower

reopened. Now the number of visitors is controlled via 30-minute slots—and a massive admission charge. See "Campo dei Miracoli Admissions," above for details.

The campanile isn't the only edifice out of whack on the piazza. The same saturated, sandy soil has taken its toll on the Baptistery, which leans to the north; and if you catch the Cattedrale's facade at the correct angle, you'll see it is a few feet shy of straight. Many of Pisa's old buildings have shifted, and a couple of other *campanili* about town have been nicknamed Pisa's "other leaning towers" (San Michele degli Scalzi is perhaps even more askew than its famous cousin; see below).

only original door survives in the Museo dell'Opera (see below) and was cast by Bonnano Pisano in 1180 while he was working on the bell tower. Inside the right transept, you'll find another work that survived the fire, the **tomb of Emperor Henry VII** by Tino di Camaino (1315) surmounted by a pair of Ghirlandaio angels. Henry VII was a hero to the Ghibelline Pisans, who supported his successful bid for Holy Roman Emperor.

On the north side of the nave, Giovanni Pisano's masterpiece **pulpit ★★** (1302–11) has regained its rightful place. After the fire, the baroquies decided the nasty old Gothic pulpit was an eyesore, so they dismantled it and put it in a crate; it wasn't found and reassembled until 1926. It's the last of the famed Pisano pulpits and, along with the one in Pistoia (p. 244), the greatest.

Hanging low near the pulpit is a large **bronze lamp** that, according to legend, a bored Galileo was staring at one day during Mass, watching it sway gently back and forth, when his law of the pendulum suddenly hit him. Spoilsports like to point out the lamp was cast in 1586, a few years after Galileo's discovery, but the legend may still be salvaged: Another lamp probably hung here before this one. Beneath the frescoed oval dome is what remains of the **Cosmatesque pavement** of particolored marble designs. The **bronze angels** (1602) flanking the choir entrance and the **crucified Christ** over the altar are by the baroque master of bronze Giambologna, and on the entrance pier to the choir is Andrea del Sarto's almost Leonardesque *St. Agnes with her Lamb ★*, painted in High Renaissance style. In the apse is the last of the major survivors of the fire, an enormous 13th-century mosaic *Christ Pancrator,* completed in 1302 by Cimabue, who added the St. John the Evangelist on the right.

Piazza del Duomo. (📞 **050-835-011.** www.opapisa.it. For prices, see "Campo dei Miracoli Admissions," above. Apr–Sept Mon–Sat 10am–8pm, Sun 1–8pm; Mar Mon–Sat 10am–5:30pm, Sun 1–5:30pm; Oct Mon–Sat 10am–6:30pm, Sun 1–6:30pm; Nov–Feb Mon–Sat 10am–12:45pm and 2–4:30pm, Sun 2–4:30pm. Bus: E, 4, or LAM Rossa.

Museo delle Sinopie ★ Perhaps Pisa's saddest museum houses the *sinopie* sketches that were discovered underneath the charred remains of the Camposanto's ruined frescoes (see above). Placards reproducing Carlo Lasinio's 19th-century engravings of the finished frescoes sit in front of each *sinopie* to help you reconstruct what the final work once looked like. Note how different artists used the *sinopia* stage of the fresco process (some sketched just rough outlines to guide their later work, others went as far as shading the drapery and detailing facial features) and see where a master changed his mind between sketch and finished work.

Piazza del Duomo. (📞 **050-835-011.** www.opapisa.it. For prices, see "Campo dei Miracoli Admissions," above. Same hours as Baptistery; see above. Bus: E, 4, or LAM Rossa.

Museo dell'Opera del Duomo ★ The old Chapter House–cum-convent has been transformed into a storehouse for sculptures, paintings, and other works from the ecclesiastical buildings on Piazza del Duomo. Room 1 has **models** of the Duomo buildings and engraved glass plans showing the square's history and geometry. Room 2 is, since 2008, the home of the cathedral's last remaining 12th-century original portal, the **Door of San Ranieri ★★★**. Room 3 has delicate 12th-century carvings and intarsia marble decoration displaying a strong Moorish influence and a massive 12th-century wooden crucifix from Burgundy, with a Christ styled so medievally naive that it looks like modern art. But the main attraction is the Islamic 11th-century bronze **griffin ★**, war booty from

The Cattedrale and Baptistery on Pisa's Campo dei Miracoli.

the Crusades, which long decorated the Duomo's cupola before it was replaced by a copy.

Room 7 contains curving ranks of faded-to-facelessness 13th-century Giovanni Pisano statues from the baptistery and cathedral. The treasury (room 11) has two Pisanos: a wooden crucifix and a swaybacked **Madonna col Bambino** ★ he carved from a curving ivory tusk (1299). Also here is a precious Pisan relic, the cross that led Pisans on the First Crusade.

Upstairs, the last few rooms house the precious legacy of Carlo Lasinio, who restored the Camposanto frescoes in the early 19th century and, fortunately for posterity, made a series of **etchings** ★★ of each fresco, the prints from which were colored by his son. Not only did the original publication of these prints have an important influence on the developing pre-Raphaelite movement at the time, but they're the best record we have of the paintings that went up in flames when the Camposanto was bombed in 1944. The elevated loggia also provides a unique (rear) perspective on the Leaning Tower.

Piazza Arcivescovado 6. ✆ **050-835-011.** www.opapisa.it. For prices, see "Campo dei Miracoli Admissions," above. Same hours as Baptistery; see above. Bus: E, 4, or LAM Rossa.

Exploring the Rest of Pisa

If you go down Via Santa Maria from Piazza del Duomo and take a left on Via dei Mille, you'll come out into **Piazza Cavalieri,** possibly the site of the Roman town's forum and later the square where the citizens of the medieval city-state met to discuss political issues. Giorgio Vasari remodeled the **Palazzo dei Cavalieri** in 1562 and decorated it with recently restored and very detailed graffiti; it now houses the renowned Scuola Normale Superiore. Next to the palace is the baroque **Santo Stefano,** housing tempera paintings by the likes of Empoli, Cristofano Allori, and Vasari (✆ **050-580-814;** Mon–Sat 10am–7pm, Sun 1–7:30pm; admission 1.50€). Also on the piazza is the stubby clock tower of the **Palazzo dell'Orologio,** where Count Ugolino della Gherardesca, suspected of having betrayed his fellow Pisans in the fateful battle where Genoa decisively crushed Pisan naval might, was locked up to starve to death along with his sons and grandsons. The tragic story was immortalized by Dante in his *Inferno* and Shelley in his *Tower of Famine*. The nearby **Orto Botanico ★**, Via Luca Ghini 5 (✆ **050-560-045**) is the oldest of its kind in Europe, established in 1544 and here since 1595. There's space to relax in the shade of palm trees as the aroma of herbs washes over you. Admission costs 2.50€ for adults, 1.50€ for children aged 6 to 12. Hours are Monday to Friday from 8:30am to 5:30pm and Saturday 8:30am to 1pm.

If you continue down Via Santa Maria toward the Arno, you'll come to the millennial church of **San Nicola** (✆ **050-24-677**), with a Francesco Traini *Madonna and Child* on the first altar on the right and a 1400 St. Nicholas of Tolentino *Protecting Pisa from the Plague*. To the left of the high altar is Giovanni Pisano's gaunt *Jesus* being crucified. The church is also home to the second of Pisa's leaning towers, a 13th-century campanile whose spiral staircase inspired Renaissance architect Bramante for the stairs he installed in the Vatican. (Though the church is officially open daily 9am–noon and 5–8pm, you often need to seek out the sacristan to get in; ring the bell at the door next to the tower, though there's no guarantee you'll get an answer.)

To the northeast of Piazza Cavalieri lies **Santa Caterina** (✆ **050-552-883**), with a Gothic facade from 1330 and the tomb of Archbishop Simone Saltarelli by Nino Pisano along with Francesco Traini's *Apotheosis of St. Thomas Aquinas*. It's open daily from 8am to 1pm, as long as restoration works are complete. Southeast of this, near the city walls, **San Francesco** (✆ **050-544-091**) contains good baroque works by Empoli, Il Passignano, and Santi di Tito. The transept has 1342 frescoes by Taddeo Gaddi. It's open daily from 7:30am to noon and 4 to 7pm.

Walk west along Via San Francesco to **Borgo Stretto,** Pisa's arcaded shopping street. Off Borgo Stretto near Piazza Garibaldi is hidden the arched **Piazza Vettovaglie,** which houses a bustling **outdoor produce market** every day except Sunday. At the foot of Borgo Stretto is Pisa's best gelato stop: **La Bottega del Gelato ★**, Piazza Garibaldi 11 (✆ **050-575-467**).

East along the Arno near Ponte Fortezza is Pisa's only significant painting collection, the **Museo Nazionale di San Matteo ★★**, Piazza San Matteo in Soarta 1 (✆ **050-541-865**). To see the collection in chronological order, head immediately out into the pretty brick cloister and cross to ascend the central staircase on the opposite side. Poorly lit and sporadically labeled, the collections are constantly being rearranged, but you should be able to find the masterpieces amid the shuffle. The first large room has a *Life of St. Dominic* polptych by Turino Vanni that reads like a cartoon strip, and works by Taddeo di Bartolo and Spinello Aretino, plus a pair of Agnolo Gaddi polyptychs. One of the prides of the collections is the Sienese master Simone Martini's polyptych of the **Virgin and Child with Saints ★**. In a side room they keep the originals of the Giovanni and Nino Pisano sculptures from Santa Maria della Spina, including Nino's masterpiece, a *Madonna del Latte,* a very human mother in Gothic curving grace who smiles down at her nursing baby.

Other star works are a *St. Paul* by Masaccio (the only part of his lost *Pisa Altarpiece* still in Pisa), the greenishly aged *Madonna dell'Umiltà* by Gentile da Fabriano, and a Donatello gilded bronze reliquary *Bust of St. Rossore* (1427), an important sculptural step from medieval to Renaissance style that is held by some to be a self-portrait. Dig around some more (it's that kind of place) and you'll discover works by Ghirlandaio, Michelozzo, Fra' Angelico, and Benozzo Gozzoli. Walk or take bus no. 4, LAM Blu, or LAM Verde to get to the museum; it's open Tuesday through Saturday from 8:30am to 7pm and Sunday from 9am to 1:30pm; admission is 5€, free for children 18 and under and seniors 65 and over.

If you follow the north side of the Arno upstream about a mile past San Matteo (or take bus no. 14), you'll come to Pisa's third and perhaps most skewed "leaning tower." It almost looks as if the Pisans simply gave up on right angles when building **San Michele degli Scalzi.** Nothing stands straight up: not the outer walls, the tiers of columns dividing the nave from the aisles, the apse, the windows, or, of course, the bell tower. Take bus no. 13 (from Via San Michele degli Scalzi) back to the center.

All Pisa's truly ancient churches face the sea (the city's original source of prosperity), and that's certainly true of the jewel of the Arno's south bank, Gothic **Santa Maria della Spina ★★**, Lungarno Gambacorti (✆ **050-21-441**). The church is a collaborative Giovanni and Nino Pisano work of 1230 to 1323, dismantled and raised to current ground level (for fear of floods) in 1871. It was built to house a *spina* (thorn) from Christ's Passion crown brought back by a merchant from the Crusades. Much of the Pisano sculpture from the outside has been removed for safekeeping to the Museo Nazionale di San Matteo, as has the church's primary attraction, Nino Pisano's *Madonna del Latte.* The main architectural action is on the outside, but the inside is open Tuesday through Friday from 11am to 12:45pm and 3 to 5:45pm, Saturday and Sunday 11am to 12:45pm and 3 to 6:45pm. (Note, however, that these hours are *very* variable.) Admission costs 2€ adults, 1.50€ for children and seniors. In 2009, the city opened a nearby collection of art by painters who have worked in Pisa over the centuries, owned by CariPisa bank and displayed at the renovated **Palazzo Blu ★**, Lungarno Gambacorti 9 (✆ **050-916-950;** www.palazzoblu.org), the striking blue palace on the banks of the Arno. It houses some perhaps lesser-known Tuscan artists, such as Giovan Battista Tempesti, who often chose the city as a backdrop for their paintings, and stages contemporary shows, too. Admission is free, and it's open Tuesday to Sunday 10am to 1pm and 4 to 10pm.

Where to Stay

Pisa is such a major day-trip site that few people stay here overnight, which helps keep hotel prices down but also limits quality options in the center. The low season for most hotels in Pisa is August.

Novecento ★ Opened in late 2006, this immaculately converted colonial villa set around a courtyard garden is Pisa's best affordable boutique hotel. Rooms are small, certainly—none has a bathroom, for example, nor are there family-size units—but decor is refreshingly contemporary, with muted colors, the occasional flash of exuberance, and not an antique armoire in sight. Most peaceful and most comfortable of the rooms is the Garden Room, a self-contained unit with a small "antechamber" standing alone amid the lush subtropical greenery.

Via Roma 37, 56100 Pisa. www.hotelnovecento.pisa.it. ✆ **050-500-323.** Fax 050-220-9163. 14 units. 80€–120€ double; 90€–170€ Garden Room. Rates include breakfast. AE, MC, V. Parking on street (10€ per day). Bus: E or 4. **Amenities:** Babysitting; concierge. *In room:* A/C, TV, hair dryer, minibar, Wi-Fi (free).

A Night on the Town

The city center scene is a lively mix of young locals and students from Pisa's prestigious university who gather—on warm weekend nights especially—around the central piazzas, Garibaldi, Cairoli, and San Paolo al'Orto in particular. The bar of the minute waxes and wanes, but **Bazeel**, Lungarno Pacinotti 1 (at Piazza Garibaldi; ☎ 340-2881-113; www.bazeel.it) is ever popular for an *aperitivo*, live big-screen sports, cocktails, and DJ sets till late on weekends. At **Orzo Bruno** ★, Via Case Dipinte 6 (☎ 050-578802; www.orzobruno.it), twenty-somethings gather in animated groups to enjoy the place's artisan beer, brewed out back. Glasses cost 3€ and 4€ (slightly less between 7 and 8:30pm). Opened in 2010, **Sottobosco**, Piazza San Paolo all'Orto 3 (☎ 050-991-2364; www.facebook.com/sottobosco.libricafe; closed Mon) is a bookish cafe by day, but after dark draws an artsy, well-dressed crowd sipping cocktails and bottled beers. There's also a dinner menu and often acoustic music sets after hours. *Note:* The city is *very* quiet in August, and many places close for almost the whole month.

Relais dell'Orologio ★★ These are the best lodgings in central Pisa, a hotel of charm and grace worthy of Pisa's status as a major tourist destination. It's also one of the most tranquil hotels in the center, despite a location just yards from the city's heartbeat Piazza dei Cavalieri. This former historic mansion was constructed as a fortified tower in the 13th century, and great respect was shown for the style of the original building in its modernization. Small to midsize bedrooms are furnished with Italian flair and style, and many retain their wooden beams. You'll pay a little extra for a room overlooking the courtyard garden, perhaps the quietest spot in the city within 5 minutes' walk of the Campo. For tighter budgets, the same owners run the 12-room B&B **Relais dei Fiori**, Via Carducci 35 (www.relais deifiori.com; ☎ 050-556-054), where doubles cost between 75€ and 175€.

Via della Faggiola Ugiccione 12–14, 56126 Pisa. www.hotelrelaisorologio.com. ☎ 050-830-361. Fax 050-551-869. 21 units. 135€–375€ double; 225€–685€ suite. Rates include buffet breakfast. AE, DC, MC, V. Garage parking 30€. Bus: E or 4. **Amenities:** Restaurant; bar; babysitting; room service; Wi-Fi (free, in lobby). *In room:* A/C, TV, hair dryer, minibar.

Royal Victoria ★ ☺ "I fully endorse the above," wrote Teddy Roosevelt of this place in one of the antique guest books. It opened in 1839 as Pisa's first hotel, uniting several medieval towers and houses, and remains Pisa's most characterful traditional hotel. The rooms on the Arno tend to be larger, as do the quieter (and cooler) ones installed in the remains of a tower dating from the 980s. There are many frescoed ceilings, and one room is a triumph of *trompe l'oeil,* including fake curtains painted on the walls surrounding the bed. They have three rooms with common doors that can be turned into family suites for four—but the junior suites are more characterful and only slightly less spacious. Although some rooms are rather plain, in all you'll probably find yourself, as Ruskin did in terse simplicity, "always very comfortable in this inn."

Lungarno Pacinotti 12 (near Piazza Garibaldi), 56126 Pisa. www.royalvictoria.it. ☎ 050-940-111. Fax 050-940-180. 48 units. 40€–80€ double without bathroom; 65€–150€ double with bathroom; 150€–190€ junior suite. Rates include breakfast. AE, DC, MC, V. Garage parking 20€. Bus: 4, E, LAM Rossa, or LAM Verde. **Amenities:** Bar; babysitting; bikes; concierge; Wi-Fi (2.50€/hr.). *In room:* A/C (in some), TV.

Where to Eat

For pizza or *cecina* (a garbanzo-bean flour flatbread served warm), stop in at **Il Montino,** Vicolo del Monte (☏ 050-598-695), a favorite slice stop for Pisans. There's much good dining in and around Pisa's produce market: In addition to our favorites below, you could try **Porton Rosso ★**, Via Porton Rosso 11 (☏ 050-580-566; www.osteriadelportonrosso.com). where seafood is the house specialty. Primi cost 10€ and secondi up to 16€; it's closed Sunday and most of August.

Da Bruno ★ PISAN/SEAFOOD The decor is typical, cluttered trattoria—paintings of the Duomo, pictures of the owner with vaguely famous people, copper pots—for this is a typical trattoria that has been dignified to *ristorante* status only through its years of deserved success. It specializes in tried-and-true Pisan dishes. The *crostini misti di pesce* antipasto is as good as it comes, to be followed by *pasta e ceci* (pasta with garbanzo beans) or *zuppa pisana* (a very bready Pisan *ribollita*). Although you can order a well-turned version of *coniglio al forno* (baked rabbit), the famous secondo here is a *baccalà con porri,* salt cod cooked with leeks and tomatoes.

Via Luigi Bianchi (outside Porta a Lucca). ☏ **050-560-818.** www.dabruno.it. Reservations recommended. Primi 10€–12€; secondi 15€–25€. AE, DC, MC, V. Wed–Mon noon–3pm and 7–10:30pm. Closed 2 weeks late July to early Aug. Bus: E or 4.

La Mescita ★ PISAN/WINE BAR The marketplace location and simple decor of this popular spot belie its reputation for skillful cooking. The menu changes each month, but often includes the delicious likes of a *sformatino di melanzane* (eggplant soufflé in tomato sauce), to be followed perhaps by *ravioli di ceci con salsa di gamberetti e pomodoro fresco* (ravioli stuffed with a garbanzo bean pâté and served in shrimp-and-tomato sauce) or *strozzapreti al trevisano e Gorgonzola* (pasta curlicues in a cheesy sauce topped with shredded bitter radicchio). You can stick to tradition with your secondo by ordering the *acciughe ripieni* (stuffed anchovies). Because the place operates as an enoteca (wine cellar) after hours, the wine list is long and detailed.

Via Cavalca 2 (just off the market square). ☏ **050-957-019.** www.osterialamescitapisa.it. Reservations recommended. Primi 9€; secondi 15€. AE, DC, MC, V. Tues–Sun 7:45–11pm; Sat–Sun 1–2:30pm. Closed 20 days in Aug. Bus: 4, E, Lam Rossa, or LAM Verde.

S. Omobono ★ 🍴 PISAN Around a column surviving from the medieval church that once stood here, locals gather at this trattoria to enjoy authentic Pisan home cooking. Open with something like *brachette alla renaiaola* (an antique Pisan dish consisting of large pasta squares in a purée of turnip greens and smoked fish) or *tagliatelle alla scarpara* (in a sausage ragù). The secondi are simple and straightforward: *baccalà alla livornese* (salt cod stewed with tomatoes) or *maiale arrosto* (thinly sliced roast pork), with which you can order fried polenta slices or ultra-Pisan *ceci* (garbanzo) beans.

Piazza S. Omobono 6 (next to the market square). ☏ **050-540-847.** Reservations recommended. Primi 7€–8€; secondi 8.50€–10€. DC, MC, V. Mon–Sat 7:30–10pm. Closed Aug 8–20. Bus: 4, E, Lam Rossa, or LAM Verde.

A Monastery & a Wilderness near Pisa

Thirteen kilometers (8 miles) east of Pisa outside the village of Calci lies the largest and most interesting Carthusian monastery (or Charterhouse) in Italy, the

Certosa di Calci ★ (℃ 050-938-430). It was founded in 1366, but most of its current facade dates from the 18th and 19th centuries. You can see this huge complex of baroque frescoed chapels and cloisters during a fascinating 1-hour guided tour leading you through chapels, the main church, and a monk's "cell." The University of Pisa also keeps a **Natural History Museum** in one wing (℃ 050-221-2970; www.msn.unipi.it), with a large taxonomy collection and a tropical aquarium. The Certosa is open Tuesday through Saturday from 8:30am to 6:30pm, and Sunday from 8:30am to 12:30pm year-round. Tours cost 4€. The natural history museum is open daily 9am to 5pm (Sun 10am–7pm, but closes 2pm Mon–Fri Oct–Feb), and admission is an additional 7€ for adults, 3.50€ for children 6–18 and seniors 65 and over. The best way to get to the Certosa is by taking CPT bus no. 120 to Montemagno, which lets you off at the gates, rather than the one to Calci.

Just west of Pisa begins the **Parco Naturale Migliarino San Rossore Massaciuccoli** ★ (℃ 050-530-101; www.parcosanrossore.it). Once the summer estate of Italy's president, it is now a publicly owned park. It forms part of one of Tuscany's most precious protected wildlife areas, a coastal zone of dense pines with populations of wild deer, boar, and aquatic birds surrounding beaches and boggy wetlands. To properly explore the park's wildlife and bird-watching trails, pre-book a guided tour on foot, bike, or horseback. These depart from the visitor center in Cascine Vecchie (℃ 050-533-755; www.centrovisitesanrossore.it). Guided bike tours lasting 2½ hours cost 13€, 11€ for children 12 and under. On horseback a 1½-hour guided outing is 20€; a 2-hour guided walk costs 10€. E-mail visitesr@tin.it or call ℃ 050-530-101 to book (℃ 338-366-2431 for horse-riding). There are also around 10km (6 miles) of free flat cycling and walking trails, but access to Gombo beach (where drowned Romantic poet Percy Bysshe Shelley's body washed up in 1822) is only possible on a guided visit. The park is open (and offers bike rental) on weekends and national holidays all year.

THE VALDARNO

SAN MINIATO The most diverting Valdarno detour is a trip to **San Miniato** ★, southwest of Empoli. The tourist office is at Piazza del Popolo 1, San Miniato (℃ 0571-418-739; daily 9:30am–1pm and 3:30–7pm). The hilltop Old Town is famous these days mainly for its kite-flying festival (the Sun after Easter) and the white **truffles** hiding under the soil of the surrounding valley—the key market takes place on the last three weekends in November. San Miniato's long history, though, puts it as a former outpost of the Holy Roman Empire and countryside seat of emperors from Otto I to Frederick II. The latter left the town a 1240 **Rocca** (rebuilt after it was bombed in World War II), the taller remaining tower of which rises gracefully above the village and the shorter of which serves as the Duomo bell tower.

On Piazzetta del Castello is the **Duomo,** open daily from 8am to 12:30pm and 3 to 6:30pm. Few of its original 12th-century Romanesque features remain, save the facade, unusually inset with ceramic North African bowls. A few of those bowls have been removed and are kept next door in the **Museo Diocesano** (℃ 0571-418-071), along with a Sienese school *Maestà,* a Neri di Bicci *Madonna and Child,* a Verrocchio terra-cotta bust of the *Redeemer,* and some baroque works. Admission is 2.50€. Between April and September, it's open Thursday to Sunday 10am to 6pm; October through March, it's open the same days from 10am to 5pm. The town's other worthwhile church is **San Domenico,** Piazza del Popolo, which contains works ranging from 14th-century Masolino-school frescoes to early-20th-century Art Deco frescoes. It's open daily from 8:30am to noon and 4 to 7pm (3–7pm in winter). However,

A Central Tourist Office

The **Ufficio Turistico Intercomunale,** Via della Torre 11, Vinci (© 0571-568-012; www.terredelrinascimento.it), is the central tourism office for **Vinci** and **Empoli.** March through October, it's open daily from 10 to 7pm; the winter closing time is 3pm Monday through Friday and 6pm on weekends.

the number-one reason to visit the town is to stock up from one of Tuscany's great butchers, **Sergio Falaschi** ★, Via Augusto Conti 18–20 (© 0571-43-190; www.sergiofalaschi.it), where you'll find fresh and cured meats, salami made from the Cinta Senese breed of pig, homemade ragù made with veal, rabbit, and countless other animals, and much more. The shop is closed on Sunday afternoon and all day Wednesday. If you're in town over lunch, **L'Upupa,** Via Augusto Conti 15 (© 0571-400-429), is a reliable trattoria serving tasty, yet simple, seasonal plates of pasta and plenty of truffle dishes. Primi cost 7€ to 9€, and secondi between 13€ and 18€. It's closed on Thursdays.

EMPOLI The modern market town of **Empoli** gave forth in 1551 a talented baroque painter christened Jacopo Chimenti but known by the name of his hometown. Although World War II bombs wreaked havoc on much of the town, the main piazza, Piazza della Propositura, is still graced with the **Collegiata di Sant'Andrea,** an 8th-century church with a harmonious green-and-white Romanesque facade. The facing is original 12th century in the bottom half, but the top was finished off in a seamless imitation style in the 19th century.

The inside doesn't live up to the exterior, but its **Museo della Collegiata** ★, Piazza della Propositura 3 (© 0571-76-284), certainly does. It was one of Tuscany's first community museums when it opened in 1859, and the collections include a detached Masolino *Pietà* fresco (1424–25), a tiny Filippo Lippi *Madonna,* and works by Lorenzo Monaco, like his 1404 *Madonna dell'Umiltà with Saints.* The museum is open Tuesday to Sunday from 9am to noon and 4 to 7pm, and the ticket costs 3€ adults, 1€ children 9 to 17 and seniors 65 and over.

VINCI Leonardo fans can take a 9km (5½-mile) detour north to visit his hometown, **Vinci.** The village honors its original Renaissance man with the 2010-renovated **Museo Leonardiano** ★, Piazza dei Guidi (© 0571-933-251; www.museoleonardiano.it), in the 13th-century castle of the Guidi counts. It has no original Leonardos but does contain, in two adjacent *palazzi,* full-size models of some of the weird and wonderful machines he invented, faithfully reproduced from Leo's *Codex Atlanticus,* alongside multimedia exhibits that science-minded older children and adults will enjoy. It's open daily from 9:30am to 6pm (until 7pm in summer), and admission costs 7€ adults, 5€ children 15 to 18 and seniors 65 and over, and 3€ children 6 to 14. You can also see the baptismal font where he was baptized

A sculpture at the Museo Leonardiano.

in **Santa Croce** church and drop by the **Biblioteca Leonardiana,** Via Giorgio la Pira 1 (☎ **0571-933-250;** www.bibliotecaleonardiana.it), which preserves copies of anything printed relating to Leonardo. The Biblioteca is open Monday through Friday from 3 to 7pm. Hike or drive 3km (2 miles) up the hill to the tiny hamlet of Anchiano to see Leonardo's modest **Birth House** (☎ **0571-56-519;** free admission; Mar–Oct daily 9:30am–7pm, Nov–Feb until 6pm).

LIVORNO & THE ETRUSCAN COAST

19km (12 miles) S of Pisa; 95km (59 miles) W of Florence; 315km (195 miles) NW of Rome

Livorno is like a blue-collar Tuscan Venice, a busy port city second only to Florence in size and graced with canals and some of the Italian peninsula's best seafood restaurants. Its seaside promenade was once the dreary banks of the port, but has seen a rebirth over the past few years with new bars and cafes opening every year. The overhauled waterfront and its centerpiece, the checkerboard **Terrazza Mascagni,** has had a profound effect on Livornese life. For one thing, bar life has gravitated south to take advantage of the emerging seaside energy. It's here you'll also find the city's best ice cream, at **Gelateria Popolare,** Via Meyer 11 (☎ **0586-260-354**).

Other than eating and hanging out, there isn't much to grab a photo-snapping tourist's attention. The city is unique in Tuscany because there are very few churches to speak of and just one significant museum—of 19th- and 20th-century paintings by artists of the Macchiaioli movement, a Tuscan forerunner of French Impressionism.

You'll see posters in town of a tower sprouting from cobalt-blue waters apparently in the middle of the sea. Actually, this watchtower, **Meloria,** is resting on a barely submerged reef about 5km (3 miles) offshore. It was here, in 1284,

Masterpiece Theater

Bohemian sculptor Amadeo Modigliani was born here in 1884. In Paris, his womanizing was notorious, and he drank himself to death at age 35. Rumor held that a despondent Modigliani had thrown some of his works into a canal on his last visit to his hometown. In 1984, several sculptures were dredged up and trumpeted as his lost works. Just before they sold for millions of dollars, some school kids appeared on national TV showing how they'd made the works themselves—one of the most successful art hoaxes of the century.

that Genoa's navy thoroughly trounced the Pisan fleet, signaling the beginning of Pisa's slow decline under Genoese maritime dominance.

Essentials

GETTING THERE By Train: The Arno valley line runs 24 trains daily from **Florence** (about 1½ hr.) through **Empoli** (55 min.) and **Pisa** (19 min.) to **Livorno Centrale,** where you can catch the no. 1 or 2 bus to Piazza Grande. There's also a regular service (Mon–Sat) down the Etruscan Coast to **Cecina** (25 min.) and **San Vincenzo** (40–50 min.), with a sparser service also calling at **Castiglioncello** (18 min.).

By Car: There's a highway from Florence (the *FI-PI-LI*) that runs straight into town. From Pisa, the fastest way is to zip down the A12 or the SS1. Driving in the center can be a little chaotic, however; we either take public transportation or park as soon as we arrive: There's pay parking by the train station in Piazza Dante, along the Fosse Reale, and in Piazza Unità d'Italia.

By Bus: The train is almost always better, but **CPT** buses (© 050-884-111; www.cpt.pisa.it) do run from **Pisa** to Piazza Grande. **ATL** buses (© 0586-884-262; www.atl.livorno.it) run from Piazza Grande to service **Livorno's province** down the coast, including Cecina and Piombino.

VISITOR INFORMATION The helpful **tourist office** is under the arcade in Piazza del Municipio, Livorno (© 0586-820-454; www.comune.livorno.it/portale turismo), open Monday through Saturday 10am to 1pm and 2 to 5pm between November and April, daily 9am to 6pm otherwise. If you plan to explore the town, the **Livorno Card** (www.livornocard.it) offers free travel on city buses, discounts in some shops, and free entry into the Museo Civico (see below). A 1-day version costs 3€, 3 days are 5€, and children 12 and under pay nothing. The tourist office is also the place to meet for the **Tour in Battello nei Fossi Medicei** (© 348-738-2094), a sightseeing circumnavigation of the old port by canal boat. Tours, which cost around 10€ per person (8.50€ for Livorno Card holders), leave daily in good weather.

Exploring Livorno

Most of the interesting bits of Livorno are within the old **Porto Mediceo** part of town (laid out by Florentine architect Bernardo Buontalenti in 1567 on behalf of the Medici), still surrounded by its five-sided **Fosso Reale canal.** The canal is bridged in the east by an enormous vault called the Voltone, better known today as the huge rectangular **Piazza della Repubblica,** off the north of which you can

Monumento dei Quattro Mori.

see the **Fortezza Nuova,** which today is home to a popular, if somewhat down-trodden, public park (daily 10am–7pm). Just to the southwest, along the canal is Livorno's 19th-century market building, the **Mercato delle Vettovaglie ★,** still a wonderland of local flavors (closed Sun).

Via Grande leads west from Piazza della Repubblica, passing **Via Madonna** on the right, with its three baroque facades before spilling into Piazza Grande. The **Duomo** here, laid out in 1587, had to be almost entirely reconstructed after World War II bombings. The piazza used to be much longer, but a modern build-ing has separated it from what's now Largo Municipio to the north, where you'll find the bell tower and double stairs of the 1720 **Palazzo Municipale** and, to the left, the 17th-century **Palazzo di Camera.**

Beyond is the somewhat ambitiously named **Venezia Nuova** district, where the 18th-century merchants' palaces are visibly crumbling, but you'll still find plenty of character along colonial **Via Borra.** On nearby Via San Marco, spot the facade of the former **Teatro di San Marco,** where the Italian Communist Party was founded in 1921—marked by a plaque and the red flag, still flying.

On the water is the **Fortezza Vecchia,** designed by Antonio da Sangallo (1521–34) and built into a 1377 Pisan fort with the stump of the 11th-century **Torre Matilda** poking perkily above it and hiding a Roman *castrum* in its bowels. The road along the harbor gives a good glimpse into the life of a still very much alive and functioning seaport, and where it hits the other end of Via Grande com-ing down from the Duomo is Livorno's prize art sight, the Mannerist ***Monumento dei Quattro Mori ★*** (1623–26). It's the masterpiece of Giambologna's student Pietro Tacca and is much more famous for the four bronze Moorish slaves lung-ing and twisting in their bonds than the statue of Ferdinando I above them.

South of the Old Town, Livorno's modern art collections are at the **Museo Civico Giovanni Fattori.** It's housed in the Villa Mimbelli, which is surrounded by a lush public park on Via San Jacopo in Acquaviva (✆**0586-808-001;** http://pegaso.comune.livorno.it/index). The villa is a trip, designed by Liberty architect Vincenzo Micheli in 1865 for a local businessman; its sumptuous restored inte-rior contains quite an eclectic grab bag of styles. The museum is almost entirely dedicated to the only Tuscan art movement of note over the past several hundred years, the Macchiaioli, whose painters were interested in the way a viewer perceived the marks of light and color on a painting and covered canvases with their own take on French Impressionism. The museum is dedicated to one of the Macchiaioli's greatest talents and Livornese native son, Giovanni Fattori, whose work spanned the 1860s to 1908. Admission is 4€ adults, or 2.50€ for students and children. The museum is open Tuesday through Sunday from 10am to 1pm and 4 to 7pm. Take bus no. 1 or 8 here.

Where to Stay

Gennarino ★ 🏨 An extraordinary 19th-century, Liberty *faux*-castle is the setting for this comfortable hotel just south of central Livorno. The Gennarino reopened in 2008 after a head-to-toe renovation that took 2 years, and its light-bathed communal areas and color-washed walls hung with black-and white photos of old Livorno exude an air of quiet luxury. Standard guest rooms are small, but furnished and equipped to a high standard, with gleaming parquet floors; it's well worth the extra 10€ to 20€ for the larger superior rooms facing the front, some of which have small terraces and/or sea views. You'll find cheaper rates—and perhaps more bargaining scope—on weekends.

Viale Italia 301, 57123 Livorno. www.hotelgennarino.it. ℂ **0586-803-109.** Fax 0586-803-450. 23 units. 100€–140€ standard double; 130€–140€ superior double. Rates include buffet breakfast. AE, DC, MC, V. Free parking. Bus: 1. **Amenities:** Bar; airport transfer (55€); concierge. *In room:* A/C, TV, hair dryer, minibar, Wi-Fi (1 hr. free).

Gran Duca Overlooking the harbor and Pietro Tacca's *Quattro Mori,* the Gran Duca is the most characterful hotel in the center of the city. Most accommodations are medium size, with unassuming but comfortable furniture, and some rooms have futons that fold out to sleep up to four. Suites add a little luxury to the standard package. Some rooms along the front have small terraces so you can sit and watch the shipping trade at your feet. The hotel's 80 rooms were renovated in 2007.

Piazza Micheli 16–18, 57123 Livorno. www.granduca.it. ℂ **0586-891-024.** Fax 0586-891-153. 80 units. 98€–250€ double; 128€–280€ triple. Rates include breakfast. AE, DC, MC, V. Garage parking 13€. Bus: 1, 5, or 8r. **Amenities:** Restaurant; bar; concierge; outdoor pool; small gym and sauna; room service. *In room:* A/C, TV, hair dryer, kitchenette (in some), minibar, Wi-Fi (free).

Where to Eat

If you don't like seafood, you've come to the wrong town—eating is Livorno's major "sight," and is worth the journey here by itself. Livorno's king of all seafood dishes is *cacciucco,* a poor man's soup of shellfish, squid, mollusks, today's catch, prawns, and other fruits of the sea in a tomato soup base spiked with hot peppers, garlic, and red wine, poured over stale bread. There are many great seafood eateries in the city, and our favorites below in no way exhaust your options. Tasty alternatives include **Cantina Senese** ★, Borgo Cappuccini 95 (ℂ **0586-890-239;** www.ristorantecantinaseneselivorno.com; closed Sun), **La Barrocciaia,** Piazza Cavalotti 13 (ℂ**0586-882-637;** closed Sun lunch and Mon), and **Il Sottomarino** ★, Via dei Terrazzini 48 (ℂ**0586-887-025;** closed Tues and July).

L'Ancora ★ LIVORNESE/SEAFOOD The Livornese know their seafood, and this place under the brick vaults of a former canalside storehouse is popular with everyone from octogenarian grandmas to trendy twenty-somethings. Alongside the usual shellfish-and-pasta combos, primi might include a *carbonara del mare* (mixed seafood in a rich cream sauce) or *farfalle mare e monti* (pasta bows with seafood and mushrooms). For secondo, the thick, rich, spicy *cacciucco* is excellent, and there's also daily catches such as *totani* (baby cuttlefish) done *fritto* (fried), *alla griglia* (grilled), or *in forno* (baked). The ambience is traditional, but not fussily so.

Scale delle Ancore 10. ✆ **0586-881-401.** Reservations recommended. Primi 9€; secondi 8€–16€. MC, V. Wed–Mon noon–3pm and 7–10pm. Bus: 5 or 8r.

L'Angelo d'Oro ★ 🎁 LIVORNESE/SEAFOOD This corner trattoria is not on any tourist's short list, because it is utterly unnoticed and intends to remain so. Good news for the rest of us, since the *cacciucco* and the *triglie alla livornese* (red mullet in a marinara sauce) are as authentic as they come. Families gather on a Sunday, filling up its dozen tables to enjoy a plate of delicious but unassuming *spaghetti all'orata* (spaghetti with sea bream in a marinara sauce), with fresh fish that only had to make a 50m (164-ft.) hop from the port. Skip dessert for a gelato along the esplanade instead.

Piazza Mazzini 15 (on the port side). ✆ **0586-881-295.** Primi 5€–7€; secondi 10€–15€. No credit cards. Thurs–Tues noon–2:30pm and 7:30–9:30pm. Bus: 1, 5, or 8r.

Osteria del Mare ★★ LIVORNESE/SEAFOOD More of a napkin-and-table-cloth place than many in this informal port city, this small, wood-paneled dining room hung with maritime memorabilia is the setting for fine cooking complemented by attentive, even old-fashioned service. Primi usually include coastal classics like *spaghetti alle vongole* (with clams) or *riso nero* (risotto blackened with cuttlefish ink). Mains are very much catch dependent—there's nothing from the freezer here—but if you're lucky the giant house *fritto misto* (mixed seafood fry) will include baby squid and fresh anchovies.

Borgo Cappuccini 12. ✆ **0586-881-027.** Reservations recommended. Primi 7€–8€; secondi 10€–16€. AE, MC, V. Fri–Wed noon–2:30pm and 7:30–10pm. Closed 20 days in Aug–Sept. Bus: 1, 5, or 8r.

Bolgheri Wines & the Coast South of Livorno

Few foreigners frequent Tuscany's "Etruscan Riviera," south of Livorno, although it is teeming with Italian vacationers in summer. The old Roman Via Aurelia down the coast has become a modern highway (SS1), and is the gateway to much of it. There are nice spots, but you need to choose carefully, because there are some ghastly ones too. The **Bay of Quercetano** near **Castiglioncello** has the views, especially at sunset, but the beaches are narrow and rocky. **Vada** is a modern center with passable white sand.

Another 9km (5½ miles) farther down the road is the turnoff for **Bolgheri.** This is the birthplace of the so-called "Supertuscans," wines that back in the 1980s shot to prominence when quality in Chianti was at a low ebb. The most prestigious of these remains Sassicaia, its scarcity and correspondingly stratospheric price due largely to the fact that only one vineyard produces it. That estate is the **Tenuta San Guido** (www.sassicaia.com) and is still owned by the noble Incisa della Rocchetta family. The estate concentrates more on wine than tourism, which is to say they don't offer tours of the property. To tour a well-known Bolgheri estate, try **Tenuta dell'Ornellaia,** Via Bolgherese 191, Bolgheri (✆ **0565-718-242;** www.ornellaia.com), which produces the prestigious wine

The bay of Quercetano, near Castiglioncello.

of the same name and conducts tours by appointment of its giant, modern cantina, culminating in a tasting or lunch in the estate's historic buildings. Back on the coastal road, you'll find that **Marina di Bibbona** has reasonable sand, and if you don't mind crowds the busy resort of **San Vincenzo** has even longer swaths of fluffy beach. Ancient **Populonia Alta,** on its promontory beyond the scenic beach at the **Golfo di Baratti ★**, was once an important center in the Etruscan world. On sunny days you get a great coastal view from its medieval **castle** (www.castellodipopulonia.it; admission 2€; daily 10am–6pm), and the tiny town still retains bits of the walls the Etruscans built. The archaeological jewel of the Etruscan Coast, however, is the nearby **Parco Archeologico di Baratti e Populonia ★** (✆0565-226-445; www.parchivaldicornia.it). This important site consists of the remains of an **Etruscan-Roman Acropolis** (next to Populonia Alta) and, by the bay below, two sites where finds have confirmed Populonia's status as a major metalworking center in the Etruscan era. Scientifically, the most important area remains **San Cerbone,** the only Etruscan Necropolis ever found by the sea, whose intact circular tombs litter a field by the visitor center. The site is open daily until around dusk, and admission costs 9€, 13€, and 15€ to visit one, two, and all three of the sites.

At the south end of this promontory sits **Piombino,** a modern port whose only reason to visit is to catch the ferry to the island of Elba.

ELBA ★

12km (7½ miles) off the coast at Piombino; 86km (53 miles) S of Livorno; 179km (111 miles) SW of Florence; 231km (143 miles) NW of Rome

Elba is Italy's third-largest island, but at about 27 x 18km (17 x 11 miles), it's much smaller than Sicily or Sardinia. So while it has a tall, mountainous interior speckled with ancient villages, the sea is never far away. Coastal fishing and port towns in soft pastels are interspersed with some fine sandy beaches—and only the occasional overdeveloped spot.

The Greeks founded the first large-scale settlements here in the 10th century B.C., calling the island *Aethalia* after the Greek word for sparks, a reference

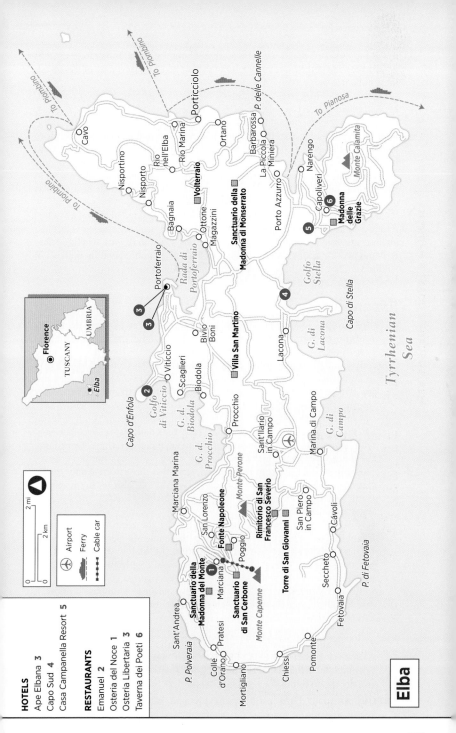

HOTELS

Ape Elbana **3**
Capo Sud **4**
Casa Campanella Resort **5**

RESTAURANTS

Emanuel **2**
Osteria del Noce **1**
Osteria Libertaria **3**
Taverna dei Poeti **6**

Elba

to the forges sailors could see winking throughout the night. Elba's forges smelted iron ore, one of the hundreds of minerals that make up the fabric of the island, for 3 millennia.

When would-be emperor of Europe Napoleon Bonaparte was first defeated, he was exiled to Elba to rule as the island's governor. Beginning May 3, 1814, the Corsican general busied himself with revamping the island's economy, infrastructure, and mining system—perhaps out of nation-building habit or merely to keep himself and his 500-man personal guard occupied. Napoleon managed to be a good boy until February 26, 1815, at which point the conquering itch grew too strong and he sailed ashore to begin the famous Hundred Days that ended in his crushing defeat at the Battle of Waterloo. The island preserves his two villas and various other mementos of its brief Napoleonic era.

These days Elba is a proletarian resort island, visited mainly by middle-class Italian youngsters, young families, and German tourists, who together fill just about every available inch of hotel and camping space in August. The best time to come is during May, when the scrubby interior is illuminated by millions of wildflowers in bloom, or late September, when the seas are still warm but the beaches are empty.

Essentials

GETTING THERE The easiest way to get to the island is by **ferry from Piombino** to Portoferraio, Elba's capital. Throughout the high season, it's best to reserve, especially if you're taking a car over. There are two major ferry companies, **Toremar** (✆ **0565-31-100** in Piombino, 0565-960-131 in Portoferraio; www.toremar.it) and **Moby** (✆ **0565-221-212** in Piombino, 0565-914-133 in Portoferraio; www.moby.it). Both run regular ferries (*traghetto* or *nave*) that take about an hour. Toremar also offers slightly faster (40 min.) but almost twice-as-expensive hydrofoils (*aliscafo*) on which you can't take a car. Toremar has the most ferry runs daily, especially off season, with hourly runs April through August and eight daily in winter. Year-round, there are three to six hydrofoils daily to Cavo, on Elba's northeast coast, plus three or four direct to Portoferraio, as well as three to eight daily ferries (fewer on Mon) linking Piombino and Rio Marina, also on the northeast coast. You can compare both companies' schedules quickly and easily at **www.traghetti.com**.

You'll find uncrowded **ticket offices** by the road as you approach Piombino and inside the port building itself (all well sign-posted). Prices for ferry tickets vary by season, starting from 10€ each way per foot passenger including tax. Cars with one person in them cost from about 40€ each way. Hydrofoils cost from about 14€ per passenger to Portoferraio or 10€ to Cavo. Hydrofoils cost about 50€ per passenger to Portoferraio or about 40€ to Cavo. You can **park** at well-signed lots by Piombino docks for 10€ to 15€ per day.

Most years there's also a limited high-season flight service connecting Elba's small airport near Campo nell'Elba with northern Italy—both Milan Malpensa Airport and Orio al Serio Airport, near Bergamo. The service is operated by **ElbaFly** (✆ **0565-977-900;** www.elbafly.com). There are usually big discounts for advance booking.

GETTING AROUND Drivers will have no problem, as the island's road system is reasonable, if a bit rutted. If you want to rent a car on Elba, the tourist office (see below) has a list of ten or so rental companies in Portoferraio. **Happy Rent,** for example, is at Viale Elba 5 (✆ **0565-914-665;** www.renthappy. it). To rent a scooter or bike—a slightly hair-raising way to tool around—try **Two Wheels Network,** Viale Elba 32 (✆ **0565-914-666;** www.twn-rent. it). Rates vary widely depending on season, but expect midpowered scooters to run about 30€ to 40€ per day and road or mountain bikes to start at 15€.

Elba is also blessed with an excellent **bus** network run by **ATL** (✆ **0565-914-392;** www.atl.livorno.it). Buses leave Portoferraio from the main terminal at Viale Elba 22 (opposite the Toremar dock), with three lines servicing the west, east, and south of the island. (If you know the name of a beach between villages where you want to be let off, tell the driver.)

VISITOR INFORMATION Elba's only year-round **tourist office** is opposite the ferry dock, at Viale Elba 4, Portoferraio (✆ **0565-914-671;** www.aptelba. it; Mon–Sat 8am–7pm, Sun 9:30am–12:30pm and 3–6pm). Note, however, the provision of tourist services is undergoing constant review, and you may find those hours only apply during the high season. For information about outdoor activities in western Elba, also contact the **Casa del Parco,** Fortezza Pisana, Marciana (✆ **0565-901-030**). It's also worth consulting private website **www.elba.org**. Note, too, that all opening hours in Elba are subject to frequent changes from season to season, and year to year.

For help in the hotel hunt, head to the **Associazione Albergatori Isola d'Elba,** upstairs at Calata Italia 26 (✆ **0565-915-555;** www.elba promotion.it; open Mon–Fri 9am–1pm and 3–6pm). Although it isn't an official body, its network does include most hotels on the island, and it'll be happy to give you a price list.

FESTIVALS & MARKETS Elba puts on a **wine festival** in September or October at Le Ghiaie beach behind Portoferraio. During the July and August high season, every town puts on some sort of **small *festa;*** in Marciana Alta, it's an August **medieval pageant** that robes the locals in costume and fills the streets with artisans offering old-fashioned crafts. Portoferraio's weekly **Friday market** is held on Viale Zambelli.

Exploring Elba

PORTOFERRAIO & AROUND Founded in 1548 by Medici grand duke Cosimo I, Portoferraio is Elba's capital and largest city. Ferries dock in the city's newer half to the west, but its core is still an old fishing village, a U-shaped theater of streets terracing up the rocky promontory. It was guarded in Medici days by two massive fortresses, the **Forte Falcone** (✆ **0565-944-024**) and the **Forte Stella** (✆ **0565-916-989**). You can explore the rambling battlements of both; the Forte Falcone to the west costs 3€ (2€ children) and between April and October is usually open daily from 9am to 7 or 8pm (closed Wed and at lunchtime Apr to mid-June and mid-Sept to Oct); the Forte Stella is free and open daily from 9am to 12:30pm and 2:30 to 6pm.

The old entrance to the city is through **Porta al Mare** at the base of Portoferraio's "U." In the town's upper reaches, by the Forte Stella, is the house where Napoleon lived in exile for 9 months: At the **Villa dei Mulini,** Piazzale Napoleone 1 (✆ **0565-915-846**) you get to wander through the emperor's sparsely furnished apartments and see the books he kept in his study—exciting for history enthusiasts only. It's open April through October

Portoferraio, Elba.

Monday and Wednesday through Saturday from 9am to 7pm, Sunday from 9am to 1pm. Admission is 3€, though the 5€ cumulative ticket also gets you into Napoleon's summer villa just outside Portoferraio (see below).

South of Portoferraio, the road divides at Bivio Boni to head east and west. A short trip west (right) then off the main road, following the signs, will lead you to the entrance to the **Villa San Martino ★** (©**0565-914-688**), the more interesting of the two villas Napoleon left on the island. The pretentious neoclassical facade wasn't the ex-emperor's idea—his step-nephew had it constructed after his death to honor him with its giant N's all over. Head to the left to be escorted up a path to Napoleon's more modest residence—for the former ruler of half the known world, he had surprisingly simple tastes. The only extravagance is the Egyptian Room, celebrating his most successful campaign with *trompe l'oeil* desert scenes glimpsed between hieroglyphic-painted walls and columns. Hours and admission are the same as Villa dei Mulini, above, but Villa San Martino is closed Monday instead of Tuesday.

EASTERN ELBA The old Spanish capital of **Porto Azzurro** contains a 1603 fortress built so well they're still using it as a prison. Today, the fortified Spanish port is one of the island's major resorts, but you can catch a whiff of the past in the shop fronts and bustle of the Old Quarter around Via d'Alarcon. From Porto Azzurro, you can see the fortified Capo Focardo across the bay, with the beach at **Naregno** leading up to it.

South of Porto Azzurro lies eastern Elba's most picturesque town, the mountainside village of **Capoliveri ★**. It's full of twisty old streets, a large terracelike main **Piazza Matteotti,** and bars where you can quaff Elba's wines or artisan beers until 2 or 3am. In fact, the town is known for its nightlife, as well as for its traditional **Thursday market,** but gets very crowded in season. Capoliveri is also home to one of the island's fine-dining highlights, the **Taverna dei Poeti ★**, Via Roma 14 (©**0565-968-306;** www.latavernadeipoeti.com), where creative primi such as *ravioli di pesce con crema di molluschi* (pasta stuffed with fish in a shellfish cream) cost around 10€ and secondi like *gulasch di pescatrice* (fisherwoman's stew) 19€. It's open at dinner only and reservations are essential.

MARCIANA The island's oldest settlement, **Marciana** ★ is also the most attractive base for exploring western Elba. It's a picturesque and very steep little town made of minuscule tree-shaded *piazze* and winding stepped-stone streets stacked atop one another. The car park above the village makes an excellent jumping-off point for the hike to the **Madonna del Monte,** a remote hermitage visited by Napoleon in 1814. Leave 1½ hours for the round-trip. For the best views on the island, catch the **Cabinovia Marciana–Monte Capanne** ★★ (℃0565-901-020) from just outside town. The 20-minute ride in an open cage to Elba's tallest peak (at 1,019m/3,343 ft.) ends in 360-degree views across the arc of the Tuscan coast from Livorno to Monte Argentario, over the Tuscan archipelago, and out to Corsica. You can ride one-way and hike down (10€; leave 1½ hr. at least) or buy an *andata e ritorno* (round-trip) for 17€ (7€ for kids ages 4 to 10). Weather permitting, the cableway is open daily 10am to 12:30pm and 2:20 to 5:30pm, with seasonal variations.

Where to Stay

To find the perfect hotel to fit your needs, you can call or drop by the **Associazione Albergatori** office (see "Essentials," above). **Seasons** on the island have seemingly infinite gradations. The highest season is August, when the island is packed with vacationing Italians and you'll find stratospheric prices and most hotels booked months in advance (and at many places at least half-pension required). Then come various midseasons in June, July, Easter, late spring, and early fall. The rest is low season, when most places are closed, while those that stay open offer deeply discounted rates.

Campers will find plenty to satisfy them. Ask at the tourist office for a catalog of campgrounds because sacking out on most beaches is frowned upon.

If you wish to stay in Portoferraio itself—for a late arrival or early ferry departure—you'll find practical, clean, unspectacular, but good-value rooms at the **Ape Elbana,** Salita Cosimo de' Medici 2 (www.ape-elbana.it; ℃0565-914-245). A simple double costs between 70€ and 160€, including parking in Piazza della Repubblica opposite the hotel. It's open year-round.

ELBA'S BEST beaches

Cut through the edge of Portoferraio's new town to the north shore, past **Le Ghiaie,** Portoferraio's only real (but not great) beach. Farther beyond are slightly better beaches at **Acquaviva** and **Viticcio.** However, the nearest really good stretch of sand is in the sheltered bay at **Biodola** ★, 7km (4½ miles) southwest of Portoferraio. The next major bay heading west, **Procchio** also has decent sand and a shallow shelf for little ones, but—like its south-coast counterpart at **Marina di Campo** ★—it's developed and can get crowded in season. Farther west still are some of Elba's best sands: At the pretty little cove of **Sant'Andrea** ★★, where there are also rock-pools, and at the idyllic crescents at **Fetovaia** ★★ and **Cavoli** ★★. Any of the three will get busy in peak periods. **Lacona** is another fluffy, but well frequented beach on the south coast. The coast west of Capoliveri has excellent sand-and-pebble beaches aligned for sunset watching, at **Zuccale, Barabarca, Morcone,** and **Innamorata** ★.

NEAR LACONA

Capo Sud ★ ☺ Set in a relatively peaceful corner of Elba, the Capo Sud makes a lasting impression with its clifftop views and friendly staff. Rooms are set in small blocks wedged into a lush slope down to a private stretch of Margidore's dark-sand beach. All units are cool, comfortable, and spacious, if a little bland (although some are due to be overhauled in time for the 2012 season). Units Il Sole and La Luna offer the best combination of seclusion and beach access, but families will need the extra space offered by rooms in Il Pino or L'Aleatico. It's well worth the extra 20€ a night to turn your outside space (standard across all units) into one with a sea view.

Via del Capo Marinaro 301, Loc. Lacona, 57031 Capoliveri, Elba (LI). www.hotelcaposud.it. ✆ **0565-964-021.** Fax 0565-964-263. 40 units. 76€–198€ double; 20€ extra per night for sea view. Rates include breakfast. MC, V. Free parking. Closed Nov–Easter. **Amenities:** 2 restaurants; 2 bars; outdoor pool; private beach; outdoor tennis court. *In room:* A/C (in some), TV, hair dryer, minibar, Wi-Fi (free).

NEAR CAPOLIVERI

Casa Campanella Resort ★ ☺ 🎁 Families make up about 90% of the clientele at this boutique apartment complex surrounded by gardens. Units in the converted 19th-century villa come in four grades, but all are simply decorated, with spacious cool rooms plus modern kitchenettes and large bathrooms. Superior and deluxe units have a little more space, but mostly you're paying for an upgrade to bathroom suites and add-ons like LCD TVs–and all guests benefit from the same thoughtful service provided by family owner-managers. Outside of midsummer, when it's weekly bookings only, apartments are bookable from 1 night upward. The complex makes extensive use of green and sustainable products, including energy.

Loc. Piano di Mola, 57031 Capoliveri, Elba (LI). www.casacampanella.it. ✆ **0565-915-740.** Fax 0565-935-533. 15 units. 80€–185€ standard apt; 120€–270€ superior apt. AE, DC, MC, V. Discounts for stays of 1 week. or more. Free parking. Closed mid-Nov to Easter. **Amenities:** Babysitting; children's play area; concierge; 2 outdoor pools; volleyball court; Wi-Fi (free). *In room:* TV, hair dryer.

Where to Eat

The best place to eat in Portoferraio itself is **Osteria Libertaria ★**, right on the harbor at Calata Matteotti 12 (✆ **0565-91-478**), where it's all about the freshest, sizzling fish and Elban specialties like *riso nero* (risotto blackened with cuttlefish ink). Portions aren't huge; primi cost 10€ and secondi between 10€ and 15€.

Emanuel ★★ SEAFOOD Behind a deceptive beach-bum bar facade snuggled into the beach at the Enfola headland, friendly family-run Emanuel excels at marrying the pick of the ocean with fresh pastas and seasonal vegetables. Reserve ahead for one of a few shaded tables in the pocket-size courtyard, just feet from the waves lapping at the pebble beach. The *garganelli branzino e verdure* (sea bass scented with rosemary and tossed with zucchini, carrots, oil, and a bit of peperoncino) is outstanding, as is the simple *tagliolini bottarga e carciofi* (thin pasta strands twirled with grated tuna roe and artichoke hearts). For a secondo, have them grill or oven-roast the catch of the day pulled in by local fishermen that morning, or try the island specialty *totani alla diavola* (small cuttlefish cooked up with oil and hot peppers).

Loc. Enfola (15 min. west of Portoferraio). ✆ **0565-939-003.** Reservations highly recommended. Primi 9€–12€; secondi 12€–18€. AE, DC, MC, V. Thurs–Tues (daily June 15–Sept 15) noon–3:15pm and 7:30–10:30pm. Closed mid-Oct to Easter.

Osteria del Noce ★ LIGURIAN/SEAFOOD It's well worth the climb up Marciana's steep stone steps to eat at this informal Elban-Ligurian seafood joint. There's no permanent menu, because diners are at the mercy of today's catch: Everything is chalked up on a board that gets passed from table to table by bustling staff. The *misto mare* is a mixed antipasto of warm, cold, and cured seafood that might include clams, octopus, anchovies, smoked tuna—or all of the above. The place's real forte, however, is secondi such as *acciughetta ligure* (anchovy, potato, and zucchini layered, baked in the oven, and served dressed with pesto) or meaty fish such as *palamita all'Elbana* (Atlantic bonito stewed with tomato, capers, olives, and potato). Booking is essential if you want a perch on the panoramic terrace.

Via della Madonna 19, Marciana Alta. ✆ **0565-901-284.** www.osteriadelnoce.it. Reservations strongly recommended. Primi 9€–10€; secondi 12€–15€. AE, MC, V. Daily noon–2pm and 7–11pm, closed Nov–Mar.

MASSA MARITTIMA

65km (40 miles) S of Volterra; 67km (41 miles) SW of Siena; 115km (71 miles) SW of Florence

Inland Massa Marittima, sitting stately atop its 356m (1,168-ft.) mount with a sweeping view over the farmland far below and Metalliferous Hills beyond, is an Etruscan grandchild. It's a medieval mining town that's heir to ancient Pupolónia. When St. Cerbone moved his bishop's seat here in the 9th century, he kicked off Massa's Middle Ages prosperity, based on mining the metal-rich hills around it. It established a republic in 1225 and grew fat on mine proceeds—unfortunately attracting the attentions of the nearby Sienese.

In 1335, Siena attacked and subdued Massa, taking the upper half of town and fortifying it as their Città Nuova (New Town). In its heyday, the city produced both religious heritage (St. Bernardino of Siena was born and died here) and civic legacy: The first mining code in European history was drawn up here in the 14th century, one of the most important legislative documents from the Middle Ages.

Massa has a fine crop of small museums and an impressive cathedral, and makes a great cultural timeout if you're holidaying by the coast. For most of the year, the two-tier town lies empty for exploration.

Essentials

GETTING THERE By Bus: By far the most regular **RAMA** (✆ **199-848-787** in Italy; www.ramamobilita.it) bus connection is with Follonica (approx. hourly; 35 min.), which itself it best reached by rail (see below); a couple every weekday continue on to Piombino (70 min.). There are a handful of other connections: Weekdays only, there are three buses to/from Grosseto (1 hr.) and two to/from Siena (1¾ hr.).

By Car: Massa sits on the SS439, 22km (13½ miles) inland from Follonica and a twisty-turny 65km (40 miles) south of Volterra. From Siena, head southwest on the SS73 then the SS441 for 67km (41½ miles). The most convenient parking is in Piazza Mazzini, costing 1€ per hour.

By Train: Massa Marittima doesn't have its own train station, but there's a stop at Follonica on the main line between Rome (11 daily; 2½ hr.) and Pisa (18 daily; 80 min.). Buses meet incoming trains for the ride to Massa.

VISITOR INFORMATION The **tourist information office** is at Via Todini 3–5 (✆ **0566-902-756;** www.altamaremmaturismo.it), down the right side of the Palazzo del Podestà. Hours are seemingly in a state of constant flux, but generally are Tuesday to Sunday from 9:30am to 1pm and 2 to 6:30pm. If you're visiting on a day trip, avoid Monday, when the town museums are all closed.

FESTIVALS & MARKETS The **Balestro del Girifalco** involves a crossbow competition, processions, and displays of flag juggling all done by the town's *terzieri* (neighborhood representatives) in 13th-century costume. It's put on twice a year, on May 20 or the following Sunday and on the second Sunday in August. Photographers can take part in workshops or just enjoy the displays at the early July **Toscana Foto Festival** (www.toscanafotofestival. net). Music lovers should make plans to be here during the first week in August for **Lirica in Piazza ★** (www.liricainpiazza.it), a short open-air opera festival featuring works by the likes of Puccini and Bizet. Tickets costing 22€ to 50€ go on sale starting in April.

Exploring Massa Marittima
CITTÀ VECCHIA

The Old Town clusters around triangular **Piazza Garibaldi ★**. Today, the medieval buildings guard over sleepy cafes with tables out on the flagstones or shaded under arcades. The square is anchored at one end by the steeply angled off-kilter steps of the **Duomo ★★**, turned slightly as if to show off its good side and bell tower (open daily 8am–noon and 3–6pm). The bulk of the building was raised in travertine in the early 13th century with Pisan-Romanesque blind arcading, but the Gothic style had hit town by the time they got to the top half of the facade, so it was crowned with an architecturally agile arcade of slender columns and pink-and-white marble. Above the main door lintel, a 12th-century Pisan sculptor carved a relief panel celebrating the miracle-ridden life of Massa's patron saint and one-time bishop, 9th-century African immigrant San Cerbone, to whom the cathedral is dedicated—spot the scene for which he's most famous, when he took a flock of geese to see the Pope.

The interior is supported by fat travertine columns with flowing Corinthian capitals. Just inside the entrance is a font carved with *St. John the Baptist* scenes by Giroldo da Como from a single block of travertine (1267). The tabernacle balancing above it is an anonymous 15th-century Sienese work. In the apse behind the altar is the **Arca di San Cerbone ★**. This marble urn sheltering the remains of the town patron is covered with reliefs depicting the saint's life carved in 1324 by little-known Sienese Gothic talent Goro di Gregorio.

Across the piazza from the Duomo is the 13th-century **Palazzo del Podestà**—recognizable by the old mayoral coats of arms. From the narrow end of Piazza Garibaldi, Via Moncini branches steeply up from Via della Libertà toward the New Town.

ATTRACTIONS

Museo d'Arte Sacra **3**
Museo degli Organi Meccanici **1**
Museo della Miniera **6**

HOTELS

La Fenice Park Hotel **2**

RESTAURANTS

La Tana del Brillo Parlante **4**
Osteria da Tronca **5**

ⓘ Information
P Parking
▪▪▪ Pedestrian Only

Massa Marittima

CITTÀ NUOVA

The upper part of town is only "new" by virtue of the fact that the conquering Sienese revamped it after 1335. You enter the New Town through the **Porta alla Silici,** part of the *cassero* fortifications built by the Sienese (1337–38). The gate's back side sprouts a narrow **flying arch** framing the trees of the tiny park beyond—though built as a viaduct for the Sienese garrisons, it was made more for show than for sound military purposes. The arch connects the fortress ramparts to the 1228 **Torre del Candeliere** (②**0566-902-289;** www.massamarittima musei.it), a clock tower since 1443 and still impressive at two-thirds of its original 60m (197 ft.). You can climb it for **views** ★ over the ramparts. April through October, it's open Tuesday to Sunday from 10am to 1pm and 3 to 6pm; November through March, it's open Tuesday to Sunday from 11am to 1pm and 2:30 to 4:30pm. Admission is 2.50€ adults, 1.50€ children 13 and under and seniors 60 and over.

Massa's art highlight is the **Museo d'Arte Sacra** ★, Corso Diaz 36 (②**0566-901-954;** www.massamarittimamusei.it), built largely to showcase **Ambrogio Lorenzetti's** *Maestà* ★★, painted in the late 1330s. Sitting at the feet of Mary nuzzling her baby is a glowing reddish Lorenzetti angel, and amid the stacks of saintly halos on the right is black-robed St. Cerbone, his geese milling about his feet. During the baroque era, which didn't care for these early "crude" paintings, the city lost track of the work, and it wasn't rediscovered until 1867, by which point it had been divided into five pieces and, nailed together, was serving as an ash bin for a stove. Elsewhere in the small collection is a fine stained-glass *Crucifixion* by Ambrogio's brother, Pietro. The museum is open Tuesday through Sunday from 10am to 1pm and 3 to 6pm (11am–1pm and 3–5pm Nov–Mar). Admission is 5€ adults and 3€ children 13 and under and seniors 60 and over.

The **Museo degli Organi Meccanici** ★★, Corso Diaz 28 (✆ **0566-940-282;** www.museodegliorgani.it), houses a unique collection of organs rescued from churches across Italy, from Bologna to Naples, and restored here in the museum. Some of the instruments date back to 1600; there's also an early *ghironda* (hurdy-gurdy) and a line of fortepianos dating from 1700s Vienna to the early 20th century. If you're lucky the proprietor will give you an improvised demo of the instruments in action—they're all in working order. June through September the museum is open 10am to 1pm and 4 to 7pm; March through May afternoon hours are 4 to 6pm; and October through mid-January it's open 10:30am to 12:30pm and 3 to 6pm. From mid-January through February, it's closed. Admission costs 4€, 3€ for children and seniors.

To learn more about the town's fascinating subterranean heritage, don your hard hat and head underground at the **Museo della Miniera** ★, Via Corridoni (✆ **0566-902-289;** www.massamarittimamusei.it), where a guided tour of 700m (2,300 ft.) of authentically reconstructed 1940s mine shaft gets you inside the life and mind of a miner in these mineral-rich hills. Tours run Tuesday to Sunday approximately hourly 10am to noon and 3 to 5:45pm (last tour 4:30pm Nov–Mar). Adults pay 5€ for the 45-minute visit; it's 3€ for children and seniors.

Where to Stay

La Fenice Park Hotel ★ Massa isn't over-endowed with standout places to stay, and this handsome shuttered *palazzo* in the Città Nuova is comfortably the best within the walls. Its large, airy rooms are every bit the match for the grand, vaulted entrance: They're equipped with traditional Tuscan dark-wood furniture and terra-cotta tiled floors. The little extra that secures you a junior suite, with a separate seating area, is money well spent.

Corso Diaz 63, 58024 Massa Marittima (GR). www.lafeniceparkhotel.it. ✆ **0566-903-941.** Fax 0566-902-202. 17 units. 90€–180€ double. Rates include breakfast. AE, DC, MC, V. Free parking. **Amenities:** Bar; babysitting; outdoor pool; Wi-Fi. *In room:* A/C, TV, hair dryer, minibar.

Where to Eat

Osteria da Tronca ★ MAREMMAN This restaurant, known by most people simply as "l'osteria," is split-level medieval—all stone walls, brick arches, and hand-hewn wood ceiling beams. An explanation of any dish begins "Oh, that's the way we make it." "We" seems to incorporate the jocular restaurateurs, the septuagenarian cook who steadfastly prepares food the way mamma taught her, and Massans in general. Kick off your meal with *tortelli alla maremmana* (ravioli stuffed with ricotta and Swiss chard in meaty ragù) or *zuppa dell'Osteria* (a cannellini bean and cabbage soup poured over toasted garlic bread). Follow with *cinghiale alla cacciatore* (wild boar huntsman style, stewed with mushrooms—but no olives, which, they sniff, are only "for making oil")—or an *arista di maiale* (slices of roast pork with potatoes).

Vicolo Porte 5 (from Via della Libertà, take left turn after Hotel Il Sole, then left again). ✆ **0566-901-991.** Reservations recommended. Primi 8€–10€; secondi 7€–12€. MC, V. Thurs–Tues 7-10:30pm. Closed Jan–Feb.

La Tana del Brillo Parlante ★★★ MODERN MAREMMAN The instant the parchment "menu book" is presented to you with the reverence of a Bible, you know you're in for a dining treat. Massa's—perhaps the Maremma's—best restaurant is a tiny, four-table dining room with thoughtful country styling, complete with stripped brick walls, hessian tablecloths, and water served in terra-cotta pots. The seasonal menu hosts plenty of familiar flavors, but they are combined with creativity and originality. A typical route through the menu might begin with *crostini con lardo di Colonnata,* followed by *chicche al cinghiale* (chestnut-flour gnocchi with a sauce made from boar marinated in red wine), then *stinco di maiale sfumato alla birra* (shin of pork stewed with herbs and beer). This is slow food, served with a flourish and not a hint of pretension.

Vicolo Ciambellano 4. ✆ **0566-901-274.** Reservations highly recommended. Primi 7€–9€; secondi 14€–17€. No credit cards. Thurs–Tues noon–2:30pm and 6:30–11pm.

En Route to Siena

The **Abbey of San Galgano** ★, about 30km (19 miles) northeast of Massa Marittima beside the SS441 close to the junction with the SS73, is an imposing, roofless Gothic structure built by Cistercian monks in the 13th century. It is accompanied by the **rotunda of Montesiepi** atop a nearby hill, held together by a dome of 24 concentric stone circles. In the middle of the floor is **the sword of Saint Galgano Guidotti** springing from a rock. After a visitation from the Archangel Michael, the saint is said to have miraculously thrust his sword into the stone, like the legend of King Arthur in reverse, in a sign of his renunciation of violence and worldly pleasures. Adorning a side-chapel are badly decayed **frescoes** by Sienese maestro Ambrogio Lorenzetti. The site is open during daylight hours, and admission is free.

THE MAREMMA

The Maremma stretches along Tuscany's coast from Cecina to Monte Argentario and extends inward (where it becomes the Alta Maremma), along flat, occasionally rolling land toward the mountainous interior. The Maremma was once the heartbeat of the Etruscan world and preserves scant remains of some of their most important cities and miles of the mysterious sunken roads (*vie cave*) they carved more than 4m (13 ft.) into the tufa. The complex canal and drainage system built by those ancient Tuscans allowed them to turn the marshy flatlands into a breadbasket—it's still a major produce-growing province.

The conquering Romans, though, weren't as able as landscape administrators, and when the neglected drainage system broke down, marshes and bogland swamped the region and brought with them the malaria mosquito. Grand Duke Leopold I was the first to seriously attempt a large-scale reclamation of the land in 1828, and his canals still form an important part of the drainage network, but it wasn't until malaria was defeated here in the 1950s that the coastal stretches of land became livable again.

Today, the Maremma puts forth a mixed image. It's part rugged new colony, where man has reconquered the land and cowboys called *butteri* watch over herds of white oxen. It's also part relic of the ancient past, where centuries of relative isolation have allowed Etruscan ruins and towns to decay romantically. You'll encounter very few other tourists as you explore archaic hill towns and grassy, mounded Etruscan tombs.

Essentials

GETTING THERE & GETTING AROUND By Train: Regular trains on the relatively slow **Rome-Livorno-Pisa** line stop at Follonica, Grosseto, and Orbetello (for Monte Argentario). There's also a minor line linking **Siena** and Grosseto, where you can change to the train or bus for other Maremman destinations.

By Bus: Maremma's **RAMA** bus network (✆ **0564/475-111;** www.ramamobilita.it) runs from Grosseto to Florence (six daily; 2¼ hr.), Siena (12 daily; 80 min.), Castiglione della Pescaia (at least hourly; 45 min.), and Pitigliano (five daily; 1¾ hr.). There are also connections with Orbetello (for Monte Argentario).

Exploring the Maremma

HITTING THE BEACH Along the southern stretch of Tuscany's coast are several beaches and resorts. **Castiglione della Pescaia** is probably the best all-around resort. The beach is passable, the prices are lower than at nearby, upscale **Punta Ala,** and it has a touch of the genteel, faded air about it, relying on an old fishing-village atmosphere and the ancient Old Town up on the hill as attractions. **Marina di Alberese** is more remote, without the beach services to be found at Castiglione, but has better, pine-backed sands and views of Isola Giglio offshore in the haze.

Tuscany's most southerly point is on the resort peninsula of **Monte Argentario,** guarded by the tiny city of **Orbetello,** which sits in the middle of a saltwater lagoon. The **Laguna di Orbetello** (✆ **0564-870-198;** www.wwf.it/orbetello.nt) is protected by the World Wildlife Fund (WWF) as a natural oasis, where an estimated 200 of the 450 species that call the country home live or pass through every year. Keen bird-watchers should pack binoculars. The main reason to visit Monte Argentario is for the Tuscan mainland's best beach, the **Tombolo della Feniglia** ★, a long, flat arc of sand, with a south-facing, shallow shelf, that stretches almost all the way back across the southern fringe of the lagoon. Head for Porto Ercole and park when you see the signs. There's plenty of natural shade under the parasol pines.

HORSEBACK RIDING & HIKING Just 15km (9 miles) southwest of Grosseto, a 15km (9-mile) stretch of hilly coastline is protected as the **Parco Naturale della Maremma** ★★ (www.parco-maremma.it; click through to their Facebook page for the most up-to-date information). One of Tuscany's few remaining wilderness areas incorporates the **Monti dell'Uccellina,** capped by crumbling medieval towers. The "Mountains of the Little Bird" are actually hills some 390m (1,279 ft.) high, covered with the almost unbroken carpet of parasol pine forest, though you'll also find ilex, oak, elms, juniper, and the occasional dwarf palm, Italy's only native-growing palm tree. Rustling around in the myrtle and juniper *macchia* brush are families of Italy's small native wild boar, herds of roe deer, foxes, crested porcupines, and the occasional feral cat. Larger critters include a famous pack of semi-wild horses and long-horned white cattle, both of which are wrangled by the Maremma's famous but dwindling breed of cowboy, the *butteri.* There are wondrous stretches of sand-dune beaches, rising to a rocky cliff toward the south and petering into marshy bog land to the north. The latter is the park's best bird-watching area, where you might even spot flamingos, peregrine falcons, and osprey among the scores of migratory and water birds that spend time here.

The park **visitor center** is at Via del Bersagliere 7, Alberese (☎ **0564-407-098**), from where an hourly shuttle bus takes you into the closed-to-traffic park and drops you at the trail heads. Trail A1 is 7.8km (4.9 miles) in its entirety and involves the most rugged, but most rewarding, hiking; it leads past the evocative ruins of the 11th-century San Rabano abbey. Trail A2 runs for 5.8km (3.6 miles) past abandoned medieval watchtowers toward the rocky coast with unforgettable vistas of the parasol pine forests along the way. Gentler Trail A3 follows 9.7km (6 miles) of sandy pine woods and visits caves once inhabited by prehistoric man. Challenging Trail A4 is 12.8km (8 miles) and takes you along wooded cliffs and down on the Cala di Forno beach. The park is open daily from 9am to dusk. Admission costs 9€ for adults, 5.50€ for children 6 to 14 and seniors 60 and over. The visitor center also offers seasonal guided visits by canoe (16€ adults, 10€ children and seniors), as well as nighttime excursions (15€ adults, 12€ children and seniors). Between June 15 and September 15, brushfire risk means that entrance to the park is by guided visit on trails A1 and A2 only (prebook by 5pm one day ahead; about 3 visits run per day, Fri afternoon tours are usually in English); prices are the same.

PITIGLIANO AND THE ALTA MAREMMA It's a substantial diversion from the coast to **Pitigliano** ★★—turn inland on the SS74 at Albinia and drive northeast on a slow road for 51km (31½ miles)—but even hill-town veterans won't be prepared for the almost Transylvanian sight of the town seemingly growing from living tufa rock. It's an unforgettable sight. The town's **tourist office** is at Piazza Garibaldi 51 (☎ **0564-617-111**), open Easter to September Tuesday through Sunday 9am to 1pm and 4 to 7pm (9:30am–12:30pm and 3–6pm the rest of the year).

Pitigliano's twisted alleys and gnarled stone staircases make for pleasant strolling, especially along **Via Roma,** which you can follow all the way to the town's oldest church, **San Rocco,** whose Romanesque interior sports a

Pitigliano.

handsome nave and aisles supported by travertine columns. It is the town's Jewish community, banished here under the Medici grand dukes, that has left the most interesting historical mark, and gave the town its nickname, *Piccola Gerusalemme* ("Little Jerusalem"). The mazelike **Jewish Museum and Synagogue ★**, Vicolo Marghera (off Via Zuccarelli; ✆**0564-616-006;** www.lapiccolagerusalemme.it), is built into the former ghetto. The ritual baths, *matzo* oven (last used for Passover in 1939), and kosher wine cellars are carved into the tufa that underpins the town. The synagogue was built in 1598, shortly after Jews were banished from Rome. This fascinating area is open Sunday through Friday 10am to 12:10pm and 3:30–6:10pm (shorter afternoon hours off season). Admission costs 3€ adults, 2€ children ages 6 to 12. If you're in town over lunchtime, **Il Grillo,** Via Cavour 18 (✆**0564-615-202**), serves good-value, rustic Maremman dishes in a traditional dining room. It's closed Tuesday.

Pitigliano also sits at the center of a network of Etruscan "sunken roads" (*vie cave*) hollowed out of the volcanic rock upon which the Alta Maremma sits. Nobody is quite sure what the *vie cave* were for—processional walkways or livestock droving paths are two theories—but these days they are free and open to anyone armed with a decent local map. Even in summer, you'll likely have the routes to yourself. The best of them is the **Via Cava di San Giuseppe ★**, 1km (under 1 mile) out of Pitigliano on the road to Sovana. Just west of Sovana is the **Tomba Ildebranda (Hildebrand's Tomb;** ✆**0564-614-074;** www.leviecave.it), the most extensive and important Etruscan burial site in the Maremma, which (in its 3rd-c. B.C. heyday) was decorated with vivid pictures of vegetables. Leave an hour at least to explore the network, including the Via Cava di Poggio which originates here. It's open daily March through September 10am to 7pm (plus weekends only until 5pm Oct). Admission costs 5€, free for children 11 and under. There are more Etruscan remains at Saturnia, but it's the **thermal springs ★** that have put the town on the map. The cascade of swirling, steaming, slightly stinky sulfur water at a constant temperature of 37°C (97°F) is a surreal place for a dip. On a sunny day the cataract cascade reflects an intense cobalt blue, looks like nothing so much as an oversize ornamental water feature, and makes for a great photo. It's just outside of Saturnia by the road to Montemerano, is completely free, but gets busy on weekends, even way out of high season.

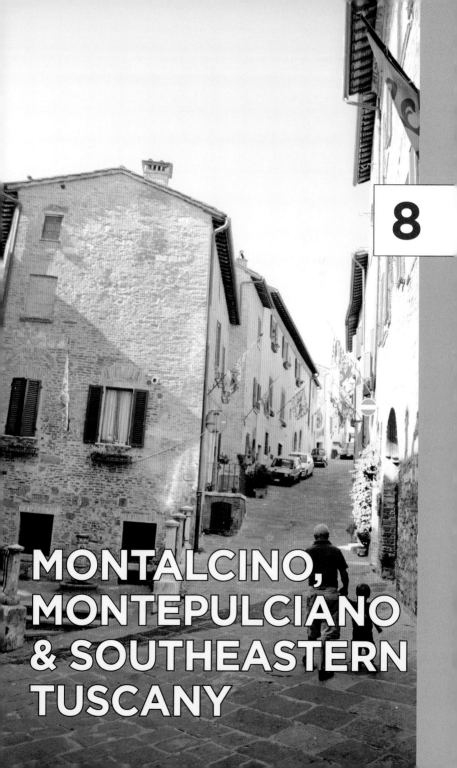

8

MONTALCINO, MONTEPULCIANO & SOUTHEASTERN TUSCANY

T he hill towns and valleys south of Siena comprise perhaps Tuscany's most enchanting and downright picturesque region. It's a land of medieval castles guarding narrow road passes, isolated farmhouses perching atop limestone ridges, stands of cypress and ribbons of plane trees against a bucolic backdrop, and thermal spas enjoyed by both the Medici and modern health-seekers. The minute you hit the dramatically scarred Crete Senesi hills just beyond Siena, the savage beauty of this region becomes apparent. A few small patches of forest stick to the steeper slopes of its river valleys, but most of it has been landscaped to a human scale over thousands of years, turning the rolling hills into farmlands and vineyards that produce Tuscany's mightiest red wines.

Southern Tuscany's cities are textbook Italian hill towns. **Chiusi** dwells deep in its Etruscan roots, still remembering a time when King Lars Porsenna was one of the few leaders of the Etruscan confederation who had the audacity to take on Rome. **Sarteano** has unique Etruscan frescoes that predate the Renaissance by millennia. Roman settlements like **Montalcino** and **Montepulciano** grew into medieval cities and today produce two of Italy's top red wines, the powerhouse Brunello di Montalcino and the subtle Vino Nobile di Montepulciano. And the gemlike village of **Pienza,** famed for its pecorino sheep's cheese, shelters within its tiny ring of walls a Renaissance core of the most perfect proportions and planning.

Much of the area is occupied by the **Val d'Orcia**—an expansive valley that glows a bright emerald green in spring, and burns to golden-brown under the fierce summer sun. Souvenir-stand postcards and cover shots of coffee-table books are snapped right here.

MONTALCINO, THE BRUNELLO VINEYARDS & THE VAL D'ORCIA

42km (26 miles) S of Siena; 112km (70 miles) S of Florence; 190km (118 miles) NW of Rome

Montalcino presents a mighty image on the approach from the valley—a walled town set high on a hill punctuated with the spires of medieval buildings and a glowering fortress at one end. Up close, it becomes a smaller, meeker place, but the precipitous medieval alleyways and stone buildings make it a day-trip delight, and the views of the valleys from which you ascended are magnificent from this height.

Paleolithic tribes and the Etruscans set up camp here, but it wasn't until the Roman era that a permanent settlement formed. By the Middle Ages, Montalcino was a bustling town and a defensive center for the surrounding

PREVIOUS PAGE: **A winding street in Montepulciano.**

farming community. Although it divided itself into four minuscule neighborhood *contrade* (neighborhoods) after the Sienese model, Montalcino was initially allied to Florence and at odds with its northerly neighbor Siena. After several skirmishes, though, the Sienese took over Montalcino in the 13th century. By 1462, the town had grown large enough to be declared a city, and in 1555 its now-cozy relations with Siena led it to harbor the 700 Sienese families who refused to submit to the Medici when Florence defeated Siena. The exiles set up the defiant "Republic of Siena at Montalcino," which lasted 4 years until the Medici grand dukes finally laid their hands on both the Sienese and Montalcino through treaty. Montalcino's loyalty is honored to this day—their standard-bearer rides in pride of place at the front of Siena's annual pre-Palio parade.

Montalcino's Medici-induced slide into obscurity began to turn around in the 1960s, when the world discovered that the sangiovese grosso grapes—known as "Brunello" to the locals, who had been quietly experimenting with them for about a century—made one of the finest red wines in the world. Today, with an annual production of more than 3.5 million bottles of **Brunello di Montalcino**— and 3 million of its lighter-weight cousin Rosso di Montalcino—Montalcino has become a rather well-to-do town, also known for its white dessert wine called Moscadello and its fine honey.

Essentials

GETTING THERE By Train: Ten trains a day on the Grosseto line out of Siena stop at Buonconvento (25 min.). From there, it's about 14km (8½ miles), or 30 minutes by bus, to Montalcino; buses generally run in sync with train arrivals.

By Car: Montalcino is about 8km (5 miles) off the SS2 Via Cassia running between Siena and Rome. There is a small parking lot next to the Fortezza just inside the walls. If it's full, you can also find pay parking ringing the walls.

By Bus: There are roughly 12 daily **TRA-IN** buses from Siena (70 min.); a few require a change at **Buonconvento.** The **bus terminus** in Montalcino is Piazza Cavour; buy your tickets at Bar Prato on the piazza or from the tourist office.

VISITOR INFORMATION The **tourist office** (©0577-849-331; www.proloco montalcino.it) is at Costa del Municipio 1, in the shadow of the bell tower. It's open Tuesday through Sunday from 10am to 1pm and 2 to 5:40pm. Between April and October, it's also open the same hours on Monday.

FESTIVALS Celebrating the opening of hunting season is the **Torneo di Apertura della Caccia,** held on the second weekend in August. The events, dating from the 14th century, include archery competitions and lots of food as everybody struts in medieval costume. The residents dust off those outfits again for a similar but much larger festival called the **Sagra del Tordo ★**, held the last weekend in October. It kicks off on Saturday with an archery competition pitting Montalcino's four *contrade* against one another. Parades, pageantry, and plenty of food follow for the next 2 days. The *festa* honors the lowly thrush, long considered a delicacy in these hills. Music lovers are also catered to: The town echoes to the sounds of everything from rock to traditional song during June's **Festa della Musica** (www.montalcinofestadella musica.com), and July sees an **International Chamber Music Festival** (www.musica-reale.com). Friday is **market** day on Viale della Libertà.

Exploring Montalcino

The dominant feature of Montalcino's skyline is the 14th-century Sienese **Fortezza (Fortress)** ★★, expanded in 1571 by Duke Cosimo I. Inside the old keep is the **Enoteca La Fortezza** wine shop (✆ **0577-849-211;** www.enoteca lafortezza.com; see "Sampling the *Vino,*" below), where you can buy tickets to circumnavigate the ramparts for panoramic views of the Val d'Orcia and Vallombrone. In one of the castle rooms, the last battle standard of the Sienese Republic is preserved. April through October, the fortress is open daily from 9am to 8pm; November through March, hours are 10am to 6pm. Admission is 4€ adults and 2€ children ages 6 to 12. A 6€ cumulative ticket also gets you into the Musei di Montalcino, but you must buy it at the museum (see below).

Walk down Via dell'Oca and turn left on Via Panfilo to **Piazza Garibaldi,** with the small 11th-century church of **Sant'Egidio.** Inside is a *Madonna and Saints* by Luca di Tommé.

Out the other end of the piazza, Costa del Municipio leads past the entrance to the **Palazzo Comunale** (1292). On the *palazzo's* exterior wall are attached rows of outsized acrylic wine labels. The town commissions one each year from a leading international designer to mark the vintage—the number of stars (up to five) on each denotes the "quality" of the year's harvest. The elongated front of the *palazzo* on Piazza del Popolo, sporting the mayoral coat of arms of past *podestà,* looks far too narrow to stand. It's nothing more than a slender clock tower with a loggia off the left side. On the slender piazza you'll find a 14th- to 15th-century **loggia** and the 19th-century cafe **Fiaschetteria Italiana** ★ (see "Sampling the *Vino,*" below), focal point of the evening *passeggiata* up Via Mazzini.

A stepped street leads uphill from Piazza del Popolo to the 14th-century church of **Sant'Agostino.** Just to the right of the church, in its former convent, is the **Musei di Montalcino** ★ (✆ **0577-846-014;** www.museisenesi. org). The museum is dedicated largely to Sienese works, including a panel by Ambrogio Lorenzetti and four extraordinary carved *Crucifixions* ★ from the 1300s. It's one of the best small-town collections in Tuscany, and has been sup-

plemented by a new archaeological section displayed in an atmospheric cellar. The museum is open Tuesday through Sunday from 10am to 1pm and 2 to 5:40pm. Admission is 4.50€ adults and 3€ for children 11 and under; a 6€ cumulative ticket also gets you into the Fortezza (see above).

A Romanesque Abbey near Montalcino

In a pocket-size vale bounded by low green hills, the Cistercian abbey of **Sant'Antimo** ★★★ (✆ **0577-835-659;** www.antimo.it) rises amid olive groves. Its church is one of the most intact Romanesque countryside temples left in Tuscany, although its monastery is mostly ruins. Since 1992, a handful of French monks have inhabited what's

The fortress at Montalcino.

Sant'Antimo.

left, and the church interior echoes with their haunting Gregorian chant seven times every day—you're welcome to attend a service; contact Montalcino's tourist office for the timetable. The first stone was supposedly laid on the order of Charlemagne in A.D. 781, but the current structure dates from 1118. Its amalgamated Lombard-French architecture has produced a building of singular beauty, with strong, simple lines of pale yellow and white stone. The fabric of the walls is studded with recycled materials, some inscribed and many with fantastic medieval (and even a few Roman) reliefs. One side of the campanile supports a medieval relief of the *Madonna and Child,* and the carvings of animals and geometric designs around the doors are worth study. Before going inside, walk around to the back; at the base of the apse is a small, round window through which you can glimpse a bit of the 9th-century crypt underneath, part of the original church where St. Antimo himself prayed.

The honey-colored travertine interior of the church, with its second-level women's gallery adapted from Byzantine models, is filled even on cloudy days with a warm, diffuse light. Several of the column capitals have intricate alabaster carvings. The second down the right aisle tells the story of *Daniel in the Lion's Den.* You can descend to the cramped crypt, where you'll find a *Pietà* fresco, and spend time admiring the carvings—a plethora of eagles and evangelists, sheep and medieval Christs—throughout the church. Behind the high altar and its 13th-century wooden crucifix is an unusual three-apsed ambulatory that gets plenty of sun—your best bet for seeing that luminous effect on the alabaster. Ask the guy at the postcard desk *"Posso vedere la sagrestia per piacere?"* (Poh-so ved-*air*-ay la sah-gres-*tee*-yah pair pee-ah-*chair*-ay) for a peek into the sacristy and its cartoonish 15th-century frescoes by Giovanni di Asciano on the *Life of St. Benedict,* interesting for their earthy details and the animal extras that often seem wonderfully oblivious to the holy events happening around them. (One scene features two blatantly amorous pigs.) Sant'Antimo is open to visitors Monday through Saturday from 10:30am to 12:30pm and 3 to 6:30pm, Sunday from 9:15 to 10:45am and 3 to 6pm. Admission is free.

Where to Stay

An excellent B&B inside the walls is the **Porta Castellana ★**, Via Santa Lucia 20, 53024 Montalcino (www.portacastellana.it; ✆**0578-839-001**), where the brick-vaulted storehouses of a former *palazzo* have been converted into three stylish rooms with plenty of exposed stone and well-chosen antiques. The garden, where breakfast is served in summer, has magical Val d'Orcia views. Doubles cost 85€ per night.

Dei Capitani ☺ The building probably once served the Sienese army as a refuge from the Florentines during their incessant wars, but these days it offers friendly service at a comfortable inn of modest refinement. The halls are carpeted, the staircase is travertine, and the rooms are mainly modern-rustic in style, with wood-beamed ceilings and terra-cotta floors. The four mini-apartments, with lofted master bedrooms and a pair of futon chairs in the living space, are

SAMPLING THE vino

Brunello di Montalcino exudes the smell of mossy, damp earth and musky berries. It tastes of dark, sweet fruits and dry vanilla. It's also the backbone of Montalcino's economy. As the deep ruby liquid mellows to garnet, the wine takes on its characteristic complex and slightly tannic aspect. Brunello is one of Italy's mightiest reds, a brawny wine that can tackle the rarest *bistecca alla fiorentina.* It's also the perfect accompaniment to game, pungent mushroom sauces, and aged cheeses.

Although Montalcino has produced wine for centuries, its flagship Brunello is a recent development, born out of late-19th-century sangiovese experiments to concentrate the grapes through strict cultivation methods. Most Brunellos are drinkable after about 4 to 5 years in the bottle, and the complex ones are best after 10 years or so (few last beyond 30 years). Bottles of 2001 are excellent. Avoid 2002, but Brunello bucked the Tuscan trend by producing good 2003s. Every vintage since 2004 is considered very good or better, with 2007, by many reviews, shaping up to be truly outstanding. Montalcino's **wine consortium** (✆ **0577-848-246;** www.consorziobrunellodimontalcino.it) is at Piazza Cavour 8, and staff members are happy to answer questions and provide information on *vini.*

In town, the best informal introduction to the deep-red liquid is some time spent at the **Enoteca La Fortezza** ★ (✆ **0577-849-211;** www.enotecalafortezza.it), inside the fortress. The stone-and-brick vaults are filled with excellent wines and grappa, as well as prosciutto, salami, pecorino cheese, and Montalcino's famous honey. The staff is adept at helping you and the wine get better acquainted, and glasses start at

4€. The Brunello generally starts at 7€. Plates of simple pasta dishes, *crostini,* or cold cuts and cheese to accompany a tasting cost around 8€. There's free shipping on mixed dozens of selected labels. The enoteca is open the same hours as the fortress (p. 306).

On the town's main square, the 19th-century cafe **Fiaschetteria Italiana,** Piazza del Popolo 6 (✆ **0577-849-043**), offers more imbibing pleasure, open Friday through Wednesday from 7:30am to midnight. A glass of wine ranges from 5€ to 12€.

If you prefer to go right to the source, many Brunello estates welcome visitors. **Poggio Antico** ★★ (✆ **0577-848-044;** www.poggioantico.com) is 4km (2½ miles) south of town along the Grosseto road (right-hand road at the fork). Its Brunellos, especially the *riserva,* are consistently voted among the top 100 wines in the world by oenological magazines—and this boutique winery often holds the number-one spot among Brunellos. Their sangiovese-cabernet "Supertuscan" Madre is elegant and velvety. *Cantina* visits are free but must be reserved at least a day in advance (more in summer). The direct-sales store is open daily to drop-ins from 10am to 5pm; you can also taste there. (Prices great for families. A drop-dead view of the Val d'Orcia and Val d'Arbia is visible from about half the rooms, the breakfast space, and the gravel-covered terrace with a tiny pool out back.

Via Lapini 6 (down the hill from Piazza Cavour), 53024 Montalcino (SI). www.deicapitani. it. ℂ **0577-847-227.** Fax 0577-847-239. 29 units. 100€–150€ double; 130€–180€ triple. Rates include breakfast. AE, DC, MC, V. Free parking. Closed Jan 8–Mar 10. **Amenities:** Bar; bikes;

range from 2€ for a Rosso di Montalcino to 22€ for all five of the estate's superlative wines.) Poggio Antico also has an excellent **restaurant** (p. 311).

Banfi (ℂ **0577-877-505;** www. castellobanfi.com) above Sant'Angelo Scalo, 10km (6¼ miles) south of Montalcino, is part of an American-owned exporting empire, an enormous ultramodern vineyard with a massive *cantine.* It's a little corporate, certainly, but there's no arguing with the outstanding quality of the wines: The *riserva* in particular is precisely balanced. Banfi also runs a small museum (4€ admission) on the history of glass and wine in its medieval castle. The huge enoteca (wine cellar) sells books, ceramics, packaged local foods, and all the Banfi wines. This is also where you go for tastings; a selection of three wines costs 15€. The enoteca and museum are open daily from 10am to 7pm (until 6pm Nov–Feb). Call ahead for an appointment (best at least a week in advance) to take a free, 1-hour guided tour of the cellars at 4pm Monday through Friday (3:30pm Nov–Feb). They also run eatery **La Taverna,** where you can pair Montalcinese cooking with multiple wine tastings (for example, three courses with three wines at 55€ per person). In 2005, the estate opened a group of 14 luxury units called **Il Borgo** ★ (ℂ **0577-877-700;** www.castellobanfiilborgo.com; 320€ double, 580€ suite), open March through October.

Fattoria dei Barbi ★ (ℂ **0577-841-111;** www.fattoriadeibarbi.it), 5km (3 miles) south of town on the road to Castelnuovo, makes a mean Brunello di Montalcino *riserva,* Vigna del Fiore. The *cantina* also sells Moscadello and vin santo and is open Monday through Friday from 10am to 1pm and 2:30 to 6pm, weekends from 2:30 to 6pm. The slightly refined **Taverna** (ℂ **0577-841-200**) serves good meat and pasta using their own farm products (olive oil, cheeses, and, of course, wine) at a middlin' price, open Thursday through Tuesday from 12:30 to 2:30pm and 7:30 to 9:30pm. *Cantina* tours cost 5€ per person and are given Monday through Friday at 10am, and 1, 3, and 4pm; booking is required. You can buy their delicious cheeses and salami from a separate on-site outlet weekdays from 8am to noon and 1 to 5pm (closed 4pm Fri).

Smaller wineries tend to offer a more personalized service, and also require booking in advance. Among our favorite Brunello producers happy to receive visitors is **Sesta di Sopra** (ℂ **0577-835-698;** www.sestadisopra. it), just west of Castelnuovo dell'Abate.

If you're merely looking for a decent wine to drink on the terrace at your *agriturismo,* you'll find a great selection in every price bracket at roadside bottle-shop **Bruno Dalmazio,** Via Traversa dei Monti 214 (ℂ **0577-849-019;** www.dalmazio.com). It's just outside the center beside the road to San Quirico.

Brunello vineyards outside Montalcino.

concierge; outdoor pool (May–Sept); room service. *In room:* A/C, TV, hair dryer, minibar, Wi-Fi (free).

Palazzina Cesira ★ Spacious rooms dressed with antique furniture, 17th-century frescoes on the walls, a prime location in the *centro storico,* and a warm welcome from knowledgeable hosts: This place has the essence of a Tuscan historic B&B distilled perfectly. (Plus you can order eggs for breakfast, cooked the way you like them.) Each unit is a good size, with firm beds and quality fittings, but it's well worth the 20€ to upgrade to the monster-sized "suites" overlooking the house's rear courtyard. Bookings are taken for 2 nights at a minimum, but if you turn up without a reservation and there's a free room, they will accommodate a single-night booking.

Via Soccorso Saloni 2, 53024 Montalcino (SI). ©/fax **0577-846-055.** www.montalcinoitaly. com. 5 units. 95€–120€ double; 115€–140€ suite. Rates include breakfast. No credit cards. Free street parking with permit. Usually closed mid-Jan to mid-Mar, but dates vary, so inquire. *In room:* A/C, TV, hair dryer, Wi-Fi (free).

Where to Eat

Pick up excellent pastries at **Mariuccia** ★, Piazza del Popolo 29 (©**0577-849-319**), where since 1935 they've turned out homemade *torrone, panforte* (including an unusual "white" version), Sienese cookies, and the formidable *cioccolatoni di Mariuccia* (giant chocolate truffles filled variously with cream, caramel, coffee, grappa, or walnut cream). The *baccio di Montalcino* is best described as a semi-frozen "death, burial, and several weeks of mourning" by chocolate. Central, cavelike **Re di Macchia,** Via Saloni 21 (©**0577-846-116**), serves a reliable introduction to typical Montalcinese cooking, which makes ample use of meat, especially wild boar. Primi cost 9€ and secondi 16€. Reservations are recommended (closed Tues).

Al Giullare ★ 🛉 MODERN TUSCAN This contemporary-styled bistro owned by the Padelletti winemaking family opened in 2009. The flavors are very much Montalcinese, but presentation keeps one eye on modern cooking trends. Handmade pastas and meats are the menu's strengths: Start with *gnocchi al Brunello* (with a rich butter and Brunello wine reduction) or the house special *la geometria di Giullare* (five different handmade ravioli), then follow it up with a mixed grill of rib, steak, and sausage all sourced from farms surrounding the family estate. There's a fine selection of vintages to choose from. If you just want to snack and sip, there are cheese and salami tasting plates in various combinations, and unobtrusive background music for added atmosphere.

Via Panfilo dell'Oca 11–13 (a block from the Fortezza). ℂ **0577-847-207.** Reservations recommended. Primi 7€–14€; secondi 9€–15€. MC, V. Daily 11am–midnight.

Il Pozzo 🍴 SOUTHERN TUSCAN This is the definition of so-called *cucina casalinga,* or "housewife cuisine," where Paola and her sisters serve up homemade *pinci* and *ribollita* in a simple and cozy atmosphere in a magical hilltop village. Although the ragù and porcini sauces are not particularly intricate, they are deeply satisfying. Locals flock here for the *fiorentina* steak or *coniglio con olive* (rabbit with olives), enjoyed with an honestly priced Brunello. If you're only interested in wine tasting, try the expertly run enoteca next door, **Enoteca Il Leccio** (ℂ **0577-843-016**).

Piazza Castello, Sant'Angelo in Colle (a hill town south of Montalcino). ℂ **0577-844-015.** Primi 7€–9€; secondi 7€–12€. MC, V. Wed–Mon 12:30–2pm and 7:30–9:30pm.

Ristorante di Poggio Antico ★★ TUSCAN The most refined dining around Montalcino is offered in these converted stalls surrounded by the vineyards of an award-winning wine estate. Bouquets of fresh wildflowers sit on each table, the staff is informative, and the tiny flavored rolls are freshly baked. The best deal is the *menù degustazione,* small samplings of the restaurant's specialties, including a ravioli stuffed with wild boar and a selection of desserts. The *parfait di fegatini in salsa di moscadello* (mousse of chicken livers prepared as foie gras in a sweet sauce of reduced Moscadello wine) is excellent, and the *ravioli alle erbette* (ricotta-and-herb ravioli in butter sauce with grated black truffles) are fine as well. For a second course, try the *piccione disossato con vin santo* (deboned pigeon with a sweet liqueur) or the *tagliata alle erbette* (thick short strips of prime beef).

Loc. i Poggi (south of town). ℂ **0577-849-200.** www.poggioantico.com. Reservations highly recommended. Primi 12€–15€; secondi 18€–22€; *menù degustazione* without wine 30€–60€. MC, V. Tues–Sun 12:30–2:30pm and 7:30–9:30pm (closed Sun evening Nov–Mar). Closed Jan 8–Feb 4. Follow Grosseto road 3.6km (2¼ miles) south of Montalcino to signposted turnoff on right.

The Val d'Orcia

The Via Cassia SS2 meets the SS146 toward Pienza at **San Quirico d'Orcia** ★; the town's tourist office is inside the Palazzo Chigi, Via Dante Alighieri, 53027 San Quirico d'Orcia (ℂ **0577-897-211**), open April through October Thursday to Tuesday from 10am to 1pm and 3:30 to 6:30pm This market town with its 12th-century Romanesque **Collegiata** ★ makes a good half-hour diversion. The honey-colored, travertine church has three elaborate medieval portals. The front entrance is the oldest and most intricate, a Lombard-style affair with animal heads as capitals, a receding stack of carved arches, friezes of dueling fantasy animals, and columns made of four slender poles knotted in the middle. To the right side is the second portal, perhaps by Giovanni Pisano, with telamon columns posing atop lions' backs. Another kneeling telamon supports a nearby window arch. The smaller, final portal dates to 1298. Inside is a Sano di Pietro polyptych and a set of 15th-century intarsia choir stalls by Antonio Barili that were originally set up in a chapel of Siena's Duomo. Down the block in the main square, Piazza della Libertà, is the entrance to the (alas, slightly neglected) **Horti Leonini,** a Renaissance Italianate garden (1580) with geometric box-hedge designs and shady holm oaks, originally a resting spot for holy pilgrims on the Francigena road from Canterbury to Rome. It's open daily from sunrise to sunset. For a taste of 21st-century Tuscany, stop in at **Birrificio San Quirico** ★, Via Dante Alighieri

Val d'Orcia.

The Collegiata in San Quirico.

93a (© **0577-898-193;** www.birrificiosanquirico.it). Tuscany's artisan brewing industry is flourishing, and this little place is among the best. They create unfiltered blonde and amber beers. A tasting is free; bottles cost 10€ to 12€.

Five kilometers (3 miles) south signposted off the SS2 is **Bagno Vignoni ★**, little more than a group of houses surrounding one of the most memorable *piazze* in Tuscany. The Medici harnessed the naturally hot sulfur springs percolating from the ground by building a giant outdoor pool that fills the spot where the main square ought to be; it's lined with stone walls and finished with a pretty loggia at one end. Even St. Catherine of Siena, when not performing religious and bureaucratic miracles, relaxed here with a sulfur cure. To see the springs in their more natural state, take the second turnoff on the curving road into town and pull over when you see the tiny sulfurous mountain on your right. The waters bubble out here in dozens of tiny rivulets, gathering in a pool at the bottom, and there's a fairy-tale view, especially on misty days, of the **Rocca d'Orcia.** From the 11th to the 14th century, the castle was a stronghold and strategic watchtower of the Aldobrandeschi clan, formidable toll collectors along the Francigena pilgrim road through these parts.

Eighteen kilometers (11 miles) farther down the SS2, in a landscape dotted with dramatically eroded swathes of *Crete,* **Radicofani** glowers from atop its basalt outcropping. The remains of the town's **Fortezza** (© **339-743-7394;** www.radicofani-heritagecentre.com) stand high above a medieval warren of steep streets and houses in stony gray basalt; all were seriously damaged by earthquakes in the 18th century. The castle, built by Hadrian IV—the only English pope—is most famous as the base of operations of the "gentle outlaw" Ghino di Tacco, immortalized by both Dante in his *Inferno* (*Purgatorio,* Canto VI) and Boccaccio in the *Decameron* (day 10, tale 2). Ghino was something of a Robin Hood figure, robbing from the rich to give to the poor—and taking a hefty share himself. It's open April through September daily from 9am to 7pm, weekends only during daylight hours otherwise. Admission is 4€ for adults, 3€ for children 3 to 16 or those 65 and over.

There are some **della Robbia terra cottas** in Radicofani's churches of San Pietro and Sant'Agata, and the views from Radicofani of the surrounding rugged farmscape can be especially evocative when there's a morning mist melting shadows into soft relief. The locals call the region the Mare di Sassi ("Seas of Stones")—an assessment with which Dickens, Montaigne, and other grand tourists heartily agreed. Those intrepid early travelers stayed at **La Posta,** a hotel converted from Grand Duke Ferdinando I's hunting lodge along the road south out of town down to the Via Cassia. The 1584 structure was designed by Buontalenti, but these days it sadly crumbles by the roadside across from a 1603 **Medici fountain.**

PIENZA ★

24km (15 miles) E of Montalcino; 55km (34 miles) SE of Siena; 125km (78 miles) S of Florence; 177km (110 miles) NW of Rome

Surveying the rolling farmland of Tuscany's Val d'Orcia, from a little natural balcony, the village of Pienza sits as a testament to one man's ambition and ego. At the height of the 15th-century Renaissance, humanist Sienese Pope Pius II, with the help of Florentine architect Bernardo Rossellino, converted the tiny village in which he had been born into a vision of the ideal Renaissance city. The "city" began and ended with the new central square and its buildings—the plan to cover the surrounding area with a grid of streets never materialized. The village of Pienza, however, retains its remarkable city-size piazza, one of the grandest achievements of Renaissance architecture and the only intact example of a city-planning scheme from the era. Director Franco Zeffirelli was so taken by the village's look that he dethroned Verona as the city of the Montagues and Capulets and filmed his *Romeo and Juliet* in Pienza. Pienza was also used in the Oscar-winning epic, *The English Patient.*

But for all Pius's dreams, Pienza never became more than a village. Today, its 2,500 inhabitants put up with the stream of day-trippers with good humor, lots of craft stands, and a surfeit of food stores. The main drag, **Corso Rossellino,** goes in one end of town and out the other in less than 4 minutes at a stroll. There are a handful of narrow side streets within Pienza's proud little walls, and modest new developments surround the burg on three sides (the fourth, southern side is saved for a memorable Val d'Orcia **view ★★★**). Pienza will take no more than half a day in your schedule, time enough to admire the palaces, Sienese art collection, and Duomo at the town's perfect core; nibble on the famous sheep's milk cheeses and honey; and take a short walk to the odd, isolated medieval churches in the countryside outside the walls. Its environs also make a good base for discovering most of the places in this chapter.

Essentials

GETTING THERE By Car: Pienza is on the SS146 between San Quirico d'Orcia and Montepulciano. From Montalcino, take the road toward Torrenieri and the SS2; take the SS2 south 7km (4⅓ miles) to San Quirico d'Orcia, where the SS146 runs east for 10km (6¼ miles) to Pienza. From Siena, take the SS2 south to the SS146 (or the slower, but more dramatic SS438 south through Asciano and via Monte Oliveto Maggiore). You can park along the streets surrounding the walls.

By Bus: TRA-IN buses (© 0577-204-111; www.trainspa.it) run from **Siena** (six daily; 1¼ hr.) and **Montepulciano** (10 daily; 20 min.) In Pienza, buy tickets at the corner bar in Piazza Dante.

VISITOR INFORMATION The **tourist office** is inside the Palazzo Vescovile on Piazza Pio II, Corso Rossellino 30, 53026 Pienza (© 0578-749-905; www.

comunedipienza.it). Between mid-March and October, it's open Wednesday through Monday 10am to 1pm and 3 to 6pm; through the rest of the year, it's weekends only. You can also find more about the city online at **www.pienza.info**.

FESTIVALS & MARKETS On the first weekend in September, Pienza celebrates its peerless pecorino sheep's milk cheese in the **Fiera di Cacio** with a low-key medieval festival. **Market** day is Friday.

Exploring Pienza

When local boy Enea Silvio Piccolomini was elevated from cardinal to Pope Pius II in 1458, he decided to play God with his hometown of Corsignano and rebuild the village based on High Renaissance ideals. The man he hired for the job was Bernardo Rossellino, a protégé of Florentine architect Leon Battista Alberti. Rossellino leveled the old center and built in its place **Piazza Pio II ★★**, a three-dimensional realization of the "Ideal City" ideas drawn up by such artists as Piero della Francesca.

The square is flanked by the cathedral and three palaces: one for the government, one for the bishop, and one (of course) for Pius II. The pope liked the result so much he felt the village needed a new name for its new look, and he modestly decided to rename it after himself: Pienza ("Pio's Town"). As with modern big productions, Rossellino's civic face-lift came in both late and way over budget. (He fudged the account books so Pius wouldn't realize how deep the architect was dipping into the papal purse for funding.) Pius, aware of the duplicity but still immensely pleased with his new burg, reportedly reduced Rossellino to tears by saying, "You did well, Bernardo, in lying to us about the expense. . . . Your deceit has built these glorious structures, which are praised by all except the few consumed with envy." When the pope went on tour to try to drum up support for a Crusade to the Holy Land, he left a papal bull that said, in refined Latin, "Don't touch anything until I get back." He died in the same year as Rossellino, 1464, trying to raise his army in Ancona, and Pienza dutifully kept the cathedral and palaces exactly as Pius II left them in the 15th century—the only Renaissance town center in Italy to survive the centuries perfectly intact.

Pius II liked the Austrian churches he'd seen in his travels, so he had Rossellino grace one side of the piazza with a syncretic **Duomo ★★** whose

A farm outside Pienza.

Renaissance facade hides a Gothic interior. The gigantic coat of arms gloating above the rose window is that of Pius II's Piccolomini family. Not above letting everyone know who was financing all this, Pius II had the family *cinque lune* (five moons) device repeated more than 400 times throughout the church. The apse is set right on the cliff's edge so that sunlight can stream through its tall Gothic windows unencumbered by surrounding buildings, making this the best-lit church in Tuscany. Alas, the site has proved none too stable, and dangerous cracks have appeared in the fabric; you'll notice the slope as you walk toward the apse. With no good way yet found to shore up the structure, the altar end of the church threatens to slide down the slope without warning.

Unusually for Tuscany, the **five altarpieces** painted specifically for the cathedral by Sienese masters (1460–62) are still in situ; they make a good study of how the mid-15th-century artists worked a theme: Four of the five paintings are *Madonna and Child with Saints* (the other is an *Assumption*). First, on your right, is Giovanni di Paolo's take, where angels cluster around Mary to coo at the baby. A young Matteo di Giovanni rendered the scene next, his Mary accompanied by Saints Catherine of Siena, Matthew, Bartholomew, and Lucy (the last carrying an awful lot of her martyrs' eyeballs on a plate). The following chapel has a marble **tabernacle** by Bernardo Rossellino (there's a bit of St. Andrew's head inside), and after the choir stalls comes Vecchietta's *Assumption,* in which it takes quite a number of angels to boost Mary up to Heaven. The final two are by Sano di

Pienza's Piazza Pio II.

Pietro and a later altarpiece by Matteo di Giovanni. The Duomo is open daily 7am to 1pm and 2:30 to 7pm. Admission is free.

Opposite the Duomo, you'll see the travertine portico of the **Palazzo Comunale,** also by Rossellino and another odd hybrid—this time Renaissance architecture masquerading as a medieval Tuscan town hall. To your right is the **Palazzo Vescovile,** built by Cardinal Rodrigo Borgia, who later became Pope Alexander VI. It's the home of both the tourist office and the **Museo Diocesano** (© 0578-749-905), entered at Corso Rossellino 30, which collects treasures of Sienese art from the churches of Pienza and small towns in the area. One of its most important works is the early-14th-century Cape of Pius II, a silk papal garment embroidered with gold, saintly portraits, and colorful scenes from the Life of the Virgin. The 14th-century school of Bartolo di Fredi produced a portable triptych that reads like a comic strip, and the master himself is responsible for the *Madonna della Misericordia* (1364), in which Mary protects a kaleidoscope of tiny saints under her shawl. Il Vecchietta's altarpiece of the *Madonna and Child with Saints, Annunciation* lunette, and predella show off the peculiar grace and intent perspective of his flowing lines. From March 15 to October 31, the museum is open Wednesday through Monday from 10am to 1pm and 3 to 6pm; November through mid-March, it's open weekends only from 10am to 1pm and 3 to 5pm. Admission is 4.10€ adults and 2.60€ ages 8 to 13 and 65 and over.

Across the piazza, past Rossellino's Renaissance well, is the architect's finest palace (and Pius II's Pienza digs). The **Palazzo Piccolomini ★★** (© 0578-748-503; www.palazzopiccolominipienza.it) was inspired by Alberti's Palazzo Rucellai in Florence, but Rossellino added an Italianate hanging garden out the left side of the inner courtyard. Pius particularly liked his small patch of box hedges backed by a triple-decker loggia. It's perched on the edge of Pienza's tiny bluff and offers postcard views across the rolling cultivated hills of the wide Val d'Orcia to Monte Amiata. Half-hourly tours take you through the pope's private apartments and out on the loggia to see the gardens Tuesday through Sunday from 10am to 6pm (4pm Oct 16–Mar 14). Admission is 7€ adults and 5€ students. Members of the

Piccolomini family lived here until the 1960s but kept the Renaissance look in the pope's bedroom, the library, and a heavily armed great hall. The palace is closed the last 2 weeks in November and January 7 through February 14.

Shopping for Wine, Crafts & Cheese

Even though it's tinier than neighboring towns, Pienza has about the same number of wine shops. The main difference is that these stores aren't tied to a single estate or producer (in Montalcino and Montepulciano, most *enoteche* are thinly disguised branches of local vineyards). Here you can often get a more well-rounded tasting experience, plus less biased advice. It's not a place to pick up an everyday bottle, but **L'Enoteca di Ghino ★**, Via del Leone 16 (© **0578-748-057;** www.enotecadighino.it), has the best high-end range of bottles for miles around—including a couple of boutique labels from the emerging wine area around Chiusi.

Any food store in town usually doubles as an outlet for other regional specialties, including the king of all sheep cheeses, Pienza's own **pecorino ★** (or *cacio*). You can get it *fresco* (fresh), *semistagionato* (partially aged), or *stagionato* (aged and suitable for grating, though it really needs a few extra months for that). Many *pecorini* are also dusted with ground materials to keep them soft and alter the taste slightly. Most popular are *cenerato* or *sottocenere* (an ash coating that's mainly a softening technique), *peperocinato* (hot peppers), and *tartufato* (truffles). A few producers even mix ingredients directly into the cheese (*tartufi* are a favorite), but others claim this mars the purity of the pecorino. Luckily, you can judge for yourself, as pecorino tasting is even more popular here than wine tasting. Two of the best places are **La Bottega del Cacio,** Corso Rossellino 66 (© **0578-748-713**), and tiny **La Bottega del Naturista,** Corso Rossellino 16 (© **0578-748-760**).

On Corso Rossellino, you'll find ceramics stores and the showroom for **Biagiotti** (© **0578-748-666**), a family of artisans at no. 69 who specialize in *ferro battuto* (cast iron). Its workshop and foundry is on SS146 on the way to Montepulciano. **Calzoleria Pientina,** down a side street at Via Gozzante 22 (© **0578-749-040** or 0578-748-195), handcrafts leather shoes to measure as well as bags and purses. Right opposite, at the **Bottega Linda Bai,** Via Gozzante 33 (© **0578-749-507;** www.ceramiche bai.it), ceramics are painted in the workshop and displayed for sale inside an atmospheric 11th-century cave.

Where to Stay

Giardino Segreto, Via Condotti 13, 53026 Pienza (www.ilgiardinosegre-topienza.it; © **0578-748-539**) rents simple, central **rooms and mini-apartments** around a peaceful herb garden, all with bathrooms, TVs, and Wi-Fi (but no phones), for 55€ to 70€ for a double or 105€ to 125€ for a unit sleeping four. It's closed for a month from mid-January to mid-February. Also in the center, **Città Ideale**

The interior of Pienza's Duomo.

Suites, Piazza San Carlo Borromeo 4 (www.cittaidealesuites.com; ✆ **366-931-1051**), has three elegant, well equipped B&B suites. Prices range from 120€ to 160€ per night.

Castello di Ripa d'Orcia ★ This oasis of tranquility in the countryside occupies an early medieval castle mentioned as far back as 1218. The Piccolomini family—who've owned it since 1484—transformed several of the buildings into a hotel in 1990. The fairy-tale views sweep across forested hillsides (protected as a nature preserve) capped with other medieval castles, and the 10-minute dirt road that winds its way out here only enhances the feeling of solitude and quiet. In fact, they emphasize relaxation: The rooms, which require at least a 2-night stay, have phones but no TVs or other worldly temptations. The rooms are enormous country affairs, with antique furnishings and very comfy beds surrounded by thick stone walls and heavily beamed ceilings. There's a reading room with a fireplace and chessboard in the former granary, a quite good restaurant below the rooms (closed Mon), and they have installed an enoteca in the old *cantina*.

Loc. Ripa d'Orcia (signposted from San Quirico), 53023 San Quirico d'Orcia (SI). www.castello ripadorcia.com. ✆ **0577-897-376.** Fax 0577-898-038. 14 units (6 rooms, 8 apts. sleeping 2–4). 110€–150€ double (2-night minimum); 110€–155€ apt for 2 (3-night minimum); 175€–190€ apt for 4 (4-night minimum). Rates for rooms (not apts) include breakfast. MC, V. Free parking. Closed Nov to mid-Mar. **Amenities:** Restaurant (closed Mon, dinner only); bikes; outdoor pool. *In room:* Hair dryer, kitchenette (in apts), minibar.

Hotelito Lupaia ★★ 🏚 The ultimate in quirky, boho luxury and romantic rural seclusion, these eight rooms built imaginatively into a traditional farm complex amid magical countryside combine the best of the B&B, hotel, and *agriturismo* ethos. Intimacy complements authenticity in the eclectic, midsize hippie-chic meets country-manor styled rooms, which make full use of original architectural details, soothing colors, and natural fabrics. Although none is huge, standard rooms have space for a third bed, and all units except the Blue Suite have a terrace or mini-garden. Lunch and dinner (38€ fixed-price menu) are served in summer.

Loc. Lupaia 74, 53049 Torrita di Siena (SI). www.lupaia.com. ✆ **0578-668-028.** 8 units. 270€ standard double; 320€ deluxe double; 360€ suite. Rates include breakfast. Free parking. AE, MC, V. Closed Nov–Mar. Follow SS146 6km (3½ miles) northeast from Pienza, then turn north toward Torrita di Siena; hotel signposted from road shortly after turnoff. **Amenities:** Restaurant; bar; bikes (free); concierge; outdoor pool; Internet (free). *In room:* A/C, TV, hair dryer, minibar (free).

Il Chiostro di Pienza ★ Even though this hotel in a 15th-century Franciscan convent faces no real competition within Pienza's walls, the staff still strives to maintain a high level of comfort with a keen attention to detail. The interior atmosphere—frescoes on a few walls, the enlarging of old monks' cells to make larger rooms—owes much to the building's 19th-century incarnation as a seminary, but most of the rooms feature modern touches like glass-topped tables and bright fabrics. A few rooms have a more antique charm, with simple peasant-style furniture made of old wood. The garden outside the breakfast room/restaurant (which offers refined Tuscan food) has sweeping views of the Val d'Orcia and breakfast and bar service in summer.

Corso Rossellino 26, 53026 Pienza (SI). www.relaisilchiostrodipienza.com. ✆ **0578-748-400.** Fax 0578-748-440. 37 units. 70€–250€ double; 150€–500€ suite. Rates include breakfast. AE, DC, MC, V. Open weekends only Jan to mid-Mar. **Amenities:** Restaurant; bar; babysitting; bikes; concierge; outdoor pool; room service; Wi-Fi (free). *In room:* A/C, TV, hair dryer, minibar.

Where to Eat

La Botte Piena ★★ 🏨 SOUTHERN TUSCAN Upstairs under the eaves of this village osteria-cum-enoteca, browsing a leather-bound wine list that's as hefty as a Bible, is our little piece of Tuscan heaven. Cooking is "refined rustic," and the atmosphere intimate without being intimidating. Dishes have the Val d'Orcia drizzled all over them: the pasta is *pici*, the cheese pecorino, and the salami made only from Cinta Senese pigs or boar, species native to these hills. A simple pairing such as *salsiccia grigliata* (grilled pork sausage) with *radicchio* (bitter endive) takes on new dimensions with quality ingredients like these. The menu caters as equally to weekend lunchtime *bruschetta* snackers as to romantic diners.

Piazza Cinughi 12, Montefollonico (signposted off SP15 10km/6 miles NE of Pienza). ⓒ **0578-669-481.** www.labottepiena.com. Reservations highly recommended. Primi 7€–9€; secondi 9€–14€. AE, MC, V. Thurs–Tues 7:30–10pm; Sat–Sun also 12:30–2pm. Closed sporadically, so call ahead.

Latte di Luna ★ ☺ SOUTHERN TUSCAN This easygoing trattoria in central Pienza has captured a following of everyone from art students to local *carabinieri*. To enter, thread through the wedge of outdoor tables and past the cage of Willy, a merlin who squawks *"Ciao"* and *"Come stai?"* at each passerby. Inside, brick and yellow stucco are the backdrop for your *pici all'aglione* (with spicy tomato-and-garlic sauce) or *zuppa di pane* (a local variant on *ribollita*, with more cabbage and no extra day of cooking). You can follow this up with *vitello girello* (thin slices of veal, with or without mushrooms) or the specialty, *maialino arrosto* (roast suckling pig). For dessert, the restaurant makes its own *semifreddi* flavored with seasonal ingredients.

Via San Carlo 2–4 (at Porta al Ciglio end of Corso Rossellino). ⓒ **0578-748-606.** Reservations recommended. Primi 6€–9€; secondi 7€–16€. MC, V. Wed–Mon 12:15–2:15pm and 7:15–9:15pm. Closed Feb–Mar 15 and July.

La Porta ★ SOUTHERN TUSCAN Service tends to the "relaxed," but the food's worth waiting for at this remote borgo *osteria* long recommended by savvy guidebooks. Classic southern Tuscan primi include *gnocchi al cacio e pepe* (with local pecorino and black pepper) and *pici all'anatra* (hand-rolled pasta strands with goose ragù). Ingredients in such secondi as *tagliata di manzo al Vino Nobile* (Valdichiana beef in Vino Nobile wine) and *faraona al vinsanto con patate arrosto* (guinea hen in sweet wine sauce with roast potato) are as traditional and local as they come, but the combinations and presentation show modern influences. You'll have to book ahead to secure one of just six tables on the stunning terrace-with-view. (**Note:** Smoking is allowed on outdoor terraces, even in restaurants.)

Via del Piano 1, Monticchiello (6km/3½ miles SE of Pienza on *strada bianca;* inquire for directions). ⓒ/fax **0578-755-163.** www.osterialaporta.it. Reservations recommended. Primi 10€–13€; secondi 12€–20€. MC, V. Fri–Wed 9am–midnight. Closed Jan 10–Feb 5 and 1 week in June–July.

MONTEPULCIANO ★★

13km (8 miles) E of Pienza; 67km (41 miles) SE of Siena; 124km (77 miles) SE of Florence; 186km (116 miles) N of Rome

The biggest and highest of southern Tuscany's hill towns, steeply graded Montepulciano, with its medieval alleyways and plethora of Renaissance palaces and churches, has just enough city feel and tourist infrastructure to make it perhaps the best base for visiting the region. The fields around the town produce a violet-scented, orange-speckled ruby wine called **Vino Nobile di Montepulciano.** This area has been known since at least the 8th century for its superior wine, and in the 17th century, when Francesco Redi wrote his *vino*-praising poem, *Bacchus in Tuscany,* he described the Noble Wine of Montepulciano as "the king of all wines." Vino Nobile is known as Tuscany's number-two red because it's slightly less beefy than Montalcino's Brunello. But for our money, its high quality and mellow character make it a better all-around wine, good to age and save for special occasions but also to toss back on a picnic.

The locals call themselves Poliziani after the Roman name for the town, and Poliziano is also the name that the local classical scholar/humanist Angelo Ambrogini took when he went to Florence to hold discourses with Lorenzo de' Medici, tutor Lorenzo's sons, and write some of the most finely crafted Renaissance poetry of the era—some say his *Stanze per la Giostra* inspired Botticelli's mythological paintings, such as the *Birth of Venus* and *Allegory of Spring.*

Essentials

GETTING THERE   By Train: From Florence, take one of the 30 daily trains on the main **Rome-Florence** line, alighting at Chiusi–Chianciano Terme station (80 min.–2¼ hr. from Florence). From Siena, the bus is more convenient (see below); however several daily trains ply a secondary **Siena-Chiusi** line (1¼ hr.). Alternatively, get off at the stop called Montepulciano Stazione; it's about as far from Montepulciano as the Chiusi stop. Buses to Montepulciano itself from either are coordinated with the trains' arrival.

By Car: From Siena, the quickest, most scenic route is south on the SS2 to San Quirico d'Orcia, where you get the SS146 eastbound through Pienza to Montepulciano. From Florence, take the A1 south to the Chianciano Terme exit, and then take SS146 (direction Chianciano) for 18km (11 miles). As in most Tuscan hill towns, you will need to park at one of the public lots outside the historic center. The handiest is the small lot just below Porta al Prato, although you'll need to arrive early to secure a space in that one.

By Bus: Six **TRA-IN** buses (*©* **0577-204-111;** www.trainspa.it) run daily from Siena (1½ hr.), most coming through Pienza (20 min.) en route. **LFI** (*©* **0578-31-174**) buses run approximately hourly from Chiusi (1 hr.) through Chianciano Terme (25 min.), and three times daily (none on Sun) from Florence to Bettolle, where you transfer for the bus to Montepulciano (2¼ hr. total). In Montepulciano, buy **bus tickets** at the tourist office (see below).

VISITOR INFORMATION   Montepulciano's pro-loco **tourist office** is in the little parking lot just below Porta al Prato (*©* **0578-757-341;** www.proloco montepulciano.it). It's open daily from 9:30am to 12:30pm and 3 to 6pm (until 8pm in summer); it's closed Sunday afternoons, but not for *riposo* in August.

FESTIVALS & MARKETS   Poliziani in general are still adept wordsmiths and poets. The tradition of popular theater, which had its roots in extemporaneous performances on threshing-room floors, is carried on by a company of locals who write lyric plays on themes of religion, local legends, and chivalric romances. During the annual **Bruscello,** the townspeople perform their homespun musicals out on the *piazze* on the days running up to August 15 (Assumption Day, or *ferragosto*).

Poliziani also used to gallop horses pell-mell through the streets in an annual palio, but for safety reasons this has been reduced in modern times to the **Bravio delle Botti ★★**. In this only slightly less perilous race, the locals don 14th-century costumes as teams from the traditional *contrade* (neighborhoods) roll barrels weighing more than 79 kilograms (175 lb.) toward the finish line. (Oh, yeah: It's uphill.) To witness the hernias and join in the pageantry before the race and the feast after, drop by town on the last Sunday in August.

Montepulciano's **market** day is Thursday.

Exploring Montepulciano

Outside the city walls below Porta al Prato squats the church of **Sant' Agnese,** with a striped 1935 facade surrounding a 14th-century portal. Inside, the first chapel on the right (hit the free light switch) has a frescoed *Madonna* by Simone Martini. Ring at the door to the right of the altar for access to the pretty cloister. Die-hards can make the 1.6km (1-mile) trek down Viale Calamandrei to **Santa Maria delle Grazie,** with *Mary of the Graces* and *Annunciation* figures by Giovanni della Robbia on the second altar and a rare late-16th-century organ with cypress wood pipes to which musicians from all over the world travel to play.

You'll see architecture by Antonio Sangallo the Elder before you even get inside the walls. **Porta al Prato** was reconstructed in the 1500s on his designs, and the Medici balls above the gate hint at Montepulciano's long association with Florence. One block up Via Gracciano nel Corso, a Florentine Marzocco lion reigns from atop a **column.** (It's a copy of a 1511 original, now in the town museum.) To the right (no. 91) is the massive **Palazzo Avignonesi,** with grinning lions' heads, and across the street is the **Palazzo Tarugi** (no. 82). Both are by Vignola, the late Renaissance architect who designed Rome's Villa Giulia. A bit higher up on the left is the **Palazzo Cocconi** (no. 70) by Sangallo; the top floor looks out of place because it was added in the 1890s. In lieu of an Etruscan museum, Montepulciano has the **Palazzo Bucelli** (no. 73), the sort of place that makes archaeologists grimace—the lower level of the facade is embedded with a patchwork of Etruscan reliefs and funerary urns. Most probably came from the Chiusi area, and they represent the collection of 18th-century antiquarian scholar and former resident Pietro Bucelli.

Next on the right is **Sant'Agostino ★**, with a facade by Michelozzo in a style mixing late Gothic with early Renaissance. The first altar on the right has a *Resurrection of Lazarus* by Alessandro Allori. Over the high altar is a wooden crucifix by Donatello, and,

Bags for sale in Montepulciano.

behind it, the entrance to the choir of an older church on this spot, with frescoes and an Antonio del Pollaiolo crucifix. On the right as you leave is a painted *Crucifixion* by Leonardo da Vinci's protégé Lorenzo di Credi. On Piazza Michelozzo in front of the church stands the **Torre di Pulcinella,** a short clock tower capped with a life-size Pulcinella, the black-and-white clown from Naples, who strikes the hours. It was left by a philandering Neapolitan bish-op who was exiled here for his dalliances. At the next corner on the left is the **Palazzo Burati-Bellarmino** (no. 28), where the door is kept open so you can admire the Federico Zuccari frescoes on the ceiling inside.

Take the Bus

Montepulciano's Corso is *very steep indeed.* If you are unfit, or suffer from health problems, **take the bus.** Little orange *pollicini* connect the junction just below the Porta al Prato and Piazza Grande in about 8 minutes. The official point of origin is "the fifth tree on the right above the junction." Tickets cost 1€ each way for all passengers above 1m (3¼ ft.) tall. Buses run every 20 minutes.

The road now rises steeply to Piazza delle Erbe and the **Logge del Grano,** a *palazzo* designed in the 15th century by Vignola with an arcaded porch and the Medici balls prominent above the entrance. The main road (it takes a left here) now becomes Via di Voltaia nel Corso, passing **Il Capriccio,** at no. 14 (📞 **0578-717-006**), the town's best gelato vendor, then the grandiose **Palazzo Cervini** (no. 21) on the left, probably designed by Antonio Sangallo the Younger (Sangallo the Elder's nephew) for Cardinal Marcello Cervini just before he was elevated to the papacy. One of the shortest-lived pontiffs, Pope Marcellus II died 21 days into office. Climbing farther, you'll pass the 19th-century **Caffè Poliziano ★,** which serves snacks and pastries in elegant, Liberty surrounds. Next comes the rough facade of the baroque **Chiesa del Gesù** (the little *trompe l'oeil* cupola on the dome inside is courtesy of Andrea Pozzo) and, much farther on—the street's name is now Via del Poliziano—the **house where Poliziano was born** stands at no. 5. A scholar, writer, and philosopher, Angelo Ambrogini (called Poliziano after the Latin name of his hometown) had an enormous impact on the Florentine humanist movement as a friend of Lorenzo de' Medici and tutor to his children. Just before his house, Via delle Farine leads left to **Porta delle Farine,** an excellent and intact example of a 13th-century Sienese double gate.

The main road now passes out of the city walls, wrapping around the **Medici fortress** (now private) and passing the seldom-open **Santa Maria dei Servi,** with another late-17th-century interior by Andrea Pozzo and a *Madonna and Child* by the Duccio school (inserted into another panel in the third altar on the left).

Back inside the walls, you come to Montepulciano's historic and civic heart, **Piazza Grande.** On the left is the **Palazzo Comunale ★,** designed by Michelozzo as a late-14th-century homage in travertine to Florence's Palazzo Vecchio. (Teens may recognize it from the 2009 vampire movie *Twilight: New Moon*—filmed here, despite being set in Volterra.) Daily from 10am to 6pm, you can wander through civic offices to climb the tower for a great view of the surrounding countryside. (It's 2€ to climb, free for children 12 and under; watch your head.) Back on terra firma, to your left is the **Palazzo Nobili-Tarugi,** with an arcaded loggia on the corner facing a **well** topped by the Medici arms flanked by two Florentine lions and two Poliziani griffins. Both the palace and well are

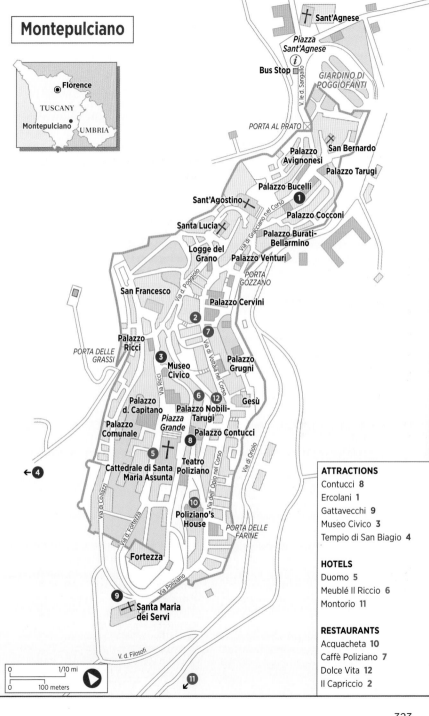

Montepulciano

TUSCANY
Florence
Montepulciano
UMBRIA

Sant'Agnese
Piazza Sant'Agnese
Bus Stop
V. le d. Sangallo
GIARDINO DI POGGIOFANTI

PORTA AL PRATO

San Bernardo
Palazzo Avignonesi
Palazzo Tarugi
Palazzo Bucelli ❶

Sant'Agostino
Via di Gracciano nel Corso
Palazzo Cocconi

Santa Lucia
Palazzo Burati-Bellarmino

Logge del Grano
Palazzo Venturi
PORTA GOZZANO

Via d. Poggiolo
San Francesco
Palazzo Cervini ❷
❼
Palazzo Ricci
PORTA DELLE GRASSI
❸
Museo Civico
Via di Voltaia nel Corso
Palazzo Grugni
Via Ricci
❻ ⓬
Palazzo d. Capitano
Piazza Grande
Palazzo Nobili-Tarugi
Gesù
Palazzo Comunale
Palazzo Contucci ❽
Via di Oriolo
❺
Cattedrale di Santa Maria Assunta
Teatro Poliziano
Via dell'Opio nel Corso

⓾
Poliziano's House
PORTA DELLE FARINE
Via di Collazzi
Via d. Fortezza

Fortezza
❹

❾
Santa Maria dei Servi
Via Poliziano

V. d. Filosofi

0   1/10 mi
0   100 meters

❶❶

ATTRACTIONS
Contucci **8**
Ercolani **1**
Gattavecchi **9**
Museo Civico **3**
Tempio di San Biagio **4**

HOTELS
Duomo **5**
Meublé Il Riccio **6**
Montorio **11**

RESTAURANTS
Acquacheta **10**
Caffè Poliziano **7**
Dolce Vita **12**
Il Capriccio **2**

the design of Antonio Sangallo the Elder, as is the **Palazzo Contucci** across from the Palazzo Comunale.

The last side of Piazza Grande is taken up by the rambling brick nonfacade of the 17th-century **Cattedrale di Santa Maria Assunta ★**, a somewhat embarrassing reminder to Poliziani that, after building so many palaces and fitting so many of them with travertine, the city ran out of money to finish the ambitious plans for rebuilding the cathedral and had to leave it faceless. To the left of the church, the suspiciously 1950s-looking bell tower is actually the oldest thing on the piazza, dating from the 14th century and the cathedral of Santa Maria that once stood here. Inside, the Duomo makes up for its plain facade with two important works. The first takes some explaining because it's scattered in pieces around

underground **TUNNELS & NOBLE WINE**

The local wine consortium, the **Consorzio del Vino Nobile di Montepulciano** (www.consorziovinonobile.it), has a **showroom and tasting center** in the basement of the Palazzo del Capitano on Piazza Grande where you can sample the wares of every member (which means most Vino Nobile vineyards) Monday through Friday from 10am to 1pm and 3 to 6pm, Saturday from 10am to 3pm. In the same building, the **Strada del Vino Nobile** office (✆ **0578-717-484**; www.stradavinonobile.it) can arrange wine tours in the vineyards, most of which lie to the northeast of the town. Hours for both can be erratic—especially out of season, when you may be lucky to find either open at all.

Montepulciano has more *enoteche* and *cantine* (wine cellars) than you can shake a wine bottle at, most offering the chance to sample local products: pecorino cheese, salami, honey, olive oil, and, of course, Vino Nobile di Montepulciano. Many shops also let you descend into their *cantine*, often a linked maze of basements, underground tunnels that once connected the palaces, and older grottoes carved into the tufa of the mountain. Calling the grottoes "Etruscan tombs," as the signs in the stores proclaim, may not be far from the truth—the earliest foundations of a city on this site are still contested.

The *cantine* with the most attention-grabbing tunnels include **Ercolani,** Via Gracciano nel Corso 82 (✆ **0578-716-764**; www.pulcino.com), which boasts a *città sotteranea* (or "underground city") in its lengthy cellars, featuring a "medieval torture room," an Etruscan tomb, and a collec-

tion of iron implements found here—medieval weapons, household tools, and even a chastity belt. The **Gattavecchi ★** *cantine,* Via di Collazzi 74 (✆ **0578-757-110;** www.gattavecchi.it), burrow under Santa Maria dei Servi (see below), with moldy tunnels and a staircase leading down to an even moldier chapel-like structure carved out of the rock—no one knows when it dates from or what it was, but it's intriguingly and suggestively located directly below the altar end of the church. Bottles such as their Riserva dei Padri Serviti and 100% sangiovese Parceto have been well received worldwide. Tasting is free, and a few euros gets you a tasting plate of meats and cheeses to accompany the superlative wine. At Piazza Grande, the **Contucci** winery (✆ **0578-757-006;** www.contucci.it), presided over by knowledgeable, gregarious winemaker Adamo, occupies the 13th-century cellars of the Palazzo Contucci.

Montepulciano's Palazzo Comunale (right) and Duomo in Piazza Grande.

the church. Between 1427 and 1436, Michelozzo carved a monumental tomb for Bartolomeo Aragazzi, secretary to Pope Martin V. In the 18th century it was disassembled and the pieces lost until they were discovered under the altar of the Duomo in 1815. Two of the figures were stolen and found their way to London, but the rest remain here. Because no indication of what the monument originally looked like exists and the supporting architecture is gone, the various figures are distributed throughout the church. They start with a reclining statue of the deceased to the right of the central entrance door (he's the one with the hood) and two bas-reliefs on the first two columns on either side of the nave. The Greco-Roman-influenced statues flanking the high altar and the putti frieze above it, along with a statue in a niche to the right of the altar, are the other main pieces.

The gold-heavy triptych on the high altar is by Taddeo di Bartolo (1401) and depicts the *Assumption of the Virgin with Saints* topped by *Annunciation* and *Crowning of the Virgin* pinnacles, and is banded with a *Passion* cycle in the predella. Bartolo was one of the Sienese artists of the generation after the 1348 Black Death, and this is one of his greatest works. (We particularly enjoy the predella panel where one child is shinning up a tree to get a better view of Christ entering Jerusalem.) On a pilaster to the right of the altar is a *schiacciato* bas-relief tabernacle by Vecchietta. Also inside the Duomo, as you walk out on the right, is an almond-eyed *Madonna and Child* (1418) by Sano di Pietro, located on the pilaster between the first two chapels. In the last chapel stands a 14th-century baptismal font with bas-relief and caryatid figures and, on the wall, della Robbia's *Gigli Altar* surrounding a gilded marble bas-relief of the *Madonna and Child* by Benedetto di Maiano.

Down the hill opposite the Duomo is Montepulciano's modest **Museo Civico Pinacoteca Crociani,** Via Ricci 10 (©**0578-717-300**), whose star attractions are two blockbuster painted terra-cotta altars by Andrea della Robbia. Admission costs 5€, or 3€ for children 18 and under and those 65 and over. Opening hours are complex, but you should find it open Tuesday through Sunday most weeks outside quiet winter months, when it may be open on Fridays and weekends only.

Continue down Via Ricci to the intersection with Via del Paolino, where you can cut back to the left on Via de' Grassi. Outside the walls is Antonio da Sangallo the Elder's **Tempio di San Biagio** ★★ (1518–34), one of the undisputed masterpieces of High Renaissance architecture. It became fashionable in the High Renaissance to build a church, usually on a Greek cross plan, just outside a city so that the classically inspired architecture would be unimpaired by surrounding buildings and the church could be appreciated from all angles. Todi and Prato each have their own version, but Montepulciano's is the best of the lot, a pagan temple built entirely of travertine, dedicated to the gods of mathematical and architectural purity and only nominally to any saint. Two bell towers were to have been fitted into the corners at the front, but the right one reached only 4.5m (15 ft.). The interior, while as peaceful and elegantly restrained as the overall structure, has nothing to hold you. Sangallo also designed the companion canon's house nearby, which was built after his death.

Where to Stay

If you're touring southern Tuscany, the roadside **Locanda del Vino Nobile ★**, Via dei Lillà 3, 53045 Sant'Albino (www.lalocandadelvinonobile.it; ✆ **0578-798-064**), 5km (3 miles) outside Montepulciano on the road to Chianciano, offers convenience, stylish rooms, a great buffet breakfast and refined Tuscan restaurant, and a warm welcome from gregarious owner-managers. The location is unspectacular, although the value is quite the opposite: Double rooms generally range from 80€ to 100€.

Duomo ★ This friendly, family-run joint is the most pleasant full-service hotel in the center. The very firm beds have thick floral-print quilts and pleasingly simple cast-iron frames, and the furniture, while mostly unobtrusively modern, includes a few writing tables and fat armoires made of old wood. All the bathrooms were redesigned in 2007. There's a sitting area with a fireplace and a cozy TV room that opens onto a small terra-cotta–tiled courtyard where you can take your coffee and rolls in the morning. It's also the only hotel in town with an elevator.

Via San Donato 14 (next to the Duomo), 53045 Montepulciano (SI). www.albergoduomo montepulciano.it. ✆/fax **0578-757-473.** 13 units. 75€–95€ double; 115€ triple. Rates include breakfast. Free parking. AE, MC, V. Closed 2 weeks in Jan or Feb. **Amenities:** Bar. *In room:* A/C (in some), TV, hair dryer, minibar, Wi-Fi (free).

Meublé Il Riccio This hotel's name comes from the *ricci* (hedgehogs) that were carved on the wooden supports once adorning the outside of this 13th-century house. They now decorate the rooms, which are comfortable with functionally modern furniture and whitewashed walls. The mosaics in the small colonnaded entrance courtyard come from the school founded by the hotel proprietor's

---

 The Best Pecorino Around

Artisan sheep's-milk cheese maker **Cugusi ★**, Via della Boccia 8 (2km/1 ¼ miles outside Montepulciano on the road to Pienza; ✆ **0578-757-558**; www.caseificiocugusi.it), which supplies Acquacheta (see below) among other local restaurants, sells direct to customers from the farm. The vast range includes pecorino at every aging stage (from *fresco* to *stagionato*) as well as whole or part cheeses wrapped in hazelnut leaves, or herbs and oil, or infused with grapes (known as *ubriaco*, or "drunk"). The farm store is open daily (closing between 1 and 3pm for lunch) and accepts credit cards. They will wrap it *sotto vuoto* (in thick plastic shrink-wrap) for long-life storage.

father. Guests share the pretty sitting room, which has floral-print couches, and a rooftop terrace where the views stretch over the Valdichiana and even get in the top of the Palazzo Comunale's tower. It's a two-story walk-up with no elevator.

Via Talosa 21 (a few steps off Piazza Grande), 53045 Montepulciano (SI). www.ilriccio.net. ℂ/fax **0578-757-713.** 6 units. 100€ double; 116€ triple. Breakfast 8€. MC, V. Free parking. **Amenities:** Bar; bike rental. *In room:* A/C, TV, hair dryer, minibar.

Montorio ★★ Opened in 2000, these five spacious mini-apartments sit atop a hill overlooking the Tempio di San Biagio and the countryside just outside Montepulciano's walls. All save the smallest of the sumptuously homey accommodations combine the best of countryside tradition with modern amenities such as full kitchens and complimentary wine upon arrival (everything in the stocked minifridges is free as well); the smallest unit is more like a suite with a kitchenette. The only drawbacks: Montorio is a stiff 20-minute walk uphill into town and there's a minimum 3-night stay in high season.

The same owners also renovated the nearby hotel **Villa Poggiano ★★** (www.villapoggiano.com; ℂ **0578-758-292**), which is exceptionally quiet and has views of sheep-dotted hillsides 1.6km (1 mile) along the road to Pienza. It now boasts 11 enormous suites, inheriting the wildly dramatic and elegant touches of its 1930s owner. These luxurious suites range from 220€ to 330€ per night including breakfast; it's open April through October only. Children 8 and up are welcome.

Strada per Pienza 2, 53045 Montepulciano (SI). www.montorio.com. ℂ **0578-717-442.** Fax 0578-715-635. 100€–170€ for 2-person apt; 200€–250€ for 4-person apt. Discounted weekly rates available. MC, V. Free parking. Closed Jan 7–Feb 15. *In room:* TV, hair dryer, minibar, Wi-Fi (free).

Where to Eat

To accompany their celebrated Vino Nobile, the Poliziani concentrate their culinary energies on grilled and roasted meats (beef, duck, and pork) and handmade pasta, especially *pici* (fat, chewy spaghetti rolled out between the palms so they're irregular and hold a ragù well). If all you're seeking is a salad, simple primo, or fat *bruschettone* with Tuscan toppings to accompany a glass or two of Vino Nobile, don't overlook wine-bar-with-food **La Dolce Vita,** Via Voltaia nel Corso 80 (www.enotecaladolcevita.it; ℂ **0578-758-760**). It's open continuously from midday till 9pm daily except Saturday (when it closes at 5pm).

Acquacheta ★★★ ✦ SOUTHERN TUSCAN/GRILL This outstanding cellar eatery is strictly for carnivores: *"bistecca numero uno"* is how Adamo, the winemaker at Contucci, describes it. The style is informal and rustic, fussily so—they insist you drink water and wine from the same beaker—but they take produce very seriously: Meat is sold by weight and brought to your table by a cleaver-wielding chef for your approval before it goes onto the brick-built flamegrill (only briefly . . . if you like your steak anything but rare, holler). Pair their excellent beef with a simple side like baked pecorino cheese served with a cold, sliced pear. If a plate of cow isn't for you, there's a lengthy specials list, too, plus three pastas and five sauces to combine any way you please. Everything is local, and oozes flavor as a result. You won't regret or forget a meal here.

Via del Teatro 22 (down right side of Palazzo Contucci from Piazza Grande). ℂ **0578-717-086.** www.acquacheta.eu. Reservations essential. Primi 5€–8€; secondi 7€–18€. MC, V. Wed–Mon noon–3pm and 7:30–10:30pm. Closed mid-Jan to mid-Mar.

Fattoria Pulcino ★ TUSCAN/GRILL If you could mark a spot for a perfect panorama of Montepulciano, your X would come down somewhere near the terrace at Pulcino. This former monastery is now the headquarters of a *tipico* produce empire selling Vino Nobile, organic olive oil, and salami *della casa* from the roadside. The large, informal restaurant's cooking is almost beside the point, but a menu of pasta and grilled meats is perfectly executed, if limited. The "local" choice is *pici di Montepulciano*, a thick, hand-rolled spaghetti. Ordering from the grill (the free-range chicken half and veal steak are especially succulent) means a longer wait; everything here is cooked to order from scratch.

Via SS146 per Chianciano 35 (3km/2 miles SE of town). ✆ **0578-758-711.** www.pulcino.com. Primi 8€–12€; secondi 10€–16€. AE, MC, V. Daily noon–10pm; winter hours vary, so call ahead.

CHIUSI & SARTEANO

21km (13 miles) SE of Montepulciano; 89km (55 miles) SE of Siena; 151km (94 miles) SE of Florence; 165km (103 miles) N of Rome

One of southern Tuscany's smaller hilltop cities, Chiusi doesn't transport you to the Middle Ages or wow you with the Renaissance. You come to Chiusi for one thing: Etruscans.

Alternately spelled *Camars* or *Clevsins,* the Etruscan center here was of considerable importance in the 7th and 6th centuries B.C. One of the more powerful among the Etruscan 12-city confederation, it was ruled in the late 500s B.C. by the

---

A FAMOUS spa town EN ROUTE TO CHIUSI

Take the SS146 about 7km (4⅓ miles) southeast out of Montepulciano to **Chianciano Terme** (✆ **0578-68-111;** www.termechianciano.it), one of Italy's most famous spas. You can drink the thermal mineral waters of **Acqua Santa,** Piazza Martiri Perugini (✆ **0578-68-411**), supposedly to clean out your liver (daily 8am–2pm; Mar–Nov also 4–6pm; 7.50€–9.50€). Those of **Acqua Sillene,** Piazza Marconi (✆ **0578-68-551**), are used for thermal and mud baths and other treatments (daily 8am–6pm Apr–Oct; from 13€). The cold springs of **Acqua Fucoli,** Piazza Martiri Perugini (✆ **0578-68-411;** daily 8am–6pm Apr–Oct; 5.50€), are usually drunk in the afternoon (allegedly to clean out the digestive system). Apparently, it takes 12 days to see any real benefits from taking the waters. For details about spa packages, call the helpful **tourist office,** Piazza Italia 67, Chianciano Terme (✆ **0578-671-122;** www.vivichiancianoterme.it; daily 8am–2pm and 3:30–7:30pm).

The modern spa town and the Old Town are of the same *comune* but really separate communities, about 2km (just over 1 mile) apart, connected only by an umbilical cord of serviceable hotels called Viale della Libertà. Old Chianciano is compact, with a "lived-in" feel, if a little unremarkable, although it possesses genuine links to Nobel Literature Laureate Luigi Pirandello, who set a couple of his tales here. There are fine views over the Valdichiana from Via Casini, in the shadow of a Medici-built clock tower. The **Museo della Collegiata,** Piazzolina dei Soldati (✆ **0578-30-378;** Tues–Sat 10am–noon), has some good Sienese panel paintings from the 13th to the 18th centuries. Admission is 2€; ring the bell for the custodian.

---

lucumo (king) Lars Porsenna, who was famous for attacking Rome from 507 to 506 B.C. Like Cortona just up the Valdichiana (see chapter 9 for more information), the lowlands around Chiusi are a treasure-trove of tombs, some of which you may visit with a guide. And the less famous ones are open to anyone armed with a good map, a few oranges in their pocket, and half a day to explore the valley on their own. Chiusi's excellent restaurants await you after a hard day's tomb hunting.

Essentials

GETTING THERE By Train: Chiusi–Chianciano Terme station, in the "new" town of Chiusi Scalo, is a major stop on the main **Rome-Florence** line (which passes through Arezzo) and is also the terminus of a secondary line that originates in **Siena** (13 trains daily; 80 min.). A short bus ride will carry you up to the *centro storico*.

By Car: From Montepulciano, follow the SS146. From **Florence,** take the A1 to the Chiusi exit. From **Siena,** take the SS326 toward Sinalunga to the A1 south to the Chiusi exit. You can **park** off Via della Pietriccia and Via dei Longobardi.

By Bus: Because Chiusi has one of the main train stations in the region, most towns run several **LFI buses** (www.lfi.it) here daily. Sixteen buses depart daily from Montepulciano (50 min.) that stop in Chianciano Terme (25 min.) along the way. Eight daily buses connect Chiusi's center with Sarteano. Ask to get off at the *centro storico* or you'll end up in the meatpacking town of Chiusi Scalo down below.

By Bike: The best way to see the land of the Etruscans up close is by bike, specifically by riding a **bicycle path** called the **Sentiero della Bonifica** that stretches about 60km (37 miles) between Chiusi and **Arezzo.** It crosses historic bridges and passes friendly farms that offer a true taste of the region. The gravelly path is better suited for mountain bikes and hybrids than for fancy road bikes, and can be an arduous trek under the hot sun. For more instructions and for a good map, see **www.sentierodellabonifica.it**.

VISITOR INFORMATION The **tourist office** is at Via Porsenna 79, 53043 Chiusi (✆ **0578-227-667;** www.prolocochiusi.it). April through September it's open Monday to Saturday from 9am (10am Sept) to 1pm and 3 to 6pm, and Sunday from 9am (10am Sept) to 1pm only. October hours are daily 10am to 2pm; November through March it's open daily 10am to 1pm.

Exploring Chiusi

Although a huge portion of Chiusi's rich Etruscan patrimony was carried off by early archaeologists to museums in Orvieto and elsewhere, the city's **Museo Archeologico Nazionale ★★**, in Via Porsenna (✆ **0578-20-177**), has no mean share of what's left. The collections inside this neoclassical building are in eternal rearrangement. There are plenty of the rectangular Etruscan cinerary urns, in which the deceased's ashes were kept in a box topped by a lid carved with the man or woman's reclining likeness. Keep on the lookout for a winged version of the split-tailed siren—the mythological symbol of sex and fertility, which pops up as late as the Middle Ages on Christian buildings like Pienza's Pieve. Also here is a 6th-century B.C. funerary sphinx carved from a local limestone called *pietra fetida,* as well as sarcophagi in travertine and alabaster. Another of the museum's

Chiusi's Duomo.

greatest treasures is a set of **painted urns** dating back to the 2nd century B.C. on which the polychrome decorations are still marvelously intact.

Another Etruscan funerary vehicle on display is the anthropomorphic canopic jar, made of terra cotta and sometimes bronze with a carved human head for a lid and handles like arms. Occasionally an entire statue would top off the affair, as in the 7th-century-B.C. example from Dolciano. The deceased, perched on the lid, is apparently orating, surrounded by stylized griffins whose heads are raised high, crying out. Aside from the prehistoric and Villanovan bits, the imported Attic black- and red-figure vases, and some ebony-toned 7th- to 6th-century-B.C. *bucchero* ceramics, keep your eyes peeled for the marble portrait of Augustus and the 3rd-century-A.D. mosaic of a boar hunt. The museum is open daily from 9am to 8pm. Admission is 4€ for adults, 2€ ages 18 to 25, and free for E.U. citizens 18 and under and those 65 and over.

A short block up from the museum, **Piazza del Duomo** opens off to your left, past a medieval tower converted to Christian purposes in the 16th century as the bell tower to San Secondiano cathedral. The piazza, with its loggia running down one side, is a small but striking square of light-gray cut stone that matches the facade of the 12th-century **Duomo** at one end. The inside was restored in the late 19th century but retains its recycled columns and capitals pilfered from local Roman buildings. On closer inspection, you'll note those seemingly early medieval "mosaics" covering every inch of the nave and apses are actually made of paint—an 1887-to-1894 opus by Arturo Viligiardi (take a .50€ coin for the lights).

The entrance to the **Museo della Cattedrale** (© **0578-226-490**) is to the right of the Duomo's doors under the arcade. The first floor has some uninspired paleo-Christian and Lombard remains, but the museum's main attraction is upstairs—a series of 21 **antiphonals** from the abbey of Monte Oliveto Maggiore that were illuminated by artists like Francesco di Giorgio Martini and Liberale da Verona in the 15th century. The entire set was stolen in 1972, but miraculously all save one and a few pages of another were recovered. The museum is open daily from June to October 15 from 9:30am to 12:45pm and 4 to 6:30pm and from October 16 to May from 9:30am to 12:45pm (Sun also 3:30–6:30pm, but Jan–Mar only open Tues, Thurs, and Sat–Sun). Admission is 2€ for adults, 1€ for school-age children.

Meet at the museum desk for the obligatory guided tour of the **Labirinto di Porsenna (Labyrinth of Porsenna)** ★ (☎ **0578-226-490** for reservations), a jaunt through a painstakingly excavated portion of the tunnel system carved under the city by the Etruscans. The cathedral museum and gardens in the square above were once the bishop's palace, and the tunnels were used as a refuse dump. They were rediscovered in the 1920s by some kids who decided to start cleaning them out. The good-hearted teenagers kept at their task, eventually becoming a volunteer society of amateur archaeologists, and slowly the tunnels were reopened. A good stretch of the *cunicoli* (water sewers) was opened to the public in 1995. The narrow passages were apparently part of a vast plumbing system that once supplied the entire Etruscan city, as well as medieval firefighters, from a huge underground lake. As a bonus to the tour, the cathedral bell tower sits right on top of this well, and the climb to the top is worth it for the sweeping city and countryside vista. The half-hour tours cost 3€ (or 4€ combined with Museo), 2€ for school-age children, and leave about every 40 minutes during museum hours.

Of the **Etruscan tombs** ★★ in the surrounding area, especially to the north and northeast toward the small Lake Chiusi (a remnant of the once widespread Valdichiana marshes), currently only the **Tomba della Pellegrina** (with 4th-c.-B.C. sarcophagi and 3rd-c.-B.C. cinerary urns still in place) and **Tomba del Leone** (still showing a bit of color on its walls) are open to visitors with a valid ticket for the Museo Archeologico Nazionale (see above). On Tuesday, Thursday, and Saturday, you can also book ahead; space is limited for two visits a day at 11am and 4pm (11am and 2:30pm Nov–Feb) to see the famous painted **Tomba della Scimmia.** The fee is 2€, but free for E.U. citizens 18 years and under or 65 and over. To visit any of the tombs, contact the archaeological museum desk (☎ **0578-20-177**). You must have your own car, in which the custodian accompanies you.

A detail of an urn at the Museo Archeologico Nazionale.

You must also have wheels to visit the local 3rd- to 5th-century-A.D. **paleo-Christian catacombs.** Prebook to meet the guide Tuesday, Thursday, or Saturday at 11am at the cathedral museum (in summer also Sun at 4:30pm). The visit costs 5€.

Few other sights in town hold much interest, but on a stroll you might pass through the market square of **Piazza XX Settembre,** anchored at one end by the 13th-century **Santa Maria della Morte,** with its tall, flat tower and with a 14th-century loggia along one side. At the square's other end sprouts a **clock tower,** near which is the medieval **San Francesco.** Via Petrarca leads from Via Porsenna to a **panorama** over the Valdichiana from Piazza Olivazzo.

Where to Stay

If our favorites below are full, **La Sfinge,** Via Marconi 2, 53043 Chiusi (www. albergolasfinge.it; ©0578-20-157) offers a guaranteed welcome right in the center. Rooms are unremarkable, but are clean and a very good value. Two have panoramic terraces with Valdichiana views. Doubles range from 65€ to 85€. It's closed February through early March and 1 week in November.

Casa Toscana B&B ★ 💼 This handsome Liberty villa in a quiet location in the old center was completely renovated and opened in 2011. It's now an upscale bed-and-breakfast with a sun terrace facing San Francesco, which combines modern, hotel-style amenities with an eye for design: Good-size rooms are color-washed in rich Tuscan tones, mattresses are firm, and furniture is modern but modeled on antique styles. Oliva is comfortably the largest unit, but comes at no extra cost if you request it.

Via Baldetti 37, 53043 Chiusi Città (SI). www.bandbcasatoscana.it. ©**0578-222-227.** 8 units 90€ double; 110€ quad (5% discount for bookings of 2 nights or more). Rates include breakfast. AE, DC, MC, V. Free parking. *In room:* A/C, TV, hair dryer, minibar, Wi-Fi (free).

La Fattoria 💼 The rooms at this 1850s lakeside farmhouse are fitted out in full country-inn style, with dark wood furniture and floral-patterned fabrics. Most are fairly large, and a few have a view out over the lake (two have their own terrace). In summer, you can dine on an open lake-view terrace and toast the view with a *torta al limone* (in this case, an American-style lemon meringue pie) for dessert.

Via Lago di Chiusi (5km/3 miles east of Chiusi on the lake), 52043 Chiusi (SI). www.la-fattoria. it. ©**0578-21-407.** Fax 0578-20-644. 8 units. 85€–95€ double. Half and full pension available. Rates include breakfast. AE, DC, MC, V. Free parking. Closed Jan 10–Feb 10. **Amenities:** Restaurant; bikes; room service. *In room:* A/C, TV, hair dryer, minibar.

Where to Eat

Chiusi's unique local specialty is lake fish. The best place to sample dishes like *tegamaccio* (lake-fish stew) and *persico* (perch) is down by Lake Chiusi at **Pesce d'Oro ★**, Via Sbarchino 26 (©**0578-21-403;** www.ristorantepescedoro.it). Lake fish secondi cost around 10€; you should book ahead on sunny weekends.

La Solita Zuppa ★ TUSCAN An ex-theater couple runs this excellent restaurant, where the atmosphere is a strange mix of country trattoria and refined *boîte,* with Ella Fitzgerald and Louis Armstrong as the musical accompaniment. You'll be served a delicious assortment of warm *crostini* and sliced salami and an aperitif while you decide between the likes of *pici* or *lasagne al cinghiale* (lasagne layered with cheese and wild boar), cooked in a ceramic casserole. Some of the

"Same Old Soups" of the restaurant's name include *porri e patate* (potato leek), *fagioli e farro* (bean and emmer), and a peasant *lenti e castagne* (lentils and chestnuts). For secondi, the chef makes a mean *faraona pere ed arancio* (guinea hen with pear and orange).

Via Porsenna 21. ℂ **0578-21-006.** www.lasolita zuppa.it. Reservations recommended. Primi 8€; secondi 11€. AE, DC, MC, V. Tues–Sun 12:30–2:30pm and 7:30–9:45pm.

Zaira ★★ SOUTHERN TUSCAN Regarded as the best restaurant in a city where the competition is tough, Zaira was refitted in 2010—but mercifully, the menu remains little changed. Try *trota in carpione* (marinated trout) as an appetizer before passing on to the justifiably famous house specialty, the tasty *pasta del lucumone* (ziti baked with cooked ham and three types of cheese in a ceramic casserole). The *lucumone* is a tough act to follow, but

An Etruscan tomb in the Pianacce complex, outside Sarteano.

you can try with *coniglio al limone* (rabbit kissed with lemon) or *anatra al Vino Nobile* (duck cooked in red wine) plus a side of *carciofi ripieni* (artichokes stuffed with bread crumbs and pancetta). Ask to visit the rambling wine cellars, dug right into the rock, which house more than 20,000 bottles.

Via Arunte 12. ℂ **0578-20-260.** www.zaira.it. Reservations recommended. Primi 8€–9€; secondi 8€–16€. AE, DC, MC, V. Daily noon–2:45pm and 7–10:30pm (closed Mon mid-Jan to June and Oct–Nov). Closed 15 days in Nov.

A Side Trip to Sarteano

The lively little market town of **Sarteano** ★ is one of our favorite corners of southern Tuscany for whiling away a morning—especially a Saturday morning, the only day its incredibly precious Etruscan sight is open to the public. The tiny, friendly **tourist office** at Corso Garibaldi 9, 53047 Sarteano (ℂ**0578-269-204** or 0578-265-312; www.prolocosarteano.it) is open weekends (and sometimes Wed or Fri) 10am to noon. Driving by car is the easiest way to reach the town, which lies 12km (7½ miles) southwest of Chiusi and is well signposted off the SS146 Chiusi-Montepulciano road. Eight buses a day from Chiusi (25 min.) and a similar number from Montepulciano (45 min.) also connect with the town.

Hands down the best Etruscan sight for miles around is the town's **Tomba della Quadriga Infernale (Tomb of the Demon Charioteer)** ★★★. The tomb itself is just one part of a complex numbering at least 14, and inside contains vivid frescoes dating from around 330 B.C. The most striking image shows the eponymous charioteer driving two lions and two griffins—the only known painting of its kind in Etruscan art. Visits inside are limited to 40 people per week, on Saturdays only. In summer e-mail museo@comune.sarteano.siena.it a few weeks in advance to book; at other times a few days' notice usually suffices. The visit is conducted in Italian, but there's an English handout. You'll need a car to drive the 2km (just over 1 mile) to the site, known as **Pianacce,** where several tombs are cut into the travertine bedrock on a ridge with stupendous views of the Valdichiana. At other times, the site (and its other tombs) are open for free exploration. Tomb visits are run by Sarteano's **Museo Civico,** Via Roma 24 (② **0578-269-261**) which displays finds including *attica* and *bucchero* pottery from Etruscan necropoli at Mulin Canale, Solaia, and Poggio Rotondo, a wealth of finds from Pianacce, as well as a realistic reconstruction of part of the Tomba della Quadriga's wall art. The museum is open April through October Tuesday to Sunday 10:30am to 12:30pm and 4 to 7pm; it's open the same hours on weekends only during other months. Admission costs 4€ adults, 3€ ages 6 to 18 and those 65 and over; a ticket covering the museum and the Tomba della Quadriga costs 7€ and 5€ respectively.

Elsewhere in town, seek out the **Chiesa di San Martino,** Piazza San Martino (no phone), whose boxy little interior is graced by one of the masterpieces of Sienese Renaissance painter Domenico Beccafumi, a 1546 ***Annunciation*** ★ swept by his trademark light and shadow. If the church is locked, as it often is in low season, inquire at the tourist office (they hold a key).

Sarteano's best food is served in the small dining room at **Da Gagliano** ★, Via Roma 5 (② **0578-268-022**), where the menu closely follows the waxing and waning of the seasons—very little produce is sourced from outside the local hills. Primi cost 7.50€ to 9€, and delightful secondi such as *coniglio al tegame con lardo e finocchio selvatico* (pan-fried rabbit with cured ham fat and wild fennel) range from 9€ to 13€. Between April and October it's open Thursday through Monday for lunch and dinner (daily Aug and over Christmas); in the off season it's open on weekends only. Reservations are highly recommended.

9

AREZZO & NORTHEASTERN TUSCANY

The province of Arezzo, bounding Tuscany's northeast corner, is a land of castle-dominated hill towns, misty blue mountains, and Apennine forests. Snowy-white cattle graze in the wide Chiana Valley, while light industry toils at the edges of medieval centers. In the reaches of the mountains lie tranquil hermitages such as **La Verna,** St. Francis's favorite spot to pray, where tradition holds he became the first human to receive the stigmata.

This is the region where the brawny, humanist Renaissance of Florence meets and melds with the intangible, hazy spirituality of Umbria's green hills. This hybrid is perfectly displayed in the works of the region's two most famous artistic sons, Piero della Francesca and Luca Signorelli, both masters of mathematical proportion and of rarefied moods and landscapes in painting. Piero is the focus of his native **Sansepolcro,** and one of the main draws in **Arezzo,** a low-key city of amiable citizens and modest art treasures. Art-rich **Cortona,** Luca Signorelli's hometown, is an ancient Etruscan hill town that doesn't quite fill up its medieval walls; much of the space is occupied by oversize gardens.

Arezzo province has also given us the great poet Petrarch, whose classical studies and humanist philosophy rang in the Renaissance and earned him the moniker "the first modern man," and Giorgio Vasari, architect of the Uffizi, court painter to Cosimo I, and the Western world's first art historian. Vasari brought Petrarch's movement full circle by literally writing the book on the Renaissance. It's no surprise the ultimate Florentine of the Renaissance era, Michelangelo, was born in the forested hills east of Arezzo.

AREZZO ★★

85km (53 miles) SE of Florence; 246km (153 miles) N of Rome

Arezzo is a medium-size Tuscan city, an agricultural center clambering up a low hill, best known for its artistic masterpieces by **Piero della Francesca** and stained-glass marvels by **Guillaume de Marcillat.** As Arretium, Arezzo was an important member of the 12-city Etruscan confederation, and it was famous in Roman times for its mass-produced *corallino* ceramics. The Ghibelline medieval *comune* ran afoul of Florence's Guelphs, and the city's armies were soundly trounced by Florence in the 1289 Battle of Campaldino. (The Florentine forces counted a young Dante Alighieri among the foot soldiers.) More recently, the city's gotten some international face time as the setting for Roberto Benigni's 1999 Oscar-winning film *La Vita è Bella (Life Is Beautiful).*

Arezzo has produced an unusual number of cultural giants. Guido Monaco (or Guido d'Arezzo), born around A.D. 995, invented the modern musical scale and notation. The poet Petrarch (1304–74) helped found the humanist movement that was the basis for the entire cultural Renaissance. Spinello Aretino (1350–1410) was one of the great *trecento* masters of Italian fresco. Pietro

PREVIOUS PAGE: **Cortona's countryside.**

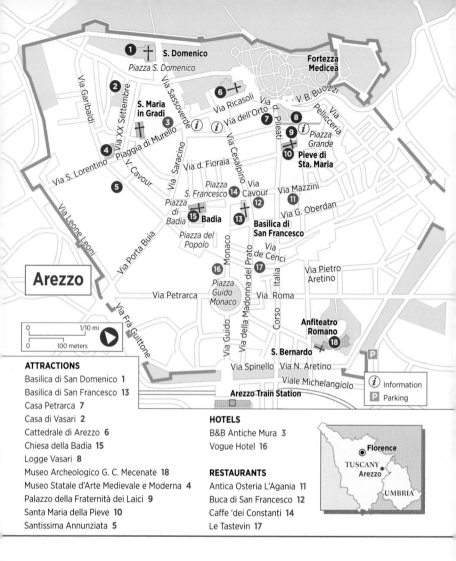

Arezzo

ATTRACTIONS

Basilica di San Domenico **1**
Basilica di San Francesco **13**
Casa Petrarca **7**
Casa di Vasari **2**
Cattedrale di Arezzo **6**
Chiesa della Badia **15**
Logge Vasari **8**
Museo Archeologico G. C. Mecenate **18**
Museo Statale d'Arte Medievale e Moderna **4**
Palazzo della Fraternità dei Laici **9**
Santa Maria della Pieve **10**
Santissima Annunziata **5**

HOTELS

B&B Antiche Mura **3**
Vogue Hotel **16**

RESTAURANTS

Antica Osteria L'Agania **11**
Buca di San Francesco **12**
Caffe 'dei Constanti **14**
Le Tastevin **17**

Aretino (1492–1566), a gifted poet, was capable of writing the most vituperative, scandal-causing verses. Another towering Aretine was Giorgio Vasari (1512–74), a mediocre painter, a much more talented architect, and, with his book *Lives of the Artists*—a collection of biographies of masters from Cimabue and Giotto through Michelangelo—the unwitting author of the first art history text.

Essentials

GETTING THERE By Train: The main line between **Rome** (hourly; 2 hr.–2 hr., 55 min.; 13€–23€) and **Florence** (45 trains daily; 40–90 min; 5.80€–10€) also passes **Chiusi/Chianciano Terme** (28 trains daily; 45 min; 4.70€–8€) and **Orvieto** (15 trains daily; 1 hr.–1 hr., 50 min; 6.70€–13€) on its way to Arezzo. You can transfer at Terontola/Cortona for the dozen daily trains to

Perugia (2¼ hr. total riding time) and **Assisi** (2 hr., 40 min.). The **train station** (☏ 0575-20-553) is at Piazza della Repubblica just southwest of the city walls. All hotels are within a few blocks' walk.

By Car: The quickest route from Florence or Rome is the **A1 auto-strada.** Follow the **parking** signs to the walls of the old city; Parcheggio Eden (1.25€ per hr.) is along Via Niccolò Aretino just inside the southwest corner of the walls, and there's more space at Via B. Alberti, behind the train station. There's free parking on Via Pietri and Via XXV Aprile.

By Bus: SITA buses (☏ 0575-749-818; www.sitabus.it) from **Florence** (1 hr., 20 min.–2 hr.) and **LFI** buses (☏ 0575-324-294; www. lfi.it) from **Siena** (1½ hr.) let you off in front of the train station.

VISITOR INFORMATION An **APT information office** (www.turismoprovincia. arrezzo.it) is located at Palazzo Comunale (☏ 0575-401-945; Mon–Fri 11am–1pm and 2–4pm, and Sat-Sun 11am–4pm).

FESTIVALS & MARKETS In the last week of August or early September, Guido Monaco's musical traditions are carried on in a series of choral concerts called the **Concorso Polifonico Internazionale Guido d'Arezzo (International Polyphonic Competition).**

On the third Sunday in June and the first Sunday in September, Arezzo pulls out the stops for a full-fledged medieval jousting tournament, the **Giostra del Saracino** ★★, dating from at least the 16th century. After an afternoon of complex flag-tossing and pageantry, mounted, armored riders thunder across dirt-lined Piazza Grande with their lances aimed at the effigy of a Saracen warrior. The twist is that when the "knights" strike a blow on his shield, the Saracen swivels, and his other arm is carrying a whip. Hitting the shield's bull's-eye is only half the trick—the other is dodging the whip.

On the first Saturday and Sunday of every month, Piazza Grande is filled with more than 500 dealers in one of Italy's leading **antiques fairs** ★. The dealers specialize in 19th-century furniture and 17th- to 19th-century glass, but items dating from the Renaissance are well represented (as are items from the 1950s and 1960s). It draws serious collectors from around the world. In winter, the fair runs from 7:30am to 3pm (in summer as late as 7 or 9pm).

A market in Arezzo.

Don't miss the special local **farmers' market,** held in Piazza Sant'Agostino every first Saturday of the month.

Exploring Arezzo

Arezzo's main square, **Piazza Grande** ★, is charmingly off-kilter. Since 1200, it has listed alarmingly to one side, creating a slope crowned with the graceful **Logge Vasari** ★ designed in 1573 by local boy Giorgio Vasari. Perpendicular to where the cafe-filled tunnel-like loggia runs out of the square sits the composite **Palazzo della Fraternità dei Laici.** The Gothic lower half (1377) has a detached Spinello Aretino fresco of the *Pietà* and a Bernardo Rossellino *Madonna della Misericordia* (1434) in bas-relief above the door. The upper loggia was built in 1460, and the clock bell tower added by Vasari in 1552. One palace down to the left is the arcaded apse of Santa Maria della Pieve (see below).

Basilica di San Domenico The interior of this 13th-century church contains several engaging 14th-century **fresco fragments** and one real gem. Over the high altar is a justly lauded *Crucifix* ★, painted by Cimabue in the 1260s, then brilliantly restored and returned to this place of honor in early 2003. It's classic Cimabue, a work marking the start of the long transition from Byzantine triumphalism to Renaissance Humanism.

On the entrance wall are frescoes of the *Crucifixion* and the *Life of St. Nicholas of Bari* by Parri di Spinello. On the right wall, under a Gothic canopy, Luca di Tommé painted a very young *Christ with the Doctors of the Church* in the Sienese style. The chapel to the right of the high altar contains a 14th-century stone *Madonna and Child* and a delicate fresco of the *Annunciation* by Spinello Aretino. More faded frescoes line the church's left wall, and the last one on your right as you leave is a 15th-century *St. Vincent Ferrer*. According to Giorgio Vasari, this is the only known work by his grandfather, Lazzaro Vasari. Note that the church interior is very dark, but to the left and right of the altar are fuse boxes where you can switch on the lights.

Piazza San Domenico. ☏ **0575-22-906.** Free admission. Nov–Mar daily 9am–6:30pm; Apr–Oct daily 9am–7pm.

Basilica di San Francesco ★★ One of the greatest fresco cycles by one of the greatest artists of the Renaissance holds court in this 14th-century church. Piero della Francesca's *Legend of the True Cross* ★★★, completed in 1466 inside the **Capella Maggiore,** has drawn art-loving pilgrims from around the world for centuries. Piero's work features perfect perspective and hauntingly ethereal, woodenly posed figures that nonetheless convey untold depths of emotion. The entire cycle was gorgeously restored from 1985 to 2000 to fix the extensive damage wreaked by 500 years of fires, earthquakes, Napoleonic troops, and creeping dampness in the plaster. You can see them from the ropes at the base of the altar steps, about 10m (33 ft.) away, but it is well worth paying for a ticket to get up close. To get tickets, you must make **reservations.** Twenty-five people are admitted every 30 minutes, and are required to leave at the end of the time slot. Go online to the website listed below, or call the phone line. Note that you're required to pick up your tickets at least a half-hour before your entry time or you risk losing your space on the tour. If you just turn up and there's space (unlikely in the summer), staff will probably (and reluctantly) arrange tickets on the spot.

Spend some time admiring the rest of the church, though the remaining frescoes are a lot more faded and damaged than Francesca's masterpiece. French master Guillaume de Marcillat painted the **rose window** in 1520, and for a peek

Piero della Francesca's *Legend of the True Cross*.

at what Piero's assistant Lorentino d'Andrea was capable of, check out the first altar on the right. Here in 1463, Lorentino frescoed a scene of San Bernardino leading the Aretines out of this very church on a good old-fashioned pagan-smashing day trip to destroy the cultish temple of Fons Tecta. Just beyond it is a *Sacred Conversation* by Niccolò Soggi and, in the second chapel niche, scenes from the *Life of St. Bartholomew* by another of Piero's followers. Spinello Aretino painted the *Annunciation* at the end of the right aisle.

Piazza San Francesco. © **0575-20-630;** required reservation for Piero cycle tickets at © **0575-352-727** or www.pierodellafrancesca.it. Admission to church free; Piero cycle 6€ including the booking fee. Church Mon–Sat 8:30am–noon and 2:30–6:30pm, Sun 9:45–10:45am and 1–5pm. Piero cycle by 30-min. guided tour only, leaving on the half-hour Nov–Mar Mon–Fri 9am–5:30pm, Sat 9am–5pm, Sun 1–5pm; Apr–Oct Mon–Fri 9am–6:30pm, Sat 9am–5:30pm, Sun 1–5:30pm.

Casa Petrarca (Petrarch's House) Legend has it that lauded scholar and master poet Francesco Petrarca (Petrarch) was born in this house in 1304 to Florentine parents living in exile. Other than soaking up the powerful sense of history and chatting to the enthusiastic docents (ask about directions to the "Pozzo del Boccaccio," the nearby well which features in Boccaccio's *Decameron*), there's not much to see as the building remains the home of the stuffy **Accademia Petrarca**—the academy's extensive library of rare books is usually open. There's also a well-stocked bookshop.

Via dell'Orto 28. © **0575-182-2770.** www.accademiapetrarca.it. Admission 4€ adults, 3€ students 6–25, 65 and over, free for 5 and under. Apr–Oct daily 9:30am–6:30pm; Nov–Mar daily 10am–12:30pm and 3–5pm.

Casa di Vasari (Vasari's House) Giorgio Vasari (1511–74), bought this house in 1540 and decorated it with rather bland, semi-Mannerist paintings with the help of his contemporaries and students. There are works by Il Poppi, Alessandro Allori, Santi di Tito, and, of course, Giorgio himself. The best of the Vasari pieces are a *Deposition* in the second room and a painting in the first room of **Virtue, Envy, and Fortune** duking it out on the ceiling. It features a nifty optical trick: The figure that appears to be on top changes as you view it from different perspectives. Vasari's precious **archives**—which includes correspondence from five popes and the Medici rulers of Florence, as well as 17 handwritten letters from

Michelangelo—are also here, despite ongoing (and highly controversial) attempts by the private owners to sell them.

Via XX Settembre 55. ℂ **0575-409-040.** Admission 2€ adults, 1€ ages 18–25, free 17 and under. Wed–Sat and Mon 9am–7pm; Sun 9am–1pm.

Cattedrale di Arezzo At the highest point in town, surrounded by the Parco il Prato with its 16th-century Medici fortress ruins, Arezzo's cathedral was slowly agglomerated between 1278 and 1510, though it took until 1859 to raise the neo-Gothic bell tower and until 1935 to finish the simple facade. Among the masterpieces inside, the greatest may be the seven **stained-glass windows** ★ (1516–24) by the undisputed master of the form, the French immigrant **Guillaume de Marcillat.** This is one of the few complete cycles of his work in Italy that hasn't been destroyed, and it includes the *Pentecost* rose window in the facade; the *Calling of St. Matthew,* the *Baptism of Christ,* the *Expulsion of Merchants from the Temple,* the *Adulteress,* and the *Raising of Lazarus* along the right wall; and *Saints Silvester and Lucy* in the chapel to the left of the apse. De Marcillat also painted the first three **ceiling vaults** of the nave.

There are fine Gothic tombs throughout the church, and the city's patron saint, San Donato (martyred here in 363), is commemorated by the beautifully sculpted 14th-century Gothic **high altar.** At the end of the left aisle, on the wall next to the sacristy door, is a scraggly-haired but still magnificent *Mary Magdalene* frescoed by Piero della Francesca in around 1459. Next to this is the venerated monument to **Pope Gregory X** (1210–76), who died in Arezzo and is buried in the cathedral.

Sienese sculptors Agostino da Giovanni and Agnolo di Ventura, who worked on the high altar, created the Gothic stone comic book of the **tomb of Bishop Guido Tarlati** (d. 1327) in the left aisle. The 14th-century relief panels depict scenes from the life of the warrior bishop with Aretine landscapes in the background. The mammoth 1535 *cantoria* beyond it was Vasari's first go at architecture.

The large **Cappella della Madonna del Conforto** in the left aisle near the church entrance preserves several Andrea della Robbia terra cottas, including an *Assumption,* a *Crucifixion,* and a pretty *Madonna and Child.* In the small **baptistery** is a **font** bearing Donatello-school *schiacciato* relief panels—the *Baptism of Christ* scene may have been carved by Donatello himself.

Piazza del Duomo. ℂ **0575-23-991.** Free admission. Daily 7am–12:30pm and 3–6:30pm.

Chiesa della Badia In 1565, Giorgio Vasari performed a Mannerist architectural overhaul on this 13th-century church. He did such a good job that in 1865, church officials hijacked what Vasari had intended to be his and his family's tomb, installed in the Pieve di Santa Maria, and reassembled it here in the Badia as the church's **high altar.** Vasari's paintings adorning the altar include a 1551 *Calling of St. Peter* in cotton-candy pastels and a watery classical background. On the inside entrance wall of the church is a 1476 fresco by Bartolomeo della Gatta, who painted a remarkably lifelike face of *St. Lawrence* in a *trompe l'oeil* niche. Past the third altar on the right is a 1320 *Crucifix* by Segna di Bonaventura. Above the transept is the restored *trompe l'oeil* dome painted on canvas (1702) by the baroque master of perspective illusion, Andrea Pozzo. There actually is a dome there, but it's a shallow one—Pozzo was hired to make it look mightier. The best effect isn't from directly underneath but from the little bronze marker in the aisle near the front of the pews.

Piazza di Badia. ℂ **0575-356-612.** Free admission. Mon–Sat 8am–noon and 4–7pm; Sun 7:15–9:15am and 10:15am–12:30pm.

Museo Archeologico G. C. Mecenate Arezzo has made a small park and absorbing museum out of the remains of its **Roman amphitheater** (entered from Via Crispi) and adjacent ex Convento di S. Bernardo. After some 6th-century-B.C. bronzes and a red-figure amphora from the 5th century B.C., rooms 6 to 8 contain the museum's pride, a collection of the mass-produced *corallino pottery* that made Roman Arezzo famous from 50 B.C. to A.D. 70. These waxy brick-red ceramics were decorated with stamped reliefs and depressions, and the tools and styles of various production studios are didactically laid out. Room 8 contains the remnants of the famed Atelus workshop, which at its height had branch ateliers in Pisa and Lyons. Upstairs are some relics from the Chiusi area, including an unusually anthropomorphic 7th-century-B.C. urn with human arms and a lid shaped like a human head. Don't miss the highly refined tiny **portrait of a toga-wearing man** incised on gold and silver leaf and protected by a glass disk. This remarkably realistic artistry dates from the early 3rd century A.D.

Via Margaritone 10. © **0575-20-882.** Admission 4€ adults, 2€ ages 18–25 (E.U. citizens), free for ages 17 and under and seniors 65 and over (E.U. citizens). Daily 8:30am–7:30pm.

Museo Statale d'Arte Medievale e Moderna Every epoch of Aretine and imported artistry from the Middle Ages to the Macchiaioli (a Tuscan school of the mid-19th c.), is represented in the large, moderately interesting collections here, housed in the Palazzo Bruni-Ciocchi. A room off the ground-floor courtyard has **medieval sculptures** ranging from 11th-century capitals to 14th-century *Madonna*s rescued from various town gates and defunct churches. On the first floor are a Byzantine-style 13th-century painting of *St. Francis* by Margaritone d'Arezzo and an early-Sienese-school *Madonna* embedded with baubles. The 15th-century frescoes of Spinello Aretino's pupil Giovanni d'Agnolo di Balduccio dominate room 2. In the next room, the master weighs in with a **Trinità,** accompanied by his son Parri's *Sconfitta di Massenzio,* a battle scene discovered in the Badia during World War II cleanup. Historic tournament armor is preserved in room 5 in the form of loads of 17th-century weapons of death. There are two paintings by Bartolomeo della Gatta here of **St. Roch**—one shows a medieval Arezzo in the background but doesn't reveal that the city is in the throes of the Black Death. This work was part of an offering to the saint begging him to intercede to stop the disease.

The museum also has a fine collection of 14th- to 18th-century **majolica ceramic** works from Faenza, Gubbio (including one precious plate by the famous Mastro Giorgio), and Deruta, along with some Andrea della Robbia terra cottas. The first-floor collections contain Mannerist and baroque canvases by Il Poppi, Empoli, and Salimbeni, plus several by Vasari—the best is his large, crowded 1548 **Supper for the Marriage of Esther.** The second floor has a gathering of small Macchiaioli paintings and a pair of Luca Signorelli *Madonna with Child* paintings (1518–22) but sputters out into insipid baroque pieces.

Via San Lorentino 8. © **0575-409-050.** Admission 4€ adults, 2€ ages 18–25, free for children 17 and under and seniors 65 and over. Tues–Sun 8:30am–7pm.

Santa Maria della Pieve ★ This 12th-century church is Lombard Romanesque architecture at its most beautiful, with a craggy, eroded **facade** ★ of stacked arcades in luminous beige stone. The spaces between the columns of the arcades get narrower at each level, which, along with the setting on a narrow street, only adds to the illusion of great height. The fat 36m (118-ft.) **bell tower** "of the hundred holes," with its bifore windows (mullioned windows with two lights), is a 1330 addition. The medieval reliefs lining the main doorway depict the months of the year, including the two-faced pagan god Janus sitting in for the month of January (named after him).

The arches in the relatively simple interior are just starting to get plucked to Gothic pointiness, and dozens of windows light the place. On the high altar above the raised crypt is a 1320 **polyptych of the *Madonna and Child with Saints* ★**—all wearing gorgeously worked fabrics—by Sienese master Pietro Lorenzetti. In the crypt, with its carved medieval capitals, is an elegant reliquary bust of Arezzo's patron saint, San Donato, made by Aretine goldsmiths in the 14th century.

Corso Italia 7. ✆ **0575-22-629.** Free admission. May–Sept daily 8am–7pm; Oct–Apr daily 8am–noon and 3–6pm.

Santissima Annunziata This church was built to house a miraculous terra-cotta statue of the Virgin Mary (the **Madonna delle Lacrime,** or "Our Lady of Tears"), attributed to Michele da Firenze in 1425. The statue is said to have shed real tears in 1490, and today it is still venerated in the central niche of the marble altar, designed by Bernardo Buontalenti and completed in 1600. The main artistic attractions of the handsome Renaissance interior—designed by Bartolomeo della Gatta and Giuliano and Antonio da Sangallo the Elder—are a series of **stained-glass windows** by Guillaume de Marcillat. Just inside to the right is what may be his masterpiece, the *Marriage of the Virgin.* Behind the high altar is an *Assumption,* and saints are depicted in windows along the aisles. The church also retains some good baroque works, as well as Niccolò Soggi's restored 1522 *Nativity* to the left of the high altar, and, on the first altar on the left, a painting of the *Deposition* that an 18-year-old Giorgio Vasari painted based on a Rosso Fiorentino cartoon.

Via Garibaldi 185. ✆ **0575-26-774.** Free admission. Daily 7:30am–12:30pm and 3:30–7pm.

Where to Stay

Hotels in Arezzo are nothing to write home about—they cater mainly to business-people passing through—though there are a handful of smaller and more appealing B&Bs and guesthouses. Accommodations in the surrounding hills are more inviting, assuming you have a car. The **Poggio del Drago ★★★**, Localita Poggio del Drago 18, near Ponticino on the SR69 (www.poggiodeldrago.it; ✆ 331-549-8767), is a gorgeous country house just 9km (5 ½ miles) from the city, offering simple but spotless rooms with flatscreen TVs, free Wi-Fi, a swimming pool, and communal breakfast. Doubles range from 70€ to 100€. Large groups should consider **Casa Pippo ★★**, Lignano 6, (www.casapippo.it; ✆ 0575-365-555), an enchanting stone-built *agriturismo* overlooking the city, with room for at least eight people (rates from 2,875€ per week).

Badia di Pomaio ★★ This luxurious hotel is actually high above the city and best for those with their own transport, though the hotel shuttle bus will pick up train travelers at the station. The elegant main building was constructed in 1645 as a religious retreat, and though the holy orders have long gone, the same sense of tranquility pervades the whole site, with gasp-inducing views of Arezzo and soothing forests of chestnut all around. Many guests choose to spend at least one day simply lounging by the pool. Room sizes vary, but most feature Renaissance-themed furnishings and bedspreads and all the usual modern amenities.

Località Badia a Pomaio 4, 52100 Arezzo. www.badiadipomaio.it. ✆ **0575-371-407.** Fax 0575-

The forested mountains of the Casentino, the region encompassing the upper valley of the River Arno, have been a hotbed of spirituality for centuries. The area is crammed with atmospheric mountain towns and historic sights, easily explored by car on day trips from Florence or Arezzo. For information on the region, call ℰ **0575-593-098** or visit www.turismo.intoscana.it.

An enticing target is the medieval hill town of **Poppi**, whose **Castello dei Conti Guidi** (ℰ **0575-520-516**) is visible for miles. This castle, started in 1274, was the seat of the Guidi counts who ruled the Casentino until 1440, when it came under the control of Florence. It's open daily from 10am to 6pm (last ticket 5:30pm). Admission is 5€ for adults, and 4€ for children 6–12 (free for 5 and under). Audio guides are 1€. The rest of diminutive Poppi is fun to explore. Many of the medieval buildings have retained their wooden porticos, and a slightly sleepy village atmosphere prevails.

You can branch off at Bibbiena, just 7km (4⅓ miles) down the road from Poppi, onto the SS208 and travel a winding 25km (16 miles) to the **Santuario Francescano della Verna** ★ (ℰ **0575-5341;** www.santuariolaverna. org), around 3km (1 ¾ miles) from the

village of **Chuisi della Verna. Francis of Assisi** loved to meditate here—a vision had informed him that the odd rents in the rocky ground were caused by the earthquakes that occurred when Christ was crucified. On his last trip here, the night of September 14, 1224, he was visited by a seraph who left him with a wholly new mark of sanctity—the stigmata of Christ's wounds. The small **mud-hut monastery** he founded has grown and is still a pilgrimage site for the devout. Surrounded by giant beech trees at a height of around 1,128m (3,700 ft.), it's also a wonderfully serene place with spectacular views.

In the main **Basilica di Santa Maria Assunta,** Andrea della Robbia left some of the greatest, most spiritual examples of his glazed terra-cotta works, like an *Ascension* and a beautifully simple *Annunciation.* The adjacent **Cappella**

371-409. 17 units. 95€–130€ double. Rates include breakfast. AE, DC, MC, V. Free parking. **Amenities:** Restaurant; bar; concierge; room service. *In room:* A/C, TV, hair dryer, minibar, Wi-Fi (free).

B&B Antiche Mura ★★ This remarkable guesthouse is plugged into the old city walls in rooms that date back to the 1200s—much of it feels like a plush museum, with walkways over glass-covered foundations, an olive press, and ancient drains. Each room is named and styled after a famous woman in literature or the movies, from Madame Bovary's period decor to the sensual reds used in the Marilyn Monroe room—all are comfy and feature exposed brick walls and wood-beam ceilings. It's just a short walk from the cathedral.

Piaggia di Murello 35, 52100 Arezzo. www.antichemura.info. ℰ **0575-20-410.** Fax 0575-016-2231. 6 units. 75€ double. Rates include breakfast vouchers for use in nearby cafes. AE, DC, MC, V. Free parking nearby. **Amenities:** Concierge. *In room:* A/C, TV, Wi-Fi (free).

Vogue Hotel Best of the standard hotels in town, with sleek doubles set in a beautifully renovated space, though, like most Aretines, the hosts are perhaps better known for their artistic prowess and business acumen than any down-home hospitality. Though service can be hit-and-miss, the location is perfect, the di Santa Maria degli Angeli, begun while the saint was alive, has another Andrea della Robbia *Assumption,* a *Pietà* and a *Nativity.* The **Museo della Verna** (Sat–Sun 10am–noon and 2–5pm, daily Jul–Aug; donation requested) next door houses some interesting bits and pieces, including the interior of an old apothecary and an ancient monk's habit fashioned from sackcloth. From the basilica you can walk along the **Corridor of the Stigmata,** lined with 17th-century murals detailing key moments in the life of St. Francis, to the scene of the miracle itself, now protected by the tiny **Capella delle Stimmate** (daily 8am–5pm; 7pm in summer; free). Scramble up to the summit of **La Penna** (1283m/4209 ft. 45 min.) for even more spectacular views. The sanctuary is open daily from 6pm to 7:30pm (9:30pm in summer). Admission is free (parking 2€ for 2 hr.).

Another 12km (7½ miles) south of Verna, **Michelangelo Buonarroti** was born in the hamlet of Caprese on March 6, 1475. Caprese has never forgotten this portentous event and even changed its name to **Caprese Michelangelo** after the boy grew up to become one of the greatest artists the world has ever known. His birthplace and ruined Castello di Caprese above the town have been converted into the serene **Museo Michelangiolesco** (✆ 0575-793-776; www.capresemichelangelo. net). The museum comprises two core 14th-century buildings: the Palazzo del Podestà (considered the most likely birthplace, as Michelangelo's father was mayor in 1475), and the Corte Alta, home to an intriguing ensemble of 19th-century Italian sculptures and casts of Michelangelo's greatest works. Opening times vary throughout the year (see website), but it's usually open Tuesday to Sunday from 11am to 5pm (Nov–Mar Fri–Sun only). Admission is 4€ for adults, 2.50€ ages 7 to 14, and free for children 6 and under. The location is stunning, and you can grab a rustic Tuscan meal at **Buca di Michelangelo** ★ (✆ 0575-793-921; www.bucadi michelangelo.it), nearby at Via Roma 51.

bathrooms are spacious and luxurious (huge tubs and rainforest showers), and the breakfasts are pretty filling.

Via Guido Monaco 56, 52100 Arezzo. www.voguehotel.it. ✆ **0575-24-361.** 26 units. 165€–220€ double. Rates include breakfast. AE, DC, MC, V. Garage parking 30€ per day. **Amenities:** Bar; babysitting; concierge; Internet (free in lobby); smoke-free rooms; room service (bar). *In room:* A/C, TV, minibar, Wi-Fi (3€ per hr.).

Where to Eat

Arezzo is a great place to eat, with plenty of *osteria*s and bars offering relatively cheap eats compared to other Tuscan towns. Be sure to grab a coffee and pastry at the venerable **Caffe 'dei Constanti** ★ (✆ **0575-182-4075;** Wed–Sun 7:30am–2am, also open Mon Apr–Sep), Piazza San Francesco 19 (opposite San Francesco church), which was featured in Roberto Benigni's *Life Is Beautiful* (there's a small still from the movie at the door). Founded in 1805, the cafe is also the best place in town for an *aperitivo* (from 6pm).

Antica Osteria L'Agania ★ TUSCAN This small joint doesn't bother with a wine list; a staff member plunks down a bottle of the eminently quaffable house chianti (just 5€). The locals pack into this long, wood-paneled room especially for the thick rib-sticking *ribollita* (minestrone with bread chunks), but you can also mix and match gnocchi, tagliatelle, and creamy polenta with the basic Tuscan sauces. The trattoria proudly offers the lovely "local dishes" foreign visitors rarely order, such as tripe *(trippa)* and the very fatty *grifi e polenta* (chunks of veal stomach in polenta). You may find your taste buds more attuned to the *polpette* (meatballs) or *uova con tartufo,* fried eggs topped with generous shavings of dried truffles.

Via Mazzini 10 (near San Francesco). ☎ **0575-295-381.** www.agania.com. Reservations recommended for dinner in high season. Primi 6€–10€; secondi 7€–10€. AE, DC, MC, V. Tues–Sun noon–3pm and 7–10:30pm. Closed last 2 weeks of June.

Buca di San Francesco ★ TUSCAN The Buca resides in the frescoed cellar of a 14th-century *palazzo* and has been run by the same family for over 70 years. Try the respectable *ribollita* or good *bringoli casalinghi con il sugo finto* (homemade spaghetti in chunky tomato sauce). For a secondo, order *la saporita di bonconte,* a plate piled with portions of all the restaurant's specialties—tripe, roasted sausages, baked rabbit, and others—a dish from the days when an army on the march had to make a communal stew out of what each man could muster (it comes with a commemorative plate). They'll keep pouring the *vin santo* until you run out of *cantucci* or fall off your chair, and they love sending you off with a bag of little goodies.

Via San Francesco 1 (next door to San Francesco). ☎ **0575-23-271.** www.bucadisanfrancesco.it. Reservations recommended. Primi 8€–16€; secondi 15€–22€. AE, DC, MC, V. Mon noon–2:30pm; Wed–Sun noon–2:30pm and 7–9:30pm. Closed 2 weeks in July.

Le Tastevin TUSCAN Tastevin is a chic and haughty spot that serves up Aretine dishes as well as plenty of more innovative foods, too. The *rigatoni alla amatriciana* is a hearty version with tomato sauce and cured chicken, while the very good *fusilli al ferretto* comes with duck ragout. Or you can try a variety of fish dishes or a fabulous *ossobuco di chianina* (beef *osso buco* cooked in fine chopped vegetables). But beware: If you're not a regular, service can verge on rude.

Via de' Cenci 9 (btw. Via Madonna del Prato and Corso Italia). ☎ **0575-28-304.** www.letastevin .it. Reservations recommended. Primi 8€–15€; secondi 12€–21€. AE, DC, MC, V. Tues–Sun 12:30–3pm and 7–10pm.

SANSEPOLCRO

37km (23 miles) NE of Arezzo; 15km (9 miles) N of Città di Castello; 122km (76 miles) E of Florence; 240km (149 miles) N of Rome

The medieval walled town of Sansepolcro is another key destination for anyone enamored of the art of **Piero della Francesca,** the monumentally important painter who was born here around 1412 or 1415. The small village established here around A.D. 1000 was so proud of the bits of the Holy Sepulcher a couple of pilgrims brought back that the town was named Borgo San Sepolcro, long after the alleged relics had been lost. Since then it's also been the birthplace of painters Raffaellino del Colle (1490–1566) and Santi di Tito (1536–1603), and more prosaically, of the Buitoni pasta empire, founded by Giulia Buitoni in 1827.

Essentials

GETTING THERE By Train: Unless you're coming from Umbria, the train is not an option. Sansepolcro anchors one end of the private FCU train line, with about 20 trains daily from **Perugia** (80 min.–2 hr.; 3.95€). Seven trains a day run from **Rome** to Terni, where you can switch to this FCU line (3½ hr. total if you hit the layover right). Sansepolcro station (✆ **0575-742-094**) is just outside the city walls at Piazza Battisti.

By Car: Sansepolcro lies where the SS73 from Arezzo intersects with the E45/SS3bis from Perugia. You can park outside Porta Fiorentina along Viale Vittorio Veneto to the east, or north outside Porta del Castello (around .70€ per hr.).

By Bus: BASCHETTI buses (✆ **0575-736-083;** www.baschetti.it) arrive and leave at the traffic circle off Via G. Marconi (at the west end of Via Aggiunti). Buses serve **Arezzo** (1 hr.) and **Città di Castello** (25 min.). **SULGA** runs a daily bus from Rome's Fiumicino airport (2:30pm) via Tiburtina bus station.

VISITOR INFORMATION The helpful **tourist office** is at Via Matteotti 8, just off the main piazza (✆/fax **0575-740-536;** www.comune.sansepolcro.ar.it; daily 9am–1pm and 3:30–7pm).

FESTIVALS On the second Sunday in September, the **Palio della Balestra** allows Sansepolcro a crossbow rematch with its traditional rivals from Gubbio (Umbria; p. 394). This medieval test of archery skill is highlighted with a display from Sansepolcro's famous *sbandieratori* (flag tossers). They perform their medieval act of juggling colorful banners dressed in Renaissance costumes lifted straight from Piero paintings. Call ✆ **0575-75-827,** or visit www.balestrierisansepolcro.it for more info. Don't miss the **markets** on Tuesday and Saturday mornings, and the excellent "high quality" market every third Saturday of the month.

Exploring Sansepolcro

Sansepolcro boasts a handsome old town but the only outstanding sight is the Museo Civico (see below), housed in the 14th-century **Palazzo dei Conservatori.** An outdoor staircase runs to the former main entrance, now a glassed-in doorway where you can see into one of the museum's main halls. There you can gaze on Piero della Francesca's masterpieces at any time of day or night—regardless of whether you buy a ticket to the museum. If you have more time, take a break from art at the **Aboca Museum,** Via Aggiunti 75 (✆ 0575-733-589, www.aboca museum.it; Apr–Sep daily 10am–1pm and 3–7pm; Oct–Mar Tues–Sun 10am–1pm and 2:30–6pm; adults 8€, 4€ children 10–14 and 65 and over, free children 9 and under), a slickly presented history of medicinal herbs, replete with fittingly rich aromas and pots of dried chamomile, mustard, and the like.

Museo Civico ★★ Though most famous for its remarkable **Piero della Francesca** works, Sansepolcro's museum also has a small collection of **prehistoric remains** (mostly ceramics and funerary goods) and elaborate medieval locks, as well as a room of church vestments and reliquary busts in the **vaulted cellars.**

In the main galleries, **Room 1** sports a 19th-century terra-cotta bust of Piero della Francesca. Among the 17th-century works in **Room 2** is a late Mannerist *Crucifixion* painted by il Passignano or someone in his circle. Stairs here lead up to a pair of rooms housing detached 15th-century frescoes by mostly unknown local artists, some with their fascinating *sinopie* (preliminary sketches).

Room 3 houses Piero's ***Polyptych della Misericordia*** ★ (1445–62), reassembled without its frame. The Mary of Mercy spreads her cloak around kneeling donors (the one to the left of her, looking up, is believed by some to be a self-portrait by Piero), while a sleepy-eyed St. John the Baptist and other saints look on. The central panel and Saints John and Sebastian are certainly from Piero's brush, as are the Crucifixion and the Angel and Virgin Annunciate panels flanking it. The rest were probably worked on by assistants or a miniaturist.

Room 4 starts with two detached frescoes by Piero, one **San Ludovico da Tolosa** (1460, and attributed by some to Piero's student Lorentino), and a famous partial fresco of **San Giuliano** ★ (1455–58). At the end of the room is one of Piero's indisputable masterpieces, the ***Resurrection of Christ*** ★★★. Painted in 1463, this work made Piero's modern reputation—art historians began paying attention to it and Piero in general after 1925, when Aldous Huxley dubbed it the "best picture in the world." The fresco-and-tempera work displays a resounding naturalism in its perfect perspective and the almost uncanny modeling of the figures and faces. At the same time it's imbued with an eerie spirituality, or rather supernaturalness, in the deadpan gaze of the risen Christ—here, truly a god in human form—and in the soldiers who look less asleep than under a magic spell of suspended animation. Piero lets the power of his art speak through his incomparable technique, leaving the religious symbolism to be relayed simply through the background. The second sleeping soldier on the left in the brown armor is thought to be a self-portrait of Piero. This fresco may be one of the few pieces of art that actually did save its city from destruction. In 1944, a British commanding officer had orders to bomb Nazi troops occupying the city. The officer, having read Huxley's words, held off the attack until the Germans withdrew on their own.

Room 5 has a 16th-century Umbrian-school *Annunciation* and Matteo di Giovanni's 1440 cathedral altarpiece, missing the central *Baptism of Christ* panel by Piero (it's in London's National Gallery). **Room 6** has two paintings by Raffaellino del Colle, a huge 1526 *Assumption and Coronation of the Virgin* and a detached fresco of *St. Leo I* (1520–30). The last few rooms are filled with Mannerist and baroque canvases, including a whole room dedicated to Santi di Tito.

The *Resurrection of Christ* at the Museo Civico.

Via Aggiunti 65 (back side of the former Palazzo Comunale on Piazza Garibaldi). ✆ **0575-732-218.** www.museocivicosansepolcro.it. Admission 6€ adults, 4.50€ seniors 65 and over and students 19–25, 3€ children 10–18, free children 9 and under. Mid-June to mid-Sept daily 9:30am–1:30pm and 2:30-7-pm; mid-Sept to mid-June daily 9:30am–1pm and 2:30–6pm.

BEAUTY IN GEOMETRY—ON THE TRAIL OF
PIERO della francesca

One of the leading lights of the early Renaissance, Piero della Francesca took the perspective obsession of Florentine masters Masaccio and Paolo Uccello and mixed it with the ethereal posed beauty of the Umbrian school to create a haunting style all his own. Piero's figures are at once hyper-posed masses of precision Euclidean geometry and vehicles for a profound expressive naturalism and astute psychological studies. His backgrounds, even those of the countryside, are masterpieces of architectural volume. His painting has so fascinated the modern world that the connect-the-dots loop of cities preserving his works has become known as the **Piero della Francesca Trail,** a pilgrimage route of sorts for art lovers. Arezzo and Sansepolcro are the main sites, but some 25km (16 miles) from Arezzo lies **Monterchi.** This is the home of Piero della Francesca's **Madonna del Parto ★★,** which you can see in the **Museo della Madonna del Parto,** built especially for it at Via Reglia 1 (© **0575-70-713**). This psychologically probing fresco depicts the Virgin Mary 9 months pregnant with Jesus, shown to us by a pair of angels who hold back the intricately embroidered flaps of a tent. Mary here is heavy with child, with one eyelid drooping and a hand on her swollen belly. She emanates a solemnity that's at once human yet regal, reflecting the grave import of becoming the mother of the Savior. The museum is open Monday to Friday from 9am to 1pm and 2 to 7pm, and Saturday and Sunday from 9am to 7pm (until 5pm daily Oct–Mar). Admission is 3.50€ for adults and 2€ for students 14 and over; children 13 and under are free.

When Piero's eyesight began to fail later in life, he wrote two treatises, *On the Five Regular Bodies* and *On Perspective in Painting,* which together set the rules for his universe of perspective and logic, broke down the human body into a geometric machine of perfect proportions, and became required reading for almost every Renaissance artist. He died near his hometown of Sansepolcro in 1492.

Where to Stay

Casa Mila ★★ This enchanting 14th-century property is smack in the middle of town, yet its surrounding gardens ensure complete serenity inside. You can rent the simple double room on a B&B basis (with en suite bathroom and shared sitting room), or two full apartments with one, two or three bedrooms, modern bathrooms and a kitchen/dining room. Furnishings are modern, but all the ceilings are timbered and the floors are original terra-cotta tiles. Guests can use the barbecue grill in the garden.

Via della Firenzuola 49, 52037 Sansepolcro (AR). www.casamila.it. ©/fax **0575-788-548.** 3 units. 80€ double (B&B); 80€–90€ apartment (1 bed); 105€–135€ apartment (2 beds); 150€–195€ apartment (3 beds). B&B rate includes breakfast. AE, DC, MC, V. Free parking nearby. **Amenities:** Wi-Fi (free). *In room:* A/C, TV, hair dryer, kitchen.

Locanda del Giglio (Ristorante Fiorentino) ★★ Don't confuse this welcoming place with the Albergo Fiorentino next door (much older and less appealing)—the Locanda features just four modern, cozy rooms, all equipped with DVD players and satellite TV, some with antique furnishings, and all are spotless, with bleached oak floors and soft LED lighting. La Lilla has the most historic character, while La Torre has a subtle Japanese theme. And you never have to leave the building for the best restaurant in town (see Ristorante Fiorentino, below).

Via L. Pacioli 60, 52037 Sansepolcro (AR). www.ristorantefiorentino.it/Locanda.aspx. ©/fax **0575-742-033.** 4 units. 77€ double. Rates include breakfast. MC, V. Free parking nearby. **Amenities:** Restaurant. *In room:* A/C, minibar, TV, Wi-Fi (free).

Where to Eat

Da Ventura ★ TUSCAN Service at this unpretentious trattoria, in its third generation of Tofanelli family management, is truly "by the cart." Under rough-hewn wood ceilings and arches made of wine bottles, you can mix and match your own antipasto with selections from a wheeled cart. Another cart bears fresh homemade tagliatelle so you can choose the sauce of your choice to top it. (The ragù is a tasty bet.) The *bistecca di vitello* (thick veal steak) and the *maialino in porchetta* (roast suckling pig) are also accompanied by a gurney of *contorni* so that you can sample several side dishes. Of course, it's all capped off with a cart of homemade desserts. Upstairs are five plain rooms with bathrooms that rent for 65€ per double.

Via Aggiunti 30 (a few blocks west of the Museo Civico). ©/fax **0575-742-560.** www.albergo daventura.it. Reservations recommended. Primi 8€–15€; secondi 8.50€–39€. AE, DC, MC, V. Tues–Sat 12:30–2:15pm and 7:30–9:30pm; Sun 12:30–2:15pm. Closed Jan 1–10 and Aug 1–20.

Ristorante Fiorentino ★★ TUSCAN This very traditional 2-centuries-old place with coffered wood ceilings has a mélange of trattoria artifacts crowding the walls. The genial owner, Alessio, would rather recite what the kitchen is most proud of that night than break out an impersonal menu. Everything is fresh, the pasta is made by hand, and though the kitchen sticks to antique recipes, it does trim meats lean, and they won't look askance if you order a *porzione ridotto* (small portion). The *cappelli d'Alpino con pasta verde* (ricotta and veggies stuffed into spinach ravioli) is the primo to order. Afterward, try the veal stewed with pears or duck roasted with wild fennel.

Via L. Pacioli 60. © **0575-742-033.** www.ristorantefiorentino.it. Reservations recommended. Primi 8€–8.50€; secondi 9€–14€. DC, MC, V. Thurs–Tues 12:30–3pm and 7:30–10:30pm. Closed Jan 20–30 and last 2 weeks of July.

A Side Trip to Castiglion Fiorentino

From Sansepolcro, it's a 15km (9-mile) jaunt across the border to **Umbria** (see chapters 10 and 11 for more information). If you haven't finished with Tuscany, you can head back toward Arezzo, turning south on the SS71 to **Castiglion Fiorentino,** a fortified medieval town dominated by a pronglike tower, the **Torre del Cassero.**

The **tourist office** (© **0575-658-278;** www.prolococastiglionfiorentino.it; Mon 9:30–11:30, Tues–Sat 9:30am–11:30am and 4–6pm) is at Piazza Risorgimento 19 next to a parking lot (1€ for 1 hr.), near the 13th-century Porta Fiorentina.

From here the center of town is a short climb along Corso Italia to the **Piazza del Municipio,** bordered by the 16th-century **Loggiato Vasariano,** supposedly remodeled by Giorgio Vasari in the 1560s—the views across the valley from here are sensational. Just above this at Via del Cassero 6 is the deconsecrated church of Sant'Angelo, now the entrance to the **Pinacoteca Comunale,** Piazza del Municipio 12 (© **0575-657-466**). Its well-labeled collections include some medieval gilded copper crosses, a Taddeo Gaddi *Madonna and Child,* and an odd Bartolomeo della Gatta *St. Francis Receiving the Stigmata.* (Tradition holds the other friars nearby weren't awake when Francis was visited by the seraph, but here one clearly is.) The museum is open April to October Tuesday to Sunday from 10am to 12:30pm and 4 to 6:30pm, and November to March Tuesday to Sunday 10am to 12:30pm and 3:30 to 6pm. Admission is 3€ for adults; 2€ for students 17 and over and adults 65 and over; and .50€ for children 16 and under; or 5€, 3€, and 1€ if you want to tack on a visit to any of the town's other museums. Just around the corner at Via Tribunale 8 is the **Palazzo Pretorio** and the **Museo Archeologico,** a tiny collection of Etruscan remains found in the area (same hours and fees as the Pinacoteca). The *palazzo* borders the **Area Monumental de Cassero** (daily 8am–7pm; free admission), the remains of the 14th-century Perugian fortress that contains the **Torre del Cassero.** You can only climb the tower itself May to September, usually on holidays and the day before holidays from 10am to 1pm and 4 to 7pm (adults 1.50€). Call © **0575-659-457** to confirm.

Also worth calling on is the somber **Collegiata di San Giuliano** (daily 8am–6pm; free admission), some 300m (984 ft.) below on Piazza San Giuliano, completed in 1853 on the site of a much older church (the bell tower actually dates from 1930). Inside is a *Madonna Enthroned with Saints* by Bartolomeo della Gatta on the third altar on the right, Lorenzo di Credi's *Adoration of the Child* in a chapel to the right of the high altar, and a huge *Maestà* by Segna di Bonaventura in the left transept. The **Museo delle Pieve di San Giuliano** next door (with the same hours and fees as Pinacoteca) preserves a *Deposition* by Signorelli's school.

CORTONA ★★

34km (22 miles) S of Arezzo; 105km (63 miles) SE of Florence; 194km (120 miles) N of Rome

Cortona sits majestically on a green mountainside above terraced olive groves, stony yet inviting. It's a steep medieval city where cut-stone staircases take the place of many streets, and views over the wide Chiana Valley stretch south to Umbria's Lake Trasimeno. Cortona has truly punched above its artistic weight; it spawned (among others) the great pre-Michelangelo painter Luca Signorelli and the early-17th-century painter/architect Pietro da Cortona.

Cortona was already a thriving city by the 4th century B.C., when it was one of 12 cities that formed the Etruscan confederation. New finds at Melone II, one of several Etruscan tombs dotting the hillside and valley below the town, suggest it may have been an even more important center than previously believed.

Even though it was long in a fairly undervisited corner of Tuscany, Cortona never succumbed to the all-too-common fate of becoming a dusty abandoned backwater. It retained a good bit of *passeggiata* action most evenings on the **Rugapiana** ("flat street," a nickname for Via Nazionale, the only road in town that even comes close to fitting that description), and in summer the city hosts a modest outdoor film festival in the Parterre Gardens behind San Domenico. Its art treasures have always ensured a steady stream of tourists, but the huge popularity of Frances Mayes's book *Under the Tuscan Sun* (1996), about finding love while buying and renovating a villa just outside town, hurled Cortona from relative obscurity to the forefront of Tuscan tourism, especially after the tear-jerking movie starring Diane Lane was released in 2003. Expect serious crowds, especially in summer.

Essentials

GETTING THERE By Train: Cortona doesn't have its own station, but two stops on the main Rome-Arezzo line serve it. The nearer one, Camucia/Cortona (✆ 0575-603-018), is just 5km (3 miles) from town, but only local trains stop here. More trains stop at Terontola (✆ 0575-67-034) station, 11km (7 miles) from town. It's about a 25-minute ride from Arezzo (26 trains daily; 3.10€), 1 hour (2 hr. on the slow line) from Florence (24 trains daily; 7.90€), and 2 to 3 hours from Rome (15 trains daily; 10.20€). To save time, you can buy tickets at Cortona's tourist office.

From both stations, buses leave about every 30 minutes for Cortona. At Camucia you can buy tickets at the bar outside the station or, if it's closed, the *tabacchi* up the street near the next bus stop.

By Car: From Arezzo (24km/15 miles), take the SS71 and turn off for Cortona at Il Sodo (especially for Il Falconiere hotel) or Camucia. From Florence or Rome, take the A1 to the Valdichiana exit and follow the Raccordo Perugia-A1 (direction: Perugia) until the Cortona exit. This same highway originates in Siena. When the road divides just below Cortona, turn right and **park** for free in the lot on your right. From there, an escalator whisks you up the worst of the hill.

By Bus: Roughly hourly **LFI buses** (✆ 0575-39-881; www.lfi.it) from Arezzo (50 min.) terminate in Piazzale Garibaldi, by the gate.

VISITOR INFORMATION The **APT office** is at Piazza Signorelli 9, in the courtyard beyond the Museo dell'Accademia Etrusca ticket office (✆ 0575-637-223; infocortona@apt.arezzo.it). October through mid-May, it's open

Typical wares for sale in Cortona.

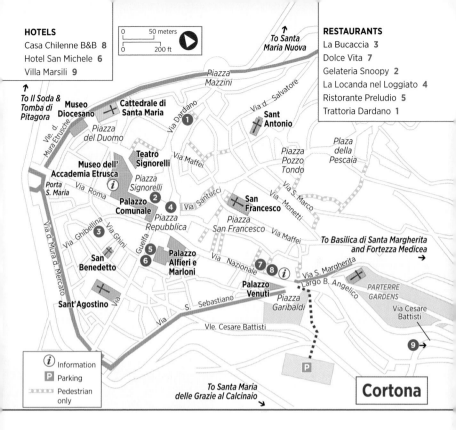

HOTELS
Casa Chilenne B&B **8**
Hotel San Michele **6**
Villa Marsili **9**

RESTAURANTS
La Bucaccia **3**
Dolce Vita **7**
Gelateria Snoopy **2**
La Locanda nel Loggiato **4**
Ristorante Preludio **5**
Trattoria Dardano **1**

To Santa Maria Nuova

To Il Soda & Tomba di Pitagora

Museo Diocesano

Cattedrale di Santa Maria **1**

Piazza Mazzini

Via Dardano

Via d. Salvatore

Sant Antonio

Piazza del Duomo

Vle d. Mura Etrusche

Teatro Signorelli

Museo dell' Accademia Etrusca

Porta S. Maria

Via Maffei

Piazza Signorelli

Via Roma

Palazzo Comunale **2**

Piazza Repubblica

Via Santucci

San Francesco

Piazza Pozzo Tondo

Plaza della Pescaia

Via S. Marco

Via Monetti

4

Piazza San Francesco

Via Maffei

To Basilica di Santa Margherita and Fortezza Medicea →

Via Ghibellina

Via Ghini

Via Guelfa

3

5
6

San Benedetto

Palazzo Alfieri e Marloni

Via Nazionale

7 8 i

Via S. Margherita

Largo B. Angelico

PARTERRE GARDENS

Via Cesare Battisti

Via d. Mura d. Mercato

Sant'Agostino

Via

S. Sebastiano

Palazzo Venuti

Piazza Garibaldi

9 →

Vle. Cesare Battisti

i Information
P Parking
Pedestrian only

P

To Santa Maria delle Grazie al Calcinaio ↘

Cortona

0 — 50 meters
0 — 200 ft

9am to 1pm and 3 to 6pm Monday to Friday, 9am to 1pm only on Saturdays. Mid-May to November it's open Monday to Saturday 9am to 1pm and 3 to 6pm, and Sunday 9am to 1pm.

FESTIVALS & MARKETS On a Sunday in late May, the town turns out in late-14th-century costume for crossbow competitions in the annual **Giostra dell'Archidado.** At the end of July, Cortona takes part in the **Umbria Jazz festival** (Umbria is just across the border), and a well-regarded **antiques fair** is held in late August/early September (©**0575-630-610** for info). From August 14 to August 15, Cortona celebrates the mighty Chiana Valley beefsteak with a **Sagra della Bistecca,** holding a huge communal barbecue in the Parterre Gardens. **Market** day is Saturday.

Exploring Cortona

Basilica di Santa Margherita ★★ High above the town, this important pilgrimage site contains the revered remains of St. Margaret, the patron saint of Cortona. **Margaret of Cortona** (1247–97) became a humble follower of St. Francis relatively late in life, but by 1277 she began attracting attention thanks to her alleged ability to communicate directly with God. She spent the rest of her life looking after the sick and indigent of Cortona, and was canonized in 1728. Most of the church is 19th century, and though grand, of little artistic merit—come instead to see Margaret's embalmed remains, displayed in a lavish 14th-century Gothic tomb above the main altar. You can park by the basilica, or make a very steep ascent from town.

Piazzale Santa Margherita 1. © **0575-603-116.** www.santamargheritadacortona.org. Free admission. Daily 10:30am–1:30pm and 2:30–6pm.

Cattedrale di Santa Maria The Duomo's High Renaissance barrel-vaulted interior from the 16th century contains many mediocre 17th-century works and decorations alongside good pieces. You'll see Raffaello Vanni's *Transfiguration,* with a rather effeminate Christ (second altar on the right), and local boy Lorenzo Berrettini's *Death of St. Joseph* (fourth altar), a touching scene where a frightened, dying Joseph turns to Jesus and grasps his son's hand for reassurance. Behind the high altar, in the choir, is a collection of 16th- and early-17th-century paintings. In the middle of the right wall is Andrea Commodi's richly detailed *Consecration of the Basilica of San Salvatore* (1607). The back wall has a thematic link from right to left, starting with Luca Signorelli's badly deteriorated *Crucifixion,* then Francesco Signorelli's *Incredulity of St. Thomas,* who pokes his finger suspiciously into the risen Christ's wound. Thomas doubts again in Alessandro Allori's *Madonna of the Holy Girdle.* The only work of note on the choir's left wall is Andrea del Sarto's *Assumption.* As you leave the church, pause at the third altar on your right to see local baroque master Pietro (Berrettini) da Cortona's *Adoration of the Shepherds* (1663).

Piazza del Duomo 1 (at the end of Via Casali).
© **0575-603-256.** Free admission. Summer daily 7:30am–1pm and 3:30–6:30pm; winter daily 8am–12:30pm and 3–5:30pm (hours tend to vary).

Fortezza Medicea di Girifalco ★★ Cortona's major secular highlight is all uphill. The best route to the Fortezza Medicea di Girifalco follows the wall from Piazza Garibaldi along Via Santa Margherita, the **Via Crucis ★**. This torturous, stepped ascent is enlivened by 15 mosaics depicting the Stations of the Cross by Cortonese Futurist Gino Severini. By the second time Christ falls, you'll feel like doing the same. Pause for a restorative drink at the bar by the Basilica Santa Margherita. Built in 1556 by a relative of Pope Pius IV, the four surviving bastions of the Fortezza have unmatched views as far as Castiglione del Lago, Arezzo, and the colossal Monte Amiata. The interior primarily serves as an exhibition venue for cultural events—check at the tourist office to see what's on.

Via Santa Margherita 2. © **0575-637-235.** Admission 3€ adults, 1.50€ ages 6–12. Daily 10:30am–1:30pm and 2:30–6pm.

The Palazzo Communale in Cortona.

Museo dell'Accademia Etrusca

★★ Cortona was one of the 12 cities of the Etruscan confederation, and the proliferation of artifacts discovered in the area led to the founding of an Etruscan Academy in 1727. Their illuminating collections are now housed in the Palazzo Casali, a 13th-century mansion built for the city's governors; the original upper floors evoke the medieval period, while the lower galleries received a smart, contemporary overhaul in 2008. Allow at least 2 hours to see it all.

Fra' Angelico's *Annunciation* in the Museo Diocesano.

The **lower galleries** primarily tackle the Etruscan and Roman history of Cortona, enlivened by some spectacular finds, mostly from excavated tombs in the area. Exceptional pieces grace each of the 14 galleries, but don't miss the enigmatic **"banquet and symposium"** statues and **Bettole gold jewelry** (including an extraordinary gold-leaf diadem) in Room 7. Roman Cortona (rooms 10 to 14), is less absorbing, though the mosaics in Room 14 have been wonderfully preserved.

The sprawling **upper floors** are devoted to the vast collection of miscellaneous objects collected by the Accademia Etrusca over the years, including a rare **Etruscan oil lamp chandelier** from the late 4th century B.C. decorated with human heads, allegorical figures, and a few virile Pans playing their pipes, all surrounding a leering Gorgon's head on the bottom. On the walls hang **paintings** spanning the Renaissance and baroque periods, and the famous *Musa Polimnia,* an encaustic (pigmented wax on wood) portrait that has of late been accused of being an 18th-century fake rather than a 1st-century-A.D. Roman original.

The Sala Severini is devoted to the work of **Gino Severini** (1883–1966), Cortona's most recent artistic master. Severini's goal apparently was to paint at least one piece in every major artistic style and movement from the first half of this century, though he was ostensibly a die-hard Futurist.

If this museum has piqued your interest in Etruscan archeology, ask here about visiting excavation sites in the surrounding countryside (p. 357).

Piazza Signorelli 9. ℂ **0575-630-415** or 0575-637-235. www.cortonamaec.org. Admission 8€ adults, 4€ children 6–12, students 2€ (joint ticket with Museo Diocesano 10€, 6€). Daily 10am–7pm (Tues–Sun 10am–5pm Nov–Mar).

Museo Diocesano del Capitolo ★★

Across from the cathedral, in the deconsecrated Chiesa del Gesù (Church of Jesus), is a little museum where almost every work is a masterpiece.

Rooms 2 and 3, in the old church hall and sacristy dating from 1505, contain some of the best works, but don't overlook the elaborate painted wood **ceiling,** carved by a local maestro Mezzanotte ("Midnight") in 1536. Inside you'll see a crucified *Christ* (1320) gushing blood, by a young Pietro Lorenzetti; and a *Madonna and Child with Saints* (1435) by Sassetta (another possible Cortonan) in which Mary looks with surprising tenderness (for early-15th-c. art) at her baby.

In Bartolomeo della Gatta's ***Assumption*** (1475), Mary, surrounded by a host of heavenly musicians and russet cherubim, dangles her girdle almost suggestively to the incredulous Thomas below.

This section's true treasures are the Fra'Angelicos. The polyptych ***Madonna Enthroned with Four Saints*** (1437), in bright primaries, stands out against the gold-leaf background. Over the altar is the theme at which Angelico was the master, an ***Annunciation*** (1436). The delicate feathers on Gabriel's wings and carpet of wildflowers show Angelico's command of minute detail, and the composition demonstrates his deep understanding of meaning in the Bible stories he illustrated so well. In the background is the finale of man's fall from grace, the expulsion of Adam and Eve from Eden; the theme is brought full circle in the foreground's Annunciation of the birth of Christ, the beginning of man's salvation. The sacristy behind the altar has a Pietro Lorenzetti *Madonna and Child* and a damaged 13th-century *St. Margaret of Cortona* by the Aretine school.

Room 4 or the Sala Signorelli, just off the entrance, gives you a chance to appreciate how skilled the Cortona-born master was in comparison to his workshop, his school (painters who imitated him), or even his nephew. **Luca Signorelli** himself painted the ***Deposition*** (1502), with the crucifixion, the resurrection, and a surreal city by a lake all in the background, and in the foreground a swooning Mary, a well-modeled Christ, and a saint pocketing a crucifixion nail and the crown of thorns—presumably destined for numerous Italian reliquaries. Vasari tells us the face of Christ is actually a portrait of Luca's son, who died during the 1502 plague. Luca also signed the ***Communion of the Apostles*** (1512), painted with a very strong sense of perspective and liberal use of bright primaries and illusionistic marble floor panels (notice Judas in the foreground—ashamed of his imminent betrayal, he can't swallow the Host and instead hides it in his purse as he turns away).

Downstairs, **Room 6** is the old Oratory, decorated by florid frescoes of Old Testament scenes designed by Vasari and executed by one of his pupils in around 1554. There's a terra-cotta *Pietà* dating from around 1520 at the altar.

Rooms 7 and 8 contain less interesting religious vestments and artifacts, though the incredibly ornate 15th-century **Vagnucci Reliquary** is worth lingering over.

Piazza del Duomo 1. ✆ **0575-62-830.** Admission 5€ adults, 3€ ages 6–14, 1€ students (joint ticket with Museo dell'Accademia Etrusca 10€ adults, 6€ children). Apr–Oct Tues–Sun 10am–7pm; Nov–Mar Tues–Sun 10am–5pm.

San Domenico ★ When you've finished with the main sights above, you might want to visit other attractions like San Domenico, near Piazza Garibaldi (the first square in town you come to by car or bus), with its faded *Fra'Angelico* under glass above the door and Luca Signorelli's *Madonna and Saints* (1515) to the left of the altar. The 15th-century altarpiece by Lorenzo di Niccolò Gerini is a cross between a Gothic composition and a classic early Renaissance style, plus—unlike many large altarpieces across Italy that have been broken up over the ages—it's completely intact, pinnacles, predella, and all.

Largo Beato Angelico 1. ✆ **0575-603-217.** Free admission. Daily 8am–12:30pm and 3–5:30pm.

San Francesco ★ The second Franciscan church ever built (begun around 1247), and the burial place of the saint's main disciple, **Brother Elias,** is a quiet, contemplative space, despite being a relatively important place of worship. The high altar contains the **Reliquary of the Holy Cross**, an ornate 10th-century

tomb hunting: THE PARCO ARCHEOLOGICO DI CORTONA

The countryside around Cortona is dotted with so-called **"Meloni,"** Etruscan burial-mounds. Most are looked after by the Museo dell'Accademia Etrusca under the collective heading **Parco Archeologico di Cortona;** three of the most intriguing tombs are located on the slopes just below the Cortona walls. You could walk down, but it's a lot easier going back up by car.

Heading down the hill on the main road to Camucia, you'll come upon a turnoff to the right for the **Tanella di Pitagora,** a charming 2nd-century-B.C. Etruscan tomb. It's on a circular plan with a vaulted roof that a 19th-century "restoration" left bare of its probable earth covering (but surrounded with solemn cypresses). The tomb is normally open all day (no admission).

Farther down follow the signs to the hamlet known as Il Sodo (just off the SS71 to Arezzo), and park at the **Tumulo I del Sodo ★**, open April to October Tuesday, Friday, and Sunday 9:30am to 12:30pm (admission 2€). The passage and chambers inside this 6th-century-B.C. Etruscan tomb are in excellent condition, due in no small part to the fact that the bits that were missing were replaced by brick guesswork after it was discovered in 1909. The walls are made of tufa from Orvieto (how the rock got all the way here is anybody's guess), and there's an Etruscan inscription (read right to left) above a small passage between two of the burial chambers. The inscription explains this side door: The chambers were the final resting places of a husband and wife; the passage was there in case they felt like visiting each other during eternity.

From tomb 1 a signposted footpath leads to the **Tumulo II del Sodo ★★**, open Tuesday to Sunday from 8:30am to 1:30pm (free admission), dating back at least to the late 7th century B.C. The tomb catapulted to the fore of Etruscan archaeological interest after the chance discovery in the early 1990s of a 6th-century-B.C. altar sticking out of one side of the circular tumulus. Subsequent excavations have unearthed more bits from the altar, which is reached by a monumental stairway flanked by two sphinxes biting the heads off warriors who are simultaneously stabbing the animals in the side, thought to represent the battle between life and death. The digs have also revealed at least 17 more tombs in the ground around the tumulus. Some of these predate the altar, but most are from the Hellenistic and Roman eras, all the way to the 1st century A.D. For more information, call ☎ **0575-630-415** or 0575-637-235, or ask at the Museo dell'Accademia Etrusca (p. 355).

ivory tablet, said to contain a fragment of Christ's cross, gifted to Elias by the Byzantine emperor in 1244. The chapel to the left contains three holy relics linked to **St Francis** (his tunic, a New Testament, and a cushion). In terms of art work, the chapel to the right of the altar contains a 14th century fresco of *Madonna and Child,* while the *Immacolata Concezione* (1609) by Commodi dominates the third altar on the right. **Pietro da Cortona**'s last work, an *Annunciation* in the third chapel on the left, was completed around 1669. **Luca Signorelli,** who died in Cortona in 1523, may also be buried in the church's crypt.

Piazza San Francesco, Via Berrettini 4. ☎ **0575-603-205.** Free admission. Daily 9am–6:45pm.

Santa Maria delle Grazie al Calcinaio ★ Just below the city walls, on the hillside carpeted with olive trees, sits Cortona's tribute to High Renaissance architecture: Santa Maria delle Grazie al Calcinaio. It was built between 1485 and 1513 and is the masterpiece (and only definitely attributable work) of Francesco di Giorgio Martini. He designed it on a Latin cross plan to mark the spot where a worker in a limekiln (*calcinaio*) saw a miraculous image of the Virgin appear on the rock wall. The harmonious Brunelleschian interior has a rose window in stained glass by the French master of that art, Guillaume de Marcillat, as well as a late-16th-century *Madonna and Saints* by Florentine artist Alessandro Allori in the right transept.

Loc. Calcinaio 227. ✆ **0575-604-830.** Free admission. Daily 9am–noon and 3–5pm.

Where to Stay

Besides the hotels below, Cortona contains some real B&B gems. **Casa Chilenne B&B** ★★★, Via Nazionale 65 (www.casachilenne.com; ✆/fax **0575-603-320**), and **Casa Bellavista** ★★★, Località Creti 40 (www.casabellavista.it; ✆ **0575-610-311**), both offer stunning accommodations, friendly hosts, and free Internet. Casa Chilenne is located in the heart of town (rooms for 100€), while Bellavista offers a more rustic experience a short drive west in the village of Creti (120€–140€). Book way in advance, as rooms in both are limited (four rooms are available in Bellavista and five in Casa Chilenne).

If you really want to soak up the sun in this now-famous countryside, you can also try an *agriturismo* outside of town. The tourist office publishes a list of them, or visit **www.apt.arezzo.it** for additional choices. A luxurious option is the **Villa di Piazzano** ★★, Località Piazzano (www.villadipiazzano.com; ✆ **075-826-226**), 6km (3 ¾ miles) southeast of Cortona. This fabulous property dates back to 1464, but boasts modern amenities, large rooms, a pool, and flowery gardens—breakfast includes a huge spread of homemade cakes, fresh fruit, and baked goods, served on a sun-swept terrace. Rates in high season range from 205€ to 340€.

Finally, fans of *Under the Tuscan Sun* will be thrilled to learn that the actual house that served as "Villa Bramasole" in the movie is now a rental property known as **Villa Laura,** just outside town. Originally built in 1504, the site contains the main villa and adjacent farmhouse, with nine bedrooms with en suite bathrooms, air-conditioning, a swimming pool and hot tub, and Wi-Fi. Contact Villa Vacations (www.villavacations.com; ✆ **800-261-4460**) for more details.

Hotel San Michele ★ This 15th-century palace offers High Renaissance Brunelleschian style with off-white plaster walls and vaulted ceilings accented by arches in gray *pietra serena.* It's the best place to stay in the center of town. None of the rooms are overly spacious, but that just renders ones like no. 250, in the tower, more cozily romantic (and it has great views to boot). The breakfast spread is generous, with fruit and ham, and there are two bar lounges, one of them frescoed, to relax in after dinner at Ristorante Preludio next door (under separate management; see below).

They also run the excellent **Residence Borgo San Pietro** (www.borgo sanpietro.com; ✆ **0575-612-402**), 4km (2½ miles) outside town in San Pietro a Cegliolo, with 14 rooms and 5 apartments each with a kitchenette. Doubles start at around 130€, including free Wi-Fi.

Via Guelfa 15 (just off Piazza della Repubblica), 52044 Cortona (AR). www.hotelsanmichele.net. ✆ **0575-604-348.** Fax 0575-630-147. 43 units. 89€ standard double; 98€ superior double; 109€

triple. Rates include buffet breakfast. AE, DC, MC, V. Garage parking 20€ per day. Closed Jan 6–Mar 6. **Amenities:** Babysitting; bikes; concierge; room service; Wi-Fi (free in public areas). *In room:* A/C, TV, hair dryer, minibar.

Relais Il Falconiere ★★ Riccardo and Silvia Baracchi have turned a series of 17th-century buildings into a countryside idyll overlooking their own olive grove to the Valdichiana. The rooms are scattered between the main villa, two flanking the little chapel, and seven very large rooms and minisuites in a series of stone buildings a bit removed from the rest of the complex for some privacy. Each guest room is different, but many have worn terra-cotta–tiled floors, cast-iron canopied bed frames, hand-woven linens, antique-style furnishings, timbered ceilings, hydromassage tubs, and frescoes on some of the walls. The old *limonaia* (lemon house) has been converted into one of the best restaurants in the area, serving refined Tuscan food in an elegant setting with classical music in the background (daily 1–2pm and 8–10pm; closed Mon–Tues afternoon Jan–Feb; closed several days in Jan).

Loc. San Martino 370 (3km/2 miles north of Cortona), 52044 Cortona (AR). www.ilfalconiere.it. ✆ **0575-612-616** or 0575-612-679. Fax 0575-612-927. 19 units. 270€ classic double; 360€ deluxe double; 460€ junior suite; 570€ suite. Rates include breakfast. AE, DC, MC, V. Free parking. Follow directions to Cortona listed earlier and turn to head up toward the city at the Il Sodo intersection of the SS71; the main road to town immediately curves up to the right, but follow instead the small road veering left (a blue sign reads SAN MARTINO IN BOCENA). **Amenities:** Restaurant; babysitting; free bikes; concierge; 2 pools; room service; Wi-Fi (free in public areas). *In room:* A/C, TV, hair dryer, Internet, minibar, Jacuzzi (in deluxe rooms and suites).

Villa Marsili ★★★ Cortona's most enchanting and tranquil hotel lies a short, but steep, hike down from the old center, set in a sensitively converted 18th-century villa. Frescoes from the 14th-century church that once stood here have been artfully blended into the property. Rooms are beautifully decked out in antique and period furnishings, many offering panoramic views of Lake Trasimeno in the distance (deluxe rooms come with a Jacuzzi). Breakfasts are especially high quality. The only real downsides are the hike uphill to town and the long walk to the nearest free parking (valet parking is also available).

Viale Cesare Battisti 13, 52044 Cortona (AR). www.villamarsili.net. ✆ **0575-605-252.** Fax 0575-605-618. 27 units. 165€ standard double; 210€–230€ superior double; 350€ suite. Rates include buffet breakfast. AE, DC, MC, V. Free parking. **Amenities:** Bar; babysitting; concierge; room service; Wi-Fi (free in public areas). *In room:* A/C, TV, hair dryer, Internet (free), minibar.

Where to Eat

Even if you are not staying in Cortona, try and snag at least one meal at the charming Relais Il Falconiere (see above). Newcomer **Dolce Vita ★**, Via Nazionale 71 (✆ **0575-630-102;** www.gelateriadolcevita.it), wins the gelato stakes with its exotic (papaya) and quirky (Lion bar, Coca-Cola) flavors, but **Gelateria Snoopy** opposite MAEC at Piazza Signorelli 29 is a decent standby.

La Bucaccia ★★ TUSCAN Cortona's most popular restaurant just about deserves the plaudits, set in a series of gorgeous stone-wall cellars that form part of the 13th-century Palazzo Cattani. While the dining room is entertained by ebullient manager Romano Magi, Chef Agostina draws upon local olive oils and meats to create traditional soups and homemade pastas and desserts. Secondi are the real highlight here, especially the beef fillets and steaks cooked in red wine and other luscious Tuscan sauces; try the boar with apple and almonds if it's on the menu.

Via Ghibellina 17. ℂ **0575-606-039.** www.labucaccia.it. Reservations recommended. Primi 8€–15€; secondi 9€–17€. AE, DC, MC, V. Wed–Mon 12:30–2:30pm and 7–10pm. Closed Jan 7 to mid-Feb and 1st week of July.

La Locanda nel Loggiato ITALIAN/TUSCAN Piazza della Repubblica is your dining backdrop if you plunk down the extra money for one of the alfresco tables under this restaurant's namesake little loggia overlooking the main square. If you choose to sit indoors, you'll be dining amid 16th-century stone-and-brick wine cellars. It's all very touristy of course and service can be a little cold, but the surroundings are hard to beat. The food is good, too; *verdure grigliate* (grilled vegetable slices under oil) as an antipasto will make you feel healthy even if you order the succulent *bistecca fiorentina* as a secondo (it goes excellently with roast potatoes). In between, consider the ravioli *gnudi alla fonduta di tartufo*, "naked ravioli"—just the ricotta and spinach stuffing—which is good even if the fondue sauce masks the delicate flavor of the truffles.

Piazza di Pescheria 3 (above Piazza della Repubblica). ℂ **0575-630-575.** www.locandanel loggiato.it. Reservations recommended. Primi 8€–10€; secondi 7€–31€. AE, DC, MC, V. Thurs–Tues 12:15–2:30pm and 7:15–9:30pm. Closed Jan.

Ristorante Preludio ★ TUSCAN In a town otherwise steeped in tradition, Preludio draws crowds for its unique nouvelle twist on Tuscan cooking. The white walls, high ceilings, and gray stone accents give the restaurant a Renaissance look, even though the lunette frescoes are modern. The *bruschette miste* (toasted bread sliced and topped with tomatoes, liver pâté, or cheese and arugula) makes a tasty start, followed by *ravioli di caciotta ai pomodorini* (homemade ravioli stuffed with fresh sheep's cheese and spinach and topped with barely cooked tomatoes and garlic). The *carpaccio alla rucola* is a classic secondo, but even better is the *petto d'anatra ai quattro pepi* (rich, delicate slices of duck served in a sauce laden with four types of softened peppercorn). One piece of advice: Order bottled wine rather than the limp house red.

Via Guelfa 11 (next to the Hotel San Michele). ℂ **0575-630-104.** www.ilpreludio.net. Reservations recommended. Primi 8€–10€; secondi 13€–18€. AE, DC, MC, V. June–Oct Tues–Sun 12:30–3:30pm and 7:30–10pm; early Nov and Dec 16–May Tues–Sun 7:30–10pm, Sun noon–2pm. Closed Nov 15–Dec 15.

Trattoria Dardano ★ 🍴 TUSCAN Of the several good *casalinga* (home cooking) *trattorie* along this street, this one merits singling out if only for its heavenly tiramisù, made the old-fashioned way. It's also justly famous for its *crostini neri* with chicken liver, and thick *ribollita*—Cortonans ask for hot pepper to sprinkle over it, but you can just drizzle on olive oil if that's more your style. There's always lots of fresh porcini mushrooms in season, and a tasty boar pasta, but when it comes to secondi, Dardano specializes in roasts over a charcoal fire: Try *pollo* (chicken), *anatra* (duck) or *faraona* (guinea hen)—or go for a modest splurge with a *bistecca alla fiorentina* (this being the valley whence comes Tuscany's best beef).

Via Dardano 24. ℂ **0575-601-944.** www.trattoriadardano.com. Reservations recommended. Primi 5€–7€; secondi 5€–8€; fixed-price menu without wine 13€. No credit cards. Thurs–Tues noon–2:45pm and 6:40–10pm. Closed Jan–Feb.

THE WESTERN valdichana

The eastern side of the wide Valdichiana (Chiana Valley) falls primarily within Arezzo province and is dominated by Cortona (discussed earlier), but with more time it pays to explore the less touristy western side, bordering Siena province. **Monte San Savino** (www.comune.monte-san-savino.ar.it; see picture below) is a scenic walled hill town 43km (27 miles) from Arezzo on the SS73; the main attractions here are associated with ceramic artist **Andrea Sansovino** (1460–1529), who eventually took up sculpture and became a master Renaissance carver. You can see two of his ceramic pieces in the church of **Santa Chiara;** his altarpiece of the *Madonna and Child with Saints* was probably glazed by Andrea or Giovanni della Robbia, and the unglazed *Saints Lorenzo, Roch, and Sebastian* was one of his earliest masterpieces. The **Pieve,** farther along Corso Sangallo on the right, was built in 1100 and remodeled in the 18th century; it contains some early Sansovino works, including a sarcophagus (1498) just inside the main door. On Piazza di Monte is the disintegrating Sansovino door on **Sant'Agostino.** Andrea Sansovino designed the double loggia against the inside front wall of this church, as well as the cloister (1528), entered from a door to the left of the facade on the piazza outside. The artist's simple tomb slab was discovered in 1969 under the pulpit.

A byroad from here leads 8km (5 miles) south to the tiny elliptical burg of **Lucignano** (www.comune.lucignano.ar.it), a popular aerial photo on posters in area tourist offices. The focuses of the town's four concentric ellipses are the **Collegiata,** with its pretty oval staircase, and the **Palazzo Comunale,** with its small museum (✆ **0575-836-128**). The collections include two Signorelli works, 15th-century frescoes, a triptych by Bartolo di Fredi, and a beautifully crafted gold reliquary more than 2.4m (8 ft.) high called the *Tree of Lucignano* (1350–1471). The museum is open November to March Monday 10am to 1pm, Wednesday through Friday from 10am to 1pm and 2 to 5pm, and Saturday and Sunday 10am to 1pm and 2 to 6pm. April to October the museum is open until 6pm on weekdays (closed Tues), and 7pm on weekends. Admission is 5€ adults, 3€ children and seniors.

Consider spending the night at the **Castello di Gargonza** ★★ (www.gargonza.it; ✆ **0575-847-021**), nestled among the forested mountains 8km (5 miles) west of Monte San Savino, a 13th-century walled hamlet complete with a fairy-tale, crenellated castle tower. Count Riccardo Guicciardini, whose family has owned the property for 300 years, decided to save the abandoned village from decay in the 1960s by converting it in its entirety into a guest "residence." It's not a hotel, but a wonderfully evocative and isolated retreat. The former peasant houses contain self-catering apartments, complete with kitchenettes and working fireplaces, and the Tuscan restaurant is so good you needn't venture out for your meals. Doubles range from 140€ to 190€ in high season.

10

PERUGIA, ASSISI
& NORTHERN
UMBRIA

Consistently overshadowed by its culturally mega-rich neighbor, **Northern Umbria** is nevertheless brimming with gorgeous medieval hill towns, plenty of art treasures of its own, and an olive-growing industry that's been thriving for thousands of years.

The capital city, **Perugia,** is the birthplace of the Umbrian style of painting, which took form during the Renaissance in the work of Perugino and his students Pinturicchio and Raphael. Perugia gets hip each fall with one of Europe's greatest jazz festivals and spends the rest of its time selling Baci chocolates to the world.

At Umbria's spiritual heart is **Assisi,** a place of pilgrimage second only to Rome—not just the birthplace of Italy's patron saint but also of Western art in the form of Giotto's frescoes covering the Basilica di San Francesco.

Northern Umbria was the stronghold of the ancient Umbri tribes, neighbors to the Etruscans and even more mysterious. Their strange half-forgotten culture continues to manifest itself in colorful pagan festivals such as the Corso dei Ceri in the stony northern border town of **Gubbio.** Up here in the far north is a landscape of contemplation, and a historic core of overgrown villages surrounded by wild corners of the Apennines where wolves still roam and roads don't go.

PERUGIA ★★

164km (102 miles) SE of Florence; 176km (109 miles) N of Rome

Perugia is a capital city in a medieval hill town's clothing—a town of Gothic palaces and jazz cafes, where ancient alleys of stone drop precipitously off a 19th-century shopping promenade. It produced and trained some of Umbria's finest artists, including Gentile da Fabriano and Perugino (born Pietro Vannucci in nearby Città della Pieve), from whose workshop emerged Pinturicchio, Lo Spagna, and Raphael. In addition to one the finest art galleries in Italy, there are several important churches and smaller museums to see, but it's this combination of shops, bars, and sights—the juxtaposition of medieval and contemporary Umbria—that makes the city so appealing. Perugia is also a respected university town, whose student population ensures a lively cultural calendar.

Perugia was one of the 12 cities of the Etruscan confederation, and though it submitted to general Roman authority in 310 B.C., it remained a fractious place, always allying itself with a different Roman faction. It chose the losing side in Octavian's war with Marc Antony, and when the future emperor defeated Marc Antony's brother here in 40 B.C., a panicked Perugian noble set fire to his house in a suicide attempt. The flames spread quickly, and most of Perugia burned to the ground. Soon after, Octavian, now Emperor Augustus, rebuilt the city as Augusta Perusia. Throughout the Dark Ages, Perugia held its own against the likes of the Goths, but it became subject to the Lombard Duchy of Spoleto in the later 6th century.

By the Middle Ages, Perugia was a thriving trade center and had begun exhibiting the bellicose tendencies, vicious temper, violent infighting, and

FACING PAGE: **A Giotto fresco in Assisi.**

penchant for poisons that would earn it such a sunny reputation among contemporary chroniclers. The Oddi and Baglioni were just two of the noble families who waged secret vendettas and vied with the middle-class burghers for absolute power. Burgher Biordo Michelotti, egged on by the pope, managed to seize power in 1393 by murdering a few rivals from the Baglioni family. Five years later, his despotic rule ended with a knife in the back. A period of relative calm came in 1416 with the stewardship of Braccio Fortebraccio ("Arm Strongarm"), under whose wise and stable rule the city's small empire expanded over the Marches region. In the end, he was done in by a fellow Perugian while he was besieging L'Aquila in 1424. And then there were the Baglioni.

When their rivals, the Oddi, were run out of town in 1488, the field was more or less clear for the Baglioni to reign in all their horrible glory. The family turned assassination, treachery, and incest into gruesome art forms. When not poisoning their outside rivals, they killed siblings on their wedding nights, kept pet lions, tore human hearts out of chests for lunch, and married their sisters. In a conspiracy so tangled it's almost comic in its ghastliness, the bulk of the family massacred one another on a single day in August 1500.

The last of the surviving Baglioni, Rodolfo, tried to assassinate a papal legate in response to his uncle's murder at the hands of the pontiff. All that did was anger Pope Paul III, who upped the salt tax a year after promising otherwise. The rebellion Paul was trying to provoke ensued, giving the pope the excuse he needed to subdue the city. Papal forces quickly quashed the city's defenses and leveled the Baglionis' old neighborhood. After riding triumphantly into town, the pope had all Perugia's nuns line up to kiss his feet, an experience he reported left him "very greatly edified."

The enormous Rocca Paolina fortress he built to keep an eye on the city quelled most rebellious grumblings for a few hundred years, during which time the Perugini slowly mellowed. Since Italian unification in 1860, Perugia has thrown its energies into becoming the most cosmopolitan medieval city in the world. It's home to one of Italy's largest state universities as well as the Università per Stranieri, the country's most prestigious school teaching Italian language and culture to foreigners. Local industry's biggest name is Perugina, purveyor of Italy's famous Baci chocolates, and the city stages an urbane and stylish *passeggiata* stroll every evening and one of Europe's most celebrated jazz festivals every summer.

Essentials

GETTING THERE By Air: Six weekly **Ryanair** (✆ **0871/246-0000;** www.ryanair.com) flights connect London Stansted with Perugia's **Aeroporto Internazionale dell'Umbria** (✆ **075-592141;** www.airport.umbria.it), 10km (6 miles) east of the city at San Egidio. The airport has an ATM, cafe, and four car rental desks: Europcar (✆ 075-692-0615), Hertz (✆ 075-592-8590), Maggiore (✆ 075-692-9276) and Avis (✆ 075-692-9796). Ryanair flights are usually met by a minibus outside the terminal, taking you to Perugia train station and Piazza Italia (30–40 min.; 3.50€), but heading back there are just three buses per day, so check times in advance (just one Sat and Sun). Taxis cost around 25€.

By Train: Two railways serve Perugia. The state railway (✆ 199-303-060; www.trenitalia.it) station serves **Rome** (11€–26€, 2–3 hr.; most trains require a change at Foligno) and **Florence** (11€, 2¼ hr.; most trains require a change at Terontola) every couple of hours. There are also hourly trains to **Assisi** (2.40€, 20–30 min.) and **Spoleto** (4.80€, 1¼ hr.). The station is

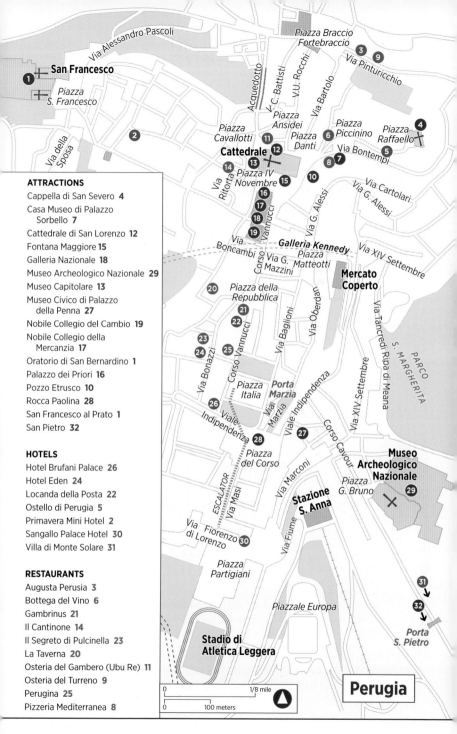

Perugia

a few kilometers southwest of the center at Piazza Vittorio Veneto (✆ **147-888-088**), but well connected with buses to/from Piazza Italia, at the foot of Corso Vannucci (1€). Minimetrò trains (see below) will also whisk you into the center (near Piazza Matteotti) from the adjacent Fontivegge station (1.50€). A taxi will cost at least 10€. Europcar (✆ 075-501-8115) and Hertz (✆ 075-500-2439) have offices near the station.

The station for the **Umbria Mobilità-operated regional railway** (✆ **800-512-141;** www.fcu.it), Sant'Anna, is closer, in Piazzale Bellucci (near the bus station). These tiny trains serve **Città di Castello** (3.05€) and **Todi** (2.55€) every couple of hours.

By Car: Perugia is bisected by three fast, and free, roads. The Raccordo Perugia-A1 runs east–west between the A1, Lago Trasimeno, and Perugia, bypassing the city to link with the E45 (aka SS3bis). The E45 runs north to Città di Castello and south to Todi and Terni (for Rome). Heading southeast, the SS75bis connects the E45 at Perugia with Assisi and Spoleto. From **Florence,** take the A1 autostrada south to the Valdichiana exit and the raccordo to Perugia. The SS326 also leads to this interchange from Siena. From **Rome,** exit the A1 north at Orte to take the SS204 to the E45/SS3bis north.

Parking is fairly abundant, with the most convenient being the underground pay lot at **Piazza Partigiani.** The best way there is via the Raccordo "PERUGIA PREPO" exit: to park, head for "Centro," then look for Partigiani signs. Regular charges are 1.40€ for the first hour and 1.70€/hour thereafter (8pm–2am 2€; maximum daily 15€). Escalators (*scale mobili*) whisk you up to the Corso Vannucci. The **Piazzale Europa** parking lot (signposted from the same highway exit), a bit farther down the hill, is 1€ for the first hour, 1.40€/hour thereafter or 15€/day. A further option is to park in the outskirts

THE CITY OF cioccolato

Perugia is a chocoholics paradise, with the **Baci** brand of chocs made here and a weeklong **Eurochocolate Festival** held annually from mid- to late October. Hour-by-hour festivities are held throughout town, staged by chocolate manufacturers from all over the world. You can witness a chocolate-carving contest, when the scraps of 1,000-kilogram (455-lb.) blocks are yours for sampling, and entire multiple-course menus are created around the chocolate theme. Half-day lessons from visiting chefs are also available. For details, contact the **Eurochocolate Organization,** Via D'Andreotto 19, 06124 Perugia (✆ **075-502-5880;** fax 075-502-5889; www.euro chocolate.com).

You don't have to visit the festival or the *Baci* museum (p. 378) to enjoy Perugia's famed **chocolate: Perugina ★** (✆ **075-573-4760;** Mon 2:30–7:45pm, Tues–Sat 9:30am–7:45pm, Sun 9:30am–1:30pm, and 3–7:45pm) has a shop selling all the major chocolate products at Corso Vannucci 101, but you shouldn't miss the handmade chocolates and

sensational *gelato* (1.80€–2.80€) at **Augusta Perusia ★★**, Via Pinturicchio 2 (✆ **075-573-4577;** www.cioccola toaugustaperusia.it; Mon–Sat 10:30am–8:30pm, Sun 10:30am–1pm and 4–8pm). More convenient is **Gambrinus** at Via Luigi Bonazzi 3 (just off the Corso), with tempting *gelato* flavors for 1.70€ to 4.20€. It's open daily from 11am to 1am.

for free and take the **Minimetrò** in and out of the center; you can reach free parking at Piazzale Porta Nova via the Madonna Alta exit (direction Stadio), and take the metro to Pincetto station in the old center (1.50€; see below). Note that since 2008 all tour buses have been required to park here, so the service can get very busy at peak times. For more information about parking in Perugia (and Todi), visit **www.sipaonline.it**.

By Bus: SULGA lines (✆ **075-500-9641**; www.sulga.it) also has one bus (Mon and Fri) from **Florence**, (6pm; 2 hr.), six or seven daily from **Assisi** (30 min.) and **Todi** (40 min.), and around six a day from **Rome** (2½ hr.); the morning buses usually stop at the airport. **Umbria Mobilità** (✆ **800/512-141**; www.umbriamobilita.it), buses connect Perugia with **Assisi** (six buses daily; 50 min.), **Gubbio** (six buses daily; 1 hr., 10 min.), **Todi** (six buses daily; 1 hr., 15 min.), and **Chiusi** (three to five buses daily; 1 hr., 25 min.). The **bus station** in Perugia is in Piazza Partigiani (above the parking lot), an escalator ride below Piazza Italia. The stand there sells tickets for all lines (Mon–Sat 6:15am–8pm, Sun 7:30am–7:30pm).

GETTING AROUND Perugia is a walking city, and once you've arrived at the compact center you should be able to stroll to most of the sights. Perugia's 3km (1¾ miles) one-line Minimetrò is primarily designed to get people in and out of the city, rather than as a sightseeing tool. The service runs Monday to Saturday 7am to 9:20pm, and Sunday 8:30am to 8:30pm, every 15 minutes, from Pian de Massiano at the Porta Nova parking lot to Pincetto station, just below Piazza Matteotti in the old center. Fares are 1.50€. It also stops at Fontivegge, next to the main train station.

VISITOR INFORMATION The tourist office is at Piazza Matteotti 18 (✆ 075-573-6458; fax 075-573-9386; www.regioneumbria.eu). It's open daily from 8:30am to 6:30pm. You can also pick up a copy of *Viva Perugia* (1€) at newsstands to find out what's going on around town. The **Città Museo** (✆ 075-577-2805; www.perugiacittamuseo.it) pass covers 12 of Perugia's cultural attractions, and gives discounts at shops and the Partigiani car park. Visiting any five within a 48-hour period costs 10€ (plus free entry for one child 17 and under); a 35€ family card gets you into all 12 sights for 1 year for a family of four. Buy the pass from any participating sight and many hotels.

FESTIVALS & MARKETS Perugia is something of a musical nucleus for central Italy. The fun starts with the rather tame **Rockin' Umbria** festival at the end of June. For information, contact ARCI-Perugia, Via della Viola 1 (✆ **075-573-1074**; www.rockinumbria.it). It's followed by one of Europe's most important jazz festivals, **Umbria Jazz ★★**, which usually runs for 2 weeks in mid-July. Established in 1973, it draws top international names to town for concerts, and instructors from Boston's prestigious Berklee School of Music hold seminars and workshops. It's so popular that a smaller version, **Umbria Jazz Winter,** takes place from December 29 to January 5 in nearby Orvieto. It includes a traditional New Year's Eve banquet and all-night jazz parties. For information, contact the **Associazione Umbria Jazz–Perugia,** Piazza Danti 28, Casella Postale 228 (✆ **075-573-2432**; fax 075-572-2656; www.umbriajazz.com).

During the second and third weeks of September, Perugians celebrate music of a different sort in the **Sagra Musicale Umbra,** an international festival of classical music that has, since 1937, become one of the top musical events of its kind in Italy. For more information, contact the **Associazione Sagra Musical Umbra-Perugia,** Via Podiani 11 (© **075-572-1374;** fax 075-572-7614; www.perugiamusicaclassica.com). The summer-long gig is rounded out the last week of September with **Perugia Classico,** a classical music festival that includes an antique-instrument market, concerts, shows, musical workshops, and chamber-music performances throughout town. Contact the Comitato Promotore Perugia Classico, c/o Comune di Perugia, Ripartizione XVI Economia e Lavoro, Via Eburnea 9 (© **075-577-2253;** fax 075-572-4252).

On July 29 and 30, the cathedral shows off the **marriage ring of the Virgin** that 15th-century Perugini swiped from rival Chiusi. You might drop by town the last week of October for the **antiques market** held in the Rocca Paolina. From November 1 to November 5, the town holds secular celebrations for the **Fiera dei Morti** in honor of All Saints' Day. (Contact the *comune* at © **075-577-3898.**)

Market days are Tuesday and Saturday on Via Ercolano and Saturday at Pian di Massiano. There's also a daily covered market off Piazza Matteotti.

Exploring Perugia

Perugia's public living room is **Corso Vannucci ★**, a wide promenade that's the stage for one of Italy's most lively and decorous evening *passeggiate.* One end of Corso Vannucci is anchored by the 19th-century **Piazza Italia** (see "Perugia's Medieval Pompeii," below), while another end cuts into Perugia's superb main square, **Piazza IV Novembre.** The centerpiece of the piazza is the **Fontana Maggiore ★★**, one of Italy's prettiest public fountains, with panels and figures carved between 1278 to 1280 by Gothic master sculptors Nicola Pisano and his son Giovanni.

Palazzo dei Priori One of the largest town halls in Italy, this *palazzo* was started in the 1290s and expanded in 1443. Inside are the Collegio del Cambio and the Galleria Nazionale (see below). The far end of the building has the oldest **facade,** with an off-center main portal (opposite the cathedral), from which spills a fan of steps. At their top are a small terrace and the *palazzo*'s first entryway, topped by bronze copies of the Perugian griffin and the Guelph lion. Through the door is the **Sala dei Notari,** a long rectangular room supported by eight large arches, formerly a citizens' assembly chamber and now used for public lectures and concerts. Matteo Tassi repainted much of it in 1860 with the coats of arms of Perugia's *podestà* (mayors) from 1297 to 1424, but in the spandrels of the arches remain the Old Testament and mythological scenes painted in 1297 by a follower of the Roman master Pietro Cavallini.

Piazza IV Novembre. © **075-572-8599.** Free admission. Tues–Sun 9am–1pm and 3–7pm (also Mon June–Sept), when not in use.

Galleria Nazionale ★★★ One of central Italy's top museums, Perugia's National Gallery houses the largest and finest collection of Umbrian art in the world, including plenty of Perugino paintings. Like most galleries in the region, it is heavy on religious iconography and paintings between the 13th and 16th centuries, though later works are also included. The galleries begin chronologically on the third floor, though **Room 1** houses larger frescoes from various periods.

Palazzo dei Priori.

Rooms 2 and 3 show the development of 13th-century Perugian painting. It was heavily influenced by the artists working on Assisi's Basilica di San Francesco and therefore torn between the local traditional eastern influences and the classicism of the new Florentine masters, Cimabue and Giotto. The highlight in Room 2 is a *Madonna* by Sienese master **Duccio di Buoninsegna,** painted for Perugia's San Domenico church around 1310.

Room 4 is full of 14th-century painting and sculpture, with the Sienese influence represented by more works from Duccio, Luca di Tommè, and Bartolo di Fredi. On the left wall is a tiny parchment painting of the *Madonna and Child with the Crucifixion* by Puccio Capanna, one of the most modern and skilled of Giotto's followers.

Rooms 5 to 7 are devoted to early-15th-century altarpieces from the brushes of Bartolo di Fredi, Ottaviano Nelli, and Bicci di Lorenzo. Among them, in Room 6, is Gentile da Fabriano's tiny gemlike *Madonna and Child* ★ (1405), an International Gothic masterpiece. Gentile used layers of transparent paints, plenty of gold, and a sure, delicate hand to produce this unique work. Look out also for **Taddeo di Bartolo**'s *Pentecost* ★ of 1403 (Room 5) and **Iacopo Salimbeni**'s monochrome *Crucifixion* ★ of 1420 (Room 6), the first for its radical composition, the second for a display of facial emotion that wouldn't become the norm for decades.

Room 8 is entirely dedicated to the finely detailed *Guidalotti Polyptych* crafted by Beato Angelo around 1448, while **Room 9** contains canvasses and frescoes by Giovanni Boccati and **Room 10** an altarpiece from Benozzo Gozzoli.

 Take a Tour

The **Perugia City Tour** (☏ 075-5757) open-top minibus (6 to 7 times daily Apr–Oct 10:30am–7pm) can be an easy way to see the city for those with tired feet. A full circuit from Plaza Italia (buy tickets at the booth here) takes around 50 minutes and costs 14€ for adults, 7€ for children 3 to 12 (there's commentary in English). Book ahead to be sure of getting seats.

Room 11 contains the museum's greatest masterpiece, Piero della Francesca's *Polyptych of Sant'Antonio* ★★★. The master from Sansepolcro probably painted this large altarpiece in the mid-1460s, with a Madonna enthroned in a classical niche surrounded by solid-bodied saints. The most arresting portion, though, is the pinnacle's *Annunciation* scene, worked with a delicacy and sense of perspective unheard of at the time. The scene is all the more engrossing for the illusory hole punched straight through the center of it by a receding arched colonnade that puts a gulf between the angel Gabriel and Mary. **Rooms 12** and **13** show lesser-known work from the region.

The vaults are all that remain of Perugia's Rocca Paolina (see p. 371).

Room 14 houses large canvases by Benedetto Bonfigli, a fairly talented painter of the Perugian Renaissance. These works inspired H. V. Morton to dub the museum a "haunt of exquisite musical angels," and their cityscapes and background buildings offer us a glimpse of Perugia in the 1400s. **Rooms 15 to 17** explore the Renaissance period in more detail—don't miss the **Treasury** (Room 17), with its priceless collection of goldwork and ivory carvings. **Rooms 18 to 21** cover the 16th century and the development of Mannerism in Perugia, including the beautiful **Priori Chapel** frescoed by Benedetto Bonfigli (Room 21).

Rooms 22 to 26 contain what many visitors come here for—the 15th- and 16th-century art starring large **altarpieces by Perugino** ★. He may have been assisted on the 1505 *Monteripido Altarpiece* background by his young pupil Raphael (Room 23). His later works here, especially the *Polyptych of St. Augustine* (which he worked on for 20 years and was still unfinished at his death), show how he eventually developed a more transparent, spatially spare style with delicate landscapes and crafted pastel figures. **Rooms 27 to 36** house the remaining 16th-century Mannerist collection, while **Room 37** covers 17th-century classicism and **Rooms 38 to 40** a far less absorbing ensemble of florid 18th-century rococo works.

Palazzo dei Priori, Corso Vannucci 19. ✆ **075-574-1247.** www.gallerianazionaleumbria.it. Admission 6.50€ adults, 3.25€ ages 18–25 (E.U. citizens only), free for children 17 and under and seniors 65 and over (E.U. citizens only). Mon 9:30am–7:30pm; Tues–Sun 8:30am–7:30pm.

Nobile Collegio del Cambio ★★ The meeting rooms of Perugia's Moneychanger's Guild, just to the left of the National Gallery, make up one of the best-preserved "office suites" of the Renaissance. Perugino was hired in 1496 to fresco their **Sala dell' Udienza** with a style and scenery illustrating the humanist marriage of Christianity and classicism. It's perhaps his masterpiece in the medium, replete with a studied naturalism and precise portraiture, and a virtual catwalk of late-15th-century fashion. Perugino frescoed a superlative self-portrait on the pilaster of the left wall, looking sternly out of violet eyes set in a chubby, double-chinned face topped by a red cap. Perugino's less-talented student Giannicola di Paolo frescoed the adjacent **Capella di San Giovanni Battista** from 1509 to 1529. Don't overlook the tiny collection of old gold and silver coins and 550 coin-weights between the two rooms, a fitting memorial to the activity that once took place here.

A few doors down at no. 15 (to the right of the National Gallery), is the single chamber of the **Nobile Collegio della Mercanzia ★** (*©* **075-573-0366**), home to the Perugian Merchants' Guild since 1390—the guild still operates as a charitable institution out of the *palazzo*. In the 15th century, the walls and ceilings were swathed in remarkable woodwork delicately carved and inlaid by anonymous craftsmen, probably northern European. Note that it's open the same hours as the Collegio del Cambio, but it closes at 1pm instead of at 12:30pm.

Palazzo dei Priori, Corso Vannucci 25. *©* **075-572-8599.** Admission 4.50€ adults, 2.50€ seniors 65 and over, free for children 12 and under, 5.50€ for joint ticket (Collegio della Mercanzia only 1.50€). Dec 20–Jan 6 Tues–Sat 9am–12:30pm and 2:30–5:30pm, Sun 9am–1pm; Mar 1–Oct 31 Mon–Sat 9am–12:30pm and 2:30–5:30pm, Sun 9am–1pm; Nov 1–Dec 19 and Jan 7–Feb 28 Tues–Sat 8am–2pm, Sun 9am–12:30pm.

PERUGIA'S MEDIEVAL pompeii

To cow the insurgent Perugini into submission after he put down their rebellion against his salt tax, Pope Paul III demolished more than one-quarter of the city in 1530, pointedly including the palaces of the fractious former leaders, the Baglioni family. He then ordered Antonio da Sangallo the Younger to build him a fortress, the **Rocca Paolina ★**, in the gaping empty space. By 1543, the massive bastion was complete, and it helped uphold papal domination over Perugia for more than 300 years. At the Italian unification in 1860, when Perugia was finally freed from the pope's yoke, workers came to dismantle the fortress. They found themselves outnumbered, however, as almost every man, woman, and child in the city descended with grim faces on the hated *rocca* and began to tear it apart stone by stone with pickaxes, shovels, and their bare hands.

Sangallo didn't merely raze all the buildings, however. The land sloped away from Perugia's ridge here in all three directions; to make a flat plain on which to build the fortress, he leveled the field, using the houses, towers, and churches in the area as supports for the *rocca,* aided by brick pillars and vaults. In the process, a whole neighborhood of the medieval town was preserved, intact but eerily silent and still, buried beneath the newer streets above. The vaults of the *rocca* now serve as a **public exhibition space,** and stretches of the subterranean streets are interspersed with the escalators that connect Piazza Italia, which partially takes up the space the dismantled fortress left, with the parking lots below. An underground "Via

Baglioni" leads through a section of this almost-forgotten city, with dozens of houses and churches abandoned for hundreds of years. The mid-20th-century travel writer H. V. Morton called it a medieval Pompeii and imagined its narrow alleys and ruined buildings inhabited by covens of witches brewing Perugia's notorious poisons. You can clamber through doorless entrances, climb the remains of stairways, walk through empty rooms, and wander at will through the maze of mute walls.

You can enter the underground city daily (no admission fee) from the escalators at Piazza Italia (daily 6:15am–1:45am), through the Porta Marzia on Via Marzia, or by riding the escalators up from Piazza Partigiani.

Cappella di San Severo ★ Before he set off for Florence and Rome, a young Perugino protégé named Raphael Sanzio made his first attempt at fresco in this 14th-century chapel in 1505. Though damaged, the upper half of this work, with the *Holy Trinity* surrounded by saints seated on clouds, shows the germ of Raphael's budding genius and his eye for composition and naturalism. By 1521, Raphael had died young, and his now-septuagenarian teacher, Perugino—just 2 years from the grave himself, with his talent fading—finished the scene with six posed saints along the bottom. The rest of the church, which was founded in the 11th century by Camaldulensian monks, and reconstructed in the mid-1700s, is usually closed.

Piazza Raffaello. ☎ **075-573-3864.** Admission 3€ adults, 2€ seniors 65 and over, 1€ children 7–14, free for children 6 and under; includes admission to Pozzo Etrusco (see below), valid 1 week. May–July, Sept and Oct Tues–Sun 10am–1:30pm and 2:30–6pm; Nov–Mar Tues–Sun 11am–1:30pm and 2:30–5pm; Apr and Aug daily 10am–1:30pm and 2:30–6pm.

Casa Museo di Palazzo Sorbello ★ Just around the corner from the cathedral, this historic home provides a rare window into 18th-century Perugia. The mansion dates back to the 16th century, though it was purchased by the aristocratic Marchesi Bourbon di Sorbello in 1785, and is lavishly furnished with period furniture. Ornate frescoes, a library of aging tomes, and the family's rare porcelain collection round out the experience.

Piazza Piccinino 9. ☎ **075-571-6233.** www.casamuseosorbello.org. Admission 5€, children 10 and under free. Mon noon–1:30pm; Tues–Sun 11am–1:30pm.

Cattedrale di San Lorenzo For a major Italian city and provincial capital, Perugia has a pretty disappointing cathedral, at least from the outside. First raised in the early 14th century on the Gothic model of the German hall churches, it didn't take its present form until the 16th century. Unsure whether the front on Piazza Danti or the flank facing Piazza IV Novembre should be the facade, Perugians slapped a bit of desultory decoration on both.

The **interior** is a bit gaudy (those columns are painted, not real marble), but there is a handful of good paintings. The first chapel on the left aisle is the **Cappella del Sant'Anello,** where a gilded reliquary protected by 15 locks supposedly holds the wedding ring of the Virgin Mary, stolen from Chiusi in 1473. Church officials solemnly take out the ring—set with a pale gray agate whose color they swear changes, mood-ring style, to reveal the character of the person wearing it—to show the crowds on July 29 and 30.

In the **Cappella di San Bernardino** (first on the right aisle) is baroque painter Frederico Barocchio's finest work, a tumultuous *Descent from the Cross* painted in 1567. Against the third pillar of the right aisle is the *Madonna della Grazie,* whose hallowed status is given away by dozens of ex-votos and burning candles surrounding it. It's attributed to Perugino's early-16th-century student Giannicola di Paolo. Just beyond it on the right aisle, in the **Cappella del Sacramento,** Luca Signorelli's 1484 *Madonna* altarpiece is provisionally installed.

The cathedral cloisters and former clergy dorms contain the mildly interesting **Museo Capitolare** (☎ **075 5720-4853;** adults 3.50€, 2.50€ 12 to 26 years and 65 and over; free for children 12 and under), open Tuesday to Sunday 10am to 12:30pm and 3 to 5:30pm (use the separate entrance on the far corner of Piazza IV Novembre at no. 6), with its collection of rare religious artifacts, paintings by Luca Signorelli and Benedetto Bonfigli, and Etruscan/Roman funerary art excavated from the city's ancient necropolis.

Piazza IV Novembre/Piazza Danti. ☎ **075-572-3832.** Free admission. Daily 10am–1pm and 3–6pm.

Museo Archeologico (Archaeology Museum)

Museo Archeologico (Archaeology Museum) Among the precious collections here, really for aficionados only, you'll find a 2nd-century-A.D. well head carved with a frieze of Greeks battling Amazons; a rare 6th-century-B.C. Etruscan sphinx discovered near Cetona; and plenty of Etruscan funerary urns sculpted with intricate relief scenes. Among the collection's prizes are a travertine cippus known as the *Inscription of Perugia.* It's the longest document yet discovered written in the Etruscan language—apparently by lawyers. (It seems to resolve a property dispute.)

Inside **San Domenico church** itself is Italy's second-largest stained-glass window (Milan's Duomo beats it), assembled in the 15th century, and a Gothic monument marking the tomb of **Pope Benedict XI,** carved in the early 14th century—the pope died in Perugia suddenly in 1304.

Piazza G. Bruno 10 (in the cloisters of San Domenico). ☎ **075-572-7141.** www.archeopg.arti. beniculturali.it. Admission 4€ adults, 2€ ages 18–25 and seniors 65 and over. Tues–Sun 8:30am–7:30pm; Mon 10am–7:30pm.

Museo Civico di Palazzo della Penna

Museo Civico di Palazzo della Penna ★ Art fans should check out this tranquil 16th-century mansion, loaded with lesser known but intriguing collections that cover the baroque period, 19th-century works from the "Pietro Vannucci" Academy of Fine Arts, and the Modernist oeuvre of Gerardo Dottori and Joseph Beuys.

Via Podiani 11. ☎ **075-571-6233.** Admission 3€ adults, 1€ children 7–14, free for children 6 and under. Nov–Mar Tues–Sun 10:30am–1pm and 4–6:30pm; May–July and Sept–Oct Tues–Sun 10:30am–1pm and 3:30–6pm; Apr, Aug daily 10am–1pm and 4–7pm.

Pozzo Etrusco (Etruscan Well)

Pozzo Etrusco (Etruscan Well) When the 3rd-century-B.C. Etruscans needed water, they sank a 5.4m-wide (18-ft.) shaft more than 35m (115 ft.) into the pebbly soil under Perugia. To support the cover over the well, they built two massive trusses of travertine that have stood the test of more than 2,000 years. You can climb down past the dripping, moss-smothered walls to a bridge across the bottom.

Piazza Danti 18 (at the end of the tunnel). ☎ **075-573-3669.** Admission 3€ adults, 2€ seniors 65 and over, 1€ children 7–14, free for children 6 and under; includes admission to Cappella di San Severo (see above), valid 1 week. Apr–Oct Tues–Sun 10am–1:30pm and 2:30–6:30pm; Nov–Mar Tues–Sun 11am–1pm and 2:30–5pm.

San Bernardino and San Francesco

San Bernardino and San Francesco The grassy lawn at the bottom of the Via dei Priori, a lounging spot for university students on sunny days, is bordered by two of the finest church facades in Perugia. On the left is the small **Oratorio di San Bernardino,** whose facade is layered with bas-reliefs and sculptures (created 1457–61, and beautifully restored in the 1990s) by Florentine sculptor Agostino di Duccio. Inside are a 1464 processional banner by Benedetto Bonfigli and a carved 4th-century paleo-Christian sarcophagus serving as the altar. The oratory's lumbering big brother next door is 13th-century **San Francesco al Prato,** with an unusual, vaguely Moorish geometric facade. It is undergoing a lengthy restoration and currently closed, but will eventually serve as a concert space.

Piazza San Francesco (at the bottom of Via dei Priori). Free admission. Daily 8am–12:30pm and 3–6pm.

San Pietro

San Pietro ★ This Benedictine monastery at Perugia's edge, its pointed **Gothic tower** a city landmark, was founded in the late 900s. Inside the first courtyard is the Romanesque entrance to the monastery's San Pietro church. The church's old **facade** was uncovered in the 1980s, revealing 14th-century Giottesque **frescoes** between the arches—the enthroned three-headed woman on the right may represent the Holy Trinity. The 16th-century **interior** is supported by ancient granite and marble columns (pilfered from a pagan temple) and is heavily decorated—wallpapered with 16th-and 17th-century canvases, frescoed with grotesques, and filled with Renaissance and baroque paintings. The first altarpiece on the right is a colorful 16th-century *Madonna with Saints* by Eusebio da San Giorgio. Toward the end of the right aisle is the door to the sacristy (track down a monk to open it), which contains five **small Perugino paintings of saints** that were stolen in 1916 but found their way back here by 1993. Also here are two small Caravaggiesque works: The *Santa Francesca Romana with an Angel* is attributed by some to Caravaggio himself, and the *Christ at the Column* copperplate sketch is a copy, perhaps of a lost Caravaggio original.

Ask the sacristan also to light up the choir so you can see the incredible **wooden choir stalls ★**, some of the finest examples of wood intarsia in all of Italy, produced in 1526 by a workshop under the direction of Bernardino Antonibi and Stefano Zambelli. In 1536, Stefano's brother Fra' Damiano inlaid the masterpiece door at the back, whose panels could hold their own against any painting of the Renaissance.

At the altar end of the left aisle are a strikingly medieval Pietà scene painted by Fiorenzo di Lorenzo in 1469 and paintings of *St. Peter* and *St. Paul* attributed to Il Guercino. The **Cappella Vibi** houses a gilded marble tabernacle by Mino da Fiesole, and in the **Cappella Ranieri** next door hangs Guido Reni's *Christ in the Garden.* Continuing down the left aisle, before the third altar, is another Eusebio da San Giorgio painting, this one of the *Adoration of the Magi* (1508). Between the second and first altars is a late *Pietà* by Perugino.

Down Corso Cavour, out Porta San Pietro, and to the end of Borgo XX Giugno. ✆ **075-30-482.** Free admission. Daily 8am–noon and 4pm–sunset.

Where to Stay

Most Perugian hotels are flexible about rates, which dive 40% to 50% below posted prices in the off season, so it always pays to ask. Reserve well in advance if you plan to visit during the booked-solid Umbria Jazz season (discussed earlier). If you have a car, there are plenty of romantic and historic *agriturismos* and rental apartments in the surrounding countryside; the best of the latter is the **Villa Nuba Apartments ★★**, just 1.5km (1 mile) outside town (Eugubina 70, Collegiorgio II, 06125 Perugia; www.villanuba.com; ✆ **075-572-5765**), with rates as low as 50€ per night. Families or groups should consider **Le Torri di Bagnara ★★** (Strada della Bruna 8, Località Pieve San Quirico; www.letorri dibagnara.it; ✆ **075-579-2001**), one of Umbria's most popular and romantic *agriturismo* options. The grounds are gorgeous, the apartments are spacious, with stupendous views, and are located inside a medieval tower, while the other rooms occupy the 11th-century abbey nearby. It's just 18km (11 miles) north of Perugia and 4km (2½ miles) from the E45 "RESINA" exit. Doubles are 130€ to 200€, and apartments 790€ to 1,390€ per week (free Wi-Fi is included).

VERY EXPENSIVE

Hotel Brufani Palace ★ Where the bastions of the papal Rocca Paolina once glowered, Perugia's bastion of luxury now rises, built in 1883 by a Grand Tour guide as an inn for his English clients. It offers standardized comforts and (from most rooms) spectacular views. Most accommodations are done in a modernized classic style—or, in the newer ones, a gilded 18th-century decor to match the original marble statues in the public areas—all with fresh carpets and wall fabrics, heavy curtains, and sparkling bathrooms with marble sinks; some have Jacuzzi tubs. The first-floor rooms are older and grander—a few even have high, frescoed ceilings and the original furnishings.

Piazza Italia 12, 06100 Perugia. www.brufanipalace.com. © **075-573-2541.** Fax 075-572-0210. 94 units. 325€ double; 460€ junior suite; 850€–980€ suite. AE, DC, MC, V. Garage parking 31€. **Amenities:** Collins Restaurant/American Bar (tables on the piazza in summer); babysitting; concierge; small exercise room; indoor pool; room service. *In room:* A/C, TV, VCR and fax in suites, hair dryer, minibar, Wi-Fi (6€ per hr.).

EXPENSIVE

Villa di Monte Solare ★★ This gorgeous luxury hotel lies 25 minutes outside Perugia, up in the hills. There are nightly classical music concerts in the villa's frescoed chapel, a huge range of spa treatments in a converted *limonaia*, and Michelin-worthy dinners in a jacket-and-tie restaurant led by local chef Nicola Fanfano. The main house is impeccably furnished in period chairs and paintings with ancient terra-cotta floors, while the surrounding farm buildings where most of the guests stay are fitted with ultramodern furnishings. The hotel offers walking tours of the historic property and of the surrounding towns, as well as cycling tours and cooking classes. On rainy days you can spend time in the reading room on the top floor of the main house, which has books, games for the children, and sweeping views of the valley all the way to Lake Trasimeno.

Via Montali, 7 Colle San Paolo (near Panicale). www.villamontesolare.com. © **075-832-376.** Fax 075-835-5462. 21 units. 200€–240€ double; 240€–280€ superior double; 300€–350€ suite. Rates include breakfast. AE, DC, MC, V. Free parking. **Amenities:** Formal restaurant; bar; concierge; pool; spa. *In room:* A/C, TV, hair dryer, minibar, Wi-Fi (10€ per day).

MODERATE

Locanda della Posta ✦ This hotel is right in the heart of the action on Corso Vannucci, a few palaces down from the National Gallery and in the midst of the *passeggiata*. Although pricey, rather characterless, and not particularly friendly, it offers comfort as solid as the Brufani (see above) at a better rate. The Posta was the only hotel in Perugia when it opened in the late 1700s and has entertained Goethe, Frederick III of Prussia, and Hans Christian Andersen. The small breakfast room retains its frescoed ceiling, yet most of the property was redecorated in the early 1990s in mainly dark, muted colors; only a few canvases on corridor walls remain of the 18th-century decor. The sizable accommodations now include padded fabric-lined walls, matching Art Nouveau floral prints on the quilts and chair upholstery, and modern wood furniture.

Corso Vannucci 97, 06121 Perugia. www.locandadellaposta.com. © **075-572-8925.** Fax 075-573-2562. 39 units. 134€–170€ double; 167€–201€ suite. Rates include breakfast. AE, DC, MC, V. Parking 20€ in garage or free in front of Brufani nearby. **Amenities:** Concierge; room service. *In room:* A/C, TV, hair dryer, minibar, Wi-Fi (free).

Sangallo Palace Hotel ☺ Ranking just under Hotel Brufani (see above), this palace is right below the historic center—it sits atop the Partigiani garage, so it's just a 10-minute walk and a few escalator rides from Corso Vannucci. The hotel is modern, elegant, and preferred by business types in town for conferences.

Over each bed is a framed reproduction of a Perugino or Pinturicchio. The medium-size to spacious guest rooms come with amenities like private safes, an interactive television, and wide beds with firm mattresses, and they often open onto panoramic countryside views. In summer, breakfast is served on the (noisy) terrace.

Via Masi 9, 06121 Perugia. www.sangallo.it. ✆ **075-573-0202.** Fax 075-573-0068. 93 units. 126€–178€ double; 169€–222€ suite. Rates include breakfast. AE, DC, MC, V. Garage parking 15€/day. **Amenities:** Restaurant; babysitting; small children's center; small exercise room; Internet (2.50€ per hr.); Jacuzzi; small indoor heated pool; room service; tennis courts (1km/⅔ mile away). *In room:* A/C, TV, hair dryer, minibar.

INEXPENSIVE

Travelers watching their purse strings might want to forgo the more expensive choices above for a quiet hotel in the medieval streets east of Corso Vannucci. Otherwise, the city's decent youth hostel, **Ostello di Perugia** (www.ostello .perugia.it; ✆**075-572-2880**) has beds for 15€ at Via Bontempi 13.

Hotel Eden ★ 🍃 This cozy three-star property, in a completely renovated building dating back to the 13th century, is a great deal considering the central location, especially out of season. Most rooms come with stupendous views over the countryside and the old town—compact but stylish, the furnishings are simple and contemporary, with not a medieval antique in sight. Even the art on the walls is modern. Expect exceptionally friendly staff and service.

Via Cesare Caporali 9, 06123 Perugia. www.hoteleden.perugia.it. ✆ **075-572-8102.** Fax 075-572-0342. 12 units. 65€–95€ double. Rates include breakfast. MC, V. Garage parking 25€. **Amenities:** Bar. *In room:* A/C; TV, hair dryer, Wi-Fi (free).

Primavera Mini Hotel A small, homey place, with spotless, modern rooms that are fairly roomy (though the otherwise fabulous showers are a bit of a squeeze). Most come with fine views across the rooftops and it's just a short walk to the center of town. Like Hotel Eden (see above), this is a small, family-owned place housed in a medieval building but with immaculate, modern interiors. Though it's not as close to the Corso and the rooms are a bit smaller than at the Hotel Eden, it's generally about 20€ to 30€ cheaper and offers free parking passes. The owners are also incredibly welcoming and helpful—and speak excellent English. Note that you'll have to climb 47 steps up to the entrance (someone will help with your bags if required). Breakfast is extra but comes with the added bonus of eating on the roof terrace.

Via Vincioli 8, 06123 Perugia. www.primaveraminihotel.it. ✆/fax **075-572-1657.** 8 units. 65€–90€ double; 95€–105€ standard triple. Breakfast 6€. MC, V. **Amenities:** Bar/lounge; room service; Wi-Fi (free). *In room:* TV, hair dryer, minibar.

Where to Eat

Dining in Perugia is polarized: There are several worthy fine restaurants and plenty of cheap *pizzerie* supported by the vast student population, but very few *trattorie* in between. Of the *pizzerie,* the best is **Il Segreto di Pulcinella,** Via Larga 8, off Via Bonazzi and a short walk from Plaza della Repubblica (✆**075-573-6284**). Pizzas are 4€ to 7€. It's open Tuesday through Sunday from 12:10 to 2:30pm and 8:30pm to midnight. **Pizzeria Mediterranea** (✆**075-572-1322;** daily 12:30–2:30pm and 7:30–11pm), at Piazza Piccinino 11–12 near the cathedral, is a basic pizza joint with decent pies and slices.

EXPENSIVE

Bottega del Vino ★ UMBRIAN Bottega del Vino is one of Perugia's best and most popular dining spots. The focus here is fresh produce from the farms around Perugia, with homemade Umbrian pastas, cured ham, and even beef angus steaks. The melted cheese appetizers are addictive treats, and there's a huge choice of local wine—no surprise, given that the restaurant also doubles as a wine bar. The terrace is one of the best places in town for evening *aperitivo*.

Via del Sole 1. ℰ **075-571-6181.** Reservations recommended. Primi 8.50€; secondi 13€. DC, MC, V. Tues–Sun noon–3pm and 7pm–midnight. Closed Jan.

MODERATE

Il Cantinone UMBRIAN On a side street just a few yards off Piazza IV Novembre, this low-key restaurant is set in a medieval mélange of vaulted ceilings and stone walls. The wall art is of questionable merit, but the food is good. Both the ravioli (covered in spinachy cream sauce) and the *gnocchi al pomodoro* (potato dumplings in tomato sauce) are made from scratch, and the *grigliata mista* (mixed grilled meats) and *torello alla Perugina* (veal smothered in chicken liver pâté) are good secondi. Il Cantinone is known as one of the cheaper choices in town, and their pizza menu has been expanding over the years.

Via Ritorta 6 (near the Duomo). ℰ **075-573-4430.** Reservations recommended. Primi 6.50€–14€; secondi 10€–18€; pizza 4€–7.50€. No credit cards. Wed–Mon 12:30–2:30pm and 7:30–10:30pm. Closed Dec 22–Jan 5.

La Taverna ★★ UMBRIAN The best restaurant in town, candlelit La Taverna is removed from the hubbub (but still central; just follow the signs). Couples meet for a romantic meal and families celebrate special occasions under the brick barreled vaults or outside in the tiny courtyard. Chef Claudio Brugalossi should recommend the best pick of the day. If they're available and you have an appetite, go for the *caramelle rosse al Gorgonzola,* a zola-soaked plate of homemade ravioli filled with juicy beets. Follow that up with *medaglioni alle punte di asparagi,* which are cuts of filet, smothered in a creamy asparagus sauce and scalloped potatoes. The outdoor seating is limited, so call ahead for one of the tables.

Via delle Streghe 8 (near Corso Vannucci's Piazza Repubblica). ℰ **075-572-4128.** Reservations recommended. Primi 8€–10€; secondi 9€–16€. AE, DC, MC, V. Tues–Sun 12:30–2:30pm and 7:30–11pm.

Osteria del Gambero (Ubu Re) ★ UMBRIAN/SEAFOOD Ubu Re feels a bit like a posh private home, with modern art prints, soft jazz, and a small, intimate dining room well off the main drag. This has become one of the best restaurants in Perugia, with contemporary riffs on local cuisine—it can be a little heavy for lunch, unless you plan to doze for a couple of hours. The tasty breads, pasta, and desserts are made on-site, and seasonal dishes grace the menu, anything from *mousse tepida di piccione* (pigeon soufflé in black truffle sauce) to lamb and potato pudding—their pastas with squid or Sagrantino are always sensational. They offer a good-value fixed-price menu for 30€, and a seafood menu for 32€.

Via Baldeschi 8/a (behind the Duomo). ℰ **075-573-5461.** Reservations recommended. Primi 9.50€–10€; secondi 14€. MC, V. Tues–Sun 7:30–11:30pm. Closed 2 weeks in Jan and 2 weeks in July.

Osteria del Turreno ★ 🍴 UMBRIAN/ITALIAN This *tavola calda* diner opposite the cathedral has been serving basic lunches with a Perugian twist for decades. The day's dishes are displayed canteen style; pick what you fancy, pay at the till, and take it to your table, inside or out. Options always include simple pasta (such as lasagne, 4.10€), grilled meats, and plenty of salad and veg. Desserts are a bit scarce—but beer and wine (3€ for ¼ liter) aren't!

Piazza Danti 16. ☏ **075-572-1976.** Primi 4€–5€; secondi 6€–7€. Sun–Fri 9am–3pm.

Side Trips from Perugia

Casa del Cioccolato Perugina ★ Some 3km (2 miles) southwest of Perugia, the Casa del Cioccolato is the home of Perugia's iconic chocolate factory. The creator of Baci ("kisses") started in 1907 selling sugared almonds and now pumps out 120 tons of the brown stuff a day, including 1½ million gianduja-and-hazelnut kisses. The site includes the **Museo Storico Perugina,** a small museum, where you can learn about the company's products and key moments in its history—it was purchased by Nestlé in 1988—including an actual-size reproduction of the world's biggest chocolate, the BaciOne. Weighing in at 5,980 kilograms (13,150 lb.), the monster choc was made in 2003 for the Eurochocolate festival, and apparently wolfed down by the crowds in just 4 hours.

To take a far more enjoyable **factory tour,** you'll need to phone and make reservations in advance—English tours are available, but call to check times during the hours listed below. Guides run through the museum before leading groups on a walkway loop above the vast factory floor. Tours used to be free, but considering the piles of free chocolate on offer at the end (you can literally eat as much as you like), the new charge is probably justified. A gift store selling all the products rounds off the experience. *Note:* The factory shuts down production May through July (domestic demand drops off in the summer), so you won't see any activity in the factory at this time. The complex occasionally opens on Saturdays, but always confirm in advance. Call also about classes (from 1 hr. and up) at the on-site **School of Chocolate.**

Via San Sisto 42, San Sisto (SS220; take Madonna Alta Perugia exit from the Raccordo A1-Perugia). ☏ **075-527-6796.** www.perugina.it. Free admission to museum and shop; tours 5€ adults, groups of 10 or more 3€, free for children 12 and under. Mon–Fri 9am–1pm and 2–5:30pm.

TORGIANO

The sleepy old town of Torgiano, 15km (9⅓ miles) south of Perugia via the E45, is celebrated for its fine wines, considered the best in Umbria. (The town produces one of just two DOCG wines in Umbria, and Montefalco produces the other.) The top label is the complex red **Rubesco Riserva** ★★, produced by the local estates of the **Fondazione Lungarotti** (www.lungarotti.it), whose vintages were formulated by contemporary wine guru Giorgio Lungarotti. Although he used modern techniques and experimental methods to concoct his excellent reds and vin santo, Lungarotti was also in touch with the region's oenological roots and founded a **Museo del Vino (Wine Museum),** in the Palazzo Baglioni at Corso Vittorio Emanuele 31 (☏ **075-988-0200;** www.vino.lungarotti.biz). It's one of the best didactic collections of its kind (perhaps the only one, come to think of it), fascinating even for those mildly interested in viticulture. Admission is 4.50€ for adults and 2.50€ for students (free for children 6 and under) and includes a hand-held audiovisual guide in English. It's open daily from 10am to 1pm and 3 to 6pm (until 7pm in summer). There's no actual wine here. For that, go next door to the Lungarotti-owned **Osteria del Museo** (daily 8am–1pm and 2–6:30pm, 7pm in summer),where everything from the basic, slightly fizzy white Brezza to the San Giorgio is all good.

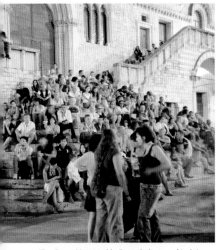

The Corso Vannucci in Perugia is one of Italy's most lively evening *passeggiate*.

An exhibit at the Museo del Vino.

The **Museo dell'Olivo e dell'Olio,** Via Garibaldi 10 (✆ **075-988-0300;** www.olio.lungarotti.biz), a short walk across the old town, continues the agricultural theme; displays include an illuminating collection of ancient olive oil lamps. It follows the same hours as the wine museum (though it is usually closed on Tuesday), and tickets also cost the same (joint tickets 7€ for adults, 4.50€ for students). To **visit wineries** in the area, check the **tourist office** at Piazza della Repubblica 9 (✆ **075-988-6037** or www.stradadeivinidelcantico.it).

DERUTA

Another 5km (3 miles) down the road from Torgiano is a ceramic production center that has been one of Italy's most famous since the 14th century, the crafts town of **Deruta ★★**. The small **tourist office** in Piazza dei Consoli (✆ **075-971-1559;** www.proderuta.it or www.comune.deruta.pg.it) has some good info and maps. It's usually open Tuesday to Sunday 10am to 5pm (with a break for lunch), and Monday 10am to 1pm.

Large modern factories now crank out huge numbers of assembly-line plates, bowls, and vases in traditional colors and patterns, and that is what's hawked behind the plate-glass windows of the large showrooms forming a phalanx along the new town's main drag below the highway. The merchandise is usually pretty good quality, but if you explore the back roads in the **Old Town,** you can find true artisans hand-painting ceramics they've tossed on foot-powered wheels. Our favorites are the traditionalists **Deruta Placens,** with shops at Via B. Michelotti 25 (✆ **075-972-277**) and Via Umberto I 16 (✆ **075-972-4027**); and **Miriam,** where at Marcella Favaroni's Via Umberto I 15 shop (✆ **075-971-1452**) she paints vividly colorful and intricate patterns at half the prices most shops charge. Her husband's shop at Piazza dei Consoli 26 (✆ **075-971-1210**) carries more traditional pieces and quality Renaissance reproductions. To get a sense of the evolution of ceramics, visit the extensive **Museo Regionale della Ceramica (Regional Museum of Ceramics),** Largo San Francesco (✆ **075-971-1000;** www.museoceramicaderuta.it), which houses a precious collection of Deruta ceramics of various periods from the Middle Ages to the 1930s. April through September, it's open daily from 10:30am to 1pm and 3 to 6pm; October through March, hours are Wednesday through Monday 10:30am to 1pm and 3:30 to 7pm. Admission is 7€ adults; 5€ ages 15 to 25 and seniors 65 and over; 2€ ages 7 to 14; and free for children 6 and under.

ASSISI ★★★

27km (17 miles) E of Perugia; 190km (118 miles) SE of Florence; 175km (109 miles) N of Rome

Arrive early in the morning, before the first tour buses, and you'll soon see that Assisi is a special place—the rising sun behind Monte Subasio, often shrouded in mist, cuts massive silhouettes behind this medieval city of miracles. A peculiar blend of romance, architecture, and devotion make it the quintessential Umbrian hill town—the absolutely essential stop on any Umbrian tour. For Christian pilgrims the magic is all about **St. Francis,** patron saint of Italy, founder of one of the world's largest monastic orders, and generally considered just about the holiest person to walk the earth since Jesus. The biggest secular draw is the giant **Basilica di San Francesco,** built to honor the saint but now almost as much a temple to pre-Renaissance painter **Giotto.** The rest is an ideally sited hill town, hardly spoiled by its pesky traffic and tat shops, and absorbing its millions of annual tourists and pilgrims with a quiet ease. Though inevitably commercial, Assisi has avoided an invasion of tack that's all too apparent in parts of Tuscany, and it's not hard to find a backstreet all to yourself.

Essentials

GETTING THERE By Train: From **Perugia,** there are about 20 trains daily (25–30 min.; 2.40€). From **Florence** (2–3 hr.; 12€), there are trains every 2 hours or so, though some require a transfer at Terontola. Coming from **Rome,** there are nine daily trains (most via Foligno or Terontola; 2–3 hr. total; 9.30€–24€). The **station** (© **075-804-0272**) is in the modern valley town of Santa Maria degli Angeli, about 5km (3 miles) from Assisi, with bus connections to Assisi every 20 minutes (1€), or you can take a **taxi** for about 15€ to 20€.

    By Car: Assisi is 18km (11 miles) east of Perugia, off the SS75bis. Driving the center's steep streets is forbidden for tourists. The best strategy is to **park** in Piazza Matteotti (1.15€/hr.), keep walking west, and finish at the basilica; it's all downhill. Below the basilica, in Piazza Giovanni Paolo II, catch the half-hourly bus (Linea C) back to Piazza Matteotti. The adjacent *tabacchi* sells tickets (1€; 1.50€ if you pay on the bus). Dependable alternatives are the Mojano multistory (1.05€ first 2 hr., 1.45€/hr. thereafter) or Piazza Giovanni Paolo II itself (1.05€ first hr.; 1.45€ thereafter).

    For the best **free parking,** arrive early and drive to the north side of town, up along the ridge above the city, where there's plenty of space in the lot near the cemetery off Viale Albornoz behind the walls; even better are the spaces lining Via della Rocca just inside the walls near the Rocca (enter through Porta Perlici off Viale Albornoz and take the first right within the walls).

    By Bus: Eight **Umbria Mobilità** buses (© **800-512-141;** www. umbriamobilita.it) run the route seven times daily (Mon–Fri) between **Perugia** and Assisi's Piazza Matteotti (50 min.; 3.20€, 4€ if you pay on the bus). Most also pass by the lower half of Piazza San Pietro (at the bottom of

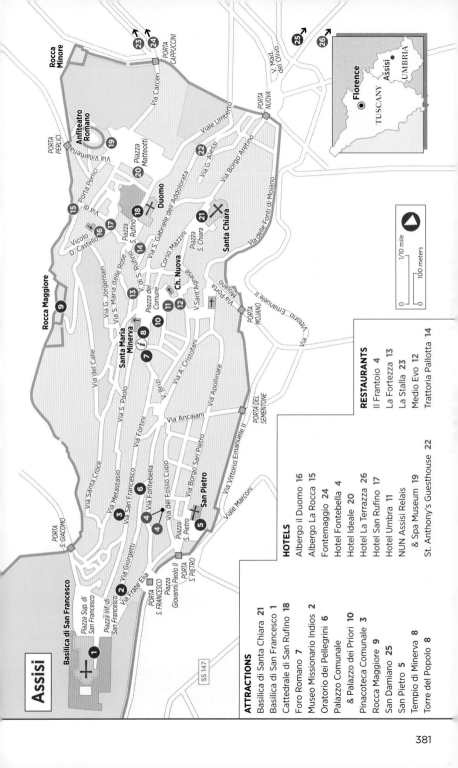

Assisi

ATTRACTIONS

Basilica di Santa Chiara 21
Basilica di San Francesco 1
Cattedrale di San Rufino 18
Foro Romano 7
Museo Missionario Indios 2
Oratorio dei Pellegrini 6
Palazzo Comunale
& Palazzo dei Priori 10
Pinacoteca Comunale 3
Rocca Maggiore 9
San Damiano 25
San Pietro 5
Tempio di Minerva 8
Torre del Popolo 8

HOTELS

Albergo il Duomo 16
Albergo La Rocca 15
Fontemaggio 24
Hotel Fontebella 4
Hotel Ideale 20
Hotel La Terrazza 26
Hotel San Rufino 17
Hotel Umbra 11
NUN Assisi Relais
& Spa Museum 19
St. Anthony's Guesthouse 22

RESTAURANTS

Il Frantoio 4
La Fortezza 13
La Stalla 23
Medio Evo 12
Trattoria Pallotta 14

SS 147

the big traffic curve) at the other end of town. They also run about five buses from **Gubbio** (1¾ hr.). **Sulga** (☎ **075-500-9641;** www.sulga.it) runs two buses daily from **Rome**'s Tiburtina station, taking about 3 hours, and one daily trip from Piazza Adua in **Florence,** which takes about 2½ hours. In Assisi, buy tickets in any *tabacchi* or at the tourist office.

VISITOR INFORMATION The **tourist office** (☎ **075-812-534;** fax 075-813-727; www.comune.assisi.pg.it) is in the Palazzo S. Nicola on Piazza del Comune, 06081 Assisi. It's open summer daily from 8am to 6:30pm, winter Monday through Saturday from 8am to 2pm and 3 to 6pm, Sunday from 9am to 1pm. The private websites **www.assisionline.com** and **www.assisiweb.com** also have good info. **Taxi** fares start at 3.10€ in Assisi (plus .05€ per 35m/115 ft.), but you should always try to negotiate a rate in advance when heading to sights outside the city walls.

FESTIVALS & MARKETS In the city of St. Francis, all **church holidays** are pilgrim-ridden, solemn religious rites. Processions and church ceremonies—occasionally mixed with some livelier restaurant feasts—are celebrated throughout Easter Week and on Corpus Domini (early June), Festa del Voto (June 22), Festa del Perdono (Aug 1 and 2), Festa di San Rufino (Aug 11), Festa di Santa Chiara (Aug 12), Ascension Day (around Aug 15), Festa di San Francesco (Oct 3 and 4), and Christmas Eve and Day (Dec 24 and 25).

But for the **Calendimaggio** ★★ spring celebration, the first weekend (starting Thurs) after May 1, Assisi goes totally pagan. The town divides itself into "upper" and "lower" factions that date to the 1300s. The festivities, with processions, medieval contests of strength and skill, and late-night partying—all in 14th-century costume, of course—go back much further to the pre-Roman rites of spring. The winner of the contests gets to have the fair damsel of his choice declared Lady Spring. The whole shebang ends with a singing duel on the main piazza. Call ☎ **075-812-534** for info.

The regular **weekly market** takes place on Saturday along Via Alessi and Via San Gabriele dell'Addolorata.

Seeing the Basilica

Basilica di San Francesco ★★★ Although Assisi's basilica is first and foremost a site of Christian pilgrimage, it's also a masterpiece of medieval architecture and the home of some exuberant medieval art. The almost simultaneous construction of huge Lower (1228) and Upper (1230) Churches in contrasting Romanesque and Gothic styles had no peer or precedent. Franciscan Brother Elias, the probable architect, built the basilica to house Francis's recently sanctified bones. Today it still moves the devout to tears and art lovers to fits of near-religious ecstasy.

The Lower Church Entered through a Gothic portal under a Renaissance porch on Piazza Inferiore di San Francesco (the lower of the two squares abutting the church), the basilica's bottom

Dress Appropriately

San Francesco and Santa Chiara, like many other churches throughout Italy, have a strict **dress code:** Entrance to the basilica is *forbidden* to those wearing shorts or miniskirts or showing bare shoulders. You also must remain silent and cannot take photographs in the Upper Church of San Francesco.

Basilica di San Francesco.

half is a low-ceilinged, extremely dim cryptlike church. It's full of masterpieces of the early Sienese school of painting, but they're poorly lit, mainly by beautiful but unfortunately not very transparent stained-glass windows, many of which are as old as the church itself.

There's a 1422 fresco of the *Madonna Enthroned with Saints* by Eugubine master Ottaviano Nelli just past the tiny decorated chapel on the left as you enter, plus some fine Gothic tombs along the right wall. Across the nave, the first chapel on the left is the **Cappella di San Martino ★★**, frescoed with that saint's life by the Sienese genius Simone Martini (1312–15). Martini amply displays both his penchant for boldly patterned fabrics—not unusual in an artist from a textile center—and his mastery of the medieval forms and themes of late Gothic Sienese painting. The scene on the right wall, *St. Martin Is Knighted by Emperor Julian,* sums up the chivalric medieval ideal perfectly: the ceremony of a king strapping on a knight's sword and a squire slipping on his spurs; the noble sports of the hunt and falconry; and the love of good music and singing of the bel canto. The portrait of Julian, by the way, is probably accurate; Martini based it on the official profiles stamped on Roman coins from the emperor's era.

Halfway up the nave on either side are stairs descending to the **crypt** containing the venerated **stone coffin of St. Francis** surrounded by the graves of four of his followers—for pilgrims this is the most sacred part of the church, despite the endless stream of tourists filing up and down the steps.

Up the nave again, the **Cappella della Santa Maria Maddalena ★**, the last chapel on the right, was frescoed with the *Life of St. Mary Magdalene* by Giotto and his assistants (1303–09). For two of the more dramatic scenes—the *Raising of Lazarus,* where bystanders dramatically cover their noses at the stench of Lazarus's rotting flesh, and a *Noli Me Tangere,* where Christ appears almost to hitch up his robes as he scurries from the Magdalene's touch—Giotto borrowed the compositions from the same scenes he'd recently finished in his fresco cycle for Padua's Scrovegni Chapel.

In the **left transept's barrel vault** and on its walls, early Sienese master Pietro Lorenzetti left one of his masterpieces. A 1320 cycle of *Christ's Passion* ends with a huge and colorful, but sadly damaged, *Crucifixion* ★★, and on the wall is a touching and dynamic *Deposition,* featuring a gaunt Christ and whimpering Mary.

The **barrel vault of the right transept ★** was originally frescoed in 1280 by Giotto's master, Cimabue, but only his *Madonna Enthroned with Four Angels* *and St. Francis* survives, containing what has become the most popular portrait of the saint. This panel sticks out like a sore thumb amid the early-14th-century frescoes on the *Childhood of Christ* painted by Giotto's assistants under his direction—though the master himself apparently took his brush to the *Crucifixion* scene. Beneath the Cimabue fresco is the tomb of five of Francis's original followers, above which Pietro Lorenzetti frescoed their portraits. To the left of the door and on the end wall are half-length figures of the *Madonna* and seven saints (including St. Clare) by Simone Martini.

Stairs lead up from the lower church's two transepts to the upper level of a 15th-century **cloister.** More stairs lead from here to the **Upper Church,** but you may want to take a minute to zip through the **gift shop** and the **Museo del Tresoro** (see opening times below). Its best works are a 15th-century altar frontal, a Flemish tapestry of *St. Francis,* and a 1290 silver chalice with an enameled portrait of Pope Nicholas IV. Beyond the treasury museum is the **Collezione F.M. Perkins** of paintings by Lorenzo Monaco, Taddeo di Bartolo, Pietro Lorenzetti, and Pier Francesco Fiorentino, among others.

The Upper Church The tall, light-filled Gothic interior of the upper church is a striking contrast to its downstairs neighbor. Though it's best to start with the lower church (so you can view the art chronologically) you could also enter the upper one through the plain medieval facade with its double portal (common in pilgrimage churches) and large rose window behind a small grassy park called Piazza Superiore di San Francesco. However, assuming you're coming up from the lower church you'll begin with the oldest frescoes in the upper church, those in the **transept.** The **choir** is lined with early-16th-century inlaid stalls, including a papal throne—the only one outside the Vatican. Above them are large frescoed scenes whose weird photo-negative quality is the result of oxidation in the pigments. As with most of the frescoes in this church, no one can agree on the attribution of these works. Some hold the opinion that Cimabue did them all (with the help of assistants) in 1277; others allow him only the masterful and dramatic composition of the *Crucifixion* ★ and pin the rest on his Roman assistants (Jacopo Torriti, Rustici, and possibly Pietro Cavallini).

By 1288, the artist or artists had moved on to the upper register of the nave, filling the top half of the left wall (standing at the altar and facing the main entrance) with stories from the Old Testament and the upper-right wall with scenes from the New Testament. Among Cimabue's assistants working here was a young Giotto, who's now given credit for the two red-heavy scenes in the second bay of the left wall depicting *Isaac Blessing Jacob* and *Esau Before Isaac.*

The lower register of the nave, with 28 scenes of the **Life of St. Francis** ★★★, is what most art aficionados have traveled here to see: the frescoes of Giotto. These frescoes were fully restored in 2002, 5 years after the earthquake that shattered them. Again, there were probably assistants at work here, and there's strong evidence that one pupil, the anonymous Maestro di Santa Cecilia, finished the final four compositionally crowded scenes and may have touched up the first. But most of the attempts to find some additional unknown master can be written off as mere iconoclasm—everyone from Giotto's contemporaries to Vasari to many modern-day art historians accepts Giotto as the primary author of the cycle.

The frescoes pick up the story (at the transept end of the right aisle) as Francesco's initial glimmers of saintliness begin to appear, running through all the most famous incidents of his life, from renouncing his father's inheritance (and taking off all his clothes), to the appearance of stigmata in 1472. On the entrance wall is perhaps the most famous and charming of the scenes, where Francis preaches to the birds. Francis taught that, because God was present in all life, everything from the animals to the trees to the smallest bird is worthy of love and respect.

Piazza Superiore di San Francesco/Piazza Inferiore di San Francesco. ℂ **075-819-001.** www. sanfrancescoassisi.org. Free admission. Lower church daily 6am–6:45pm; upper church daily 8:30am–6:45pm. Treasury and Perkins Collection Easter–Oct Mon–Sat 9:30am–7pm. You may visit church for Mass on Sun morning (before 2pm), but purely touristic visits at this time are frowned on.

Exploring the Rest of Assisi

The main square in town is **Piazza del Comune.** The medieval edition of what may have been the old Roman forum (see below) is most famous for the six gleaming white Corinthian columns and tympanum of the **Tempio di Minerva,** a 1st-century-B.C. Roman temple the Assisians sensibly recycled into the church of **Santa Maria sopra Minerva** (daily 6:45am–8pm; free), with a thoroughly uninteresting baroque interior. This was the first object in all of Italy that Goethe—traveling the peninsula for the sole purpose of communing with the ruins of ancient Rome—showed anything but contempt for in his *Italian Journey:* "Lo and behold!—there it stood . . . so perfect in design . . . one could never tire of looking at the facade. . . . I cannot describe the sensations which this work

THE LIFE OF st. francis

With mesmerizing art all around, it's sometimes easy to forget that Assisi (and much of the surrounding region) pays homage primarily to **St. Francis,** one of the most important saints in the Catholic Church and the patron saint of Italy since 1939. When it comes to the details of his life, it's sometimes hard to separate the myth from reality, but it's generally agreed that he was born around 1181 in Assisi. Francesco, the son of a wealthy local cloth merchant and his French wife, spent much of his youth carousing, drinking, gambling, and going off to wars with his buddies—he even spent a year stewing in Perugia's dungeons as a prisoner of war in 1201. Restless and bored, the youth began to suspect there was more to life. He started hanging out in remote, lonely places, and finally renounced his father and all his possessions (famously removing his fine clothes), after Christ spoke to him at San Damiano (p. 389). He spent the next few years living as a beggar, before restoring several churches, notably the **Porziuncola** outside Assisi (p. 389). In 1210 he officially founded the **Franciscan Order,** dedicated to a life of service, poverty, and preaching the Gospels. From then on Francis travelled widely to preach simplicity and a return to kindness and the basics (one of his adventures included a famous encounter with the Egyptian Sultan in 1219).

Praying on **Mt. Verna** in 1224, Francis is said to have been visited by a heavenly seraph who imparted to him a singular honor, the **stigmata** of Christ's wounds. Although later saints were also blessed with the stigmata, Francis was the first, and the miracle pretty much cinched his sainthood. After a life spent traveling as far as Spain, Morocco, Egypt, and Palestine, Francis died near his hometown in 1226. Within 2 years, he was made a saint.

aroused in me, but I know they are going to bear fruit forever." He didn't give the frescoes in San Francesco the time of day.

Next door to the temple is the tall 13th-century **Torre del Popolo,** with the coeval mayor's palace next to that. Across the piazza are the Gothic piles of the **Palazzo Comunale** and connected **Palazzo dei Priori** (both closed to the public).

Basilica di Santa Chiara ★ The resting place of St. Clare and St. Francis's miraculous crucifix is fronted by a lively terrace-like piazza with views over the valley and some shady trees. The 1260 church is early Gothic. The facade, done in strong bands of Assisian pink and white, is set with a giant wagon wheel of a rose window and stabilized by the unwieldy wings of two cumbersome flying buttresses.

The vast interior is dark and perennially crowded with people filing down into the neo-Gothic crypt to see the original stone **tomb of St. Clare.** Born to a local minor noble family in 1193, Chiara (anglicized to Clare) was a friend of Francis who followed the mystic's example against her parents' wishes. In 1211, she abandoned her parental household and ran off to meet Francis, who clothed her in sackcloth after his own fashion and hacked off her hair, signaling Clare's renunciation of earthly goods and the beginning of her quest for spiritual enlightenment. This path she pursued with a vengeance, adopting the rule of St. Benedict tempered with Francis's preaching of poverty. She soon gathered a large enough female following at San Damiano that Francis urged her to set up a convent there, and she became abbess. (The order she founded, the Poor Clares, didn't move into town until after her death.)

Chiara's miracles accumulated as Francis's did, and she became adept at using the Eucharist (the communion wafer) to ward off Assisi invaders as diverse as the Saracens (1240) and local thug Vitale d'Aversa (1241). Bedridden and less than a year from death, on Christmas Eve 1252 Clare was upset that her illness was keeping her from the Franciscans' singing of Mass in the new basilica of St. Francis in town. Suddenly, she was blessed with a vision of the Mass, both hearing and seeing it miraculously from several miles away. In 1958, the pope latched onto the audiovisual aspect of the miracle and granted Clare the rather dubious honor of becoming the patron saint of television.

Off the right wall of the church built to house her tomb is the **Oratorio del Crocifisso,** preserving the venerated 12th-century crucifix that spoke to St. Francis at San Damiano and set him on his holy path. Against this oratory's back wall are some holy relics, including tunics worn by Francis and Clare, a shirt she embroidered, and some of the hair Francis sheared from her head. The chapel divided from this one by glass walls is the **Cappella del Sacramento,** with frescoes by Pace di Bartolo and a triptych of the *Madonna and Saints* by Puccio Capanna. Of the frescoes that covered the interior of the church until the 17th century, only some colorfully intense 13th-century ones by an anonymous follower of Giotto remain, up in the transept.

Piazza Santa Chiara. ✆ **075-812-282.** Free admission. Daily 6:30am–noon and 2–7pm (6pm in winter).

Cattedrale di San Rufino Assisi's cathedral is off a quiet walled piazza that receives some historians' votes as the true site of Assisi's Roman forum. The first church on this spot may have been raised as early as the 5th century. In 1028, the town's bishop witnessed an unrecorded miraculous event and had the old church torn down and a Romanesque one built to replace it, accompanied by a fat bell tower built over a Roman cistern. In 1134, however, another bishop had an even greater miraculous vision, and the poor church was flattened to make way for the present structure, saving only the bell tower. Alas, in the more than 100 years it took to build the church, the Romanesque styling of the lower two-thirds of the facade—including highly decorative friezes, Lombard lions, and griffins at the doors, stone-spoked rose windows, and a classical dividing arcade of thin columns—gave way to Gothic fashion. The top third was finished with a jarring pointed blind arch set in the tympanum.

The interior was remodeled in 1571, following structural damage, and deserves your attention only if you're interested in the font in which St. Francis, St. Clare, and Emperor Frederick II were baptized (to the right as you enter), and the newer memorials to Pope John Paul II. A small shrine to the late Pope lies to the left as you enter, and in a special gallery on the right side of the nave is an exhibition of paintings of the now beatified John Paul by Italian artist Giuseppe Afrune. At the altar are two canvases by Dono Doni—a *Deposition* on the right and *Crucifixion* on the left. You can enter the **Museo Diocesano e Cripta di San Rufino** (C 075-812-712), from the entrance outside the church; the crypt's rough vaulting and Ionic columns are, along with the bell tower, the only surviving bits of the 11th-century cathedral. The beautifully presented museum section preserves detached frescoes by Puccio Capanna, more works by Dono Doni, and triptychs by L'Alunno and Matteo da Gualdo.

Piazza San Rufino. C **075-812-283.** www.assisimuseodiocesano.com. Free admission to the church; Museo Diocesano e Cripta 3€ adults, 2.50€ children 12–18 and seniors, 1.50€ children 8–11, free for children 7 and under. Church Mon–Fri 7:30am–12:30pm and 2:30pm–7pm; Sat–Sun and Aug daily 7am–7pm. Museo Diocesano e Cripta Mar 16–Oct 15 Thurs–Tues 10am–1pm and 3–6pm (Aug 10am–6pm); Oct 16–Mar 15 Thurs–Tues 10am–1pm and 2:30–5:30pm.

Foro Romano ★ Assisi's secular highlight is a little underwhelming for non-history buffs, but the remnants of this Roman Forum can still hold some magic. An entrance room (the old crypt of San Nicolò Church) houses inscribed tablets and headless statues, but the main passage leading off from here preserves a tiny piece of 2nd-century B.C. Asisium—a slice of the old forum some 3.9m (13 ft.) below 21st-century Piazza del Comune. There isn't much to see beyond more tablets and the foundations (with English labels) of what would have been grand Roman buildings, but it's enough to stir a curious imagination. The plain stone rectangular slab in the middle was probably used as an altar for votive statues. Farther along the corridor, ongoing excavations have revealed the bases of some Roman buildings, probably shops.

Via Portica 2 (on the edge of Piazza del Comune). C **075-815-5077.** Admission 4€ adults; 2.50€ students, children 8–17, and seniors 65 and over; free for children 7 and under; joint ticket with Rocca Maggiore and Pinacoteca Comunale 8€ and 5€. June–Aug daily 10am–1pm and 2.30–7pm; Mar–May, Sept, and Oct daily 10am–1pm and 2.30–6pm; Nov–Feb daily 10.30am–1pm and 2–5pm.

Museo Missionario Indios Assisi's newest museum is also the most atypical, though it still retains a religious link, this time via the Capuchin religious order (an offshoot of the Franciscans). The museum is testimony to the order's missionary work with the native tribes of Amazonia (along the upper Solimões River, Brazil), displaying photos, instruments, masks, and handicrafts from the region. This isn't what most visitors associate with Assisi, but it makes an intriguing break from all things St. Francis.

Via San Francesco 19. ℂ **075-812-480.** www.mumamuseo.it. Free admission. Tues–Sat 10am–6:30pm; Sun 3-6:30pm.

Oratorio dei Pellegrini ★ The white-robed sisters are often kneeling inside praying, so you'll most likely only be able to poke your head through the heavy curtains and automatic glass doors for a respectfully quick glance at the 15th-century frescoes inside this tiny chapel. Matteo da Gualdo, who was responsible for the painting on the outside wall, frescoed the scenes on the altar wall, and Pierantonio Mezzastris took care of the ceiling and side walls in 1477, with mir acle scenes of *St. Anthony Abbot* on the left and *St. James* on the right. The three saints frescoed on the entrance wall were once attributed to a young Perugino, but these days it seems more likely that L'Ingegno did them.

Via San Francesco 13. ℂ **075-812-267.** Free admission. Mon–Sat 9am–noon and 3–6pm, except during prayers.

Pinacoteca Comunale The town's art gallery is nothing overly special, existing mainly to preserve the faded remains of frescoes from street tabernacles. The collection includes some 13th-century knights on horseback detached from the Palazzo del Capitano del Popolo, and a *Crucifix* by the Maestro Espressionista di Santa Chiara. Pace di Bartolo also did some nice works here, including a *Madonna and Child with Angels,* on whose backside Giotto's student Puccio Capanna painted *St. Francis and Child.* Of later works, there's a *Madonna della Misericordia* with St. Biagio by L'Alunno and a Dono Doni *Annunciation.*

Via San Francesco 10. ℂ **075-815-5234.** Admission 3€ adults, 2€ children 8–18 and seniors 65 and over, free for children 7 and under. Mar–May and Sept–Oct daily 10am–1pm and 2:30–6pm; June–Aug daily 10am–1pm and 2:30–7pm; Nov–Feb daily 10:30am–1pm and 2–5pm. Closed Jan 1 and Dec 25.

Rocca Maggiore ★★ The bleached yellow bones of this fortress glower high above the city, a reminder of the hated Cardinal Albornoz, who built the 14th-century version we see today to establish papal authority over Assisi. A young Frederick II, future Holy Roman Emperor, spent his earliest childhood within the walls of the short-lived 12th-century fortress that stood here, on an Umbri burial site. Beyond the circular rampart added in the 16th century by Pope Paul III, you can enter the outer walls to visit the restored keep and soldiers' quarters. Inside, the castle is a warren of rooms and halls highlighting costumes, arms, and festivals of medieval Assisi. A very long corridor lit by repeating arrow slits leads to a polygonal watchtower, with a panoramic view that's not lit at all. The warning sign at the corridor's base is no joke—a spiral staircase in the pitch dark can be quite a challenge for those who don't come equipped with a flashlight. From the top of the keep is a stunning view to Assisi below—indeed, the best part of a visit here is the walk up the hill through ever narrowing streets.

Rocca Maggiore.

Piazzale delle Libertà Comunali, at the top of town, at the ends of Via della Rocca, Via del Colle, and the stepped Vicolo San Lorenzo off Via Porta Perlici. © **075-815-292.** Admission 5€ adults; 3.50€ students, children 8–18, and seniors 65 and over; free for children 7 and under; joint ticket with Foro Romano and Pinacoteca Comunale 8€ and 5€. June–Aug daily 9am–8pm; Apr–May and Sept–Oct daily 10am–6:30pm; Nov–Feb daily 10am–4:30pm; Mar 10am–5:30pm.

Exploring Outside the Walls

Basilica di Santa Maria Degli Angeli ★ It's impossible to miss this enormous Mannerist-style church, dominating the valley below Assisi. Constructed between 1569 and 1679 to preserve the 9th-century chapel known as **Porziuncola,** where St. Francis established his order in 1209 (Benedictine monks gifted the chapel to him), it also contains the **Cappella del Transito** (where Francis died in 1226), and the **Cappella delle Rose,** on the site of the saint's former mud hut. The basilica tends to be visited by busloads of Catholic pilgrims rather than tourists, but the altar screen of Prete Ilario da Viterbo (1393) in the Porziuncola is definitely worth a peek even for nonbelievers, and the sheer monumental aspect to the place is certainly awe-inspiring.

The **Museo della Porziuncola** (Tues–Sun 9:30am–12:30pm and 3–6pm, 7pm in summer) chronicles the history of the site and the church, and displays works by Cimabue, Pisano, and Andrea della Robbia.

Via Protomartiri Francescani, S.M. degli Angeli. © **075-805-1430.** www.porziuncola.org. Free admission; Museo della Porziuncola 2.50€ adults, 1.50€ children 11–18, free for children 10 and under. Daily 6:15am–12:30pm and 2:30–7:30pm. Walk (4km/2½ miles along the La Strada Mattonata, pilgrim's pathway), drive or take a bus (1€) to S.M. degli Angeli from Piazza Giovanni Paolo II (taxis 15€–20€).

Eremo delle Carceri & Monte Subasio ★ The Via Eremo delle Carceri runs ever more steeply from Assisi's Porta Cappuccini along the oak- and ilex-covered slopes of **Mt. Subasio.** Nestled at the head of a tree-smothered gorge 4km (2½ miles) along the road, is the peacefully isolated **Eremo delle Carceri** (hermitage), built on the site where St. Francis often withdrew to meditate and pray with his followers. St. Francis started coming here in 1205 (when there was already a tiny Benedictine chapel), but the core of the buildings you see today were built in the early 15th century by St. Bernardino of Siena. The monks living here will sometimes show you around, but you are otherwise free to explore the public areas. You'll have to negotiate some tiny, rock-hewn passages to see the rocky bed where Francis slept, and a few worn frescoes in tiny chapels. Along a shady path, dramatic sculptures mark the site where Francis caused water to gush from the rocks, and beyond this a wooden cross and stone altar marking the spot where the saint preached his sermons to the birds.

The hermitage also makes a good starting point for walks in the woods, though the walk here along the road from Assisi is already fairly strenuous (you can drive and park here for free instead). Mt. Subasio is a protected regional park, and there are plenty of marked trails to follow. (Maps are available in town.)

Via Eremo delle Carceri (4km/2½ miles from Porta Cappuccini). © **075-812-301.** www.eremo carceri.it. Free admission. Eremo delle Carceri daily 6:30am–7pm Easter–Oct, rest of year 6:30am–6pm; sanctuary daily 8:30am–5:30pm. Walk (4km/2½ miles, steep in parts), drive, or take taxi (6€ per person, with 1 hr. wait), from Piazza Santa Chiara or Piazza Matteotti.

San Damiano San Damiano is where it all began, a dilapidated old church that in 1205 housed a 12th-century painted crucifix before which young and restless

Religious icons on display in Assisi.

Francesco was praying one day when the Christ on it spoke to him. Francis first acted on its "rebuild my church" injunction in literal terms: He decided Jesus wanted him to shore up this decaying building, and reconstructed the church stone by stone. The church later became a favorite retreat for Francis and his followers. St. Clare founded her order of the Poor Clares here, lived out her life as its abbess, and passed away within these walls. The pretty little church is still—in a city filled with garish and monumental memorials to the saint—a pleasingly simple and rudimentary place, with rustic wooden choir stalls and a few simple frescoes on the walls. The monastery, with its quiet 15th-century cloister, is also usually open to visitors.

Via San Damiano (1.5km/1 mile from Porta Nuova). ℂ **075-812-273.** Free admission. Daily 10am–12:30pm and 2–6pm. Taxis charge 8€ per person with 1 hr. wait, plus a visit to Eremo delle Carceri.

Where to Stay

Book ahead, book ahead, book ahead. Never show up in Assisi, especially from Easter to fall, without a reservation. If you do, you'll spend half your morning at the tourist office calling hotels, only to find yourself stuck overnight in one of the hideous large constructions 4km (2½ miles) away in Santa Maria degli Angeli. If you plan to visit at Easter or the first weekend in May, book at least 6 months in advance. Behind only Rome and Bethlehem (tellingly, Assisi's sister city) as a Christian pilgrimage site, Assisi fills up for any religious holiday. On the bright side, it has more guest beds per square meter than any other town in Umbria. The official central booking office is **Consorzio Albergatori ed Operatori Turistici di Assisi,** Via A. Cristofani 22a (ℂ **075-816-566;** www.visitassisi.com).

Besides the larger, more standard hotels, dozens of smaller board-rated one- and two-star outfits offer six to 10 rooms each. Additionally, families often have a few rooms to rent (*affittacamere*; ask at the tourist office), and many of the religious orders in town will let you play at being a nun or a monk for a few nights at a very low price (usually with many rules about curfew, noise, and bunkmates).

At **Fontemaggio,** hidden in the woods about 1.6km (1 mile) east of town at Via Eremo delle Carceri 8 (www.fontemaggio.it; ℂ **075-813-636**), are a campground, a hostel, and a hotel complex with one of the best countryside restaurants in Umbria (La Stalla; p. 393). The campground has 950 sites and costs 6€ per person, plus 5.50€ per tent and 3€ per car. The hostel has 16 rooms, six of which are doubles, costing 20€ per person. There are 15 rooms in the hotel portion, with a bathroom, phone, and views of the valley, costing 52€ per double with breakfast.

Brigolante Guest Apartments ★ ☺ If you have a car, skip Assisi's overpriced central hotels in preference for this rural gem—still only 5 minutes' drive from town in the foothills of Monte Subasio. The 16th-century *agriturismo,* once part of a castle, offers three self-catering apartments featuring terra-cotta floors, hand-painted tiles, antiques, and period furniture. Host Rebecca and her family are especially welcoming and the apartments are perfect for families, with a large outdoor space, sandpit, and playground.

Via Costa di Trex 31, 06081 Assisi, 6km (4 miles) east of Assisi. www.brigolante.com. ✆ 075-802-250. 3 units. 370€–550€/week; daily rates available Nov–Mar (except mid-Dec to early Jan). AE, MC, V. Free parking. **Amenities:** Playground, bikes. *In apartment:* A/C, TV, full kitchen.

Hotel Fontebella ☺ The spacious rooms in this 17th-century Illuminati family *palazzo* are fitted with contemporary furnishings done in a Renaissance style and rich yellow, gold, and green fabrics. The rooms without wood floors have knobby carpets, and the proprietors jokingly refer to the smallish singles as their "Franciscan cells." The suites are bi-level, lofted affairs good for families, and there are a few attractive little rooms with wood-beam ceilings in a small annex across the back alley from the main building.

Via Fontebella 25 (btw. the basilica and Piazza del Comune), 06081 Assisi. www.fontebella.com. ✆ **075-812-883.** Fax 075-812-941. 46 units. 72€ standard double; 90€ "valley view" double; 230€ suite. Rates include continental breakfast. AE, DC, MC, V. Free parking in front, otherwise 10€ per day. **Amenities:** Restaurant (Il Frantoio, recommended below); concierge; room service (bar); Wi-Fi in public areas (free). *In room:* A/C, TV, hair dryer, Internet (2€/hr.), minibar.

Hotel Ideale ★ The Hotel Ideale is an excellent deal in the center of town, with spotless rooms, off-street parking, and a relatively substantial breakfast buffet. Every room comes with a sensational view (10 with balconies), there's a gorgeous garden (where breakfast is served in the summer), and a large deck with more magnificent views of the valley.

Piazza Matteotti 1, 06081 Assisi. www.hotelideale.it. ✆ **075-813-570.** Fax 075-813-020. 12 units. 60€–90€ double. Buffet breakfast included. AE, MC. V. Free parking. **Amenities:** Bar. *In room:* A/C, TV, hair dryer, minibar, Wi-Fi (free).

 CHEAP sleep

Long a pilgrim destination, Assisi is accustomed to travelers on a tight budget and is consequently one of the few places in Central Italy where you can spend under 60€ per person on accommodations. Solid budget options include three properties owned by the local Roberti family since the 1950s: **Hotel San Rufino,** on the main street at Via Porta Perlici 7 (www.hotelsanrufino.it; ✆ **075-812-803**), where doubles go for 57€ plus 8€ for breakfast (for two), and **Albergo La Rocca,** Via Porta Perlici 27 (www.hotelarocca.it; ✆/fax **075-812-284**), in the dizzying heights of town on the road to the castle. Prices there run around 58€ for a double (66€ with two breakfasts). The San Rufino also manages cheap doubles from 52€ (plus 8€ for breakfast for two) at the adjacent annex of **Albergo il Duomo** (same contacts).

For a stay with a religious order, **St. Anthony's Guesthouse,** Via G. Alessi 10 (✆ **075-812-542;** fax 075-813-723; atoneassisi@tiscalinet.it), is run by the Franciscan Sisters of Atonement, an American order of nuns. They offer hotel-like rooms with bathrooms from 60€ for a double with breakfast (singles are 40€). They're open March through October, have a minimum stay of 2 nights, and usually require a deposit in advance (parking is 5€ per day).

Hotel La Terrazza ★ 🦢 Located some 800m (10–15 min. on foot) from the center of Assisi and surrounded by olive trees, this is another justly popular choice, with comfy and clean if fairly standard rooms. The friendly owners, stunning views, on-site Castae Aquae Wellness Centre, and swimming pool are enticing extras, however, and the rates are an extremely good value. The restaurant provides solid Umbrian cuisine, with homemade pastas and decent wine.

Via Fratelli Canonichetti, 06081 Assisi. www.laterrazzahotel.it. ℭ **075-812-368.** Fax 075-816-142. 26 units. 110€–130€ double; half-board and full-board plans available. Rates include breakfast. AE, DC, MC, V. Free parking. **Amenities:** Restaurant; bar; concierge; room service; pool; spa; Wi-Fi in lobby (free). *In room:* A/C, TV, minibar, Internet (free).

Hotel Umbra ★★ Antiques buffs will feel right at home in the collection of 13th-century houses from which the Umbra was converted, thanks to agreeable old furniture like 19th-century dressers, 18th-century desks, and 17th-century armoires. Many rooms have views over the rooftops and valley, some have balconies, and the hotel is graced with little hidden panoramic terraces. Ask to see the basement kitchen and laundry rooms, where the town's Roman walls make up part of the foundations. The restaurant is well regarded for its Umbrian food and makes use not only of standard black truffles but also of Gubbio's rare white variety when in season. In summer, the tables are moved out onto a terrace for lamplit dinners in a pretty vine-shaded garden.

Via Delgli Archi 6 (off the west end of Piazza del Comune), 06081 Assisi. www.hotelumbra.it. ℭ **075-812-240.** Fax 075-813-653. 24 units. 110€ standard double; 125€ superior double. Rates include breakfast. AE, DC, MC, V. Garage parking 10€ per day. Closed mid-Jan to Easter. **Amenities:** Restaurant; bar; babysitting; bikes; concierge; room service. *In room:* A/C, TV, hair dryer, minibar, Wi-Fi (free).

NUN Assisi Relais & Spa Museum ★★ This slick boutique offers an elegant blend of medieval Italy and contemporary style, with rooms decked out in crisp white designer furniture. The renovated building once formed part of St. Catherine's 13th-century nunnery, with original vaulted ceilings and frescoes sprinkled throughout the rooms. The "museum" is actually a posh spa set atmospherically among Roman foundations. The breakfast buffets are a delicious minibanquet. Note that some rooms still have problems receiving decent Wi-Fi.

Eremo delle Carceri 1A, 06081 Assisi. www.nunassisi.com. ℭ **075-815-5150.** Fax 075-816-580. 8 units. 260€ double. Breakfast included. AE, DC, MC, V. Garage parking 25€ per day. **Amenities:** Restaurant; bar; concierge; indoor pool; room service; spa (free). *In room:* A/C, TV, minibar, Wi-Fi (free).

Where to Eat

Several of Assisi's restaurants serve a local flatbread called ***torta al testa,*** usually split and stuffed with cheeses, sausages, and vegetables (spinach is popular). The breads make good snacks and appetizers, and are best at La Stalla. For a posh picnic, visit **La Bottega dei Sapori,** Piazza del Comune 34 (ℭ **075-812-294;** www.labottegadeisapori.com), a family-business selling delicious truffle spreads, vinegars, and panini sandwiches.

Il Frantoio UMBRIAN This restaurant occupies a 17th-century olive-press building with modernized interiors, a lovely garden terrace with stunning views across the valley, and a stony medieval room below the Hotel Fontebella. Specialties include *tortelloni frantoio* (ricotta-and-spinach-filled pasta in a sauce of creamlike mascarpone cheese, sausage, and sage) and *stringozzi paesani* (homemade thick spaghetti with tomatoes, artichokes, and a pinch of hot pepper). Secondi are dominated by the house tenderloin steaks and grilled meats, best eaten with mushrooms or truffles, and the wine list is practically a book.

Vicolo Illuminati (can enter at Via Fontebella 25). ☏ **075-812-977.** Reservations recommended. Primi 8€–14€; secondi 9€–23€. Set menus 17€–27€. AE, DC, MC, V. Tues–Sun noon–2:30pm and 7–9:30pm. **Note:** Hours and even closing days are subject to change.

La Fortezza ★★ 🏫 UMBRIAN This is one of Assisi's great hidden treasures. Since 1960, the Chiocchetti family has offered refined *ristorante* service and inspired cuisine at trattoria prices, and all just a few steps above the main piazza. The *cannelloni all'Assisiana* are scrumptious (fresh pasta sheets wrapped around a veal ragù, all baked under parmigiana), as is the *gnocchi alla Fortezza* (homemade gnocchi tossed with a garden of chopped vegetables: tomatoes, mushrooms, zucchini, peas, onions, and more). For a secondo, try the *coniglio in salsa di mele* (rabbit in a sort of curry of white wine, saffron, and apples) or marinated wild boar in sweet and sour sauce.

Vicolo della Fortezza/Piazza del Comune (up the stairs near the Via San Rufino end). ☏ **075-812-993.** www.lafortezzahotel.com. Reservations recommended. Primi 7€–10€; secondi 10€–13€. MC, V. Fri–Wed 12:30–2:30pm and 7:30–9:30pm. Closed Feb and 1 week in July.

La Stalla ★★ TRADITIONAL UMBRIAN This is about as rustic as it gets, a series of former livestock stalls made of stone walls and low-beamed ceilings thoroughly blackened by smoke. The smoke still rises tantalizingly from the open wood-fire grill. It's noisy and chaotic (there's also a sunny terrace if you crave more air), but it just may be one of your most memorable and authentic Umbrian meals. Start with the *assaggini di torta al testo,* small samplers of Assisian flatbread, split and stuffed with prosciutto and cheese or spinach and sausage. Next up: the *trittico,* a scooped-out wooden platter laden with a trio of the house specialty primi, usually *strangozzi, gnocchi* (both in tomato sauce), and *bigoli* (a ricotta-and-spinach log dusted with Parmesan). For secondi, you have a wide range of choices, all barbecued on the grill, from *bistecca di vitello* (grilled veal) to *spiedino di cacciagione* (grilled game). Their *salsicce* (sausages) are out of this world.

Via Eremo delle Carceri 24 (1.6km/1 mile east of town). ☏ **075-812-317.** www.fontemaggio.it. Reservations strongly recommended (but not always accepted). Primi 5€–5.50€; secondi 7€–12€. MC, V. Tues–Sun 12:30–2:30pm and 7:30–10pm. Head out Porta Cappuccini; the turnoff is about 1km/⅔ mile along on the right (follow the signs for the Fontemaggio campground/hostel complex).

Medio Evo ★ ITALIAN/UMBRIAN Down a steep S-curve from the center of town, Medio Evo offers well-spaced tables set with flowers beneath magnificent stone-vaulted ceilings that truly deserve the title of medieval. Meat is sourced exclusively from Umbrian and Tuscan farms, olive oil is 100% Umbrian, and the pasta is made fresh daily; try the tortellini stuffed with pheasant. Menus are seasonal, but in summer secondi might include roast lamb chops with cheese and mushrooms, or rabbit stewed in Montefalco red wine. Don't overlook the desserts, with a fabulous chocolate mousse and classic tiramisù on offer.

Via Arco dei Priori 4B (a dogleg down from Piazza del Comune). ☏ **075-813-068.** www.ristorante medioevoassisi.it. Reservations strongly recommended. Primi 8€–18€; secondi 10€–18€. AE, DC, MC, V. Tues–Sun 12:30–3pm and 7:30–10:45pm.

Trattoria Pallotta UMBRIAN Pallotta's pair of brightly lit stone-and-plaster rooms sees its share of tourists siphoned off from the nearby Piazza del Comune, but it hasn't wavered from serving good Umbrian food at fair prices. The *antipasto misto* is a meal in itself, with Assisi's *torta al testo, crostini,* sliced meats, and more. The *strangozzi alla Pallotta* are served with a pesto of olives, mushrooms, and some peperoncino for kick, and the *ravioloni al burro e salvia* come in a light butter-and-sage sauce. Move on to the *coniglio alla cacciatore* (rabbit in tomato sauce with a side of plain *torta al testo*) or the *scaloppina al vino bianco* (breaded chicken in white wine sauce). Although the *menù turistico* includes wine, the tasting menu offers better food choices.

Vicolo della Volta Pinta 3. ℰ **075-812-649.** www.pallottaassisi.it. Reservations recommended. Primi 5€–18€; secondi 9€–15€; *menù turistico* with wine 16€; tasting menu without wine 25€, 37€ with wine. AE, MC, V. Wed–Mon 12:15–2:30pm and 7:15–9:30pm. Closed 1 week in late Feb.

A Side Trip from Assisi

With its ruined castle and small piazza high above the Vale of Spoleto, the warm-pink glow of **Spello** ★★ is visible for miles. The town makes an essential half-day for art-lovers (just 14km/9 miles south of Assisi), with the best Pinturicchio you can see for free, and one of Umbria's most charming festivals; each Corpus Christi (60 days after Easter), the streets are carpeted in murals made with fresh petals for the **Infiorate** ★ (www.infioratespello.it), literally "flower decorations." The **tourist office** (ℰ**0742-301-009;** www.comune.spello.pg.it) is at Piazza Matteotti 3. It's open daily 9:30am to 12:30pm and 3:30 to 5:30pm all year.

The major highlight here is the church of **Santa Maria Maggiore** ★ (daily 8:30am–noon and 3–7pm; free admission), in Piazza Matteotti. To the left and right of the altar a *Madonna and Child* and a *Pietà* by Perugino neatly book-end the life of Christ. The spectacular **Cappella Baglioni** ★, frescoed like Siena's Piccolomini Library (p. 197), is by Pinturicchio. It's on the left as you walk in; take 1€ to turn on the lights. The vaulted ceiling depicts four sibyls (pre-Christian prophetesses). The three main panels read left to right: an *Annunciation,* followed by a *Nativity* and *Christ's Dispute with the Doctors.* At the far end of the first panel, a Pinturicchio self-portrait appears to hang on the wall like a painting (but it's just part of the mural). Also worth a look is the **Mosaci Villa Romana** (Tues–Sun 10:30am–12:30pm and 3–5pm; 3€), a group of delicate 4th-century Roman mosaics protected beneath a futuristic dome on the outskirts of the old town (at Via Porta Consolare). It looks a bit ordinary from the outside, but the large panoramic garden at **Bar Bonci** (ℰ**0742-651-397**), Via Garibaldi 10, is an ideal spot to take a break in Spello. You can share plates of local salami, cheeses, and *torta al testo.* It's open 7am to 10pm and to midnight March to October (closed Wed).

GUBBIO ★★★

39km (24 miles) NE of Perugia; 170km (106 miles) SE of Florence; 200km (124 miles) N of Rome

Gubbio is every inch the classical Umbrian hill town, a magical, medieval city of sharp-edged fortress-like buildings, stacked at the base of a monumental tree-covered pyramid of a mountain. Gubbio is proud of its patron saint, medieval palaces, and homespun school of painting. And its hill-town cocoon of Gothic silence occasionally bursts open with the spectacular color and noise of some of the region's most deeply ingrained traditional **festivals.**

Traces of both Neanderthals and early *Homo sapiens* have been found around here, proving that Gubbio has been prime hominid real estate for well over 30,000 years. But the Umbri tribes that established their city in the 3rd century

Gubbio, a classic Umbrian hill town.

B.C. probably lived on the valley floor, with their backs against the mountainside. They allied themselves with the Etruscans, then with the encroaching Romans, and, as the Roman municipium Iguvium, lived wholly on the valley floor. It was a modestly prosperous city during Roman times, but the fact that the Roman Via Flaminia skipped it helped keep Gubbio out of the limelight, and many of its Etruscan neighbors were subjected and Latinized in more fundamental ways.

The Eugubium of the Dark Ages suffered its share of Gothic sacking, but by the 11th century it emerged as a bustling trade center. The smooth talking of its incorruptible and wise bishop **Ubaldo** is said to have saved the town from Barbarossa in the 1150s, and after dutifully sanctifying the man soon after his death (he was canonized in 1192), the medieval city went about building walls and attacking its neighbors in grand Umbrian style.

Though a worthy antagonist to warlike Perugia down the road, Gubbio never neglected its spiritual side. It welcomed **St. Francis,** and later his monastic cult, and became particularly beholden to the saintly Assisian after one visit. Francis, on hearing of the problem the Eugubines were having with a voracious wolf, went out into the woods and had a serious tête-à-tête with the offending lupine. Francis returned to town with the giant black wolf trotting at his heels and, in front of the townsfolk, made a pact with the wolf that it would no longer attack the local sheep and men if the town would feed it regularly; the deal was sealed with a paw-shake.

In the early 14th century, riding high, Gubbio built its monumental center and the best of its palaces. In 1384, however, began the long, boring, but basically benevolent reign of the Urbino counts, and later dukes, of Montefeltro. During this time, Gubbio became widely known for the high-quality glazed ceramics and majolica that came out of its workshops, especially that of Maestro **Giorgio Andreoli** (ca. 1472–1554), an innovator and one of the world's greatest masters of the craft. In 1625 the Duchy of Urbino along with Gubbio was annexed by the Papal States, and ruled by the Popes until Italian unification in the 1860s. These days Gubbio is thriving once more, with a revival of traditional industries fed by a steady stream of tourists—within Italy it's also famous as the location of hit TV series *Don Matteo*. The ugly cement factory owned by Cementerie Aldo Barbetti on the edge of town employs just about everyone else.

Essentials

GETTING THERE By Train: The closest **station** is at Fossato di Vico (℡ **075-919-230**), 19km (12 miles) away on the Rome-Ancona line. Ten trains run daily from **Rome** (2¼ hr.; 11€), and nine daily from **Spoleto** (45–60 min.; 4.80€). Nine daily buses (six on Sun) connect the train station with Gubbio (30 min.) for around 2€.

By Car: The SS298 branches north from Perugia, off the E45, through rugged scenery. To park in Gubbio, follow the "P" signs on the road from Perugia: turn left at the second mini-roundabout and right at the next two to reach the Teatro Romano free car park. Marginally closer, at Piazza

40 Martiri, there is some pay parking .80€/first hr.; .30€/20 min. thereafter; Gubbio hotel guests pay 8€/24 hr.). Metered parking here is .80€ per hour.

By Bus: There are eight or nine daily **Umbria Mobilità** buses (© **800-512-141;** www.umbriamobilita.it) from **Perugia** (4.60€; 5.50€ if you pay onboard) to Piazza 40 Martiri (1 hr., 10 min.). Three Umbria Mobilità buses run to Gubbio from **Città di Castello** daily (6:40am, 1:50pm, 5:45pm).

From **Florence,** you'll have to take the daily 6pm **SULGA** bus (©**075-500-9641;** www.sulga.it) to Perugia, you can connect (hopefully) with the 8pm Umbria Mobilità bus to Gubbio. Monday through Saturday, there's a 4pm SULGA bus from **Rome**'s Tiburtina station (arriving in Gubbio around 7pm).

Buses to Gubbio arrive at and leave from Piazza 40 Martiri. **Tickets** are available at the newsstand on the piazza.

VISITOR INFORMATION The **tourist office** is at Via della Repubblica 15, 06024 Gubbio (©**075-922-0693** or 075-922-0790; www.comune.gubbio.pg.it). It's open Monday through Friday from 8:30am to 1:45pm and 3:30 to 6:30pm, Saturday from 9am to 1pm and 3:30 to 6:30pm, and Sunday from 9:30am to 1pm and 3 to 6pm; October through March, all afternoon hours are 3 to 6pm.

FESTIVALS & MARKETS Gubbio's biggest annual bash, the **Corso dei Ceri ★★★**, held on May 15 to honor St. Ubaldo, is one of Italy's top five traditional festivals. Three teams of burly young men in colorful silk shirts carry three 15-foot-long wooden battering ram–like objects called *ceri,* or "candles"; the festivities involve three giant painted ceramic jars full of water being tossed from the candles into the surrounding crowds (the shards are collected to signify good luck for the next year), before the *ceri* are boisterously paraded through the city streets. After an enormous seafood banquet and a solemn religious procession of the relics of St. Ubaldo and the *ceri,* the day ends with a race between the candle-carrying teams—the finish lies more than 300m (984 ft.) of vertical elevation along a switchbacked road at the mountainside basilica of Sant'Ubaldo. The real contest is to see how many times the runners let their candle fall; those that touch ground the fewest times are the real winners of the day.

The last Sunday in May marks part one of the annual face-offs between the archers of Gubbio and those of rival Sansepolcro in the **Palio della Balestra ★**. At 5:30pm, before the main crossbow competition begins, *sbandieratori* come out to practice their mesmerizing flag-tossing. At 7pm, there's a procession through the streets, which are lined with people in colorful medieval costumes. (The return match takes place in Sansepolcro in September; p. 347.)

The **Gubbio Festival** brings performers of international status to town for 3 weeks of mainly classical instrumental music in late July. During the **Torneo dei Quartieri** on August 14, the city's crossbow sharpshooters duke it out, and there's flag-tossing and a historic procession—a warm-up for the competition in Sansepolcro 3 weeks later. Gubbio shows off its revered albino tuber at the **White Truffle and Agricultural Fair** from October 29 to November 2.

The *Guinness Book of World Records* votes are in: Gubbio is home to the **World's Largest Christmas Tree,** formed by more than 800 lights

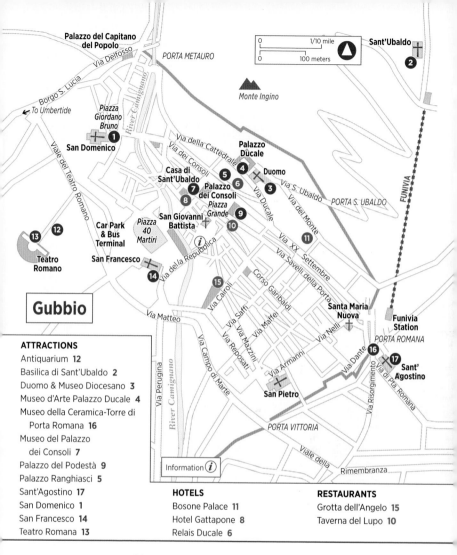

0   1/10 mile
0   100 meters

Gubbio

ATTRACTIONS

Antiquarium **12**
Basilica di Sant'Ubaldo **2**
Duomo & Museo Diocesano **3**
Museo d'Arte Palazzo Ducale **4**
Museo della Ceramica-Torre di
  Porta Romana **16**
Museo del Palazzo
  dei Consoli **7**
Palazzo del Podestà **9**
Palazzo Ranghiasci **5**
Sant'Agostino **17**
San Domenico **1**
San Francesco **14**
Teatro Romana **13**

HOTELS

Bosone Palace **11**
Hotel Gattapone **8**
Relais Ducale **6**

RESTAURANTS

Grotta dell'Angelo **15**
Taverna del Lupo **10**

zigzagging up Gubbio's mountainside to a star at the top (though places that have real trees dispute this title). Every December 7 since 1981, the town's forces of good taste have failed to keep someone from throwing the switch on this monstrosity, and it's left on until January 10.

On the last Sunday of every month, there's an **antiques market** on Piazza 40 Martiri, where the regular **weekly market** is also held on Tuesday (8am–1pm).

Exploring Gubbio

Gubbio's main square is the brick-paved terrace of **Piazza Grande,** a medieval minimalist space open on the south side to a panoramic sweep over the lower part of town and across the wide valley beyond. If you want to avoid the climb, take the free elevator at the junction of Via Repubblica and Via Baldassini (daily 7:45am–7pm).

The plaza is bounded on the longer north side by the orange neoclassical **Palazzo Ranghiasci** (mostly 19th c.), while on the southeast end of the plaza, the **Palazzo del Podestà** (still city hall) sits suffering from the curse of a few too many architectural rearrangements that have left it looking entirely unfinished.

Duomo On your way up Via Montefeltro toward the cathedral, peek through the grate over the basement storeroom of the Palazzo dei Canonici, where sits the huge **Botte dei Canonici** (15th-c. wine barrel), boggling the mind with its 19,350-liter (5,112-gal.) capacity. Those that would prefer to skip the climb can take the free elevator, just off Piazza Grande on Via XX Settembre (daily 10am–6pm).

The interior of the 13th-century **cathedral** (aka Basilica dei Santi Mariano e Giacomo Martiri) is striking for its "wagon vaulting," a receding series of pointed arches defining the graceful bulk and space of the single central nave. Most of the art on the nave altars is by local talent, including multiple works by Virgilio Nucci, Benedetto Nucci, Sinibaldo Ibi, and Antonio Gherardi. In the third niche on the right is a *Pietà* by Dono Doni, who also painted the *Way to Calvary* in the seventh niche. In between the two, the fourth niche on the right opens up to the florid baroque **Capella San Sacramento** (1644–72) by Francesco Allegrini and Gherardi. Don't miss the *Nativity* in the left aisle's sixth niche, a rare work by Giuliano Presutti.

Via Montefeltro. ⓒ **075-922-0904.** Free admission. Jan 1–Mar 31 daily 10am–4:30pm; Apr 1–Sept 30 daily 10am–5pm.

Museo d'Arte Palazzo Ducale While Renaissance-era Gubbio was under the fairly benevolent ducal rule of nearby Urbino, Duke Federico da Montefeltro commissioned Francesco di Giorgio Martini to build him this palace in the 1470s. Although the sumptuous decorations have mostly been stripped away— the entire studio of *intarsia* wood paneling was moved to New York's Metropolitan Museum of Art—a few furnishings, painted ceilings, and simple terra-cotta flooring survive. You enter through a stunning Renaissance courtyard of pink brick accented in gray *pietra serena.* Past the ticket booth, a spiral staircase leads down to **foundations** of the structures that stood on this site as long ago as the 10th century, along with countless ceramic shards. The ground-floor rooms are hung with permanent exhibits, primarily **paintings** ranging from 16th-century portraits to landscapes of the 17th century. The vast **Salone di Corte** contains an intriguing holographic installation featuring an actor playing Duke Frederico, but there's nothing labeled in English.

Farther down Via Montefeltro at Via della Cattedrale, a portcullis gate leads into the **Piano Voltone,** the palace's **hanging gardens,** open in summer. Snacks and drinks are provided by Snack Bar Giardini Pensili (pizza slices 2€; focaccia 3.50€), and there are dazzling views over medieval Gubbio to the valley floor.

Via Montefeltro. ⓒ **075-927-5872.** www.madgubbio.it. Admission 5€ adults, 2.50€ ages 18–25, free for children 17 and under and seniors 65 and over. Tues–Sun 8:30am–7:30pm; closed Dec 25–Jan 1. Ticket office closes 30 min. before museum.

Museo della Ceramica-Torre di Porta Romana The 13th-century Porta Romana is the only survivor of the six identical defensive towers that guarded

Gubbio's entrances. Its private owners are serious history buffs who have restored the gate tower and set up an eclectic but worthy ceramics museum inside. The museum's most valuable installation is a collection of more than 250 **majolica** pieces spanning local production from 1500 to 1950. In the central display case are two **Maestro Giorgio** plates signed and dated 1530, another one attributed to him, and eight pieces by his son and workshop. (The city itself owns only one of Maestro Giorgio's works.)

The old guard tower above is equipped with lances, crossbows, axes, and a 19th-century suit of armor. The owners are inordinately proud of their chastity belt collection, and preserve an odd crossbowlike sling with which nobles once stoned birds. The gaping hole in the floor was defensive, used to pour boiling water down on attackers—hot oil, Hollywood siege scenes notwithstanding, was much too expensive to waste in this manner.

Porta Romana (Via Dante 24). ✆ **075-922-1199.** www.museoportaromana.it. Free admission. Daily 9am–1pm and 3:30–7:30pm (until 8pm in summer).

Museo Diocesano The beautifully restored Palazzo dei Canonici just below the cathedral contains the small Museo Diocesano, with archaeological exhibits dating from the Roman era and early Middle Ages, and a respectable collection of devotional paintings including those by Mello, Cristoforo Roncalli (Pomarancio), G.B. Salvi (Sassoferrato), and Giusto di Gand (if you take the elevator from Piazza Grande, you'll pass the back entrance first). The Botte dei Canonici (see above) dominates the lower level. You can buy a joint ticket here (6€) for two more churches, only really worthwhile for aficionados—**Santa Maria dei Laici** (at the end of the Logge dei Tiratori) on Piazza 40 Martiri, and **Santa Maria Nuova,** close to the Porta Romana on Via Savelli della Porta (the churches are otherwise 2€ to visit). The latter contains the revered **Madonna of the Belvedere,** a master work of Ottaviano Nelli.

Via Montefeltro. ✆ **075-922-0904.** www.museogubbio.it. Admission 3€ adults, 2€ children 14–18, free for children 13 and under. Thurs–Sun 10am–5pm. Closed Dec 25–Feb 28.

Museo del Palazzo dei Consoli ★★ Facing the Piazza Grande is Gubbio's imposing Palazzo dei Consoli, whose square Guelph crenellations and off-center 91m (299-ft.) bell tower dominate Gubbio from afar. The tongue of a staircase sprouting from the raised central door to the piazza below adds a touch of delicate grace to the Gothic solidity. Eugubine master architect Gattapone designed the *palazzo* in 1332.

Inside the vast and poorly lit barrel vault of the main hall, used for public assemblies of the medieval commune, is the town museum, with the largest collection of Roman materials in Umbria. There are dozens of broken statues, stretches of cornice, and other architectural fragments, inscriptions, sarcophagi, and amphorae, all leaning against the walls as if someone just set them down temporarily—it's been this way for decades. The *ceri* used in the **Corso dei Ceri** are also sometimes on display here.

At the base of the staircase are a few rooms with small objects such as coins and metal implements and, in a back room, the seven **Eugubine Tables** ★—the only existing record of the Umbri language transposed in Etruscan and Latin letters (ancient Umbria's **Rosetta Stone**). The tablets were inscribed on bronze from 200 to 70 b.c., and mainly detail the finer points of religious divination—they're thought to be priestly textbooks to help find the will of the gods through animal sacrifice and watching the flight patterns of birds. These are the single-most detailed set of religious instructions and explanations that survive from any antique culture and are of incalculable value for the insights they offer into the religious and social life of the ancient world. A local farmer turned up the tablets while he was plowing his fields in 1444, and the city convinced him to sell them for 2 years' worth of grazing rights.

Upstairs is a small **majolica and porcelain collection,** including plates painted by Maestro Giorgio in the 16th century. Take the narrow "secret corridor" from here, past a row of medieval toilets, and up another stair to the small **pinacoteca** gallery of minor paintings, mainly 13th- to 16th-century Eugubine works. Note the unique fountain system up here that once required an ingenious mechanism to supply it with water. There's also access to an outdoor **loggia** with stupendous views across town.

Museo del Palazzo dei Consoli.

Piazza Grande. © **075-927-4298.** Admission 5€ adults, 2.50€ children 7-25, free for children 6 and under and seniors. Apr–Sept daily 10am–1pm and 3–6pm; Oct–Mar daily 10am–1pm and 2–5pm.

Sant'Agostino ★ The entire interior of this 13th-century church was once covered with frescoes. Remaining today are the exquisitely detailed and colored **cycle of the *Life of St. Augustine,*** covering the walls and vaulting in the apse, and a *Last Judgment* on the arch outside it. The work was carried out by Eugubine master Ottaviano Nelli and his assistants in the 1420s. Nelli's brush also whipped up the *St. Ubaldo and Two Saints* fresco on the fifth altar of the right aisle, while Felice Damiani took care of *St. Ambrogio Baptizing St. Augustine* at the third altar.

Just outside Porta Romana (Via Dante 24). Free admission. Daily 7:30am–noon and 4–7pm.

San Domenico Via dei Priori crosses the river into Piazza G. Bruno and the 14th-century church of San Domenico. The interior was remodeled in 1765, but some 15th-century frescoes remain in the first two chapels on the right and the first on the left. Piles of books were left lying around in wood intarsia on the 16th-century lectern in the choir. The left aisle has a run of good baroque works, including Giovanni Baglione's early-17th-century *Mary Magdalene* in the sixth chapel, *St. Vincent Ferrer* in the fifth chapel by Ottaviano Nelli's follower Tomasso, and a *Madonna and Child* fresco (1546) attributed to Raffaellino del Colle in the fourth chapel.

Piazza G. Bruno. No phone. Free admission. Daily 7:30am–noon and 4–7pm.

San Francesco One of the earliest churches built in honor of St. Francis, this bulky structure with three Gothic apses and an octagonal bell tower was raised in the mid–13th century. Inside, all three apses were painted with high-quality frescoes by the Eugubine school. (There's a free light switch behind the speaker next to the confessional on the left aisle to illuminate the chapels.)

The chapel to the right of the main apse was frescoed in the 14th century on two levels with the *Life of St. Francis* in the upper half and a gaggle of saints in the lower. The main apse has some ceiling-scraping, 13th-century frescoes of *Christ Enthroned with Saints,* while the chapel to the left contains a deteriorating but well-painted cycle on the *Life of the Virgin* by Gubbio's early-15th-century master Ottaviano Nelli. Some fine 17th-century altarpieces line the right aisle, and a 16th-century *Crucifixion* by Benedetto Nelli hides in the sacristy. A cloister behind the apse (enter around the back at Piazza 40 Martiri no. 4) preserves a 14th-century *Crucifixion* fresco and pieces of a 3rd-century-A.D. Roman floor mosaic that still show some color.

Piazza 40 Martiri. No phone. Free admission. Daily 7:30am–noon and 4–7pm.

Teatro Romana and Antiquarium Just outside Gubbio's city walls lies a well-preserved circular Roman theater, a mini Colosseum in surprisingly good shape. You can actually wander up to the gate and get a fairly good look at the ruin for free, but to get up close you'll need to buy a ticket at the nearby **Antiquarium,** a small museum housing some carefully restored Roman artifacts, pots, and mosaics.

Via del Teatro Romano. ✆ **075-922-0992.** www.archeopg.arti.beniculturali.it. Admission 3€ adults, 1.50€ children 5–18. Daily 10am–7pm.

A Side Trip to Monte Ingino

Outside Porta Romana, a left up Via San Gerolamo leads to the base of the *funivia,* a ski-lift contraption that dangles you in a little blue cage as you ride up the side of Mt. Ingino (see below for hours and cost; you can also walk up steep Via San Ubaldo from behind the Duomo, a vertical elevation of 300m/984 ft.). It lets you off just below the **Basilica di Sant'Ubaldo.** The current structure is a 16th-century incarnation over whose high altar the withered corpse of the local patron saint, Ubaldo, is preserved in a glass casket. Usually stored in the aisle are the three giant wooden *ceri* used during the annual Corso dei Ceri (see "Festivals & Markets," earlier).

You can take a path leading from the sanctuary farther up the mountainside to the traces of the 12th-century **rocca** fortress, sitting on the pinnacle of the 908m (2,952-ft.) mountain. The virtually unspoiled wide Saonda Valley lies beyond Gubbio, but even more spectacular is the **panorama ★★** that opens up east across the surprisingly wild Apennine Mountains and the snowy peaks of Monte Cucco National Park at the Marches' border in the distance. A few trails run off here if you want to do some backwoods exploring.

The **Funivia Colle Eletto** (✆ **075-927-3881**) runs daily, but with excruciatingly complicated hours: November through February from 10am to 1:15pm and 2:30 to 5pm; March from 10am to 1:15pm and 2:30 to 5:30pm (Sun 9:30am–1:15pm and 2:30–6pm); April through May from 10am to 1:15pm and 2:30 to 6:30pm (Sun 9:30am–1:15pm and 2:30–7pm); June from 8:30am to 1:15pm and 2:30 to 7pm (Sun 9am–7:30pm); July through August from 8:30am to 7:30pm (to 8pm Sun); September from 9:30am to 7pm (Sun 9am–7:30pm); and October from 10am to 1:15pm and 2:30 to 5:30pm. Round-trip tickets are 5€ adults, 4€ children 4 to 13; one-way tickets are 4€ adults, 3€ children.

Where to Stay

Gubbio contains some decent hotels, but if you have a car you'll find much better accommodations in the surrounding countryside. Romantic and tranquil, **La Cuccagna,** Fraz. S. Cristina 22 (www.lacuccagna.com; ℭ **075-920-317**) is a justly popular B&B in the hills south of Gubbio (doubles 70€–90€). For something cheapish in town, **Hotel Gattapone,** Via Beni 11 (www.hotel gattapone.net; ℭ **075-927-2489;** fax 075-927-2417), is a solid, centrally located medium-range choice; official rates range from 110€ to 125€ in high season, but online deals start at around 60€.

Bosone Palace ★★ This property occupies the 14th-century Palazzo Raffaelli, once the home of the influential Bosone Raffaelli (to whom Petrarch dedicated a sonnet, "Spirito Gentil"). Splurge on one of the Renaissance suites, which have 17th-century frescoes. (Try for no. 212, which has the larger bathroom and frescoes in both rooms.) Even if you opt for the standard doubles, you aren't sacrificing. The breakfast room sports 18th-century grotesques and stuccoes. The hotel's official restaurant isn't the recommendable Bosone Garden underneath, but the Taverna del Lupo (see "Where to Eat," below), a few blocks downhill.

Via XX Settembre 22 (near Piazza Grande), 06024 Gubbio (PG). www.hotelbosone.com. ℭ **075-922-0688.** Fax 075-922-0552. 30 units. 80€ double; 130€ 4-person junior suite; 155€ 4-person Renaissance suite. Rates include breakfast. AE, DC, MC, V. Free parking nearby. **Amenities:** Concierge; room service; Wi-Fi (free) in public areas. *In room:* TV, hair dryer, minibar.

Relais Ducale ★★ You simply can't get more central than the 14th century and Renaissance guest quarters of Duke Montefeltro's palace. The mansard rooms, with their sloping ceilings, are a bit cheaper, but spring for a room on the upper floors with a panorama over the jumble of rooftops and Piazza Grande, to the stitched-together fields of the green valley beyond. But even Foresteria rooms on the first and second floors are memorable—a pair inhabits long barrel-vaulted rooms of rough ancient stone. The Caffè Ducale attached to the hotel opens directly onto the center of Piazza Grande, and on summer mornings guests can breakfast on the square. You can even take summer dinners by candlelight on a small hanging garden—or opt for a half-pension deal at the Taverna del Lupo (see below).

Via Galeotti 19/Viale Ducale 2, 06024 Gubbio. www.relaisducale.com. ℭ **075-922-0157.** Fax 075-922-0159. 32 units. 85€ double; 115€ deluxe double. Rates include breakfast. AE, DC, MC, V. Free parking in public lots nearby. **Amenities:** Restaurants (family owns 3 nearby, including Taverna del Lupo, recommended below, for which pension plans are available); babysitting; bikes; concierge; room service; Wi-Fi (free) in public areas. *In room:* A/C, TV, VCR on request, hair dryer, minibar.

Where to Eat

Gubbio is especially known for its white and black truffles, served in a variety of ways throughout the town. To buy them fresh (or arrange a delivery), visit **La Grotta del Tartufo** (ℭ **347-230-5452;** www.papatartufi.it) at Via Picardi 1, just off Piazza 40 Martiri.

Grotta dell'Angelo ★ ITALIAN/UMBRIAN This cavernous space of tunnels and wine caves has been a thriving osteria for about 700 years, but the best place to sit in spring and summer is the vine-shaded terrace outside (in the winter time, grab a seat in the long, barrel-vaulted dining room and ask for a tour of the cellar). The Cecchini family has run the restaurant for the last half-century and rarely deviates from the tried and true Umbrian favorites. Local meats are grilled on a wood fire, such as *anatra e porchetta,* a goose and pork combination served with fennel. The homemade gnocchi is the house specialty. The adjacent hotel offers bright, rustic doubles for 60€.

Via Gioia 47. ☏ **075-927-3438.** www.grottadellangelo.it. Primi 6.50€–8€; secondi 9€–14€. AE, DC, MC, V. Wed–Mon 12:30–2:30pm and 7:30–11pm. Closed Jan 7–Feb 7.

Taverna del Lupo ★ UMBRIAN Each of the five tunnels of vaulted stonework that make up this 30-year-old Eugubine culinary landmark feels like a little medieval trattoria. This is the home of the truffle, black and white, and storied chef Claudio Ramacci blends the delicacy into a variety of dishes—it's not cheap, and is probably best as a dinner venue for most budgets. The *frittatina gentile con lamelle di tartufo* (cheese omelet under a shower of white truffle flakes) is excellent, as is the *sfogliatina del Lupo con tartufo* (a light lasagne made with cheese, bits of ham and mushrooms, and white truffle shavings). To stay with the precious white mushroom, you can order as a secondo the *scallopina affogato di tartufo* (a tender veal scallop "drowning" in truffles) or the simple and juicy *agnellino* (charcoal-grilled Umbrian lamb).

Via Ansidei 21 (on the corner of Via Repubblica, a few blocks uphill from Piazza 40 Martiri). ☏ **075-927-4368.** www.tavernadellupo.it. Reservations strongly recommended. Primi and secondi 7€–25€; tasting menus without wine 20€–46€. AE, DC, MC, V. Tues–Sun noon–3pm and 7pm–midnight (July–Aug open daily).

CITTÀ DI CASTELLO

56km (35 miles) N of Perugia; 128km (80 miles) SE of Florence; 234km (145 miles) N of Rome

Up in the far north of Umbria, 42km (26 miles) from Gubbio, the main point of interest is Città di Castello, a working place quite unlike the hilltowns elsewhere on the tourist trail. In the Middle Ages it was known as Castrum Felicitatis, the "Town of Happiness." More recently, as a tobacco, printing, and textile center, it developed an artisan aura that's only reluctantly fading. There's no distinguished piazza and little medieval masonry, so you'll have to settle for enough art treasures to satisfy an expert, and perhaps the ugliest cathedral in Umbria—a magnificent pile that has to be seen to be believed.

Essentials

GETTING THERE By Train: The hourly FCU train (☏**075-575-4034;** www. fcu.it) takes 1¼ hour from Perugia and costs 3.05€.

    By Car: Northern Umbria is sliced in two by the E45 (SS3bis), making access to Città very easy. From Perugia, exit the E45 at "Città di Castello" (not the first "sud" exit), turn right at the first and second roundabouts, and you'll eventually pass the free Parcheggio Ferri, 3 minutes from the Duomo via the *scala mobile* (escalators) over the road.

    By Bus: Umbria Mobilità buses (p. 367) between Gubbio and Città run around three times a day (6:20am, 1:40pm, 5:35pm), and take a little over 1 hour.

VISITOR INFORMATION The helpful **tourist office** (☏**075-855-4922;** 8:30am–1:30pm and 3:30–6:30pm Mon–Fri; 9:30am–12:30pm and 3:30–6:30pm Sat; 9:30am–12:30pm Sun) is under the Logge Bufalini in Piazza Matteotti.

Exploring Città di Castello

The center of Città's old town is anchored by Piazza Matteotti, a modest, workaday square, and the unmissable 16th-century **Duomo** (Mon–Sat 8am–noon and 3:30–7:15pm; Sun 8:30am–1pm and 3:30–7:30pm; free admission) a short walk along Corso Cavour—its cylindrical campanile seems lifted from a Breton château and grafted onto an architectural mess. The cool, tranquil interior is a cavernous space with a stunning roof and 18th-century frescoed dome, though the art on display is nothing special. On Thursday and Saturday mornings, the **local market** ★ fills the streets around here; be sure to grab a luscious *porchetta panino* (2.50€) from the stalls by the Duomo.

If your Italian's up to it, the best way to pass 45 minutes is a guided tour (minimum two people) of **Tipografia Grifani-Donati** ★ (✆ **075-855-4349;** grifanidonati@libero.it; Mon–Fri 9am–12:30pm and 3–7pm, Sat 9am–1pm; 10€) at Corso Cavour 4. This family printer has occupied the former church of San Paolo since 1799; you'll see lithographs and engravings printed in the original workshops, still in use. You can also visit the site on your own for 3.50€. If time doesn't allow for a tour, pop into the shop farther along the street (no. 5b; Tues–Sun 9am–1pm and 3–7pm) to buy a postcard (1€) with a difference—Ex-libris images designed by Grifani.

The best known of Città's art galleries is the **Pinacoteca Comunale** (✆ **075-852-0656;** www.cdcnet.net/pinacoteca; Apr–Oct Tues–Sun 10am–1pm and 2:30–6:30pm, Nov–Mar Tues–Sun 10am–1pm and 3–6pm), in a fine Renaissance *palazzo* on Via della Cannoniera, with 30 rooms tracing the development of Umbrian art from its early roots to the 1900s. Sadly, despite Raphael and Luca Signorelli both being active in Città, only one work from each remains—a damaged Holy Trinity by Raphael and Signorelli's 1498 *Martyrdom of St. Sebastian,* not one of his classics. Best of the rest is Room 16, dedicated to Raffaellino dal Colle ★. Ask for the English-language handout; explanations are the most detailed and academic anywhere in Umbria. Admission is 6€ for adults, 2€ to 4€ for children 6 to 14 years, and free for children 5 and under.

An otherwise dry **Museo del Duomo** in Piazza Gabriotti, next to the Duomo (✆ **075-855-4705;** www.museoduomocdc.it; Oct–Mar Tues–Sun 10am–1pm and 3–6:30pm; Apr–Sept Tues–Sun 9:30am–1pm and 2:30–7pm) is enlivened by the 6th-century **Treasure of Canoscio** (a precious collection of 25 silver articles), an embossed, 12th-century silver altar front, the **Paliotto** ★, illustrating scenes from the New Testament, and Rosso Fiorentino's dark *Cristo in Glory*.

Signorelli's *Martyrdom of St. Sebastian.*

Admission is 6€ for adults, 4€ for students, and 2€ for schoolchildren (free for those 5 and under).

Completing the trinity is a modern art museum, the **Collezione Burri** (*075-855-4649*; www.fondazioneburri.org; Tues–Sat 9:30am–1pm and 3–6pm, Sun 10:30am–12:30pm and 3–6pm), in the Palazzo Albizzini at Via Albizzini 1. Burri's hometown has an unmatched collection of his textured, abstract art, including his 1963 *Grande Plastica*—not something Raphael could have dreamed up. Admission is 6€ for adults, 4€ for university students, and 2€ for schoolchildren.

Where to Eat

Trattoria Lea ★ ♦ UMBRIAN/CLASSIC ITALIAN This cozy, traditional restaurant down a backstreet not far from the Duomo has a decent menu of all the favorites and plenty of local Umbrian ingredients. There's no tourist menu here (there are few tourists, after all), but pastas include a very tasty ravioli, and there's a magnificent *gnocchi ai funghi porcini*. The secondi are equally enticing, but do leave room for the cheese plates (3€) and some tiramisù (5€). Bottles of the house wine are a reasonable 5€.

Via San Florido 38a. *075-852-1678.* Primi 4.50€–7€; secondi 5€–14€. AE, MC, V. Tues–Sun 12:30–3pm and 7:30–10pm.

ORVIETO, SPOLETO & SOUTHERN UMBRIA

More than anywhere else in the region, life in southern Umbria remains governed by the rhythms of the sun and the path of the seasons. It's a land of historic villages, family vineyards and sunny slopes thick with olive groves, ideal territory for escaping to a secluded villa or farmhouse. The food is richer, the traffic slower, and life in general much more laid-back. Within an hour's drive of Rome's outskirts, the popular culture and architectural legacy of this region draw threads from its many epochs, from the Stone Age through early Umbri settlers, powerful Etruscan colonists, haughty Roman conquerors, iron-fisted Lombard dukes, and centuries of politically active scheming popes who used Spoleto and Orvieto as homes away from the Vatican.

Etruscan **Orvieto** is the pearl of the south, Umbria's magnificent cathedral *città* and wine center at the meeting point of Lazio and Tuscany, while **Todi** offers the stoniest medieval town within Rome's reach. **Spoleto** plays down its Roman theater, medieval remains, and Renaissance art to promote instead its urbane attitude—exemplified by the annual **Spoleto Festival,** one of Europe's most important and anticipated carnivals of contemporary music, art, dance, and theater.

SPOLETO ★★

63km (39 miles) SE of Perugia; 212km (132 miles) SE of Florence; 126km (78 miles) N of Rome

A sleepy repository of Roman ruins and medieval buildings, **Spoleto** is terraced up a high hill backed by the deep-green forested slopes of a sacred mountain. Dreamed up in 1958 by the Italian-American composer Gian Carlo Menotti, the **Festival dei Due Mondi** (aka **Spoleto Festival**) brings heavy-duty culture to Spoleto every June, in the form of music, dance, and theater showcased by premier Italian and international performers. Though an ongoing legal dispute between the old and new organizers (the government took the festival away from the Menotti family in 2008) has marred the festivities somewhat, the event still attracts high-quality artists.

Although it often seems to revolve around it, Spoleto doesn't begin and end with the festival. A forgotten small city in the 1950s when Menotti chose it as the festival site, Spoleto started out as a Bronze Age Umbri settlement. Strategically situated on the ancient Via Flaminia from Rome to the late imperial capital of Ravenna, Spoleto became the capital of the Lombards' empire in the 8th century A.D. At the turn of the 12th century, Spoleto fell into papal hands, and its twilight began.

FACING PAGE: **Relief panels on Orvieto's Duomo.**

In the 12th century, Spoleto was the birthplace of Alberto Sotio, the earliest known Umbrian painter, and Lo Spagna, a pupil of Perugino. But the city's main nonmusical treasures are Roman and medieval. Only the Duomo, containing Filippo Lippi's last fresco cycle, and the graceful Ponte delle Torri really stands out, but the town as a whole makes for a good day's diversion.

Essentials

GETTING THERE **By Train:** Spoleto is a main station on the Rome-Ancona line, and all 16 daily trains from **Rome** stop here (about 1½ hr.; 8€). From **Perugia** (4.15€), take one of the 20 daily trains to Foligno (25 min.) to transfer to this line for the final 20-minute leg. From outside the station, take bus A, B, or C to Piazza Carducci on the edge of the old town. Bus tickets (1€) are sold at the Centro Servizi Stazione on the platform. Ask the driver if the bus is going toward the *centro storico.*

By Car: The town sits on the old Roman Via Flaminia, now the SS3. There's usually plenty of parking, but the easiest option is to make for the Spoletosfera parking garage, signposted from the SS3 "SPOLETO SUD" exit (1€/1 hr.). It's a 10-minute walk via underground moving walkways to Piazza della Libertà.

By Bus: SSIT (℗0742-670-746; www.spoletina.com) runs buses into Piazza della Vittoria from **Perugia** (two afternoon runs, weekdays only; 1 hr.) and several regional destinations, including **Spello** and **Montefalco.**

VISITOR INFORMATION The **information center** at Piazza della Libertà 7 (℗0743-220-773; www.visitspoleto.it) hands out heaps of info and an excellent map. It's open Monday to Friday from 9am to 1:30pm and 2 to 7pm, Saturday 9am to 1pm, and Sunday 10am to 1pm and 3:30 to 6:30pm. The alternative is the **Pro Loco di Spoleto visitor center** (℗0743-46484; www.prospoleto.it), Via Minervio 2, open Tuesday, Thursday, and Saturday 10am to 1pm, and Wednesday and Friday 4 to 7pm.

FESTIVALS & MARKETS Spoleto's be-all and end-all annual event bridges the end of June and early July. The **Spoleto Festival ★★** (www.festival dispoleto.it) offers 3 weeks of world-class drama, music, and dance held in evocative spaces like an open-air restored Roman theater and the pretty piazza fronting the Duomo. For details, see the "Calendar of Events," in chapter 2. The festival's cultural beacon keeps the arts alive here for part of the rest of the year. A secondary **"Spoleto Estate"** season of music, art, and theater runs from just after the festival ends through September. (Contact the tourist office for info.) The "A. Belli" **opera and experimental musical theater** season runs from late August to October (℗0743-221-645; fax 0743-222-930; www.tls-belli.it). The **weekly market** is held Fridays on Piazza del Mercato and Piazza Garibaldi.

Exploring Spoleto

The Duomo and the Ponte delle Torri are Spoleto's only real attention-grabbers, so if you're pressed for time, skip the lower town (most of which was rebuilt after extensive bombing during World War II) and head straight for the highlights of upper Spoleto.

THE LOWER TOWN

The thoroughly unattractive bus depot and gathering spot called Piazza Garibaldi flows seamlessly into **Piazza della Vittoria.** At the end of the piazza is the 11th-century Romanesque **San Gregorio di Maggiore** (✆ **0743-44-140**), which replaced an earlier oratory here in a cemetery of Christian martyrs. (You'll see bits from the 700s incorporated into the structure.) The church's namesake saint was killed in a spectacle at the nearby amphitheater in A.D. 304, as were a supposed 10,000 lesser-known martyrs whose bones symbolically reside beneath the altar. Passing under the portico (a 16th-c. addition), you'll see how a 1950s restoration carefully returned the interior to its medieval state, removing most baroque additions to reveal the Romanesque architecture and 14th-century frescoes by local artists. The presbytery, full of architectural *spoglio* (salvage) from differing epochs—a 6th-century Byzantine capital here, some medieval cosmatesque pavement there—is raised above a crypt of slender columns. It opens daily from 8am to noon and 4 to 6pm, and admission is free.

Spoleto Shopping

For an excellent selection of olive oil and local wines, visit **Bartolomei Orvieto** at 97 Corso Cavour (✆ **0763 344550**; www.oleificiobartolomei.it), where you can taste and drink the products before buying.

On the east side of the SS3, a 15-minute hike northeast of Piazza Garibaldi, **Basilica San Salvatore ★** gathers dust (✆ **0743-49-606**). It's one of Italy's oldest churches, built in the late 4th or early 5th century A.D. The simple facade shows Byzantine influences and the remains of what must once have been spectacularly carved doorways. Much of the musty interior incorporates scavenged materials taken from Roman temples, including Corinthian columns and a presbytery fitted together in a complicated late classical architectural fantasy. The patches of frescoes date from the 13th to 18th centuries. It's open daily from 7am to 5pm (until 7pm May–Aug, and 6pm Mar, Apr, Sept and Oct). Admission is free.

The quickest route to the upper town from Piazza della Vittoria is up the arrow-straight, shop-lined *passeggiata* drag, **Corso Garibaldi,** which becomes the steeply curving medieval **Via di Porta Fuga** before ducking under the 13th-century **Porta Fuga** into **Piazza Torre dell'Olio,** with its slender 13th-century defensive tower.

THE UPPER TOWN

Spoleto's other main drag, **Corso Giuseppe Mazzini,** leads up to the first of the three main squares in the Upper Town, **Piazza della Libertà. Piazza del Mercato,** the second main piazza and probable site of the old Roman forum, is a bustling spot lined with grocers and fruit vendors' shops.

Casa Romana Under Spoleto's Palazzo Comunale lies the Casa Romana, a 1st-century-A.D. patrician house that supposedly belonged to Vespasia Polla, the mother of the Emperor Vespasian. The intricate monochromatic patterns in the mosaic floors are well preserved, and you can also see the marble well cap and the bases of a few carved columns supporting the display cases of smaller excavated materials.

Via di Visiale. ✆ **0743-234-350.** Admission 2.50€ adults, 2€ ages 15–25 and seniors 65 and over, 1€ children 7–14, free for children 6 and under. Daily 10:30am—5:30pm.

Cattedrale di Santa Maria dell'Assunta ★★ Towards the top end of Via Saffi, the low, graded steps of Via dell'Arringo flow down to the left into Piazza del Duomo, the third and most beautiful main square in Spoleto, with the cathedral backed by a rocca-crowned green hill; the small **Santa Maria della Manna d'Oro** is to the left of the stairs. The main attraction is the dazzling facade of the 12th-century Duomo, with a 1207 mosaic by Solsterno surrounded by eight rose windows. The bell tower was pieced together using stone looted from Roman temples, and the porch is a 1492 addition.

The Duomo's interior retains its original pavement, but the rest was redecorated in a lavish baroque style in the 17th century for Pope Urban VII, who's commemorated with a Gian Lorenzo Bernini bust high above the central door inside. The first chapel on the right, **Cappella di San Leonardo,** has a not-quite-finished **fresco** (1497) by a 17-year-old Pinturicchio lit by a light box, which also illuminates the early-16th-century frescoes by Jacopo Siculo adorning the **Capella dell'Assunta** next door.

The right transept is home to a *Madonna and Child with Saints* (1599) by baroque master Annibale Carracci as well as a monument to Filippo Lippi, designed by his son, Filippino, at the request of Lorenzo de' Medici. According to Vasari, Lorenzo couldn't convince the Spoleteans to return the body to Florence when the irascible painter died just before completing his fresco cycle here. Though a monk, Filippo was quite the womanizer, and when he died, rumors

San Pietro (see "A Walk in the Spoleto Woods" on p. 413).

ran wild that he'd been poisoned by the enraged family of a local girl whose honor he had compromised. Filippo's bones mysteriously disappeared a few centuries later, and some say they were removed and scattered by her still-indignant descendants.

Another small coin in a light box will buy you enough time to admire the *Life of the Virgin* ★ fresco cycle covering the **apse.** Begun by Filippo Lippi in 1467, the frescoes were almost finished by 1469 when the master suddenly died, at the height of his powers. The cycle was finished by his assistants, Fra' Diamante and Pier Matteo d'Amelia. The first scene on the left, the *Annunciation,* is believed to be almost entirely from the master's hand, as is the magnificently colored *Incoronation of the Virgin* in the curving space above, with God taking the place of Jesus and a rainbow of saints and Old Testament figures surrounding Mary's richly patterned gown. The central panel, the *Dormition of the Virgin,* is also mainly from Lippi's brush and contains on the right several portraits by way of signature. Filippo is the man in the black hat, turned toward us and wearing for the last time the white monk's habit that seemed so inappropriate throughout his sensualistic philandering life. Lippi placed portraits of his assistants behind him and that of his 11-year-old son Filippino Lippi, who was already becoming a painting prodigy, in front as a candle-holding angel. The final *Nativity* scene was completed by Filippo's assistants.

As you leave the Duomo, you'll pass the entrance to the **Cappella delle Reliquie (Reliquary Chapel)** on the left aisle, restored in 1993. They include 16th-century intarsia wood cupboards, a 14th-century painted wooden *Madonna and Child,* and a rare letter written and signed by St. Francis. (Assisi has the only other bona fide signature.) The last altar before the exit has a colorful **Crucifix,** painted and signed in 1187 by Alberto Sotio.

Piazza del Duomo. ✆ **0743-231-063.** Free admission. Daily 8:30am—12:30pm and 3:30—5:30pm (until 7pm Apr–Oct).

Museo Archeologico/Teatro Romano ★ At the edge of Piazza della Libertà, Via Apollinare leads down to the entrance of Spoleto's 1st-century-A.D.

Roman theater. Partly destroyed and buried over the ages, it was all but forgotten until 1891, when local archaeologist Giuseppe Sordini began excavating. Extensively restored in the 1950s, it now serves as an evocative venue for the Spoleto Festival.

The attached Museo Archeologico (which can be visited using the same admission ticket) preserves relics from a 7th-century-B.C. warrior's tomb and materials recovered from the theater area, including the torso of a young boy and 1st-century-A.D. portrait busts of Julius and Augustus Caesar. The final main room contains the *Lex Spoletina.* These two tablets, inscribed after 241 B.C., were set up to protect the *lucus* ("sacred groves") of the wooded Monteluco behind the city from woodcutters. In no-nonsense terms, they warn, "These sacred woods, no one may violate. Do not remove or strip away that which belongs to the forest. . . . Whosoever transgresses will offer to Jupiter an ox as placation. If one does it knowingly and with evil intent, to Jupiter he must offer a placating ox plus pay a 300 assi fine."

Via di Sant'Agata 18A. ✆ **0743-223-277.** Admission 4€ adults, 2€ ages 18–25, free for children 18 and under and seniors 65 and over. Daily 8:30am—7:30pm.

Museo Diocesano e Basilica di Sant'Eufemia ★ This museum and old church lies within the **Palazzo Arcivescovado,** built atop the 8th-century palace of the Lombard dukes. The palace courtyard incorporates the facade of the 12th-century Basilica di Sant'Eufemia. The simple Romanesque stone interior has a second-story *matroneum* (women's gallery), 15th-century frescoes on some of the columns, and a 1200s cosmatesque altar, inherited from the Duomo. The double stairs in the courtyard lead up to the Museo Diocesano. Room 1 has a *Madonna and Child with Angels* (1315) and a 15th-century triptych lifted from Sant'Eufemia and attributed to Bartolomeo da Miranda. In room 2 is the Sienese Domenico Beccafumi's 16th-century baroque *Adoration of the Child,* and among the sculptures in room 3 is a 14th-century *Madonna del Cholera.* Room 5 has one of Filippino Lippi's less inspired paintings, a 1485 *Madonna and Child with Sts. Montano and Bartolomeo,* and Neri di Bicci's damaged *Madonna della Neve with Sts. Sebastian and Nicholas.*

Via A. Saffi 13. ✆ **0743-231-022.** Admission 3€ adults, 2.50€ ages 15–25 and seniors 65 and over, 2€ children 7–14, free for children 6 and under. Wed–Fri 11am—1pm and 2:30—5:30pm (to 6pm Apr–Oct); Sat and Sun 11am–5pm.

Museo del Tessile e del Costume Spoleto's museum of textiles and costumes from the 14th to the 20th century makes a pleasant diversion from churches and frescoes. The eclectic collection covers everything from old hats, ties and chains of gold, to church vestments, wall tapestries (some from the collection of Queen Christina of Sweden), historic flags, and even a rare 17th-century Persian carpet.

Palazzo Rosari Spada, Piazza Sordini. ✆ **0743-45-940.** Admission 3€ adults, 2.50€ ages 15–25 and seniors 65 and over, 1.50€ children 7–14, free for children 6 and under. Wed–Mon 3-6pm.

Palazzo Collicola Arti Visive-Museo Carandente Contemporary art fans might want to check out this lavish tribute to local and international modern artists. In addition to work by the likes of Spoleto-born sculptor Leoncillo Leonardi (1915–1968), Alexander Calder's models for his 1962 sculpture *Teodelapio* (outside the train station) are here, as is a tiny 1960 Pomodoro sculpture.

Palazzo Collicola 1. ✆ **0743-46-434.** www.palazzocollicola.it. Admission 4€ adults, 3€ ages 15–25 and seniors 65 and over, 1.50€ children 7–14, free for children 6 and under. Wed–Mon 10:30am–1pm and 3:30-7pm.

Rocca Albornoziana ★★ ☺ Up Via A. Saffi from the Duomo is the shady **Piazza Campello** and the 1642 **Fontana del Mascherone,** a bit of baroque silliness marking the end of the old Roman aqueduct (see the Ponte delle Torri in "A Walk in the Spoleto Woods," below). Also here is the entrance to the **Rocca Albornoziana,** a fierce-looking castle built from 1359 to 1362 by Gubbio's

A WALK IN THE SPOLETO woods

There's plenty to explore on foot or mountain bike on the wooded slopes around Spoleto, but an easy introduction is the 1-hour circuit starting by the gatehouse of the **Rocca Albornoziana** (see above). Walk along the right flank of this fortress, Via del Ponte, and around the bend (grab a quick drink at La Portella cafe), will swing into view the stately **Ponte delle Torri** ★★ (see picture below). This bridge's nine tall pylons separating graceful, narrow arches span the sheer walls of the valley behind Spoleto, a gorge swimming in the dense green of an ilex forest. The 80m-high (262-ft.) and 236m-long (748-ft.) bridge was most likely raised by Eugubine architect Gattapone in the 13th century, though the two most central pylons contain traces of older masonry, supporting the long-held theory that the bridge was built on a Roman aqueduct. The span received the hard-won praise of Goethe in 1786 (apparently because he thought the whole shebang was Roman) and is named after the 13th-century towers that are crumbling at its opposite end.

At the far end of the bridge lie the wooded slopes of **Monteluco** ★. As the *Lex Spoletina* cippus stones in the Archaeology Museum record, the Romans held these woods sacred, as did the medieval Christians—St. Francis and St. Bernardino were both fond of meditating in the holy greenery. Michelangelo himself came here to unwind from the pressures of Rome's papal court, writing to Vasari in 1556, "I found great pleasure in visiting those hermits in the mountains of Spoleto . . . indeed peace is not to be found elsewhere than in the woods." The left path at the bridge's end puts you on the road toward the 795m (2,608-ft.) summit, passing the 12th-century **San Giuliano,** the small convent St. Francis founded, and the tiny old resort village of Monteluco.

The right trail at the tower will take you along a tree-shaded path that eventually branches off toward the ancient church of **San Pietro** ★

(✆ **0743-49-796**). Its latest reconstruction dates from the 13th century, but the facade incorporates reliefs full of medieval symbolism from its 12th-century Lombard predecessor. The interior, much less interesting since it was subjected to a baroque overhaul in 1699, is usually open daily from 9am to noon and 3:30 to 5pm (to 6:30pm in summer). From the church, cross the busy road and take the second right. Straight ahead (5 minutes) is Piazza della Libertà.

master architect, Gattapone, for the papal watchdog, Cardinal Albornoz. The *rocca* rests atop the site of the oldest prehistoric settlement in Spoleto and was used as a prison until 1982—inmates included members of the Red Brigades terrorist organization and Mehmet Ali Agca, who tried to assassinate Pope John Paul II in 1981.

Much of the interior is now occupied by the **Museo Nazionale del Ducato di Spoleto** (✆ 0743-223-055), which chronicles the history of the city from Roman times to the Renaissance, with an ensemble of richly inscribed sarcophagi, mosaics, and plenty of religious art and statuary. Don't miss the **frescoes** in the Camera Pinta, inside the Torre Maestra. Uncovered during a recent restoration, they were commissioned by governor Marino Tomacelli around 1400—the artist is unknown.

Piazza Campello. ✆ **0743-224-952.** Admission 7.50€ adults; 6.50€ ages 15–25, 3.50€ children 7–14, free for children 6 and under. Tues–Sun 8:30am–7:30pm (last ticket 6:45pm).

San Domenico Straight up Via Leone Pierleone from Piazza Torre dell'Olio is the pink- and white-banded 13th-century San Domenico. The first altar on the right preserves an early-15th-century fresco of the *Triumph of St. Thomas Aquinas,* with tiny monks, prelates, and scholars discussing the theologian's writings. There are more 15th-century frescoes in the presbytery and transept chapels, plus a painted crucifix from the 1300s above the main altar. The Cappella Benedetti di Montevecchio in the left transept is said to conserve not just any nail from the True Cross but one that pierced the Lord's hands. On the left wall is a moving 14th-century fresco of the *Pietà.*

Piazza San Domenico, Via Leone Pierleone. ✆ **0743-223-240.** Free admission. Daily 9:30am–noon and 3:30–5pm (until 6pm Apr–Oct).

Where to Stay

Accommodations are tight during the Spoleto Festival (reserve by Mar), so here are a few places to try in addition to the choices below if you have trouble finding a room. The **Hotel dei Duchi,** Viale G. Matteotti 4 (www.hoteldeiduchi.com; ✆ **0743-44-541;** fax 0743-44-543), has 49 modern rooms in a bland 1959 brick building just south of Piazza Libertà, but the rooms are spacious, the views are spectacular, and all the amenities are included (including free Wi-Fi). Online rates range from 75€ to 100€ per double. Cheaper and simpler are the six spacious doubles above the restaurant (under separate ownership) **Il Panciolle,** Via del Duomo 3–7 (www.ilpanciolle.it; ✆/fax **0743-45-677**). They have tiled floors, soft beds, clean bathrooms, TVs, phones, Wi-Fi, and minibars, and cost 45€ to 85€. One of the most appealing options outside town is the **Le Logge di Silvignano,** Frazione Silvignano 14 (www.leloggedisilvignano.it; ✆ **0743-274-098**), a gorgeous palace complex in the hills southeast of Spoleto. Rentals are usually by the week only, starting at 500€ to 700€ for a two-person suite.

Hotel Charleston ★ Many of the rooms in this friendly hotel are quite large and have a 1970s artist's loft feel (despite being refurbished in 2011), with good use of available space and antique-style furnishings. Rough-hewn chestnut-beam ceilings mirror the parquet floors (some are carpeted), and the walls are hung with modern art prints and original works. If you're feeling particularly hedonistic, you can cough up 20€ for a trip to the basement sauna, or just cozy up on a cushy sofa before the wintertime fire crackling between the TV and sitting lounges. They also organize all sorts of specialized tours (cooking classes, horseback rides, truffle hunts, and so on).

Piazza Collicola 10 (near San Domenico), 06049 Spoleto. www.hotelcharleston.it. © **0743-220-052.** Fax 0743-221-244. 21 units. 95€–120€ double; 120€–135€ triple. Rates include breakfast. AE, DC, MC, V. Garage parking 10€ per day. **Amenities:** 2 bars; winery; bikes; concierge; massage; room service (breakfast and bar); sauna; Wi-Fi (6€ per hr.). *In room:* A/C, TV, hair dryer, minibar, Wi-Fi (in some rooms).

Hotel Gattapone ★ Spoleto's most stratospheric hotel is a clutch of 17th-century buildings clinging to the cliff behind the *rocca*—isolated and surrounded by nature but still only a 3-minute stroll from the Duomo. It was formerly the home of 19th-century artist Francesco Santoro, and its interiors were remodeled to maximize views of the valley and the remarkable bridge nearby. Most of the wood-floored accommodations have plenty of elbow room, and while the styling dates from the hotel's birth in the 1960s, it has aged well. The standard rooms aren't as large or well appointed as the superiors, but are still recommendable. The small terrace off the conference room overlooks the full splendor of the bridge, and terraced gardens off the other end of the buildings, where the view, alas, is marred by a highway.

Via del Ponte 6 (near the *rocca* at the top of town), 06049 Spoleto. www.hotelgattapone.it. © **0743-223-447.** Fax 0743-223-448. 15 units. 120€–170€ standard double; 170€–230€ superior double. Rates include breakfast. AE, DC, MC, V. Free parking. **Amenities:** Babysitting; bikes; concierge; massage; room service; Wi-Fi (free in reading room). *In room:* A/C, TV, hair dryer, minibar.

Hotel Palazzo Leti ★★ Staying in this elegant and artfully restored hotel really is like being in a palace. It was built by the noble Letti family in the late 13th century, and has been enlarged many times since. All rooms have a view of the Monteluco hills, and even the cheapest standard doubles come with antique beds, rugs, and closets. The classical art and style is ramped up in the deluxe rooms, where you'll find more space, and wood-beam or beautifully engraved ceilings. The breakfasts here are truly sumptuous. Helpful owners Gianpaulo and Anna-Laura speak a little English, and the hotel is within walking distance of all the main sights.

Via degli Eremiti 10,06049 Spoleto. www.palazzoleti.com. © **0743-224-930.** Fax 0743-202-623. 12 units. 130€–200€ double. Rates include breakfast. AE, DC, MC, V. Free parking. **Amenities:** Bar; babysitting; bikes; concierge; room service; spa. *In room:* TV, hair dryer, minibar, Wi-Fi (free).

Hotel San Luca ★★ ☺ This is a wonderful, family-friendly hotel, and just a short walk from the historic center. The building dates back to the mid–19th century, when it was used as a tannery. The tranquil courtyard, replete with fountain and tables, is a pleasant place to relax, while the lounge features real log fires in winter. The spacious rooms are well equipped with all the extras, including heated bathrooms finished in Carrara marble and—unusual in this part of the world—real soundproofing. The lavish buffet breakfast will set you up well for the day.

Via Interna delle Mura 21, 06049 Spoleto. www.hotelsanluca.com. © **0743-223-399.** Fax 0743-223-800. 35 units. 100€–150€ standard double; 195€–240€ superior double. Rates include buffet breakfast. AE, DC, MC, V. Garage parking (13€ per day). **Amenities:** Restaurant (groups only); bar; babysitting; bikes; concierge; room service (bar); solarium. *In room:* A/C, TV, minibar, hair dryer, Wi-Fi (2€ per hr.).

Where to Eat

Its location at the Piazza Vittoria end of Viale Trento e Trieste (no. 29) isn't exactly convenient, but **Colder Gelateria** ★★ (© **0743-235-015**) serves some of the best gelato (notably "bread and chocolate" flavor) in Umbria, created by local artisans Crispini. Its open daily from 12:30pm to midnight.

La Torretta ★★ SPOLETINA This historic wine cellar oozes charm and excels at what the Italians call *"rustico-chic."* Run by the indefatigable Salvucci brothers, most of its menu is sourced locally and Umbrian dishes (and truffles) are the focus—highlights from the kitchen include the *Lo sformatino di riso tartufato* (baked rice cooked in a broth, with a butter, onion, and truffle sauce), and the *strangozzi alla Spoletina* (traditional homemade pasta, with tomato, garlic, red pepper, and parsley sauce). Outdoor seating is available during the summer.

Via Filitteria 43. ✆ **0743-44-954.** www.trattorialatorretta.com. Reservations recommended. Primi 8€–13€; secondi 9€–16€. AE, DC, MC, V. Wed–Mon 12:30–2:30pm and 7:45–10:45pm (closed Sun evening).

Osteria del Matto ★ UMBRIAN Eating here is certainly an interesting experience, though perhaps not for everyone. There's no menu to choose from, just a blackboard telling you what you're going to eat, and waiters telling you when you're going to eat it—dinners often last 3 to 4 hours. Your host-*cum*-entertainer in chief is the gregarious Filippo Matto (a former butler for composer Gian Carlo Menotti), who carves meats, welcomes guests, and generally goofs around. Load up on the small plates of meats, onion frittata wedges, artichokes, and *crostini,* usually followed by a single pasta dish—and if you're lucky, the farro stew made with sausage, wine, and peperoncini (Tuscan peppers).

Vicolo del Mercato 3 (under the big arch on the south side of Piazza del Mercato). ✆ **0743-225-506.** Reservations not necessary. Full meal 18€ without wine. MC, V. Wed–Mon 11am–3pm and 5pm–2am.

Osteria del Trivio ★ ITALIAN/UMBRIAN It's worth trudging down steep streets and steps for lunch in this proper Umbrian trattoria. The menu changes daily, but if you can, try the stuffed artichokes or divine *funghi sanguinosi,* "bloody mushroom" pasta (named after its bright-red color and usually served in the fall). Whenever you visit, you'll have a choice of hearty plates of homemade gnocchi, tagliatelle, and ravioli, and plenty of rich, filling mains such *pollo alla cacciatore* ("hunter's chicken stew"). A full meal with wine shouldn't cost more than 30€.

Via del Trivio 16. ✆ **0743-44-349.** www.osteriadeltrivio.it. Reservations recommended. Primi 8€–13€; secondi 8€–16€. AE, MC, V. Wed–Mon 12:30–2:30pm and 7–10pm.

Trattoria del Festival ☺ UMBRIAN The cavernous pair of vaulted brick rooms here are large enough to host the festival hordes yet still leave room for die-hard locals who come for the best fixed-priced menus in town. The two more "expensive" of these are the ones to order, because they let you sample a pair of primi (the chef's surprise, but one is assured to involve truffles) and include all the incidentals, save wine. Start with a foot-long *bruschetta al pomodoro* with a couple of cream-stuffed veal rolls before sinking your fork into the *tagliatelle tartufate* (a particularly successful use of the elusive black mushroom). The secondi also tend to be very simple but good. If you don't care for the excellent *frittata al tartufo* (mixed meat fried with truffles), try the *salsicce alle brace* (charcoal-grilled Italian sausages) or the *pollo arrosto* (roast chicken with lemon and rosemary).

Via Filippo Brignone 8 (near Piazza della Libertà). ✆ **0743-220-993.** www.trattoriadelfestival .com. Reservations recommended. Primi 7€–13€; secondi 7€–10€; fixed-price menu without wine 17€. AE, DC, MC, V. Thurs–Tues noon–3pm and 7pm–midnight. Closed Feb.

MONTEFALCO ★

18km (11 miles) NW of Spoleto; 149km (93 miles) SE of Florence; 112km (70 miles) N of Rome.

Looming some 475m (1,558 ft.) over the Vale of Spoleto, the enticing hill town of Montefalco surveys a 360-degree scene of wine trellises and olive groves. It's a handsome place, and usually attracts far fewer tourists than larger towns in the region, though the real highlight here is wine: the town's **Sagrantino di Montefalco ★★**, made from an indigenous grape and qualifying as a DOCG (p. 43). Truly great years, such as 2003, can improve in the bottle for a further 15 years, leaving a rich, velvety wine quite unlike neighboring Tuscany's robust reds.

Essentials

GETTING THERE By Car: Parking is plentiful and free around the walls; the main spot is the Parcheggio Ex Campo Sport, on the right, just off the road from Foligno and Perugia (SP444). The town holds a small market here every Monday morning.

By Bus: The small bus station is at the Parcheggio Ex Campo Sport on the edge of town. Mondays to Fridays there are three to four buses a day from Perugia (11am–6pm; 5.20€) and four to five buses from Spoleto (7:20am–5pm; 3.20€).

VISITOR INFORMATION The **tourist office** is on Via Ringhiera Umbra, just down from the piazza (✆ **0742-847-570**; www.promontefalco.com; Mon–Fri 11am–1pm and 2–6pm), while the Strada del Sagrantino wine trail office also doubles as a **tourist information center** (✆ **0742-378-490**; www.montefalcodoc.it; Mon 2:30–5:30pm, Tues–Sat 10:30am–1pm and 2:30–5:30pm, Sun 10:30am–1pm). It's at Piazza del Comune 17.

 ### On the Sagrantino Wine Trail

Montefalco is surrounded by a plethora of ravishing vineyards producing the region's famed Sagrantino wine—almost all of them have on-site stores where you can taste the wines before you buy. You can get a full list at the tourist offices in Montefalco (see above or visit www.stradadelsagrantino.it). One of the most respected producers is **Antonelli** ★ in the village of San Marco, a few kilometers west of the town (✆ **0742-379-158**; www.antonellisanmarco.it), open Monday to Saturday 8:30am to 12:30pm and 2:30 to 6:30pm. For a more intimate tasting experience, visit family-owned **Colle del Saraceno** ★★★ in Pietrauta (✆ **0742-379-500**; www.cantinabotti.com), where the

Bettoni family will provide a comprehensive introduction to their Sagrantino (16€), white Grechetto (9€), and the highly-prized sweet Passito (25€). They usually accept visitors Monday to Friday 9am to 6pm. For full tours of any of the vineyards, you'll have to call ahead. Plenty of stores in Montefalco also sell the local vino—most places double as wine bars. **Enoteca L'Alchimista** at Piazza del Comune 14 (✆ **0742-378-558**; www.montefalcowines.com; Thurs–Tues 9am–11pm) is a convenient and friendly choice with a wide selection. The other safe bet is **Enoteca di Benozzo**, at Piazza del Comune 10 (daily 9am–12:30pm and 1:30–11pm).

Exploring Montefalco

Montefalco is anchored by the fine hexagonal **Piazza del Comune,** whose 13th-century palazzo is tastefully embellished with a simple loggia. Other than visiting the superb Museo San Francesco, there's little to do but wander the enchanting streets and sample the wines.

Museo San Francesco ★ The frescoed apse of this former church was the first major commission of **Benozzo Gozzoli,** completed in 1452; it saw him step from the shadows of Lorenzo Ghiberti and Fra' Angelico, with whom he'd long collaborated. Today the church is part of a museum complex that begins with a series of small galleries showing minor 14th- and 15th-century works. In the church itself, Gozzoli's awe-inspiring *The Life of St. Francis* ★★ is the undoubted star, a series of 12 scenes covering the central apse (read left to right, from bottom to top). Gozzoli also frescoed the **Capella di San Girolamo,** while near the old main door, **Perugino**'s 1503 *Annunciation*

Gozzoli's frescoes in the Museo San Francesco.

and *Nativity* ★, as much about Umbrian landscapes as it is a devotional work, shows his mastery of skin tone and composition. Downstairs is a comparatively dreary archaeological collection (mostly funerary urns and sculpted stone), and the former monks' wine cellars replete with aging wine-making equipment.

Via Ringhiera Umbra 6. ✆ **0742-379-598.** www.benozzogozzoli.it. Admission 6€ adults, 4€ ages 19–25, 2€ children 11–18, free for children 10 and under. MC, V. June–July daily 10:30am–1pm and 3–7pm; Aug daily 10:30am–1pm and 3–7:30pm; Mar–May and Sept–Oct daily 10:30am–1pm and 2–6pm; Nov–Feb Tues–Sun 10:30am–1pm and 2:30–5pm.

Where to Stay & Eat

The best hotel in town is the central and extremely plush **Palazzo Bontadosi** (www.hotelbontadosi.com; ✆ **0742-379-357**), Piazza del Comune 19, offering spa and boutique comforts from 160€ for a double.

Brizi ★★ UMBRIAN Brizi is an enticing B&B and trattoria, but at its heart is an olive oil business run by the Brizi family since 1915. The family restaurant retains a commitment to seasonal food and simple Umbrian cooking, while the guesthouse upstairs (cash only) has just three individually named rooms, all with private bathrooms, and a panoramic communal terrace. Visit the on-site shop to sample the family's pride, but don't be fooled by the price (7.50€ for 500ml): This is a serious olive oil, made only from hand-picked fruit. Brizi also sells small Sagrantino wine producers (bottles from 7€) and a microbrew (www.birra camiano.com), created locally by a German expat.

Via S Chiara 34-60. www.frantoiobrizi.it. ℂ **0742-379-165.** 3 units. 70€–80€ double. Rates include buffet breakfast. AE, DC, MC, V. Free parking. **Amenities:** Restaurant; bar. Shop open Mon-Sat 10am–12:30pm and 2:30–5:30pm; restaurant open Mon–Sat 12:30am–2:30pm and 7–10pm.

Coccorone ★★ UMBRIAN Umbrian and local dishes are cooked and presented perfectly here, the service is attentive without being annoyingly hovering, and the wine list would make a Michelin-starred restaurant proud. For the daring there's beef in Sagrantino wine, lamb with truffles or snail kebabs—truffles feature in several dishes and their strangozzi pasta is excellent. Although the outdoor cover charge is a bit steep (3€ per person), the best spot is under the parasols on the terrace—book ahead or arrive early.

Largo Tempestivi (behind Palazzo del Comune). ℂ **0742-379-535.** www.coccorone.com. Reservations accepted. Primi 7.50€–13€; secondi 10€–20€. MC, V. Thurs–Tues 12:30–2:30pm and 7:30–10pm (plus Wed in summer).

TODI ★

43km (27 miles) W of Spoleto; 40km (25 miles) S of Perugia; 203km (126 miles) S of Florence; 130km (81 miles) N of Rome

One of the most picturesque Umbrian hill towns, Todi is a warren of narrow medieval streets twisting and plunging off at every angle, with many alleys whose graceful sets of shallow stairs flow down the center. It's a cobble of mottled grays accented with brick, all surrounding a picture-perfect central square justly celebrated as one of the finest medieval spaces on the peninsula.

A backwater for the past 500 years or so, Todi headed its own small Umbrian empire for a while in the early 13th century, and during the long Dark Ages of Lombard rule in central Italy, the *comune* apparently maintained its independence from the Lombard dukes in Spoleto. Todi claims a 2nd-century-A.D. martyr to prove it was Christianized early; while only a few bits of the 42 B.C. Roman Tuder survive, traces of the Etruscan border town Tutare are scarcer still. Even the Etruscans were relative newcomers, having conquered the city from an Umbri tribe that probably had displaced the Iron Age squatters who occupied the site in 2700 B.C.

Todi doesn't harbor much great art, with the exception of one jewel of High Renaissance architecture. People come here mainly just to look; to drink in the vistas from the town's terraces and the medieval character of its alleyways; to nap, picnic, and play in the public gardens; and to sit on the Duomo steps and stare at the Gothic public palaces across the way. Todi's once-upon-a-time atmosphere hasn't gone unnoticed. It sees its share of film crews and English-speaking expats, property speculators, and Italian businessmen, who have taken advantage of its relative proximity to Rome to buy medieval palazzi. Yet Todi remains a showcase hill town, and a refreshing break from a culture-heavy Italian tour.

Essentials

GETTING THERE By Train: Todi is on the private FCU train line (ℂ **075-575-401;** www.fcu.it), not the state-run FS rail routes. About a dozen trains leave daily from **Perugia**'s FCU stations (45 min.; 2.55€). From **Spoleto,** take the train to Terni (22 daily trains; 20–30 min; 2.70€) and transfer to the FCU line (14 trains per day; 2.55€; about 1 hr. total travel time). There are about eight runs daily from **Rome** to Terni (6.30€) that meet up with an

FCU train (about 2 hr. total). At Todi, get off at Ponte Rio (not Ponte Naia) station (✆ **075-894-2092** or 075-882-092), where a bus will be waiting to take you the 5km (3 miles) up to town.

By Car: Todi is 40km (25 miles) south of Perugia, off the E45 superstrada. For the quickest route into town, take the "Todi-Orvieto" exit and turn right by the orange building immediately after Ponterio; it heads straight up to Todi's Porta Perugiana. Don't park here—turn right again for the **Porta Orvietana** parking lot (.90€/first hr., .60€/hr. thereafter; 6.60€/day; daily 7am–midnight). A single-car **funicular** (free) whizzes you up to Via Ciuffelli.

By Bus: Umbria Mobilità buses (✆ **800-512-141;** www.umbria mobilita.it) stop in the center, on Piazza della Consolazione and sometimes Piazza Jacopone; the only useful connection is with **Perugia** (1¼ hr.), with four to eight runs daily.

VISITOR INFORMATION The central **tourist office** is under the arches at Palazzo del Popolo 38-39, 06059 Todi (✆ **075-894-2526;** www.comune.todi. pg.it/fap). It's open Monday through Saturday from 9:30am to 1pm and 3:30 to 7pm, Sunday 10am to 1pm and 3:30 to 7pm (in winter it closes at 6pm, and is not open Sun afternoons).

FESTIVALS & MARKETS For a decade, the town has put on the classy **Todi Festival,** 10 days at the end of August showcasing theater, music, and ballet, often surprisingly cutting edge. For information, contact **Teatro Comunale,** Via Mazzini (✆ **075-894-2206** or 075-894-3933; www.todiartefestival .com). The weekly **market** is Saturdays at the sports fields south of the center, while an annual **antiques fair** is held at the Palazzo Landi Corradi towards the end of April (www.rassegnaantiquariaditalia.it).

Exploring Todi

Piazza del Popolo ★★ is not only the center of Todi but also the center of an ideal: A balance of secular and religious buildings in transitional Romanesque-Gothic style that epitomizes the late medieval concept of a self-governing *comune*. On the south end of the piazza squats the brick-crenellated marble bulk of the **Palazzo dei Priori,** started in 1293 and finished in 1339 with the crowning touch of a bronze eagle, Todi's civic symbol. The paired Gothic structures running along the piazza's side are the battlemented **Palazzo del Popolo** (1213) and the **Palazzo del Capitano** (1290). They're linked in the middle by a grand medieval staircase onto which you might expect Errol Flynn to come swashbuckling down at any moment.

Cisterne Romane Remnants of the Roman era can be found in these excavated water tanks, ancient cisterns that form part of 5km (3 miles) of tunnels under Todi. You can enter just behind Piazza del Popolo. Descending below ground, you walk through a few of the two dozen parallel water-storage cells. There's not a whole lot to see, per se, but engineering enthusiasts will appreciate the ingenious way in which runoff was collected and stored for future use.

Piazza del Popolo. ✆ **075-894-4148.** Admission 2€ adults; 1.50€ students 15–25, children 6–14, and seniors; free for children 5 and under. Apr–Oct Tues–Sun 10am–1:30pm and 3–6pm; Nov–Mar Sat–Sun 10:30am–1pm and 2:30–5pm; closed Dec 25–Jan 1.

Duomo ★ At the north end of the main piazza rises the Duomo's facade, which ran the stylistic gamut from Romanesque through the Renaissance but still came out blessedly simple in the end. Inside on the entrance wall, framing a gorgeous rose window, is a **Last Judgment** ★ frescoed by Ferraù di Faenza in 1596 that owes about 80% of its figures and design directly to Michelangelo's *Last Judgment* in Rome's Sistine Chapel. Art critics tend to hate it, but it's stunning nevertheless, and the highlight of the cathedral. In the right aisle, under the sprightly thin-columned Gothic arcade added in the 1300s, are a 1507 marble font, what's left of a *Trinity* (1525) by Lo Spagna (here he's cribbing from Masaccio), and an early-16th-century tempera altarpiece by Giannicola di Paolo. To see the **crypt** and tiny **Museo di Lapidario** (which contains a small collection of Roman and Etruscan remains and medieval statuary), you must pay 1€.

Piazza del Popolo. ☎ **075-894-3041.** Free admission. Daily 8:30am–12:30pm and 2:30–6:30pm.

Museo Pinacoteca Todi's art gallery and history museum occupies the Palazzo del Popolo's fourth floor (elevator under the central arches), and features a modest lot of local 16th- and 17th-century pictures, plus the exuberant *Incoronation of the Virgin* (1507–11) by Lo Spagna that copies a Ghirlandaio work; Lo Spagna (nickname for the Spanish-born Giovanni di Pietro) seldom bothered coming up with anything original. The museum portion covers the history of the town with rooms devoted to Etruscan archeology, coins, textiles, and ceramics.

Palazzo del Popolo, Piazza del Popolo. ☎ **075-894-4148.** Admission 5€ adults, 3€ ages 15-25 and seniors, 2.50€ children 6-14, free for children 5 and under. Combined tickets with Cisterne Romane and Campanile di San Fortunato 7.50€, 6€, and 5€. Apr–Oct Tues–Sun 10:30am–1:30pm and 3–6pm; Nov–Mar Tues–Sun 10:30am–1pm and 2:30–5pm.

San Fortunato ★ From Piazza del Popolo, going around the right side of Palazzo dei Priori then taking a right at Piazza Jacopone will lead you to Todi's second major sight. The massive Franciscan shrine of San Fortunato was begun in 1291, but finishing touches dragged on to 1459. Cross the gardens to see the central doorway carvings, testament to the greatness the rest of the facade could have had. It's a late-Gothic tangle of religious, symbolic, and just plain naked figures clambering around vines or standing somberly under teensy carved Gothic canopies. Inside, the church is remarkably bright, as Italian churches go, and the whitewashed walls of the chapels sport many bits and pieces of what must once have been spectacular, colorful 14th- and 15th-century frescoes. The oldest of the surviving fragments are Masolino's 1432 *Madonna and Child with Angels,* in the **Capella de San Michele Arcangelo** (on the right), and the 1340 *Banquet of Herod* in the **Capella del Santissimo Crocifisso** (on the left). Todi's main Franciscan mystic, **Fra' Jacopone** (see the box below, "Monks & Christmas Carols: Fra' Jacopone"), lies in a tomb created in 1596 in a specially designed section of the crypt (steps lead down in front of the altar). A monument to the 13th-

Santa Maria della Consolazione.

Monks & Christmas Carols: Fra' Jacopone

Jacopone da Todi (1230–1306) started life in grand Umbrian style, living a fun, sometimes debauched, materialistic existence. But when his young wife died in his arms (a floor collapsed under her), he had a spiritual crisis, and from about 1268 he wandered Umbria as an indigent monk for 10 years. At around this time the Franciscan order had become divided between those who favored an extreme ascetic life, and those who took a more lenient attitude—Jacopone joined the former group, eventually bringing him into conflict with Pope Boniface VIII, who favored the latter. Jacopone responded by telling off, in verse form, the reprehensible pope (the written jibes got him excommunicated and 5 years in a Roman dungeon, between 1298 and 1303). He also wrote catchy late-medieval poetry, *laudi,* set to music that became, for all intents and purposes, the world's first Christmas carols. Jacopone died in Collazzone, a village between Perugia and Todi, but is still revered in his hometown today.

century poet and ascetic monk stands outside, back on Via Ciuffelli. The statue at the altar is of **San Fortunato** (a 6th-c. bishop of Todi and now its patron saint), finished in 1643—his arm is supposedly preserved in a silver reliquary in the Capella di San Fortunato, on the left. Paid tickets are required to climb the **Campanile di San Fortunato** (bell tower), with its gasp-inducing views over the city.

Piazza Umberto I, Via Ciuffelli. ℂ **0743-224-952.** Free admission to the church; Campanile di San Fortunato admission 2€ adults; 1.50€ ages 15-25, seniors and children 6-14; free for children 5 and under. Church Apr-Oct daily 9am-1pm and 3-7pm; Nov-Mar daily 10am-1pm and 2:30-5pm. Campanile di San Fortunato Apr-Oct Tues-Sun 10am-1pm and 3-6:30pm; Nov-Mar Tues-Sun 10:30am-1pm and 2:30-5pm (closed Dec 25-Jan 1).

One of Todi's medieval streets.

Tempio di Santa Maria della Consolazione ★★ At the southwestern end of the town, just outside the walls on Viale della Consolazione, lies Todi's High Renaissance masterpiece. Construction began in 1508 under Cola da Caprarola, who may have had Donato Bramante's help in the design. Before it was finished in 1607, its register of architects included Antonio Sangallo the Younger, Vignola, and Peruzzi, among others. It reposes in quiet, serious massiveness on a small, grassy plot. Although huge (its main dome its 70m/230 ft. high), it carries its mass compactly, with all lines curving inward and the domes and rounded transept apses keeping the structure cubically centered. The interior, however, is nothing special.

Viale della Consolazione. No phone. Free admission. Daily 9:30am-12:30pm and 2:30-6:30pm.

Where to Stay

There are a handful of convenient hotels in Todi itself, though as always, the choices in the surrounding countryside are more appealing if you have a car. We recommend **Country House Entropia** ★★ Via Loreto Grutti 6, Loreto (www.progettoentropia.it; ✆ **075-885-2249**), a wonderfully tranquil B&B just 6km (3¾ miles) from Todi. Doubles range from 70€ to 100€, with breakfast, Wi-Fi, and use of the pool included.

Larger groups or families might consider **La Torriola** ★, in Pian di San Martino (www.torriola.com; ✆ **333-495-0860**), a gorgeous farmhouse with five self-catering apartments 2km (just over 1 mile) from the E45 Todi-Orvieto exit on SS448. Apartments are normally rented on a weekly basis, but exceptions can be made if you book well in advance (especially off season; doubles are 100€–140€).

Fonte Cesia ★ The first hotel to open in Todi's historic center, the Fonte Cesia successfully melds modern architectural glass and wood elements with a 16th-century *palazzo*. Each of the suites has a small balcony or terrace and is unique—and worth the splurge, especially when the high-season cost of a double brings the prices close. The "Novecento" has 19th-century antiques, the "Jacopone" has Wassily chairs and a claw-foot tub, and the "Venturini" has a canopy bed. In summer, breakfast is served on a huge palm-shaded terrace that sits atop the hotel's 17th-century namesake fountain.

Via Lorenzo Leonj 3 (off Piazza S. Jacopo), 06059 Todi. www.fontecesia.it. ✆ **075-894-3737.** Fax 075-894-4677. 42 units. 120€–150€ double. Rates include breakfast. AE, DC, MC, V. Garage parking 10€ per day. **Amenities:** Restaurant; bar; babysitting; concierge; room service (during restaurant hours); smoke-free rooms. *In room:* A/C, TV, hair dryer, minibar, Wi-Fi (3€ per hr.).

San Lorenzo Tre ★★ This is what many people come to Umbria to experience—a simple, historic guesthouse that drips with character and doesn't break the bank. Decked out in the style of a late 19th-century middle class family (only the bathrooms are modern), rooms feature period furniture, linens and wood-beam ceilings. There are no TVs or phones, but plenty of books lying around. It's a short walk from the Duomo and very popular—book well ahead.

Via San Lorenzo 3, 06059 Todi. www.sanlorenzo3.it. ✆/fax **075-894-4555.** 6 units. 75€–100€ double. Rates include breakfast. AE, MC, V. Free parking. *In room:* Wi-Fi (free).

Where to Eat

Todi is a small town, so good and affordable restaurant options are fairly limited. For a more rustic lunch break, drive down the slopes south of Todi to **La Mulinella** at Ponte Naia 2 (✆ **075-894-4779;** Thurs–Tues 12:30–2:30pm and 7:30–11:30pm), an exceptional restaurant set within a lovely Umbrian house and garden full of blossoms. There's a small swing, lots of room for kids to run around, stunning views back up to the town, and a menu of hearty Umbrian classics.

Antica Hosteria de la Valle ★ UMBRIAN A small restaurant with fabulous food, full of locals most nights, with a shady canopy above just a handful of outside tables. The menu often changes, but standards are consistently high, despite the cozy, laid-back atmosphere. It's a place to try something different: fresh tagliatelle with carrot and olives (an addictive combo), or anything with roasted guinea fowl. Don't overlook the varied wine list, which often features some real bargains.

Via Augusto Ciuffelli 19. ✆ **075-894-2737.** Reservations strongly recommended. Primi 8€–14€; secondi 10€–20€. AE, DC, MC, V. Wed–Mon 12:30–2:30pm and 7:30–10:30pm.

Pane e Vino ★★ PIZZA/UMBRIAN This exceptional spot for lunch or dinner, just 50m (164 ft.) or so from the top of Todi's funicular, is tucked away in a lovely nook between two medieval stone buildings. You'll find all the basics here but the real specialty is black Noria truffles: Thick, Umbrian *strangozzi* pasta with truffles, and beef or spiced lamb with truffles are our favorites. Vegetarians (or meat-eaters) shouldn't miss the pumpkin and saffron risotto.

Via Augusto Ciuffelli 33. 🕐 **075-894-5448.** www.panevinotodi.com. Reservations recommended for dinner. Primi 9.50€–10€; secondi 12€–16€. MC, V. Thurs–Tues noon–2:30pm and 7–10pm.

ORVIETO ★★★

45km (28 miles) W of Todi; 87km (54 miles) W of Spoleto; 86km (53 miles) SW of Perugia; 152km (95 miles) S of Florence; 121km (75 miles) N of Rome

The defining feature of southern Umbria's most touristy town is its cathedral, with its dazzling facade: day-trippers come to Orvieto from as far as Florence and Rome to see it. The rest of town looks much as it did 500 years ago—a preserved medieval center stuck high on a volcanic plug some 315m (1,033 ft.) above the plain, visible for miles in every direction. This impenetrable perch ensured that Etruscan "Velzna" was among the most powerful members of the *dodecapoli* (Etruscan confederation of 12 cities); its Etruscan heritage has left an underground world that's just as much fun.

It was a close enough threat to the Romans that they attacked and leveled it in 265 B.C., driving the Etruscans to settle on the shores of nearby Lake Bolsena. The Romans built a port on the Tiber to ship home a steady supply of the famous wine produced in the area—still much in demand today as **Orvieto Classico,** one of Italy's finest whites (see "Orvieto's Liquid Gold," later). As a medieval *comune,* the city expanded its empire in all directions until the Black Death decimated the population in the 14th century. Soon after, Orvieto became part of the Papal States and a home away from home to some 32 popes.

The city seems not so much to rise as to grow out of the flat top of its butte. The buildings are made from blocks of the same *tufo* volcanic rock (tufa, or more accurately, tuff, in English), on which Orvieto rests, giving the disquieting feeling that the town evolved here of its own volition. A taciturn, solemn, almost cold feeling emanates from its stony walls, and the streets nearly always turn at right angles, confounding your senses of direction and navigation. Of course, a goodly dose of wine with lunch can make the whole place seem very friendly indeed, and the stoniness is greatly relieved by the massive Duomo rising head and shoulders above the rest of the town, its glittering mosaic facade visible for miles around.

Essentials

GETTING THERE By Train: Fourteen trains on the main **Rome-Florence** line stop at Orvieto daily (1 hr., 45 min. from Florence; 11€–19€; 1 hr., 20 min. from Rome; 7.10€–15€). From **Perugia,** take the train to Terontola (16 trains daily) for this line heading south toward Rome (1¼ hr. total train time; 7.10€ total). From **Todi,** it's easiest to take the bus (see below).

Orvieto's **station** is in the dreary new town of Orvieto Scalo in the valley. To reach the city, cross the street and take the **funicular** (www.atcterni.it;

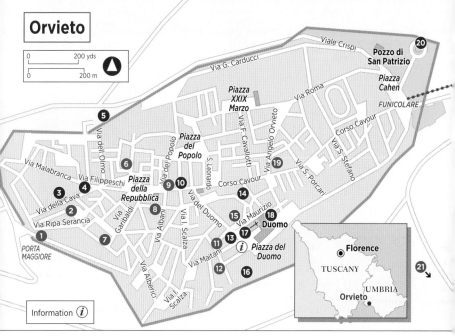

Orvieto

| 0 | 200 yds |
| 0 | 200 m |

ATTRACTIONS

Duomo **18**

Grotte della Rupe
(Etruscan Orvieto Underground) **16**

Museo Archeologico Nazionale **18**

Museo Claudio Faina e Civico **13**

Museo delle Maioliche Medievali **4**

Museo dell'Opera del Duomo
& Museo Emilio Greco **17**

Necropoli Etrusca di Crocifisso del Tufo **5**

Pozzo della Cava **3**

Pozzo di San Patrizio **20**

Teatro Mancinelli **14**

Torre del Moro **10**

HOTELS

Casa Flavia **19**

Hotel Duomo **15**

Hotel La Badia **21**

Palazzo Piccolomini **2**

Ripa Medici Bed & Breakfast **7**

RESTAURANTS

Al San Francesco **12**

Caffè Montanucci **9**

La Palomba **8**

Le Grotte del Funaro **1**

Tipica Trattoria Etrusca **11**

Trattoria dell'Orso **6**

every 10 min. 7:20am–8:30pm), a modern version of the steep cog railway that ran on hydraulic power in the 19th century. The funicular ticket is 1€, and is also valid on the minibuses (otherwise it's also 1€; accompanied children 9 and under ride free) that head into the center from the top of the funicular (Piazza Cahen). The "A" bus heads to Piazza del Duomo, the "B" bus to central Piazza della Repubblica via Piazza XXIX Marzo (it then doubles back to the Duomo). Both run every 10 minutes from 7am to 8pm. Or you may wish to get the ***Carta Unica*** cumulative ticket covering the funicular, bus, and museums (see "The Orvieto All-in-One Card," below).

By Car: Orvieto is straightforward to reach by car, especially from southern Tuscany: It's right by the A1. The main link to the rest of Umbria is the SS448 to Todi (40 min.). There's free (white) and pay (blue) parking

Tufa rock in Orvieto.

spaces (1€/hr., .10€ per 5 min.) in Piazza Cahen, the first major square as you arrive in town.

By Bus: From **Todi,** there's one ATC (www.atcterni.it) bus daily at 5:50am (a scenic twisting ride; about 2 hr.). The bus returns at 2:05pm. There's one daily SULGA bus to (3:15pm) and from (8am) **Rome**'s Tiburtina station (1½ hr.). From other cities, it's best to take the train. For bus information, call ✆**0763-301-234** or visit the tourist office.

VISITOR INFORMATION The **tourist office** is opposite the Duomo at Piazza Duomo 24, 05018 Orvieto (✆**0763-341-772;** fax 0763-344-433; www. comune.orvieto.tr.it or www.regioneumbria.eu). It's open Monday through Friday from 8:15am to 1:50pm and 4 to 7pm, Saturday from 10am to 1pm and 3:30 to 7pm, and Sunday from 10am to noon and 4 to 6pm.

FESTIVALS & MARKETS Florentines are wimps—they use a little fake bird to set off the cart of fireworks in front of their cathedral at Easter. The Orvietani use the real thing in **La Palombella ★.** On Pentecost Sunday, an unlucky white dove is tied to a frame encircled with flares, which slides down a steel cable and, amid much cheering and doubtless a few animal-rights protests, ignites the fireworks and sparklers strapped to a giant Gothic canopy placed outside the Duomo. Assuming the poor thing doesn't have a heart attack, the dove is then given to the couple last married in the Duomo to be cared for until its natural death.

 The Orvieto All-in-One Card

The useful **Carta Unica** cumulative ticket (www.cartaunica.it) for 18€ adults and 15€ students and seniors 60 and over gets you into the Duomo's Cappella San Brizio, the Musei Archeologici Faina e Civico, the Torre del Moro, and the Orvieto Underground tour—plus either one funicular plus one bus ride *or* 5 hours in the ex–Campo della Fiera parking lot. Buy the ticket from the funicular car park (✆ **0763-302-378**) in Orvieto Scalo, any participating sight, or the Carta Unica office (10am–6pm daily in summer, shorter hours in winter) next to Orvieto's tourist office at Piazza Duomo 23. It's valid for a year.

Umbria Jazz moves from Perugia to Orvieto for the winter, celebrating the last 5 days of the year with wine tastings and jazz artists from around the world. Call ✆ **075-573-3363** or visit www.umbriajazz.com for info. There are weekly **morning markets** on Thursday and Saturday in Piazza del Popolo.

Exploring Orvieto

Orvieto's most striking sight is, without a doubt, the facade of its Duomo. The overall effect—with the sun glinting off the gold of 17th- to 19th-century mosaics in the pointed arches and intricate Gothic stone detailing everywhere—has led some to call it a precious (or gaudy) gem and others to dub it the world's largest triptych. It is, to say the least, mesmerizing.

DUOMO ★★

Orvieto's Duomo was ordered built in 1290 by Pope Nicholas IV to celebrate the miracle that had occurred 27 years earlier at nearby Bolsena. Work was probably begun by Arnolfo di Cambio, but the structure ran through its share of architects over the next few hundred years—including Florentine Andrea Orcagna; a couple of Pisanos; and, most significantly, Sienese Lorenzo Maitani (1310–30). Maitani not only shored up the unsteady structure with his patented buttresses but also left a Gothic stamp on the building, especially the facade. Here he executed, with the help of his son, Vitale, and Niccolò and Meo Nuti, the excellent carved marble **relief panels ★★** in the lower register (protected by Plexiglas after many vandalism incidents). The scenes on the left are stories from Genesis; God fishes around inside Adam's rib cage with an "I know I left an Eve in here somewhere" look on His face. The far right panels are a Last Judgment preamble for the Signorelli frescoes inside. The most striking is the lower-right panel, a jumble of the wailing faces of the damned and the leering grins of the demonic tormentors dragging them to eternal torture. The anguish and despair are intense, possibly because the damned didn't realize Hell would contain quite so many snakes. The controversial (mainly because they're contemporary) **bronze doors** were cast in 1970 by Sicilian sculptor Emilio Greco.

Orvieto's Duomo.

Capella del Corporale Save for the 1426 *Madonna* fresco by Gentile Fabriano just inside the doors on the left, there's nothing to grab you in the boldly striped interior of the Duomo until you get to the altar end. The handsome **choir** behind the main altar was frescoed by Ugolino di Prete Ilario in the 14th century, while the left transept houses the Cappella del Corporale (1357–64), also by Ugolino and his workshop. The left wall depicts various miracles performed by communion wafers throughout the ages, while the right wall highlights the **Miracle of Bolsena.**

In 1263, a young priest who doubted the miracle of transubstantiation—the transformation of the communion wafer and wine into the actual body and blood of Christ—was saying Mass at Bolsena, on the shores of a lake a few dozen miles south of Orvieto. As he raised the Host toward the heavens, it began dripping blood onto the *corporale* (cloth covering the altar). The altar cloth instantly became a relic; today it resides in a huge gilded silver case designed in 1339 to mimic the cathedral facade and set with scenes of the Miracle of Bolsena and life of Christ in enameled panels inlaid with silver.

Cappella San Brizio To the right of the high altar is the Cappella San Brizio, containing one of the Renaissance's greatest **fresco cycles ★★★**. Fra' Angelico started the job in 1447 but finished only two of the vault triangles: *Christ as Judge* and a gold-backed stack of *Prophets*. The Orvietan council brought in pinch-hitter Pinturicchio in 1490, but the Perugian painter inexplicably cut out after just 5 days. It wasn't until 1499 that Cortonan Luca Signorelli strode into town, with the council hailing him as Italy's most famous painter and practically throwing at him the contract to finish the paintings. After completing the ceiling vaults to Fra' Angelico's designs, Signorelli went into hyperdrive with his own style on the walls. By 1504, the Duomo had some of the most intense studies ever seen of the naked human body, plus a horrifically realistic and fascinating rendition of the **Last Judgment.** Michelangelo, master of the male nude, who was most impressed, made many sketches of the figures, and found a prime inspiration for his own *Last Judgment* in the Sistine Chapel.

The first fresco on the left wall is *The Preaching of the Antichrist,* a highly unusual subject in Italian art. The Devil-prompted Antichrist discourses in the center, Christians are martyred left and right, soldiers scurry about a huge temple in the background, and the Antichrist and his followers get their angelic come-uppance on the left. The prominent whore in the foreground reaching back to accept money for her services is a bit of painterly revenge—it's a portrait of a girl-friend who had recently dumped Signorelli. On the far left is Signorelli's "signature": two black-robed figures bearing portraits of Signorelli and his skullcapped predecessor Fra' Angelico standing behind.

On the right wall, the first fresco shows the *Resurrection of the Flesh,* in which the dead rise from an eerily flat, gray plane of earth—Signorelli apparently didn't want any background detailing to clutter his magnificently detailed anatomical studies of nudes. The muscular bodies struggling out of the ground seem oblivious to the bright-winged angelic trumpeters standing on the clouds above.

In the arch to the left of the altar, angel musicians summon the lucky ones in the *Calling of the Chosen.* Italian last judgments tend to have infinitely more interesting "damned in Hell" scenes than "blessed in Paradise" ones, and Signorelli's is no exception. His *Crowning of the Chosen* on the left wall, however, is one of the few versions worth pausing over, again mainly because of its studies of nudes. This is a painterly festival of well-turned calves, modeled thighs, rounded bellies, and firm buttocks.

Then there's how the other half dies. To the right of the altar is *The Entrance to Hell*, filled with Dantean details such as a group of the indolent being led off by a devil bearing a white banner, and a man raising his fists to curse God as he sees Charon rowing across the Styx for him. Two rather militant angels oversee the whole process as if to make sure no one scrambles over the arch to the "Chosen" side. This fresco sets you up for the last and most famous scene: the writhing, twisting, sickly colored mass of bodies, demons, and horror of *The*

ORVIETO'S LIQUID gold

The plains and low hills around Orvieto grow the grapes—verdello, grechetto, and Tuscan varietals trebbiano and malvasia—that go into one of Italy's great wines, a pale straw-colored DOC white called simply **Orvieto Classico.** A well-rounded and judiciously juicy white (often with a hint of crushed almonds), it goes great with lunch and has one of the longest documented histories of any wine in Italy. Orvieto's wine trade is still a cornerstone of the area's economy. Most Orvieto Classico you'll run across is *secco* (dry), but you can also find bottles of the more traditional *abboccato* (semidry/semisweet), *amabile* (medium sweet), and *dolce* (sweet) varieties. The *secco* was created for export to satisfy the general public accustomed to the taste of bad chardonnay, and the sweeter varieties are treats seldom exported, so try them while you can. You may want to steer clear of big-name labels like Bigi—a perfectly fine wine, but one widely exported abroad—in favor of the smaller producers you can get only here.

To sample a glass (or buy a bottle) with a pastry or *panino,* drop by the **Cantina Foresi,** Piazza Duomo 2 (✆ **0763-341-611**). Ask to see the small, moldy cellar carved directly into the *tufo.* You can also tipple on a visit to one of Orvieto's friendliest shopkeepers at his enoteca/trattoria above the Pozzo della Cava excavations (see "Tunnels in the Tufo," below) at **La Bottega del Buon Vino,** Via della Cava 26 (✆ **0763-342-373;** www.pozzodellacava.it)—it sells its own bottles for 7€. To **visit a vineyard,** pick up a copy of the Strada dei Vini brochure at the tourist office or at the **Enoteca Barberani** at Via Maitani 1 (✆ **0763-341-532;** www.barberani.it); it lists the wineries along with the hours of tours and contact numbers.

Damned in Hell. Signorelli didn't pull any punches here. Tightly sinewed, particolored demons attack and torture the damned while a few of their comrades, menaced by heavily armed angels in full plate mail, toss humans down from the sky. One winged devil is making off with a familiar blonde on his back—the jilted artist's ex-mistress again—but there's also a gray-haired electric-blue devil in the center of the squirming mass, grasping an ample-bosomed woman and looking out at us from the chaos with a rather sad expression (another self-portrait?).

Piazza del Duomo. ✆ **0763-341-167.** www.museomodo.it. Admission 3€ including Cappella di San Brizio, 5€ with Museo dell'Opera del Duomo, free for children 10 and under. Apr–Oct Mon–Sat 9.30am–7pm, Sun 1–5.30pm (to 6:30pm July–Sept); Nov–Mar Mon–Sat 9.30am–1pm and 2.30–5pm Mon–Sat (Sun to 5.30pm).

Grotte della Rupe (Etruscan Orvieto Underground) ★★ The Orvieto *comune* has opened some of the tunnels under the city, with guided tours providing a taster of the vast network honeycombing the *tufo* subsoil (15m/45 ft. below the surface). The visit can be overly didactic, but you do get to see an underground 14th-century olive press (the constant temperature of 14°C was great for oil making). You can also peer down a few claustrophobically narrow Etruscan-era wells, wander around a subterranean quarry for *pozzolano* (a volcanic stone powdered to make cement mix) in use as late as the 19th century, and tour a series of Etruscan pigeon coops (no, seriously) carved out of the cliff-side rock. Note that the tour involves a steep climb up and down 55 steps, along a narrow rock-hewn passage.

Piazza Duomo 23 (next to the tourist info office; open daily 10:30am–5:30pm). ✆ **0763-344-891.** www.orvietounderground.it. Admission (by guided tour only, 45 min.–1 hr.) 6€ adults, 5€ students and seniors. Tours daily at 11am and 12:15, 3, 4, and 5:15pm (other times can be arranged); Sat–Sun only in Feb. English tours usually at 11:15am, but check in advance.

Museo Claudio Faina e Civico ★ The core of this Etruscan museum dates from a private collection started in 1864 and contains almost as much material from Chiusi and the Perugia area as it does from Orvieto area tombs. The highlights include an intriguing collection of **Etruscan black *bucchero* ware** from the 6th and the 5th century B.C., and some **Attic black-figure** (6th-c.-B.C.) and **red-figure** (5th-c.-B.C.) vases and amphorae that originated in Athenian workshops and were bought by discriminating Etruscan collectors. The museum even has three black-figure **amphorae by Greek master Exekias** (540 B.C.) that were fished out of the Crocifisso del Tufo necropolis (see Necropoli Etrusca di Crocifisso del Tufo, below). Of local manufacture is a celebrated group of 4th-century **pots depicting Vanth,** the Etruscan winged goddess of the netherworld, who has snakes wrapped around her arms and carries keys, a torch, or a scroll inscribed with her name.

The ground floor contains Etruscan material from the Cannicella tomb and Temple of Belvedere. These include a famous marble **"Venus"** (530–520 B.C.), the remarkably realistic **head of a bearded old man** (4th c. B.C.), a well-turned **warrior's torso** (late 5th c. B.C.), and a genuinely frightening **Gorgon's head.** The last room contains an enormous helmeted warrior's head carved in the late 6th century B.C. with some Etruscan script scrawled across it, and a 4th-century-B.C. **polychrome sarcophagus** found in nearby Torre San Severo. Its reliefs depict soldiers leading naked prisoners to be garroted and winged women carrying scepters and snakes (Vanth again).

Piazza del Duomo 29. ✆ **0763-341-511** or 0763-341-216. www.museofaina.it. Admission 4.50€ adults; 3€ ages 7–12, seniors 65 and over, and families of 4 or more. MC, V. Apr–Sept daily 9:30am–6pm; Oct–Mar 10am–5pm; closed Mon Nov–Mar.

Museo delle Maioliche Medievali This museum offers another insight into Orvieto's underground world, this time preserving a rare 14th-century kiln *in situ*, in addition to wells, wine cellars, and other remnants of medieval structures cut from the *tufo* rock. Display cases highlight various ceramic and majolica wares (most of it made here). It's especially worth considering if you can't take the underground tour (see above).

Via della Cava 8. ✆ **0763-344-149.** www.ceramicunderground.org. Admission 5€ adults, 3€ students, 1€ schoolchildren, free for children 5 and under. Daily 10am–1pm and 3–8pm.

Museo dell'Opera del Duomo and Museo Archeologico Nazionale
Housed in the yellow tufa 13th-century Palazzi Papali complex to the right of the Duomo, the Museo dell'Opera del Duomo preserves some of the fragile art once on display in the cathedral. The collection includes a rare *Madonna and Child* by Coppo di Marcovaldo (1270), two polyptychs by Simone Martini, and a touching *Mary Magdalene* by Luca Signorelli (1504).

In the adjacent Palazzo Soliano is the **Museo Emilio Greco** (© 0763-344-605; admission with Museo dell'Opera del Duomo; same hours), dedicated to the sculpture of the sometimes controversial contemporary artist who cast the Duomo's bronze doors.

Also in the Palazzi Papali complex (separate entry), the **Museo Archeologico Nazionale** (© 0763-341-039; www.archeopg.arti.beniculturali.it), contains desultory finds from Etruscan tombs in the area dating from the 7th to 4th centuries B.C., but unless you're a real aficionado, the Museo Claudio Faina e Civico (see above) provides a better introduction to Orvieto's ancient history.

Palazzi Papali, Piazza del Duomo 26. © **0763-343-592.** www.museomodo.it. Museo dell'Opera del Duomo: admission 5€ (includes Duomo/Cappella San Brizio), free for children 7 and under. Museo Archeologico Nazionale: admission 3€ adults, 1.50€ ages 18-25, free for children 18 and under and seniors; combined ticket with Necropoli Etrusca 5€. Museo dell'Opera del Duomo: Nov–Mar Wed–Mon 9:30am–1pm and 3–5pm; Apr–Oct daily 9:30am–7pm. Museo Archeologico Nazionale: Daily 8:30am–7:30pm.

Necropoli Etrusca di Crocifisso del Tufo ★ This 4th-century-B.C. necropolis of houselike stone tombs lies about halfway around the north edge of town off Viale Crispi (leading out of Piazza Cahen). On some tombs you can still see Etruscan script, written from right to left, on the door lintels, but the funerary urns and other relics found inside have long since been carted off to museums. What makes this site unique compared to similar necropolises in Etruria is that Etruscan Velzna, at least for a sizable period, apparently practiced some measure of democracy. None of the tombs is larger or otherwise set apart to denote the status of the occupants; rather, the whole affair is laid out in neat rows of uniform measure, indicating that citizens of differing ranks and occupations were interred side by side.

Viale Crispi (SS71). © **0763-343-611.** www.archeopg.arti.beniculturali.it. Admission 3€ adults, 1.50€ ages 18–25 and seniors, free for children 17 and under. Apr–Oct Mon–Sat 8:30am–7:30pm; Nov–Mar Mon–Sat 8:30am–5pm.

Pozzo di San Patrizio (St. Patrick's Well) ★ ☺ Orvieto's main military problem throughout history has been a lack of water. Fleeing Emperor Charles V's army in 1527, Pope Clement VII took shelter in the city. He hired Antonio Sangallo the Younger to dig a new well that would ensure an abundant supply in case the pope should have to ride out another siege. Sangallo set about sinking a shaft into the tufa at the lowest end of town. His design was unique: He equipped the well with a pair of wide spiral staircases, lit by 72 internal windows, forming a double helix so that mule-drawn carts could descend on one ramp and come back up the other without colliding.

Although Clement and Charles V reconciled in 1530, the digging continued. Eventually, workers did strike water—almost 10 years later, at which point Clement was dead and the purpose moot. The shaft was nicknamed St. Patrick's Well when some knucklehead suggested that it vaguely resembled the cave into which the Irish saint was wont to withdraw and pray. What you get for descending the 248 steps (62m/203 ft.) is a close-up view of that elusive water, a good echo, and the sheer pleasure of climbing another 248 steps to get out.

Viale San Gallo (near the funicular stop on Piazza Cahen). *© **0763-343-768.** Admission 5€ adults, 3.50€ students. May–Aug daily 9am–7:45pm; Mar–Apr and Sept–Oct daily 9am–6:45pm; Nov–Feb daily 10am–4:45pm.

Teatro Mancinelli Completed in 1844, this fine neoclassical theater is dedicated to Orvieto local boy Luigi Mancinelli. Even if you don't see a show here (check the website), it's worth a visit to admire the four stories of gilded box seats, the ornate chandelier, and bold ceiling frescoes and painted curtain by Cesare Fracassini. The latter is a romantic imagining of Belisarius liberating Orvieto from the siege of the Goths in the 6th century.

Corso Cavour 122. *© **0763-340-422.** www.teatromancinelli.it. Admission 2€ adults, 1€ students. Mar–Oct Tues–Sun 10am–6pm.

Torre del Moro This 45m-high (148-ft.) civic project from the late 13th century was built to keep on eye on Orvietan territory. In the 19th century it served as a main cistern for the city's new aqueduct system, then became the bell-ringing communal timekeeper when a mechanical clock was installed in 1876. You can clamber up for a sweeping view of the city and, on clear days, the countryside as far as Mts. Cetona and Amiata. If you don't fancy climbing all 236 steps, a lift whizzes you up the first 100 or so.

---

tunnels IN THE TUFO

The Orvietani have been burrowing into the soft *tufo* (tufa) and *pozzolano* stone under their feet for thousands of years. The Etruscans hollowed out cisterns to collect rainwater, sank wells to seek out groundwater, and carved public plumbing systems into the rocky foundations. The practice was continued by the Romans, the people of the Middle Ages (who also used some defunct wells as rubbish dumps), and even Renaissance Pope Clement VII.

Through the ages, the man-made cavern system has also been used for wine and oil production and storage, artisan workshops, escape tunnels for nobility, and quarries for tufa building blocks and the *pozzolano* dust to cement them with. The last tunneling and the closing of the last *pozzolano* mine occurred in the late 19th century.

Besides the *comune*-run **Grotte della Rupe** caverns and privately owned **Museo delle Maioliche Medievali** (see listings above), many shops and other private buildings sit atop underground excavations—scholars suspect the military base covering a fifth of the city (and closed to visitors) hides some of the finest. Perhaps the best accessible ones are under an enoteca, the **Pozzo della Cava**, Via della Cava 28 (*© **0763-342-373;** www.pozzodellacava.it). The excavations consist of six caves containing, among other things, a few medieval refuse shafts and a kiln from 1300, an Etruscan cistern, and, of course, a well almost 4.5m (15 ft.) in diameter and more than 30m (98 ft.) deep, first used by the Etruscans and later enlarged by Pope Clement VII. It's open Tuesday through Sunday from 9am to 8pm. Admission is 3€ for adults and 2€ for students, seniors, and holders of tickets to Pozzo Patrizio or the funicular parking tokens.

At the intersection of Via Duomo and Corso Cavour. ☎ **0763-344-567.** Admission 2.80€ adults, 2€ students and seniors, free for children 10 and under. Nov–Feb daily 10:30am–1pm and 2:30–5pm; Mar–Apr and Sept–Oct daily 10am–7pm; May–Aug daily 10am–8pm.

Shopping

You'll see the **Michelangeli** clan's **wood sculptures,** puppets, and stacked-contour reliefs all over town, while their showroom (☎ **0763-342-660;** www.michelangeli.it) is at Via Gualverio Michelangeli 3, just off the Corso. One of the top **antiques shops** in town is **Carlo & Cesare Bianchini,** Via Duomo 37 (☎ **0763-344-626**), which is filled with gorgeous *pietra dure* tabletops inlaid with semiprecious stones and marbles. Whether an antique or made by a local artisan, the wares here don't come cheap! Another popular stop is **Duranti Profumerie,** Via del Duomo 13-15 (☎ **0763-344-606**) which sells local perfumes and beauty products for men and women. For **wine shops,** see "Orvieto's Liquid Gold," p. 429.

Where to Stay

The hotel situation in Orvieto is fairly uninspiring. Most inns are of a consistently bland modern motel style, and the price doesn't come close to justifying the accommodations. The more pleasant choices are profiled below. If you have a car, you might want to try **Inncasa ★★★**, Località San Giorgio 6 (www.inncasa.eu; ☎ **0763-393-682**), 5km (3 miles) or so north of Orvieto on SR79bis, one of the best hotels in the region. Lavish rooms ("junior penthouses") start at 183€ in high season. You could also go the self-catering route: The best apartment in the city is **Casa Flavia ★★**, Via Angelo da Orvieto 12 (www.casa-flavia.it; ☎ **0763/341-821**), which rents for 60€ to 80€ per night. There's a kitchen, dining-living room, bathroom, space for up to four or five beds, and a sunny terrace.

Hotel Duomo ★★ 🌿 This three-star, modern hotel offers an excellent price for the central location, with comfortable rooms and all the usual amenities. The interior was designed and decorated by local artist Livio Orazio Valentini, and his bold, contemporary paintings light up the interior. The rooms are elegant but fairly standard, enhanced only by a couple of Valentini prints and mosaics on the lamps. A few rooms overlook the cathedral's striped flank, and there's a small garden out front for alfresco breakfasts in summer.

Vicolo di Maurizio 7 (near the Duomo), 05018 Orvieto. www.orvietohotelduomo.com. ☎ **0763-341-887.** Fax 0763-394-973. 18 units. 100€–130€ double; 120€–160€ junior suite. Rates include breakfast. AE, DC, MC, V. Garage parking 10€ per day. **Amenities:** Concierge; room service; Internet (free in public areas). *In room:* A/C, TV, hair dryer, minibar, Wi-Fi (5€ per hr.).

Hotel La Badia ★ This 12th-century abbey has been a hotel since 1968 and is one of Orvieto's best accommodations, albeit out of the town proper. The property is undeniably atmospheric, but it's not for everyone. Some rooms are palatial, others quite cramped; a few even have lofts and can sleep families without crowding, but the smallest rooms are best avoided. The suites are roomy, and those in the outbuilding connected to the church have Jacuzzis and a view of Orvieto up on its rocky perch. Bathrooms on the first floor have been renovated, but the older ones throughout La Badia carry their age well. Make sure you duck into the Romanesque church to see the frescoes and gorgeous cosmatesque-style floor.

Loc. La Badia 8 (about 3km/2 miles south of town off the road to Bagnoregio), 05019 Orvieto. www.labadiahotel.it. ☎ **0763-301-959.** Fax 0763-305-396. 27 units. 180€ double; 270€ junior suite. Rates include breakfast. AE, MC, V. Free parking. Closed Jan–Feb. **Amenities:** Restaurant; concierge; massage; outdoor pool (June–Sept); room service (bar); outdoor tennis court; Wi-Fi (free in public areas). *In room:* A/C, TV, hair dryer, minibar.

Palazzo Piccolomini ★★ Converted from a 16th-century *palazzo*, the family-run Piccolomini is the most inviting hotel in the center of town. It retains some palatial grandeur in echoey salons and the remnants of decorative frescoes, but the rooms tend toward the elegantly simple, with missionary-style wood furnishings, compact bathrooms, and modernized comforts (some suites have plush touches like heated towel racks and canopied beds). The ground-floor rooms have high vaulted ceilings, while those on the upper floors often have views across lichen-splayed roof tiles to the countryside.

Piazza Ranieri 36 (2 blocks down from Piazza della Repubblica), 05018 Orvieto. www.hotel piccolomini.it. ✆ **0763-341-743.** Fax 0763-391-046. 32 units. 154€ double; 196€ triple; 244€ suite. AE, MC, V. Rates include breakfast. Parking 15€ in main public lot next door. **Amenities:** Restaurant; babysitting; concierge; room service; Wi-Fi (free in public areas). *In room:* A/C, TV, hair dryer, minibar.

Ripa Medici Bed & Breakfast ★★★ 🍴 This gem of a B&B is an incredibly good value, right in the heart of town—there's just two rooms, though (it's more like an apartment rental), with a shared living room, two modern bathrooms, and a shared kitchen. The whole property is decked out in period furnishings, wood floors, and rugs. The views across the old town are fabulous and your host, Sabrina, is a font of local knowledge. Her mother also offers Italian home-cooking lessons.

Vicolo Ripa Medici 14, 05018 Orvieto. www.ripamedici.it. ✆ **0763-341-343.** 2 units. 65€ double. AE, DC, MC, V. Rates include breakfast. Free parking. *In room:* A/C, TV, hair dryer, Wi-Fi (free).

Where to Eat

Orvieto's unofficial pasta is *umbrichelli,* simple flour-and-water spaghetti rolled out unevenly by hand and somewhat chewy—similar to the *pici* of southern Tuscany, but not as thick. For a cappuccino and a cake, try **Caffè Montanucci,** Corso Cavour 21–23 (✆ **0763-341-261**), which has sold excellent local marmalades and a vast assortment of chocolate against a backdrop of Michelangeli wood reliefs since 1913. It's open Thursday through Tuesday from 6:30am to midnight and has public computers for Internet access. Sit in the garden at the back for maximum tranquility.

If you're in a hurry or on a budget and want to skip the restaurants below, try the cafeteria-style **Al San Francesco,** Via B. Cerretti 10 (✆ **0763-343-302;** www.ristorantealsanfrancesco.it), off Via Maitani near the Duomo. You can get a full meal with wine for well under 20€ (pastas 5€, meat and fish dishes 6€). The restaurant is open daily from noon to 3pm and 7 to 10:30pm (in winter, it closes Sun evenings). Self-service customers must sit inside.

La Palomba 🍴 ORVIETANA A giant wooden Pinocchio marks the entrance to this unpretentious place, a solid choice for a memorable meal of good home cooking. Try one of the specialty homemade *umbrichelli* dishes, either *tartufati* (in light butter-and-truffle sauce with fresh truffle grated on top) or *all'arrabbiata* (if it isn't *piccante* enough for you, add peperoncini-spiked olive oil). You can cool your mouth afterward with a simple omelet stuffed with cheeses or order the divine *filetto alla cardinale* (beef filet cooked in cardinal-colored red wine).

Via Cipriano Menente 16 (1st left under the arch at Piazza della Repubblica). ✆ **0763-343-395.** Reservations recommended. Primi 8€–12€; secondi 9€–14€. AE, DC, MC, V. Thurs–Tues 12:30–2:15pm and 7:30–10pm. Closed 20 days in July and/or Aug.

Le Grotte del Funaro ★ UMBRIAN Dating from at least the 1100s, when the eponymous *funaro* (rope maker) had his workshop here, these grottoes carved into the tufa draw Italians and tourists alike. The *bruschette miste Umbre* give their Tuscan *crostini* cousins a run for the money, but save room for the *ombrichelli del Funaro* (in a heavy sauce of tomatoes, sausage, artichokes, and mushrooms). For a sampling platter of the best grilled meats, order the *grigliata mista* (suckling pig, lamb, sausage, and yellow peppers). The wine cellar offers just about every Orvieto Classico. After 10pm, the restaurant transforms into a piano bar; if you're here for lunch, retire outside to digest with the aid of the spectacular view from the terrace-like piazza.

Via Ripa Serancia 41 (at the west end of town near Porta Maggiore; well signposted). ✆ **0763-343-276.** www.grottedelfunaro.it. Reservations recommended. Primi 9€–15€; secondi 10€–13€; pizza 5.50€–8.50€; fish-tasting menu without wine 32€; minimum 2 people. AE, DC, MC, V. Tues–Sun noon–3pm and 7pm–midnight. Closed 1 week in July.

Tipica Trattoria Etrusca ★ ORVIETANA Squirreled away under a 15th-century palace, this trattoria features vaulted ceilings, magnificent tufa arches, a massive column at the center, and modern art on the walls. Start with *umbrichelli dell'Orvietana* (in a spicy hot tomato sauce mixed with *pancetta*) or the homemade gnocchi. The *coniglio all'Etrusca* (rabbit in a green sauce of herbs and spices) is the house special secondo, but don't rule out the *abbacchio a scottadito* (lamb so piping hot it'll "burn your fingers"). Desserts tend toward antique Orvietan sweets, including fresh ricotta dusted with sugar, cinnamon, and a sweet berry sauce. Ask to see the wine cellars, carved from the living tufa beneath.

Via Lorenzo Maitani 10 (1 block from the Duomo). ✆ **0763-344-016.** Reservations recommended. Primi 7€–15€; secondi 7€–15€. AE, DC, MC, V. Daily noon–3pm and 7:15–10pm. Closed Mon in winter, and every day Jan 7–Feb 7.

Trattoria dell'Orso ★★ UMBRIAN Chef Gabriele di Giandomenico uses the freshest local ingredients and traditions (mixed with those of his native Abruzzo) to create memorable dishes that change daily, which is why his Neapolitan partner, Ciro Cristiano, prefers to recite them to you in delectable detail rather than break out the printed menu. In the tiny rooms surrounded by Michelangeli wood sculptures—including a remarkably realistic "lacy" curtain—you can sample fresh homemade tagliatelle, served perhaps with mushrooms and truffles, with broccoli, or with baby tomatoes, basil, and shredded scamorza cheese. The local specialty secondo is chicken with olives, or you can try Gabriele's *faraona* (game hen) stuffed with truffles.

Via della Misericordia 18–20. ✆ **0763-341-642.** Reservations recommended. Primi 7€–12€; secondi 8€–16€. AE, DC, MC. Wed–Sun noon–2pm and 7:30–10pm. Closed Feb, July, and Nov.

12

PLANNING YOUR TRIP TO TUSCANY & UMBRIA

A s with any trip, a little preparation is essential before you start your journey to Florence, Tuscany, and Umbria. This chapter provides a variety of planning tools, including information on how to get there and the fastest and easiest ways to travel around; tips on accommodations and dining; and quick, on-the-ground resources.

GETTING THERE
By Plane

Many visitors choose to fly into Rome's **Fiumicino Airport (FCO;** ✆**06-65951;** www.adr.it) or Milan's **Linate Airport (LIN;** ✆**02-7485-2200;** www.sea-aeroportimilano.it) or **Malpensa Airport (MXP;** ✆**02-2680-0613;** www.sea-aeroportimilano.it), and then transfer to Florence, Tuscany, or Umbria either via another flight or by train or car.

Flying directly to Tuscany or Umbria is obviously the most convenient option, but it's nearly impossible if you want to fly non-stop from another continent. One exception to this rule, however, is the non-stop New York to Pisa flight on **Delta,** which runs from JFK to Aeroporto Galileo Galilei (summer only), otherwise known as **Pisa International Airport (PSA;** ✆**800-018-849;** www.pisa-airport.com). Flying directly to Pisa is much more convenient than arriving in Rome or Milan and then taking a car or train.

You might consider flying to another Italian or European hub, and then transferring to a flight to Pisa. **Iberia, British Airways, Air France,** and **Lufthansa** service Pisa airport. Pisa airport is also serviced by budget airlines such as **easyJet** and **Ryanair** from a variety of locations in Europe and the U.K.

The other major airport in Tuscany is Florence's airport, known as **Amerigo Vespucci Airport,** but best known locally as **Peretola (FLR;** www.aeroporto.firenze.it), after the neighborhood where it resides. There are only a dozen airlines that fly into it, none of them major international budget carriers, but it might make sense for you to arrive somewhere else in Europe and transfer to Florence on **Air France, Alitalia,** or **Lufthansa.** While it might be more expensive to fly directly to Florence, you will most likely save money on the trains or taxis you would have taken to get there.

The only major airport in Umbria is just outside Perugia, the **Aeroporto Internazionale dell'Umbria S. Egidio** (✆**075-592-141;** www.airport.umbria.it). It's a small airport that only serves a handful of destinations, the most useful being London Stansted (via **Ryanair**) and Milan Malpensa (via **Skybridge AirOps**).

To find out which airlines travel to Tuscany and Umbria, please see "Airline Websites," p. 458.

GETTING TO TUSCANY OR UMBRIA FROM ROME'S AIRPORTS

Most international flights to Rome will arrive at **Fiumicino Airport (FCO).** Some inter-European and transatlantic charter flights may land at **Ciampino**

FACING PAGE: **A Vespa in Tuscany.**

Airport (CIA), which is closer to the center, but not connected by an express train. You can connect to a plane at either to take you to Pisa's or Florence's airport, but it's often simpler, almost as fast in the long run, and cheaper to take the train. You can also **rent a car** at either airport.

Fiumicino (✆ 06-659-51; www.adr.it) is 30km (19 miles) from Rome's center. You can take the **Leonardo Express train** (14€) from Fiumicino to Rome's central train station, Termini. A taxi to the station costs 40€. From Termini, you can grab one of many daily trains to Florence, Pisa, and most other destinations. If you happen to fly into **Ciampino Airport** (✆ 06-7934-0297), 15km (9¼ miles) south of the city, a COTRAL bus (1€) will take you to the Ciampino Città Metro station every 30 minutes, where you can take the Metro to Termini (15 minutes). A taxi to Rome's center from Ciampino is 30€.

Information on getting to most major Tuscan and Umbrian cities and towns from Rome **by train** is included under each destination throughout this book.

GETTING TO TUSCANY OR UMBRIA FROM MILAN'S AIRPORT

Flights to Milan land at either **Linate Airport** (**LIN**; ✆ 02-7485-2200; www.sea-aeroportimilano.it), about 8km (5 miles) southeast of the city, or **Malpensa Airport** (**MXP**; ✆ 02-2680-0613), 45km (28 miles) from downtown—closer to Lake Maggiore than to Milan itself. Some budget airlines also serve **Bergamo-Orio al Serio Airport** or Milan-Bergamo, some 45km (28 miles) from Milan, but a lot more inconvenient.

From **Malpensa,** the 30-minute **Malpensa Express** (www.malpensa express.it) train departs half-hourly to the Cadorna train station in western Milan rather than to the larger and more central Stazione Centrale from which most trains onward to Tuscany will leave (you'll have to take the Metro to get there). This train costs 11€. Alternatively, slower (50 min.) and cheaper (7€) trains run every hour direct to Stazione Centrale. To grab a bus instead, which will also take you directly to the central downtown rail station, take the **Malpensa Shuttle** (✆ 02-5858-3185) for 7€, which leaves two or three times per hour for the 50-minute ride to the east side of Milan's Stazione Centrale. A taxi to the city center runs about 70€.

From **Linate, Starfly buses** (✆ 02-5858-7237) make the 25-minute trip to Milan's Stazione Centrale every 30 minutes daily from 6:10am to 11:30pm for 5€ (6:30am–10pm weekends). The slightly slower **ATM** (✆ 800-808-181) city bus no. 73 leaves hourly for the S. Babila Metro stop downtown (1.05€ for a regular bus ticket bought from any newsagent inside the airport, but not onboard).

From Milan's Stazione Centrale, you can get regular high-speed trains to Florence (see "Getting There," in chapter 4).

By Bus

Italy is connected by **Eurolines** (✆ 055-357-059 in Italy, 08705-143-219 in the U.K.; www.eurolines.com), long-distance buses to a variety of European countries. Though fares are relatively cheap, budget airlines can be just as competitive and far less time-consuming. For example, London to Milan can take 26 hours, involve a change at Paris, and cost 70€.

By Car

Tuscany and Umbria are most accessible by car. In fact, one of the most common and convenient ways to take a tour of this area is to fly or take a train into

Florence, see the city, then pick up a rental car to wind your way through Tuscany and Umbria toward Rome, where you can drop off the car and fly home.

Getting to Tuscany and Umbria by car isn't hard from either Milan or Rome. The A1 *autostrada* runs straight down the peninsula, connecting Milan, Bologna, Florence, Rome, and Naples in a straight shot. The trick is getting to it. Both city beltways (in Rome it is the *Grande Raccordo Anulare*; in Milan, the *tangenziale*) feed right onto it, but getting onto the GRA or the *tangenziale* can be nightmarish procedures for an out-of-towner. Insist on specific, detailed directions from the car-rental agencies or make use of a GPS. Drivers used to the traffic in L.A., New York, or London should have few concerns about Italian roads, but driving in Italy can still be nerve-racking—for both the winding roads and the Italian penchant for driving a Fiat like a Ferrari. (And driving a Ferrari like one, too, for that matter.)

Officially, it is a legal requirement for all foreigners driving in Italy to obtain an **International Driver's Permit** (IDP; not to be confused with the International Drivers License), though in practice few rental companies will ask to see anything more than your home driving license and a credit card. Nevertheless, should you be stopped by police, they'll expect to see an IDP. In the U.S., only the **American Automobile Association** (AAA; ✆ 800/222-1134 or 407/444-4300; www.aaa.com) and the American Automobile Touring Alliance (through the National Automobile Club; www.nationalautoclub.com) are authorized to issue IDPs (usually $15). In Canada, the permit is available from the Canadian Automobile Association (CAA; ✆ 613/247-0117; www.caa.ca). If you have an E.U. driving license it's not usually necessary to obtain an IDP.

Italy's equivalent of AAA is the **Automobile Club d'Italia (ACI),** a branch of the Touring Club Italiano. They're the people who respond when you place an emergency call to ✆ 803-116 for road breakdowns, though they do charge for this service if you're not a member. If you wish, you may join online at www.aci.it or at one of the club's regional offices (in Florence, Viale Amendola 36, ✆ 055-24-861; in Rome, Via C. Colombo 261, ✆ 06-514-971). For information on car rentals and gasoline (petrol) in Tuscany and Umbria, see "Getting Around: By Car," below.

By Train

Traveling around Tuscany by train may not always be the most convenient option, but getting there on a train from Rome or Milan couldn't be easier. The high-speed **Frecciarossa** and **Frecciargento** trains stop in Florence (some stop in Arezzo as well), and the slower trains make stops in the smaller cities. It is the best route to Florence from airports in Milan (1¾ hr./53€) and Rome (1½ hr./45€). From Milan you can be in **Paris** in 7 hours, and **London** (via the Channel Tunnel) in around 10 hours by train. Another option from Paris is the Artesia overnight sleeper train (www.artesia.eu); it departs Gare de Bercy at 6:54pm and pulls into Florence at 7:13am the next morning. The cheapest tickets range from 76€ for a bed in a 6-couchette compartment, to 140€ for a bunk in a 2-bed sleeper compartment.

Getting to **Perugia** from Rome and Milan by train takes a lot longer, although southern Umbrian towns—Orvieto, for example—are under 2 hours and just a few euros from Rome.

For more information about train travel in Tuscany and Umbria, see "Getting Around," below.

GETTING AROUND
By Car

Contrary to the Italian stereotype, Tuscan and Umbrian drivers tend to be very safe and alert—if a bit more aggressive than many visitors are used to. If someone races up behind you and flashes his lights, that's the signal for you to slow down so he can pass you quickly and safely. Stay in the right lane on highways; the left is only for passing and for cars with large engines and the pedal to the metal. If you see someone in your rearview mirror speeding up with his hazard lights blinking, get out of the way because it means his Mercedes is opened up full throttle. On a two-lane road, the idiot passing someone in the opposing traffic who has swerved into your lane expects you to veer obligingly over into the shoulder so three lanes of traffic can fit—he would do the same for you. (Plus, the alternative is not pretty.)

Autostrade are superhighways, denoted by green signs and a number prefaced with an A, like the A1 from Rome to Florence. A few aren't numbered and are simply called *raccordo,* a connecting road between two cities or highways (such as Florence-Siena and Perugia-A1). On longer stretches, *autostrade* often become toll roads. **Strade Statali** are state roads, usually two lanes wide, indicated by blue signs. Their route numbers are prefaced with an SS or an S, as in the SS222 from Florence to Siena. On signs, however, these official route numbers are used infrequently. Usually, you'll just see blue signs listing destinations by name with arrows pointing off in the appropriate directions. Even if it's just a few kilometers down on the road, often the town you're looking for won't be mentioned on the sign at the appropriate turnoff. It's impossible to predict which of all the towns that lie along a road will be the ones chosen to list on a particular sign. Sometimes, the sign gives only the first minuscule village that lies past the turnoff; at other times it lists the first major town down that road; and some signs mention only the major city the road eventually leads to, even if it's hundreds of kilometers away. It pays to study the map before coming to an intersection.

The **speed limit** on roads in built-up areas around towns and cities is 50kmph (31 mph), 90kmph (56 mph) on secondary and local roads, 110kmph (68 mph) on main roads outside urban areas, and 130kmph (80 mph) per hour on highways. Italians have an astounding disregard for these limits, mostly because the limits are only enforced if the offense is egregious. However, police can ticket you and collect the fine on the spot. The blood-alcohol limit in Italy is 0.05%, often achieved with just two drinks. Clearly drunk drivers can expect to be arrested. The wearing of **seat belts** is compulsory for front and back seat passengers as well as for the driver.

As far as ***parcheggio*** (parking) is concerned, on **streets** white lines indicate free public spaces and blue lines pay public spaces. (Never park in yellow-lined spaces, which are for residents or local business owners only.) Meters don't line the sidewalk; rather,

 Dealing with Strikes

It's always a good idea in Italy to double-check the official hours that museums and sites are open, and to confirm airline, train, and bus reservations the day before traveling. What's open or running today may be closed tomorrow, as strikes can close attractions and shut down public transportation without much warning. For information on pending strikes, visit www.slowtrav.com/blog/italy_transport_strikes.

there's one machine on the block where you punch in how long you want to park. The machine spits out a ticket that you leave on your dashboard. Sometimes streets will have an attendant who'll come around and give you your timed ticket (pay him or her when you get ready to leave). If you park in an area marked **PARCHEGGIO DISCO ORARIO,** root around in your rental car's glove compartment for a cardboard parking disc (or buy one at a gas station). With this device, you dial up the hour of your arrival (it's the honor system) and display it on your dashboard. You're allowed *un ora* (1 hr.) or *due ore* (2 hr.), according to the sign. If you don't have a disc, find a piece of blank paper and write *"Arrivo:"* followed by the time you arrived, then display it on the dashboard. **Parking lots** have ticket dispensers, but booths are not usually manned as you exit. Take your ticket with you when you park; when you return to the lot to get your car and leave, first visit the office or automated payment machine to exchange your ticket for a paid receipt that you then use to get through the automated exit.

CAR RENTAL All the major international rental companies are represented in Tuscany and Umbria, with desks at all the airports listed above, and offices in major towns such as Florence and Perugia. **Hertz** (www.hertz.com) and **Europcar** (www.europcar.com) tend to be the most popular. Rates vary according to the season and length of rental, and can range from 40€ to 100€ per day for the smallest car. Book in advance for the cheapest rates. Basic mandatory insurance is always included (collision damage waiver and theft waiver). See "Getting There" above for driving license requirements.

ROAD SIGNS Here's a brief rundown of the road signs you'll most frequently encounter. A **speed limit** sign is a black number inside a red circle on a white background. The **end of a speed zone** is just black and white, with a black slash through the number. A red circle with a white background, a black arrow pointing down, and a red arrow pointing up means **yield to oncoming traffic,** while a point-down red-and-white triangle means **yield ahead.** In town, a simple white circle with a red border, or the words *zona pedonale* or *zona a traffico limitato,* denotes a **pedestrian zone** (you can sometimes drive through only to drop off baggage at your hotel); a white arrow on a blue background is used for Italy's many **one-way streets;** a mostly red circle with a horizontal white slash means **do not enter.** Any image in black on a white background surrounded by a red circle means that image is **not allowed** (for instance, if the image is two cars next to each other: no passing; a motorcycle means no Harleys permitted; and so on). A circular sign in blue with a red circle-slash means **no parking.**

GASOLINE Like most of Western Europe, *benzina* (gas or petrol) in Italy is much more expensive than in the U.S. (and most parts of Canada). Even a small rental car guzzles 50€ to 70€ for a fill-up (equivalent to $7–$8 a gallon). There are many pull-in gas stations along major roads and on the outskirts of town, as well as 24-hour rest stops along the *autostrada* highways, but in towns some stations are small sidewalk gas stands where you parallel park to fill up. Almost all stations are closed for *riposo* and on Sundays, but the majority of them now have a pump fitted with a machine that accepts bills so you can self-service your tank at 3am. Unleaded gas is *senza piombo,* but most locally-rented cars take *gasolio* (diesel). Be sure to check before filling up.

By Train

Italy has one of the best train systems in Europe, and even traveling on a regional level through Tuscany and Umbria, you'll find many destinations connected. There are four major rail arteries in Tuscany. The most important and quickest is the Milan-Florence-Arezzo-Orvieto-Rome line that parallels the A1 highway; the second is the coastal Genoa-Pisa-Livorno-Rome line. The third and fourth connect those two: the Florence-Viareggio route stops in Prato, Pistoia, Montecatini Terme, and Lucca, and the Florence-Pisa line has principal intermediate halts in Empoli and Pontedera. The slower the train, the smaller the towns where it will stop.

Most lines are administered by the state-run **Ferrovie dello Stato** or **FS** (© **892-021** for national train info, or 199-166-177 to buy tickets; www.tren italia.com), but servicing the Casentino and western Valdichiana in Tuscany is a private line called **LFI,** and northern Umbria is serviced by the private **FCU.** About the only difference you'll notice is that these private lines don't honor special discount cards or passes (see "Special Passes & Discounts," below).

Italian trains are clean and reasonably comfortable. First class (*prima classe*) is usually only a shade better than second class (*seconda classe*), with four to six seats per *couchette* instead of six to eight. The only real benefit of first class comes if you're traveling overnight, in which case four berths per compartment are a lot more comfortable than six.

Few visitors are prepared for how **crowded** Italian trains can sometimes get, though with the increase in automobile travel, they're not as crowded as they were in decades past. An Italian train is only full when the corridors are packed solid and there are more than eight people sitting on their luggage in the little vestibules by the doors. Overcrowding is usually only a problem on Friday evenings and weekends, especially in and out of big cities, and just after a strike. In summer the crowding escalates, and any train going toward a beach in August bulges like an overstuffed sausage.

Italian trains come in varieties based on how often they stop. The **Frecciarossa (ES)** is the high-speed train that zips back and forth between Salerno, Naples, Rome, Milan, and Turin, stopping at Florence along the way. It's the fastest but most expensive option; it has its own ticket window at the stations and *requires* a seat reservation. Other **Eurostar/Frecciabianca/Frecciargento (ES)** trains connect most Italian cities; these are the speediest of Italian trains, offering both first and second class and always requiring a supplement; **Eurocity (EC)** and **Euronotte (EN)** trains connect Italy with international destinations; **Intercity (IC)** trains offer both first and second class seating and require a smaller supplement, but are slower (sometimes *much* slower) than a high-speed train. Regular trains that don't require supplements are called **Regionale (R)** or (slightly quicker) **Regionale Veloce (RV)** trains.

When buying a **regular ticket,** ask for either *andata* (one-way) or *andata e ritorno* (round-trip). If the train you plan to take is a high-speed service, ask for the ticket *con supplemento rapido* (with speed supplement) to avoid on-train penalty charges. On a trip under 200km (124 miles), your ticket is good to leave within the next 6 hours; over 200km (124 miles) you have a full day. (This code isn't rigorously upheld by conductors, but don't push your luck.) On round-trip journeys of less than 250km (155 miles), the return ticket is valid only for 3 days. This distance-time correlation continues, with an extra day added to your limit for each 200km (124 miles) above 250km (155 miles) (the maximum is 6 days). If you board a regular train without a ticket (or board an IC/ES without the supplement), you'll have to pay a hefty "tax" on top of the ticket or supplement, which the conductor will sell you. Most conductors also get extremely crabby if you forget to **stamp your ticket in the little yellow box** on the platform before boarding the train. You are liable for a fine.

Schedules for all lines running through a given station are printed on posters tacked up on the station wall. *Binario (bin.)* means track. You can also get official schedules (and more train information, some even in English) on the Web at **www.trenitalia.com**.

By Taxi

In small towns throughout Tuscany and Umbria, taxis don't wait for arriving trains or buses. To avoid having to call for a cab, arrange transportation with your hotel in advance. Similarly, you won't be able to hail cabs in the street—always arrange rides in advance or rely on other forms of transport. In small towns taxis rarely use meters—prices will usually be fixed in advance (often by the local authorities). Note that taking a taxi for longer rides between towns is very expensive and rarely worth the money, even for groups.

Stations tend to be well run, with luggage storage facilities at all but the smallest and usually a good bar attached that serves surprisingly palatable food. If you pull into a dinky town with a shed-size or nonexistent station, find the nearest bar or *tabacchi,* and the person behind the counter will most likely sell you tickets.

SPECIAL PASSES & DISCOUNTS To buy the **Eurail Italy Pass,** available only outside Italy, contact **Rail Europe** (www.raileurope.com). You have 2 months in which to use the train a set number of days; the base number of days is 3, and you can add up to 7 more. For adults, the first-class pass starts at $278, second class is $227. Additional days cost roughly $30 more for first class, $25 for second class. For Youth tickets (25 and younger), a 3-day pass is $183 and additional days about $20 each. Saver passes are available for groups of two to five people traveling together at all times, extending a discount of about $20 off an adult pass. Be aware, however, that you have to do a fair amount of traveling to make a pass financially worthwhile. Trenitalia.com allows you to price your journeys, so take a moment to do the math before buying a pass.

When it comes to regular tickets, if you're **25 and under,** you can buy at any Italian train station a 40€ **Carta Verde (Green Card)** that gets you a 10% discount for domestic trips and 25% on international connections on all FS tickets for 1 year. Present it each time you go to buy a ticket. A similar deal is available for anyone **60 and over** with the **Carta d'Argento (Silver Card):** 15% off domestic and 25% off international, for 30€. The card costs 30€, but is free to anyone 75 or over. Children 11 and under always ride half price (and can get the passes mentioned above at half price), and kids 3 and under ride free.

By Bus

Regional intertown buses are called *pullman,* though *autobus,* the term for a city bus, is also sometimes used. When you're getting down to the kind of small-town travel this guide describes, you'll probably need to use regional buses at some point. You can get just about anywhere through a network of dozens of local, provincial, and regional lines (see below), but schedules aren't always easy to come by or to figure out—the local tourist office usually has a photocopy of the schedule, and in cities the local companies have offices. Bus company websites have been poor in the past, but are slowly improving, and you can usually root out at least a downloadable PDF of the timetable somewhere. Buses exist mainly to shuttle workers and schoolchildren, so the most runs are on weekdays, especially early in the morning and before and after the lunchtime *riposo*. *"Feriale"* on a timetable denotes a weekday (which in Italy includes Sat.); Sundays (*"festivi"*) are best avoided on the buses, because few run.

A town's bus stop is usually either the main piazza or, more often, a large square on the edge of town or the bend in the road just outside the main city gate. You should always try to find the local ticket vendor—if there's no office, it's invariably the nearest newsstand or *tabacchi* (signaled by a sign with a white T), or occasionally a bar—but you can usually also buy tickets on the bus. You can also flag a bus down as it passes on a country road, but try to find an official stop (a small sign tacked onto a telephone pole). Tell the driver where you're going and ask him courteously if he'll let you know when you need to get off. When he says *"È la prossima fermata,"* that means yours is the next stop. *"Posso scendere?"* (*Poh*-so *shen*-dair-ay?) is "May I please get off?"

For shorter trips within the region—Perugia to Assisi, or Florence to Siena, for example—there's no need to buy tickets in advance, but when traveling longer distances try to buy tickets at least the day before, just to be sure of a seat.

TUSCAN & UMBRIAN BUS LINES The ticketing offices and depots of most Tuscan bus lines based in Florence are very near the main train station, Santa Maria Novella.

Lazzi, Via Mercadante 2, Florence (✆ **055-363-041;** www.lazzi.it), and **SITA,** Viale dei Cadorna 105, Florence (✆ **055-478-21** or 800-373-760 in Italy; www.sitabus.it), service all of Italy.

The following companies service northern Tuscany: **CAP,** Largo Alinari 11, Florence (✆ **055-214-637** or 055-292-268; www.capautolinee.it); **VaiBus** (www.vaibus.com), Via Gaetano Luporini 895, in Lucca, a result of the merger between Lazzi and CLAP; and **Lazzi/COPIT** buses (✆ **0573-363-243;** www.blubus.it), in Pistoia. **CPT,** Via Nino Bixio, Pisa (✆ **050-505-511** or 800-012-773 in Italy; www.cpt.pisa.it), services Pisa province. **LFI,** Via Guido Monaco 37, Arezzo (✆ **0575-324-294** or 0575-39-881; www.lfi.it), services Arezzo province and the Valdichiana. **RAMA,** Via Topazio 12, Grosseto (✆ **0564-475-111;** www.griforama.it), services the Maremma and southern Tuscany. **TRAIN,** Piazza San Domenico, Siena (✆ **0577-204-111** or 0577-204-246; www.trainspa.it), services Siena province.

In Umbria, **ATC,** Piazzale della Rivoluzione Francese, Terni (✆ **0744-492-711;** www.atcterni.it), services southern Umbria and Orvieto. **Umbria Mobilità** (✆ **800-512-141;** www.umbriamobilita.it), services Perugia, Assisi, Todi, and northern Umbria. **SSIT,** Piazza della Vittoria, Spoleto (✆ **0743-212-208;** www.spoletina.com), services the Spoleto area. And **SULGA/ACAP,** Pian di Massimo, Perugia (✆ **075-500-9641** or 075-74-641; www.sulga.it), has service to Perugia, Assisi, Todi, and northern Umbria.

TIPS ON ACCOMMODATIONS

Italy ceased to be the country of the cheap *pensione* a long time ago. In fact it takes some searching these days to find a hotel room with a shared bathroom.

Hotels are **rated** by regional boards on a system of one to five stars. Prices aren't directly tied to the star system, but for the most part, the more stars a hotel has, the more expensive it'll be—but a four-star in a small town may be cheaper than a two-star in Florence. The number of stars awarded a hotel is based strictly on the amenities offered—not how clean, comfortable, or friendly a place is.

A few of the four- and five-star hotels have their own private **garages,** but most city inns have an agreement with a local garage. In many small towns, a garage is unnecessary because public parking, both free and pay, is widely available and never too far from your hotel. Parking costs and procedures are indicated under each hotel, and the rates quoted are per day (overnight). The provision of **smoke-free rooms** is a legal requirement.

The **high season** throughout most of Tuscany and Umbria runs from Easter to early September or October—peaking June through August—and from December 24 to January 6. One major exception to this is **Florence**—and to a lesser degree, Pisa—where August is low season for hotels. You can almost always bargain for a cheaper rate if you're traveling in the shoulder season (early spring and late fall) or winter off season (not including Christmas). In rural Tuscany, it's common to find a hotel closes for all or part of the off season (November through February or March). Even in cities, family-run hotels or guesthouses tend to close for a month. In hotel reviews, we usually quote a range of prices (see below). If there is one figure only, that represents the maximum. Prices vary so wildly these days depending entirely on availability, that sometimes the only dependable figure is the highest the hotel is allowed to charge. The moral of the story: If it seems like availability is high, you should be getting a discount.

Throughout this book, we've separated hotel listings into several broad categories: **Very Expensive,** 300€ and up; **Expensive,** 200€ to 300€; **Moderate,** 100€ to 200€; and **Inexpensive,** under 100€ for a double.

If your hotel quotes the price for **breakfast** separately from the room, be aware that you can almost certainly get the same breakfast, perhaps even better, for a few euros at the bar down the block. Most, however, quote an inclusive B&B price these days.

Agriturismo (Staying on a Farm)

Tuscany and Umbria are at the forefront of the *agriturismo* movement in Italy, whereby a working farm or agricultural estate makes available accommodations for visitors who want to stay out in the countryside. The supply of such places has exploded perhaps even more quickly than demand. The rural atmosphere is ensured by the fact that an operation can call itself *"agriturismo"* only if (a) it offers fewer than 30 beds total and (b) the agricultural component of the property brings in a larger economic share of profits than the hospitality part—in other words, the property has to remain a farm and not become just a rural hotel. That's why you'll almost always be offered homemade sausages, home-pressed olive oil, home-produced wine, and so on.

Agriturismi can be a crapshoot. The types of accommodations can vary dramatically. Most, though, are mini-apartments, usually rented out with a minimum stay of 3 days, or even a week in high season. Sometimes you're invited to eat big country dinners at the table with the family; other times you cook for yourself. Rates can vary from 60€ for two per day to 250€ and beyond—as much as a board-rated four-star hotel in town. We've reviewed a few really choice ones throughout this book, but there are hundreds more.

Villa Rentals

Each summer, thousands of visitors become temporary Tuscans by renting an old farmhouse or "villa," a marketing term used to inspire romantic images of manicured gardens, a Renaissance mansion, and glasses of chianti, but in reality guaranteeing no more than four walls and most of a roof.

Actually, finding your countryside Eden isn't that simple, and if you want to ensure a romantic and memorable experience, brace yourself for a lot of research and legwork. Occasionally you can go through the property owners themselves, but the vast majority of villas are rented out via agencies (see below).

Root around on travel forums (like the one at Frommers.com), search sites like Tripadvisor (though take the opinions posted there with a pinch of salt!), Google for reviews and photos, and find out exactly where the property is (check it out on Google Maps before you go).

Alternative Accommodations

Sustainable and eco-friendly travel is possible in Tuscany and Umbria, with companies such as **Responsiblevacation.com** (www.responsiblevacation.com) offering a range of tour options (walking holidays, for example), and a list of organic farmstays in Umbria and Tuscany.

For a more adventurous type of vacation, **Tourdust** (www.tourdust.com) uses local businesses in Tuscany to combine accommodations and activities in one trip (from cooking to ballooning). If you crave peace and tranquility, **Monastery Stays** (www.monasterystays.com) specializes in accommodations in monasteries and convents all over Tuscany and Umbria, including Florence and Assisi.

TOP SIX *AGRITURISMI* WEBSITES

Tuscany Tourism (www.turismo.intoscana.it): Probably the most comprehensive resource in English, with databases of hundreds of farmstays, searchable both by text or by clickable map down to the locality level, with info about each property, a photo or two, and a direct link to each *agriturismo's* own website.

Agriturist (www.agriturist.it): Easiest site to navigate, since you click on a region (Tuscany or Umbria) on the map or text list, and the next page gives you the option of continuing in English.

Italy Farm Holidays (www.italyfarmholidays.com): U.S.-based agency representing many of the more upscale *agriturismo* properties in Tuscany and Umbria.

Terranostra (www.terranostra.it): Features handy maps and 400 choices in Tuscany and 69 in Umbria (in Italian, but understandable enough).

Turismo Verde (www.turismoverde.it): Italian only—click on *"Scegli il tuo Agriturismo"* for a high-quality selection.

Untours (www.untours.com): For apartment, farmhouse, or cottage stays of 2 weeks or more, this site provides exceptional vacation rentals for a reasonable price.

TOP 10 RENTAL AGENCIES

Cottages to Castles (www.cottagesto castles.com): U.K.-based agency specializing in luxury rentals.

Holidaylettings.co.uk (www.holiday lettings.co.uk): One of the best U.K.-based agencies for Tuscan rentals.

Homeabroad.com (www.homeabroad. com): Handles hundreds of rather upscale properties.

HomeAway Vacation Rentals (www. HomeAway.com): Global agency with an excellent Italian selection.

Homelidays (www.homelidays.com): European specialist.

Insider's Italy (www.insidersitaly.com): Small, upscale outfit run by a very per-

sonable agent who's thoroughly familiar with all of her properties and with Italy in general.

Owners Direct (www.ownersdirect. co.uk): Huge worldwide selection and extensive coverage in Tuscany and Umbria.

Rentvillas.com (www.rentvillas.com): California-based agency with loads of experience tracking down the best villas.

To Tuscany Villas (www.to-tuscany. com): Tuscany specialists.

Tuscany Vacation Rentals (www. tuscanyholidayrent.com): Tuscan rentals for all budgets.

FAST FACTS: TUSCANY & UMBRIA

Area Codes The country code for Italy is **39.** Every city and its surrounding towns have a separate city code. The code for most of the Florence area is **055;** Livorno is **0586;** Lucca is **0583;** Perugia is **075;** and Pisa is **050.**

Business Hours General open hours for stores, offices, and churches are from 9:30am to noon or 1pm and again from 3 or 3:30pm to 7pm. That early-afternoon shutdown is the *riposo,* the Italian siesta. Most stores close all day Sunday and many also on Monday (morning only or all day). Some services and business offices are open to the public only in the morning. Traditionally, museums are closed Mondays, and although some of the biggest stay open all day long, many close for *riposo* or are only open in the morning (9am–2pm is popular). Banks tend to be open Monday through Friday from 8:30am to 1:30pm and 2:30 to 3:30pm or 3 to 4pm.

Car Rental See "Getting Around: By Car," earlier in this chapter.

Cellphones See "Mobile Phones," below.

Crime See "Safety," later in this section.

Customs What You Can Bring into Italy Foreign visitors can bring along most items for personal use duty-free, including merchandise up to $800, such as fishing tackle, a pair of skis, two tennis rackets, a baby carriage, two hand cameras with 10 rolls of film or a digital camera, computer, CD player with 10 CDs, tape recorder, binoculars, personal jewelry, portable radio set (subject to a small license fee), and 400 cigarettes and a quantity of cigars or pipe tobacco not exceeding 500 grams (1 lb.). A maximum of two bottles of wine and one bottle of hard liquor per person may be brought in duty-free.

What You Can Take Home from Italy Each U.S. tourist may bring back to the U.S. $400 worth of goods duty-free. Only 1 liter of alcohol (less than 2 bottles of wine) is allowed duty-free, though many tourists successfully ignore this rule and "smuggle" more booze back in their luggage. Bear in mind that if you are unlucky enough to get searched, U.S. Customs may not only confiscate the goods, but also slap you with a hefty fine. The good news is that duty is usually not that high: generally 3% of value (keep your receipts!), plus IRS excise tax of between 21 to 31 cents per 750ml bottle of wine. There are no federal limits on the total amount of alcohol you can bring back (these are set by states, but are usually quite high). Brits and other E.U. citizens can bring as much alcohol and tobacco home as they can carry duty-free, as long as it's not obviously for re-sale. For detailed information on what you're allowed to bring home, contact one of the following agencies:

U.S. Citizens: **U.S. Customs & Border Protection** (CBP), 1300 Pennsylvania Ave., NW, Washington, DC 20229 (✆ **877/287-8667;** www.cbp.gov).

Canadian Citizens: **Canada Border Services Agency** (✆ **800/461-9999** in Canada, or 204/983-3500; www.cbsa-asfc.gc.ca).

U.K. Citizens: **HM Customs & Excise** at ✆ **0845/010-9000** (from outside the U.K., 020/8929-0152), or consult their website at www.hmrc.gov.uk.

Australian Citizens: **Australian Customs Service** at ✆ **1300/363-263,** or log on to www.customs.gov.au.

New Zealand Citizens: **New Zealand Customs,** The Customhouse, 17–21 Whitmore St., Box 2218, Wellington (✆ **04/473-6099** or 0800/428-786; www.customs.govt.nz).

Disabled Travelers A few museums and churches have installed ramps at the entrances, and a few hotels have converted first-floor rooms into accessible units by widening the doors and bathrooms. Other than that, don't expect to find much of Tuscany and Umbria easy to tackle. Builders in the Middle Ages and the Renaissance didn't have wheelchairs or mobility impairments in mind when they built narrow doorways and spiral staircases, and preservation laws keep modern Italians from being able to do much about this. Older buses and trains can cause problems as well, with high, narrow doors and steep steps at entrances—though the gradual updating of fleets is slowly removing some of these impediments. There are, however, seats reserved on public transportation for travelers with disabilities. One organization that helps travelers with disabilities in Tuscany is **Accessible Italy** (✆ **378-0549-9411;** www.accessible italy.com). It provides travelers with information about accessible tourist sites and places to rent wheelchairs, as well as offering organized "Accessible Tours" around Italy. Additionally, this non-profit organization invests its proceeds in Italy's infrastructure, to make the country more accessible.

Doctors See "Hospitals," below.

Drinking Laws There is no legal drinking age in Italy in the sense that a young person of any age can legally consume alcohol, but a person must be 16 years old in order to be served alcohol in a restaurant or a bar. Similarly, laws in other countries that exist in order to stamp out public drunkenness simply aren't quite as necessary in Italy where binge-drinking is unusual. (In fact, it doesn't take a very keen observer in Florence to note that most of the loud drunks at night aren't Italian.) Noise is the primary concern to city officials, and so bars generally close at 2am at the latest, although alcohol is commonly served in clubs after that. Bars in Florence will stop take-out sales at midnight. Supermarkets generally carry beer, wine, and sometimes spirits.

Driving Rules See "Getting Around," earlier in this chapter.

Electricity Italy operates on a 220 volts AC (50 cycles) system (equivalent to the U.K., Ireland, Australia, and New Zealand), as opposed to the United States' 110 volts AC (60 cycle) system. You'll need a simple adapter plug (to make flat pegs fit their round holes) and, unless your appliance is dual-voltage (as most electronic devices are), an electrical currency converter. You can pick up the hardware at electronics, travel specialty stores, luggage shops, airports, and from Magellan's catalog (www.magellans.com).

Embassies & Consulates The **U.S. Embassy** is in Rome at Via Vittorio Veneto 121 (☏ **06-46-741;** fax 06-488-2672; http://italy.usembassy.gov). The **U.S. consulate** in Florence—for passport and consular services but not for visas—is at Lungarno Vespucci 38 (☏ **055-266-951;** fax 055-284-088; http://florence.usconsulate.gov), open to drop-ins Monday through Friday from 9am to 12:30pm. Afternoons 2 to 4:30pm, the consulate is open by appointment only; call ahead. The **U.K. Embassy** is in Rome at Via XX Settembre 80a (☏ **06-4220-0001;** fax 06-4220-2334; http://ukinitaly.fco.gov.uk/it), open Monday through Friday from 9:15am to 1:30pm. The **U.K. consulate** in Florence is at Lungarno Corsini 2 (☏ **055-284-133;** fax 055-219-112). It's open Monday to Friday from 9:30am to 12:30pm and 2:30 to 4:30pm.

Of English-speaking countries, only the United States and Great Britain have consulates in Florence. Citizens of other countries must go to their consulates in Rome for help: The **Canadian consulate** in Rome is at Via Zara 30, on the fifth floor (☏ **06-445-981** or 06-85444-3937; www.canadainternational.gc.ca/italy-italie), open Monday through Friday from 8:30am to 12:30pm and 1:30 to 4pm. **Australia's consulate** in Rome is at Via Antonio Bosio 5 (☏ **06-852-721;** fax 06-8527-2300; www.italy.embassy.gov.au). The consular section is open Monday through Thursday from 8:30am to noon and 1:30 to 4pm. The immigration and visa office is open Monday to Thursday from 10am to noon; telephone hours are from 10 to 11:30am. **New Zealand's consulate** in Rome is at Via Clitunno 44 (☏ **06-853-7501;** fax 06-440-2984; www.nzembassy.com/italy), open Monday through Friday from 8:30am to 12:45pm and 1:45 to 5pm.

Emergencies If you experience an emergency, dial ☏ **113,** Italy's general emergency number. For an ambulance, call ☏ **118.** You can also call ☏ **112** for the *carabinieri* (police), or ☏ **115** for the fire department. If your car breaks down, dial ☏ **116** for roadside aid courtesy of the Automotive Club of Italy.

Family Travel Italy is still a family-oriented society, and kids have free rein just about anywhere they go. A crying baby at a dinner table is greeted with a knowing smile rather than with a stern look. Children under a certain age almost always receive discounts, and maybe a special treat from the waiter, but the availability of such accouterments as child seats for cars and dinner tables is more the exception than the norm. There's plenty of parks, offbeat museums, markets, ice-cream parlors, and vibrant streetlife to amuse even the youngest children. **Prénatal** (www.prenatal.com) is the premier toddler and baby chain store in Italy, with branches in Arezzo, Florence, Lucca, Perugia, Pisa, Siena, and many other towns. You can buy Huggies and Pampers (ask for *pannolini*) at most supermarkets, and a decent selection of formula (powdered milk) at pharmacies. To locate accommodations, restaurants, and attractions that are particularly kid-friendly, refer to the "Kids" icon throughout this guide.

Gasoline See "Getting Around: By Car," earlier in this chapter.

Health There are no special health risks you'll encounter in Tuscany and Umbria. The tap water is safe, and medical resources are high quality. With Italy's universal health-care system, you can usually stop by any hospital emergency room with an ailment, get swift and courteous service, receive a diagnosis and a prescription, and be sent on your way with a wave and a smile—without filling out a single sheet of paperwork. However, the benefits of Italy's partially socialized medicine strictly speaking only apply to E.U. citizens, so those from elsewhere should be prepared to pay medical bills upfront. Before leaving home, find out what medical services your **health insurance** covers. Your health insurance in your home country may not cover any extended treatment abroad. However, even if you don't have insurance, you will be seen and treated in an emergency room, just as you would at home.

Pharmacies in Italy are ubiquitous (look for the green cross) and offer essentially the same range of generic drugs available all over the developed world. Pharmacies are also the only place you'll find simple stuff such as aspirin and run-of-the-mill cold medicines: You won't find Tylenol at any old corner store (even if there were such a thing as a corner store). Pharmacies in Florence and other cities take turns doing the night shift. Normally there is a list posted at the entrance of each pharmacy, telling customers which pharmacy is open which night of the week.

Hospitals Thanks to its tax-funded universal health care (*Servizio Sanitario Nazionale*), you can walk into almost any Italian hospital when ill and get taken care of speedily with no insurance questions asked, no forms to fill out, and no fee charged. They'll just give you a prescription and send you on your way. The **Tuscan Health Service** is the regional authority (✆ **800-556-060;** www.salute.toscana.it). In Florence, the most central hospital is **Santa Maria Nuova,** a block northeast of the Duomo on Piazza Santa Maria Nuova (✆ **055-27-581**), open 24 hours. For a free translator to help you describe your symptoms, explain the doctor's instructions, or aid in medical issues in general, call the volunteers at the **Associazione Volontari Ospedalieri** (**AVO;** ✆ **055-234-4567;** www.federavo.it) Monday, Wednesday, and Friday from 4 to 6pm and Tuesday and Thursday from 10am to noon.

Insurance Italy may be one of the safer places you can travel in the world, but accidents and setbacks can and do happen, from lost luggage to car crashes.

For information on traveler's insurance, trip cancelation insurance, and medical insurance while traveling, visit **www.frommers.com/planning**.

Internet & Wi-Fi Cybercafes are in healthy supply in most Italian cities. In smaller towns you may have a bit of trouble, but increasingly hotels are offering Wi-Fi throughout the rooms, although those in rural areas are not as likely to have a high-speed connection. In a pinch, hostels, local libraries, and, sometimes, bars will have some sort of terminal for access. For getting online in Florence, see its own "Fast Facts" section in chapter 4. More and more hotels, resorts, airports, cafes, and retailers are offering Wi-Fi, for a small fee or for free. Most hotels and lots of wine bars and Irish pubs in Florence have wireless Internet access, as do many hotels throughout Tuscany and Umbria.

If you are bringing your own computer, keep in mind the outlets are 220 volts in Italy, and you will need an adapter for a U.K. or North American plug—the same one used for France and most of the rest of the Continent.

Language Italians may not be quite as polished with their English as some of their European counterparts, but Tuscany and Umbria in particular have been hosting Anglophones for a long time now, and English is a regular part of any business day. In Florence and other cities, you will probably be the 20th English-speaking tourist they've spoken with that day. In very rural parts, slow and clear speech, a little gesticulating, and a smile will go a long way—but learn a few words of Italian and you will always receive a better response. A handy reference guide is Frommer's *Italian PhraseFinder & Dictionary*.

Legal Aid   Your embassy or consulate can provide a list of foreign attorneys should you encounter legal problems in Italy. In criminal cases, if you cannot afford an attorney, the local court will provide one for you.

LGBT Travelers   Italy as a whole, and northern and central Italy in particular, are gay-friendly. Homosexuality is legal, and the age of consent is 16. Luckily, Italians are already more affectionate and physical than Americans in their general friendships, and even straight men occasionally walk down the street with their arms around each other—however, kissing anywhere other than on the cheeks at greetings and good-byes will certainly draw attention. As you might expect, smaller towns tend to be less permissive and accepting than cities. Florence has the largest and most visible homosexual population (not that that's saying much), though university cities such as Pisa also take gayness in stride. Elba's beaches are Tuscany's big gay-vacation destination. Italy's national association and support network for gays and lesbians is ARCI-Gay/ARCI-Lesbica. The national website is **www.arcigay.it**, but they also have a Tuscany-specific one at **www.gaytoscana.it**. There are other offices in Pisa, Via San Lorenzo 38 (©/fax 050-555-618; www.arcigaypisa.it); in Livorno (© 320-817-1758; www.arcigay livorno.it); and in Grosseto, Via Parini 7/e (© 0564-490-565; www.grossetogay.it). Their cousin association in Florence is called **Ireos** (www.ireos.org), in the Oltrarno at Via dei Serragli 3, Firenze (© 055-216-907). For info on Siena, check out **www.siena gay.net**.

Mail   At press time, the cost of sending a postcard or letter up to 20 grams, or a little less than an ounce, was .39€ to other European countries, and .41€ everywhere else. Sending via the Premium service is much faster—rates are .52€ and .62€ respectively. For a full table of prices and weights, visit www.poste.it; there is an English version available for translations.

Mobile Phones   The three letters that define much of the world's wireless capabilities are GSM (Global System for Mobile communications), a big, seamless network that makes for easy cross-border cellphone use throughout Europe and dozens of other countries worldwide. GSM phones function with a removable plastic SIM card, encoded with your phone number and account information. If your cellphone is on a GSM system, and you have a world-capable multiband phone such as many Sony Ericsson, Motorola, or Samsung models, iPhone/smartphone, or Blackberry, you can make and receive calls in Tuscany and Umbria. In the U.S. this means that Verizon customers (including iPhone users) will not be able to make calls in Italy (Verizon uses the CDMA system); AT&T users should be okay, although international rates for iPhones can be very expensive. All U.K. networks have roaming agreements with their Italian counterparts. Just call your wireless operator and ask for "international roaming" to be activated on your account. Unfortunately, per-minute charges can be high—usually $1 to $1.50 in Italy. Coverage with major carriers is excellent in Tuscan and Umbrian cities, like Florence, but can be spotty sometimes in the region's less populated countryside.

Buying an Italian SIM card or phone can be economically attractive, as Italy has relatively cheap prepaid phone programs; TIM, Vodafone, Wind, and Tre have very cheap, entry-level pay-as-you-go rates. Once you arrive at your destination, stop by a local cellphone shop and get the cheapest package; you'll pay less than 35€ for a phone and a starter calling card, and just 5€ for a SIM card. The best deals will probably be in Rome and Milan, if you're flying into one of those cities. Both cities' principal train stations, Stazione Centrale in Milan and Termini in Rome, in the lower level shopping center, have cellular stores. Local calls may be as low as 15¢ per minute, (international calls 50¢–60¢ per minute), and all incoming calls are free, including international ones. Data, of course, will be *much* cheaper than roaming rates (2€ per week for up to 500MB was fairly standard at the time of writing).

Money & Costs Frommer's lists prices throughout this guide in the local currency. (US$ are sometimes used for overseas tour operators, denoted with a "$"). The currency conversions provided were correct at press time. However, rates fluctuate, so before departing consult a currency exchange website such as **www.oanda.com/currency/converter** to check up-to-the-minute rates.

THE VALUE OF THE EURO VS. OTHER POPULAR CURRENCIES

€	AUS$	CAN$	NZ$	UK£	US$
1	A$1.36	C$1.40	NZ$1.75	£0.88	$1.43

Despite the ongoing financial crisis in much of the world, Tuscany is as popular as ever and it remains a relatively expensive destination. In Florence, you can expect to find roughly the same prices for services as you would in Rome and Milan, which are generally lower than London, New York, and Paris, but higher than the rest of Southern Europe. Like anywhere else, prices for everyday goods and services like groceries and haircuts will always be greater in a high-rent city like Florence than in the countryside. Still, travelers from North America and the U.K. will be giddy about the savings on what they might consider luxuries but are basic staples in Italy—fine wine, cheese, cold cuts, and an impeccable cappuccino that costs less than two euros.

Euro coins are issued in denominations of .01€, .02€, .05€, .10€, .20€, and .50€ as well as 1€ and 2€; bills come in denominations of 5€, 10€, 20€, 50€, 100€, 200€, and 500€.

Traveler's checks, while still the safest way to carry money, are going the way of the dinosaur. The aggressive evolution of international computerized banking and consolidated ATM networks has led to the triumph of plastic throughout the Italian peninsula—even if cold cash is still the most trusted currency, especially in smaller towns or cheaper mom-and-pop joints, where credit cards may not be accepted.

You'll get the best rate if you exchange money at a bank or one of its ATMs. The rates at "Cambio/change/wechsel" exchange booths are invariably less favorable but still a good deal better than what you'd get exchanging money at a hotel or shop (a last-resort tactic only). The bill-to-bill changers you'll see in some touristy places exist solely to rip you off.

The easiest and best way to get cash away from home is from an **ATM,** referred to in Italy as a "Bancomat." ATMs are easily found in the cities of Tuscany and Umbria, but are not as common in smaller towns and villages. While every town usually has one, it's good practice to fuel up on cash in urban centers, ideally during business hours. (International circuits seem to go off-line on occasion late at night and on weekends.) The **Cirrus** (*©* **800/424-7787;** www.mastercard.com) and **PLUS** (*©* **800/843-7587;** www.visa.com) networks span the globe. Go to your bank card's website to find ATM locations in Florence, Tuscany, or Umbria. Be sure to check with your bank that your card is valid for international withdrawal, and that you have a four-digit PIN. (Most ATMs in Italy will not accept any other number of digits.) Also, be sure you know your daily withdrawal limit before you depart. ***Note:*** Many banks impose a fee every time you use a card at another bank's ATM, and that fee can be higher for international transactions (up to $5 or more) than for domestic ones (where they're rarely more than $2). In addition, the bank from which you withdraw cash may charge its own fee, although this is not common practice in Italy. For international withdrawal fees, ask your bank. If at the ATM you get a message saying your card isn't valid for international transactions, don't panic: It's most likely the bank just can't make the phone connection to check it (occasionally this can be a citywide epidemic) or else simply doesn't have the cash. Try another ATM or another town.

WHAT THINGS COST IN FLORENCE	€
Taxi (from the train station to Santa Croce)	15.00
Public bus (to any destination)	1.20
Continental breakfast (cappuccino and croissant standing at a bar)	3.00
Glass of wine	2.50–7.00
Coca-Cola (standing/sitting in a bar)	2.00/3.50
Cup of espresso (standing/sitting in a bar)	1.00/1.75

Credit cards are widely accepted in Tuscany and Umbria these days, especially in hotels and larger establishments. However, it is always a good idea to carry some cash since some small businesses may only accept cash or may claim that their credit card machine is broken to avoid paying fees to the credit card companies. Visa and Master-Card are almost universally accepted at hotels, plus most restaurants and shops; the majority of them also accept American Express. Diners Club is gaining some ground, especially in Florence and in more expensive establishments throughout the region. ***Note:*** It is an unfortunately common practice among many restaurants in Italy to claim that the credit card machine is down when, in fact, it is more often the case that the owner simply doesn't want to pay the merchant fees. On more than one occasion we've insisted that they try it just in case, as we had no cash, and—surprise—it's been instantly fixed! The best way to avoid this chicanery is to inform the waitstaff upfront that you intend to use a credit card. If they tell you it's broken, you have the option of finding a restaurant where the machine "works."

Chip and PIN cards represent a change in the way that credit and debit cards are used. The program is designed to cut down on the fraudulent use of credit cards. More and more banks—across Europe—are issuing customers Chip and PIN versions of their debit or credit cards. In the future, more and more vendors will be asking for a four-digit personal identification number or PIN, which will be entered into a keypad near the cash register. For now, traditional "swipe" cards are commonly accepted in central Italy even though they are being phased out elsewhere, and "chip" cards are also commonly accepted.

Finally, be sure to let your bank know that you'll be traveling abroad to avoid having your card blocked after a few days of big purchases far from home. Note that many banks now assess a 1% to 3% "transaction fee" on all charges you incur abroad (whether you're using the local currency or your native currency). Check with your bank before departing to avoid any surprise charges on your statement.

For help with currency conversions, tip calculations, and more, download Frommer's convenient Travel Tools app for your mobile device. Go to **www.frommers.com/go/mobile** and click on the "Travel Tools" icon.

Newspapers & Magazines The *International Herald Tribune* (published by the *New York Times* and with news catering to Americans abroad) and *USA Today* are available at just about every newsstand, even in smaller towns. You can find the *Wall Street Journal Europe,* European editions of *Time* and *Newsweek,* the *Economist,* and just about any major European newspaper or magazine at the larger kiosks. Tuscany's major Italian-language daily is *La Nazione,* although you'll find *Il Tirreno* more widely read in the western part of the region. For local events guides in English, see each individual city's "Visitor Information" listing.

Packing For helpful information on packing for your trip, download our convenient Travel Tools app for your mobile device. Go to **www.frommers.com/go/mobile** and click on the "Travel Tools" icon.

Passports Anyone traveling to Italy from outside the Schengen Agreement countries will need a passport to enter. The Schengen Area comprises Iceland, Norway, Switzerland and all of the E.U. except the U.K., Ireland, Bulgaria, Cyprus, and Romania. You technically do not need a passport to travel within the Schengen Area (typically there are no customs checks at land borders, and flights within the area are treated as domestic), although you are required to present one to authorities upon request, as they are commonly looking for fugitives from justice or illegal immigrants. You are required to present a passport at hotel desks in Italy for the same reason. Note also that some checks between the French and Italian borders were re-instated in 2011 due to illegal immigration fears.

E.U. nationals (including U.K. and Irish passport holders) have the right to both live and work in Italy; however, after 90 days, they must obtain a residence certificate *(certificato di residenza)* at the *anagrafe* of the local town hall, by providing some proof of employment or financial resources. Citizens of the United States, Canada, Australia, and New Zealand are allowed to stay in Italy for 90 days visa-free; after that period, they are required to apply for a visa or obtain a *permesso di soggiorno* (permit of stay).

Australia Australian Passport Information Service (✆ **131-232,** or visit www.passports.gov.au).

Canada Passport Office, Department of Foreign Affairs and International Trade, Ottawa, ON K1A 0G3 (✆ **800/567-6868;** www.ppt.gc.ca).

Ireland Passport Office, Setanta Centre, Molesworth Street, Dublin 2 (✆ **01/671-1633;** www.foreignaffairs.gov.ie).

New Zealand Passports Office, Department of Internal Affairs, 47 Boulcott St., Wellington, 6011 (✆ **0800/225-050** in New Zealand or 04/474-8100; www.passports.govt.nz).

United Kingdom Visit your nearest passport office, major post office, or travel agency or contact the **Identity and Passport Service (IPS),** 89 Eccleston Square, London, SW1V 1PN (✆ **0300/222-0000;** www.homeoffice.gov.uk/agencies-public-bodies/ips).

United States To find your regional passport office, check the U.S. State Department website (http://travel.state.gov/passport) or call the **National Passport Information Center** (✆ **877/487-2778**) for automated information.

Petrol Please see "Getting Around: By Car," earlier in this chapter.

Police For emergencies, call ✆ **113.** Italy has several different police forces, but there are only two you'll most likely ever need to deal with. The first is the urban *polizia,* whose city headquarters is called the *questura* and who can help with lost and stolen property. The most useful branch—the cops to go to for serious problems and crimes— is the *carabinieri* (✆ **112**), a national order-keeping, crime-fighting civilian police force.

Safety Tuscany and Umbria are remarkably safe regions, and you generally won't encounter the pickpockets that sometimes frequent touristy areas and public buses in Rome and Naples. There are, of course, thieves in central Italy, as there are everywhere, so be smart; don't leave anything valuable in your rental car overnight, and leave nothing visible in it at any time to avoid tempting a would-be thief. If you do happen to be robbed, you can fill out paperwork at the nearest police station, but this is mostly for insurance purposes—don't expect them to actually hunt down the perpetrator or find your lost valuables. In general, avoid public parks at night and public squares in the wee hours of the morning, situations that attract the seediest elements looking to prey on late-night partyers.

Italy for centuries was and, to a large degree, still is a homogenous culture. Add to that the fact that issues of race here are discussed so frankly and openly—there's apparently no taboo to saying, in a loud voice, "That black guy over there . . ." More-over, the reality is that most people of **African descent** in Italy are working as street vendors, not bankers. All this may make travelers with darker skin feel—correctly at times—as if they're being singled out. Pockets of racism do exist in Italy just like any-where else in the world, but on the whole, it is an extremely warm and tolerant coun-try. For issues specific to female travelers, see "Women Travelers" below.

Senior Travel Italy is a multigenerational culture that doesn't tend to marginalize its seniors, and older people are treated with a great deal of respect and deference throughout Italy. But there are few specific programs, associations, or concessions made for them. The one exception is on admission prices for museums and sights, where those ages 60 or 65 and older will often get in at a reduced rate or even free. There are also special train passes and reductions on bus tickets and the like in various towns (see "Getting Around," earlier in this chapter). As a senior in Italy, you're *un an-ziano* (*una anziana* if you're a woman), or "ancient one"—consider it a term of respect and let people know you're one if you think a discount may be in order.

Smoking Smoking was banned in public places in Italy, including all restaurants and bars, offices, clubs (discos), as well as most hotels, in 2005. That said, there are still smokers in Italy, and they tend to take the outside tables. Be aware that if you are keen on an outdoor table, you are essentially choosing a seat in the smoking section, and requesting that your neighbor not smoke may not be politely received.

Student Travel The **Florence Student Point** (Via San Gallo 25; ✆ **055-282-770;** www.studentpointfirenze.it) is like a junior tourist office that caters to students; its staff can help you find a reasonable place to stay and can assist you with any other tourism-related dilemma you might be facing. The best reason to stop by, though, is the free Student Card, available to students of any age with some proof of their aca-demic status; it offers discounts on museums, trains, restaurants, bars, and more.

Taxes There's no sales tax added onto the price tag of your purchases, but there is a 20% value-added tax (in Italy: IVA) automatically included in just about everything. For major purchases, you can get this refunded. A very small number of hotels still don't include the special 10% hotel IVA in their quoted prices. Ask when making your reservation.

Telephones If you want to stay in touch, it is a good idea to use a cellphone on your visit to Tuscany and Umbria. Pay phones have not entirely gone by the wayside, but these days there are very few pay phones in central Italy—a place where there are far more cellular numbers than land-line numbers.

To call Tuscany/Umbria

1. Dial the international access code: 011 from the U.S.; 00 from the U.K., Ireland, or New Zealand; or 0011 from Australia.
2. Dial the country code: 39.
3. Dial the city code (for Florence: 055) and then the number. (Do not drop the initial 0 as you might in other European countries.) Even when calling within Italy, you always need to dial the city code first.

To make international calls from Italy First dial 00 and then the country code (U.S. or Canada 1, U.K. 44, Ireland 353, Australia 61, New Zealand 64). Next you dial the area code and number. For example, if you wanted to call the British Embassy in Washington, D.C., you would dial 00-1-202-588-7800.

For directory assistance Each cellphone carrier has its own directory assistance number, which is listed automatically in the address book of your SIM card. For Telecom Italia, and its mobile carrier, TIM, the directory assistance number is ✆ **412.**

For operator assistance For operator assistance in making either a domestic or international call from a Telecom Italia land line, call ✆ **170.**

Toll-free numbers Numbers in Italy beginning with 800 or 877, and a few others beginning with 8, are toll-free, but calling a 1-800 number in the States from Italy is not toll-free. In fact, it costs the same as an overseas call.

Time All of Italy is in the same Western European time zone; that is, GMT plus 1 hour (plus 2 hr. in officially designated "summertime," between late March and late October). For help with time translations, and more, download our convenient Travel Tools app for your mobile device. Go to **www.frommers.com/go/mobile** and click on the "Travel Tools" icon.

Tipping In **hotels,** a service charge is usually included in your bill. In family-run operations, additional tips are unnecessary and sometimes considered rude. In fancier places with a hired staff, however, you may want to leave a .50€ daily tip for the maid, pay the bellhop or porter 1€ per bag, and a helpful concierge 2€ for his or her troubles. In **restaurants,** 10% to 15% is almost always included in the bill—to be sure, ask *"è incluso il servizio?"*—but you can leave up to an additional 10%, especially for good service. At **bars and cafes,** tipping the barman is not expected; if you sit at a table, leave 10% to 15% only if the service is good. **Taxi** drivers in cities expect 10% to 15%.

For help with tip calculations, currency conversions, and more, download our convenient Travel Tools app for your mobile device. Go to **www.frommers.com/go/mobile** and click on the "Travel Tools" icon.

Toilets Public toilets in Tuscany and Umbria are practically nonexistent except at the train stations and highway gas stations, where they are sometimes pay toilets (.50€ usually does the trick). Standard practice in Italy is to pay for a .90€ cup of coffee at a bar and then ask to use the toilet—although it's best to ask for both simultaneously as the restrooms in heavily touristed parts of Florence, Tuscany, and Umbria are sometimes "out of order."

VAT See "Taxes," above.

Visas Travelers from Australia, Canada, New Zealand, and the U.S. can visit Italy for up to 90 days without a visa, and can enter Italy with a valid passport. Visits of more than 90 days may require a visa, but the requirements vary depending on the purpose of your visit. U.S., Canadian, Australian, and New Zealand citizens with a valid passport don't need a visa to enter Italy if they don't expect to stay more than 90 days and don't expect to work there. If, after entering Italy, you find you want to stay more than 90 days, you can apply for a permit for an extra 90 days, which, as a rule, is granted immediately. Go to the nearest *questura* (police headquarters) or your home country's consulate.

E.U. nationals (including U.K. and Irish passport holders) have the right to both live and work in Italy, so long as they have a valid passport; however, after 90 days, they must obtain a residence certificate *(certificato di residenza).* For more information on visas to visit or stay in Italy, go to the Foreign Ministry's English-language page at www.esteri.it/visti/index_eng.asp.

Visitor Information See "Visitor Information" in each of this book's destination chapters for local websites and resources. For Tuscany in general, visit www.turismo.intoscana.it; for Umbria visit www.umbria-turismo.it.

Water Although most Italians take mineral water with their meals, tap water is safe everywhere. (Unsafe sources will be marked *acqua non potabile.*) In fact, many cities are now urging their citizens to cut back on their plastic-wasting ways and to turn back to the tap. If the water comes out cloudy, it's only the calcium or other minerals inherent in a water supply that often comes untreated from fresh springs. Also, the water from fountains in public parks is not only potable, it's often the best water you've ever tasted.

Wi-Fi See "Internet & Wi-Fi," earlier in this section.

Women Travelers It is hard not to notice that, on the streets of Florence, young foreign women far outnumber any other category of people. Women feel remarkably welcome in Tuscany and Umbria, and the stereotype of the young Italian male—out to prove himself the most irresistible lover on the planet—applies more to Rome and the South. Having said that, the more exotic you look to an Italian—statuesque blondes, ebony-skinned beauties, or simply an American accent—the more attention you can expect to get, especially at night. This will almost certainly be of the mild flirtatious type; take your cue from Italian women, who usually ignore the men around them entirely unless it's someone they're already walking with. Although most foreign women report feeling far safer wandering the deserted streets of an Italian city to their hotels at 2am than they do in their own neighborhoods back home, use some common sense. Rape is much rarer in Italy than in the United States, but it does happen.

A more subtle issue—one you are unlikely to encounter on a short stay—concerns Italian stereotypes of foreign women (especially northern European and American students) as uninhibited and passionate sex kittens. Not only does this tend to encourage would-be Romeos, it can have far more sinister overtones, as the troubling case of U.S. student **Amanda Knox** suggests. Convicted of murdering her English roommate in Perugia in 2007, Knox was sentenced to 26 years in prison after a highly emotive trial. The tabloids went into overdrive as "Foxy Knoxy" became demonized as the symbol of licentious American female behavior, guilty or not (she had an Italian boyfriend at the time). Knox was released and returned to the U.S. after winning her appeal against the conviction in 2011.

AIRLINE WEBSITES

MAJOR AIRLINES

Air France
www.airfrance.com

Alitalia
www.alitalia.com

American Airlines
www.aa.com

British Airways
www.british-airways.com

Continental Airlines
www.continental.com

Delta Air Lines
www.delta.com

EgyptAir
www.egyptair.com

Iberia Airlines
www.iberia.com

Lufthansa
www.lufthansa.com

Swiss Air
www.swiss.com

United Airlines
www.united.com

Virgin Atlantic Airways
www.virgin-atlantic.com

BUDGET AIRLINES

Aer Lingus
www.aerlingus.com

Air Berlin
www.airberlin.com

Air One
www.flyairone.it

BMI Baby
www.bmibaby.com

CityJet
www.cityjet.com

easyJet
www.easyjet.com

Jet2.com
www.jet2.com

Meridiana Fly
www.meridiana.it

Ryanair
www.ryanair.com

Skybridge AirOps
www.skybridgeairops.com

INDEX

465

PHOTO CREDITS